THE MODERN LIBRARY

OF THE WORLD'S BEST BOOKS

EIGHT FAMOUS ELIZABETHAN PLAYS

EIGHT FAMOUS ELIZABETHAN PLAYS

INTRODUCTION BY

ESTHER CLOUDMAN DUNN

THE MODERN LIBRARY · NEW YORK

Random House IS THE PUBLISHER OF

THE MODERN LIBRARY

BENNETT A. CERF · DONALD S. KLOPFER · ROBERT K. HAAS

Manufactured in the United States of America

Printed by Parkway Printing Company   Paper by Richard Bauer & Co.

Bound by H. Wolff

CONTENTS

INTRODUCTION

The Elizabethans were spiritual geographers. They charted the countries of the mind as well as remapped the earth. The desire to enlarge life was strong in them; for they risked the little security of their souls to discover new emotions and ideas, and came home staggering under the load.

That is why their literature is chiefly dramatic. Drama shows men doing and feeling and Elizabethan drama presented an enlarged realm of acting and suffering. The contemporary audience saw in it a glorification of its own desires. We still find their plays spacious: for three hundred years of attempting and discovering has not dwarfed their accomplishment or contracted their vision. We rely upon their virility and daring outlook.

Eight plays by eight different men, written at intervals across forty years in the reigns of three sovereigns as distinct as Elizabeth, James and Charles; in various patterns of tragedy, comedy, melodrama and new blends of all three, would make uneasy company within the covers of a single book; if it were not for a kind of integrity, truth to a certain view of life which belongs to them all. In the midst of differences in the personalities of the authors, their material, the effect they were aiming for, all eight of these plays intensify life. They grasp its indestructible core through the thin veil of everydayness and its quintessence beats near the surface. They know that underneath a veneer of order lie violent powers, uncontrolled by experience, controlling it. This sense of life was the possession of all kinds of authors, bungling, competent or superb; it might be found in any class of society, for the Elizabethans had discovered that all sorts of men are sometimes aware of infinity.

They loved the surface of life too, the events and accidents which may at any moment bring out its essence. That is why their plays are so full of story; everybody down to the servant and nurse has his story, till the modern reader holds his head and cries for mercy. Even when the hero's happy or unhappy tale is ended, the greatest writers cannot resist carrying the play along till the minor stories are finished, the jewels disposed of, the remains of the unfinished feast distributed to the beggars. Thus the series of events through which man gambles with life becomes important for itself.

Marlowe's *Faustus* comes first in time in this gesticulating noisy company and it is first in quality. It is as great as any play of the period, not excluding Shakespeare's. The reason for this is clear: Faustus' desire is the apotheosis of Renaissance desire. He goes after the essence of life and fails gloriously in the effort to transcend human limitations. Marlowe used a legend of the Middle Ages and kept a good deal of the old machinery, the Good and Evil Angel, the Seven Deadly Sins, the hierarchy of Hell. But he used it to represent pictorially the inward conflict of men like himself, whose spirit "lift upward and divine" found no earthly arena large enough for his struggle but plunging toward infinity by illicit paths, with his mortal body still about him, glimpsed and lost its glory. No other play of the eight is a tragedy in this cruel Elizabethan sense of the word.

The play of *Faustus* goes on in the limbo which lies between earth and hell. The field for action is imaginatively enlarged to match the temper of the hero. Italy was another such limbo outside the bounds of commonplace English existence. England had been impressed by Italy from the time of Henry VII; the light of modernism had risen there first, and slowly mounting above the Alps, had cast a pale reflection upon Tudor England. The subjects of Elizabeth and James still felt provincial beside Italians, gauche in the presence of cosmopolitanism. They admired Italy for the intellectual and artistic achievements of the humanists and for the cut of a sleeve, the studding of a dagger handle. The turbulent city-states, each with its small court where beauty and crime went hand in hand, were accepted as part of the picture. Italian political and religious corruption were not censored as they would have been, if an enchantment had not blinded English eyes. It was a far away world where cruelty and torture lost their reality and became the picturesque accompaniment of existence, purely for imaginative consumption and at a safe distance. Jonson gave *Volpone* an Italian setting in 1605 and Webster's two best plays, written in the second decade of the seventeenth century, are laid in Italy. Both Jonson and Webster had the creative dexterity to put on the garment of this imagined world and wear it easily.

Volpone, though it is called a comedy, belongs in a deeper category near tragedy. It is a story of those vicious figures, the legacy-hunters, who in the time of Nero and after, tried to secure from a rich old man at his death, the reversion of his estate. Juvenal and Lucian had scourged them in their satires. Jonson moved the vice forward to Renaissance Italy. It took root easily, and no doubt seemed more convincingly horrible to the English play-goer for the change. It is a fine piece of sustained imagination. Jonson creates a realm where perverted intellectual cunning panders to inhuman lust for wealth, power, pleasure in deceiving others. He shows the greedy expectation of hangers-on, themselves men of no mean ability, who simulate the decencies, friendship, generosity, affectionate regard, while underneath they plot with relentless art to get Volpone's fortune. Once this unreal world is granted, Jonson makes it vivid. One is fascinated by the enormity of wickedness. It nourished the imagination of the Northerners at the same time that they abjured it and it was not so much the unnaturalness of Italian villainy that stirred them as its vigor. They saw something whole-hearted and strong. The machinations were brilliantly conceived; the daring was superb. Though vice is punished in the end of *Volpone,* we scarcely remember it, for Volpone and his crew belong to a world where justice is alien and clever villainy its own reward.

The Duchess of Malfi is laid in the same superworld. The wicked Cardinal and his scheming brother, Ferdinand, are such creatures as belong right off the map. To create them and put them in action is the business of a strong imagination which must at every point resist the imitation of familiar humanity, for in their strangeness, under the guise of familiar appearance, lies their appeal. They release the reader from the restrictions of his mere humanity. Webster is a good showman. By the slow accretion of one strange hint upon another he builds a towering terror. The play has hardly opened when Bosola, the paid creature of the Cardinal, says of him and his brother, Ferdinand:

> He and his brother are like plum trees that grow
> crooked
> Over standing pools; they are rich and o'er laden
> with
> Fruit, but none but crows, pies and caterpillars
> feed
> On them.

As a foil to their evil, Webster creates their beautiful and sentimental sister, the Duchess. With the introduction of this sort of character, Webster forfeits that integrity which keeps Jonson's play virile and credibly incredible in its superhuman villains and their relentless intrigue. Webster makes his Duchess too white against her brothers' blackness. The opposition of the groups is theatrical, effective at the moment but not gripping. It has the dazzling beauty of momentary melodrama but as a whole the play is not even fantastically real. The lady is elegant, stately, a beautiful woman of position, and for the duration of the play we feel an aching pity for her innocence, tortured and wracked by her demoniacal brothers. But when the play is over and we reflect, we can grant her scarcely any of the nobility which goes with a real woman meeting bravely a real dilemma. She marries her good platitudinous steward and invites ruin by this act which her brothers have forbidden. But it is a sentimental union: she is lonely, he is good and the marriage has the small glamour of being forbidden. This marriage, then, which sets the whole rout of Hell loose, is a theatrical device, not a glowing necessity like the marriage of Othello and Desdemona. But the villains of the play are magnificently sustained and the Duchess is forgiven her sentimentality for the exquisite moments when crossing the path of her brothers' grand evil, she makes them cry out, in quick poetry, from the far regions of their torment and remorse.

The vigorous imagination to sustain a villain's point of view, which Jonson has in *Volpone* and Webster in a lesser degree in *The Duchess,* weakened as the seventeenth century grew older. The strongest minds, like Milton's, were working in other forms than drama, forms more suited to the accent of another age. Yet Italian plays kept being produced. Ford's *'Tis Pity She's a Whore* in 1633 keeps the tradition weakly. Banditti, friars, confessions, all the furniture of Italian story, is badly grafted on a play of English sentiment. Only in the handling of the main theme of incestuous love is there the old intellectual and spiritual temerity working freely without consciousness that it works in a forbidden realm. Ford writes of the love of a brother and sister with some effective sentiment. He is sure of the individual's right to emotional adventure, in fact the social ties of blood-relationship are so tenuous that he scarcely feels their weight.

Heywood's *A Woman Killed with Kindness,* a sentimental melodrama of middle-class provincial people, acted in the same year with the first printed text of *Hamlet* (1603), seems an odd companion for the plays we have been describing.

But under its differences of setting and social type, it has a strong sense of the incalculability of life which all good plays of that age emphasized. No group of artists were more aware of the mystery of man's life, the strange conjunction of everyday incident and infinite spiritual adventure than the Elizabethan playwrights. The media and formulæ of their plays were various, but this essential ingredient they all shared. It was the peculiar angle of their world upon life.

In *A Woman Killed with Kindness* a wife commits adultery with her husband's best friend and house guest; a young country gentleman fights in duels, gets his friend into debt, sends him to languish in prison, while he tries to seduce his sister. In the end every one forgives his enemy. The would-be seducer marries the girl and when the wife's sin is discovered, her husband kills her with his kind penance and forgives her in a sentimental death-scene. The plot is sentimental and the characterization is undistinguished. But one reads it still: for now as then, though we think we are grown wondrous wise about the hidden springs of conduct, yet the surprises of life, the unexpected plunge into terror, the equally unexpected righting of the situation, the pathetically jumbled sequence of things still presses on us. Nobody knew how to play upon this quality better than Heywood. Good character and plotting might go hang; he wanted only this poignant pattern of fluctuation in human moods which he elaborates, in this play, as if it were a theme in music. He tortures the wronged husband with the unfaithful lady's lute which she has left behind her at her banishment. As a symbol of lost harmony, it serves to lead out sorrow for a pretty exhibition. The husband sends it after the lady to reproach her and she breaks it against her coach's wheel, to mark the discord of her broken life. Though its shoddy theatricality is clear to an analytic mood, the incident is effective in the theatre, for in life itself some deep sense of the pity of things might be called up by just such an obvious circumstance.

The play that fits least easily into this group and is, I think, least Elizabethan of them all is Beaumont and Fletcher's *Maid's Tragedy*. The thing that makes it un-Elizabethan is the social attitude of the authors and the ideas which they portray. Though in date it comes in the height of the period (Shakespeare's *Lear* had been first acted about two years before) it is one of the early signs of a different view of life, both in the authors and in the audience. Beaumont and Fletcher were Jacobean gentlemen, cavaliers in the seventeenth century sense of the word, writing plays for an audience unlike the public which saw *Faustus* twenty years earlier. They "understood the language of gentlemen" better than Marlowe or Jonson, in the sense that they were more aware of the earmarks of their own class, more conscious of a set for which they wrote. They were masters of "good theatre," knew how to calculate their effects and what kinds of scenes were admired.

The Maid's Tragedy is distinctly a gentleman's play, full of passion and pathos, duels and suicides. The conversation is all about honor, that sophisticated sort of honor which is routed in dishonor. Evadne, beautiful and passionate, a court lady and the King's mistress, marries Amintor by the King's arrangement in order to cloak the royal amour. Thus a marriage which is a marriage only in name becomes the central force for the whole play. How does Amintor behave in the circumstances? How should he behave? Where lies the line between his duty to his King and his treatment of the lady? The action proceeds from the confused motives of a world which holds fashionable honor and romantic love equally dear. Evadne displays a variety of high moods: the scornful bride, the wronged woman whose hatred drives her to murder, the penitent wife who when rebuffed by the man she does *not* love, commits suicide. The only clear-headed person in the play is Melantius: successful officer, romantic friend, with a clear boyish code of honor which makes him the refuge of complicated ladies and worldly gentlemen. The play is set off with a marriage masque and delicate songs sung by a fragile lady who is dying of love. These clever young men did indeed "understand the conversation of gentlemen." Their play with its problems of a society-world has many modern counterparts and invites the reader with a sense that it is all familiar while many a better play goes dusty and unread. But the *Maid's Tragedy* has none of that large sense of life and courage to take it in the raw which mark the majority of Elizabethan plays.

Dekker's *Shoemaker's Holiday,* written in 1599 when the old Queen had still three years to live, comes out of the heart of the Elizabethan world on its obvious gay side. It is based on a popular middle-class novel about a master shoemaker who becomes a Lord Mayor, and a Lord Mayor's daughter who marries a titled gentleman after a rough course of true love. It has no poignant melodrama, no satiric comedy, for the social foibles are too gently handled and their purpose is decorative, not corrective. It does not belong among the romantic comedies, for the people and events are too commonplace. Perhaps the real secret of its popularity is this: that in the midst of everyday London, with its plainness and hardness, the obstacles and defeats of real life are finally removed. Things happen as they should happen, not as they do happen. Life's tyranny is relaxed in *The Shoemaker's Holiday,* and life as they dreamed it actually goes forward in the midst of flowers and sunshine and jollity.

The narrative form of story which was the immediate source of a great number of Elizabethan plays, was changed into drama because the vivid sense in that age of action and reflection running together in life made drama the only fit vehicle for its transmission. But even in the best examples of Elizabethan dramatic technique, there lingers, often to the detriment of the effect, some remnant of the story-telling emphasis. In Massinger's *A New Way to Pay Old Debts,* written when the seventeenth century was a quarter over, the story-telling emphasis is so strong that it practically spoils the piece as a play. *A New Way* should have been an eighteenth century novel. The qualities which have made it a hardy perennial on the stage ever since it was written are the qualities of a good story rather than a play. Massinger thought his Overreach was a sinister villain of the type of Jonson's Volpone or Webster's Cardinal but such a character was far from his ability to create and far from his taste, for that matter. The story revolves around two country families of rank from Nottinghamshire whose fortune and estates have been or are about to be taken from them by a merchant-extortioner, Sir Giles Overreach. His sharp practice, greed and feeling of inferiority which comes out in a desire to make the gentle suffer, are hackneyed vices bestowed upon the shadow of a villain. Sir Giles is a necessary evil in a story where a sentimental widow marries the neighboring squire; a proud young man reduced to beggary gets his land again and all live happily. The villain, Overreach, goes mad for his vices but it is a very tame madness. The country servants, old houses and parks, family coaches rumbling along the muddy roads, the village ale-house with its bawdy practice are like an eighteenth century setting. The moral chat, too, suggests comparison with those reflective introductions to the chapters of Fielding.

In fact if Massinger had been able to put into prose paragraphs his comment upon character and situation, his story would have had distinction. His peculiar gift for generalizing upon life finds no appropriate place in his play. It falls flat in the mouths of characters who should be about their dramatic business of acting or reflecting upon the scene. But the tyranny of dramatic form imposed itself upon artists who did not see life dramatically. Massinger could not illumine the meaning of existence by the lightning flash of a stage moment. He had a valid emphasis for his presentation of life but the dramatic frame set off his picture badly.

In any series of Elizabethan plays, even when it is chosen for variety and range, there is amid diversity in form, matter and personality of the author, a kind of integrity which marks them all. It is awareness of the indestructible essence of life, incalculable, cruel or unbearably beautiful, revealed in both exotic and commonplace circumstances. No period in English literature, before or since, has been obsessed by this quality in the same immediate and simple way. It dwarfed individuality while it emphasized the individual as the object most full of this precious essence. Even failure and wickedness became incidents in the revelation of life.

Esther Cloudman Dunn

Smith College
April 1932

THE TRAGICAL HISTORY OF
DOCTOR FAUSTUS

by

CHRISTOPHER MARLOWE

[PERSONS IN THE PLAY

CHORUS
DOCTOR FAUSTUS
WAGNER, *his Servant*
GOOD, *and* EVIL ANGEL
VALDES *and* CORNELIUS, *Conjurors*
Three Scholars
MEPHISTOPHILIS, *a Devil*
THE CLOWN
BALIOL, BELCHER, LUCIFER, BELZEBUB *and Other Devils*
THE SEVEN DEADLY SINS
THE POPE
CARDINAL OF LORRAIN
FRIARS
ROBIN, *the Ostler*
RAFE
A VINTNER
THE EMPEROR
A KNIGHT *and Attendants*
SPIRITS OF ALEXANDER *and his* PARAMOUR
A HORSE-COURSER
THE DUKE *of* VANHOLT *and his* DUCHESS
AN OLD MAN
The Spirit of HELEN OF TROY

SCENE: Mainly the Study of Doctor Faustus; otherwise a Grove, the Pope's Privy-Chamber at Rome, the Courts of the Emperor and the Duke of Vanholt and elsewhere.]

THE TRAGICAL HISTORY OF DOCTOR FAUSTUS

Enter CHORUS

Chorus. Not marching now in fields of Trasimene,
Where Mars did mate the Carthaginians;
Nor sporting in the dalliance of love,
In courts of kings where state is overturned;
Nor in the pomp of proud audacious deeds,
Intends our Muse to vaunt his heavenly verse:
Only this, gentlemen—we must perform
The form of Faustus' fortunes, good or bad;
To patient judgments we appeal our plaud,
And speak for Faustus in his infancy.
Now is he born, his parents base of stock,
In Germany, within a town called Rhodes;
Of riper years to Wittenberg he went,
Whereas his kinsmen chiefly brought him up.
So soon he profits in divinity,
The fruitful plot of scholarism graced,
That shortly he was graced with doctor's name,
Excelling all whose sweet delight disputes
In heavenly matters of theology;
Till swollen with cunning, of a self-conceit,
His waxen wings did mount above his reach,
And, melting, heavens conspired his overthrow;
For, falling to a devilish exercise,
And glutted now with learning's golden gifts,
He surfeits upon cursèd necromancy.
Nothing so sweet as magic is to him,

Which he prefers before his chiefest bliss.
And this the man that in his study sits!

Exit

[SCENE I]

Enter FAUSTUS *in his Study*

Faust. Settle thy studies, Faustus, and begin
To sound the depth of that thou wilt profess;
Having commenced, be a divine in show,
Yet level at the end of every art,
And live and die in Aristotle's works.
Sweet Analytics, 'tis thou hast ravished me—

[*Reads*]

Bene dissere est finis logices.
Is to dispute well logic's chiefest end?
Affords this art no greater miracle?
Then read no more, thou hast attained the end;
A greater subject fitteth Faustus' wit:
Bid ὄν καὶ μὴ ὄν farewell; Galen come,
Seeing *Ubi desinit philosophus ibi incipit medicus;*
Be a physician, Faustus, heap up gold,
And be eternized for some wondrous cure.

[*Reads*]

Summum bonum medicinæ sanitas,
The end of physic is our body's health.
Why, Faustus, hast thou not attained that end?
Is not thy common talk sound aphorisms?
Are not thy bills hung up as monuments,
Whereby whole cities have escaped the plague,
And thousand desperate maladies been eased?
Yet art thou still but Faustus and a man.
Wouldst thou make men to live eternally,
Or, being dead, raise them to life again,
Then this profession were to be esteemed.
Physic, farewell.—Where is Justinian?

[*Reads*]

Si una eademque res legatur duobus, alter rem, alter valorem rei, etc.

A pretty case of paltry legacies!

[*Reads*]

Exhæreditare filium non potest pater nisi, etc.

Such is the subject of the Institute
And universal body of the law.
His study fits a mercenary drudge,
Who aims at nothing but external trash;
Too servile and illiberal for me.
When all is done divinity is best;
Jerome's Bible, Faustus, view it well.

[*Reads*]

Stipendium peccati mors est. Ha! *Stipendium,* etc.
The reward of sin is death. That's hard

[*Reads*]

Si peccasse negamus, fallimur, et nulla est in nobis veritas.
If we say that we have no sin we deceive ourselves, and there's no truth in us. Why, then, belike we must sin, and so consequently die.
Ay, we must die an everlasting death.
What docrine call you this, *Che sera sera,*
What will be, shall be? Divinity, adieu!
These metaphysics of magicians
And necromantic books are heavenly:
Lines, circles, scenes, letters, and characters:
Ay, these are those that Faustus most desires.
O, what a world of profit and delight,
Of power, of honor, of omnipotence
Is promised to the studious artisan!
All things that move between the quiet poles
Shall be at my command: emperors and kings
Are but obeyèd in their several provinces,
Nor can they raise the wind or rend the clouds;
But his dominion that exceeds in this

Stretcheth as far as doth the mind of man,
A sound magician is a mighty god:
Here, Faustus, try thy brains to gain a deity.
Wagner!

Enter WAGNER

Commend me to my dearest friends,
The German Valdes and Cornelius;
Request them earnestly to visit me.

Wag. I will, sir. *Exit*

Faust. Their conference will be a greater help to me
Than all my labors, plod I ne'er so fast.

Enter the Good Angel *and the* Evil Angel

G. Ang. O Faustus! lay that damnèd book aside,
And gaze not on it lest it tempt thy soul,
And heap God's heavy wrath upon thy head.
Read, read the Scriptures: that is blasphemy.

E. Ang. Go forward, Faustus, in that famous art,
Wherein all Nature's treasure is contained:
Be thou on earth as Jove is in the sky,
Lord and commander of these elements.
Exeunt [Angels]

Faust. How am I glutted with conceit of this!
Shall I make spirits fetch me what I please,
Resolve me of all ambiguities,
Perform what desperate enterprise I will?
I'll have them fly to India for gold,
Ransack the ocean for orient pearl,
And search all corners of the new-found world
For pleasant fruits and princely delicates;
I'll have them read me strange philosophy
And tell the secrets of all foreign kings;
I'll have them wall all Germany with brass,
And make swift Rhine circle fair Wittenberg,
I'll have them fill the public schools with silk,

Wherewith the students shall be bravely clad;
I'll levy soldiers with the coin they bring,
And chase the Prince of Parma from our land,
And reign sole king of all the provinces;
Yea, stranger engines for the brunt of war
Than was the fiery keel at Antwerp's bridge,
I'll make my servile spirits to invent.

Enter VALDES *and* CORNELIUS

Come, German Valdes and Cornelius,
And make me blest with your sage conference.
Valdes, sweet Valdes, and Cornelius,
Know that your words have won me at the last
To practise magic and concealèd arts:
Yet not your words only, but mine own fantasy
That will receive no object; for my head
But ruminates on necromantic skill.
Philosophy is odious and obscure,
Both law and physic are for petty wits;
Divinity is basest of the three,
Unpleasant, harsh, contemptible, and vile:
'Tis magic, magic that hath ravished me.
Then, gentle friends, aid me in this attempt;
And I that have with concise syllogisms
Gravelled the pastors of the German church,
And made the flowering pride of Wittenberg
Swarm to my problems, as the infernal spirits
On sweet Musæus, when he came to hell,
Will be as cunning as Agrippa was,
Whose shadows made all Europe honor him.

Vald. Faustus, these books, thy wit, and our experience
Shall make all nations to canònize us.
As Indian Moors obey their Spanish lords,
So shall the spirits of every element
Be always serviceable to us three;
Like lions shall they guard us when we please;

Like Almain rutters with their horsemen's staves
Or Lapland giants, trotting by our sides;
Sometimes like women or unwedded maids,
Shadowing more beauty in their airy brows
Than have the white breasts of the queen of love:
From Venice shall they drag huge argosies,
And from America the golden fleece
That yearly stuffs old Philip's treasury;
If learnèd Faustus will be resolute.

Faust. Valdes, as resolute am I in this
As thou to live; therefore object it not.

Corn. The miracles that magic will perform
Will make thee vow to study nothing else.
He that is grounded in astrology,
Enriched with tongues, well seen in minerals,
Hath all the principles magic doth require.
Then doubt not, Faustus, but to be renowned,
And more frequented for this mystery
Than heretofore the Delphian Oracle.
The spirits tell me they can dry the sea,
And fetch the treasure of all foreign wracks,
Ay, all the wealth that our forefathers hid
Within the massy entrails of the earth;
Then tell me, Faustus, what shall we three want?

Faust. Nothing, Cornelius! O, this cheers my soul!
Come show me some demonstrations magical,
That I may conjure in some lusty grove,
And have these joys in full possession.

Vald. Then haste thee to some solitary grove,
And bear wise Bacon's and Albanus' works,
The Hebrew Psalter and New Testament;
And whatsoever else is requisite
We will inform thee ere our conference cease.

Corn. Valdes, first let him know the words of art;
And then, all other ceremonies learned,
Faustus may try his cunning by himself.

Vald. First I'll instruct thee in the rudiments,
And then wilt thou be perfecter than I.

Faust. Then come and dine with me, and after meat,
We'll canvass every quiddity thereof;
For ere I sleep I'll try what I can do:
This night I'll conjure tho' I die therefore.

Exeunt

[SCENE II]

[*Before Faustus' House*]

Enter two Scholars

1 *Schol.* I wonder what's become of Faustus that was wont to make our schools ring with *sic probo?*

2 *Schol.* That shall we know, for see here comes his boy.

Enter WAGNER

1 *Schol.* How now, sirrah! Where's thy master?

Wag. God in heaven knows!

2 *Schol.* Why, dost not thou know?

Wag. Yes, I know. But that follows not.

1 *Schol.* Go to, sirrah! leave your jesting, and tell us where he is.

Wag. That follows not necessary by force of argument, that you, being licentiate, should stand upon't: therefore acknowledge your error and be attentive.

2 *Schol.* Why, didst thou not say thou knewest?

Wag. Have you any witness on't?

1 *Schol.* Yes, sirrah, I heard you.

Wag. Ask my fellow if I be a thief.

2 *Schol.* Well, you will not tell us?

Wag. Yes, sir, I will tell you; yet if you were not dunces, you would never ask me such a question; for is not he *corpus naturale?* and is not that *mobile?* then wherefore should you ask me such a question? But that I am by nature phlegmatic, slow to wrath, and prone to lechery (to love, I would say), it were not for you to come within forty feet of the place of execution, although I do not doubt to see you both hanged the next sessions. Thus having triumphed over you, I will set my countenance like a precisian, and begin to speak thus: Truly, my dear brethren, my master is within at dinner, with Valdes and Cornelius, as this wine, if it could speak, would inform your worships; and so the Lord bless you, preserve you, and keep you, my dear brethren, my dear brethren.

Exit

1 *Schol.* Nay, then, I fear he has fallen into that damned art, for which they two are infamous through the world.

2 *Schol.* Were he a stranger, and not allied to me, yet should I grieve for him. But come, let us go and inform the rector, and see if he by his grave counsel can reclaim him.

1 *Schol.* O, but I fear me nothing can reclaim him.

2 *Schol.* Yet let us try what we can do.

Exeunt

[SCENE III]

Enter FAUSTUS *to conjure* [*in a grove*]

Faust. Now that the gloomy shadow of the earth
Longing to view Orion's drizzling look,
Leaps from the antarctic world unto the sky,
And dims the welkin with her pitchy breath,
Faustus, begin thine incantations,
And try if devils will obey thy hest,
Seeing thou hast prayed and sacrificed to them.
Within this circle is Jehovah's name,
Forward and backward anagrammatized,
The breviated names of holy saints,
Figures of every adjunct to the heavens,
And characters of signs and erring stars,
By which the spirits are enforced to rise:
Then fear not, Faustus, but be resolute,

And try the uttermost magic can perform.
Sint mihi dei Acherontis propitii! Valeat numen triplex Jehovæ! Ignei, aerii, aquatani spiritus, salvete! Orientis princeps Belzebub, inferni ardentis monarcha, et Demogorgon, propitiamus vos, ut appareat et surgate Mephistophilis. Quid tu moraris? per Jehovam, Gehennam, et consecratam aquam quam nunc spargo, signumque crucis quod nunc facio, et per vota nostra, ipse nunc surgat nobis dicatus Mephistophilis!

Enter [MEPHISTOPHILIS,] *a Devil*

I charge thee to return and change thy shape;
Thou art too ugly to attend on me.
Go, and return an old Franciscan friar;
That holy shape becomes a devil best.

Exit DEVIL

I see there's virtue in my heavenly words;
Who would not be proficient in this art?
How pliant is this Mephistophilis,
Full of obedience and humility!
Such is the force of magic and my spells:
Now, Faustus, thou are conjuror laureat,
That canst command great Mephistophilis:
Quin regis Mephistophilis fratris imagine.

Enter MEPHISTOPHILIS [*like a Franciscan Friar*]

Meph. Now, Faustus, what would'st thou have me to do?
Faust. I charge thee wait upon me whilst I live,
To do whatever Faustus shall command,
Be it to make the moon drop from her sphere,
Or the ocean to overwhelm the world.
Meph. I am a servant to great Lucifer,
And may not follow thee without his leave:
No more than he commands must we perform.
Faust. Did not he charge thee to appear to me?
Meph. No, I came hither of mine own accord.

Faust. Did not my conjuring speeches raise thee? Speak.
Meph. That was the cause, but yet *per accidens;*
For when we hear one rack the name of God,
Abjure the Scriptures and his Saviour Christ,
We fly in hope to get his glorious soul;
Nor will we come, unless he use such means
Whereby he is in danger to be damned:
Therefore the shortest cut for conjuring
Is stoutly to abjure the Trinity,
And pray devoutly to the Prince of Hell.
Faust. So Faustus hath
Already done; and holds this principle,
There is no chief, but only Belzebub,
To whom Faustus doth dedicate himself.
This word "damnation" terrifies not him,
For he confounds hell in Elysium;
His ghost be with the old philosophers!
But, leaving these vain trifles of men's souls,
Tell me what is that Lucifer thy lord?
Meph. Arch-regent and commander of all spirits.
Faust. Was not that Lucifer an angel once?
Meph. Yes, Faustus, and most dearly loved of God.
Faust. How comes it then that he is prince of devils?
Meph. O, by aspiring pride and insolence;
For which God threw him from the face of heaven.
Faust. And what are you that live with Lucifer?
Meph. Unhappy spirits that fell with Lucifer,
Conspired against our God with Lucifer,
And are for ever damned with Lucifer.
Faust. Where are you damned?
Meph. In hell.
Faust. How comes it then that thou are out of hell?
Meph. Why this is hell, nor am I out of it:
Think'st thou that I who saw the face of God,
And tasted the eternal joys of heaven,
Am not tormented with ten thousand hells,

In being deprived of everlasting bliss?
O Faustus! leave these frivolous demands,
Which strike a terror to my fainting soul.
Faust. What, is great Mephistophilis so passionate
For being deprivèd of the joys of heaven?
Learn thou of Faustus manly fortitude,
And scorn those joys thou never shalt possess.
Go bear these tidings to great Lucifer:
Seeing Faustus hath incurred eternal death
By desperate thoughts against Jove's deity,
Say he surrenders up to him his soul,
So he will spare him four and twenty years,
Letting him live in all voluptuousness;
Having thee ever to attend on me;
To give me whatsoever I shall ask,
To tell me whatsoever I demand,
To slay mine enemies, and aid my friends,
And always be obedient to my will.
Go and return to mighty Lucifer,
And meet me in my study at midnight,
And then resolve me of thy master's mind.
Meph. I will, Faustus. *Exit*
Faust. Had I as many souls as there be stars,
I'd give them all for Mephistophilis.
By him I'll be great Emperor of the world,
And make a bridge thorough the moving air,
To pass the ocean with a band of men:
I'll join the hills that bind the Afric shore,
And make that country continent to Spain,
And both contributory to my crown.
The Emperor shall not live but by my leave,
Nor any potentate of Germany.
Now that I have obtained what I desire,
I'll live in speculation of this art
Till Mephistophilis return again. *Exit*

[SCENE IV]

[*Before* FAUSTUS' *house*]

Enter WAGNER *and* CLOWN

Wag. Sirrah, boy, come hither.

Clown. How, boy! Swowns, boy! I hope you have seen many boys with such pickadevaunts as I have; boy, quotha.

Wag. Tell me, sirrah, hast thou any comings in?

Clown. Ay, and goings out too. You may see else.

Wag. Alas, poor slave! see how poverty jesteth in his nakedness! The villain is bare and out of service, and so hungry that I know he would give his soul to the Devil for a shoulder of mutton though 'twere blood-raw.

Clown. How? My soul to the Devil for a shoulder of mutton, though 'twere blood-raw! Not so, good friend. By'r-lady, I had need have it well roasted and good sauce to it, if I pay so dear.

Wag. Well, wilt thou serve me, and I'll make thee go like *Qui mihi discipulus?*

Clown. How, in verse?

Wag. No, sirrah; in beaten silk and stavesacre.

Clown. How, how, Knave's acre! Ay, I thought that was all the land his father left him. Do you hear? I would be sorry to rob you of your living.

Wag. Sirrah, I say in stavesacre.

Clown. Oho! Oho! Stavesacre! Why then belike if I were your man I should be full of vermin.

Wag. So thou shalt, whether thou beest with me or no. But, sirrah, leave your jesting, and bind yourself presently unto me for seven years, or I'll turn all the lice about thee into familiars, and they shall tear thee in pieces.

Clown. Do you hear, sir? You may save that labor: they are too familiar with me already: swowns! they are as bold with my flesh as if they had paid for their meat and drink.

Wag. Well, do you hear, sirrah? Hold, take these guilders. [*Gives money*]

Clown. Gridirons! what be they?

Wag. Why, French crowns.

Clown. Mass, but in the name of French crowns, a man were as good have as many English counters. And what should I do with these?

Wag. Why, now, sirrah, thou art at an hour's warning, whensoever and wheresoever the Devil shall fetch thee.

Clown. No, no. Here, take your gridirons again.

Wag. Truly I'll none of them.

Clown. Truly but you shall.

Wag. Bear witness I gave them him.

Clown. Bear witness I give them you again.

Wag. Well, I will cause two devils presently to fetch thee away—Baliol and Belcher!

Clown. Let your Baliol and your Belcher come here, and I'll knock them, they were never so knocked since they were devils! Say I should kill one of them, what would folks say? "Do you see yonder tall fellow in the round slop—he has killed the devil." So I should be called Kill-devil all the parish over.

Enter two Devils: *the* Clown *runs up and down crying*

Wag. Baliol and Belcher! Spirits, away!

Exeunt [Devils]

Clown. What, are they gone? A vengeance on them, they have vile long nails! There was a he-devil, and a she-devil! I'll tell you how you shall know them; all he-devils has horns, and all she-devils has clifts and cloven feet.

Wag. Well, sirrah, follow me.

Clown. But, do you hear—if I should serve you, would you teach me to raise up Banios and Belcheos?

Wag. I will teach thee to turn thyself to anything; to a dog, or a cat, or a mouse, or a rat, or anything.

Clown. How! a Christian fellow to a dog or a cat, a mouse

or a rat! No, no, sir. If you turn me into anything, let it be in the likeness of a little pretty frisking flea, that I may be here and there and everywhere. O, I'll tickle the pretty wenches' plackets; I'll be amongst them, i' faith.

Wag. Well, sirrah, come.

Clown. But, do you hear, Wagner?

Wag. How! Baliol and Belcher!

Clown. O Lord! I pray, sir, let Banio and Belcher go sleep.

Wag. Villain—call me Master Wagner, and let thy eye be diametarily fixed upon my right heel, with *quasi vestigiis nostris insistere.*

Exit

Clown. God forgive me, he speaks Dutch fustian. Well, I'll follow him: I'll serve him, that's flat. *Exit*

[SCENE V]

Enter FAUSTUS *in his Study*

Faust. Now, Faustus, must
Thou needs be damned, and canst thou not be saved:
What boots it then to think of God or heaven?
Away with such vain fancies, and despair:
Despair in God, and trust in Belzebub;
Now go not backward: no, Faustus, be resolute:
Why waver'st thou? O, something soundeth in mine ears
"Abjure this magic, turn to God again!"
Ay, and Faustus will turn to God again.
To God?—He loves thee not—
The God thou serv'st is thine own appetite,
Wherein is fixed the love of Belzebub;
To him I'll build an altar and a church,
And offer lukewarm blood of new-born babes.

Enter GOOD ANGEL *and* EVIL

G. Ang. Sweet Faustus, leave that execrable art.

Faust. Contrition, prayer, repentance! What of them?

G. Ang. O, they are means to bring thee unto heaven.

E. Ang. Rather, illusions—fruits of lunacy,
That makes men foolish that do trust them most.

G. Ang. Sweet Faustus, think of heaven and heavenly things.

E. Ang. No, Faustus, think of honor and of wealth.

Exeunt [Angels]

Faust. Of wealth!
Why the signiory of Embden shall be mine.
When Mephistophilis shall stand by me,
What God can hurt thee? Faustus, thou are safe:
Cast no more doubts. Come, Mephistophilis,
And bring glad tidings from great Lucifer;
Is't not midnight? Come, Mephistophilis;
Veni, veni, Mephistophile!

Enter MEPHISTOPHILIS

Now tell me, what says Lucifer, thy lord?

Meph. That I shall wait on Faustus whilst he lives,
So he will buy my service with his soul.

Faust. Already Faustus hath hazarded that for thee.

Meph. But, Faustus, thou must bequeath it solemnly,
And write a deed of gift with thine own blood,
For that security craves great Lucifer.
If thou deny it, I will back to hell.

Faust. Stay, Mephistophilis! and tell me what good
Will my soul do thy lord.

Meph. Enlarge his kingdom.

Faust. Is that the reason why he tempts us thus?

Meph. *Solamen miseris socios habuisse doloris.*

Faust. Why, have you any pain that tortures others?

Meph. As great as have the human souls of men.
But tell me, Faustus, shall I have thy soul?
And I will be thy slave, and wait on thee,
And give thee more than thou hast wit to ask.

Faust. Ay, Mephistophilis, I give it thee.
Meph. Then, Faustus, stab thine arm courageously,
And bind thy soul that at some certain day
Great Lucifer may claim it as his own;
And then be thou as great as Lucifer.
Faust. [*stabbing his arm*] Lo, Mephistophilis, for love of thee,
I cut mine arm, and with my proper blood
Assure my soul to be great Lucifer's,
Chief lord and regent of perpetual night!
View here the blood that trickles from mine arm,
And let it be propitious for my wish.
Meph. But, Faustus, thou must
Write it in manner of a deed of gift.
Faust. Ay, so I will. [*Writes*] But, Mephistophilis,
My blood congeals, and I can write no more.
Meph. I'll fetch thee fire to dissolve it straight.
Exit
Faust. What might the staying of my blood portend?
Is it unwilling I should write this bill?
Why streams it not that I may write afresh?
Faustus gives to thee his soul. Ah, there it stayed.
Why should'st thou not? Is not thy soul thine own?
Then write again, *Faustus gives to thee his soul.*

Enter MEPHISTOPHILIS *with a chafer of coals*

Meph. Here's fire. Come, Faustus, set it on.
Faust. So now the blood begins to clear again;
Now will I make an end immediately. [*Writes*]
Meph. O, what will not I do to obtain his soul.
[*Aside*]
Faust. *Consummatum est:* this bill is ended,
And Faustus hath bequeathed his soul to Lucifer.
But what is this inscription on mine arm?
Homo, fuge! Whither should I fly?
If unto God, he'll throw me down to hell.

My senses are deceived; here's nothing writ—
I see it plain; here in this place is writ
Homo, fuge! Yet shall not Faustus fly.
Meph. I'll fetch him somewhat to delight his mind.
Exit

Enter MEPHISTOPHILIS *with* DEVILS, *giving crowns and rich apparel to* FAUSTUS, *and dance, and then depart*

Faust. Speak, Mephistophilis, what means this show?
Meph. Nothing, Faustus, but to delight thy mind withal,
And to show thee what magic can perform.
Faust. But may I raise up spirits when I please?
Meph. Ay, Faustus, and do greater things than these.
Faust. Then there's enough for a thousand souls.
Here, Mephistophilis, receive this scroll,
A deed of gift of body and of soul:
But yet conditionally that thou perform
All articles prescribed between us both.
Meph. Faustus, I swear by hell and Lucifer
To effect all promises between us made.

Faust. Then hear me read them: *On these conditions following. First, that Faustus may be a spirit in form and substance. Secondly, that Mephistophilis shall be his servant, and at his command. Thirdly, that Mephistophilis shall do for him and bring him whatsoever. Fourthly, that he shall be in his chamber or house invisible. Lastly that he shall appear to the said John Faustus, at all times, in what form or shape soever he please. I, John Faustus, of Wittenberg, Doctor, by these presents do give both body and soul to Lucifer, Prince of the East, and his minister, Mephistophilis: and furthermore grant unto them, that twenty-four years being expired, the articles above written inviolate, full power to fetch or carry the said John Faustus, body and soul, flesh, blood, or goods, into their habitation wheresoever. By me,*
John Faustus.

Meph. Speak, Faustus, do you deliver this as your deed?

Faust. Ay, take it, and the Devil give thee good on't!

Meph. Now, Faustus, ask what thou wilt.

Faust. First will I question with thee about hell.
Tell me where is the place that men call hell?

Meph. Under the heavens.

Faust. Ay, but whereabout?

Meph. Within the bowels of these elements,
Where we are tortured and remain for ever;
Hell hath no limits, nor is circumscibed
In one self place; for where we are is hell,
And where hell is there must we ever be:
And, to conclude, when all the world dissolves,
And every creature shall be purified,
All places shall be hell that is not heaven.

Faust. Come, I think hell's a fable.

Meph. Ay, think so still, till experience change thy mind.

Faust. Why, think'st thou then that Faustus shall be damned?

Meph. Ay, of necessity, for here's the scroll
Wherein thou hast given thy soul to Lucifer.

Faust. Ay, and body too; but what of that?
Think'st thou that Faustus is so fond to imagine
That, after this life, there is any pain?
Tush; these are trifles, and mere old wives' tales.

Meph. But, Faustus, I am an instance to prove the contrary.
For I am damnèd, and am now in hell.

Faust. How! now in hell?
Nay, an this be hell, I'll willingly be damnèd here;
What? walking, disputing, etc.?
But, leaving off this, let me have a wife,
The fairest maid in Germany;
For I am wanton and lascivious,
And cannot live without a wife.

Meph. How—a wife?

I prithee, Faustus, talk not of a wife.

Faust. Nay, sweet Mephistophilis, fetch me one, for I will have one.

Meph. Well—thou wilt have one. Sit there till I come: I'll fetch thee a wife in the Devil's name.

Exit

Re-enter MEPHISTOPHILIS *with a* DEVIL *dressed like a woman, with fireworks*

Meph. Tell me, Faustus, how dost thou like thy wife?

Faust. A plague on her for a hot whore!

Meph. Tut, Faustus,
Marriage is but a ceremonial toy;
And if thou lovest me, think no more of it.
I'll cull thee out the fairest courtesans,
And bring them every morning to thy bed;
She whom thine eye shall like, thy heart shall have,
Be she as chaste as was Penelope,
And as wise as Saba, or as beautiful
As was bright Lucifer before his fall.
Here, take this book, peruse it thoroughly:

[*Gives a book*]

The iterating of these lines brings gold;
The framing of this circle on the ground
Brings whirlwinds, tempests, thunder and lightning;
Pronounce this thrice devoutly to thyself,
And men in armor shall appear to thee,
Ready to execute what thou desir'st.

Faust. Thanks, Mephistophilis; yet fain would I have a book wherein I might behold all spells and incantations, that I might raise up spirits when I please.

Meph. Here they are, in this book.

There turn to them

Faust. Now would I have a book where I might see all characters and planets of the heavens, that I might know their motions and dispositions.

Meph. Here they are too.

Turn to them

Faust. Nay, let me have one book more—and then I have done—wherein I might see all plants, herbs, and trees that grow upon the earth.

Meph. Here they be.

Faust. O, thou art deceived.

Meph. Tut, I warrant thee.

Turn to them. [*Exeunt*]

[SCENE VI]

Enter FAUSTUS *in his Study, and* MEPHISTOPHILIS

Faust. When I behold the heavens, then I repent,
And curse thee, wicked Mephistophilis,
Because thou hast deprived me of those joys.

Meph. Why, Faustus,
Think'st thou heaven is such a glorious thing?
I tell thee 'tis not half so fair as thou,
Or any man that breathes on earth.

Faust. How prov'st thou that?

Meph. 'Twas made for man, therefore is man more excellent

Faust. If it were made for man, 'twas made for me; I will renounce this magic and repent.

Enter GOOD ANGEL *and* EVIL ANGEL

G. Ang Faustus, repent; yet God will pity thee.

E. Ang. Thou art a spirit; God cannot pity thee.

Faust. Who buzzeth in my ears I am a spirit?
Be I a devil, yet God may pity me;
Ay, God will pity me if I repent.

E. Ang. Ay, but Faustus never shall repent.

Exeunt [Angels]

Faust. My heart's so hardened I cannot repent.

Scarce can I name salvation, faith, or heaven,
But fearful echoes thunder in mine ears
"Faustus, thou are damned!" Then swords and knives,
Poison, gun, halters, and envenomed steel
Are laid before me to dispatch myself,
And long ere this I should have slain myself,
Had not sweet pleasure conquered deep despair.
Have not I made blind Homer sing to me
Of Alexander's love and Œnon's death?
And hath not he that built the walls of Thebes
With ravishing sound of his melodious harp,
Made music with my Mephistophilis?
Why should I die then, or basely despair?
I am resolved: Faustus shall ne'er repent—
Come, Mephistophilis, let us dispute again,
And argue of divine astrology.
Tell me, are there many heavens above the moon?
Are all celestial bodies but one globe,
As is the substance of this centric earth?

Meph. As are the elements, such are the spheres
Mutually folded in each other's orb,
And, Faustus,
All jointly move upon one axle-tree
Whose terminine is termed the world's wide pole;
Nor are the names of Saturn, Mars, or Jupiter
Feigned, but are erring stars.

Faust. But tell me, have they all one motion both, *situ et tempore?*

Meph. All jointly move from east to west in twenty-four hours upon the poles of the world; but differ in their motion upon the poles of the zodiac.

Faust. Tush!
These slender trifles Wagner can decide;
Hath Mephistophilis no greater skill?
Who knows not the double motion of the planets?
The first is finished in a natural day;

The second thus: as Saturn in thirty years; Jupiter in twelve; Mars in four; the Sun, Venus, and Mercury in a year; the moon in twenty-eight days. Tush, these are freshmen's suppositions. But tell me, hath every sphere a dominion or *intelligentia?*

Meph. Ay.

Faust. How many heavens, or spheres, are there?

Meph. Nine: the seven planets, the firmament, and the empyreal heaven.

Faust. Well, resolve me in this question: Why have we not conjunctions, oppositions, aspects, eclipses, all at one time, but in some years we have more, in some less?

Meph. Per inœqualem motum respectu totius.

Faust. Well, I am answered. Tell me who made the world.

Meph. I will not.

Faust. Sweet Mephistophilis, tell me.

Meph. Move me not, for I will not tell thee.

Faust. Villain, have I not bound thee to tell me anything?

Meph. Ay, that is not against our kingdom; but this is. Think thou on hell, Faustus, for thou art damned.

Faust. Think, Faustus, upon God that made the world.

Meph. Remember this.

Exit

Faust. Ay, go, accursèd spirit, to ugly hell.
'Tis thou hast damned distressèd Faustus' soul.
Is't not too late?

Enter GOOD ANGEL *and* EVIL ANGEL

E. Ang. Too late.

G. Ang. Never too late, if Faustus can repent.

E. Ang. If thou repent, devils shall tear thee in pieces.

G. Ang. Repent, and they shall never raze thy skin.

Exeunt [Angels]

Faust. Ah, Christ my Saviour,
Seek to save distressèd Faustus' soul!

Enter LUCIFER, BELZEBUB, *and* MEPHISTOPHILIS

Luc. Christ cannot save thy soul, for he is just;
There's none but I have interest in the same.
Faust. O, who art thou that look'st so terrible?
Luc. I am Lucifer,
And this is my companion-prince in hell.
Faust. O Faustus! they are come to fetch away thy soul!
Luc. We come to tell thee thou dost injure us;
Thou talk'st of Christ contrary to thy promise;
Thou should'st not think of God: think of the Devil.
Belz. And his dam, too.
Faust. Nor will I henceforth: pardon me in this,
And Faustus vows never to look to heaven,
Never to name God, or to pray to him,
To burn his Scriptures, slay his ministers,
And make my spirits pull his churches down.
Luc. Do so and we will highly gratify thee. Faustus, we are come from hell to show thee some pastime: sit down, and thou shalt see all the Seven Deadly Sins appear in their proper shapes.
Faust. That sight will be as pleasing unto me,
As Paradise was to Adam the first day
Of his creation.
Luc. Talk not of Paradise nor creation, but mark this show: talk of the Devil, and nothing else: come away!

Enter the SEVEN DEADLY SINS

Now, Faustus, examine them of their several names and dispositions.
Faust. What art thou—the first?
Pride. I am Pride. I disdain to have any parents. I am like to Ovid's flea: I can creep into every corner of a

wench; sometimes, like a periwig, I sit upon her brow; or like a fan of feathers, I kiss her lips; indeed I do—what do I not? But, fie, what a scent is here! I'll not speak another word, except the ground were perfumed, and covered with cloth of arras.

Faust. What art thou—the second?

Covet. I am Covetousness, begotten of an old churl in an old leathern bag; and, might I have my wish, I would desire that this house and all the people in it were turned to gold, that I might lock you up in my good chest. O, my sweet gold!

Faust. What art thou—the third?

Wrath. I am Wrath. I had neither father nor mother; I leapt out of a lion's mouth when I was scarce half an hour old; and ever since I have run up and down the world with this case of rapiers, wounding myself when I had nobody to fight withal. I was born in hell; and look to it, for some of you shall be my father.

Faust. What art thou—the fourth?

Envy. I am Envy, begotten of a chimney-sweeper and an oyster-wife. I cannot read, and therefore wish all books were burnt. I am lean with seeing others eat. O, that there would come a famine through all the world, that all might die, and I live alone! then thou should'st see how fat I would be. But must thou sit and I stand! Come down with a vengeance!

Faust. Away, envious rascal! What art thou—the fifth?

Glut. Who, I, sir? I am Gluttony. My parents are all dead, and the devil a penny they have left me, but a bare pension, and that is thirty meals a day and ten bevers—a small trifle to suffice nature. O, I come of a royal parentage! My grandfather was a Gammon of Bacon, my grandmother was a Hogshead of Claret wine; my godfathers were these, Peter Pickle-herring, and Martin Martlemas-beef; O, but my god-mother, she was a jolly gentlewoman, and well beloved in every good town and city; her name was Mistress

Margery March-bee. Now, Faustus, thou hast heard all my progeny, wilt thou bid me to supper?

Faust. No, I'll see thee hanged: thou wilt eat up all my victuals.

Glut. Then the Devil choke thee!

Faust. Choke thyself, glutton! Who art thou—the sixth?

Sloth. I am Sloth. I was begotten on a sunny bank, where I have lain ever since; and you have done me great injury to bring me from thence: let me be carried thither again by Gluttony and Lechery. I'll not speak another word for a king's ransom.

Faust. What are you, Mistress Minx, the seventh and last?

Lechery. Who, I, sir? I am the one that loves an inch of raw mutton better than an ell of fried stock-fish; and the first letter of my name begins with L.

Luc. Away to hell, to hell! *Exeunt the Sins*

Now, Faustus, how dost thou like this?

Faust. O, this feeds my soul!

Luc. Tut, Faustus, in hell is all manner of delight.

Faust. O, might I see hell, and return again,
How happy were I then!

Luc. Thou shalt; I will send for thee at midnight.
In meantime take this book; peruse it throughly,
And thou shalt turn thyself into what shape thou wilt.

Faust. Great thanks, mighty Lucifer!
This will I keep as chary as my life.

Luc. Farewell, Faustus, and think on the Devil.

Faust. Farewell, great Lucifer! Come, Mephistophilis.

Exeunt omnes

Enter WAGNER *solus*

Wag. Learned Faustus,
To know the secrets of astronomy,
Graven in the book of Jove's high firmament,

Did mount himself to scale Olympus' top,
Being seated in a chariot burning bright,
Drawn by the strength of yoky dragons' necks.
He now is gone to prove cosmography,
And, as I guess, will first arrive at Rome,
To see the Pope the manner of his court,
And take some part of holy Peter's feast,
That to this day is highly solemnized.

Exit WAGNER

[SCENE VII]

[*The Privy-Chamber of the Pope*]

Enter FAUSTUS *and* MEPHISTOPHILIS

Faust. Having now, my good Mephistophilis,
Passed with delight the stately town of Trier,
Environed round with airy mountain tops,
With walls of flint, and deep entrenchèd lakes,
Not to be won by any conquering prince;
From Paris next, coasting the realm of France,
We saw the river Maine fall into Rhine,
Whose banks are set with groves of fruitful vines;
Then up to Naples, rich Campania,
Whose buildings fair and gorgeous to the eye,
The streets straight forth, and paved with finest brick,
Quarter the town in four equivalents:
There saw we learned Maro's golden tomb,
The way he cut, an English mile in length,
Thorough a rock of stone in one night's space;
From thence to Venice, Padua, and the rest,
In one of which a sumptuous temple stands,
That threats the stars with her aspiring top.
Thus hitherto has Faustus spent his time:
But tell me, now, what resting-place is this?
Hast thou, as erst I did command,

Conducted me within the walls of Rome?

Meph. Faustus, I have; and because we will not be unprovided, I have taken up his Holiness' privy chamber for our use.

Faust. I hope his Holiness will bid us welcome.

Meph. Tut, 'tis no matter, man, we'll be bold with his good cheer.

And now, my Faustus, that thou may'st perceive
What Rome containeth to delight thee with,
Know that this city stands upon seven hills
That underprop the groundwork of the same:
Just through the midst runs flowing Tiber's stream,
With winding banks that cut it in two parts:
Over the which four stately bridges lean,
That make safe passage to each part of Rome:
Upon the bridge called Ponte Angelo
Erected is a castle passing strong,
Within whose walls such store of ordnance are,
And double cannons framed of carved brass,
As match the days within one complete year;
Besides the gates, and high pyramides,
Which Julius Cæsar brought from Africa.

Faust. Now, by the kingdoms of infernal rule,
Of Styx, of Acheron, and the fiery lake
Of ever-burning Phlegethon, I swear
That I do long to see the monuments
And situation of bright-splendent Rome:
Come, therefore, let's away.

Meph. Nay, Faustus, stay; I know you'd fain see the Pope,
And take some part of holy Peter's feast,
Where thou shalt see a troop of bald-pate friars,
Whose *summum bonum* is in belly-cheer.

Faust. Well, I'm content to compass them some sport,
And by their folly make us merriment.
Then charm me, Mephistophilis, that I

May be invisible, to do what I please
Unseen of any whilst I stay in Rome.

[MEPHISTOPHILIS *charms him*]

Meph. So, Faustus, now
Do what thou wilt, thou shalt not be discerned.

Sound a sennet. Enter the POPE *and the* CARDINAL *of* LORRAIN *to the banquet, with* FRIARS *attending*

Pope. My Lord of Lorrain, wilt please you draw near?

Faust. Fall to, and the devil choke you an you spare!

Pope. How now! Who's that which spake?—Friars, look about.

Friar. Here's nobody, if it like your Holiness.

Pope. My lord, here is a dainty dish was sent me from the Bishop of Milan.

Faust. I thank you, sir. [*Snatches it*]

Pope. How now! Who's that which snatched the meat from me? Will no man look? My Lord, this dish was sent me from the Cardinal of Florence.

Faust. You say true; I'll ha't. [*Snatches the dish*]

Pope. What, again! My lord, I'll drink to your grace.

Faust. I'll pledge your grace. [*Snatches the cup*]

C. of Lor. My Lord, it may be some ghost newly crept out of purgatory, come to beg a pardon of your Holiness.

Pope. It may be so. Friars, prepare a dirge to lay the fury of this ghost. Once again, my lord, fall to.

The POPE *crosseth himself*

Faust. What, are you crossing of yourself?
Well, use that trick no more I would advise you.

Cross again

Well, there's the second time. Aware the third,
I give you fair warning.

Cross again, and FAUSTUS *hits him a box of the ear; and they all run away*

Come on, Mephistophilis, what shall we do?

Meph. Nay, I know not. We shall be cursed with bell, book, and candle.

Faust. How! bell, book, and candle—candle, book, and bell,
Forward and backward to curse Faustus to hell!
Anon you shall hear a hog grunt, a calf bleat, and an ass bray,
Because it is Saint Peter's holiday.

Enter all the FRIARS *to sing the Dirge*

Friar. Come, brethren, let's about our business with good devotion. *Sing this*

Cursed be he that stole away his Holiness' meat from the table! *Maledicat Dominus!*

Cursed be he that struck his Holiness a blow on the face! *Maledicat Dominus!*

Cursed be he that took Friar Sandelo a blow on the pate! *Maledicat Dominus!*

Cursed be he that disturbeth our holy dirge! *Maledicat Dominus!*

Cursed be he that took away his Holiness' wine! *Maledicat Dominus! Et omnes sancti! Amen!*

[MEPHISTOPHILIS *and* FAUSTUS] *beat the* FRIARS, *and fling fireworks among them: and so exeunt*

Enter CHORUS

Chorus. When Faustus had with pleasure ta'en the view
Of rarest things, and royal courts of kings,
He stayed his course, and so returnèd home;
Where such as bear his absence but with grief,
I mean his friends, and near'st companions,
Did gratulate his safety with kind words,
And in their conference of what befell,
Touching his journey through the world and air,

They put forth questions of astrology,
Which Faustus answered with such learnèd skill,
As they admired and wondered at his wit.
Now is his fame spread forth in every land;
Amongst the rest the Emperor is one,
Carolus the Fifth, at whose palace now
Faustus is feasted 'mongst his noblemen.
What there he did in trial of his art,
I leave untold—your eyes shall see performed. *Exit*

[SCENE VIII]

[*An Inn-yard*]

Enter ROBIN *the Ostler with a book in his hand*

Robin. Oh, this is admirable! here I ha' stolen one of Doctor Faustus' conjuring books, and i' faith I mean to search some circles for my own use. Now will I make all the maidens in our parish dance at my pleasure, stark-naked before me; and so by that means I shall see more than e'er I felt or saw yet.

Enter RAFE *calling* ROBIN

Rafe. Robin, prithee, come away; there's a gentleman tarries to have his horse, and he would have his things rubbed and made clean: he keeps such a chafing with my mistress about it; and she has sent me to look thee out prithee, come away.

Robin. Keep out, keep out, or else you are blown up; you are dismembered, Rafe: keep out, for I am about a roaring piece of work.

Rafe. Come, what dost thou with that same book? Thou can'st not read.

Robin. Yes, my master and mistress shall find that I can read, he for his forehead, she for her private study; she's born to bear with me, or else my art fails.

Rafe. Why, Robin, what book is that?

Robin. What book! Why, the most intolerable book for conjuring that e'er was invented by any brimstone devil.

Rafe. Can'st thou conjure with it?

Robin. I can do all these things easily with it; first, I can make thee drunk with ippocras at any tabern in Europe for nothing; that's one of my conjuring works.

Rafe. Our Master Parson says that's nothing.

Robin. True, Rafe; and more, Rafe, if thou hast any mind to Nan Spit, our kitchen-maid, then turn her and wind her to thy own use as often as thou wilt, and at midnight.

Rafe. O brave Robin, shall I have Nan Spit, and to mine own use? On that condition I'd feed thy devil with horse-bread as long as he lives, of free cost.

Robin. No more, sweet Rafe: let's go and make clean our boots, which lie foul upon our hands, and then to our conjuring in the devil's name. *Exeunt*

[SCENE IX]

[*The Same*]

Enter ROBIN *and* RAFE *with a silver goblet*

Robin. Come, Rafe, did not I tell thee we were for ever made by this Doctor Faustus' book? *ecce signum,* here's a simple purchase for horse-keepers; our horses shall eat no hay as long as this lasts.

Rafe. But, Robin, here comes the Vintner.

Robin. Hush! I'll gull him supernaturally.

Enter VINTNER

Drawer, I hope all is paid: God be with you; come, Rafe.

Vint. Soft, sir; a word with you. I must yet have a goblet paid from you, ere you go.

Robin. I, a goblet, Rafe; I, a goblet! I scorn you, and you are but a, etc. I, a goblet! search me.

Vint. I mean so, sir, with your favor. [*Searches him*]

Robin. How say you now?

Vint. I must say somewhat to your fellow. You, sir!

Rafe. Me, sir! me, sir! search your fill. [*Vintner searches him.*] Now, sir, you may be ashamed to burden honest men with a matter of truth.

Vint. Well, t'one of you hath this goblet about you.

Robin. You lie, drawer, 'tis afore me. [*Aside*]—Sirrah you, I'll teach you to impeach honest men—stand by—I'll scour you for a goblet!—stand aside you had best, I charge you in the name of Belzebub.—Look to the goblet, Rafe. [*Aside to* RAFE]

Vint. What mean you, sirrah?

Robin. I'll tell you what I mean. [*Reads from a book*] *Sanctobulorum Periphrasticon*—nay, I'll tickle you, Vintner. Look to the goblet, Rafe. [*Aside to* RAFE]

[*Reads*] *Polypragmos Belseborams framanto pacostiphos tostu, Mephistophilis, etc.*

Enter MEPHISTOPHILIS, *sets squibs at their backs, and then exit. They run about*

Vint. *O nomine Domini!* what meanest thou, Robin? thou hast no goblet.

Rafe. *Peccatum peccatorum.* Here's thy goblet, good Vintner.

[*Gives the goblet to Vintner, who exit*]

Robin. *Misericordia pro nobis!* What shall I do? Good Devil, forgive me now, and I'll never rob thy library more.

Enter to them MEPHISTOPHILIS

Meph. Monarch of hell, under whose black survey
Great potentates do kneel with awful fear,
Upon whose altars thousand souls do lie,
How am I vexed with these villains' charms!
From Constantinople am I hither come

Only for pleasure of these damnèd slaves.

Robin. How, from Constantinople! You have had a great journey: will you take six-pence in your purse to pay for your supper, and begone?

Meph. Well, villains, for your presumption I transform thee into an ape, and thee into a dog and so begone.

Exit

Robin. How, into an ape; that's brave! I'll have fine sport with the boys. I'll get nuts and apples enow.

Rafe. And I must be a dog.

Robin. I'faith thy head will never be out of the pottage pot. *Exeunt*

[SCENE X]

[*The Court*]

Enter EMPEROR, FAUSTUS, *and a* Knight *with* Attendants

Emp. Master Doctor Faustus, I have heard strange report of thy knowledge in the black art, how that none in my empire nor in the whole world can compare with thee for the rare effects of magic; they say thou hast a familiar spirit, by whom thou canst accomplish what thou list. This, therefore, is my request, that thou let me see some proof of thy skill, that mine eyes may be witnesses to confirm what mine ears have heard reported; and here I swear to thee by the honor of mine imperial crown, that, whatever thou doest, thou shalt be no ways prejudiced or endamaged.

Knight. I'faith he looks much like a conjuror. *Aside*

Faust. My gracious sovereign, though I must confess myself far inferior to the report men have published, and nothing answerable to the honor of your imperial majesty, yet for that love and duty binds me thereunto, I am content to do whatsoever your majesty shall command me.

Emp. Then, Doctor Faustus, mark what I shall say.
As I was sometimes solitary set

Within my closet, sundry thoughts arose
About the honor of mine ancestors,
How they had won by prowess such exploits,
Got such riches, subdued so many kingdoms
As we that do succeed, or they that shall
Hereafter possess our throne, shall
(I fear me) ne'er attain to that degree
Of high renown and great authority;
Amongst which kings is Alexander the Great,
Chief spectacle of the world's pre-eminence,
The bright shining of whose glorious acts
Lightens the world with his reflecting beams,
As when I hear but motion made of him
It grieves my soul I never saw the man.
If therefore thou by cunning of thine art
Canst raise this man from hollow vaults below,
Where lies entombed this famous conqueror,
And bring with him his beauteous paramour,
Both in their right shapes, gesture, and attire
They used to wear during their time of life,
Thou shalt both satisfy my just desire,
And give me cause to praise thee whilst I live.

Faust. My gracious lord, I am ready to accomplish your request so far forth as by art, and power of my spirit, I am able to perform.

Knight. I'faith that's just nothing at all. *Aside*

Faust. But, if it like your grace, it is not in my ability to present before your eyes the true substantial bodies of those two deceased princes, which long since are consumed to dust.

Knight. Ay, marry, Master Doctor, now there's a sign of grace in you, when you will confess the truth. *Aside*

Faust. But such spirits as can lively resemble Alexander and his paramour shall appear before your grace in that manner that they best lived in, in their most flourishing estate; which I doubt not shall sufficiently content your imperial majesty.

Emp. Go to, Master Doctor, let me see them presently.

Knight. Do you hear, Master Doctor? You bring Alexander and his paramour before the Emperor!

Faust. How then, sir?

Knight. I'faith that's as true as Diana turned me to a stag!

Faust. No, sir, but when Actæon died, he left the horns for you. Mephistophilis, begone. *Exit* MEPH.

Knight. Nay an you go to conjuring, I'll begone.

Exit Knight

Faust. I'll meet with you anon for interrupting me so. Here they are, my gracious lord.

Enter MEPHISTOPHILIS *with* [Spirits *in the shape of*] ALEXANDER *and his Paramour*

Emp. Master Doctor, I heard this lady while she lived had a wart or mole in her neck: how shall I know whether it be so or no?

Faust. Your highness may boldly go and see.

Emp. Sure these are no spirits, but the true substantial bodies of those two deceased princes. [*Exeunt Spirits*]

Faust. Will't please your highness now to send for the knight that was so pleasant with me here of late?

Emp. One of you call him forth! [*Exit Attendant*]

Enter the Knight *with a pair of horns on his head*

How now, sir knight! why I had thought thou had'st been a bachelor, but now I see thou hast a wife, that not only gives thee horns, but makes thee wear them. Feel on thy head.

Knight. Thou damnèd wretch and execrable dog,
Bred in the concave of some monstrous rock,
How darest thou thus abuse a gentleman?
Villain, I say, undo what thou hast done!

Faust. O, not so fast, sir; there's no haste; but, good, are you remembered how you crossed me in my conference with the Emperor? I think I have met with you for it.

Emp. Good Master Doctor, at my entreaty release him; he hath done penance sufficient.

Faust. My gracious lord, not so much for the injury he offered me here in your presence, as to delight you with some mirth, hath Faustus worthily requited this injurious knight; which, being all I desire, I am content to release him of his horns: and, sir knight, hereafter speak well of scholars. Mephistophilis, transform him straight. [MEPHISTOPHILIS *removes the horns*] Now, my good lord, having done my duty I humbly take my leave.

Emp. Farewell, Master Doctor; yet, ere you go,
Expect from me a bounteous reward. *Exit Emperor*

[SCENE XI]

[*A Green, then* FAUSTUS' *house*
Enter FAUSTUS *and* MEPHISTOPHILIS]

Faust. Now, Mephistophilis, the restless course
That Time doth run with calm and silent foot,
Shortening my days and thread of vital life,
Calls for the payment of my latest years:
Therefore, sweet Mephistophilis, let us
Make haste to Wittenberg.

Meph. What, will you go on horse-back or on foot?

Faust. Nay, till I'm past this fair and pleasant green,
I'll walk on foot.

Enter a Horse-Courser

Horse-C. I have been all this day seeking one Master Fustian: mass, see where he is! God save you, Master Doctor!

Faust. What, Horse-Courser! You are well met.

Horse-C. Do you hear, sir? I have brought you forty dollars for your horse.

Faust. I cannot sell him so: if thou likest him for fifty, take him.

Horse-C. Alas, sir, I have no more.—I pray you speak for me.

Meph. I pray you let him have him: he is an honest fellow, and he has a great charge, neither wife nor child.

Faust. Well, come, give me your money. [Horse-Courser *gives* FAUSTUS *the money*] My boy will deliver him to you. But I must tell you one thing before you have him; ride him not into the water at any hand.

Horse-C. Why, sir, will he not drink of all waters?

Faust. O, yes, he will drink of all waters, but ride him not into the water: ride him over hedge or ditch, or where thou wilt, but not into the water.

Horse-C. Well, sir.—Now am I made man for ever: I'll not leave my horse for twice forty: if he had but the quality of hey-ding-ding, hey-ding-ding, I'd make a brave living on him: he has a buttock as slick as an eel. [*Aside*] Well, God buy, sir, your boy will deliver him me: but hark you, sir; if my horse be sick or ill at ease, if I bring his water to you, you'll tell me what it is?

Faust. Away, you villain; what, dost think I am a horse-doctor? *Exit* Horse-Courser

What are thou, Faustus, but a man condemned to die?
Thy fatal time doth draw to final end;
Despair doth drive distrust unto my thoughts:
Confound these passions with a quiet sleep:
Tush, Christ did call the thief upon the cross;
Then rest thee, Faustus, quiet in conceit. *Sleeps in his chair*

Re-enter Horse-Courser, *all wet, crying*

Horse-C. Alas, alas! Doctor Fustian quotha? Mass, Doctor Lopus was never such a doctor. Has given me a purgation has purged me of forty dollars; I shall never see them more. But yet, like an ass as I was, I would not be ruled by him, for he bade me I should ride him into no water. Now I, thinking my horse had had some rare quality that he would not have had me known of, I, like a venturous youth, rid him into the deep pond at the town's end. I was no sooner in the middle of the pond, but my horse vanished away, and I sat upon a bottle of hay, never so near drowning in my life. But I'll seek out my Doctor, and have my forty dollars again, or I'll make it the dearest horse!—O, yonder is his snipper-snapper.—Do you hear? you hey-pass, where's your master?

Meph. Why, sir, what would you? You cannot speak with him.

Horse-C. But I will speak with him.

Meph. Why, he's fast asleep. Come some other time.

Horse-C. I'll speak with him now, or I'll break his glass windows about his ears.

Meph. I tell thee he has not slept this eight nights.

Horse-C. An he have not slept this eight weeks I'll speak with him.

Meph. See where he is, fast asleep.

Horse-C. Ay, this is he. God save you, Master Doctor, Master Doctor, Master Doctor Fustian!—Forty dollars, forty dollars for a bottle of hay!

Meph. Why, thou seest he hears thee not.

Horse-C. So-ho, ho!—so-ho ho! (*Hollas in his ear*) No, will you not wake? I'll make you wake ere I go. (*Pulls him by the leg, and pulls it away*) Alas, I am undone! What shall I do?

Faust. O, my leg, my leg! Help, Mephistophilis! call the officers. My leg, my leg!

Meph. Come, villain, to the constable.

Horse-C. O lord, sir, let me go, and I'll give you forty dollars more.

Meph. Where be they?

Horse-C. I have none about me. Come to my ostry and I'll give them you.

Meph. Begone quickly. [Horse-Courser *runs away*

Faust. What, is he gone? Farewell he! Faustus has his leg again, and the horse-courser, I take it, a bottle of hay for his labor. Well, this trick shall cost him forty dollars more.

Enter WAGNER

How now, Wagner, what's the news with thee?

Wag. Sir, the Duke of Vanholt doth earnestly entreat your company.

Faust. The Duke of Vanholt! an honorable gentleman, to whom I must be no niggard of my cunning. Come, Mephistophilis, let's away to him. *Exeunt*

[SCENE XII]

[*Court of the Duke*]

Enter the DUKE *and the* DUCHESS
[FAUSTUS, *and* MEPHISTOPHILIS]

Duke. Believe me, Master Doctor, this merriment hath much pleased me.

Faust. My gracious lord, I am glad it contents you so well.—But it may be, madam, you take no delight in this. I have heard that great bellied women do long for some dainties or other: what is it, madam? tell me, and you shall have it.

Duchess. Thanks, good Master Doctor; and for I see your courteous intent to pleasure me, I will not hide from you the thing my heart desires; and were it now summer, as it is January and the dead time of the winter, I would desire no better meat than a dish of ripe grapes.

Faust. Alas, madam, that's nothing! Mephistophilis, begone. [*Exit* MEPHISTOPHILIS] Were it a greater thing than this, so it would content you, you should have it.

Enter MEPHISTOPHILIS *with the grapes*

Here they be, madam; wilt please you taste on them?

Duke. Believe me, Master Doctor, this makes me wonder above the rest, that being in the dead time of winter, and in the month of January, how you should come by these grapes.

Faust. If it like your grace, the year is divided into two circles over the whole world, that, when it is here winter with us, in the contrary circle it is summer with them, as in India, Saba, and farther countries in the East; and by means of a swift spirit that I have I had them brought hither, as you see.—How do you like them, madam; be they good?

Duchess. Believe me, Master Doctor, they be the best grapes that e'er I tasted in my life before.

Faust. I am glad they content you so, madam.

Duke. Come, madam, let us in, where you must well reward this learned man for the great kindness he hath showed to you.

Duchess. And so I will, my lord; and, whilst I live, rest beholding for this courtesy.

Faust. I humbly thank your grace.

Duke. Come, Master Doctor, follow us and receive your reward. *Exeunt*

[SCENE XIII]

[FAUSTUS' *Study*]

Enter WAGNER *solus*

Wag. I think my master means to die shortly,
For he hath given to me all his goods
And yet, methinks, if that death were [so] near,
He would not banquet, and carouse and swill
Amongst the students, as even now he doth,
Who are at supper with such belly-cheer
As Wagner ne'er beheld in all his life.
See where they come! belike the feast is ended.

Enter FAUSTUS, *with two or three* Scholars
[*and* MEPHISTOPHILIS]

1 *Schol.* Master Doctor Faustus, since our conference about fair ladies, which was the beautifullest in all the world, we have determined with ourselves that Helen of Greece was the admirablest lady that ever lived: therefore, Master Doctor, if you will do us that favor, as to let us see that peerless dame of Greece, whom all the world admires for majesty, we should think ourselves much beholding unto you.

Faust. Gentlemen,
For that I know your friendship is unfeignèd,
And Faustus' custom is not to deny
The just requests of those that wish him well,
You shall behold that peerless dame of Greece,
No otherways for pomp and majesty,
Than when Sir Paris crossed the seas with her,
And brought the spoils to rich Dardania.
Be silent, then, for danger is in words.

Music sounds and HELEN *passeth over the stage*

2 *Schol.* Too simple is my wit to tell her praise,
Whom all the world admires for majesty.

3 *Schol.* No marvel though the angry Greeks pursued
With ten years' war the rape of such a queen,
Whose heavenly beauty passeth all compare.

1 *Schol.* Since we have seen the pride of Nature's works,
And only paragon of excellence,

Enter an Old Man

Let us depart; and for this glorious deed
Happy and blest be Faustus evermore.

Faust. Gentlemen, farewell—the same I wish to you.

Exeunt Scholars [*and* WAGNER]

Old Man. Ah, Doctor Faustus, that I might prevail
To guide thy steps unto the way of life,

By which sweet path thou may'st attain the goal
That shall conduct thee to celestial rest!
Break heart, drop blood, and mingle it with tears,
Tears falling from repentant heaviness
Of thy most vile and loathsome filthiness,
The stench whereof corrupts the inward soul
With such flagitious crimes of heinous sins
As no commiseration may expel,
But mercy, Faustus, of thy Saviour sweet,
Whose blood alone must wash away thy guilt.

Faust. Where art thou, Faustus? wretch, what hast thou done?
Damned art thou, Faustus, damned; despair and die!
Hell calls for right, and with a roaring voice
Says, "Faustus! come! thine hour is [almost] come!"
And Faustus now will come to do thee right.

MEPHISTOPHILIS *gives him a dagger*

Old Man. Ah stay, good Faustus, stay thy desperate steps!
I see an angel hovers o'er thy head,
And, with a vial full of precious grace,
Offers to pour the same into thy soul:
Then call for mercy, and avoid despair.

Faust. Ah, my sweet friend, I feel
Thy words do comfort my distressèd soul.
Leave me a while to ponder on my sins.

Old Man. I go, sweet Faustus, but with heavy cheer,
Fearing the ruin of thy hopeless soul. *Exit*

Faust. Accursèd Faustus, where is mercy now?
I do repent; and yet I do despair;
Hell strives with grace for conquest in my breast:
What shall I do to shun the snares of death?

Meph. Thou traitor, Faustus, I arrest thy soul
For disobedience to my sovereign lord;
Revolt, or I'll in piecemeal tear thy flesh.

Faust. Sweet Mephistophilis, entreat thy lord

To pardon my unjust presumption.
And with my blood again I will confirm
My former vow I made to Lucifer.
Meph. Do it then quickly, with unfeignèd heart,
Lest greater danger do attend thy drift.
[FAUSTUS *stabs his arm and writes on a paper with his blood*]
Faust. Torment, sweet friend, that base and crookèd age,
That durst dissuade me from thy Lucifer,
With greatest torments that our hell affords.
Meph. His faith is great: I cannot touch his soul;
But what I may afflict his body with
I will attempt, which is but little worth.
Faust. One thing, good servant, let me crave of thee,
To glut the longing of my heart's desire—
That I might have unto my paramour
That heavenly Helen, which I saw of late,
Whose sweet embracings may extinguish clean
These thoughts that do dissuade me from my vow,
And keep mine oath I made to Lucifer.
Meph. Faustus, this or what else thou shalt desire
Shall be performed in twinkling of an eye.

Enter HELEN

Faust. Was this the face that launched a thousand ships
And burnt the topless towers of Ilium?
Sweet Helen, make me immortal with a kiss. [*Kisses her*]
Her lips suck forth my soul; see where it flies!—
Come, Helen, come, give me my soul again.
Here will I dwell, for heaven be in these lips,
And all is dross that is not Helena.
I will be Paris, and for love of thee,
Instead of Troy, shall Wittenberg be sacked
And I will combat with weak Menelaus,
And wear thy colors on my plumèd crest:
Yea, I will wound Achilles in the heel,

And then return to Helen for a kiss.
O, thou art fairer than the evening air
Clad in the beauty of a thousand stars;
Brighter art thou than flaming Jupiter
When he appeared to hapless Semele:
More lovely than the monarch of the sky
In wanton Arethusa's azured arms:
And none but thou shalt be my paramour! *Exeunt*

Enter the Old Man

Old Man. Accursèd Faustus, miserable man,
That from thy soul exclud'st the grace of heaven,
And fly'st the throne of his tribunal seat!

Enter Devils

Satan begins to sift me with his pride:
As in this furnace God shall try my faith,
My faith, vile hell, shall triumph over thee.
Ambitious fiends! see how the heavens smile
At your repulse, and laugh your state to scorn!
Hence, hell! for hence I fly unto my God. *Exeunt*

[SCENE XIV]

[*The Same*]

Enter Faustus *with the* Scholars

Faust. Ah, gentlemen!

1 *Schol.* What ails Faustus?

Faust. Ah, my sweet chamber-fellow, had I lived with thee, then had I lived still! but now I die eternally. Look, comes he not, comes he not?

2 *Schol.* What means Faustus?

3 *Schol.* Belike he is grown into some sickness by being over solitary.

1 *Schol.* If it be so, we'll have physicians to cure him. 'Tis but a surfeit. Never fear, man.

Faustus. A surfeit of deadly sin that hath damned both body and soul.

2 *Schol.* Yet, Faustus, look up to heaven: remember God's mercies are infinite.

Faust. But Faustus' offence can ne'er be pardoned: the serpent that tempted Eve may be saved, but not Faustus. Ah, gentlemen, hear me with patience, and tremble not at my speeches! Though my heart pants and quivers to remember that I have been a student here these thirty years, O, would I had never seen Wittenberg, never read book! And what wonders I have done, all Germany can witness, yea, all the world; for which Faustus hath lost both Germany and the world, yea heaven itself, heaven, the seat of God, the throne of the blessed, the kingdom of joy; and must remain in hell for ever, hell, ah, hell, for ever! Sweet friends! what shall become of Faustus being in hell for ever?

3 *Schol.* Yet, Faustus, call on God.

Faust. On God, whom Faustus hath abjured! on God, whom Faustus hath blasphemed! Ah, my God, I would weep, but the Devil draws in my tears. Gush forth blood instead of tears! Yea, life and soul! O, he stays my tongue! I would lift up my hands, but see, they hold them, they hold them!

All. Who, Faustus?

Faust. Lucifer and Mephistophilis. Ah, gentlemen, I gave them my soul for my cunning!

All. God forbid!

Faust. God forbade it indeed; but Faustus hath done it: for vain pleasure of twenty-four years hath Faustus lost eternal joy and felicity. I writ them a bill with mine own blood: the date is expired; the time will come, and he will fetch me.

1 *Schol.* Why did not Faustus tell us of this before, that divines might have prayed for thee?

Faust. Oft have I thought to have done so: but the Devil threatened to tear me in pieces if I named God; to fetch both body and soul if I once gave ear to divinity: and now 'tis too late. Gentlemen, away! lest you perish with me.

2 *Schol.* O, what shall we do to [save] Faustus?

Faust. Talk not of me, but save yourselves, and depart.

3 *Schol.* God will strengthen me. I will stay with Faustus.

1 *Schol.* Tempt not God, sweet friend; but let us into the next room, and there pray for him.

Faust. Ay, pray for me, pray for me! and what noise soever ye hear, come not unto me, for nothing can rescue me.

2 *Schol.* Pray thou, and we will pray that God may have mercy upon thee.

Faust. Gentlemen, farewell: if I live till morning I'll visit you: if not——Faustus is gone to hell.

All. Faustus, farewell. *Exeunt* Scholars

The clock strikes eleven

Faust. Ah, Faustus,
Now hast thou but one bare hour to live,
And then thou must be damned perpetually!
Stand still, you ever-moving spheres of heaven,
That time may cease, and midnight never come;
Fair Nature's eye, rise, rise again and make
Perpetual day; or let this hour be but
A year, a month, a week, a natural day,
That Faustus may repent and save his soul!
O lente, lente, currite noctis equi!
The stars move still, time runs, the clock will strike,
The Devil will come, and Faustus must be damned.
Oh, I'll leap up to my God! Who pulls me down?
See, see where Christ's blood streams in the firmament!
One drop would save my soul—half a drop: ah, my Christ!
Ah, rend not my heart for naming of my Christ!
Yet will I call on him: O, spare me, Lucifer!—
Where is it now? 'tis gone; and see where God

Stretcheth out his arm, and bends his ireful brows!
Mountain and hills come, come and fall on me,
And hide me from the heavy wrath of God!
No! no!
Then will I headlong run into the earth;
Earth gape! O, no, it will not harbor me!
You stars that reigned at my nativity,
Whose influence hath allotted death and hell,
Now draw up Faustus like a foggy mist
Into the entrails of yon laboring clouds,
That when you vomit forth into the air,
My limbs may issue from their smoky mouths,
So that my soul may but ascend to heaven,

The clock strikes [the half hour]

Ah, half the hour is past! 'twill all be past anon!
O God!
If thou wilt not have mercy on my soul,
Yet for Christ's sake whose blood hath ransomed me,
Impose some end to my incessant pain;
Let Faustus live in hell a thousand years—
A hundred thousand, and—at last—be saved!
O, no end is limited to damnèd souls!
Why wert thou not a creature wanting soul?
Or why is this immortal that thou hast?
Ah, Pythagoras' metempsychosis! were that true,
This soul should fly from me, and I be changed
Unto some brutish beast! all beasts are happy,
For, when they die,
Their souls are soon dissolved in elements;
But mine must live, still to be plagued in hell.
Curst be the parents that engendered me!
No, Faustus: curse thyself; curse Lucifer
That hath deprived thee of the joys of heaven.

The clock strikes twelve

O, it strikes, it strikes! Now, body, turn to air,
Or Lucifer will bear thee quick to hell.

Thunder and lightning

O soul, be changed into little water-drops,
And fall into the ocean—ne'er be found.
My God! my God! look not so fierce on me!

Enter Devils

Adders and serpents, let me breathe awhile!
Ugly hell, gape not! come not, Lucifer!
I'll burn my books!—Ah Mephistophilis!

Exeunt with him

Enter Chorus

Cho. Cut is the branch that might have grown full straight,
And burnèd is Apollo's laurel bough,
That sometime grew within this learnèd man.
Faustus is gone; regard his hellish fall,
Whose fiendful fortune may exhort the wise
Only to wonder at unlawful things,
Whose deepness doth entice such forward wits
To practise more than heavenly power permits. *Exit*

Terminat hora diem; terminat auctor opus.

THE SHOEMAKER'S HOLIDAY

OR A PLEASANT COMEDY OF THE GENTLE CRAFT

by

THOMAS DEKKER

THE FIRST THREE-MAN'S SONG

O the month of May, the merry month of May,
  So frolick, so gay, and so green, so green, so
    green!
O, and then did I unto my true love say:
  'Sweet Peg, thou shalt be my summer's queen!

'Now the nightingale, the pretty nightingale,
  The sweetest singer in all the forest's choir,
Entreats thee, sweet Peggy, to hear thy true love's
    tale;
  Lo, yonder she sitteth, her breast against a brier.

'But O, I spy the cuckoo, the cuckoo, the cuckoo;
  See where she sitteth: come away, my joy;
Come away, I prithee: I do not like the cuckoo
  Should sing where my Peggy and I kiss and toy.'

O the month of May, the merry month of May,
  So frolick, so gay, and so green, so green, so
    green!
And then did I unto my true love say:
  'Sweet Peg, thou shalt be my summer's queen!'

THE SECOND THREE-MAN'S SONG

This is to be sung at the latter end.

Cold's the wind, and wet's the rain,
  Saint Hugh be our good speed:
Ill is the weather that bringeth no gain,
  Nor helps good hearts in need.

Trowl[1] the bowl, the jolly nut-brown bowl,
  And here, kind mate, to thee:
Let's sing a dirge for Saint Hugh's soul,
  And down it merrily.

Down a down heydown a down,
[Close with the tenor boy.]
  Hey derry derry, down a down!
Ho, well done; to me let come!
  Ring compass,[2] gentle joy.

Trowl the bowl, the nut-brown bowl,
  And here, kind mate, to thee: &c.
[Repeat as often as there be men to drink; and at last when all have drunk, this verse:

Cold's the wind, and wet's the rain,
  Saint Hugh be our good speed:
Ill is the weather that bringeth no gain,
  Nor helps good hearts in need.

[1] Send round.
[2] (?) Come full circle.

THE PROLOGUE

AS IT WAS PRONOUNCED BEFORE THE QUEEN'S MAJESTY

As wretches in a storm (expecting day),
With trembling hands and eyes cast up to heaven,
Make prayers the anchor of their conquered hopes,
So we, dear goddess, wonder of all eyes,
Your meanest vassals, through mistrust and fear
To sink into the bottom of disgrace
By our imperfect pastimes, prostrate thus
On bended knees, our sails of hope do strike,
Dreading the bitter storms of your dislike.
Since then, unhappy men, our hap is such,
That to ourselves ourselves no help can bring,
But needs must perish, if your saint-like ears
(Locking the temple where all mercy sits)
Refuse the tribute of our begging tongues:
Oh grant, bright mirror of true chastity,
From those life-breathing stars, your sun-like eyes
One gracious smile: for your celestial breath
Must send us life, or sentence us to death.

DRAMATIS PERSONÆ.[1]

THE KING
THE EARL OF CORNWALL
SIR HUGH LACY, *Earl of Lincoln*
ROWLAND LACY, *otherwise* HANS, } *His Nephews*
ASKEW, }
SIR ROGER OTELEY,[2] *Lord Mayor of London*
Master HAMMON, }
Master WARNER, } *Citizens of London*
Master SCOTT, }
SIMON EYRE, *the Shoemaker*
ROGER, *commonly called* HODGE, }
FIRK, } EYRE'S *Journeymen*
RALPH, }
LOVELL, a *Courtier*
DODGER, *Servant to the* EARL OF LINCOLN
A DUTCH SKIPPER
A BOY
Courtiers, Attendants, Officers, Soldiers, Hunters, Shoemakers, Apprentices, Servants
ROSE, *Daughter of* SIR ROGER
SYBIL, *her Maid*
MARGERY, *Wife of* SIMON EYRE
JANE, *Wife of* RALPH

SCENE.—London and Old Ford

[1] Added by Fritsche (1862).
[2] Spelt also Otley and Otly in the quartos.

THE SHOEMAKER'S HOLIDAY

Act The First

[SCENE I]

[*A Street in London*]

Enter the Lord Mayor *and the* Earl of Lincoln

Lincoln. My lord mayor, you have sundry times
Feasted myself and many courtiers more:
Seldom or never can we be so kind
To make requital of your courtesy.
But leaving this, I hear my cousin Lacy
Is much affected to your daughter Rose.

Lord Mayor. True, my good lord, and she loves him so well
That I mislike her boldness in the chase.

Lincoln. Why, my lord mayor, think you it then a shame,
To join a Lacy with an Oteley's name?

Lord Mayor. Too mean is my poor girl for his high birth;
Poor citizens must not with courtiers wed,
Who will in silks and gay apparel spend
More in one year than I am worth, by far:
Therefore your honour need not doubt my girl.

Lincoln. Take heed, my lord, advise you what you do
A verier unthrift lives not in the world,
Than is my cousin; for I'll tell you what:
'Tis now almost a year since he requested
To travel countries for experience;
I furnished him with coin, bills of exchange,
Letters of credit, men to wait on him,

Solicited my friends in Italy
Well to respect him. But to see the end:
Scant had he journeyed through half Germany,
But all his coin was spent, his men cast off,
His bills embezzled,[1] and my jolly coz,
Ashamed to show his bankrupt presence here,
Became a shoemaker in Wittenberg,
A goodly science for a gentleman
Of such descent! Now judge the rest by this:
Suppose your daughter have a thousand pound,
He did consume me more in one half year;
And make him heir to all the wealth you have,
One twelvemonth's rioting will waste it all.
Then seek, my lord, some honest citizen
To wed your daughter to.

Lord Mayor. I thank your lordship.
[*Aside*] Well, fox, I understand your subtilty.—
As for your nephew, let your lordship's eye
But watch his actions, and you need not fear,
For I have sent my daughter far enough.
And yet your cousin Rowland might do well,
Now he hath learned an occupation;
And yet I scorn to call him son-in-law.

Lincoln. Ay, but I have a better trade for him:
I thank his grace, he hath appointed him
Chief colonel of all those companies
Mustered in London and the shires about,
To serve his highness in those wars of France.
See where he comes!—

Enter LOVELL, LACY, *and* ASKEW

Lovell, what news with you?

Lovell. My Lord of Lincoln, 'tis his highness' will,
That presently your cousin ship for France

[1] Squandered.

With all his powers; he would not for a million,
But they should land at Dieppe within four days.

Lincoln. Go certify his grace, it shall be done.

Exit LOVELL

Now, cousin Lacy, in what forwardness
Are all your companies?

Lacy. All well prepared.
The men of Hertfordshire lie at Mile-end,
Suffolk and Essex train in Tothill-fields,
The Londoners and those of Middlesex,
All gallantly prepared in Finsbury,
With frolic spirits long for their parting hour.

Lord Mayor. They have their imprest,[1] coats, and furniture;[2]
And, if it please your cousin Lacy come
To the Guildhall, he shall receive his pay;
And twenty pounds besides my brethren
Will freely give him, to approve our loves
We bear unto my lord, your uncle here.

Lacy. I thank your honour.

Lincoln. Thanks, my good lord mayor.

Lord Mayor. At the Guildhall we will expect your coming. *Exit*

Lincoln. To approve your loves to me? No subtilty!
Nephew, that twenty pound he doth bestow
For joy to rid you from his daughter Rose.
But, cousins both, now here are none but friends,
I would not have you cast an amorous eye
Upon so mean a project as the love
Of a gay, wanton, painted citizen.
I know, this churl even in the height of scorn
Doth hate the mixture of his blood with thine.
I pray thee, do thou so! Remember, coz,
What honourable fortunes wait on thee:

[1] Advance of pay. [2] Weapons.

Increase the king's love, which so brightly shines,
And gilds thy hopes. I have no heir but thee,—
And yet not thee, if with a wayward spirit
Thou start from the true bias of my love.

Lacy. My lord, I will for honour, not desire
Of land or livings, or to be your heir,
So guide my actions in pursuit of France,
As shall add glory to the Lacys' name.

Lincoln. Coz, for those words here's thirty Portuguese,[1]
And, Nephew Askew, there a few for you.
Fair Honour, in her loftiest eminence,
Stays in France for you, till you fetch her thence.
Then, nephews, clap swift wings on your designs:
Begone, begone, make haste to the Guildhall;
There presently I'll meet you. Do not stay:
Where honour beckons, shame attends delay. *Exit*

Askew. How gladly would your uncle have you gone!

Lacy. True, coz, but I'll o'erreach his policies.
I have some serious business for three days,
Which nothing but my presence can dispatch.
You, therefore, cousin, with the companies,
Shall haste to Dover; there I'll meet with you:
Or, if I stay past my prefixèd time,
Away for France; we'll meet in Normandy.
The twenty pounds my lord mayor gives to me
You shall receive, and these ten Portuguese,
Part of mine uncle's thirty. Gentle coz,
Have care to our great charge; I know, your wisdom
Hath tried itself in higher consequence.

Askew. Coz, all myself am yours: yet have this care,
To lodge in London with all secrecy;
Our uncle Lincoln hath, besides his own,
Many a jealous eye, that in your face
Stares only to watch means for your disgrace.

[1]A gold coin, varying in value from £3 5*s*. to £4 10*s*.

Lacy. Stay, cousin, who be these?

Enter SIMON EYRE, MARGERY *his wife,* HODGE, FIRK, JANE, *and* RALPH *with a piece*[1]

Eyre. Leave whining, leave whining! Away with this whimpering, this puling, these blubbering tears, and these wet eyes! I'll get thy husband discharged, I warrant thee, sweet Jane; go to!

Hodge. Master, here be the captains.

Eyre. Peace, Hodge; husht, ye knave, husht!

Firk. Here be the cavaliers and the colonels, master.

Eyre. Peace, Firk; peace, my fine Firk! Stand by with your pishery-pashery,[2] away! I am a man of the best presence; I'll speak to them, an they were Popes.—Gentlemen, captains, colonels, commanders! Brave men, brave leaders, may it please you to give me audience. I am Simon Eyre, the mad shoemaker of Tower Street; this wench with the mealy mouth that will never tire is my wife, I can tell you; here's Hodge, my man and my foreman; here's Firk, my fine firking [3] journeyman, and this is blubbered Jane. All we come to be suitors for this honest Ralph. Keep him at home, and as I am a true shoemaker and a gentleman of the Gentle Craft,[4] buy spurs yourselves, and I'll find ye boots these seven years.

Margery. Seven years, husband?

Eyre. Peace, midriff, peace! I know what I do. Peace!

Firk. Truly, master cormorant, you shall do God good service to let Ralph and his wife stay together. She's a young new-married woman; if you take her husband away from her a night, you undo her; she may beg in the daytime; for he's as good a workman at a prick and an awl, as any is in our trade.

[1] i.e. a piece of work; here a pair of shoes.

[2] Chatter. [3] Frisking.

[4] cf. Greene. *George-a-Green* (1592), 'You shall be no more called Shoemakers, but you and yours to the world's end shall be called the trade of the Gentle Craft.'

Jane. O let him stay, else I shall be undone.

Firk. Ay, truly, she shall be laid at one side like a pair of old shoes else, and be occupied [1] for no use.

Lacy. Truly, my friends, it lies not in my power:
The Londoners are pressed, paid, and set forth
By the lord mayor, I cannot change a man.

Hodge. Why, then you were as good be a corporal as a colonel, if you cannot discharge one good fellow; and I tell you true, I think you do more than you can answer, to press a man within a year and a day of his marriage.

Eyre. Well said, melancholy Hodge; gramercy, my fine foreman.

Margery. Truly, gentlemen, it were ill done for such as you, to stand so stiffly against a poor young wife; considering her case, she is new-married, but let that pass: I pray, deal not roughly with her; her husband is a young man, and but newly entered, but let that pass.

Eyre. Away with your pishery-pashery, your pols and your edipols! [2] Peace, midriff; silence, Cicely Bumtrinket! Let your head speak.

Firk. Yea, and the horns too, master.

Eyre. Too soon, my fine Firk, too soon! Peace, scoundrels! See you this man? Captains, you will not release him? Well, let him go; he's a proper shot; let him vanish! Peace, Jane, dry up thy tears, they'll make his powder dankish. Take him, brave men; Hector of Troy was an hackney [3] to him, Hercules and Termagant [4] scoundrels, Prince Arthur's Round-table—by the Lord of Ludgate—ne'er fed such a tall, such a dapper swordsman; by the life of Pharaoh, a brave resolute swordsman! Peace, Jane! I say no more, mad knaves.

[1] cf. *2 Henry IV,* II, iv. 160.
[2] Various forms of asseveration.
[3] i.e. a common drudge.
[4] An imaginery deity whom the Mohammedans were supposed to worship; represented in mystery plays as a violent, overbearing personage.

Firk. See, see, Hodge, how my master raves in commendation of Ralph!

Hodge. Ralph, th' art a gull, by this hand, an thou goest not.

Askew. I am glad, good Master Eyre, it is my hap
To meet so resolute a soldier.
Trust me, for your report and love to him,
A common slight regard shall not respect him.

Lacy. Is thy name Ralph?

Ralph. Yes, sir.

Lacy. Give me thy hand;
Thou shalt not want, as I am a gentleman.
Woman, be patient; God, no doubt, will send
Thy husband safe again; but he must go,
His country's quarrel says it shall be so.

Hodge. Th' art a gull, by my stirrup, if thou dost not go. I will not have thee strike thy gimlet into these weak vessels; prick thine enemies, Ralph.

Enter DODGER

Dodger. My lord, your uncle on the Tower-hill
Stays with the lord mayor and the aldermen,
And doth request you with all speed you may,
To hasten thither.

Askew. Cousin, come let's go.[1]

Lacy. Dodger, run you before, tell them we come.—

Exit DODGER

This Dodger is mine uncle's parasite.
The arrant'st varlet that e'er breathed on earth;
He sets more discord in a noble house
By one day's broaching of his pickthank tales,[2]
Than can be salved again in twenty years,
And he, I fear, shall go with us to France,

[1] Cousin, let's go. 1600.
[2] Tales told to curry favour.

To pry into our actions.

Askew. Therefore, coz,
It shall behove you to be circumspect.

Lacy. Fear not, good cousin.—Ralph, hie to your colours.

Ralph. I must, because there is no remedy;
But, gentle master and my loving dame,
As you have always been a friend to me,
So in my absence think upon my wife.

Jane. Alas, my Ralph.

Margery. She cannot speak for weeping.

Eyre. Peace, you cracked groats,[1] you mustard tokens,[2] disquiet not the brave soldier. Go thy ways, Ralph!

Jane. Ay, ay, you bid him go; what shall I do
When he is gone?

Firk. Why, be doing with me or my fellow Hodge; be not idle.

Eyre. Let me see thy hand, Jane. This fine hand, this white hand, these pretty fingers must spin, must card, must work; work, you bombast-cotton-candle-quean; [3] work for your living, with a pox to you.—Hold thee, Ralph, here's five sixpences for thee; fight for the honour of the Gentle Craft, for the gentlemen shoemakers, the courageous cordwainers, the flower of St. Martin's, the mad knaves of Bedlam, Fleet Street, Tower Street and Whitechapel; crack me the crowns of the French knaves; a pox on them, crack them; fight, by the Lord of Ludgate; fight, my fine boy!

Firk. Here, Ralph, here's three twopences: two carry into France, the third shall wash our souls at parting, for sorrow is dry. For my sake, firk the *Basa mon cues*.[4]

Hodge. Ralph, I am heavy at parting; but here's a shilling for thee. God send thee to cram thy slops with French crowns, and thy enemies' bellies with bullets.

[1] Worthless coins.
[2] Coupons given to purchasers of mustard.
[3] Bombast is another name for cotton; a cotton candle is one with a cotton wick.
[4] Thrash the Mounseers.

Ralph. I thank you, master, and I thank you all.
Now, gentle wife, my loving lovely Jane,
Rich men, at parting, give their wives rich gifts,
Jewels and rings, to grace their lily hands.
Thou know'st our trade makes rings for women's heels:
Here take this pair of shoes, cut out by Hodge,
Stitched by my fellow Firk, seamed by myself,
Made up and pinked[1] with letters for thy name.
Wear them, my dear Jane, for thy husband's sake,
And every morning, when thou pull'st them on,
Remember me, and pray for my return.
Make much of them; for I have made them so,
That I can know them from a thousand mo.

Drum sounds. Enter the LORD MAYOR, *the* EARL OF LINCOLN, LACY, ASKEW, DODGER, *and* Soldiers. *They pass over the stage;* RALPH *falls in amongst them;* FIRK *and the rest cry 'Farewell,' &c., and so exeunt.*

ACT THE SECOND

[SCENE I]

[*A Garden at Old Ford*]

Enter ROSE, *alone, making a garland*

Rose. Here sit thou down upon this flow'ry bank,
And make a garland for thy Lacy's head.
These pinks, these roses, and these violets,
These blushing gilliflowers, these marigolds,
The fair embroidery of his coronet,
Carry not half such beauty in their cheeks,
As the sweet countenance of my Lacy doth.
O my most unkind father! O my stars,
Why lowered you so at my nativity,

[1] Punched.

To make me love, yet live robbed of my love?
Here as a thief am I imprisonèd
For my dear Lacy's sake within those walls,
Which by my father's cost were builded up
For better purposes; here must I languish
For him that doth as much lament, I know,
Mine absence, as for him I pine in woe.

Enter SYBIL

Sybil. Good morrow, young mistress. I am sure you make that garland for me; against I shall be Lady of the Harvest.

Rose. Sybil, what news at London?

Sybil. None but good; my lord mayor, your father, and master Philpot, your uncle, and Master Scot, your cousin, and Mistress Frigbottom by Doctors' Commons, do all, by my troth, send you most hearty commendations.

Rose. Did Lacy send kind greetings to his love?

Sybil. O yes, out of cry,[1] by my troth. I scant knew him; here 'a wore a scarf; and here a scarf, here a bunch of feathers, and here precious stones and jewels, and a pair of garters,—O, monstrous! like one of our yellow silk curtains at home here in Old Ford house, here in Master Bellymount's chamber. I stood at our door in Cornhill, looked at him, he at me indeed, spake to him, but he not to me, not a word; marry go-up, thought I, with a wanion![2] He passed by me as proud—Marry foh! are you grown humorous, thought I; and so shut the door, and in I came.

Rose. O Sybil, how dost thou my Lacy wrong!
My Rowland is as gentle as a lamb,
No dove was ever half so mild as he.

Sybil. Mild? yea, as a bushel of stamped crabs.[3] He looked upon me as sour as verjuice. Go thy ways, thought I; thou may'st be much in my gaskins, but nothing in my

[1] Beyond measure. [2] Vengeance. [3] Crushed crab-apples.

nether-stocks.[1] This is your fault, mistress, to love him that loves not you; he thinks scorn to do as he's done to; but if I were as you, I'd cry: Go by, Jeronimo, go by! [2]
I'd set mine old debts against my new driblets,
And the hare's foot against the goose giblets,[3]
For if ever I sigh, when sleep I should take,
Pray God I may lose my maidenhead when I wake.

Rose. Will my love leave me then, and go to France?

Sybil. I know not that. but I am sure I see him stalk before the soldiers. By my troth, he is a proper man; but he is proper that proper doth. Let him go snick up,[4] young mistress.

Rose. Get thee to London, and learn perfectly,
Whether my Lacy go to France, or no.
Do this, and I will give thee for thy pains
My cambric apron and my Romish gloves,
My purple stockings and a stomacher.
Say, wilt thou do this, Sybil, for my sake?

Sybil. Will I, quoth a? At whose suit? By my troth, yes I'll go. A cambric apron, gloves, a pair of purple stockings, and a stomacher! I'll sweat in purple, mistress, for you; I'll take anything that comes a God's name. O rich! a cambric apron! Faith, then have at 'up tails all'.[5] I'll go jiggy-joggy to London, and be here in a trice, young mistress.
Exit

Rose. Do so, good Sybil. Meantime wretched I
Will sit and sigh for his lost company. *Exit*

[1] I find this unintelligible; if we read 'thy' for 'my' in both places, it would mean, 'You may have a fair exterior, but you are nothing when stripped.'

[2] 'Hieronimo beware! Go by, go by!'—Kyd's *Spanish Tragedy* iv, a line contemporary dramatists made endless fun of.

[3] A proverbial phrase for setting one thing off against another; cf. Dekker's *Westward Ho,* v. iv.

[4] Go and be hanged!

[5] i.e. Start with alacrity.

[SCENE II]

[*A Street in London*]

Enter ROWLAND LACY, *like a Dutch Shoemaker*

Lacy. How many shapes have gods and kings devised,
Thereby to compass their desired loves!
It is no shame for Rowland Lacy, then,
To clothe his cunning with the Gentle Craft,
That, thus disguised, I may unknown possess
The only happy presence of my Rose.
For her have I forsook my charge in France,
Incurred the king's displeasure, and stirred up
Rough hatred in mine uncle Lincoln's breast.
O love, how powerful art thou, that canst change
High birth to baseness, and a noble mind
To the mean semblance of a shoemaker!
But thus it must be. For her cruel father,
Hating the single union of our souls,
Hath secretly conveyed my Rose from London,
To bar me of her presence; but I trust,
Fortune and this disguise will further me
Once more to view her beauty, gain her sight.
Here in Tower Street with Eyre the shoemaker
Mean I a while to work; I know the trade,
I learnt it when I was in Wittenberg.
Then cheer thy hoping spirits, be not dismayed,
Thou canst not want: do Fortune what she can,
The Gentle Craft is living for a man. *Exit*

[SCENE III]

[*An open Yard before Eyre's House*]

Enter EYRE, *making himself ready*

Eyre. Where be these boys, these girls, these drabs, these scoundrels? They wallow in the fat brewis [1] of my bounty, and lick up the crumbs of my table, yet will not rise to see my walks cleansed. Come out, you powder-beef [2] queans! What, Nan! what, Madge Mumble-crust! Come out, you fat midriff-swag-belly-whores, and sweep me these kennels that the noisome stench offend not the noses of my neighbours. What, Firk, I say; what, Hodge! Open my shop-windows! What, Firk, I say!

Enter FIRK

Firk. O master, is't you that speak bandog [3] and Bedlam this morning? I was in a dream, and mused what madman was got into the street so early; have you drunk this morning that your throat is so clear?

Eyre. Ah, well said, Firk; well said, Firk. To work, my fine knave, to work! Wash thy face, and thou'lt be more blest.

Firk. Let them wash my face that will eat it. Good master, send for a souse-wife,[4] if you will have my face cleaner.

Enter HODGE

Eyre. Away, sloven! avaunt, scoundrel!—Good-morrow, Hodge; good-morrow, my fine foreman.

Hodge. O master, good-morrow; y'are an early stirrer. Here's a fair morning.—Good-morrow, Firk, I could have slept this hour. Here's a brave day towards.

Eyre. Oh, haste to work, my fine foreman, haste to work.

Firk. Master, I am dry as dust to hear my fellow Roger talk of fair weather; let us pray for good leather, and let clowns and ploughboys and those that work in the fields pray for brave days. We work in a dry shop; what care I if it rain?

[1] Bread soaked in broth. [2] Salt beef.
[3] A dog kept tied up. [4] Woman who pickled pigs' faces.

Enter Margery

Eyre. How now, Dame Margery, can you see to rise? Trip and go, call up the drabs, your maids.

Margery. See to rise? I hope 'tis time enough, 'tis early enough for any woman to be seen abroad. I marvel how many wives in Tower Street are up so soon. Gods me, 'tis not noon,—here's a yowling! [1]

Eyre. Peace, Margery, peace! Where's Cicely Bumtrinket, your maid? She has a privy fault, she f—ts in her sleep. Call the quean up; if my men want shoe-thread, I'll swinge her in [2] a stirrup.

Firk. Yet, that's but a dry beating; here's still a sign of drought.

Enter Lacy, *as* Hans, *singing*

Hans. Der was een bore van Gelderland
Frolick sie byen;
He was als dronck he cold nyet stand,
Upsolce sie byen.
Tap eens de canneken,
Drincke, schone mannekin.[3]

Firk. Master, for my life, yonder's a brother of the Gentle Craft; if he bear not Saint Hugh's bones,[4] I'll forfeit my

[1] Bawling.

[2] i.e. with. Cf. *Philaster* iv. ii. 'He shall shoot in a stone-bow for me.'

[3] There was a boor from Gelderland,
Jolly they be;
He was so drunk he could not stand,
Half-seas-over (?) they be:
Tap once the cannikin,
Drink, pretty mannikin!

[4] Hugh, a prince of Britain, learnt the Gentle Craft in his travels and worked for a year as an apprentice; falling in love with a Christian damsel, he adopted her faith and was martyred under Diocletian. His brother shoemakers took his bones from the gibbet and made them into tools for their trade.

bones; he's some uplandish [1] workman: hire him, good master, that I may learn some gibble-gabble; 'twill make us work the faster.

Eyre. Peace, Firk! A hard world! Let him pass, let him vanish; we have journeymen enow. Peace, my fine Firk!

Margery. [*Sarcastically*] Nay, nay, y' are best follow your man's counsel; you shall see what will come on't: we have not men enow, but we must entertain every butter-box;[2] but let that pass.

Hodge. Dame, 'fore God, if my master follow your counsel, he'll consume little beef. He shall [3] be glad of men, an he can catch them.

Firk. Ay, that he shall.

Hodge. 'Fore God, a proper man, and I warrant, a fine workman. Master, farewell; dame, adieu; if such a man as he cannot find work, Hodge is not for you.

Offers to go

Eyre. Stay, my fine Hodge.

Firk. Faith, an your foreman go, dame, you must take a journey to seek a new journeyman; if Roger remove, Firk follows. If Saint Hugh's bones shall not be set a-work, I may prick mine awl in the walls, and go play. Fare ye well, master; good-bye, dame.

Eyre. Tarry, my fine Hodge, my brisk foreman! Stay, Firk!—Peace, pudding-broth! By the Lord of Ludgate, I love my men as my life. Peace, you gallimafry![4]—Hodge, if he want work, I'll hire him. One of you to him; stay,—he comes to us.

Hans. Goeden dach, meester, ende u vro oak.[5]

Firk. Nails, if I should speak after him without drinking, I should choke. And you, friend Oake, are you of the Gentle Craft?

Hans. Yaw, yaw, ik bin den skomawker.[6]

[1] Country.
[2] A contemptuous term for a Dutchman.
[3] Ought to.
[4] A dish of different hashed meats.
[5] Good day, master, and you, mistress, too.
[6] Yes, yes, I am a shoemaker.

Firk. Den skomaker, quoth a! And hark you, skomaker, have you all your tools, a good rubbing-pin, a good stopper, a good dresser, your four sorts of awls, and your two balls of wax, your paring knife, your hand- and thumb-leathers, and good St. Hugh's bones to smooth up your work?

Hans. Yaw, yaw; be niet vorveard. Ik hab all de dingen voour mack skooes groot and cleane.[1]

Firk. Ha, ha! Good master, hire him; he'll make me laugh so that I shall work more in mirth than I can in earnest.

Eyre. Hear ye, friend, have ye any skill in the mystery of cordwainers?

Hans. Ik weet niet wat yow seg; ich verstaw you niet.[2]

Firk. Why, thus, man: [*Imitating by gesture a shoemaker at work.*] Ich verste u niet, quoth a.

Hans. Yaw, yaw, yaw; ick can dat wel doen.[3]

Firk. Yaw, yaw! He speaks yawing like a jackdaw that gapes to be fed with cheese-curds. Oh, he'll give a villanous pull at a can of double-beer; but Hodge and I have the vantage, we must drink first, because we are the eldest journeymen.

Eyre. What is thy name?

Hans. Hans—Hans Meulter.

Eyre. Give my thy hand; th' art welcome.—Hodge, entertain him; Firk, bid him welcome; come, Hans. Run, wife, bid your maids, your trullibubs,[4] make ready my fine men's breakfasts. To him, Hodge!

Hodge. Hans, th' art welcome; use thyself friendly, for we are good fellows; if not, thou shalt be fought with, wert thou bigger than a giant.

[1] Yes, yes; be not afraid. I have everything to make shoes big and little.

[2] I know not what you say; I understand you not.

[3] Yes, yes, yes; I can do that well.

[4] A cant term for anything very trifling.—*Nares.*

Firk. Yea, and drunk with, wert thou Gargantua. My master keeps no cowards, I tell thee.—Ho, boy, bring him an heel-block, here's a new journeyman.

Enter Boy

Hans. O, ich wersto you; ich moet een halve dossen cans betaelen; here, boy, nempt dis skilling, tap eens freelicke.[1]

Exit Boy

Eyre. Quick, snipper-snapper, away! Firk, scour thy throat, thou shalt wash it with Castilian liquor.

Enter Boy

Come, my last of the fives,[2] give me a can. Have to thee, Hans; here, Hodge; here, Firk; drink, you mad Greeks, and work like true Trojans, and pray for Simon Eyre, the shoemaker.—Here, Hans, and th' art welcome.

Firk. Lo, dame, you would have lost a good fellow that will teach us to laugh. This beer came hopping in well.

Margery. Simon, it is almost seven.

Eyre. Is't so, Dame Clapper-dudgeon?[3] Is't seven a clock, and my men's breakfast not ready? Trip and go, you soused conger, away! Come, you mad hyperboreans; follow me, Hodge; follow me, Hans; come after, my fine Firk; to work, to work a while, and then to breakfast! *Exit*

Firk. Soft! Yaw, yaw, good Hans, though my master have no more wit but to call you afore me, I am not so foolish to go behind you, I being the elder journeyman.

Exeunt

[SCENE IV]

[*A Field near Old Ford*]

Holloaing within. Enter Master WARNER *and* Master HAMMON, *attired as Hunters*

[1] O, I understand you; I must pay for a half-dozen cans; here, boy, take this shilling, tap once freely.
[2] A small size of last. [3] Cant term for a beggar.—*Nares.*

Hammon. Cousin, beat every brake, the game's not far.
This way with wingèd feet he fled from death,
Whilst the pursuing hounds, scenting his steps,
Find out his highway to destruction.
Besides, the miller's boy told me even now,
He saw him take soil,[1] and he halloaed him,
Affirming him to have been so embost [2]
That long he could not hold.

Warner. If it be so,
'Tis best we trace these meadows by Old Ford.

A noise of Hunters within. Enter a Boy

Hammon. How now, boy? Where's the deer? speak, saw'st thou him?

Boy. O yea; I saw him leap through a hedge, and then over a ditch, then at my lord mayor's pale. Over he skipped me, and in he went me, and 'holla' the hunters cried, and 'there, boy; there, boy!' But there he is, 'a mine honesty.

Hammon. Boy, God amercy. Cousin, let's away;
I hope we shall find better sport to-day. *Exeunt*

[SCENE V]

[*Another part of the Field*]

Hunting within. Enter Rose *and* Sybil

Rose. Why, Sybil, wilt thou prove a forester?

Sybil. Upon some, no [3]; forester, go by; no, faith, mistress. The deer came running into the barn through the orchard and over the pale; I wot well, I looked as pale as a new cheese to see him. But whip, says goodman Pinclose, up with his flail, and our Nick with a prong, and down he fell, and they upon him, and I upon them. By my troth,

[1] Take to the water. [2] Exhausted.
[3] No indeed; formed apparently on the analogy of, upon my word, upon my soul, &c. Cf. upon some, ay, *inf.*

we had such sport; and in the end we ended him; his throat we cut, flayed him, unhorned him, and my lord mayor shall eat of him anon, when he comes. *Horns sound within*

Rose. Hark, hark, the hunters come; y' are best take heed,
They'll have a saying to you for this deed.

Enter Master HAMMON, Master WARNER, *Huntsmen, and* Boy

Hammon. God save you, fair ladies.
Sybil. Ladies! O gross![1]
Warner. Came not a buck this way?
Rose. No, but two does.
Hammon. And which way went they? Faith, we'll hunt at those.
Sybil. At those? upon some, no: when, can you tell?
Warner. Upon some, ay.
Sybil. Good Lord!
Warner. Wounds! Then farewell!
Hammon. Boy, which way went he?
Boy. This way, sir, he ran.
Hammon. This way he ran indeed, fair Mistress Rose;
Our game was lately in your orchard seen.
Warner. Can you advise, which way he took his flight?
Sybil. Follow your nose; his horns will guide you right.
Warner. Th' art a mad wench.
Sybil. O, rich!
Rose. Trust me, not I.
It is not like that the wild forest-deer
Would come so near to places of resort;
You are deceived, he fled some other way.
Warner. Which way, my sugar-candy, can you shew?
Sybil. Come up, good honeysops, upon some, no.
Rose. Why do you stay, and not pursue your game?

[1] Stupid.

Sybil. I'll hold my life, their hunting-nags be lame.

Hammon. A deer more dear is found within this place.

Rose. But not the deer, sir, which you had in chase.

Hammon. I chased the deer, but this dear chaseth me.

Rose. The strangest hunting that ever I see.
But where's your park? *She offers to go away*

Hammon. [My park?] 'Tis here: O stay!

Rose. Impale me [in't], and then I will not stray.

Warner. They wrangle, wench; we are more kind than they.

Sybil. What kind of hart is that dear heart, you seek?

Warner. A hart, dear heart.

Sybil. Who ever saw the like?

Rose. To lose your heart, is't possible you can?

Hammon. My heart is lost.

Rose. Alack, good gentleman!

Hammon. This poor lost heart would I wish you might find.

Rose. You, by such luck, might prove your hart a hind.

Hammon. Why, Luck had horns, so have I heard some say.

Rose. Now, God, an't be his will, send Luck into your way.

Enter the Lord Mayor *and Servants*

Lord Mayor. What, Master Hammon? Welcome to Old Ford!

Sybil. Gods pittikins, hands off, sir! Here's my lord.

Lord Mayor. I hear you had ill luck, and lost your game.

Hammon. 'Tis true, my lord.

Lord Mayor. I am sorry for the same.
What gentleman is this?

Hammon. My brother-in-law.

Lord Mayor. Y' are welcome both; sith Fortune offers you
Into my hands, you shall not part from hence,

Until you have refreshed your wearied limbs.—
Go, Sybil, cover the board!—You shall be guest
To no good cheer, but even a hunter's feast.

Hammon. I thank your lordship.—Cousin, on my life,
For our lost venison I shall find a wife. *Exeunt*

Lord Mayor. In, gentlemen; I'll not be absent long.—
This Hammon is a proper gentleman.
A citizen by birth, fairly allied;
How fit an husband were he for my girl!
Well, I will in, and do the best I can,
To match my daughter to this gentleman. *Exit*

Act The Third

[SCENE I]

[*A Room in Eyre's House*]

Enter Hans, Skipper, Hodge, *and* Firk

Skipper. Ick sal yow wat seggen, Hans; dis skip, dat comen from Candy, is al vol, by Got's sacrament, van sugar, civet, almonds, cambrick, end alle dingen, towsand towsand ding. Nempt it, Hans, nempt it vor v meester. Daer be de bils van laden. Your meester Simon Eyre sal hae good copen. Wat seggen yow, Hans? [1]

Firk. Wat seggen de reggen, de copen slopen—laugh, Hodge, laugh!

Hans. Mine liever broder Firk, bringt Meester Eyre tot det signe vn Swannekin; daer sal yow finde dis skipper end me. Wat seggen yow, broder Firk? Doot it, Hodge.[2] Come, skipper. *Exeunt* Hans *and* Skipper

[1] I'll tell you what, Hans; this ship that comes from Candia, is all full, by God's sacrament, of sugar, civet, almonds, cambric, and all things, a thousand, thousand things. Take it, Hans, take it for your master. There are the bills of lading. Your master, Simon Eyre, shall have a good bargain. What say you, Hans?

[2] My dear brother Firk, bring Master Eyre to the sign of the Swan; there shall you find this skipper and me. What say you, brother Firk? Do it, Hodge.

Firk. Bring him, quoth you? Here's no knavery, to bring my master to buy a ship worth of lading of two or three hundred thousand pounds. Alas, that's nothing; a trifle, a bauble, Hodge.

Hodge. The truth is, Firk, that the merchant owner of the ship dares not shew his head, and therefore this skipper that deals for him, for the love he bears to Hans, offers my master Eyre a bargain in the commodities. He shall have a reasonable day of payment; he may sell the wares by that time, and be an huge gainer himself.

Firk. Yea, but can my fellow Hans lend my master twenty porpentines as an earnest penny?

Hodge. Portegues,[1] thou wouldst say; here they be, Firk; hark, they jingle in my pocket like St. Mary Overy's bells.[2]

Enter EYRE *and* MARGERY

Firk. Mum, here comes my dame and my master. She'll scold, on my life, for loitering this Monday; but all's one, let them all say what they can, Monday's our holiday.

Margery. You sing, Sir Sauce, but I beshrew your heart, I fear, for this your singing we shall smart.

Firk. Smart for me, dame; why, dame, why?

Hodge. Master, I hope you'll not suffer my dame to take down your journeymen.

Firk. If she take me down, I'll take her up; yea, and take her down too, a button-hole lower.

Eyre. Peace, Firk; not I, Hodge; by the life of Pharaoh, by the Lord of Ludgate, by this beard, every hair whereof I value at a king's ransom, she shall not meddle with you.—Peace, you bombast-cotton-candle-quean; away, queen of clubs; quarrel not with me and my men, with me and my fine Firk; I'll firk you, if you do.

Margery. Yea, yea, man, you may use me as you please;

[1] i.e. Portuguese, see note on p. 59.
[2] i.e. St. Mary of the Bank-side; now incorporated in St. Saviour's, Southwark.

but let that pass.

Eyre. Let it pass, let it vanish away; peace! Am I not Simon Eyre? Are not these my brave men, brave shoemakers, all gentlemen of the Gentle Craft? Prince am I none, yet am I nobly born,[1] as being the sole son of a shoemaker. Away, rubbish! vanish, melt; melt like kitchen-stuff.

Margery. Yea, yea, 'tis well; I must be called rubbish kitchen-stuff, for a sort[2] of knaves.

Firk. Nay, dame, you shall not weep and wail in woe for me. Master, I'll stay no longer; here's an inventory of my shop-tools. Adieu, master; Hodge, farewell.

Hodge. Nay, stay, Firk, thou shalt not go alone.

Margery. I pray, let them go; there be more maids than Mawkin, more men than Hodge, and more fools than Firk.

Firk. Fools? Nails! if I tarry now, I would my guts might be turned to shoe-thread.

Hodge. And if I stay, I pray God I may be turned to a Turk, and set in Finsbury[3] for boys to shoot at.—Come, Firk.

Eyre. Stay, my fine knaves, you arms of my trade, you pillars of my profession. What, shall a tittle-tattle's words make you forsake Simon Eyre?—Avaunt, kitchen-stuff! Rip, you brown-bread Tannikin;[4] out of my sight! Move me not! Have not I ta'en you from selling tripes in Eastcheap, and set you in my shop, and made you hail-fellow with Simon Eyre, the shoemaker? And now do you deal thus with my journeymen? Look, you powder-beef-quean, on the face of Hodge, here's a face for a lord.

Firk. And here's a face for any lady in Christendom.

Eyre. Rip, you chitterling, avaunt! Boy, bid the tapster

[1] This, a favourite saying of Eyre's, sounds like a quotation from a contemporary dramatist.

[2] Set.

[3] A famous practising ground for archery.

[4] A diminutive of Ann, applied specially to German or Dutch girls.

of the Boar's Head fill me a dozen cans of beer for my journeymen.

Firk. A dozen, cans? O brave! Hodge, now I'll stay.

Eyre. [*Aside to the* Boy]. An the knave fills any more than two, he pays for them. [*Exit* Boy. *Aloud.*] A dozen cans of beer for my journeymen. [*Re-enter* Boy.] Here, you mad Mesopotamians, wash your livers with this liquor. Where be the odd ten? [*Aside*] No more, Madge, no more.—Well said. Drink and to work!—What work dost thou, Hodge? what work?

Hodge. I am a-making a pair of shoes for my lord mayor's daughter, Mistress Rose.

Firk. And I a pair of shoes for Sybil, my lord's maid. I deal with her.

Eyre. Sybil? Fie, defile not thy fine workmanly fingers with the feet of kitchen-stuff and basting-ladles. Ladies of the court, fine ladies, my lads, commit their feet to our apparelling; put gross work to Hans. Yark [1] and seam, yark and seam!

Firk. For yarking and seaming let me alone, an I come to 't.

Hodge. Well, Master, all this is from the bias.[2] Do you remember the ship my fellow Hans told you of? The Skipper and he are both drinking at the Swan. Here be the Portigues to give earnest. If you go through with it, you cannot choose but be a lord at least.

Firk. Nay, dame, if my master prove not a lord, and you a lady, hang me.

Margery. Yea, like enough, if you may loiter and tipple thus.

Firk. Tipple, dame? No, we have been bargaining with Skellum Skanderbag: [3] can you Dutch spreaken for a ship

[1] Thrust, sc. the awl through the leather.

[2] Off the point.

[3] German: Schelm, a scoundrel. Skanderbag, or Scander Beg (i.e. Iskander Bey), a Turkish name for George Castriota, the Albanian hero, who freed his country from the Turks (1443-67).

of silk Cyprus, laden with sugar-candy?[1]

Enter the Boy *with a velvet coat and an Alderman's gown.* Eyre *puts them on*

Eyre. Peace, Firk; silence, Tittle-tattle! Hodge, I'll go through with it. Here's a seal-ring, and I have sent for a guarded gown[2] and a damask cassock. See where it comes; look here, Maggy; help me, Firk; apparel me, Hodge; silk and satin, you mad Philistines, silk and satin.

Firk. Ha, ha, my master will be as proud as a dog in a doublet, all in beaten[3] damask and velvet.

Eyre. Softly, Firk, for rearing of the nap, and wearing threadbare my garments. How dost thou like me, Firk? How do I look, my fine Hodge?

Hodge. Why, now you look like yourself, master. I warrant you, there's few in the city, but will give you the wall, and come upon you with the right worshipful.

Firk. Nails, my master looks like a threadbare cloak new turned and dressed. Lord, Lord, to see what good raiment doth! Dame, dame, are you not enamoured?

Eyre. How say'st thou, Maggy, am I not brisk? Am I not fine?

Margery. Fine? By my troth, sweetheart, very fine! By my troth, I never liked thee so well in my life, sweetheart; but let that pass. I warrant, there be many women in the city have not such handsome husbands, but only for their apparel; but let that pass too.

Re-enter Hans *and* Skipper

Hans. Godden day, mester. Dis be de skipper dat heb

[1] He means to say a ship from Cyprus and Candia (Crete) laden with silk and sugar.—*Warnke and Proescholdt.*

[2] A gown with guards or facings.

[3] Embroidered.

de skip van marchandice; de commodity ben good; nempt it, master, nempt it.[1]

Eyre. Godamercy, Hans; welcome, skipper. Where lies this ship of merchandise?

Skipper. De skip ben in revere; dor be van Sugar, cyvet, almonds, cambrick, and a towsand towsand tings, gotz sacrament; nempt it, mester: ye sal heb good copen.[2]

Firk. To him, master! O sweet master! O sweet wares! Prunes, almonds, sugar-candy, carrot-roots, turnips, O brave fatting meat! Let not a man buy a nutmeg but yourself.

Eyre. Peace, Firk! Come, skipper, I'll go aboard with you.—Hans, have you made him drink?

Skipper Yaw, yaw, ic heb veale gedrunck.[3]

Eyre. Come, Hans, follow me. Skipper, thou shalt have my countenance in the city. *Exeunt*

Firk. Yaw, heb veale gedrunck, quoth a. They may well be called butter-boxes, when they drink fat veal and thick beer too. But come, dame, I hope you'll chide us no more.

Margery. No, faith, Firk; no, perdy, Hodge. I do feel honour creep upon me, and which is more, a certain rising in my flesh; but let that pass.

Firk. Rising in your flesh do you feel, say you? Ay, you may be with child, but why should not my master feel a rising in his flesh, having a gown and a gold ring on? But you are such a shrew, you'll soon pull him down.

Margery. Ha, ha! prithee, peace! Thou mak'st my worship laugh; but let that pass. Come, I'll go in; Hodge, prithee, go before me; Firk, follow me.

Firk. Firk doth follow: Hodge, pass out in state.

Exeunt

[1] Good day, master. This is the skipper that has the ship of merchandise; the commodity is good; take it, master, take it.

[2] The ship is in the river; there are sugar, civet, almonds, cambric, and a thousand thousand things, God's sacrament! take it, master; you shall have a good bargain.

[3] Yes, yes, I have drunk well.

[SCENE II]

[*London: a Room in Lincoln's House*]

Enter the EARL OF LINCOLN *and* DODGER

Lincoln. How now, good Dodger, what's the news in France?

Dodger. My lord, upon the eighteenth day of May
The French and English were prepared to fight;
Each side with eager fury gave the sign
Of a most hot encounter. Five long hours
Both armies fought together; at the length
The lot of victory fell on our sides.
Twelve thousand of the Frenchmen that day died,
Four thousand English, and no man of name
But Captain Hyam and young Ardington,
Two gallant gentlemen, I knew them well.

Lincoln. But, Dodger, prithee, tell me, in this fight
How did my cousin Lacy bear himself?

Dodger. My lord, your cousin Lacy was not there.

Lincoln. Not there?

Dodger. No, my good lord.

Lincoln. Sure, thou mistakest.
I saw him shipped, and a thousand eyes beside
Were witnesses of the farewells which he gave,
When I, with weeping eyes, bid him adieu.
Dodger, take heed.

Dodger. My lord, I am advised,
That what I spake is true: to prove it so,
His cousin Askew, that supplied his place,
Sent me for him from France, that secretly
He might convey himself thither.[1]

Lincoln. Is't even so?
Dares he so carelessly venture his life
Upon the indignation of a king?

[1] 'hither' in all the quartos.

Has he despised my love, and spurned those favours
Which I with prodigal hand poured on his head?
He shall repent his rashness with his soul;
Since of my love he makes no estimate,
I'll make him wish he had not known my hate.
Thou hast no other news?

Dodger. None else, my lord.

Lincoln. None worse I know thou hast.—Procure the king
To crown his giddy brows with ample honours,
Send him chief colonel, and all my hope
Thus to be dashed! But 'tis in vain to grieve,
One evil cannot a worse [one] [1] relieve.
Upon my life, I have found out his plot;
That old dog, Love, that fawned upon him so,
Love to that puling girl, his fair-cheeked Rose,
The lord mayor's daughter, hath distracted him,
And in the fire of that love's lunacy
Hath he burnt up himself, consumed his credit.
Lost the king's love, yea, and I fear, his life,
Only to get a wanton to his wife,
Dodger, it is so.

Dodger. I fear so, my good lord.

Lincoln. It is so—nay, sure it cannot be! [2]
I am at my wits' end. Dodger!

Dodger. Yea, my lord.

Lincoln. Thou art acquainted with my nephew's haunts;
Spend this gold for thy pains; go seek him out;
Watch at my lord mayor's—there if he live,
Dodger, thou shalt be sure to meet with him.
Prithee, be diligent.—Lacy, thy name
Lived once in honour, now ['tis] dead in shame.—
Be circumspect. *Exit*

[1] Fritsche's conjecture; W. and Pr. suggest 'more worse', and cite *Lear* II. ii. 155.

[2] In this line the pause takes the time of a beat.

Dodger. I warrant you, my lord. *Exit*

[SCENE III]

[*London: a Room in the Lord Mayor's House*]

Enter the LORD MAYOR *and* Master SCOTT

Lord Mayor. Good Master Scott, I have been bold with you,
To be a witness to a wedding-knot
Betwixt young Master Hammon and my daughter.
O, stand aside; see where the lovers come.

Enter Master HAMMON *and* ROSE

Rose. Can it be possible you love me so?
No, no, within those eyeballs I espy
Apparent likelihoods of flattery.
Pray now, let go my hand.

Hammon. Sweet Mistress Rose,
Misconstrue not my words, nor misconceive
Of my affection, whose devoted soul
Swears that I love thee dearer than my heart.

Rose. As dear as your own heart? I judge it right,
Men love their hearts best when th' are out of sight.

Hammon. I love you, by this hand.

Rose. Yet hands off now!
If flesh be frail, how weak and frail's your vow!

Hammon. Then by my life I swear.

Rose. Then do not brawl;
One quarrel loseth wife and life and all.
Is not your meaning thus?

Hammon. In faith, you jest.

Rose. Love loves to sport; therefore leave love, y' are best.

Lord Mayor. What? square they, Master Scott?

Scott. Sir, never doubt,
Lovers are quickly in, and quickly out.

Hammon. Sweet Rose, be not so strange in fancying me.
Nay, never turn aside, shun not my sight:
I am not grown so fond, to fond [1] my love
On any that shall quit it with disdain;
If you will love me, so—if not, farewell.

Lord Mayor. Why, how now, lovers, are you both agreed?

Hammon. Yes, faith, my lord.

Lord Mayor. 'Tis well, give me your hand.
Give me yours, daughter.—How now, both pull back?
What means this, girl?

Rose. I mean to live a maid.

Hammon. [*Aside.*] But not to die one; pause, ere that be said.

Lord Mayor. Will you still cross me, still be obstinate?

Hammon. Nay, chide her not, my lord, for doing well;
If she can live an happy virgin's life,
'Tis far more blessed than to be a wife.

Rose. Say, sir, I cannot: I have made a vow,
Whoever be my husband, 'tis not you.

Lord Mayor. Your tongue is quick; but Master Hammon, know,
I bade you welcome to another end.

Hammon. What, would you have me pule and pine and pray,
With 'lovely lady', 'mistress of my heart',
'Pardon your servant', and the rhymer play,
Railing on Cupid and his tyrant's-dart;
Or shall I undertake some martial spoil,
Wearing your glove at tourney and at tilt,
And tell how many gallants I unhorsed—
Sweet, will this pleasure you?

Rose. Yea, when wilt begin?

[1] Another spelling of 'found'.

What, love rhymes, man? Fie on that deadly sin!

Lord Mayor. If you will have her, I'll make her agree.

Hammon. Enforced love is worse than hate to me.
[*Aside.*] There is a wench keeps shop in the Old Change.
To her will I; it is not wealth I seek,
I have enough, and will prefer her love
Before the world.—[*Aloud.*] My good lord mayor, adieu.
Old love for me, I have no luck with new. *Exit*

Lord Mayor. Now, mammet,[1] you have well behaved yourself,
But you shall curse your coyness if I live.—
Who's within there? See you convey your mistress
Straight to th' Old Ford! I'll keep you straight enough.
Fore God, I would have sworn the puling girl
Would willingly accept of [2] Hammon's love;
But banish him, my thoughts!—Go, minion, in! *Exit* Rose
Now tell me, Master Scott, would you have thought
That Master Simon Eyre, the shoemaker,
Had been of wealth to buy such merchandise?

Scott. 'Twas well, my lord, your honour and myself
Grew partners with him; for your bills of lading
Shew that Eyre's gains in one commodity
Rise at the least to full three thousand pound
Besides like gain in other merchandise.

Lord Mayor. Well, he shall spend some of his thousands now.
For I have sent for him to the Guildhall.

Enter Eyre

See, where he comes. Good morrow, Master Eyre.

Eyre. Poor Simon Eyre, my lord, your shoemaker.

Lord Mayor. Well, well, it likes yourself to term you so.

[1] Doll, puppet.

[2] Fritsche's conjecture for 'accepted Hammon's' of the quartos.

Enter DODGER

Now, Master Dodger, what's the news with you?

Dodger. I'd gladly speak in private to your honour.

Lord Mayor. You shall, you shall.—Master Eyre and Master Scott,
I have some business with this gentleman;
I pray, let me entreat you to walk before
To the Guildhall; I'll follow presently.
Master Eyre, I hope ere noon to call you sheriff.

Eyre. I would not care, my lord, if you might call me
King of Spain.—Come, Master Scott.

Exeunt EYRE *and* SCOTT

Lord Mayor. Now, Master Dodger, what's the news you bring?

Dodger. The Earl of Lincoln by me greets your lordship,
And earnestly requests you, if you can,
Inform him, where his nephew Lacy keeps.

Lord Mayor. Is not his nephew Lacy now in France?

Dodger. No, I assure your lordship, but disguised
Lurks here in London.

Lord Mayor. London? is't even so?
It may be; but upon my faith and soul,
I know not where he lives, or whether he lives:
So tell my Lord of Lincoln.—Lurks in London?
Well, Master Dodger, you perhaps may start him;
Be but the means to rid him into France,
I'll give you a dozen angels for your pains:
So much I love his honour, hate his nephew.
And, prithee, so inform thy lord from me.

Dodger. I take my leave. *Exit* DODGER

Lord Mayor. Farewell, good Master Dodger.
Lacy in London? I dare pawn my life,
My daughter knows thereof, and for that cause
Denied young Master Hammon in his love.
Well, I am glad I sent her to Old Ford.

Gods Lord, 'tis late; to Guildhall I must hie;
I know my brethren stay my company. *Exit*

[SCENE IV]

[*London: a Room in Eyre's House*]

Enter FIRK, MARGERY, HANS, *and* HODGE

Margery. Thou goest too fast for me, Roger. O, Firk!

Firk. Ay, forsooth.

Margery. I pray thee, run—do you hear?—run to Guildhall, and learn if my husband, Master Eyre, will take that worshipful vocation of Master Sheriff upon him. Hie thee, good Firk.

Firk. Take it? Well, I go; an he should not take it, Firk swears to forswear him. Yes, forsooth, I go to Guildhall.

Margery. Nay, when? thou art too compendious and tedious.

Firk. O rare, your excellence is full of eloquence. [*Aside*] How like a new cart-wheel my dame speaks, and she looks like an old musty ale-bottle going to scalding.

Margery. Nay, when? thou wilt make me melancholy.

Firk. God forbid your worship should fall into that humour;—I run. *Exit*

Margery. Let me see now, Roger and Hans.

Hodge. Ay, forsooth, dame—mistress I should say, but the old term so sticks to the roof of my mouth, I can hardly lick it off.

Margery. Even what thou wilt, good Roger; dame is a fair name for any honest Christian; but let that pass. How dost thou, Hans?

Hans. Mee tanck you, vro.[1]

Margery. Well, Hans and Roger, you see, God hath blest your master, and, perdy, if ever he comes to be Master

[1] I thank you, mistress.

Sheriff of London—as we are all mortal—you shall see, I will have some odd thing or other in a corner for you: I will not be your back-friend;[1] but let that pass. Hans, pray thee, tie my shoe.

Hans. Yaw, ic sal, vro.[2]

Margery. Roger, thou know'st the length of my foot; as it is none of the biggest, so I thank God, it is handsome enough; prithee, let me have a pair of shoes made, cork, good Roger, wooden heel too.

Hodge. You shall.

Margery. Art thou acquainted with never a farthingale-maker, nor a French hood-maker? I must enlarge my bum, ha, ha! How shall I look in a hood, I wonder! Perdy, oddly, I think.

Hodge. [*Aside*] As a cat out of a pillory.—Very well, I warrant you, mistress.

Margery. Indeed, all flesh is grass; and, Roger, canst thou tell where I may buy a good hair?

Hodge. Yes, forsooth, at the poulterer's in Gracious Street.[3]

Margery. Thou art an ungracious wag; perdy, I mean a false hair for my periwig.

Hodge. Why, mistress, the next time I cut my beard, you shall have the shavings of it; but they are all true hairs.

Margery. It is very hot, I must get me a fan or else a mask.

Hodge. [*Aside.*] So you had need, to hide your wicked face.

Margery. Fie upon it, how costly this world's calling is; perdy, but that it is one of the wonderful works of God, I would not deal with it. Is not Firk come yet? Hans, be

[1] False friend.

[2] Yes, I will, mistress.

[3] A corruption of Grass-church (now Gracechurch) Street, called after St. Bennet's, known as the Grass Church from 'the Herbe market there kept'.—*Stow,* p. 214 (1603).

not so sad, let it pass and vanish, as my husband's worship says.

Hans. Ick bin vrolicke, lot see yow soo.[1]

Hodge. Mistress, will you drink a pipe of tobacco?

Margery. Oh, fie upon it, Roger, perdy! These filthy tobacco-pipes are the most idle slavering baubles that ever I felt. Out upon it! God bless us, men look not like men that use them.

Enter RALPH, *being lame*

Hodge. What, fellow Ralph? Mistress, look here, Jane's husband! Why, how now, lame? Hans, make much of him, he's a brother of our trade, a good workman, and a tall soldier.

Hans. You be welcome, broder.

Margery. Perdy, I knew him not. How dost thou, good Ralph? I am glad to see thee well.

Ralph. I would [to] God you saw me, dame, as well
As when I went from London into France.

Margery. Trust me, I am sorry, Ralph, to see thee impotent. Lord, how the wars have made him sunburnt! The left leg is not well; 'twas a fair gift of God the infirmity took not hold a little higher, considering thou camest from France; but let that pass.

Ralph. I am glad to see you well, and I rejoice
To hear that God hath blest my master so
Since my departure.

Margery. Yea, truly, Ralph, I thank my Maker; but let that pass.

Hodge. And, sirrah Ralph, what news, what news in France?

Ralph. Tell me, good Roger, first, what news in England?
How does my Jane? When didst thou see my wife?

[1] I am merry; let's see you so.

Where lives my poor heart? She'll be poor indeed,
Now I want limbs to get whereon to feed.

Hodge. Limbs? Hast thou not hands, man? Thou shalt never see a shoemaker want bread, though he have but three fingers on a hand.

Ralph. Yet all this while I hear not of my Jane.

Margery. O Ralph, your wife,—perdy, we know not what's become of her. She was here a while, and because she was married, grew more stately than became her, I checked her, and so forth; away she flung, never returned, nor said bye nor bah; [1] and, Ralph, you know, 'ka me, ka thee.' [2] And so, as I tell ye— Roger, is not Firk come yet?

Hodge. No, forsooth.

Margery. And so, indeed, we heard not of her, but I hear she lives in London; but let that pass. If she had wanted, she might have opened her case to me or my husband, or to any of my men; I am sure, there's not any of them, perdy, but would have done her good to his power. Hans, look if Firk be come.

Hans. Yaw, ik sal, vro. *Exit* HANS

Margery. And so, as I said—but, Ralph, why dost thou weep? Thou knowest that naked we came out of our mother's womb, and naked we must return; and, therefore, thank God for all things.

Hodge. No, faith, Jane is a stranger here; but, Ralph, pull up a good heart, I know thou hast one. Thy wife, man, is in London; one told me, he saw her awhile ago very brave and neat; we'll ferret her out, an London hold her.

Margery. Alas, poor soul, he's overcome with sorrow; he does but as I do, weep for the loss of any good thing. but, Ralph, get thee in, call for some meat and drink, thou shalt find me worshipful towards thee.

Ralph. I thank you, dame; since I want limbs and lands,

[1] A farewell, courteous or insulting.
[2] Serve me, and I'll serve thee.

I'll trust to God, my good friends and my hands.[1] *Exit*

Enter Hans *and* Firk *running*

Firk. Run, good Hans! O Hodge, O mistress! Hodge, heave up thine ears; mistress, smug up[2] your looks; on with your best apparel; my master is chosen, my master is called, nay, condemned by the cry of the country to be sheriff of the city for this famous year now to come. And time now being, a great many men in black gowns were asked for their voices and their hands, and my master had all their fists about his ears presently, and they cried 'Ay, ay, ay, ay',—and so I came away—

Wherefore without all other grieve
I do salute you, Mistress Shrieve.[3]

Hans. Yaw, my mester is de groot man, de shrieve.

Hodge. Did not I tell you, mistress? Now I may boldly say: Good-morrow to your worship.

Margery. Good-morrow, good Roger. I thank you, my good people all.—Firk, hold up thy hand: here's a three-penny piece for thy tidings.

Firk. 'Tis but three-half-pence, I think. Yes, 'tis three-pence, I smell the rose.[4]

Hodge. But, mistress, be ruled by me, and do not speak so pulingly.

Firk. 'Tis her worship speaks so, and not she. No, faith, mistress, speak me in the old key: 'To it, Firk', 'there, good Firk', 'ply your business, Hodge', 'Hodge, with a full mouth', 'I'll fill your bellies with good cheer, till they cry twang'.

[1] 'I'll to God, my good friends, and to these my hands,' 1600, 1610. 'I'll trust to God, my good friends, and to my hands,' the three other quartos.

[2] Smarten up.

[3] Sheriff.

[4] Firk seems to have confused the coins: from 1561 silver three-pences and three-half-pences were issued with a rose at the back of the Queen's head; the groat (4*d.*) and the half-groat had no rose.—Hawkins, *Silver Coins of England.*

Enter EYRE *wearing a gold chain*

Hans. See, myn liever broder, heer compt my meester.

Margery. Welcome home, Master Shrieve; I pray God continue you in health and wealth.

Eyre. See here, my Maggy, a chain, a gold chain for Simon Eyre. I shall make thee a lady; here's a French hood for thee; on with it, on with it! dress thy brows with this flap of a shoulder of mutton,[1] to make thee look lovely. Where be my fine men? Roger, I'll make over my shop and tools to thee; Firk, thou shalt be the foreman; Hans, thou shalt have an hundred for twenty.[2] Be as mad knaves as your master Sim Eyre hath been, and you shall live to be Sheriffs of London.—How dost thou like me, Margery? Prince am I none, yet am I princely born. Firk, Hodge, and Hans!

All Three. Ay, forsooth, what says your worship, Master[3] Sheriff?

Eyre. Worship and honour, you Babylonian knaves, for the Gentle Craft. But I forgot myself; I am bidden by my lord mayor to dinner to Old Ford; he's gone before, I must after. Come, Madge, on with your trinkets! No, my true Trojans, my fine Firk, my dapper Hodge, my honest Hans, some device, some odd crotchets, some morris, or such like, for the honour of the gentlemen shoemakers. Meet me at Old Ford, you know my mind. Come, Madge, away. Shut up the shop, knaves, and make holiday. *Exeunt*

Firk. O rare! O brave! Come, Hodge; follow me, Hans;
We'll be with them for a morris-dance. *Exeunt*

[SCENE V]

[*A Room at Old Ford*]

[1] A hood. [2] i.e. For the twenty Portuguese previously lent.
[3] 'Mistris' in the four earliest quartos.

Enter the LORD MAYOR, ROSE, EYRE, MARGERY *in a French hood,* SYBIL, *and other Servants*

Lord Mayor. Trust me, you are as welcome to Old Ford
As I myself.

Margery. Truly, I thank your lordship.

Lord Mayor. Would our bad cheer were worth the thanks you give.

Eyre. Good cheer, my lord mayor, fine cheer! A fine house, fine walls, all fine and neat.

Lord Mayor. Now, by my troth, I'll tell thee, Master Eyre,
It does me good, and all my brethren,
That such a madcap fellow as thyself
Is entered into our society.

Margery. Ay, but, my lord, he must learn now to put on gravity.

Eyre. Peace, Maggy, a fig for gravity! When I go to Guildhall in my scarlet gown, I'll look as demurely as a saint, and speak as gravely as a justice of peace; but now I am here at Old Ford, at my good lord mayor's house, let it go by, vanish, Maggy, I'll be merry; away with flip-flap, these fooleries, these gulleries. What, honey? Prince am I none, yet am I princely born. What says my lord mayor?

Lord Mayor. Ha, ha, ha! I had rather than a thousand pound,
I had an heart but half so light as yours.

Eyre. Why, what should I do, my lord? A pound of care pays not a dram of debt. Hum, let's be merry, whiles we are young; old age, sack and sugar will steal upon us, ere we be aware.

Lord Mayor. It's well done; Mistress Eyre, pray, give good counsel
To my daughter.

Margery. I hope, Mistress Rose will have the grace to take nothing that's bad.

Lord Mayor. Pray God she do; for i' faith, Mistress Eyre,
I would bestow upon that peevish girl
A thousand marks more than I mean to give her
Upon condition she'd be ruled by me.
The ape still crosseth me. There came of late
A proper gentleman of fair revenues,
Whom gladly I would call [a] son-in-law:
But my fine cockney would have none of him.
You'll prove a coxcomb for it, ere you die:
A courtier, or no man must please your eye.

Eyre. Be ruled, sweet Rose: th' art ripe for a man. Marry not with a boy that has no more hair on his face than thou hast on thy cheeks. A courtier? wash,[1] go by! stand not upon pishery-pashery: those silken fellows are but painted images, outsides, outsides, Rose; their inner linings are torn. No, my fine mouse, marry me with a gentleman grocer like my lord mayor, your father; a grocer is a sweet trade: plums, plums. Had I a son or daughter should marry out of the generation and blood of the shoemakers, he should pack; what, the Gentle Trade is a living for a man through Europe, through the world.

A noise within of a tabor and a pipe

Lord Mayor. What noise is this?

Eyre. O my lord mayor, a crew of good fellows that for love to your honour are come hither with a morris-dance. Come in, my Mesopotamians, cheerily.

Enter HODGE, HANS, RALPH, FIRK, *and other* Shoemakers, *in a morris; after a little dancing the* LORD MAYOR *speaks*

Lord Mayor. Master Eyre, are all these shoemakers?

Eyre. All cordwainers, my good lord mayor.

Rose. [*Aside*] How like my Lacy looks yond' shoemaker!

[1] Nonsense.

Hans. [*Aside*] O that I durst but speak unto my love!

Lord Mayor. Sybil, go fetch some wine to make these drink.
You are all welcome.

All. We thank your lordship.

Rose takes a cup of wine and goes to HANS

Rose. For his sake whose fair shape thou represent'st,
Good friend, I drink to thee.

Hans. Ic bedancke, good frister.[1]

Margery. I see, Mistress Rose, you do not want judgment; you have drunk to the properest man I keep.

Firk. Here be some have done their parts to be as proper as he.

Lord Mayor. Well, urgent business calls me back to London:
Good fellows, first go in and taste our cheer;
And to make merry as you homeward go,
Spend these two angels in beer at Stratford-Bow.

Eyre. To these two, my mad lads, Sim Eyre adds another; then cheerily, Firk; tickle it, Hans, and all for the honour of shoemakers. *All go dancing out*

Lord Mayor. Come, Master Eyre, let's have your company. *Exeunt*

Rose. Sybil, what shall I do?

Sybil. Why, what's the matter?

Rose. That Hans the shoemaker is my love Lacy,
Disguised in that attire to find me out.
How should I find the means to speak with him?

Sybil. What, mistress, never fear; I dare venture my maidenhead to nothing, and that's great odds, that Hans the Dutchman, when we come to London, shall not only see and speak with you, but in spite of all your father's policies[2] steal you away and marry you. Will not this please you?

[1] I thank you, good maid. [2] Devices.

Rose. Do this, and ever be assured of my love.

Sybil. Away, then, and follow your father to London, lest your absence cause him to suspect something:

To-morrow, if my counsel be obeyed,
I'll bind you prentice to the Gentle Trade.

Exeunt

Act The Fourth

[SCENE I]

[*A Street in London*]

Jane *in a Seamster's shop, working. Enter* Master Hammon, *muffled; he stands aloof*

Hammon. Yonder's the shop, and there my fair love sits.
She's fair and lovely, but she is not mine.
O, would she were! Thrice have I courted her,
Thrice hath my hand been moistened with her hand,
Whilst my poor famished eyes do feed on that
Which made them famish. I am infortunate:
I still love one, yet nobody loves me.
I muse, in other men what women see,
That I so want! Fine Mistress Rose was coy,
And this too curious! [1] Oh, no, she is chaste,
And for she thinks me wanton, she denies
To cheer my cold heart with her sunny eyes.
How prettily she works, oh pretty hand!
Oh happy work! It doth me good to stand
Unseen to see her. Thus I oft have stood
In frosty evenings, a light burning by her,
Enduring biting cold, only to eye her.
One only look hath seemed as rich to me
As a king's crown; such is love's lunacy.
Muffled I'll pass along, and by that try

[1] Fastidious.

Whether she know me.

Jane. Sir, what is't you buy?

What is't you lack, sir, calico, or lawn,
Fine cambric shirts, or bands, what will you buy?

Hammon. [*Aside*] That which thou wilt not sell.
Faith, yet I'll try;
How do you sell this handkercher?

Jane. Good cheap.

Hammon. And how these ruffs?

Jane. Cheap too.

Hammon. And how this band?

Jane. Cheap too.

Hammon. All cheap; how sell you then this hand?

Jane. My hands are not to be sold.

Hammon. To be given then!
Nay, faith, I come to buy.

Jane. But none knows when.

Hammon. Good sweet, leave work a little while; let's play.

Jane. I cannot live by keeping holiday.

Hammon. I'll pay you for the time which shall be lost.

Jane. With me you shall not be at so much cost.

Hammon. Look how you wound this cloth, so you wound me.

Jane. It may be so.

Hammon. 'Tis so.

Jane. What remedy?

Hammon. Nay, faith, you are too coy.

Jane. Let go my hand.

Hammon. I will do any task at your command;
I would let go this beauty, were I not
In mind to disobey you by a power
That controls kings: I love you!

Jane. So, now part.

Hammon. With hands I may, but never with my heart.
In faith, I love you.

Jane. I believe you do.

Hammon. Shall a true love in me breed hate in you?

Jane. I hate you not.

Hammon. Then you must love?

Jane. I do.
What are you better now? I love not you.

Hammon. All this, I hope, is but a woman's fray,
That means: come to me, when she cries: away!
In earnest, mistress,[1] I do not jest,
A true chaste love hath entered in my breast.
I love you dearly, as I love my life,
I love you as a husband loves a wife;
That, and no other love, my love requires.
Thy wealth, I know, is little; my desires
Thirst not for gold. Sweet, beauteous Jane, what's mine
Shall, if thou make myself thine, all be thine.
Say, judge, what is thy sentence, life or death?
Mercy or cruelty lies in thy breath.

Jane. Good sir, I do believe you love me well;
For 'tis a silly conquest, silly pride
For one like you—I mean a gentleman—
To boast that by his love-tricks he hath brought
Such and such women to his amorous lure;
I think you do not so, yet many do,
And make it even a very trade to woo.
I could be coy, as many women be,
Feed you with sunshine smiles and wanton looks,
But I detest witchcraft; say that I
Do constantly believe you, constant have——

Hammon. Why dost thou not believe me?

Jane. I believe you;
But yet, good sir, because I will not grieve you
With hopes to taste fruit which will never fall,
In simple truth this is the sum of all:

[1] A trisyllable.

My husband lives, at least, I hope he lives.
Pressed was he to these bitter wars in France;
Bitter they are to me by wanting him.
I have but one heart, and that heart's his due.
How can I then bestow the same on you?
Whilst he lives, his I live, be it ne'er so poor,
And rather be his wife than a king's whore.

Hammon. Chaste and dear woman, I will not abuse thee,
Although it cost my life, if thou refuse me.
Thy husband, pressed for France, what was his name?

Jane. Ralph Damport.

Hammon. Damport?—Here's a letter sent
From France to me, from a dear friend of mine,
A gentleman of place; here he doth write
Their names that have been slain in every fight.

Jane. I hope death's scroll contains not my love's name.

Hammon. Cannot you read?

Jane. I can.

Hammon. Peruse the same.
To my remembrance such a name I read
Amongst the rest. See here.

Jane. Ay me, he's dead!
He's dead! if this be true, my dear heart's slain!

Hammon. Have patience, dear love.

Jane. Hence, hence!

Hammon. Nay, sweet Jane,
Make not poor sorrow proud with these rich tears.
I mourn thy husband's death, because thou mourn'st.

Jane. That bill is forged; 'tis signed by forgery.

Hammon. I'll bring thee letters sent besides to many,
Carrying the like report: Jane, 'tis too true.
Come, weep not: mourning, though it rise from love,
Helps not the mournèd, yet hurts them that mourn.

Jane. For God's sake, leave me.

Hammon. Wither dost thou turn?
Forget the dead, love them that are alive:

His love is faded, try how mine will thrive.

Jane. 'Tis now no time for me to think on love.

Hammon. 'Tis now best time for you to think on love,
Because your loves lives not.

Jane. Though he be dead,
My love to him shall not be buried;
For God's sake, leave me to myself alone.

Hammon. 'Twould kill my soul, to leave thee drowned in moan.
Answer me to my suit, and I am gone;
Say to me yea or no.

Jane. No.

Hammon. Then farewell!
One farewell will not serve, I come again;
Come, dry these wet cheeks; tell me, faith, sweet Jane,
Yea or no, once more.

Jane. Once more I say, no;
Once more be gone, I pray; else will I go.

Hammon. Nay, then I will grow rude, by this white hand,
Until you change that cold 'no'; here I'll stand
Till by your hard heart——

Jane. Nay, for God's love, peace!
My sorrows by your presence more increase.
Not that you thus are present, but all grief
Desires to be alone; therefore in brief
Thus much I say, and saying bid adieu:
If ever I wed man, it shall be you.

Hammon. O blessed voice! Dear Jane, I'll urge no more;
Thy breath hath made me rich.

Jane. Death makes me poor.

Exeunt

[SCENE II]

[*London: a Street before Hodge's Shop*]

HODGE, *at his shop-board,* RALPH, FIRK, HANS, *and a* Boy *at work*

All. Hey, down a down, derry.

Hodge. Well said, my hearts; ply your work to-day, we loitered yesterday; to it pell-mell, that we may live to be lord mayors, or aldermen at least.

Firk. Hey, down a down, derry.

Hodge. Well said, i' faith! How say'st thou, Hans, doth not Firk tickle it?

Hans. Yaw, mester.

Firk. Not so neither, my organ-pipe squeaks this morning for want of liquoring. Hey, down a down, derry!

Hans. Forward, Firk, tow best un jolly yongster. Hort, ay, mester, ic bid yo, cut me un pair vampres vor Mester Jeffre's boots.[1]

Hodge. Thou shalt, Hans.

Firk. Master!

Hodge. How now, boy?

Firk. Pray, now you are in the cutting vein, cut me out a pair of counterfeits, or else my work will not pass current; hey, down a down!

Hodge. Tell me, sirs, are my cousin Mistress Priscilla's shoes done?

Firk. Your cousin? No, master; one of your aunts,[2] hang her; let them alone.

Ralph. I am in hand with them; she gave charge that none but I should do them for her.

Firk. Thou do for her? then 'twill be a lame doing, and that she loves not. Ralph, thou might'st have sent her to me, in faith, I would have yearked and firked your Priscilla. Hey, down a down, derry. This gear will not hold.

Hodge. How say'st thou, Firk, were we not merry at Old Ford?

Firk. How, merry? why, our buttocks went jiggy-joggy

[1] Forward, Firk, thou art a jolly youngster. Hark, ay, master, I bid you, cut me a pair of vamps for Master Jeffrey's boots. 'Vamps,' upper leathers of a shoe.

[2] A cant term for a prostitute or procuress.

like a quagmire. Well, Sir Roger Oatmeal, if I thought all meal of that nature, I would eat nothing but bagpuddings.

Ralph. Of all good fortunes my fellow Hans had the best.

Firk. 'Tis true, because Mistress Rose drank to him.

Hodge. Well, well, work apace. They say, seven of the aldermen be dead, or very sick.

Firk. I care not, I'll be none.

Ralph. No, nor I; but then my Master Eyre will come quickly to be lord mayor.

Enter SYBIL

Firk. Whoop, yonder comes Sybil.

Hodge. Sybil, welcome, i' faith; and how dost thou, mad wench?

Firk. Syb-whore, welcome to London.

Sybil. Godamercy, sweet Firk; good lord, Hodge, what a delicious shop you have got! You tickle it, i' faith.

Ralph. Godamercy, Sybil, for our good cheer at Old Ford.

Sybil. That you shall have, Ralph.

Firk. Nay, by the mass, we had tickling cheer, Sybil; and how the plague dost thou and Mistress Rose and my lord mayor? I put the women in first.

Sybil. Well, Godamercy; but God's me, I forget myself, where's Hans the Fleming?

Firk. Hark, butter-box, now you must yelp out some spreken.

Hans. Wat begaie you? Vat vod you, Frister? [1]

Sybil. Marry, you must come to my young mistress, to pull on her shoes you made last.

Hans. Vare ben your egle fro, vare ben your mistris? [2]

Sybil. Marry, here at our London house in Cornhill.

Firk. Will nobody serve her turn but Hans?

Sybil. No, sir. Come, Hans, I stand upon needles.

Hodge. Why then, Sybil, take heed of pricking.

[1] What do you want? what would you, girl?
[2] Where is your noble lady, where is your mistress?

Sybil. For that let me alone. I have a trick in my budget. Come, Hans.

Hans. Yaw, yaw, ic sall meete yo gane.[1]

Exit HANS *and* SYBIL

Hodge. Go, Hans, make haste again. Come, who lacks work?

Firk. I, master, for I lack my breakfast; 'tis munching-time and past.

Hodge. Is't so? why, then leave work, Ralph. To breakfast! Boy, look to the tools. Come, Ralph; come, Firk.

Exeunt

Enter a Serving-man

Serving-man. Let me see now, the sign of the Last in Tower Street. Mass, yonder's the house. What, haw! Who's within?

Enter RALPH

Ralph. Who calls there? What want you, sir?

Serving-man. Marry, I would have a pair of shoes made for a gentlewoman against to-morrow morning. What, can you do them?

Ralph. Yes, sir, you shall have them. But what's length her foot?

Serving-man. Why, you must make them in all parts like this shoe; but, at any hand, fail not to do them, for the gentlewoman is to be married very early in the morning.

Ralph. How? by this shoe must it be made? by this? Are you sure, sir, by this?

Serving-man. How, by this? Am I sure, by this? Art thou in thy wits? I tell thee, I must have a pair of shoes, dost thou mark me? a pair of shoes, two shoes, made by this very

[1] Yes, yes, I will go with you.

shoe, this same shoe, against to-morrow morning by four a clock. Dost understand me? Canst thou do 't?

Ralph. Yes, sir, yes—ay, ay!—I can do 't. By this shoe, you say? I should know this shoe. Yes, sir, yes, by this shoe, I can do 't. Four a clock, well. Whither shall I bring them?

Serving-man. To the sign of the Golden Ball in Watling Street; enquire for one Master Hammon, a gentleman, my master.

Ralph. Yea, sir, by this shoe, you say?

Serving-man. I say, Master Hammon at the Golden Ball; he's the bridegroom, and those shoes are for his bride.

Ralph. They shall be done by this shoe; well, well, Master Hammon at the Golden Shoe—I would say, the Golden Ball; very well, very well. But I pray you, sir, where must Master Hammon be married?

Serving-man. At Saint Faith's Church, under Paul's.[1] But what's that to thee? Prithee, dispatch those shoes, and so farewell. *Exit*

Ralph. By this shoe, said he. How am I amazed
At this strange accident! Upon my life,
This was the very shoe I gave my wife,
When I was pressed for France; since when, alas!
I never could hear of her: 'tis the same,
And Hammon's bride no other but my Jane.

Enter FIRK

Firk. 'Snails, Ralph, thou hast lost thy part of three pots, a countryman of mine gave me to breakfast.

Ralph. I care not; I have found a better thing.

Firk. A thing? away! Is it a man's thing, or a woman's thing?

Ralph. Firk, dost thou know this shoe?

[1] 'At the west end of this Jesus chapel, under the choir of Paul's, also was a parish church of St. Faith, commonly called St. Faith under Paul's.'—*Stow,* p. 331 (1603).

Firk. No, by my troth; neither doth that know me! I have no acquaintance with it, 'tis a mere stranger to me.

Ralph. Why, then I do; this shoe, I durst be sworn,
Once covered the instep of my Jane.
This is her size, her breadth, thus trod my love;
These true-love knots I pricked; I hold my life,
By this old shoe I shall find out my wife.

Firk. Ha, ha! Old shoe, that wert new! How a murrain came this ague-fit of foolishness upon thee?

Ralph. Thus, Firk: even now here came a serving-man;
By this shoe would he have a new pair made
Against to-morrow morning for his mistress,
That's to be married to a gentleman.
And why may not this be my sweet[1] Jane?

Firk. And why may'st not thou be my sweet ass? Ha, ha!

Ralph. Well, laugh and spare not! But the truth is this:
Against to-morrow morning I'll provide
A lusty crew of honest shoemakers,
To watch the going of the bride to church.
If she prove Jane, I'll take her in despite
From Hammon and the devil, were he by.
If it be not my Jane, what remedy?
Hereof I am sure, I shall live till I die,
Although I never with a woman lie. *Exit*

Firk. Thou lie with a woman, to build nothing but Cripple-gates! Well, God sends fools fortune, and it may be, he may light upon his matrimony by such a device; for wedding and hanging goes by destiny. *Exit*

[SCENE III]

[*London: a Room in the Lord Mayor's House in Cornhill*]

Enter HANS *and* ROSE, *arm in arm*

Hans. How happy am I by embracing thee!
Oh, I did fear such cross mishaps did reign,

[1] A dissyllable, as in *Hamlet,* I, iii. 8.

That I should never see my Rose again.
Rose. Sweet Lacy, since fair opportunity
Offers herself to further our escape,
Let not too over-fond esteem of me
Hinder that happy hour. Invent the means,
And Rose will follow thee through all the world.
Hans. Oh, how I surfeit with excess of joy,
Made happy by thy rich perfection!
But since thou pay'st sweet interest to my hopes,
Redoubling love on love, let me once more
Like to a bold-faced debtor crave of thee,
This night to steal abroad, and at Eyre's house,
Who now by death of certain aldermen
Is mayor of London, and my master once,
Meet thou thy Lacy, where in spite of change,
Your father's anger, and mine uncle's hate,
Our happy nuptials will we consummate.

Enter SYBIL

Sybil. Oh God, what will you do, mistress? Shift for yourself, your father is at hand! He's coming, he's coming! Master Lacy, hide yourself in my mistress! For God's sake, shift for yourselves!

Hans. Your father come, sweet Rose—what shall I do?
Where shall I hide me? How shall I escape?
Rose. A man, and want wit in extremity?
Come, come, be Hans still, play the shoemaker,
Pull on my shoe.

Enter the LORD MAYOR

Hans. Mass, and that's well remembered.
Sybil. Here comes your father.
Hans. Forware, metresse, 'tis un good skow, it sal vel dute, or ye sal neit betallen.[1]

[1] In truth, mistress, 'tis a good shoe, it shall do well, or you shall not pay.

Rose. Oh God, it pincheth me; what will you do?

Hans. [*Aside*] Your father's presence pincheth, not the shoe.

Lord Mayor. Well done; fit my daughter well, and she shall please thee well.

Hans. Yaw, yaw, ick weit dat well; forware, 'tis un good skoo, 'tis gimait van neits leither; see euer, mine here.[1]

Enter a Prentice

Lord Mayor. I do believe it.—What's the news with you?

Prentice. Please you, the Earl of Lincoln at the gate
Is newly 'lighted, and would speak with you.

Lord Mayor. The Earl of Lincoln come to speak with me?
Well, well, I know his errand. Daughter Rose,
Send hence your shoemaker, dispatch, have done!
Syb, make things handsome! Sir boy, follow me. *Exit*

Hans. Mine uncle come! Oh, what may this portend?
Sweet Rose, this of our love threatens an end.

Rose. Be not dismayed at this; whate'er befall,
Rose is thine own. To witness I speak truth,
Where thou appoint'st the place, I'll meet with thee.
I will not fix a day to follow thee,
But presently steal hence. Do not reply:
Love which gave strength to bear my father's hate,
Shall now add wings to further our escape. *Exeunt*

[SCENE IV]

[*Another Room in the same House*]

Enter the Lord Mayor *and the* Earl of Lincoln

Lord Mayor. Believe me, on my credit, I speak truth:
Since first your nephew Lacy went to France,
I have not seen him. It seemed strange to me,

[1] Yes, yes, I know that well; in truth, 'tis a good shoe, 'tis made of neat's leather; only look, sir!

When Dodger told me that he stayed behind,
Neglecting the high charge the king imposed.

Lincoln. Trust me, Sir Roger Oteley, I did think
Your counsel had given head to this attempt,
Drawn to it by the love he bears your child.
Here I did hope to find him in your house;
But now I see mine error, and confess,
My judgment wronged you by conceiving so.

Lord Mayor. Lodge in my house, say you? Trust me, my lord,
I love your nephew Lacy too too dearly,
So much to wrong his honour; and he hath done so,
That first gave him advice to stay from France.
To witness I speak truth, I let you know,
How careful I have been to keep my daughter
Free from all conference or speech of him;
Not that I scorn your nephew, but in love
I bear your honour, lest your noble blood
Should by my mean worth be dishonoured.

Lincoln. [*Aside*] How far the churl's tongue wanders from his heart!
—Well, well, Sir Roger Oteley, I believe you,
With more than many thanks for the kind love
So much you seem to bear me. But, my lord,
Let me request your help to seek my nephew,
Whom if I find, I'll straight embark for France.
So shall your Rose be free, my thoughts at rest,
And much care die which now lies in my breast.

Enter Sybil

Sybil. Oh Lord! Help, for God's sake! my mistress; oh, my young mistress!

Lord Mayor. Where is thy mistress? What's become of her?

Sybil. She's gone, she's fled!

Lord Mayor. Gone! Whither is she fled?

Sybil. I know not, forsooth; she's fled out of doors with Hans the shoemaker; I saw them scud, scud, scud, apace, apace!

Lord Mayor. Which way? What, John! Where be my men? Which way?

Sybil. I know not, an it please your worship.

Lord Mayor. Fled with a shoemaker? Can this be true?

Sybil. Oh Lord, sir, as true as God's in Heaven.

Lincoln. [*Aside*] Her love turned shoemaker? I am glad of this.

Lord Mayor. A Fleming butter-box, a shoemaker!
Will she forget her birth, requite my care
With such ingratitude? Scorned she young Hammon
To love a honnikin,[1] a needy knave?
Well, let her fly, I'll not fly after her,
Let her starve, if she will; she's none of mine.

Lincoln. Be not so cruel, sir.

Enter FIRK *with shoes*

Sybil. [*Aside.*] I am glad, she's 'scaped.

Lord Mayor. I'll not account of her as of my child.
Was there no better object for her eyes
But a foul drunken lubber, swill-belly,
A shoemaker? That's brave!

Firk. Yea, forsooth; 'tis a very brave shoe, and as fit as a pudding.

Lord Mayor. How now, what knave is this? From whence comest thou?

Firk. No knave, sir. I am Firk the shoemaker, lusty Roger's chief lusty journeyman, and I come hither to take up the pretty leg of sweet Mistress Rose, and thus hoping

[1] A term of abuse, not given in *N.E.D.*

your worship is in as good health, as I was at the making hereof, I bid you farewell, yours, Firk.

Lord Mayor. Stay, stay, Sir Knave!

Lincoln. Come hither, shoemaker!

Firk. 'Tis happy the knave is put before the shoemaker, or else I would not have vouchsafed to come back to you. I am moved, for I stir.

Lord Mayor. My lord, this villain calls us knaves by craft.

Firk. Then 'tis by the Gentle Craft, and to call one knave gently, is no harm. Sit your worship merry! [*Aside to* SYBIL] Syb, your young mistress—I'll so bob them, now my Master Eyre is lord mayor of London.

Lord Mayor. Tell me, sirrah, whose man are you?

Firk. I am glad to see your worship so merry. I have no maw to this gear, no stomach as yet to a red petticoat.

Pointing to SYBIL

Lincoln. He means not, sir, to woo you to his maid,
But only doth demand whose man you are.

Firk. I sing now to the tune of Rogero. Roger, my fellow, is now my master.

Lincoln. Sirrah, know'st thou one Hans, a shoemaker?

Firk. Hans, shoemaker? Oh yes, stay, yes, I have him. I tell you what, I speak it in secret: Mistress Rose and he are by this time—no, not so, but shortly are to come over one another with 'Can you dance the shaking of the sheets?' It is that Hans—[*Aside*] I'll so gull these diggers! [1]

Lord Mayor. Know'st thou, then, where he is?

Firk. Yes, forsooth; yea, marry!

Lincoln. Canst [2] thou, in sadness?

Firk. No, forsooth; no marry!

Lord Mayor. Tell me, good honest fellow, where he is.
And thou shalt see what I'll bestow of thee.

Firk. Honest fellow? No, sir; not so, sir; my profession

[1] i.e. Diggers for information. [2] Knowest.

is the Gentle Craft; I care not for seeing, I love feeling; let me feel it here; aurium tenus, ten pieces of gold; genuum tenus, ten pieces of silver; and then Firk is your man—[*Aside*] in a new pair of stretchers.[1]

Lord Mayor. Here is an angel, part of thy reward,
Which I will give thee; tell me where he is.

Firk. No point! [2] Shall I betray my brother? no! Shall I prove Judas to Hans? no! Shall I cry treason to my corporation? no, I shall be firked and yerked then. But give me your angel; your angel shall tell you.

Lincoln. Do so, good fellow; 'tis no hurt to thee.

Firk. Send simpering Syb away.

Lord Mayor. Huswife, get you in. *Exit* SYBIL

Firk. Pitchers have ears, and maids have wide mouths; but for Hauns-prauns, upon my word, to-morrow morning he and young Mistress Rose go to this gear, they shall be married together, by this rush, or else turn Firk to a firkin of butter, to tan leather withal.

Lord Mayor. But art thou sure of this?

Firk. Am I sure that Paul's steeple is a handful higher than London Stone [3] or that the Pissing-Conduit [4] leaks nothing but pure Mother Bunch? [5] Am I sure I am lusty Firk? God's nails, do you think I am so base to gull you?

Lincoln. Where are they married? Dost thou know the church?

Firk. I never go to church, but I know the name of it; it is a swearing church—stay a while, 'tis—Ay, by the mass, no, no,—tis—Ay, by my troth, no, nor that; 'tis—Ay, by my faith, that, that, 'tis, Ay, by my Faith's Church under Paul's Cross. There they shall be knit like a pair of stockings in

[1] Lies. [2] Not a bit!

[3] A stone now cased in the wall of St. Swithin's Church, Cannon Street, which marked the centre from which the old Roman-roads radiated.

[4] A small conduit erected about 1500 near the Stocks Market where the Mansion House now stands.—*Stow,* pp. 17, 184 (1603).

[5] Here evidently used for water—why is not apparent.

matrimony; there they'll be inconie.[1]

Lincoln. Upon my life, my nephew Lacy walks
In the disguise of this Dutch shoemaker.

Firk. Yes, forsooth.

Lincoln. Doth he not, honest fellow?

Firk. No, forsooth; I think Hans is nobody but Hans, no spirit.

Lord Mayor. My mind misgives me now, 'tis so, indeed.

Lincoln. My cousin speaks the language, knows the trade.

Lord Mayor. Let me request your company, my lord;
Your honourable presence may, no doubt,
Refrain their headstrong rashness, when myself
Going alone perchance may be o'erborne.
Shall I request this favour?

Lincoln. This, or what else.

Firk. Then you must rise betimes, for they mean to fall to their 'hey-pass and repass',[2] 'pindy-pandy, which hand will you have',[3] very early.

Lord Mayor. My care shall every way equal their haste.
This night accept your lodging in my house,
The earlier shall we stir, and at Saint Faith's
Prevent this giddy hare-brained nuptial.
This traffic of hot love shall yield cold gains:
They ban our loves, and we'll forbid their banns.[4] *Exit*

Lincoln. At Saint Faith's Church thou say'st?

Firk. Yes, by my[5] troth.

Lincoln. Be secret, on thy life. *Exit*

Firk. Yes, when I kiss your wife! Ha, ha, here's no craft in the Gentle Craft. I came hither of purpose with shoes to Sir Roger's worship, whilst Rose, his daughter, be cony-

[1] A cant word of unknown origin and meaning; perhaps 'fine, dainty.'

[2] A juggler's formula.

[3] A term used in a children's game, a small object being hidden in one of two closed hands.

[4] Spelt 'baines' in the quartos.

[5] 'Their' in the quartos.

catched by Hans. Soft now; these two gulls will be at Saint Faith's Church to-morrow morning, to take Master Bridegroom and Mistress Bride napping, and they, in the meantime, shall chop up the matter at the Savoy. But the best sport is, Sir Roger Oteley will find my fellow lame Ralph's wife going to marry a gentleman, and then he'll stop her instead of his daughter. Oh, brave! there will be fine tickling sport. Soft now, what have I to do? Oh, I know; now a mess of shoemakers meet at the Woolsack in Ivy Lane, to cozen my gentlemen of lame Ralph's wife, that's true.

Alack, alack!
Girls, hold out tack![1]
For now smocks for this jumbling
Shall go to wrack. *Exit*

Act The Fifth

[SCENE I]

[*A Room in Eyre's House*]

Enter Eyre, Margery, Hans, *and* Rose

Eyre. This is the morning, then, say,[2] my bully, my honest Hans, is it not?

Hans. This is the morning, that must make us two happy or miserable; therefore, if you——

Eyre. Away with these ifs and ans, Hans, and these et caeteras! By mine honour, Rowland Lacy, none but the king shall wrong thee. Come, fear nothing, am not I Sim Eyre? Is not Sim Eyre lord mayor of London? Fear nothing, Rose: let them all say what they can; dainty, come thou to me—laughest thou?

Margery. Good my lord, stand her friend in what thing you may.

Eyre. Why, my sweet Lady Madgy, think you Simon

[1] (?) Stand at bay. [2] 'stay' in the quartos

Eyre can forget his fine Dutch journeyman? No, vah! Fie, I scorn it, it shall never be cast in my teeth, that I was unthankful. Lady Madgy, thou had'st never covered thy Saracen's head with this French flap, nor loaden thy bum with this farthingale ('tis trash, trumpery, vanity); Simon Eyre had never walked in a red petticoat, nor wore a chain of gold, but for my fine journeyman's Portigues.—And shall I leave him? No! Prince am I none, yet bear a princely mind.

Hans. My lord, 'tis time for us to part from hence.

Eyre. Lady Madgy, Lady Madgy, take two or three of my pie-crust-eaters, my buff-jerkin varlets, that do walk in black gowns at Simon Eyre's heels; take them, good Lady Madgy; trip and go, my brown queen of periwigs, with my delicate Rose and my jolly Rowland to the Savoy; see them linked, countenance the marriage; and when it is done, cling, cling together, you Hamborow turtle-doves. I'll bear you out, come to Simon Eyre; come, dwell with me, Hans, thou shalt eat minced-pies and marchpane.[1] Rose, away, cricket; trip and go, my Lady Madgy, to the Savoy; Hans, wed, and to bed; kiss, and away! Go, vanish!

Margery. Farewell, my lord.

Rose. Make haste, sweet love.

Margery. She'd fain the deed were done.

Hans. Come, my sweet Rose; faster than deer we'll run.

Exeunt all but EYRE

Eyre. Go, vanish, vanish! Avaunt, I say! By the Lord of Ludgate, it's a mad life to be a lord mayor; it's a stirring life, a fine life, a velvet life, a careful life. Well, Simon Eyre, yet set a good face on it, in the honour of Saint Hugh. Soft, the king this day comes to dine with me, to see my new buildings; his majesty is welcome, he shall have good cheer, delicate cheer, princely cheer. This day, my fellow prentices of London come to dine with me too; they shall have fine cheer, gentlemanlike cheer. I promised the mad Cappado-

[1] Marzipan.

cians, when we all served at the Conduit together,[1] that if ever I came to be mayor of London, I would feast them all, and I'll do 't, I'll do 't, by the life of Pharaoh; by this beard, Sim Eyre will be no flincher. Besides, I have procured that upon every Shrove Tuesday, at the sound of the pancake bell,[2] my fine dapper Assyrian lads shall clap up their shop windows, and away. This is the day, and this day they shall do 't, they shall do 't.

Boys, that day are you free, let masters care,
And prentices shall pray for Simon Eyre. *Exit*

[SCENE II]

[*A Street near St. Faith's Church*]

Enter Hodge, Firk, Ralph, *and five or six* Shoemakers, *all with cudgels or such weapons*

Hodge. Come, Ralph; stand to it, Firk. My masters, as we are the brave bloods of the shoemakers, heirs apparent to Saint Hugh, and perpetual benefactors to all good fellows, thou shalt have no wrong; were Hammon a king of spades, he should not delve in thy close without thy sufferance. But tell me, Ralph, art thou sure 'tis thy wife?

Ralph. Am I sure this is Firk? This morning, when I stroked[3] on her shoes, I looked upon her, and she upon me, and sighed, asked me if ever I knew one Ralph. Yes, said I. For his sake, said she—tears standing in her eyes—and for thou art somewhat like him, spend this piece of gold. I took it; my lame leg and my travel beyond sea made me unknown. All is one for that: I know she's mine.

Firk. Did she give thee this gold? O glorious glittering gold! She's thine own, 'tis thy wife, and she loves thee; for

[1] One of the duties of apprentices was to fetch water for the household from the conduits.
[2] Rung about 11 a.m. originally to call people to confession, later as a sign that the holiday had begun.
[3] Fitted.

I'll stand to 't, there's no woman will give gold to any man, but she thinks better of him, than she thinks of them she gives silver to. And for Hammon, neither Hammon nor hangman shall wrong thee in London. Is not our old master Eyre, lord mayor? Speak, my hearts.

All. Yes, and Hammon shall know it to his cost.

Enter HAMMON, *his* Serving-man, JANE, *and others.*

Hodge. Peace, my bullies; yonder they come.

Ralph. Stand to 't, my hearts. Firk, let me speak first.

Hodge. No, Ralph, let me.—Hammon, whither away so early?

Hammon. Unmannerly, rude slave, what's that to thee?

Firk. To him, sir? Yes, sir, and to me, and others. Good-morrow, Jane, how dost thou? Good Lord, how the world is changed with you! God be thanked!

Hammon. Villains, hands off! How dare you touch my love?

All the Shoemakers. Villains? Down with them! Cry clubs for prentices!

Hodge. Hold, my hearts! Touch her, Hammon? Yea, and more than that: we'll carry her away with us. My masters and gentlemen, never draw your bird-spits; shoemakers are steel to the back, men every inch of them, all spirit.

Those of Hammon's side. Well, and what of all this?

Hodge. I'll show you.—Jane, dost thou know this man? 'Tis Ralph, I can tell thee; nay, 'tis he in faith, though he be lamed by the wars. Yet look not strange, but run to him, fold him about the neck and kiss him.

Jane. Lives then my husband? Oh God, let me go,
Let me embrace my Ralph.

Hammon. What means my Jane?

Jane. Nay, what meant you, to tell me, he was slain?

Hammon. [O] pardon me, dear love, for being misled.

[*To Ralph*] 'Twas rumoured here in London, thou wert dead.

Firk. Thou seest he lives. Lass, go, pack home with him. Now, Master Hammon, where's your mistress, your wife?

Serving-man. 'Swounds, master, fight for her! Will you thus lose her?

Shoemakers. Down with that creature! Clubs! Down with him!

Hodge. Hold, hold!

Hammon. Hold, fool! Sirs, he shall do no wrong. Will my Jane leave me thus, and break her faith?

Firk. Yea, sir! She must, sir! She shall, sir! What then? Mend it!

Hodge. Hark, fellow Ralph, follow my counsel: set the wench in the midst, and let her choose her man, and let her be his woman.

Jane. Whom should I choose? Whom should my thoughts affect
But him whom Heaven hath made to be my love?
Thou art my husband, and these humble weeds
Make thee more beautiful than all his wealth.
Therefore, I will but put off his attire,
Returning it into the owner's hand,
And after ever be thy constant wife.

Hodge. Not a rag, Jane! The law's on our side; he that sows in another man's ground, forfeits his harvest. Get thee home, Ralph; follow him, Jane; he shall not have so much as a busk-point from thee.

Firk. Stand to that, Ralph; the appurtenances are thine own. Hammon, look not at her!

Serving-man. O, 'swounds, no!

Firk. Blue coat, be quiet, we'll give you a new livery else; we'll make Shrove Tuesday Saint George's Day[1] for you. Look not, Hammon, leer not! I'll firk you! For thy head

[1] On which day a festival attended by blue-coats, or serving-men was held at St. Paul's. See Nares, *Glossary,* s.v. George, St.

now, [not] one glance, one sheep's eye, anything, at her! Touch not a rag, lest I and my brethren beat you to clouts.

Serving-man. Come, Master Hammon, there's no striving here.

Hammon. Good fellows, hear me speak; and, honest Ralph,
Whom I have injured most by loving Jane,
Mark what I offer thee: here in fair gold
Is twenty pound, I'll give it for thy Jane;
If this content thee not, thou shalt have more.

Hodge. Sell not thy wife, Ralph; make her not a whore.

Hammon. Say, wilt thou freely cease thy claim in her,
And let her be my wife?

All the Shoemakers. No, do not, Ralph.

Ralph. Sirrah Hammon, Hammon, dost thou think a shoemaker is so base to be a bawd to his own wife for commodity? Take thy gold, choke with it! Were I not lame, I would make thee eat thy words.

Firk. A shoemaker sell his flesh and blood? Oh, indignity!

Hodge. Sirrah, take up your pelf, and be packing.

Hammon. I will not touch one penny, but in lieu
Of that great wrong I offerèd thy Jane,
To Jane and thee I give that twenty pound.
Since I have failed of her, during my life,
I vow, no woman else shall be my wife.
Farewell, good fellows of the Gentle Trade:
Your morning mirth my mourning day hath made. *Exit*

Firk. [*To the Serving-man.*] Touch the gold, creature, if you dare! Y 're best be trudging. Here, Jane, take thou it. Now let's home, my hearts.

Hodge. Stay! Who comes here? Jane, on again with thy mask!

Enter the EARL OF LINCOLN, *the* LORD MAYOR, *and* Servants

Lincoln. Yonder's the lying varlet mocked us so.

Lord Mayor. Come hither, sirrah!

Firk. I, sir? I am sirrah? You mean me, do you not?

Lincoln. Where is my nephew married?

Firk. Is he married? God give him joy, I am glad of it. They have a fair day, and the sign is in a good planet, Mars in Venus.

Lord Mayor. Villain, thou toldst me that my daughter Rose
This morning should be married at Saint Faith's;
We have watched there these three hours at the least,
Yet see we no such thing.

Firk. Truly, I am sorry for 't; a bride's a pretty thing.

Hodge. Come to the purpose. Yonder's the bride and bridegroom you look for, I hope. Though you be lords, you are not to bar by your authority men from women, are you?

Lord Mayor. See, see, my daughter's masked.

Lincoln. True, and my nephew,
To hide his guilt, [now] counterfeits him lame.

Firk. Yea, truly; God help the poor couple, they are lame and blind.

Lord Mayor. I'll ease her blindness.

Lincoln. I'll his lameness cure.

Firk. [*Aside to the Shoemakers*] Lie down, sirs, and laugh! My fellow Ralph is taken for Rowland Lacy, and Jane for Mistress Damask Rose. This is all my knavery.

Lord Mayor. What, have I found you, minion?

Lincoln. O base wretch!
Nay, hide thy face, the horror of thy guilt
Can hardly be washed off. Where are thy powers?
What battles have you made? O yes, I see,
Thou fought'st with Shame, and Shame hath conquered thee.
This lameness will not serve.

Lord Mayor. Unmask yourself.

Lincoln. Lead home your daughter.

Lord Mayor. Take your nephew hence.

Ralph. Hence! 'Swounds, what mean you? Are you mad?

I hope you cannot enforce my wife from me. Where's Hammon?

Lord Mayor. Your wife?

Lincoln. What Hammon?

Ralph. Yea, my wife; and, therefore, the proudest of you that lays hands on her first, I'll lay my crutch 'cross his pate.

Firk. To him, lame Ralph! Here's brave sport!

Ralph. Rose call you her? Why, her name is Jane. Look here else; do you know her now? *Unmasking* JANE

Lincoln. Is this your daughter?

Lord Mayor. No, nor this your nehpew.
My Lord of Lincoln, we are both abused
By this base, crafty varlet.

Firk. Yea, forsooth, no varlet; forsooth, no base; forsooth, I am but mean; no crafty neither, but of the Gentle Craft.

Lord Mayor. Where is my daughter Rose? Where is my child?

Lincoln. Where is my nephew Lacy married?

Firk. Why, here is good laced mutton,[1] as I promised you.

Lincoln. Villain, I'll have thee punished for this wrong.

Firk. Punish the journeyman villain, but not the journeyman shoemaker.

Enter DODGER

Dodger. My lord, I come to bring unwelcome news.
Your nephew Lacy and your daughter Rose
Early this morning wedded at the Savoy,
None being present but the lady mayoress.
Besides, I learnt among the officers,
The lord mayor vows to stand in their defence
'Gainst any that shall seek to cross the match.

Lincoln. Dares Eyre the shoemaker uphold the deed?

[1] To lace a joint was to make incisions down the sides.

Firk. Yes, sir, shoemakers dare stand in a woman's quarrel, I warrant you, as deep as another, and deeper too.

Dodger. Besides, his grace to-day dines with the mayor;
Who on his knees humbly intends to fall
And beg a pardon for your nephew's fault.

Lincoln. But I'll prevent him! Come, Sir Roger Oteley;
The king will do us justice in this cause.
Howe'er their hands have made them man and wife,
I will disjoin the match, or lose my life. *Exeunt*

Firk. Adieu, Monsieur Dodger! Farewell, fools! Ha, ha! Oh, if they had stayed, I would have so lambed [1] them with flouts! O heart, my codpiece-point is ready to fly in pieces every time I think upon Mistress Rose; but let that pass, as my lady mayoress says.

Hodge. This matter is answered. Come, Ralph; home with thy wife. Come, my fine shoemakers, let's to our master's, the new lord mayor, and there swagger this Shrove Tuesday. I'll promise you wine enough, for Madge keeps the cellar.

All. O rare! Madge is a good wench.

Firk. And I'll promise you meat enough, for simp'ring Susan keeps the larder. I'll lead you to victuals, my brave soldiers; follow your captain. O brave! Hark, hark!

Bell rings

All. The pancake-bell rings, the pancake-bell! Trilill, my hearts!

Firk. O brave! O sweet bell! O delicate pancakes! Open the doors, my hearts, and shut up the windows! keep in the house, let out the pancakes! Oh, rare, my hearts! Let's march together for the honour of Saint Hugh to the great new hall [2] in Gracious Street-corner, which our master, the new lord mayor, hath built.

[1] Whipped.

[2] 'Simon Eyre, Draper, Mayor 1446, builded the Leaden hall for a common garner of corn to the use of this City.'—*Stow.* Maitland gives the date as 1419.

Ralph. O the crew of good fellows that will dine at my lord mayor's cost to-day!

Hodge. By the Lord, my lord mayor is a most brave man. How shall prentices be bound to pray for him and the honour of the gentlemen shoemakers! Let's feed and be fat with my lord's bounty.

Firk. O musical bell, still! O Hodge, O my brethren! There's cheer for the heavens: venison-pasties walk up and down piping hot, like sergeants; beef and brewis [1] comes marching in dry-fats,[2] fritters and pancakes come trowling in in wheel-barrows; hens and oranges hopping in porters'-baskets, collops and eggs in scuttles, and tarts and custards come quavering in in malt-shovels.

Enter more Prentices

All. Whoop, look here, look here!

Hodge. How now, mad lads, whither away so fast?

First Prentice. Whither? Why, to the great new hall, know you not why? The lord mayor hath bidden all the prentices in London to breakfast this morning.

All. Oh, brave shoemaker, oh, brave lord of incomprehensible good fellowship! Whoo! Hark you! The pancake-bell rings. *Cast up caps*

Firk. Nay, more, my hearts! Every Shrove Tuesday is our year of jubilee; and when the pancake-bell rings, we are as free as my lord mayor; we may shut up our shops, and make holiday. I'll have it called Saint Hugh's Holiday.

All. Agreed, agreed! Saint Hugh's Holiday.

Hodge. And this shall continue for ever.

All. Oh, brave! Come, come, my hearts! Away, away!

Firk. O eternal credit to us of the Gentle Craft! March fair, my hearts! Oh, rare! *Exeunt*

[1] See note on p. 68. [2] Barrels.

[SCENE III]

[*A Street in London*]

Enter the KING *and his Train over the stage*

King. Is our lord mayor of London such a gallant?

Nobleman. One of the merriest madcaps in your land.
Your grace will think, when you behold the man,
He's rather a wild ruffian than a mayor.
Yet thus much I'll ensure your majesty.
In all his actions that concern his state,
He is as serious, provident, and wise,
As full of gravity amongst the grave,
As any mayor hath been these many years.

King. I am with child,[1] till I behold this huffcap.[2]
But all my doubt is, when we come in presence,
His madness will be dashed clean out of countenance.

Nobleman. It may be so, my liege.

King. Which to prevent
Let some one give him notice, 'tis our pleasure
That he put on his wonted merriment.
Set forward!

All. On afore! *Exeunt*

[SCENE IV]

[*A Great Hall*]

Enter EYRE, HODGE, FIRK, RALPH, *and other* Shoemakers, *all with napkins on their shoulders*

Eyre. Come, my fine Hodge, my jolly gentlemen shoemakers; soft, where be these cannibals, these varlets, my officers? Let them all walk and wait upon my brethren; for my meaning is, that none but shoemakers, none but the

[1] i.e. In suspense. [2] Swaggerer.

livery of my company shall in their satin hoods wait upon the trencher of my sovereign.

Firk. O my lord, it will be rare!

Eyre. No more, Firk; come, lively! Let your fellow prentices want no cheer; let wine be plentiful as beer, and beer as water. Hang these penny-pinching fathers, that cram wealth in innocent lambskins. Rip, knaves, avaunt! Look to my guests!

Hodge. My lord, we are at our wits' end for room; those hundred tables will not feast the fourth part of them.

Eyre. Then cover me those hundred tables again, and again, till all my jolly prentices be feasted. Avoid, Hodge! Run, Ralph! Frisk about, my nimble Firk! Carouse me fathom-healths to the honour of the shoemakers. Do they drink lively, Hodge? Do they tickle it, Firk?

Firk. Tickle it? Some of them have taken their liquor standing so long that they can stand no longer; but for meat, they would eat it, an they had it.

Eyre. Want they meat? Where's this swag-belly, this greasy kitchenstuff cook? Call the varlet to me! Want meat? Firk, Hodge, lame Ralph, run, my tall men, beleaguer the shambles, beggar all Eastcheap, serve me whole oxen in chargers, and let sheep whine upon the tables like pigs for want of good fellows to eat them. Want meat? Vanish, Firk! Avaunt, Hodge!

Hodge. Your lordship mistakes my man Firk; he means, their bellies want meat, not the boards; for they have drunk so much, they can eat nothing.

Enter HANS, ROSE, *and* MARGERY

Margery. Where is my lord?

Eyre. How now, Lady Madgy?

Margery. The king's most excellent majesty is new come; he sends me for thy honour; one of his most worshipful peers bade me tell thou must be merry, and so forth; but let that pass.

Eyre. Is my sovereign come? Vanish, my tall shoemakers, my nimble brethren; look to my guests, the prentices. Yet stay a little! How now, Hans? How looks my little Rose?

Hans. Let me request you to remember me.
I know, your honour easily may obtain
Free pardon of the king for me and Rose,
And reconcile me to my uncle's grace.

Eyre. Have done, my good Hans, my honest journeyman; look cheerily! I'll fall upon both my knees, till they be as hard as horn, but I'll get thy pardon.

Margery. Good my lord, have a care what you speak to his grace.

Eyre. Away, you Islington whitepot! [1] hence, you hopperarse! you barley-pudding, full of maggots! you broiled carbonado! [2] avaunt, avaunt, avoid, Mephistophilus! Shall Sim Eyre learn to speak of you, Lady Madgy? Vanish, Mother Miniver-cap; [3] vanish, go, trip and go; meddle with your partlets [4] and your pishery-pashery, your flewes [5] and your whirligigs; go, rub, out of mine alley! Sim Eyre knows how to speak to a Pope, to Sultan Soliman, to Tamburlaine,[6] an he were here, and shall I melt, shall I droop before my sovereign? No, come, my Lady Madgy! Follow me, Hans! About your business, my frolic free-booters! Firk, frisk about, and about, and about, for the honour of mad Simon Eyre, lord mayor of London.

Firk. Hey, for the honour of the shoemakers. *Exeunt*

[1] 'A dish, made of milk, eggs, and sugar, baked in a pot.'—*Webster.*

[2] A piece of meat scored across for broiling.

[3] Fur-cap.

[4] Bands or collars.

[5] Properly the chaps of a hound; here perhaps the flaps of a hood.

[6] Dekker is thinking, no doubt, of Kyd's *Soliman and Perseda* (1599) and Marlowe's *Tamburlaine* (1590).

[SCENE V]

[*An Open Yard before the Hall*]

A long flourish, or two. Enter the KING, Nobles, EYRE, MARGERY, LACY, ROSE. LACY *and* ROSE *kneel*

King. Well, Lacy, though the fact was very foul
Of your revolting from our kingly love
And your own duty, yet we pardon you.
Rise both, and, Mistress Lacy, thank my lord mayor
For your young bridegroom here.

Eyre. So, my dear liege, Sim Eyre and my brethren, the gentlemen shoemakers, shall set your sweet majesty's image cheek by jowl by Saint Hugh for this honour you have done poor Simon Eyre. I beseech your grace, pardon my rude behaviour; I am a handicraftsman, yet my heart is without craft; I would be sorry at my soul, that my boldness should offend my king.

King. Nay, I pray thee, good lord mayor, be even as merry
As if thou wert among thy shoemakers;
It does me good to see thee in this humour.

Eyre. Say'st thou me so, my sweet Dioclesian? Then, humph! Prince am I none, yet am I princely born. By the Lord of Ludgate, my liege, I'll be as merry as a pie.[1]

King. Tell me, in faith, mad Eyre, how old thou art.

Eyre. My liege, a very boy, a stripling, a younker; you see not a white hair on my head, not a grey in this beard. Every hair, I assure thy majesty, that sticks in this beard, Sim Eyre values at the King of Babylon's ransom, Tamar Cham's [2] beard was a rubbing brush to 't: yet I'll shave it off, and stuff tennis-balls with it, to please my bully king.

King. But all this while I do not know your age.

[1] Magpie.
[2] Tamerlane (Tamburlaine), Cham, or Khan, of Tartary.

Eyre. My liege, I am six and fifty year old, yet I can cry humph! with a sound heart for the honour of Saint Hugh. Mark this old wench, my king: I danced the shaking of the sheets with her six and thirty years ago, and yet I hope to get two or three young lord mayors, ere I die. I am lusty still, Sim Eyre still. Care and cold lodging brings white hairs. My sweet Majesty, let care vanish, cast it upon thy nobles, it will make thee look always young like Apollo, and cry humph! Prince am I none, yet am I princely born.

King. Ha, ha!
Say, Cornwall, didst thou ever see his like?

Cornwall. Not I, my lord.

Enter the EARL OF LINCOLN *and the* LORD MAYOR

King. Lincoln, what news with you?

Lincoln. My gracious lord, have care unto yourself,
For there are traitors here.

All. Traitors? Where? Who?

Eyre. Traitors in my house? God forbid! Where be my officers? I'll spend my soul, ere my king feel harm.

King. Where is the traitor, Lincoln?

Lincoln. Here he stands.

King. Cornwall, lay hold on Lacy!—Lincoln, speak,
What canst thou lay unto thy nephew's charge?

Lincoln. This, my dear liege: your Grace, to do me honour,
Heaped on the head of this degenerous boy
Desertless favours; you made choice of him,
To be commander over powers in France.
But he——

King. Good Lincoln, prithee, pause a while!
Even in thine eyes I read what thou wouldst speak.
I know how Lacy did neglect our love,
Ran himself deeply, in the highest degree,
Into vile treason——

Lincoln. Is he not a traitor?

King. Lincoln, he was; now have we pardoned him.
'Twas not a base want of true valour's fire,
That held him out of France, but love's desire.

Lincoln. I will not bear his shame upon my back.

King. Nor shalt thou, Lincoln; I forgive you both.

Lincoln. Then, good my liege, forbid the boy to wed
One whose mean birth will much disgrace his bed.

King. Are they not married?

Lincoln. No, my liege.

Both. We are.

King. Shall I divorce them then? O be it far,
That any hand on earth should dare untie
The sacred knot, knit by God's majesty;
I would not for my crown disjoin their hands,
That are conjoined in holy nuptial bands.
How say'st thou, Lacy, wouldst thou lose thy Rose?

Lacy. Not for all India's[1] wealth, my sovereign.

King. But Rose, I am sure, her Lacy would forgo?

Rose. If Rose were asked that question, she'd say no.

King. You hear them, Lincoln?

Lincoln. Yea, my liege, I do.

King. Yet canst thou find i' th' heart to part these two?
Who seeks, besides you, to divorce these lovers?

Lord Mayor. I do, my gracious lord, I am her father.

King. Sir Roger Oteley, our last mayor, I think?

Nobleman. The same, my liege.

King. Would you offend Love's laws?
Well, you shall have your wills. You sue to me,
To prohibit the match. Soft, let me see—
You both are married, Lacy, art thou not?

Lacy. I am, dread sovereign.

King. Then, upon thy life,
I charge thee not to call this woman wife.

[1] 'Indians' in all the quartos.

Lord Mayor. I thank your grace.
Rose. O my most gracious lord!
Kneels
King. Nay, Rose, never woo me; I tell you true,
Although as yet I am a bachelor,
Yet I believe, I shall not marry you.
Rose. Can you divide the body from the soul,
Yet make the body live?
King. Yea, so profound?
I cannot, Rose, but you I must divide.
This fair maid, bridegroom,[1] cannot be your bride.
Are you pleased, Lincoln? Oteley, are you pleased?
Both. Yes, my lord.
King. Then must my heart be eased;
For, credit me, my conscience lives in pain,
Till these whom I divorced, be joined again.
Lacy, give me thy hand; Rose, lend me thine!
Be what you would be! Kiss now? So, that's fine.
At night, lovers, to bed!—Now, let me see,
Which of you all mislikes this harmony.
Lord Mayor. Will you then take from me my child perforce?
King. Why, tell me, Oteley: shines not Lacy's name
As bright in the world's eye as the gay beams
Of any citizen?
Lincoln. Yea, but, my gracious lord,
I do mislike the match far more than he;
Her blood is too too base.
King. Lincoln, no more.
Dost thou not know that love respects no blood,
Cares not for difference of birth or state?
The maid is young, well born, fair, virtuous,
A worthy bride for any gentleman.
Besides, your nephew for her sake did stoop

[1] 'Fair maid, this bridegroom,' in all the quartos.

To bare necessity, and, as I hear,
Forgetting honours and all courtly pleasures,
To gain her love, became a shoemaker.
As for the honour which he lost in France,
Thus I redeem it: Lacy, kneel thee down!—
Arise, Sir Rowland Lacy! Tell me now,
Tell me in earnest, Oteley, canst thou chide,
Seeing thy Rose a lady and a bride?

Lord Mayor. I am content with what your grace hath done.

Lincoln. And I, my liege, since there's no remedy.

King. Come on, then, all shake hands: I'll have you friends;
Where [1] there is much love, all discord ends.
What says my mad lord mayor to all this love?

Eyre. O my liege, this honour you have done to my fine journeyman here, Rowland Lacy, and all these favours which you have shown to me this day in my poor house, will make Simon Eyre live longer by one dozen of warm summers more than he should.

King. Nay, my mad lord mayor, that shall be thy name,
If any grace of mine can length thy life,
One honour more I'll do thee: that new building,
Which at thy cost in Cornhill is erected,
Shall take a name from us; we'll have it called
The Leadenhall,[2] because in digging it
You found the lead that covereth the same.

Eyre. I thank your majesty.

Margery. God bless your grace!

King. Lincoln, a word with you!

Enter HODGE, FIRK, RALPH, *and more* Shoemakers

[1] A dissyllable.
[2] Stow says there was a building on the site with this name at least as early as 1362.

Eyre. How now, my mad knaves? Peace, speak softly, yonder is the king.

King. With the old troop which there we keep in pay,
We will incorporate a new supply
Before one summer more pass o'er my head,
France shall repent England was injured.
What are all those?

Lacy. All shoemakers, my liege,
Sometime [1] my fellows; in their companies
I lived as merry as an emperor.

King. My mad lord mayor, are all these shoemakers?

Eyre. All shoemakers, my liege; all gentlemen of the Gentle Craft, true Trojans, courageous cordwainers; they all kneel to the shrine of holy Saint Hugh.

All the Shoemakers. God save your majesty!

King. Mad Simon, would they anything with us?

Eyre. Mum, mad knaves! Not a word! I'll do 't; I warrant you.—They are all beggars, my liege; all for themselves, and I for them all, on both my knees do entreat, that for the honour of poor Simon Eyre and the good of his brethren, these mad knaves, your grace would vouchsafe some privilege to my new Leadenhall, that it may be lawful for us to buy and sell leather there two days a week.

King. Mad Sim, I grant your suit, you shall have patent
To hold two market-days in Leadenhall,
Mondays and Fridays, those shall be the times.
Will this content you?

All. Jesus bless your grace!

Eyre. In the name of these my poor brethren shoemakers, I most humbly thank your grace. But before I rise, seeing you are in the giving vein and we in the begging, grant Sim Eyre one boon more.

King. What is it, my lord mayor?

Eyre. Vouchsafe to taste of a poor banquet that stands

[1] 'Sometimes' in the quartos.

sweetly waiting for your sweet presence.

King. I shall undo thee, Eyre, only with feasts;
Already have I been too troublesome;
Say, have I not?

Eyre. O my dear king,[1] Sim Eyre was taken unawares upon a day of shroving, which I promised long ago to the prentices of London.

For, an 't please your highness, in time past,
I bare the water-tankard, and my coat
Sits not a whit the worse upon my back;
And then, upon a morning, some mad boys,
It was Shrove Tuesday, even as 'tis now,

Gave me my breakfast, and I swore then by the stopple of my tankard, if ever I came to be lord mayor of London, I would feast all the prentices. This day, my liege, I did it, and the slaves had an hundred tables five times covered; they are gone home and vanished;

Yet add more honour to the Gentle Trade,
Taste of Eyre's banquet, Simon's happy made.

King. Eyre, I will taste of thy banquet, and will say,
I have not met more pleasure on a day.
Friends of the Gentle Craft, thanks to you all,
Thanks, my kind lady mayoress, for our cheer.—
Come, lords, a while let 's revel it at home!
When all our sports and banquetings are done,
Wars must right wrongs which Frenchmen have begun.

Exeunt

[1] Probably all this speech was originally in verse; there are many differences of reading in the quartos.

A WOMAN KILLED WITH KINDNESS

by

THOMAS HEYWOOD

[PERSONS IN THE PLAY

MASTER FRANKFORD
MISTRESS ANNE FRANKFORD, *his wife*
SIR FRANCIS ACTON, *her brother*
SIR CHARLES MOUNTFORD
MASTER MALBY
MASTER WENDOLL, *befriended by Frankford*
MASTER CRANWELL, *an old gentleman*

NICHOLAS, JENKIN, SPIGOT, *Butler*, CICELY MILKPAIL, Other serving men and women — *Household servants to Frankford*

JACK SLIME, ROGER BRICKBAT — *Country Fellows*

JOAN MINIVER, JANE TRUBKIN, ISBELL MOTLEY — *Country Wenches*

Musicians
FALCONER *and Huntsmen*
SUSAN, *Sister to Sir Charles Mountford*
SHERIFF, *Officers*, Keeper, SHAFTON

OLD MOUNTFORD, *uncle*, SANDY, *former friend*, RODER, *former tenant*, TIDY, *cousin* — *to Sir Charles*

Serving-woman and ANNE'S *two little children*
Coachman, Carters

SCENE—The House of Frankford, Chevy Chase, a Jail, Mountford's House, and elsewhere in Yorkshire.]

PROLOGUE

I come but like a harbinger,[1] being sent
To tell you what these preparations mean.
Look for no glorious state; our Muse is bent
Upon a barren subject, a bare scene.
We could afford this twig a timber-tree,
Whose strength might boldly on your favors build;
Our russet, tissue; drone, a honey-bee;
Our barren plot, a large and spacious field;
Our coarse fare, banquets; our thin water, wine;
Our brook, a sea; our bat's eyes, eagle's sight;
Our poet's dull and earthly Muse, divine;
Our ravens, doves; our crow's black feathers, white.
  But gentle thoughts, when they may give the foil,
  Save them that yield, and spare where they may spoil.

[1] The officer who precedes the court to arrange for its entertainment.

A WOMAN KILLED WITH KINDNESS

[ACT I, SCENE I]

[*Room in Frankford's House*]

Enter MASTER JOHN FRANKFORD, MISTRESS ANNE [FRANKFORD,] SIR FRANCIS ACTON, SIR CHARLES MOUNTFORD, MASTER MALBY, MASTER WENDOLL, *and* MASTER CRANWELL

Sir F. Some music, there! None lead the bride a dance?
Sir C. Yes, would she dance *The Shaking of the Sheets;*
But that's the dance her husband means to lead her.
Wen. That's not the dance that every man must dance,
According to the ballad.
Sir F. Music, ho!
By your leave, sister,—by your husband's leave,
I should have said,—the hand that but this day
Was given you in the church I'll borrow.—Sound!
This marriage music hoists me from the ground.
Frank. Ay, you may caper; you are light and free!
Marriage hath yoked my heels; pray, then, pardon me.
Sir F. I'll have you dance too, brother!
Sir C. Master Frankford,
Y'are a happy man, sir, and much joy
Succeed your marriage mirth: you have a wife
So qualified, and with such ornaments
Both of the mind and body. First, her birth
Is noble, and her education such
As might become the daughter of a prince;

Her own tongue speaks all tongues, and her own hand
Can teach all strings to speak in their best grace,
From the shrill'st treble to the hoarsest base.
To end her many praises in one word,
She's Beauty and Perfection's eldest daughter,
Only found by yours, though many a heart hath sought her.
Frank. But that I know your virtues and chaste thoughts,
I should be jealous of your praise, Sir Charles.
Cran. He speaks no more than you approve.
Mal. Nor flatters he that gives to her her due.
Anne. I would your praise could find a fitter theme
Than my imperfect beauty to speak on!
Such as they be, if they my husband please
They súffice me now I am marrièd.
This sweet content is like a flattering glass,
To make my face seem fairer to mine eye;
But the least wrinkle from his stormy brow
Will blast the roses in my cheeks that grow.
Sir F. A perfect wife already, meek and patient!
How strangely the word husband fits your mouth,
Not married three hours since! Sister, 'tis good;
You that begin betimes thus must needs prove
Pliant and duteous in your husband's love.—
Gramercies, brother! Wrought her to't already,—
'Sweet husband,' and a curtsey, the first day?
Mark this, mark this, you that are bachelors,
And never took the grace of honest man;
Mark this, against [1] you marry, this one phrase:
In a good time that man both wins and woos
That takes his wife down in her wedding shoes.
Frank. Your sister takes not after you, Sir Francis:
All his wild blood your father spent on you;
He got her in his age, when he grew civil.
All his mad tricks were to his land entailed,

[1] When.

And you are heir to all; your sister, she
Hath to her dower her mother's modesty.
Sir C. Lord, sir, in what a happy state live you!
This morning, which to many seems a burden,
Too heavy to bear, is unto you a pleasure.
This lady is no clog, as many are;
She doth become you like a well-made suit,
In which the tailor hath used all his art;
Not like a thick coat of unseasoned frieze,[1]
Forced on your back in summer. She's no chain
To tie your neck, and curb ye to the yoke;
But she's a chain of gold to adorn your neck.
You both adorn each other, and your hands,
Methinks, are matches. There's equality
In this fair combination; y'are both
Scholars, both young, both being descended nobly.
There's music in this sympathy; it carries
Consort and expectation of much joy,
Which God bestow on you from this first day
Until your dissolution,—that's for aye!
Sir F. We keep you here too long, good brother Frankford.
Into the hall; away! Go cheer your guests.
What! Bride and bridegroom both withdrawn at once?
If you be missed, the guests will doubt their welcome,
And charge you with unkindness.
Frank. To prevent it,
I'll leave you here, to see the dance within.
Anne. And so will I.
[*Exeunt* FRANKFORD *and* MISTRESS FRANKFORD]
Sir F. To part you it were sin.—
Now, gallants, while the town musicians
Finger their frets [2] within, and the mad lads
And country lasses, every mother's child,

[1] Coarse cloth.
[2] The points at which the strings are stopped on the lute.

With nosegays and bride-laces [1] in their hats,
Dance all their country measures, rounds and jigs,
What shall we do? Hark! They're all on the hoigh; [2]
They toil like mill-horses, and turn as round,—
Marry, not on the toe! Ay, and they caper,
Not without cutting; you shall see, to-morrow,
The hall-floor pecked and dinted like a mill-stone,
Made with their high shoes. Though their skill be small,
Yet they tread heavy where their hobnails fall.

Sir C. Well, leave them to their sports!—Sir Francis Acton,
I'll make a match with you! Meet to-morrow
At Chevy Chase; I'll fly my hawk with yours.

Sir F. For what? for what?

Sir C. Why, for a hundred pound.

Sir F. Pawn me some gold of that!

Sir C. Here are ten angels; [3]
I'll make them good a hundred pound to-morrow
Upon my hawk's wing.

Sir F. 'Tis a match; 'tis done.
Another hundred pound upon your dogs;—
Dare ye, Sir Charles?

Sir C. I dare; were I sure to lose,
I durst do more than that; here's my hand.
The first course for a hundred pound!

Sir F. A match.

Wen. Ten angels on Sir Francis Acton's hawk;
As much upon his dogs!

Cran. I am for Sir Charles Mountford: I have seen
His hawk and dog both tried. What! Clap ye hands,
Or is't no bargain?

Wen. Yes, and stake them down.
Were they five hundred, they were all my own.

[1] Streamers.
[2] Out of bounds.
[3] Gold coins.

Sir F. Be stirring early with the lark to-morrow;
I'll rise into my saddle ere the sun
Rise from his bed.

Sir C. If there you miss me, say
I am no gentleman! I'll hold my day.

Sir F. It holds on all sides.—Come, to-night let's dance;
Early to-morrow let's prepare to ride:
We had need be three hours up before the bride.

Exeunt

[SCENE II]

[*Yard of the Same*]

Enter NICK *and* JENKIN, JACK SLIME, ROGER BRICKBAT, *with* Country Wenches, *and two or three* Musicians

Jen. Come, Nick, take you Joan Miniver, to trace withal; Jack Slime, traverse you with Cicely Milkpail; I will take Jane Trubkin, and Roger Brickbat shall have Isbell Motley. And now that they are busy in the parlor, come, strike up; we'll have a crash [1] here in the yard.

Nick. My humor is not compendious: dancing I possess not, though I can foot it; yet, since I am fallen into the hands of Cicely Milkpail, I consent.

Slime. Truly, Nick, though we were never brought up like serving courtiers, yet we have been brought up with serving creatures,—ay, and God's creatures, too; for we have been brought up to serve sheep, oxen, horses, hogs, and such like; and, though we be but country fellows, it may be in the way of dancing we can do the horse-trick as well as the serving-men.

Brick. Ay, and the cross-point [2] too.

Jen. O Slime! O Brickbat! Do not you know that comparisons are odious? Now we are odious ourselves, too; therefore there are no comparisons to be made betwixt us.

[1] Frolic. [2] Dance steps.

Nick. I am sudden, and not superfluous;
I am quarrelsome, and not seditious;
I am peaceable, and not contentious;
I am brief, and not compendious.

Slime. Foot it quickly! If the music overcome not my melancholy, I shall quarrel; and if they suddenly do not strike up, I shall presently strike thee down.

Jen. No quarreling, for God's sake! Truly, if you do, I shall set a knave between ye.

Slime. I come to dance, not to quarrel. Come, what shall it be? *Rogero?*[1]

Jen. *Rogero?* No; we will dance *The Beginning of the World.*

Cicely. I love no dance so well as *John come kiss me now.*

Nick. I that have ere now deserved a cushion, call for the *Cushion-dance.*

Brick. For my part, I like nothing so well as *Tom Tyler.*

Jen. No; we'll have *The Hunting of the Fox.*

Slime. *The Hay, The Hay!* There's nothing like *The Hay.*[2]

Nick. I have said, do say, and will say again——

Jen. Every man agree to have it as Nick says!

All. Content.

Nick. It hath been, it now is, and it shall be——

Cicely. What, Master Nicholas? What?

Nick. *Put on your Smock a' Monday.*

Jen. So the dance will come cleanly off! Come, for God's sake, agree of something: if you like not that, put it to the musicians; or let me speak for all, and we'll have *Sellenger's Round.*

All. That, that, that!

Nick. No, I am resolved thus it shall be: First take hands, then take ye to your heels!

Jen. Why, would you have us run away?

[1] Name of dance tune.
[2] A lively dance.

Nick. No; but I would have ye shake your heels.—Music, strike up!

They dance; NICK *dancing, speaks stately and scurvily,*[1] *the rest, after the country fashion*

Jen. Hey! Lively, my lasses! Here's a turn for thee!

Exeunt

[SCENE III]

[*Chevy Chase*]

Wind horns. Enter SIR CHARLES [MOUNTFORD,] SIR FRANCIS [ACTON,] MALBY, CRANWELL, WENDOLL, Falconer, *and* Huntsmen

Sir C. So; well cast off! Aloft, aloft! Well flown!
O, now she takes her at the souse,[2] and strikes her
Down to th' earth, like a swift thunder-clap.

Wen. She hath struck ten angels out of my way.

Sir F. A hundred pound from me.

Sir C. What, falconer!

Falc. At hand, sir!

Sir C. Now she hath seized the fowl and 'gins to plume her,[3]
Rebeck [4] her not; rather stand still and check her!
So, seize her gets,[5] her jesses,[6] and her bells! Away!

Sir F. My hawk kill'd, too.

Sir C. Ay, but 'twas at the querre
Not at the mount, like mine.

Sir F. Judgment, my masters!

Cran. Yours mis'd her at the ferre.[7]

Wen. Ay, but our merlin first had plumed the fowl,

[1] Ridiculously.
[2] Swoop.
[3] Scatter feathers.
[4] Call back.
[5] Doubtless some part of the hawk's harness.
[6] Leg-straps.
[7] Perhaps at a higher point.

And twice renewed [1] her from the river too.
Her bells, Sir Francis, had not both one weight,
Nor was one semi-tune above the other.
Methinks, these Milan bells do sound too full,
And spoil the mounting of your hawk.

Sir C. 'Tis lost.

Sir F. I grant it not. Mine likewise seized a fowl
Within her talons, and you saw her paws
Full of the feathers; both her petty singles [2]
And her long singles griped her more than other;
The terrials [3] of her legs were stained with blood,
Not of the fowl only, she did discomfit
Some of her feathers; but she brake away.
Come, come; your hawk is but a rifler.[4]

Sir C. How!

Sir F. Ay, and your doys are trindle-tails [5] and curs.

Sir C. You stir my blood.
You keep not one good hound in all your kennel,
Nor one good hawk upon your perch.

Sir F. How, knight!

Sir C. So, knight. You will not swagger, sir?

Sir F. Why, say I did?

Sir C. Why, sir,
I say you would gain as much by swaggering
As you have got by wagers on your dogs.
You will come short in all things.

Sir F. Not in this!
Now I'll strike home. [*Strikes* SIR CHARLES

Sir C. Thou shalt to thy long home,
Or I will want my will.

Sir F. All they that love Sir Francis, follow me!

[1] Renewed the attack.
[2] Toes.
[3] Talons.
[4] Bungler.
[5] Curly-tailed.

Sir C. All that affect Sir Charles, draw on my part!
Cran. On this side heaves my hand.
Wen. Here goes my heart.

They divide themselves. SIR CHARLES MOUNTFORD, CRANWELL, Falconer, *and* Huntsman, *fight against* SIR FRANCIS ACTON, WENDOLL, *his* Falconer *and* Huntsman; *and* SIR CHARLES *hath the better, and beats them away, killing both of* SIR FRANCIS *his men.* [*Exeunt all but*] SIR CHARLES MOUNTFORD

Sir C. My God, what have I done! What have I done!
My rage hath plunged into a sea of blood,
In which my soul lies drowned. Poor innocents,
For whom we are to answer! Well, 'tis done,
And I remain the victor. A great conquest,
When I would give this right hand, nay, this head,
To breathe in them new life whom I have slain!—
Forgive me, God! 'Twas in the heat of blood,
And anger quite removes me from myself.
It was not I, but rage, did this vile murder;
Yet I, and not my rage, must answer it.
Sir Francis Acton, he is fled the field;
With him all those that did partake his quarrel;
And I am left alone with sorrow dumb,
And in my height of conquest overcome.

Enter SUSAN

Susan. O God! My brother wounded 'mong the dead!
Unhappy jests, that in such earnest ends!
The rumor of this fear stretched to my ears,
And I am come to know if you be wounded.
Sir C. O, sister, sister! Wounded at the heart.
Susan. My God forbid!
Sir C. In doing that thing which he forbad,
I am wounded, sister.

Susan. I hope, not at the heart.

Sir C. Yes, at the heart.

Susan. O God! A surgeon, there.

Sir C. Call me a surgeon, sister, for my soul!
The sin of murder, it hath pierced my heart
And made a wide wound there; but for these scratches,
They are nothing, nothing.

Susan. Charles, what have you done?
Sir Francis hath great friends, and will pursue you
Unto the utmost danger [1] of the law.

Sir C. My conscience hath become mine enemy,
And will pursue me more than Acton can.

Susan. O! Fly, sweet brother!

Sir C. Shall I fly from thee?
Why, Sue, art weary of my company?

Susan. Fly from your foe!

Sir C. You, sister, are my friend,
And flying you, I shall pursue my end.

Susan. Your company is as my eyeball dear;
Being far from you, no comfort can be near.
Yet fly to save your life! What would I care
To spend my future age in black despair,
So you were safe? And yet to live one week
Without my brother Charles, through every cheek
My streaming tears would downwards run so rank,[2]
Till they could set on either side a bank,
And in the midst a channel; so my face
For two salt-water brooks shall still find place.

Sir C. Thou shalt not weep so much; for I will stay,
In spite of danger's teeth. I'll live with thee,
Or I'll not live at all. I will not sell
My country and my father's patrimony,
Nor thy sweet sight, for a vain hope of life.

[1] Limit. [2] Excessively.

Enter Sheriff, *with* Officers

Sher. Sir Charles, I am made the unwilling instrument
Of your attach and apprehension.
I'm sorry that the blood of innocent men
Should be of you exacted. It was told me
That you were guarded with a troop of friends,
And therefore I come thus armed.
Sir C. O Master Sheriff!
I came into the field with many friends,
But see, they all have left me; only one
Clings to my sad misfortune, my dear sister.
I know you for an honest gentleman;
I yield my weapons, and submit to you.
Convey me where you please!
Sher. To prison, then,
To answer for the lives of these dead men.
Susan. O God! O God!
Sir C. Sweet sister, every strain
Of sorrow from your heart augments my pain;
Your grief abounds, and hits against my breast.
Sher. Sir, will you go?
Sir C. Even where it likes you best.
[*Exeunt*]

[ACT II, SCENE I]

[*Frankford's House*]

Enter FRANKFORD *in a study*

Frank. How happy am I amongst other men,
That in my mean estate embrace content!
I am a gentleman, and by my birth
Companion with a king; a king's no more.
I am possessed of many fair revénues,
Sufficient to maintain a gentleman;
Touching my mind, I am studied in all arts;
The riches of my thoughts and of my time

Have been a good proficient; but, the chief
Of all the sweet felicities on earth,
I have a fair, a chaste, and loving wife,
Perfection all, all truth, all ornament.
If man on earth may truly happy be,
Of these at once possessed, sure, I am he.

Enter NICHOLAS

Nick. Sir, there's a gentleman attends without
To speak with you.
Frank. On horseback?
Nick. Yes, on horseback.
Frank. Entreat him to alight, and I'll attend him.
Know'st thou him, Nick?
Nick. Know him? Yes; his name's Wendoll.
It seems, he comes in haste: his horse is booted
Up to the flank in mire, himself all spotted
And stained with plashing. Sure, he rid in fear,
Or for a wager. Horse and man both sweat;
I ne'er saw two in such a smoking heat.
Frank. Entreat him in: about it instantly!
[*Exit* NICHOLAS]
This Wendoll I have noted, and his carriage
Hath pleased me much; by observation
I have noted many good deserts in him.
He's affable, and seen [1] in many things;
Discourses well; a good companion;
And though of small means, yet a gentleman
Of a good house, somewhat pressed by want.
I have preferred him to a second place
In my opinion and my best regard.

Enter WENDOLL, MISTRESS FRANKFORD, *and* NICHOLAS

Anne. O, Master Frankford! Master Wendoll here

[1] Proficient.

Brings you the strangest news that e'er you heard.

Frank. What news, sweet wife? What news, good Master Wendoll?

Wen. You knew the match made 'twixt Sir Francis Acton
And Sir Charles Mountford?

Frank. True; with their hounds and hawks?

Wen. The matches were both played.

Frank. Ha? And which won?

Wen. Sir Francis, your wife's brother, had the worst,
And lost the wager.

Frank. Why, the worse his chance;
Perhaps the fortune of some other day
Will change his luck.

Anne. O, but you hear not all.
Sir Francis lost, and yet was loath to yield.
At length the two knights grew to difference,
From words to blows, and so to banding [1] sides;
Where valorous Sir Charles slew, in his spleen,
Two of your brother's men,—his falconer,
And his good huntsman, whom he loved so well.
More men were wounded, no more slain outright.

Frank. Now, trust me, I am sorry for the knight
But is my brother safe?

Wen. All whole and sound.
His body not being blemished with one wound.
But poor Sir Charles is to the prison led,
To answer at th' assize for them that's dead.

Frank. I thank your pains, sir. Had the news been better,
Your will was to have brought it, Master Wendoll.
Sir Charles will find hard friends; his case is heinous.
And will be most severely censured on.
I'm sorry for him. Sir, a word with you!
I know you, sir, to be a gentleman
In all things; your possibility but mean;
Please you to use my table and my purse;

[1] Taking.

They're yours.

Wen. O Lord, sir! I shall ne'er deserve it.

Frank. O sir, disparage not your worth too much:
You are full of quality [1] and fair desert.
Choose of my men which shall attend you, sir,
And he is yours. I will allow you, sir,
Your man, your gelding, and your table, all
At my own charge; be my companion!

Wen. Master Frankford, I have oft been bound to you
By many favors; this exceeds them all,
That I shall never merit your least favor;
But when your last remembrance I forget,
Heaven at my soul exact that weighty debt!

Frank. There needs no protestation; for I know you
Virtuous, and therefore grateful.—Prithee, Nan,
Use him with all thy loving'st courtesy!

Anne. As far as modesty may well extend,
It is my duty to receive your friend.

Frank. To dinner! Come, sir, from this present day,
Welcome to me for ever! Come, away!

[*Exeunt* FRANKFORD, MISTRESS FRANKFORD,
and WENDOLL]

Nick. I do not like this fellow by no means:
I never see him but my heart still yearns.[2]
Zounds! I could fight with him, yet know not why;
The devil and he are all one in mine eye.

Enter JENKIN

Jen. O Nick! What gentleman is that, that comes to lie [3] at our house? My master allows him one to wait on him, and I believe it will fall to thy lot.

Nick. I love my master; by these hilts, I do;
But rather than I'll ever come to serve him,
I'll turn away my master.

[1] Accomplishment.
[2] Grieves.
[3] Stay.

Enter CICELY

Cic. Nich'las! where are you, Nich'las? You must come in, Nich'las, and help the gentleman off with his boots.

Nick. If I pluck off his boots, I'll eat the spurs,
And they shall stick fast in my throat like burrs.

Cic. Then, Jenkin, come you!

Jen. Nay, 'tis no boot [1] for me to deny it. My master hath given me a coat here, but he takes pains himself to brush it once or twice a day with a hollywand.

Cic. Come, come, make haste, that you may wash your hands again, and help to serve in dinner!

Jen. You may see, my masters, though it be afternoon with you, 'tis but early days with us, for we have not dined yet. Stay but a little; I'll but go in and help to bear up the first course, and come to you again presently. *Exeunt*

[SCENE II]

[*The Gaol*]

Enter MALBY *and* CRANWELL

Mal. This is the sessions-day; pray can you tell me
How young Sir Charles hath sped? Is he acquit,
Or must he try the law's strict penalty?

Cran. He's cleared of all, spite of his enemies,
Whose earnest labor was to take his life.
But in this suit of pardon he hath spent
All the revenues that his father left him;
And he is now turned a plain countryman,
Reformed in all things. See, sir, here he comes.

Enter SIR CHARLES *and his* Keeper

Keep. Discharge your fees, and you are then at freedom.

Sir C. Here, Master Keeper, take the poor remainder

[1] Use.

Of all the wealth I have! My heavy foes
Have made my purse light; but, alas! to me
'Tis wealth enough that you have set me free.

Mal. God give you joy of your delivery!
I am glad to see you abroad, Sir Charles.

Sir C. The poorest knight in England, Master Malby;
My life has cost me all my patrimony
My father left his son. Well, God forgive them
That are the authors of my penury!

Enter SHAFTON

Shaft. Sir Charles! A hand, a hand! At liberty?
Now, by the faith I owe, I am glad to see it.
What want you? Wherein may I pleasure you?

Sir C. O me! O, most unhappy gentleman!
I am not worthy to have friends stirred up,
Whose hands may help me in this plunge of want.
I would I were in heaven, to inherit there
Th' immortal birthright which my Saviour keeps,
And by no unthrift can be bought and sold;
For here on earth what pleasures should we trust?

Shaft. To rid you from these contemplations,
Three hundred pounds you shall receive of me;
Nay, five for fail. Come, sir, the sight of gold
Is the most sweet receipt for melancholy,
And will revive your spirits. You shall hold law
With your proud adversaries. Tush! let Frank Acton
Wage, with his knighthood, like expense with me,
And he will sink, he will.—Nay, good Sir Charles,
Applaud your fortune and your fair escape
From all these perils.

Sir C. O sir! they have undone me.
Two thousand and five hundred pound a year
My father at his death possessed me of;
All which the envious Acton made me spend;

And, notwithstanding all this large expense,
I had much ado to gain my liberty;
And I have only now a house of pleasure
With some five hundred pounds reserved,
Both to maintain me and my loving sister.
Shaft. [*Aside*] That must I have, it lies convenient for me.
If I can fasten but one finger on him,
With my full hand I'll gripe him to the heart.
'Tis not for love I proffered him this coin,
But for my gain and pleasure.—Come, Sir Charles,
I know you have need of money; take my offer.
Sir C. Sir, I accept it, and remain indebted
Even to the best of my unable [1] power.
Come, gentlemen, and see it tendered down! *Exeunt*

[SCENE III]

[*Frankford's House*]

Enter WENDOLL, *melancholy*

Wen. I am a villain, if I apprehend
But such a thought! Then, to attempt the deed,
Slave, thou art damned without redemption.—
I'll drive away this passion with a song.
A song! Ha, ha! A song! As if, fond [2] man,
Thy eyes could swim in laughter, when thy soul
Lies drenched and drownèd in red tears of blood!
I'll pray, and see if God within my heart
Plant better thoughts. Why, prayers are meditations,
And when I meditate (O, God forgive me!)
It is on her divine perfections.
I will forget her; I will arm myself
Not t' entertain a thought of love to her;
And, when I come by chance into her presence,

[1] Feeble. [2] Foolish.

I'll hale [1] these balls until my eye-strings crack,
From being pulled and drawn to look that way.

Enter, over the Stage, FRANKFORD, *his* Wife, *and* NICHOLAS, [*and exit*]

O God, O God! With what a violence
I'm hurried to mine own destruction!
There goest thou, the most perfect'st man
That ever England bred a gentleman,
And shall I wrong his bed?—Thou God of thunder!
Stay, in thy thoughts of vengeance and of wrath,
Thy great, almighty, and all-judging hand
From speedy execution on a villain,
A villain, and a traitor to his friend.

Enter JENKIN [*behind*]

Jen. Did your worship call?

Wen. He doth maintain me; he allows me largely
Money to spend.

Jen. By my faith, so do not you me: I cannot get a cross [2] of you.

Wen. My gelding, and my man.

Jen. That's Sorrel and I.

Wen. This kindness grows of no alliance 'twixt us.

Jen. Nor is my service of any great acquaintance.

Wen. I never bound him to me by desert.
Of a mere stranger, a poor gentleman,
A man by whom in no kind he could gain,
And he hath placed me in his highest thoughts,
Made me companion with the best and chiefest
In Yorkshire. He cannot eat without me,
Nor laugh without me; I am to his body
As necessary as his digestion,

[1] Hold. [2] A piece of money.

And equally do make him whole or sick.
And shall I wrong this man? Base man! Ingrate!
Hast thou the power, straight with thy gory hands
To rip thy image from his bleeding heart,
To scratch thy name from out the holy book
Of his remembrance, and to wound his name
That holds thy name so dear? or rend his heart
To whom thy heart was knit and joined together?—
And yet I must. Then Wendoll, be content!
Thus villains, when they would, cannot repent.

Jen. What a strange humor is my new master in! Pray God he be not mad; if he should be so, I should never have any mind to serve him in Bedlam. It may be he's mad for missing of me.

Wen. [*Seeing* JENKIN] What, Jenkin! Where's your mistress?

Jen. Is your worship married?

Wen. Why dost thou ask?

Jen. Because you are my master; and if I have a mistress, I would be glad, like a good servant, to do my duty to her.

Wen. I mean Mistress Frankford.

Jen. Marry, sir, her husband is riding out of town, and she went very lovingly to bring him on his way to horse. Do you see, sir? Here she comes, and here I go.

Wen. Vanish! [*Exit* JENKIN]

Enter MISTRESS FRANKFORD

Anne. Y'are well met, sir; now, in troth, my husband,
Before he took horse, had a great desire
To speak with you; we sought about the house,
Hallooed into the fields, sent every way,
But could not meet you. Therefore, he enjoined me
To do unto you his most kind commends;
Nay, more: he wills you, as you prize his love,
Or hold in estimation his kind friendship,

To make bold in his absence, and command
Even as himself were present in the house;
For you must keep his table, use his servants,
And be a present Frankford in his absence.

Wen. I thank him for his love.—
[*Aside*] Give me a name, you, whose infectious tongues
Are tipped with gall and poison: as you would
Think on a man that had your father slain,
Murdered your children, made your wives base strumpets,
So call me, call me so; print in my face
The most stigmatic title of a villain,
For hatching treason to so true a friend!

Anne. Sir, you are most beholding to my husband;
You are a man most dear in his regard.

Wen. I am bound unto your husband, and you too.
[*Aside*] I will not speak to wrong a gentleman
Of that good estimation, my kind friend.
I will not; zounds! I will not. I may choose,
And I will choose. Shall I be so misled,
Or shall I purchase [1] to my father's crest
The motto of a villain? If I say
I will not do it, what thing can enforce me?
What can compel me? What sad destiny
Hath such command upon my yielding thoughts?
I will not;—ha! Some fury pricks me on;
The swift fates drag me at their chariot wheel,
And hurry me to mischief. Speak I must:
Injure myself, wrong her, deceive his trust!

Anne. Are you not well, sir, that ye seem thus troubled?
There is sedition in your countenance.

Wen. And in my heart, fair angel, chaste and wise.
I love you! Start not, speak not, answer not;
I love you,—nay, let me speak the rest;
Bid me to swear, and I will call to record
The host of heaven.

[1] Add.

Anne. The host of heaven forbid
Wendoll should hatch such a disloyal thought!
Wen. Such is my fate; to this suit was I born,
To wear rich pleasure's crown, or fortune's scorn.
Anne. My husband loves you.
Wen. I know it.
Anne. He esteems you,
Even as his brain, his eye-ball, or his heart.
Wen. I have tried it.
Anne. His purse is your exchequer, and his table
Doth freely serve you.
Wen. So I have found it.
Anne. O! With what face of brass, what brow of steel,
Can you, unblushing, speak this to the face
Of the espous'd wife of so dear a friend?
It is my husband that maintains your state;
Will you dishonor him? I am his wife,
That in your power hath left his whole affairs.
It is to me you speak.
Wen. O speak no more;
For more than this I know, and have recorded
Within the red-leaved table [1] of my heart.
Fair, and of all beloved, I was not fearful
Bluntly to give my life into your hand,
And at one hazard all my earthly means.
Go, tell your husband; he will turn me off,
And I am then undone. I care not, I;
'Twas for your sake. Perchance, in rage he'll kill me;
I care not, 'twas for you. Say I incur
The general name of villain through the world,
Of traitor to my friend; I care not, I.
Beggary, shame, death, scandal, and reproach,
For you I'll hazard all. Why, what care I?
For you I'll love, and in your love I'll die.

[1] Note book.

Anne. You move me, sir, to passion and to pity.
The love I bear my husband is as precious
As my soul's health.

Wen. I love your husband too,
And for his love I will engage my life.
Mistake me not; the augmentation
Of my sincere affection borne to you
Doth no whit lessen my regard of him.
I will be secret, lady, close as night;
And not the light of one small glorious star
Shall shine here in my forehead, to bewray
That act of night.

Anne. What shall I say?
My soul is wandering, and hath lost her way.
O, Master Wendoll! O!

Wen. Sigh not, sweet saint;
For every sigh you breathe draws from my heart
A drop of blood.

Anne. I ne'er offended yet:
My fault, I fear, will in my brow be writ.
Women that fall, not quite bereft of grace,
Have their offences noted in their face.
I blush, and am ashamed. O, Master Wendoll,
Pray God I be not born to curse your tongue,
That hath enchanted me! This maze I am in
I fear will prove the labyrinth of sin.

Enter NICHOLAS, [*behind*]

Wen. The path of pleasure, and the gate to bliss,
Which on your lips I knock at with a kiss!

Nick. I'll kill the rogue.

Wen. Your husband is from home, your bed's no blab.
Nay, look not down and blush!

[*Exeunt* WENDOLL *and* MISTRESS FRANKFORD]

Nick. Zounds! I'll stab.
Ay, Nick, was it thy chance to come just in the nick?

I love my master, and I hate that slave;
I love my mistress; but these tricks I like not.
My master shall not pocket up this wrong;
I'll eat my fingers first. What say'st thou, metal? [1]
Does not that rascal Wendoll go on legs
That thou must cut off? Hath he not ham-strings
That thou must hough? [2] Nay, mettle, thou shalt stand
To all I say. I'll henceforth turn a spy,
And watch them in their close conveyances.[3]
I never looked for better of that rascal,
Since he came miching [4] first into our house.
It is that Satan hath corrupted her;
For she was fair and chaste. I'll have an eye
In all their gestures. Thus I think of them:
If they proceed as they have done before,
Wendoll's a knave, my mistress is a —— *Exit*

[ACT III, SCENE I]

[*Sir Charles Mountford's House*]

Enter [Sir] Charles *and* Susan

Sir C. Sister, you see we are driven to hard shift,
To keep this poor house we have left unsold.
I am now enforced to follow husbandry,
And you to milk; and do we not live well?
Well, I thank God.

Susan. O, brother! here's a change,
Since old Sir Charles died, in our father's house.

Sir C. All things on earth thus change, some up, some down;
Content's a kingdom, and I wear that crown.

[1] Man of mettle, spirit.
[2] Hew.
[3] Secret doings.
[4] Snooping.

Enter SHAFTON, *with a* Sergeant

Shaft. Good morrow, morrow, Sir Charles! What! With your sister,
Plying your husbandry?—Sergeant, stand off!—
You have a pretty house here, and a garden,
And goodly ground about it. Since it lies
So near a lordship that I lately bought,
I would fain buy it of you. I will give you——

Sir C. O, pardon me; this house successively
Hath longed to me and my progenitors
Three hundred years. My great-great-grandfather,
He in whom first our gentle style [1] began,
Dwelt here, and in this ground increased this mole-hill
Unto that mountain which my father left me.
Where he the first of all our house began,
I now the last will end, and keep this house,
This virgin title, never yet deflowered
By any unthrift of the Mountfords' line.
In brief, I will not sell it for more gold
Than you could hide or pave the ground withal.

Shaft. Ha, ha! a proud mind and a beggar's purse!
Where's my three hundred pounds, besides the use?
I have brought it to execution
By course of law. What! Is my monies ready?

Sir C. An execution, sir, and never tell me
You put my bond in suit? You deal extremely.

Shaft. Sell me the land, and I'll acquit you straight.

Sir C. Alas, alas! 'Tis all trouble hath left me,
To cherish me and my poor sister's life.
If this were sold, our names should then be quite
Razed from the bead-roll [2] of gentility.
You see what hard shift we have made to keep it
Allied still to our own name. This palm you see,
Labor hath glowed within; her silver brow,

[1] Title. [2] List.

That never tasted a rough winter's blast
Without a mask or fan, doth with a grace
Defy cold winter, and his storms outface.

Susan. Sir, we feed sparing, and we labor hard;
We lie uneasy, to reserve to us
And our succession this small spot of ground.

Sir C. I have so bent my thoughts to husbandry,
That I protest I scarcely can remember
What a new fashion is; how silk or satin
Feels in my hand. Why, pride is grown to us
A mere, mere stranger. I have quite forgot
The names of all that ever waited on me.
I cannot name ye any of my hounds,
Once from whose echoing mouths I heard all music
That e'er my heart desired. What should I say?
To keep this place, I have changed myself away.

Shaft. [*To the Sergeant*] Arrest him at my suit!—Actions and actions
Shall keep thee in continual bondage fast;
Nay, more, I'll sue thee by a late appeal,
And call thy former life in question.
The keeper is my friend; thou shalt have irons,
And usage such as I'll deny to dogs.—
Away with him!

Sir C. Ye are too timorous.
But trouble is my master,
And I will serve him truly.—My kind sister,
Thy tears are of no use to mollify
This flinty man. Go to my father's brother,
My kinsmen, and allies; entreat them for me,
To ransom me from this injurious man
That seeks my ruin.

Shaft. Come, irons, irons! Come, away;
I'll see thee lodged far from the sight of day.

Exeunt [*except* SUSAN]

Susan. My heart's so hardened with the frost of grief,
Death cannot pierce it through.—Tyrant too fell!
So lead the fiends condemnèd souls to hell.

Enter [Sir Francis] Acton *and* Malby

Sir F. Again to prison! Malby, hast thou seen
A poor slave better tortured? Shall we hear
The music of his voice cry from the grate,[1]
Meat, for the Lord's sake? No, no; yet I am not
Throughly revenged. They say, he hath a pretty wench
To his sister; shall I, in mercy-sake
To him and to his kindred, bribe the fool
To shame herself by lewd, dishonest lust?
I'll proffer largely; but, the deed being done,
I'll smile to see her base confusion.

Mal. Methinks, Sir Francis, you are full revenged
For greater wrongs than he can proffer you.
See where the poor sad gentlewoman stands!

Sir F. Ha, ha! Now will I flout her poverty,
Deride her fortunes, scoff her base estate;
My very soul the name of Mountford hate.
But stay, my heart! O, what a look did fly
To strike my soul through with thy piercing eye!
I am enchanted; all my spirits are fled,
And with one glance my envious spleen struck dead.

Susan. Acton! That seeks our blood! [*Runs away*]

Sir F. O chaste and fair!

Mal. Sir Francis! Why, Sir Francis! in a trance?
Sir Francis! What cheer, man? Come, come, how is't?

Sir F. Was she not fair? Or else this judging eye
Cannot distinguish beauty.

Mal. She was fair.

Sir F. She was an angel in a mortal's shape,
And ne'er descended from old Mountford's line.

[1] Of the debtors' prison.

But soft, soft, let me call my wits together!
A poor, poor wench, to my great adversary
Sister, whose very souls denounce stern war
Each against other! How now, Frank, turned fool
Or madman, whether? But no! Master of
My perfect senses and directest wits.
Then why should I be in this violent humor
Of passion and of love? And with a person
So different every way, and so opposed
In all contractions [1] and still-warring actions?
Fie, fie! How I dispute against my soul!
Come, come; I'll gain her, or in her fair quest
Purchase my soul free and immortal rest. *Exeunt*

[SCENE II]

[*Frankford's House*]

Enter three or four Serving-men, *one with a voider* [2] *and a wooden knife, to take away; another* [*with*] *the salt and bread; another* [*with*] *the table-cloth and napkins; another* [*with*] *the carpet;* [3] JENKIN *with two lights after them*

Jen. So; march in order, and retire in battle array! My master and the guests have supped already; all's taken away. Here, now spread for the serving-men in the hall!—Butler, it belongs to your office.

But. I know it, Jenkin. What d'ye call the gentleman that supped there to-night?

Jen. Who? My master?

But. No, no; Master Wendoll, he's a daily guest. I mean the gentleman that came but this afternoon.

Jen. His name's Master Cranwell. God's light! Hark,

[1] Legal transactions (Bates).
[2] Basket.
[3] Tablecloth.

within there; my master calls to lay more billets[1] upon the fire. Come, come! Lord, how we that are in office[2] here in the house are troubled! One spread the carpet in the parlor, and stand ready to snuff the lights; the rest be ready to prepare their stomachs![3] More lights in the hall, there! Come, Nicholas.

Exeunt [*all but* NICHOLAS]

Nick. I cannot eat; but had I Wendoll's heart, I would eat that. The rogue grows impudent. O! I have seen such vild,[4] notorious tricks, ready to make my eyes dart from my head. I'll tell my master; by this air, I will; fall what may fall, I'll tell him. Here he comes.

Enter MASTER FRANKFORD, *as it were brushing the crumbs from his clothes with a napkin, as newly risen from supper*

Frank. Nicholas, what make you here? Why are not you
At supper in the hall, among your fellows?
Nick. Master, I stayed your rising from the board,
To speak with you.
Frank. Be brief then, gentle Nicholas;
My wife and guests attend me in the parlor.
Why dost thou pause? Now, Nicholas, you want money,
And, unthrift-like, would eat into your wages
Ere you had earned it. Here, sir, 's half-a-crown;
Play the good husband,[5]—and away to supper!
Nick. By this hand, an honorable gentleman! I will not see him wronged.
Sir, I have served you long; you entertained me
Seven years before your beard; you knew me, sir,
Before you knew my mistress.

[1] Logs.
[2] Service.
[3] Appetites.
[4] Vile.
[5] Husbandman.

Frank. What of this, good Nicholas?

Nick. I never was a make-bate[1] or a knave;
I have no fault but one—I'm given to quarrel,
But not with women. I will tell you, master,
That which will make your heart leap from your breast,
Your hair to startle from your head, your ears to tingle.

Frank. What preparation's this to dismal news?

Nick. 'Sblood! sir, I love you better than your wife.
I'll make it good.

Frank. Y' are a knave, and I have much ado
With wonted patience to contain my rage,
And not to break thy pate. Th' art a knave
I'll turn you, with your base comparisons,
Out of my doors.

Nick. Do, do.
There is not room for Wendoll and me too,
Both in one house. O master, master,
That Wendoll is a villain!

Frank. Ay, Saucy?

Nick. Strike, strike, do strike; yet hear me! I am no fool;
I know a villain, when I see him act
Deeds of a villain. Master, master, that base slave
Enjoys my mistress, and dishonors you.

Frank. Thou hast killed me with a weapon, whose sharp point
Hath pricked quite through and through my shivering heart.
Drops of cold sweat sit dangling on my hairs,
Like morning's dew upon the golden flowers,
And I am plunged into strange agonies.
What did'st thou say? If any word that touched
His credit, or her reputation,
It is as hard to enter my belief,
As Dives into heaven.

Nick. I can gain nothing:
They are two that never wronged me. I knew before

[1] Maker of quarrels.

'Twas but a thankless office, and perhaps
As much as is my service, or my life
Is worth. All this I know; but this, and more,
More by a thousand dangers, could not hire me
To smother such a heinous wrong from you.
I saw, and I have said.

Frank. [*Aside*] 'Tis probable. Though blunt, yet he is honest.

Though I durst pawn my life, and on their faith
Hazard the dear salvation of my soul,
Yet in my trust I may be too secure.
May this be true? O, may it? Can it be?
Is it by any wonder possible?
Man, woman, what thing mortal can we trust,
When friends and bosom wives prove so unjust?—
What instance hast thou of this strange report?

Nick. Eyes, master, eyes.

Frank. Thy eyes may be deceived, I tell thee;
For should an angel from the heavens drop down,
And preach this to me that thyself hast told,
He should have much ado to win belief;
In both their loves I am so confident.

Nick. Shall I discourse the same by circumstance?

Frank. No more! To supper, and command your fellows
To attend us and the strangers! Not a word,
I charge thee, on thy life! Be secret, then;
For I know nothing.

Nick. I am dumb; and, now that I have eased my stomach,[1]
I will go fill my stomach. *Exit*

Frank. Away! Begone!
She is well born, descendèd nobly;
Virtuous her education; her repute
Is in the general voice of all the country
Honest and fair; her carriage, her demeanor,

[1] Resentment.

In all her actions that concern the love
To me her husband, modest, chaste, and godly.
Is all this seeming gold plain copper?
But he, that Judas that hath borne my purse,
And sold me for a sin! O God! O God!
Shall I put up these wrongs? No! Shall I trust
The bare report of this suspicious groom,
Before the double-gilt, the well-hatch[ed][1] ore
Of their two hearts? No, I will lose these thoughts;
Distraction I will banish from my brow,
And from my looks exile sad discontent.
Their wonted favors in my tongue shall flow;
Till I know all, I'll nothing seem to know.—
Lights and a table there! Wife, M[aster] Wendoll,
And gentle Master Cranwell!

Enter MISTRESS FRANKFORD, MASTER WENDOLL, MASTER CRANWELL, NICHOLAS, and JENKIN with cards, carpets,[2] *and other necessaries*

Frank. O! Master Cranwell, you are a stranger here,
And often baulk [3] my house; faith y' are a churl!—
Now we have supped, a table and to cards!

Jen. A pair [4] of cards, Nicholas, and a carpet to cover the table! Where's Cicely, with her counters and her box? Candles and candlesticks, there! Fie! We have such a household of serving-creatures! Unless it be Nick and I, there's not one amongst them all that can say bo to a goose. —Well said, Nick!

They spread a carpet; set down lights and cards

Anne. Come, Mr. Frankford, who shall take my part?

Frank. Marry, that will I, sweet wife.

Wen. No, by my faith, when you are together, I sit out. It must be Mistress Frankford and I, or else it is no match.

[1] Nobly wrought.
[2] Table covers.
[3] Avoid. [4] Deck.

Frank. I do not like that match.

Nick. [*Aside*] You have no reason, marry, knowing all.

Frank. 'Tis no great matter, neither.— Come, Master Cranwell, shall you and I take them up?

Cran. At your pleasure, sir.

Frank. I must look to you, Master Wendoll; for you'll be playing false. Nay, so will my wife, too.

Nick. [*Aside*] I will be sworn she will.

Anne. Let them that are taken false, forfeit the set!

Frank. Content; it shall go hard but I'll take you.

Cran. Gentlemen, what shall our game be?

Wen. Master Frankford, you play best at noddy.[1]

Frank. You shall not find it so; indeed, you shall not.

Anne. I can play at nothing so well as double-ruff.

Frank. If Master Wendoll and my wife be together, there's no playing against them at double-hand.

Nick. I can tell you, sir, the game that Master Wendoll is best at.

Frank. What game is that, Nick?

Nick. Marry, sir, knave out of doors.

Wen. She and I will take you at lodam.

Anne. Husband, shall we play at saint?

Frank. [*Aside*] My saint's turned devil.—No, we'll none
of saint:
You are best at new-cut, wife, you'll play at that.

Wen. If you play at new-cut, I'm soonest hitter of any here, for a wager.

Frank. [*Aside*] 'Tis me they play on.—Well, you may
draw out;
For all your cunning, 'twill be to your shame;
I'll teach you, at your new-cut, a new game.
Come, come!

[1] Noddy: double-ruff, knave out of doors, lodam, saint (cent), new cut, are all games at cards familiarly known to the age. The double meaning attached to most of these terms is clear.

Cran. If you cannot agree upon the game, to post and pair! [1]

Wen. We shall be soonest pairs; and my good host,
When he comes late home, he must kiss the post.[2]

Frank. Whoever wins, it shall be to thy cost.

Cran. Faith, let it be vide-ruff,[3] and let's make honors!

Frank. If you make honors, one thing let me crave:
Honor the king and queen, except the knave.

Wen. Well, as you please for that.— Lift,[4] who shall deal?

Anne. The least in sight. What are you, Master Wendoll?

Wen. I am a knave.

Nick. [*Aside*] I'll swear it.

Anne. I am queen.

Frank. [*Aside*] A quean, thou should'st say.—Well, the cards are mine:
They are the grossest pair that e'er I felt.

Anne. Shuffle, I'll cut: would I had never dealt!

Frank. I have lost my dealing.

Wen. Sir, the fault's in me;
This queen I have more than mine own, you see.
Give me the stock! [5]

Frank. My mind's not on my game.
Many a deal I've lost; the more's your shame.
You have served me a bad trick, Master Wendoll.

Wen. Sir, you must take your lot. To end this strife,
I know I have dealt better with your wife.

Frank. Thou hast dealt falsely, then.

Anne. What's trumps?

Wen. Hearts. Partner, I rub.

Frank. [*Aside*] Thou robb'st me of my soul, of her chaste love;

[1] A popular gambling game.
[2] Be shut out.
[3] Vide is vie, evidently a betting game.
[4] Cut. [5] Deck.

In thy false dealing thou hast robbed my heart.
Booty you play; [1] I like a loser stand,
Having no heart or here, or in my hand.
I will give o'er the set, I am not well.
Come, who will hold my cards?

Anne. Not well, sweet Master Frankford?
Alas, what ails you? 'Tis some sudden qualm.

Wen. How long have you been so, Master Frankford?

Frank. Sir, I was lusty, and I had my health,
But I grew ill when you began to deal.—
Take hence this table!—Gentle Master Cranwell,
Y'are welcome; see your chamber at your pleasure!
I am sorry that this megrim takes me so,
I cannot sit and bear you company.
Jenkin, some lights, and show him to his chamber!

Anne. A nightgown [2] for my husband; quickly, there!
It is some rheum or cold.

Wen. Now, in good faith,
This illness you have got by sitting late
Without your gown.

Frank. I know it, Master Wendoll.
Go, go to bed, lest you complain like me!—
Wife, pr'ythee, wife, into my bed-chamber!
The night is raw and cold, and rhéumatic.
Leave me my gown and light; I'll walk away my fit.

Wen. Sweet sir, good night!

Frank. Myself, good night!

[*Exit* WENDOLL]

Anne. Shall I attend you, husband?

Frank. No, gentle wife, thou'lt catch cold in thy head.
Pr'ythee, begone, sweet; I'll make haste to bed.

Anne. No sleep will fasten on mine eyes, you know,
Until you come.

[1] You join in confederacy to play false.
[2] Robe.

Frank. Sweet Nan, I pr'ythee, go!—

[*Exit* ANNE]

I have bethought me; get me by degrees
The keys of all my doors, which I will mould
In wax, and take their fair impression,
To have by them new keys. This being compassed,
At a set hour a letter shall be brought me,
And when they think they may securely play,
They nearest are to danger.—Nick, I must rely
Upon thy trust and faithful secrecy.

Nick. Build on my faith!

Frank. To bed, then, not to rest!
Care lodges in my brain, grief in my breast. *Exeunt*

[SCENE III]

[*Old Mountford's House*]

Enter SIR CHARLES' Sister, OLD MOUNTFORD, SANDY, RODER *and* TIDY

Old Mount. You say my nephew is in great distress;
Who brought it to him, but his own lewd life?
I cannot spare a cross.[1] I must confess,
He was my brother's son; why, niece, what then?
This is no world in which to pity men.

Susan. I was not born a beggar, though his extremes
Enforce this language from me. I protest
No fortunes of mine own could lead my tongue
To this base key. I do beseech you, uncle,
For the name's sake, for Christianity,—
Nay, for God's sake, to pity his distress.
He is denied the freedom of the prison,
And in the hole is laid with men condemned;
Plenty he hath of nothing but of irons,

[1] Piece of money.

And it remains in you to free him thence.

Old Mount. Money I cannot spare; men should take heed.
He lost my kindred when he fell to need. *Exit*

Susan. Gold is but earth; thou earth enough shalt have,
When thou hast once took measure of thy grave.
You know me, Master Sandy, and my suit.

Sandy. I knew you, lady, when the old man lived;
I knew you ere your brother sold his land.
Then you were Mistress Sue, tricked up in jewels;
Then you sang well, played sweetly on the lute;
But now I neither know you nor your suit. *Exit*

Susan. You, Master Roder, was my brother's tenant;
Rent-free he placed you in that wealthy farm,
Of which you are possessed.

Roder. True, he did;
And have I not there dwelt still for his sake?
I have some business now; but, without doubt,
They that have hurled him in, will help him out. *Exit*

Susan. Cold comfort still. What say you, cousin Tidy?

Tidy. I say this comes of roysting, swaggering.
Call me not cousin; each man for himself!
Some men are born to mirth, and some to sorrow:
I am no cousin unto them that borrow. *Exit*

Susan. O Charity, why art thou fled to heaven,
And left all things [up]on this earth uneven?
Their scoffing answers I will ne'er return,
But to myself his grief in silence mourn.

Enter SIR FRANCIS *and* MALBY

Sir F. She is poor, I'll therefore tempt her with this gold.
Go, Malby, in my name deliver it,
And I will stay thy answer.

Mal. Fair mistress, as I understand your grief
Doth grow from want, so I have here in store
A means to furnish you, a bag of gold,

Which to your hands I freely tender you.

Susan. I thank you, heavens! I thank you, gentle sir:
God make me able to requite this favor!

Mal. This gold Sir Francis Acton sends by me,
And prays you——

Susan. Acton? O God! That name I'm born to curse.
Hence, bawd; hence, broker! See, I spurn his gold.
My honor never shall for gain be sold.

Sir F. Stay, lady, stay!

Susan. From you I'll posting hie,
Even as the doves from feathered eagles fly. *Exit*

Sir F. She hates my name, my face; how should I woo?
I am disgraced in every thing I do.
The more she hates me, and disdains my love,
The more I am rapt in admiration
Of her divine and chaste perfections.
Woo her with gifts I cannot, for all gifts
Sent in my name she spurns; with looks I cannot,
For she abhors my sight; nor yet with letters,
For none she will receive. How then? how then?
Well, I will fasten such a kindness on her,
As shall o'ercome her hate and conquer it.
Sir Charles, her brother, lies in execution
For a great sum of money; and, besides,
The appeal is sued still for my huntsmen's death,
Which only I have power to reverse.
In her I'll bury all my hate of him.—
Go seek the Keeper, Malby, bring him to me!
To save his body, I his debts will pay;
To save his life, I his appeal will stay. *Exeunt*

[ACT IV, SCENE I]

[*York Castle*]

Enter Sir Charles [Mountford,] *in prison, with irons, his feet bare, his garments all ragged and torn*

Sir C. Of all on the earth's face most miserable,
Breathe in this hellish dungeon thy laments!
Thus like a slave ragg'd, like a felon gyved,—[1]
That hurls thee headlong to this base estate.
O, unkind uncle! O, my friends ingrate!
Unthankful kinsmen! Mountsford's all too base,
To let thy name be fettered in disgrace.
A thousand deaths here in this grave I die;
Fear, hunger, sorrow, cold, all threat my death,
And join together to deprive my breath.
But that which most torments me, my dear sister
Hath left to visit me, and from my friends
Hath brought no hopeful answer; therefore, I
Divine they will not help my misery.
If it be so, shame, scandal, and contempt
Attend their covetous thoughts; need make their graves!
Usurers they live, and may they die like slaves!

Enter Keeper

Keep. Knight, be of comfort, for I bring thee freedom
From all thy troubles.
Sir C. Then, I am doomed to die:
Death is the end of all calamity.
Keep. Live! Your appeal is stayed; the execution
Of all your debts discharged; your creditors
Even to the utmost penny satisfied.
In sign whereof your shackles I knock off.

[1] Chained.

You are not left so much indebted to us
As for your fees; all is discharged; all paid.
Go freely to your house, or where you please;
After long miseries, embrace your ease.

Sir C. Thou grumblest out the sweetest music to me
That ever organ played.—Is this a dream?
Or do my waking senses apprehend
The pleasing taste of these applausive news?
Slave that I was, to wrong such honest friends,
My loving kinsman, and my near allies!
Tongue, I will bite thee for the scandal breath
Against such faithful kinsmen; they are all
Composed of pity and compassion,
Of melting charity and of moving ruth.
That which I spake before was in my rage;
They are my friends, the mirrors of this age;
Bounteous and free. The noble Mountford's race
Ne'er bred a covetous thought, or humor base.

Enter SUSAN

Susan. I can no longer stay from visiting
My woful brother. While I could, I kept
My hapless tidings from his hopeful ear.

Sir C. Sister, how much am I indebted to thee
And to thy travail!

Susan. What, at liberty?

Sir C. Thou seest I am, thanks to thy industry.
O! Unto which of all my courteous friends
Am I thus bound? My uncle Mountford, he
Even of an infant loved me; was it he?
So did my cousin Tidy; was it he?
So Master Roder, Master Sandy, too.
Which of all these did this high kindness do?

Susan. Charles, can you mock me in your poverty,
Knowing your friends deride your misery?

Now, I protest I stand so much amazed,
To see your bonds free, and your irons knocked off,
That I am rapt into a maze of wonder;
The rather for I know not by what means
This happiness hath chanced.

Sir C. Why, by my uncle,
My cousins and my friends; who else, I pray,
Would take upon them all my debts to pay?

Susan. O, brother! they are men [made] all of flint,
Pictures of marble, and as void of pity
As chasèd bears. I begged, I sued, I kneeled,
Laid open all your griefs and miseries,
Which they derided; more than that, denied us
A part in their alliance; but, in pride
Said that our kindred with our plenty died.

Sir C. Drudges too much![1] What! did they? O, known evil!
Rich fly the poor, as good men shun the devil.
Whence should my freedom come? Of whom alive,
Saving of those, have I deserved so well?
Guess, sister, call to mind, remember me!
These I have raised, they follow the world's guise,
Whom rich in honor, they in woe despise.

Susan. My wits have lost themselves; let's ask the keeper!

Sir C. Gaoler!

Keep. At hand, sir.

Sir C. Of courtesy resolve me one demand!
What was he took the burden of my debts
From off my back, stayed my appeal to death,
Discharged my fees, and brought me liberty?

Keep. A courteous knight, and called Sir Francis Acton.

Sir C. Ha! Acton! O, me! More distressed in this
Than all my troubles! Hale me back,
Double my irons, and my sparing meals

[1] Too base in their conduct.

Put into halves, and lodge me in a dungeon
More deep, more dark, more cold, more comfortless!
By Acton freed! Not all thy manacles
Could fetter so my heels, as this one word
Hath thralled my heart; and it must now lie bound
In more strict prison than thy stony gaol.
I am not free, I go but under bail.

Keep. My charge is done, sir, now I have my fees;
As we get little, we will nothing leese.[1]

Sir C. By Acton freed, my dangerous opposite! [2]
Why, to what end, on what occasion? Ha!
Let me forget the name of enemy,
And with indifference balance this high favor!
Ha!

Susan. [*Aside*] His love to me, upon my soul, 'tis so!
That is the root from whence these strange things grow.

Sir C. Had this proceeded from my father, he
That by the law of nature is most bound
In offices of love, it had deserved
My best employment to requite that grace.
Had it proceeded from my friends or his,
From them this action had deserved my life,
And from a stranger more, because from such
There is less execution of good deeds.
But he, nor father, nor ally, nor friend,
More than a stranger, both remote in blood,
And in his heart opposed my enemy,
That this high bounty should proceed from him!
O! there I lose myself. What should I say,
What think, what do, his bounty to repay?

Susan. You wonder, I am sure, whence this strange kindness
Proceeds in Acton; I will tell you, brother.
He dotes on me, and oft hath sent me gifts,
Letters, and tokens; I refused them all.

[1] Lose. [2] Enemy.

Sir C. I have enough, though poor: my heart is set,
In one rich gift to pay back all my debt. *Exeunt*

[SCENE II]

[*Frankford's House*]

Enter FRANKFORD *and* NICK *with keys, and a letter in his hand*

Frank. This is the night that I must play my part,
To try two seeming angels.—Where's my keys?
Nick. They are made, according to your mould, in wax.
I bade the smith be secret, gave him money
And here they are The letter, sir!
Frank. True, take it, there it is;
And when thou seest me in my pleasant'st vein,
Ready to sit to supper, bring it me!
Nick. I'll do't; make no more question, but I'll do't. *Exit*

Enter MISTRESS FRANKFORD, CRANWELL, WENDOLL, *and* JENKIN

Anne. Sirrah, 'tis six o'clock already struck;
Go bid them spread the cloth, and serve in supper!
Jen. It shall be done, forsooth, mistress. Where's
Spigot, the butler, to give us our salt and trenchers? *Exit*
Wen. We that have been hunting all the day
Come with preparèd stomachs.—Master Frankford,
We wish'd you at our sport.
Frank. My heart was with you, and my mind was on you.—
Fie, Master Cranwell! You are still thus sad.—
A stool, a stool! Where's Jenkin, and where's Nick?
'Tis supper time at least an hour ago.

What's the best news abroad?

Wen. I know none good.

Frank. [*Aside*] But I know too much bad.

Enter Butler *and* JENKIN, *with a tablecloth, bread, trenchers, and salt;* [*then exeunt*]

Cran. Methinks, sir, you might have that interest
In your wife's brother, to be more remiss
In his hard dealing against poor Sir Charles,
Who, as I hear, lies in York Castle, needy
And in great want.

Frank. Did not more weighty business of mine own
Hold me away, I would have labored peace
Betwixt them with all care; indeed I would, sir.

Anne. I'll write unto my brother earnestly
In that behalf.

Wen. A charitable deed,
And will beget the good opinion
Of all your friends that love you, Mistress Frankford.

Frank. That's you, for one; I know you love Sir Charles— [*Aside*]
And my wife too, well.

Wen. He deserves the love
Of all true gentlemen; be yourselves judge!

Frank. But supper, ho!—Now, as thou lov'st me, Wendoll,
Which I am sure thou dost, be merry, pleasant,
And frolic it to-night!—Sweet Mr. Cranwell,
Do you the like!—Wife, I protest, my heart
Was ne'er more bent on sweet alacrity.[1]
Where be those lazy knaves to serve in supper?

Enter NICK

Nick. Here's a letter, sir.

Frank. Whence comes it, and who brought it?

Nick. A stripling that below attends your answer,

[1] Good service.

And, as he tells me, it is sent from York.
Frank. Have him into the cellar, let him taste
A cup of our March beer; go, make him drink!
Nick. I'll make him drunk, if he be a Trojan.
Frank. [*After reading the letter*] My boots and spurs!
Where's Jenkin? God forgive me,
How I neglect my business!—Wife, look here!
I have a matter to be tried to-morrow
By eight o'clock; and my attorney writes me,
I must be there betimes with evidence,
Or it will go against me. Where's my boots?

Enter JENKIN, *with boots and spurs*

Anne. I hope your business craves no such despatch,
That you must ride to-night?
Wen. [*Aside*] I hope it doth.
Frank. God's me! No such despatch?
Jenkin, my boots! Where's Nick? Saddle my roan,
And the grey dapple for himself!—Content me,
It much concerns me.—Gentle Master Cranwell,
And Master Wendoll, in my absence use
The very ripest pleasures of my house!
Wen. Lord! Master Frankford, will you ride to-night?
The ways are dangerous.
Frank. Therefore will I ride
Appointed [1] well; and so shall Nick, my man.
Anne. I'll call you up by five o'clock to-morrow.
Frank. No, by my faith, wife, I'll not trust to that:
'Tis not such easy rising in a morning
From one I love so dearly. No, by my faith,
I shall not leave so sweet a bedfellow,
But with much pain. You have made me a sluggard
Since I first knew you.
Anne. Then, if you needs will go

[1] Armed.

This dangerous evening, Master Wendoll,
Let me entreat you bear him company.

Wen. With all my heart, sweet mistress.—My boots, there!

Frank. Fie, fie, that for my private business
I should disease [1] my friend, and be a trouble
To the whole house!—Nick!

Nick. Anon, sir! [*Exit*]

Frank. Bring forth my gelding!—As you love me, sir,
Use no more words: a hand, good Master Cranwell!

Cran. Sir, God be your speed!

Frank. Good night, sweet Nan; nay, nay, a kiss, and part! [*Aside*]
Dissembling lips, you suit not with my heart.

Exeunt [FRANKFORD *and* NICHOLAS]

Wen. [*Aside*] How business, time, and hours, all gracious prove,
And are the furtherers to my new born love!
I am husband now in Master Frankford's place,
And must command the house.—My pleasure is
We will not sup abroad so publicly,
But in your private chamber, Mistress Frankford.

Anne. [Aside] O, sir! you are too public in your love,
And Master Frankford's wife——

Cran. Might I crave favor,
I would entreat you I might see my chamber.
I am on the sudden grown exceeding ill,
And would be spared from supper.

Wen. Light there, ho!—
See you want nothing, sir, for if you do,
You injure that good man, and wrong me too.

Cran. I will make bold; good night! *Exit*

Wen. How all conspire
To make our bosom [2] sweet, and full entire!

[1] Discomfort. [2] Intimacy.

Come, Nan, I pr'ythee, let us sup within!

Anne. O! what a clog unto the soul is sin!
We pale offenders are still full of fear;
Every suspicious eye brings danger near;
When they, whose clear heart from offence are free,
Despite report, base scandals do outface,
And stand at mere defiance with disgrace.

Wen. Fie, fie! You talk too like a puritan.

Anne. You have tempted me to mischief, M[aster] Wendoll:
I have done I know not what. Well, you plead custom;
That which for want of wit I granted erst,
I now must yield through fear. Come, come, let's in;
Once o'er shoes, we are straight o'er head in sin.

Wen. My jocund soul is joyful above measure;
I'll be profuse in Frankford's richest treasure. *Exeunt*

[SCENE III]

[*Another part of the House*]

Enter Cicely, Jenkin, *and* Butler

Jen. My mistress and Master Wendoll, my master, sup in her chamber to-night. Cicely, you are preferred, from being the cook, to be chambermaid. Of all the loves betwixt thee and me, tell me what thou think'st of this?

Cic. Mum; there's an old proverb,—when the cat's away, the mouse may play.

Jen. Now you talk of a cat, Cicely, I smell a rat.

Cic. Good words, Jenkin, lest you be called to answer them!

Jen. Why, God make my mistress an honest woman! Are not these good words? Pray God my new master play not the knave with my old master! Is there any hurt in this? God send no villainy intended; and if they do sup together, pray God they do not lie together! God make my mistress chaste, and make us all his servants! What harm is there in all this? Nay, more; here is my hand, thou shalt never have my heart, unless thou say, amen.

Cic. Amen; I pray God, I say.

Enter Serving-man

Serving-man. My mistress sends that you should make less noise, lock up the doors, and see the household all got to bed. You, Jenkin, for this night are made the porter, to see the gates shut in.

Jen. Thus by little and little I creep into office. Come, to kennel, my masters, to kennel; 'tis eleven o'clock already.

Serving-man. When you have locked the gates in, you must send up the keys to my mistress.

Cic. Quickly, for God's sake, Jenkin; for I must carry them. I am neither pillow nor bolster, but I know more than both.

Jen. To bed, good Spigot; to bed, good honest serving-creatures; and let us sleep as snug as pigs in pease-straw!

Exeunt

[SCENE IV]

[*Outside the House*]

Enter FRANKFORD *and* NICHOLAS

Frank. Soft, soft! We've tied our geldings to a tree,
Two flight-shot [1] off, lest by their thundering hoofs
They blab our coming. Hear'st thou no noise?

Nick. I hear nothing but the owl and you.

Frank. So; now my watch's hand points upon twelve,
And it is just midnight. Where are my keys?

Nick. Here, sir.

Frank. This is the key that opes my outward gate;

[1] Bow-shot.

This, the hall-door; this, the withdrawing-chamber;
But this, that door that's bawd unto my shame,
Fountain and spring of all my bleeding thoughts,
Where the most hallowed order and true knot
Of nuptial sanctity hath been profaned.
It leads to my polluted bed-chamber,
Once my terrestrial heaven, now my earth's hell,
The place where sins in all their ripeness dwell.—
But I forget myself; now to my gate!

Nick. I must ope with far less noise than Cripplegate, or your plot's dashed.

Frank. So; reach me my dark lantern to the rest!
Tread softly, softly!

Nick. I will walk on eggs this pace.

Frank. A general silence hath surprised the house,
And this is the last door. Astonishment,
Fear, and amazement, beat upon my heart,
Even as a madman beats upon a drum.
O, keep my eyes, you heavens, before I enter,
From any sight that may transfix my soul;
Or, if there be so black a spectacle,
O, strike mine eyes stark blind; or if not so,
Lend me such patience to digest my grief,
That I may keep this white and virgin hand
From any violent outrage, or red murder!—
And with that prayer I enter. *Exeunt* [*into the house*]

[SCENE V]

[*The Hall of the House*]

Enter NICHOLAS

Nick. Here's a circumstance!
A man may be made a cuckold in the time
That he's about it. An the case were mine,

As 'tis my master's ('sblood! that he makes me swear!),
I would have placed his action, entered there;
I would, I would!

Enter FRANKFORD

Frank. O! O!

Nick. Master! 'Sblood! Master, master!

Frank. O me unhappy! I have found them lying
Close in each other's arms, and fast asleep.
But that I would not damn two precious souls,
Bought with my Saviour's blood, and send them, laden
With all their scarlet sins upon their backs,
Unto a fearful judgment, their two lives
Had met upon my rapier.

Nick. Master, what, have ye left them sleeping still?
Let me go wake 'em!

Frank. Stay, let me pause awhile!—
O, God! O, God! That it were possible
To undo things done; to call back yesterday;
That Time could turn up his swift sandy glass,
To untell the days, and to redeem these hours!
Or that the sun
Could, rising from the west, draw his coach backward;
Take from th' account of time so many minutes,
Till he had all these seasons called again,
Those minutes, and those actions done in them,
Even from her first offence; that I might take her
As spotless as an angel in my arms!
But, O! I talk of things impossible,
And cast beyond the moon. God give me patience;
For I will in, and wake them. *Exit*

Nick. Here's patience perforce!
He needs must trot afoot that tires his horse.

Enter WENDOLL, *running over the stage in a nightgown,* [FRANKFORD] *after him with a sword drawn; the maid in her smock stays his hand, and clasps hold on him. He pauses for awhile*

Frank. I thank thee, maid; thou, like an angel's hand,
Hast stayed me from a bloody sacrifice.[1] *Exit* Maid
Go, villain; and my wrongs sit on thy soul
As heavy as this grief doth upon mine!
When thou record'st my many courtesies,
And shalt compare them with thy treacherous heart,
Lay them together, weigh them equally,—
'Twill be revenge enough. Go, to thy friend
A Judas; pray, pray, lest I live to see
Thee, Judas-like, hang'd on an elder-tree!

Enter MISTRESS FRANKFORD *in her smock, nightgown and night-attire*

Anne. O, by what word, what title, or what name,
Shall I entreat your pardon? Pardon! O!
I am as far from hoping such sweet grace,
As Lucifer from heaven. To call you husband,—
(O me, most wretched!) I have lost that name;
I am no more your wife.
Nick. 'Sblood, sir, she swoons.
Frank. Spare thou thy tears, for I will weep for thee;
And keep thy countenance, for I'll blush for thee.
Now, I protest, I think 'tis I am tainted,
For I am most ashamed; and 'tis more hard
For me to look upon thy guilty face
Than on the sun's clear brow. What! Would'st thou speak?
Anne. I would I had no tongue, no ears, no eyes,
No apprehension, no capacity.
When do you spurn me like a dog? When tread me
Under feet? When drag me by the hair?
Though I deserve a thousand, thousand-fold,

[1] *Gen.* xxii, 10, 11.

More than you can inflict—yet, once my husband,
For womanhood, to which I am a shame,
Though once an ornament—even for his sake,
That hath redeemed our souls, mark not my face,
Nor hack me with your sword; but let me go
Perfect and undeformèd to my tomb!
I am not worthy that I should prevail
In the least suit; no, not to speak to you,
Nor look on you, nor to be in your presence;
Yet, as an abject, this one suit I crave;—
This granted, I am ready for my grave.

Frank. My God, with patience arm me!—Rise, nay, rise.
And I'll debate with thee. Was it for want
Thou play'dst the strumpet? Wast thou not supplied
With every pleasure, fashion, and new toy,—
Nay, even beyond my calling?

Anne. I was.

Frank. Was it, then, disability in me;
Or in thine eye seemed he a properer man?

Anne. O, no!

Frank. Did not I lodge thee in my bosom?
Wear thee here in my heart?

Anne. You did.

Frank. I did, indeed; witness my tears, I did.—
Go, bring my infants hither!

Enter Serving-woman *with two little children*

O Nan! O Nan!
If neither fear of shame, regard of honor,
The blemish of my house, nor my dear love,
Could have withheld thee from so lewd a fact:
Yet for these infants, these young, harmless souls
On whose white brows thy shame is charactered,
And grows in greatness as they wax in years,—
Look but on them, and melt away in tears!—

Away with them; lest, as her spotted body
Hath stained their names with stripe of bastardy,
So her adulterous breath may blast their spirits
With her infectious thoughts! Away with them!

Exit Serving-woman *with children*

Anne. In this one life, I die ten thousand deaths.

Frank. Stand up, stand up! I will do nothing rashly.
I will retire awhile into my study,
And thou shalt hear thy sentence presently. *Exit*

Anne. 'Tis welcome, be it death. O me, base strumpet,
That, having such a husband, such sweet children,
Must enjoy neither! O, to redeem mine honor,
I would have this hand cut off, these my breasts seared;
Be racked, strappadoed, put to any torment:
Nay, to whip but this scandal out, I would hazard
The rich and dear redemption of my soul!
He cannot be so base as to forgive me,
Nor I so shameless to accept his pardon.
O women, women, you that yet have kept
Your holy matrimonial vow unstained,
Make me your instance; when you tread awry,
Your sins, like mine, will on your conscience lie.

Enter Cicely, Spigot, *all the* Serving-men, *and* Jenkin, *as newly come out of bed*

All. O, mistress, mistress! What have you done, mistress?

Nick. What a caterwauling keep you here!

Jen. O Lord, mistress, how comes this to pass? My master is run away in his shirt, and never so much as called me to bring his clothes after him.

Anne. See what guilt is! Here stand I in this place,
Ashamed to look my servants in the face.

Enter Frankford *and* Cranwell; *whom seeing, she falls on her knees*

Frank. My words are registered in heaven already.
With patience hear me! I'll not martyr thee,
Nor mark thee for a strumpet; but with usage
Of more humility torment thy soul,
And kill thee even with kindness.

Cran. Master Frankford——

Frank. Good Master Cranwell!—Woman, hear thy judgment!
Go make thee ready in thy best attire;
Take with thee all thy gowns, all thy apparel;
Leave nothing that did ever call thee mistress,
Or by whose sight, being left here in the house,
I may remember such a woman by.
Choose thee a bed and hangings for thy chamber;
Take with thee every thing which hath thy mark,
And get thee to my manor seven mile off,
Where live; 'tis thine, I freely give it thee.
My tenants by shall furnish thee with wains
To carry all thy stuff within two hours;
No longer will I limit[1] thee my sight.
Choose which of all my servants thou lik'st best,
And they are thine to attend thee.

Anne. A mild sentence.

Frank. But, as thou hop'st for heaven, as thou believ'st
Thy name's recorded in the book of life,
I charge thee never after this sad day
To see me, or to meet me, or to send,
By word or writing, gift or otherwise,
To move me, by thyself, or by thy friends;
Nor challenge any part in my two children.
So farewell, Nan; for we will henceforth be
As we had never seen, ne'er more shall see.

Anne. How full my heart is, in mine eyes appears;
What wants in words, I will supply in tears.

Frank. Come, take your coach, your stuff; all must along.

[1] Allow.

Servants and all make ready; all begone!
It was thy hand cut two hearts out of one. *Exeunt*

[ACT V, SCENE I]

[*Before Sir Francis Acton's House*]

Enter SIR CHARLES [MOUNTFORD,] *gentleman-like and his Sister, gentlewoman-like*

Susan. Brother, why have you tricked me like a bride,
Bought me this gay attire, these ornaments?
Forget you our estate, our poverty?
Sir C. Call me not brother, but imagine me
Some barbarous outlaw, or uncivil kern;[1]
For if thou shutt'st thy eye, and only hear'st
The words that I shall utter, thou shalt judge me
Some staring ruffian, not thy brother Charles,
O, sister!——
Susan. O, brother! what doth this strange language mean?
Sir C. Dost love me, sister? Wouldst thou see me live
A bankrupt beggar in the world's disgrace,
And die indebted to mine enemies?
Wouldst thou behold me stand like a huge beam
In the world's eye, a bye-word and a scorn?
It lies in thee of these to acquit me free,
And all my debt I may outstrip by thee.
Susan. By me? Why, I have nothing, nothing left;
I owe even for the clothes upon my back;
I am not worth——
Sir C. O sister, say not so!
It lies in you my downcast state to raise;
To make me stand on even points with the world.
Come, sister, you are rich; indeed you are,
And in your power you have, without delay
Acton's five hundred pound back to repay.

[1] Serf.

Susan. Till now I had thought y' had loved me. By my honor
(Which I have kept as spotless as the moon),
I ne'er was mistress of that single doit [1]
Which I reserved not to supply your wants;
And d'ye think that I would hoard from you?
Now, by my hopes in heaven, knew I the means
To buy you from the slavery of your debts
(Especially from Acton, whom I hate),
I would redeem it with my life or blood!

Sir C. I challenge it, and, kindred set apart,
Thus, ruffian-like, I lay siege to thy heart.
What do I owe to Acton?

Susan. Why, some five hundred pounds· towards which, I swear,
In all the world I have not one denier.[2]

Sir C. It will not prove so. Sister, now resolve me:
What do you think (and speak your conscience)
Would Acton give, might he enjoy your bed?

Susan. He would not shrink to spend a thousand pound,
To give the Mountfords' name so deep a wound.

Sir C. A thousand pound! I but five hundred owe:
Grant him your bed, he's paid with interest so.

Susan. O, brother!

Sir C. O, sister! only this one way,
With that rich jewel you my debts may pay.
In speaking this my cold heart shakes with shame;
Nor do I woo you in a brother's name,
But in a stranger's. Shall I die in debt
To Acton, my grand foe, and you still wear
The precious jewel that he holds so dear?

Susan. My honor I esteem as dear and precious
As my redemption.

Sir C. I esteem you, sister,

[1] Farthing. [2] Penny.

As dear, for so dear prizing it.
Susan. Will Charles
Have me cut off my hands, and send them Acton?
Rip up my breast, and with my bleeding heart
Present him as a token?
Sir C. Neither, sister;
But hear me in my strange assertion!
Thy honor and my soul are equal in my regard;
Nor will thy brother Charles survive thy shame.
His kindness, like a burden, hath surcharged me,
And under his good deeds I stooping go,
Not with an upright soul. Had I remained
In prison still, there doubtless I had died.
Then, unto him that freed me from that prison,
Still do I owe this life. What moved my foe
To enfranchise me? 'Twas, sister, for your love;
And shall he not enjoy it? Shall the weight
Of all this heavy burden lean on me,
And will not you bear part? You did partake
The joy of my release; will you not stand
In joint-bond bound to satisfy the debt?
Shall I be only charged?
Susan. But that I know
These arguments come from an honored mind,
As in your most extremity of need
Scorning to stand in debt to one you hate,—
Nay, rather would engage your unstained honor,
Than to be held ingrate,—I should condemn you.
I see your resolution, and assent;
So Charles will have me, and I am content.
Sir C. For this I tricked you up.
Susan. But here's a knife,
To save mine honor, shall slice out my life.
Sir C. I know thou pleasest me a thousand times
More in thy resolution than thy grant.
Observe her love; to soothe it to my suit,

Her honor she will hazard, though not lose;
To bring me out of debt, her rigorous hand
Will pierce her heart,—O wonder!—that will choose,
Rather than stain her blood, her life to lose.
Come, you sad sister to a woful brother,
This is the gate. I'll bear him such a present,
Such an acquittance for the knight to seal,
As will amaze his senses, and surprise
With admiration all his fantasies.

Enter [SIR FRANCIS] ACTON *and* MALBY

Susan. Before his unchaste thoughts shall seize on me,
'Tis here shall my imprisoned soul set free.
Sir F. How! Mountford with his sister, hand in hand!
What miracle's afoot?
Mal. It is a sight
Begets in me much admiration.
Sir C. Stand not amazed to see me thus attended!
Acton, I owe thee money, and, being unable
To bring thee the full sum in ready coin,
Lo! for thy more assurance, here's a pawn,—
My sister, my dear sister, whose chaste honor
I prize above a million. Here! Nay, take her;
She's worth your money, man; do not forsake her.
Sir F. I would he were in earnest!
Susan. Impute it not to my immodesty.
My brother, being rich in nothing else
But in his interest that he hath in me,
According to his poverty hath brought you
Me, all his store; whom, howsoe'er you prize,
As forfeit to your hand, he values highly,
And would not sell, but to acquit your debt,
For any emperor's ransom.
Sir F. [*Aside*] Stern heart, relent,
Thy former cruelty at length repent!

Was ever known, in any former age,
Such honorable, wrested courtesy?
Lands, honors, life, and all the world forego,
Rather than stand engaged to such a foe!

Sir C. Acton, she is too poor to be thy bride,
And I too much opposed to be thy brother.
There, take her to thee; if thou hast the heart
To seize her as a rape, or lustful prey;
To blur our house, that never yet was stained;
To murder her that never meant thee harm;
To kill me now, whom once thou sav'dst from death:—
Do them at once; on her all these rely,
And perish with her spotless chastity.

Sir F. You overcome me in your love, Sir Charles.
I cannot be so cruel to a lady
I love so dearly. Since you have not spared
To engage your reputation to the world,
Your sister's honor, which you prize so dear,
Nay, all the comfort which you hold on earth,
To grow out of my debt, being your foe,—
Your honored thoughts, lo! thus I recompense.
Your metamorphosed foe receives your gift
In satisfaction of all former wrongs.
This jewel I will wear here in my heart;
And where before I thought her, for her wants,
Too base to be my bride, to end all strife,
I seal you my dear brother, her my wife.

Susan. You still exceed us. I will yield to fate,
And learn to love, where I till now did hate.

Sir C. With that enchantment you have charmed my soul,
And made me rich even in those very words!
I pay no debt, but am indebted more;
Rich in your love, I never can be poor.

Sir F. All's mine is yours; we are alike in state;
Let's knit in love what was opposed in hate!
Come, for our nuptials we will straight provide,

Blest only in our brother and fair bride. *Exeunt*

[SCENE II]

[*Frankford's House*]

Enter CRANWELL, FRANKFORD, *and* NICK

Cran. Why do you search each room about your house,
Now that you have despatched your wife away?

Frank. O, sir! To see that nothing may be left
That ever was my wife's. I loved her dearly;
And when I do but think of her unkindness,
My thoughts are all in hell; to avoid which torment,
I would not have a bodkin or a cuff,
A bracelet, necklace, or rebato wire,[1]
Nor any thing that ever was called hers,
Left me, by which I might remember her.—
See round about.

Nick. 'Sblood! master, here's her lute flung in a corner.

Frank. Her lute! O, God! Upon this instrument
Her fingers have ran quick division,[2]
Sweeter than that which now divides our hearts.
These frets have made me pleasant, that have now
Frets of my heart-strings made. O, Master Cranwell,
Oft hath she made this melancholy wood
(Now mute and dumb for her disastrous chance)
Speak sweetly many a note, sound many a strain
To her own ravishing voice; which being well strung,
What pleasant strange airs have they jointly rung!—
Post with it after her!—Now nothing's left;
Of her and hers I am at once bereft.

Nick. I'll ride and overtake her; do my message,
And come back again. *Exit*

Cran. Meantime, sir, if you please,

[1] To sustain the ruff.
[2] Variation.

I'll to Sir Francis Acton, and inform him
Of what hath passed betwixt you and his sister.

Frank. Do as you please.—How ill am I bested,[1]
To be a widower ere my wife be dead! *Exeunt*

[SCENE III]

[*Road near Mistress Frankford's Manor*]

Enter MISTRESS FRANKFORD, *with* JENKIN, *her maid* CICELY, *her* Coachman, *and three* Carters

Anne. Bid my coach stay! Why should I ride in state,
Being hurled so low down by the hand of fate?
A seat like to my fortunes let me have,
Earth for my chair, and for my bed a grave!

Jen. Comfort, good mistress; you have watered your coach with tears already. You have but two miles now to go to your manor. A man cannot say by my old master Frankford as he may say by me, that he wants manors; for he hath three or four, of which this is one that we are going to now.

Cic. Good mistress, be of good cheer! Sorrow, you see, hurts you, but helps you not; we all mourn to see you so sad.

Carter. Mistress, I see some of my landlord's men
Come riding post: 'tis like he brings some news.

Anne. Comes he from Master Frankford, he is welcome;
So is his news, because they come from him.

Enter NICHOLAS

Nick. There!

Anne. I know the lute. Oft have I sung to thee;
We both are out of tune, both out of time.

Nick. Would that had been the worst instrument that e'er you played on! My master commends him unto ye; there's all he can find was ever yours; he hath nothing left

[1] Sped.

that ever you could lay claim to but his own heart,—and he could afford you that! All that I have to deliver you is this: he prays you to forget him; and so he bids you farewell.

Anne. I thank him; he is kind, and ever was.
All you that have true feeling of my grief,
That know my loss, and have relenting hearts,
Gird me about, and help me with your tears
To wash my spotted sins! My lute shall groan;
It cannot weep, but shall lament my moan.

Enter WENDOLL [*behind*] [1]

Wen. Pursued with horror of a guilty soul,
And with the sharp scourge of repentance lashed,
I fly from mine own shadow. O my stars!
What have my parents in their lives deserved,
That you should lay this penance on their son?
When I but think of Master Frankford's love,
And lay it to my treason, or compare
My murdering him for his relieving me,
It strikes a terror like a lightning's flash,
To scorch my blood up. Thus I, like the owl,
Ashamed of day, live in these shadowy woods,
Afraid of every leaf or murm'ring blast,
Yet longing to receive some perfect knowledge
How he hath dealt with her. [*Seeing* MISTRESS FRANKFORD]
O my sad fate!
Here, and so far from home, and thus attended!
O, God! I have divorced the truest turtles
That ever lived together, and being divided,
In several places make their several moan;
She in the fields laments, and he at home.
So poets write that Orpheus made the trees
And stones to dance to his melodious harp,
Meaning the rustic and the barbarous hinds,

[1] Wendoll remains unseen during most of this scene.

That had no understanding part in them.
So she from these rude carters tears extracts,
Making their flinty hearts with grief to rise,
And draw down rivers from their rocky eyes.

Anne. [*to* NICHOLAS] If you return unto your master, say
(Though not from me, for I am all unworthy
To blast his name so with a strumpet's tongue)
That you have seen me weep, wish myself dead!
Nay, you may say, too (for my vow is past),[1]
Last night you saw me eat and drink my last.
This to your master you may say and swear;
For it is writ in heaven, and decreèd here.

Nick. I'll say you wept; I'll swear you made me sad.
Why, how now, eyes? What now? What's here to do?
I'm gone, or I shall straight turn baby too.

Wen. I cannot weep, my heart is all on fire.
Curs'd be the fruits of my unchaste desire!

Anne. Go, break this lute upon my coach's wheel,
As the last music that I e'er shall make,—
Not as my husband's gift, but my farewell
To all earth's joy; and so your master tell!

Nick. If I can for crying.

Wen. Grief, have done,
Or, like a madman, I shall frantic run.

Anne. You have beheld the wofull'st wretch on earth,—
A woman made of tears; would you had words
To express but what you see! My inward grief
No tongue can utter; yet unto your power
You may describe my sorrow, and disclose
To thy sad master my abundant woes.

Nick. I'll do your commendations.

Anne. O, no!
I dare not so presume; nor to my children!
I am disclaimed in both; alas! I am.

[1] Made.

O, never teach them, when they come to speak,
To name the name of mother: chide their tongue,
If they by chance light on that hated word;
Tell them 'tis naught; for when that word they name,
Poor, pretty souls! they harp on their own shame.

Wen. To recompense her wrongs, what canst thou do?
Thou hast made her husbandless, and childless too.

Anne. I have no more to say.—Speak not for me;
Yet you may tell your master what you see.

Nick. I'll do't. *Exit*

Wen. I'll speak to her, and comfort her in grief.
O, but her wound cannot be cured with words!
No matter, though; I'll do my best good will
To work a cure on her whom I did kill.

Anne. So, now unto my coach, then to my home,
So to my death-bed; for from this sad hour,
I never will nor eat, nor drink, nor taste
Of any cates [1] that may preserve my life.
I never will nor smile, nor sleep, nor rest;
But when my tears have washed my black soul white,
Sweet Saviour, to thy hands I yield my sprite.

Wen. [*Coming forward*] O, Mistress Frankford!

Anne. O, for God's sake, fly!
The devil doth come to tempt me, ere I die.
My coach!—This sin, that with an angel's face
Conjured mine honor, till he sought my wrack,[2]
In my repentant eye seems ugly black.

Exeunt all [*except* WENDOLL *and* JENKIN;]
the Carters whistling

Jen. What, my young master, that fled in his shirt! How come you by your clothes again? You have made our house in a sweet pickle, ha' ye not, think you? What, shall I serve you still, or cleave to the house?

Wen. Hence, slave! Away, with thy unseasoned mirth!

[1] Food. [2] Ruin.

Unless thou canst shed tears, and sigh, and howl,
Curse thy sad fortunes, and exclaim on fate,
Thou art not for my turn.

Jen. Marry, an you will not, another will! farewell, and be hanged! Would you had never come to have kept this coil [1] within our doors! We shall ha' you run away like a sprite again. *Exit*

Wen. She's gone to death; I live to want and woe,
Her life, her sins, and all upon my head.
And I must now go wander, like a Cain,
In foreign countries and remoted climes,
Where the report of my ingratitude
Cannot be heard. I'll over first to France,
And so to Germany and Italy;
Where, when I have recovered, and by travel
Gotten those perfect tongues, and that these rumors
May in their height abate, I will return:
And I divine (however now dejected),
My worth and parts being by some great man praised,
At my return I may in court be raised. *Exit*

[SCENE IV]

[*Before the Manor-house*]

Enter Sir Francis Acton, Sir Charles Mountford, Cranwell, [Malby,] *and* Susan

Sir F. Brother, and now my wife, I think these troubles
Fall on my head by justice of the heavens,
For being so strict to you in your extremities;
But we are now atoned.[2] I would my sister
Could with like happiness o'ercome her griefs
As we have ours.

Susan. You tell us, Master Cranwell, wondrous things
Touching the patience of that gentleman,
With what strange virtue he demeans his grief.

[1] Trouble. [2] Reconciled.

Cran. I told you what I was witness of;
It was my fortune to lodge there that night.
Sir F. O, that same villain, Wendoll! 'Twas his tongue
That did corrupt her; she was of herself
Chaste, and devoted well.—Is this the house?
Cran. Yes, sir; I take it, here your sister lies.[1]
Sir F. My brother Frankford showed too mild a spirit
In the revenge of such a loathèd crime.
Less than he did, no man of spirit could do.
I am so far from blaming his revenge,
That I commend it. Had it been my case,
Their souls at once had from their breasts been freed;
Death to such deeds of shame is the due meed.

Enter JENKIN *and* CICELY

Jen. O, my mistress, mistress! my poor mistress!

Cicely. Alas! that ever I was born; what shall I do for my poor mistress?

Sir C. Why, what of her?

Jen. O, Lord, sir! she no sooner heard that her brother and her friends were come to see how she did, but she, for very shame of her guilty conscience, fell into such a swoon, that we had much ado to get life in her.

Susan. Alas, that she should bear so hard a fate!
Pity it is repentance comes too late.
Sir F. Is she so weak in body?

Jen. O, sir! I can assure you there's no hope of life in her; for she will take no sustenance: she hath plainly starved herself, and now she's as lean as a lath. She ever looks for the good hour. Many gentlemen and gentlewomen of the country are come to comfort her.

[1] Lodges.

[SCENE V]

[*In the Manor-house. Mistress Frankford in her bed*]

Enter SIR CHARLES MOUNTFORD, SIR FRANCIS ACTON, MALBY, CRANWELL, *and* SUSAN

Mal. How fare you, Mistress Frankford?
Anne. Sick, sick, O, sick! Give me some air. I pray you!
Tell me, O, tell me, where's Master Frankford?
Will not [he] deign to see me ere I die?
Mal. Yes, Mistress Frankford; divers gentlemen,
Your loving neighbors, with that just request
Have moved, and told him of your weak estate:
Who, though with much ado to get belief,
Examining of the general circumstance,
Seeing your sorrow and your penitence,
And hearing therewithal the great desire
You have to see him, ere you left the world,
He gave to us his faith to follow us,
And sure he will be here immediately.
Anne. You have half revived me with the pleasing news.
Raise me a little higher in my bed.—
Blush I not, brother Acton? Blush I not, Sir Charles?
Can you not read my fault writ in my cheek?
Is not my crime there? Tell me, gentlemen.
Sir C. Alas, good mistress, sickness hath not left you
Blood in your face enough to make you blush.
Anne. Then, sickness, like a friend, my fault would hide.—
Is my husband come? My soul but tarries his arrive;
Then I am fit for heaven.
Sir F. I came to chide you, but my words of hate
Are turned to pity and compassionate grief.
I came to rate you, but my brawls,[1] you see,
Melt into tears, and I must weep by thee.—

[1] Reproaches.

Here's M[aster] Frankford now.

Enter FRANKFORD

Frank. Good morrow, brother; morrow, gentlemen!
God, that hath laid this cross upon our heads,
Might (had he pleased) have made our cause of meeting
On a more fair and more contented ground;
But he that made us, made us to this woe.

Anne. And is he come? Methinks, that voice I know.

Frank. How do you, woman?

Anne. Well, Master Frankford, well; but shall be better,
I hope, within this hour. Will you vouchsafe,
Out of your grace and your humanity,
To take a spotted strumpet by the hand?

Frank. This hand once held my heart in faster bonds
Than now 'tis gripped by me. God pardon them
That made us first break hold!

Anne. Amen, amen!
Out of my zeal to heaven, whither I'm now bound,
I was so impudent to wish you here;
And once more beg your pardon. O, good man,
And father to my children, pardon me.
Pardon, O, pardon me: my fault so heinous is,
That if you in this world forgive it not,
Heaven will not clear it in the world to come.
Faintness hath so usurped upon my knees,
That kneel I cannot; but on my heart's knees
My prostrate soul lies thrown down at your feet,
To beg your gracious pardon. Pardon, O, pardon me!

Frank. As freely, from the low depth of my soul,
As my Redeemer hath forgiven his death,
I pardon thee. I will shed tears with thee;
Pray with thee; and, in mere pity of thy weak estate,
I'll wish to die with thee.

All. So do we all.

Nick. So will not I;
I'll sigh and sob, but, by my faith, not die.
Sir F. O, Master Frankford, all the near alliance
I lose by her, shall be supplied in thee.
You are my brother by the nearest way;
Her kindred hath fall'n off, but yours doth stay.
Frank. Even as I hope for pardon, at that day
When the Great Judge of heaven in scarlet sits,
So be thou pardoned! Though thy rash offence
Divorced our bodies, thy repentant tears
Unite our souls.
Sir C. Then comfort, Mistress Frankford!
You see your husband hath forgiven your fall;
Then, rouse your spirits, and cheer your fainting soul!
Susan. How is it with you?
Sir F. How d'ye feel yourself?
Anne. Not of this world.
Frank. I see you are not, and I weep to see it.
My wife, the mother to my pretty babes!
Both those lost names I do restore thee back,
And with this kiss I wed thee once again.
Though thou art wounded in thy honored name,
And with that grief upon thy death-bed liest,
Honest in heart, upon my soul, thou diest.
Anne. Pardoned on earth, soul, thou in heaven art free;
Once more: [*Kisses him*] thy wife dies thus embracing thee.
Dies
Frank. New-married, and new-widowed.—O! she's dead,
And a cold grave must be her nuptial bed.
Sir C. Sir, be of good comfort, and your heavy sorrow
Part equally amongst us; storms divided
Abate their force, and with less rage are guided.
Cran. Do, Master Frankford; he that hath least part,
Will find enough to drown one troubled heart.
Sir F. Peace with thee, Nan!—Brothers and gentlemen,
All we that can plead interest in her grief,

Bestow upon her body funeral tears!
Brother, had you with threats and usage bad
Punished her sin, the grief of her offence
Had not with such true sorrow touched her heart.
Frank. I see it had not; therefore, on her grave
Will I bestow this funeral epitaph,
Which on her marble tomb shall be engraved.
In golden letters shall these words be filled:
Here lies she whom her husband's kindness killed.

EPILOGUE

An honest crew, disposèd to be merry,
Came to a tavern by, and called for wine.
The drawer brought it, smiling like a cherry,
And told them it was pleasant, neat and fine.
'Taste it,' quoth one. He did so. 'Fie!' (quoth he).
'This wine was good; now't runs too near the lee.'

Another sipped, to give the wine his due,
And said unto the rest, it drank too flat;
The third said, it was old; the fourth, too new;
Nay, quoth the fifth, the sharpness likes me not.
Thus, gentlemen, you see how, in one hour,
The wine was new, old, flat, sharp, sweet, and sour.

Unto this wine we do allude our play,
Which some will judge too trivial, some too grave:
You as our guests we entertain this day,
And bid you welcome to the best we have.
Excuse us, then; good wine may be disgraced,
When every several mouth hath sundry taste.

VOLPONE

OR

THE FOX

by

BEN JONSON

VOLPONE; OR, THE FOX

To the most noble and most equal sisters,

THE TWO FAMOUS UNIVERSITIES

FOR THEIR LOVE AND ACCEPTANCE SHEWN TO HIS POEM IN THE PRESENTATION,

BEN JONSON

THE GRATEFUL ACKNOWLEDGER,

DEDICATES BOTH IT AND HIMSELF.

NEVER, most equal Sisters, had any man a wit so presently excellent, as that it could raise itself; but there must come both matter, occasion, commenders, and favourers to it. If this be true, and that the fortune of all writers doth daily prove it, it behoves the careful to provide well towards these accidents; and, having acquired them, to preserve that part of reputation most tenderly, wherein the benefit of a friend is also defended. Hence is it, that I now render myself grateful, and am studious to justify the bounty of your act; to which, though your mere authority were satisfying, yet it being an age wherein poetry and the professors of it hear so ill on all sides, there will a reason be looked for in the subject. It is certain, nor can it with any forehead be opposed, that the too much license of poetasters in this time, hath much deformed their mistress; that, every day, their manifold and manifest ignorance doth stick unnatural reproaches upon her: but for their petulancy, it were an act of the greatest injustice, either to let the learned suffer, or so divine a skill (which indeed should not be attempted with unclean hands) to fall under the least contempt. For, if men will impartially, and not asquint, look toward the offices and function of a poet, they will easily conclude to themselves the impossibility of any man's being the good poet, without first being a good man. He that is said to be able to inform young men to all good disciplines, inflame grown men to all great virtues, keep old men in their best and supreme state, or, as they decline to childhood, recover them to their first strength; that comes forth the interpreter and arbiter of nature, a teacher of things divine no less than human, a master in manners; and can alone, or with a few, effect the business of mankind: this, I take him, is no subject for pride and ignorance to exercise their railing rhetoric upon. But it will here be hastily answered, that the writers of these days are other things; that not only their manners, but their natures, are inverted, and nothing remaining with them of the dignity of poet, but the abused name, which every scribe usurps; that now, especially in dramatic, or, as they term it, stage-poetry, nothing but ribaldry, profanation, blasphemy, all license of offence to God and man is practised. I dare not deny a great part of this, and am sorry I dare not, because in some men's abortive features (and would they had never boasted the light) it is over-true; but that all are embarked in this bold adventure for hell, is a most uncharitable thought, and, uttered, a more malicious slander. For my particular, I can, and from a most clear conscience, affirm, that I have ever trembled to think toward the least profaneness; have loathed the use of such foul and unwashed bawdry, as is now made the food of the scene: and, howsoever I cannot escape from some, the imputation of sharpness, but that they will say, I have taken a pride, or lust, to be bitter, and not my youngest infant but hath come into the world with all his teeth; I would ask of these supercilious politics, what nation, society, or general order or state, I have provoked? What public person? Whether I have not in all these preserved their dignity, as mine own person, safe? My works are read, allowed, (I speak of those that are intirely mine,) look into them, what broad reproofs have I used? where have I been particular? where personal? except to a mimic, cheater, bawd, or buffoon, creatures, for their insolencies, worthy to be taxed? yet to which of these so pointingly, as he might not either ingenuously have confest, or wisely dissembled his disease? But it is not rumour can make men guilty, much less entitle me to other men's crimes. I know, that nothing can be so innocently writ or carried, but may be made obnoxious to construction; marry, whilst I bear mine innocence about me, I fear it not. Application is now grown a trade with many; and there are that profess to have a key for the decyphering of every thing: but let wise and noble persons take heed how they be too credulous, or give leave to these invading interpreters to be over-familiar with their fames, who cunningly, and often, utter their own virulent malice, under other men's simplest meanings. As for those that will (by faults which charity hath raked up, or common honesty concealed) make themselves a name with the multitude, or, to draw their rude and beastly claps, care not whose living faces they intrench with their petulant styles, may they do it without a rival, for me! I choose rather to live graved in obscurity, than share with them in so preposterous a fame. Nor can I blame the wishes of those severe and wise patriots, who providing the hurts these licentious spirits may do in a state, desire rather to see fools and devils, and those antique relics of barbarism retrieved, with all other ridiculous and exploded follies, than behold the wounds of private men, of princes and nations: for, as Horace makes Trebatius speak among these,

"Sibi quisque timet, quanquam est intactus, et odit."

And men may justly impute such rages, if continued, to the writer, as his sports. The increase of which lust in liberty, together with the present trade of the stage, in all their miscelline interludes, what learned or liberal soul doth not already abhor? where nothing but the filth of the time is uttered, and with such impropriety of phrase, such plenty of solecisms, such dearth of sense, so bold prolepses, so racked metaphors, with brothelry, able to violate the ear of a pagan, and blasphemy, to turn the blood of a Christian to water. I cannot but be serious in a cause of this nature, wherein my fame, and the repuation of divers honest and learned are the question; when a name so full of authority, antiquity, and all great mark, is, through their insolence, become the lowest scorn of the age; and those men subject to the petulancy of every vernaculous orator, that were wont to be the care of kings and happiest monarchs. This it is that hath not only rapt me to present indignation, but made me studious heretofore, and by all my actions, to stand off from them; which may most appear in this my latest work, which you, most learned Arbitresses, have seen, judged, and to my crown, approved; wherein I have laboured for their instruction and amendment, to reduce not only the ancient forms, but manners of the scene, the easiness, the propriety, the innocence, and last, the doctrine, which is the principal end of poesie, to inform men in the best reason of living. And though my catastrophe may, in the strict rigour of comic law, meet with censure, as turning back to my promise; I desire the learned and charitable critic, to have so much faith in me, to think it was done of industry: for, with what ease I could have varied it nearer his scale (but that I fear to boast my own faculty) I could here insert. But my special aim being to put the snaffle in their mouths, that cry out, We never punish vice in our interludes, etc., I took the more liberty; though not without some lines of example, drawn even in the ancients themselves, the goings out of whose comedies are not always joyful, but oft times the bawds, the servants, the rivals, yea, and the masters are mulcted; and fitly, it being the office of a comic poet to imitate justice, and instruct to life, as well as purity of language, or stir up gentle affections; to which I shall take the occasion elsewhere to speak.

For the present, most reverenced Sisters, as I have cared to be thankful for your affections past, and here made the understanding acquainted with some ground of your favours; let me not despair their continuance, to the maturing of some worthier fruits; wherein, if my muses be true to me, I shall raise the despised head of poetry again, and stripping her out of those rotten and base rags wherewith the times have adulterated her form, restore her to her primitive habit, feature, and majesty, and render her worthy to be embraced and kist of all the great and master spirits of our world. As for the vile and slothful, who never affected an act worthy of celebration, or are so inward with their own vicious natures, as they worthily fear her, and think it an high point of policy to keep her in contempt, with their declamatory and windy invectives; she shall out of just rage incite her servants (who are *genus irritabile*) to spout ink in their faces, that shall eat farther than their marrow into their fames; and not Cinnamus the barber, with his art, shall be able to take out the brands; but they shall live, and be read, till the wretches die, as things worst deserving of themselves in chief, and then of all mankind.

From my House in the Black-Friars,
this 11*th day of February,* 1607.

DRAMATIS PERSONÆ

VOLPONE, *a Magnifico*
MOSCA, *his Parasite*
VOLTORE, *an Advocate*
CORBACCIO, *an old Gentleman*
CORVINO, *a Merchant*
BONARIO, *son to Corbaccio*
SIR POLITICK WOULD-BE, *a Knight*
PEREGRINE, *a Gentleman Traveller*
NANO, *a Dwarf*
CASTRONE, *an Eunuch*
ANDROGYNO, *an Hermaphrodite*

GREGE (*or Mob*)

Commandadori, *Officers of Justice*
Mercatori, *three Merchants*
Avocatori, *four Magistrates*
Notario, *the Register*
LADY WOULD-BE, *Sir Politick's Wife*
CELIA, *Corvino's Wife*
Servitori, Servants, *two* Waiting-women, *etc.*

SCENE,—Venice

THE ARGUMENT

V *olpone, childless, rich, feigns sick, despairs,*
O *ffers his state to hopes of several heirs,*
L *ies languishing: his parasite receives*
P *resents of all, assures, deludes; then weaves*
O *ther cross plots, which ope themselves, are told.*
N *ew tricks for safety are sought; they thrive; when bold,*
E *ach tempts the other again, and all are sold.*

PROLOGUE

Now, luck yet send us, and a little wit
Will serve to make our play hit;
(According to the palates of the season)
Here is rhime, not empty of reason.
This we were bid to credit from our poet,
Whose true scope, if you would know it,
In all his poems still hath been this measure,
To mix profit with your pleasure;
And not as some, whose throats their envy failing,
Cry hoarsely, All he writes is railing:
And when his plays come forth, think they can flout them,
With saying, he was a year about them.
To this there needs no lie, but this his creature,
Which was two months since no feature;
And though he dares give them five lives to mend it,
'Tis known, five weeks fully penn'd it,
From his own hand, without a co-adjutor,
Novice, journey-man, or tutor.
Yet thus much I can give you as a token
Of his play's worth, no eggs are broken,
Nor quaking custards with fierce teeth affrighted,
Wherewith your rout are so delighted;
Nor hales he in a gull old ends reciting,
To stop gaps in his loose writing;
With such a deal of monstrous and forced action,
As might make Bethlem a faction:
Nor made he his play for jests stolen from each table,
But makes jests to fit his fable;
And so presents quick comedy refined,
As best critics have designed;
The laws of time, place, persons he observeth,
From no needful rule he swerveth.
All gall and copperas from his ink he draineth,
Only a little salt remaineth,
Wherewith he'll rub your cheeks, till red, with laughter,
They shall look fresh a week after.

[ACT I, SCENE I]

[*A Room in Volpone's House*]

Enter Volpone *and* Mosca

Volp. Good morning to the day; and next, my gold!—
Open the shrine, that I may see my saint.

Mosca *withdraws the curtain, and discovers piles of gold, plate, jewels, etc.*

Hail the world's soul, and mine! more glad than is
The teeming earth to see the long'd-for sun
Peep through the horns of the celestial Ram,
Am I, to view thy splendour darkening his;
That lying here, amongst my other hoards,
Shew'st like a flame by night, or like the day
Struck out of chaos, when all darkness fled
Unto the centre. O thou son of Sol,
But brighter than thy father, let me kiss,
With adoration, thee, and every relick
Of sacred treasure in this blessed room.
Well did wise poets, by thy glorious name,
Title that age which they would have the best;
Thou being the best of things, and far transcending
All style of joy, in children, parents, friends,
Or any other waking dream on earth:
Thy looks when they to Venus did ascribe,
They should have given her twenty thousand Cupids;
Such are thy beauties and our loves! Dear saint,
Riches, the dumb god, that giv'st all men tongues,
Thou canst do nought, and yet mak'st men do all things;
The price of souls; even hell, with thee to boot,
Is made worth heaven. Thou art virtue, fame,

Honour, and all things else. Who can get thee,
He shall be noble valiant, honest, wise—
Mos. And what he will, sir. Riches are in fortune
A greater good than wisdom is in nature.
Volp. True, my beloved Mosca. Yet I glory
More in the cunning purchase of my wealth,
Than in the glad possession, since I gain
No common way; I use no trade, no venture;
I wound no earth with plough-shares, fat no beasts,
To feed the shambles; have no mills for iron,
Oil, corn, or men, to grind them into powder:
I blow no subtle glass, expose no ships
To threat'nings of the furrow-faced sea;
I turn no monies in the public bank,
Nor usure private.
Mos. No, sir, nor devour
Soft prodigals. You shall have some will swallow
A melting heir as glibly as your Dutch
Will pills of butter, and ne'er purge for it;
Tear forth the fathers of poor families
Out of their beds, and coffin them alive
In some kind clasping prison, where their bones
May be forth-coming, when the flesh is rotten:
But your sweet nature doth abhor these courses;
You lothe the widow's or the orphan's tears
Should wash your pavements, or their piteous cries
Ring in your roofs, and beat the air for vengeance.
Volp. Right, Mosca; I do lothe it.
Mos. And besides, sir,
You are not like the thresher that doth stand
With a huge flail, watching a heap of corn,
And, hungry, dares not taste the smallest grain,
But feeds on mallows, and such bitter herbs;
Nor like the merchant, who hath fill'd his vaults
With Romagnia, and rich Candian wines,
Yet drinks the lees of Lombard's vinegar:

You will lie not in straw, whilst moths and worms
Feed on your sumptuous hangings and soft beds;
You know the use of riches, and dare give now
From that bright heap, to me, your poor observer,
Or to your dwarf, or your hermaphrodite,
Your eunuch, or what other household trifle
Your pleasure allows maintenance—

Volp. Hold thee, Mosca, *Gives him money*
Take of my hand; thou strik'st on truth in all,
And they are envious term thee parasite.
Call forth my dwarf, my eunuch, and my fool,
And let them make me sport. [*Exit* Mos.] What should I do,
But cocker up my genius, and live free
To all delights my fortune calls me to?
I have no wife, no parent, child, ally,
To give my substance to; but whom I make
Must be my heir: and this makes men observe me:
To give my substance to; but whom I make
Women and men of every sex and age,
That bring me presents, send me plate, coin, jewels,
With hope that when I die (which they expect
Each greedy minute) it shall then return
Ten-fold upon them; whilst some, covetous
Above the rest, seek to engross me whole,
And counter-work the one unto the other,
Contend in gifts, as they would seem in love:
All which I suffer, playing with their hopes,
And am content to coin them into profit,
And look upon their kindness, and take more,
And look on that; still bearing them in hand,
Letting the cherry knock against their lips,
And draw it by their mouths, and back again.—
How now!

Re-enter MOSCA *with* NANO, ANDROGYNO, *and* CASTRONE

Nan. Now, room for fresh gamesters, who do will you to know,
They do bring you neither play nor university show;
And therefore do entreat you, that whatsoever they rehearse,
May not fare a whit the worse, for the false pace of the verse.
If you wonder at this, you will wonder more ere we pass,
For know, here is inclosed the soul of Pythagoras,
That juggler divine, as hereafter shall follow;
Which soul, fast and loose, sir, came first from Apollo,
And was breath'd into Æthalides, Mercurius his son,
Where it had the gift to remember all that ever was done.
From thence it fled forth, and made quick transmigration
To goldly-lock'd Euphorbus, who was killed in good fashion,
At the siege of old Troy, by the cuckold of Sparta.
Hermotimus was next (I find it in my charta)
To whom it did pass, where no sooner it was missing
But with one Pyrrhus of Delos it learn'd to go a fishing;
And thence did it enter the sophist of Greece.
From Pythagore, she went into a beautiful piece,
Hight Aspasia, the meretrix; and the next toss of her
Was again of a whore, she became a philosopher,
Crates the cynick, as it self doth relate it:
Since kings, knights, and beggars, knaves, lords, and fools gat it,
Besides ox and ass, camel, mule, goat, and brock,
In all which it hath spoke, as in the cobler's cock.
But I come not here to discourse of that matter,
Or his one, two, or three, or his great oath, BY QUATER!
His musics, his trigon, his golden thigh,
Or his telling how elements shift, but I
Would ask, how of late thou hast suffered translation,
And shifted thy coat in these days of reformation.
And. Like one of the reformed, a fool, as you see,
Counting all old doctrine heresie.

Nan. But not on thine own forbid meats hast thou ventured?
And. On fish, when first a Carthusian I enter'd.
Nan. Why, then thy dogmatical silence hath left thee?
And. Of that an obstreperous lawyer bereft me.
Nan. O wonderful change, when sir lawyer forsook thee!
For Pythagore's sake, what body then took thee?
And. A good dull mule. *Nan.* And how! by that means
Thou wert brought to allow of the eating of beans?
And. Yes. *Nan.* But from the mule into whom didst thou pass?
And. Into a very strange beast, by some writers call'd an ass;
By others, a precise, pure, illuminate brother,
Of those devour flesh, and sometimes one another;
And will drop you forth a libel, or a sanctified lie,
Betwixt every spoonful of a nativity-pie.
Nan. Now quit thee, for heaven, of that profane nation,
And gently report thy next transmigration.
And. To the same that I am. *Nan.* A creature of delight,
And, what is more than a fool, an hermaphrodite!
Now, prithee, sweet soul, in all thy variation,
Which body would'st thou choose, to keep up thy station?
And. Troth, this I am in: even here would I tarry.
Nan. 'Cause here the delight of each sex thou canst vary?
And. Alas, those pleasures be stale and forsaken;
No, 'tis your fool wherewith I am so taken,
The only one creature that I can call blessed;
For all other forms I have proved most distressed.
Nan. Spoke true, as thou wert in Pythagoras still.
This learned opinion we celebrate will,
Fellow eunuch, as behoves us, with all our wit and art,
To dignify that whereof ourselves are so great and special a part.
Volp. Now, very pretty! Mosca, this
Was thy invention?
Mos. If it please my patron,

Not else.

Volp. It doth, good Mosca.

Mos. Then it was, sir.

NANO *and* CASTRONE *sing*

Fools, they are the only nation
Worth men's envy or admiration:
Free from care or sorrow-taking,
Selves and others merry making:
All they speak or do is sterling.
Your fool he is your great man's darling,
And your ladies' sport and pleasure;
Tongue and bauble are his treasure.
E'en his face begetteth laughter,
And he speaks truth free from slaughter;
He's the grace of every feast,
And sometimes the chiefest guest;
Hath his trencher and his stool,
When wit waits upon the fool.
O, who would not be
He, he, he? *Knocking without*

Volp. Who's that? Away!

Exeunt NANO *and* CASTRONE

Look, Mosca. Fool, begone!

Exit ANDROGYNO

Mos. 'Tis signior Voltore, the advocate;
I know him by his knock.

Volp. Fetch me my gown,
My furs and night-caps; say, my couch is changing,
And let him entertain himself awhile
Without i' the gallery. [*Exit* MOSCA] Now, now, my clients
Begin their visitation! Vulture, kite,
Raven, and gorcrow, all my birds of prey,
That think me turning carcase, now they come;
I am not for them yet—

Re-enter Mosca, *with the gown, etc.*

Now now! the news?

Mos. A piece of plate, sir.

Volp. Of what bigness?

Mos. Huge,
Massy, and antique, with your name inscribed,
And arms engraven.

Volp. Good! and not a fox
Stretch'd on the earth, with fine delusive sleights,
Mocking a gaping crow? ha, Mosca!

Mos. Sharp, sir.

Volp. Give me my furs. [*Puts on his sick dress*] Why dost thou laugh so, man?

Mos. I cannot choose, sir, when I apprehend
What thoughts he has without now, as he walks:
That this might be the last gift he should give;
That this would fetch you; if you died to-day,
And gave him all, what he should be to-morrow;
What large return would come of all his ventures;
How he should worship'd be, and reverenced;
Ride with his furs, and foot-cloths; waited on
By herds of fools, and clients; have clear way
Made for his mule, as letter'd as himself;
Be call'd the great and learned advocate:
And then concludes, there's nought impossible.

Volp. Yes, to be learned, Mosca.

Mos. O, no: rich
Implies it. Hood an ass with reverend purple,
So you can hide his two ambitious ears,
And he shall pass for a cathedral doctor.

Volp. My caps, my caps, good Mosca. Fetch him in.

Mos. Stay, sir; your ointment for your eyes.

Volp. That's true;
Dispatch, dispatch: I long to have possession
Of my new present.

Mos. That, and thousands more,
I hope to see you lord of.
Volp. Thanks, kind Mosca.
Mos. And that, when I am lost in blended dust,
And hundred such as I am, in succession—
Volp. Nay, that were too much, Mosca.
Mos. You shall live,
Still, to delude these harpies.
Volp. Loving Mosca!
'Tis well: my pillow now, and let him enter. *Exit* MOSCA
Now, my feign'd cough, my phthisic, and my gout,
My apoplexy, palsy, and catarrhs,
Help, with your forced functions, this my posture,
Wherein, this three year, I have milk'd their hopes.
He comes; I hear him—Uh! [*coughing*] uh! uh! uh! O—

Re-enter MOSCA, *introducing* VOLTORE, *with a piece of Plate*

Mos. You still are what you were, sir. Only you,
Of all the rest, are he commands his love,
And you do wisely to preserve it thus,
With early visitation, and kind notes
Of your good meaning to him, which, I know,
Cannot but come most grateful! Patron! sir!
Here's signior Voltore is come—
Volp. [*faintly*] What say you?
Mos. Sir, signior Voltore is come this morning
To visit you.
Volp. I thank him.
Mos. And hath brought
A piece of antique plate, bought of St. Mark,
With which he here presents you.
Volp. He is welcome.
Pray him to come more often.
Mos. Yes.
Volt. What says he?
Mos. He thanks you, and desires you see him often.

Volp. Mosca.
Mos. My patron!
Volp. Bring him near, where is he?
I long to feel his hand.
Mos. The plate is here, sir.
Volt. How fare you, sir?
Volp. I thank you, signior Voltore;
Where is the plate? mine eyes are bad.
Volt. [*Putting it into his hands*] I'm sorry,
To see you still thus weak.
Mos. [*Aside*] That he's not weaker.
Volp. You are too munificent.
Volt. No, sir; would to heaven,
I could as well give health to you, as that plate!
Volp. You give, sir, what you can: I thank you. Your love
Hath taste in this, and shall not be unanswer'd:
I pray you see me often.
Volt. Yes, I shall, sir.
Volp. Be not far from me.
Mos. Do you observe that, sir?
Volp. Hearken unto me still; it will concern you.
Mos. You are a happy man, sir; know your good.
Volp. I cannot now last long—
Mos. You are his heir, sir.
Volt. Am I?
Volp. I feel me going; Uh! uh! uh! uh!
I'm sailing to my port, Uh! uh! uh! uh!
And I am glad I am so near my haven.
Mos. Alas, kind gentleman! Well, we must all go—
Volt. But, Mosca—
Mos. Age will conquer.
Volt. 'Pray thee, hear me:
Am I inscribed his heir for certain?
Mos. Are you!
I do beseech you, sir, you will vouchsafe

To write me in your family. All my hopes
Depend upon your worship: I am lost,
Except the rising sun do shine on me.
Volt. It shall both shine, and warm thee, Mosca.
Mos. Sir,
I am a man, that hath not done your love
All the worst offices: here I wear your keys,
See all your coffers and your caskets lock'd,
Keep the poor inventory of your jewels,
Your plate and monies; am your steward, sir,
Husband your goods here.
Volt. But am I sole heir?
Mos. Without a partner, sir; confirm'd this morning:
The wax is warm yet, and the ink scarce dry
Upon the parchment.
Volt. Happy, happy, me!
By what good chance, sweet Mosca?
Mos. Your desert, sir;
I know no second cause.
Volt. Thy modesty
Is not to know it; well, we shall requite it.
Mos. He ever liked your course, sir; that first took him.
I oft have heard him say, how he admired
Men of your large profession, that could speak
To every cause, and things mere contraries,
Till they were hoarse again, yet all be law;
That, with most quick agility, could turn,
And [re-]return; [could] make knots, and undo them;
Give forked counsel; take provoking gold
On either hand, and put it up: these men,
He knew, would thrive with their humility.
And, for his part, he thought he should be blest
To have his heir of such a suffering spirit,
So wise, so grave, of so perplex'd a tongue,
And loud withal, that would not wag, nor scarce
Lie still, without a fee; when every word

Your worship but lets fall, is a chequin!— [*Knocking without*
Who's that? one knocks; I would not have you seen, sir.
And yet—pretend you came, and went in haste:
I'll fashion an excuse——and, gentle sir,
When you do come to swim in golden lard,
Up to the arms in honey, that your chin
Is borne up stiff, with fatness of the flood,
Think on your vassal; but remember me:
I have not been your worst of clients.

Volt. Mosca!—

Mos. When will you have your inventory brought, sir?
Or see a copy of the will?—Anon!—
I'll bring them to you, sir. Away, be gone,
Put business in your face. *Exit* VOLTORE

Volp. [*Springing up*] Excellent Mosca!
Come hither, let me kiss thee.

Mos. Keep you still, sir.
Here is Corbaccio.

Volp. Set the plate away:
The vulture's gone, and the old raven's come!

Mos. Betake you to your silence, and your sleep.
Stand there and multiply. [*Putting the plate to the rest*]
Now, shall we see
A wretch who is indeed more impotent
Than this can feign to be; yet hopes to hop
Over his grave—

Enter CORBACCIO

Signior Corbaccio!
You're very welcome, sir.

Corb. How does your patron?

Mos. Troth, as he did, sir; no amends.

Corb. What! mends he?

Mos. No, sir: he's rather worse.

Corb. That's well. Where is he?

Mos. Upon his couch, sir, newly fall'n asleep.

Corb. Does he sleep well?
Mos. No wink, sir, all this night.
Nor yesterday; but slumbers.
Corb. Good! he should take
Some counsel of physicians: I have brought him
An opiate here, from mine own doctor.
Mos. He will not hear of drugs.
Corb. Why? I myself
Stood by while it was made, saw all the ingredients:
And know, it cannot but most gently work:
My life for his, 'tis but to make him sleep.
Volp. [*Aside*] Ay, his last sleep, if he would take it.
Mos. Sir,
He has no faith in physic.
Corb. Say you, say you?
Mos. He has no faith in physic: he does think
Most of your doctors are the greater danger,
And worse disease, to escape. I often have
Heard him protest, that your physician
Should never be his heir.
Corb. Not I his heir?
Mos. Not your physician, sir.
Corb. O, no, no, no,
I do not mean it.
Mos. No, sir, nor their fees
He cannot brook: he says, they flay a man,
Before they kill him.
Corb. Right, I do conceive you.
Mos. And then they do it by experiment;
For which the law not only doth absolve them,
But gives them great reward: and he is loth
To hire his death, so.
Corb. It is true, they kill
With as much license as a judge.
Mos. Nay, more;
For he but kills, sir, where the law condemns,

And these can kill him too.
Corb. Ay, or me;
Or any man. How does his apoplex?
Is that strong on him still?
Mos. Most violent.
His speech is broken, and his eyes are set,
His face drawn longer than 'twas wont—
Corb. How! how!
Stronger than he was wont?
Mos. No, sir: his face
Drawn longer than 'twas wont.
Corb. O, good!
Mos. His mouth
Is ever gaping, and his eyelids hang.
Corb. Good.
Mos. A freezing numbness stiffens all his joints,
And makes the colour of his flesh like lead.
Corb. 'Tis good.
Mos. His pulse beats slow, and dull.
Corb. Good symptoms still.
Mos. And from his brain—
Corb. I conceive you; good.
Mos. Flows a cold sweat, with a continual rheum,
Forth the resolved corners of his eyes.
Corb. Is't possible? Yet I am better, ha!
How does he, with the swimming of his head?
Mos. O, sir, 'tis past the scotomy; he now
Hath lost his feeling, and hath left to snort:
You hardly can perceive him, that he breathes.
Corb. Excellent, excellent! sure I shall outlast him:
This makes me young again, a score of years.
Mos. I was a coming for you, sir.
Corb. Has he made his will?
What has he given me?
Mos. No, sir.
Corb. Nothing! ha?

Mos. He has not made his will, sir.
Corb. Oh, oh, oh!
What then did Voltore, the lawyer, here?
Mos. He smelt a carcase, sir, when he but heard
My master was about his testament;
As I did urge him to it for your good—
Corb. He came unto him, did he? I thought so.
Mos. Yes, and presented him this piece of plate.
Corb. To be his heir?
Mos. I do not know, sir.
Corb. True:
I know it too.
Mos. [*Aside*] By your own scale, sir.
Corb. Well,
I shall prevent him, yet. See, Mosca, look,
Here, I have brought a bag of bright chequines,
Will quite weigh down his plate.
Mos. [*Taking the bag*] Yea, marry, sir.
This is true physic, this your sacred medicine;
No talk of opiates, to this great elixir!
Corb. 'Tis aurum palpabile, if not potabile.
Mos. It shall be minister'd to him, in his bowl.
Corb. Ay, do, do, do.
Mos. Most blessed cordial!
This will recover him.
Corb. Yes, do, do, do.
Mos. I think it were not best, sir.
Corb. What?
Mos. To recover him.
Corb. O, no, no, no; by no means.
Mos. Why, sir, this
Will work some strange effect, if he but feel it.
Corb. 'Tis true, therefore forbear; I'll take my venture:
Give me it again.
Mos. At no hand; pardon me:
You shall not do yourself that wrong, sir. I

Will so advise you, you shall have it all.

Corb. How?

Mos. All, sir; 'tis your right, your own: no man
Can claim a part: 'tis yours, without a rival,
Decreed by destiny.

Corb. How, how, good Mosca?

Mos. I'll tell you, sir. This fit he shall recover.

Corb. I do conceive you.

Mos. And, on first advantage
Of his gain'd sense, will I re-importune him
Unto the making of his testament:
And shew him this. *Pointing to the money*

Corb. Good, good.

Mos. 'Tis better yet,
If you will hear, sir.

Corb. Yes, with all my heart.

Mos. Now, would I counsel you, make home with speed:
There, frame a will; whereto you shall inscribe
My master your sole heir.

Corb. And disinherit
My son!

Mos. O, sir, the better: for that colour
Shall make it much more taking.

Corb. O, but colour?

Mos. This will, sir, you shall send it unto me.
Now, when I come to inforce, as I will do,
Your cares, your watchings, and your many prayers,
Your more than many gifts, your this day's present,
And last, produce your will; where, without thought,
Or least regard, unto your proper issue,
A son so brave, and highly meriting,
The stream of your diverted love hath thrown you
Upon my master, and made him your heir:
He cannot be so stupid, or stone-dead,
But out of conscience, and mere gratitude—

Corb. He must pronounce me his?

Mos. 'Tis true.

Corb. This plot
Did I think on before.

Mos. I do believe it.

Corb. Do you not believe it?

Mos. Yes, sir.

Corb. Mine own project.

Mos. Which, when he hath done, sir—

Corb. Publish'd me his heir?

Mos. And you so certain to survive him—

Corb. Ay.

Mos. Being so lusty a man—

Corb. 'Tis true.

Mos. Yes, sir—

Corb. I thought on that too. See, how he should be
The very organ to express my thoughts!

Mos. You have not only done yourself a good—

Corb. But multiplied it on my son.

Mos. 'Tis right, sir.

Corb. Still, my invention.

Mos. 'Las, sir! heaven knows,
It hath been all my study, all my care,
(I e'en grow gray withal,) how to work things—

Corb. I do conceive, sweet Mosca.

Mos. You are he,
For whom I labour here.

Corb. Ay, do, do, do:
I'll straight about it. *Going*

Mos. Rook go with you, raven!

Corb. I know thee honest.

Mos. [*Aside*] You do lie, sir!

Corb. And—

Mos. Your knowledge is no better than your ears, sir.

Corb. I do not doubt, to be a father to thee.

Mos. Nor I to gull my brother of his blessing.

Corb. I may have my youth restored to me, why not?

Mos. Your worship is a precious ass!

Corb. What say'st thou?

Mos. I do desire your worship to make haste, sir.

Corb. 'Tis done, 'tis done; I go. *Exit*

Volp. [*Leaping from his couch*] O, I shall burst!
Let out my sides, let out my sides—

Mos. Contain
Your flux of laughter, sir: you know this hope
Is such a bait, it covers any hook.

Volp. O, but thy working, and thy placing it!
I cannot hold; good rascal, let me kiss thee:
I never knew thee in so rare a humour.

Mos. Alas, sir, I but do as I am taught;
Follow your grave instructions; give them words;
Pour oil into their ears, and send them hence.

Volp. 'Tis true, 'tis true. What a rare punishment
Is avarice to itself!

Mos. Ay, with our help, sir.

Volp. So many cares, so many maladies,
So many fears attending on old age,
Yea, death so often call'd on, as no wish
Can be more frequent with them, their limbs faint,
Their senses dull, their seeing, hearing, going,
All dead before them; yea, their very teeth,
Their instruments of eating, failing them:
Yet this is reckon'd life! nay, here was one,
Is now gone home, that wishes to live longer!
Feels not his gout, nor palsy; feigns himself
Younger by scores of years, flatters his age
With confident belying it, hopes he may,
With charms, like Æson, have his youth restored:
And with these thoughts so battens, as if fate
Would be as easily cheated on, as he,
And all turns air! [*Knocking within*] Who's that there, now?
a third!

Mos. Close, to your couch again; I hear his voice:
It is Corvino, our spruce merchant.
Volp. [*Lies down as before*] Dead.
Mos. Another bout, sir, with your eyes. [*Anointing them*]
—Who's there?

Enter CORVINO

Signior Corvino! come most wish'd for! O,
How happy were you, if you knew it, now!
Corv. Why? what? wherein?
Mos. The tardy hour is come, sir.
Corv. He is not dead?
Mos. Not dead, sir, but as good;
He knows no man.
Corv. How shall I do then?
Mos. Why, sir?
Corv. I have brought him here a pearl.
Mos. Perhaps he has
So much remembrance left, as to know you, sir:
He still calls on you; nothing but your name
Is in his mouth. Is your pearl orient, sir?
Corv. Venice was never owner of the like.
Volp. [*Faintly*] Signior Corvino!
Mos. Hark.
Volp. Signior Corvino!
Mos. He calls you; step and give it to him.—He's here, sir,
And he has brought you a rich pearl.
Corv. How do you, sir?
Tell him, it doubles the twelfth caract.
Mos. Sir,
He cannot understand, his hearing's gone;
And yet it comforts him to see you—
Corv. Say,
I have a diamond for him, too.
Mos. Best shew it, sir;

Put it into his hand; 'tis only there
He apprehends: he has his feeling, yet.
See how he grasps it!
Corv. 'Las, good gentleman!
How pitiful the sight is!
Mos. Tut! forget, sir.
The weeping of an heir should still be laughter
Under a visor.
Corv. Why, am I his heir?
Mos. Sir, I am sworn, I may not shew the will
Till he be dead; but here has been Corbaccio,
Here has been Voltore, here were others too,
I cannot number 'em, they were so many;
All gaping here for legacies: but I,
Taking the vantage of his naming you,
Signior Corvino, Signior Corvino, took
Paper, and pen, and ink, and there I asked him,
Whom he would have his heir? *Corvino.* Who
Should be executor? *Corvino.* And,
To any question he was silent to,
I still interpreted the nods he made,
Through weakness, for consent: and sent home th' others,
Nothing bequeath'd them, but to cry and curse.
Corv. O, my dear Mosca! [*They embrace*] Does he not perceive us?
Mos. No more than a blind harper. He knows no man,
No face of friend, nor name of any servant,
Who 'twas that fed him last, or gave him drink:
Not those he hath begotten, or brought up,
Can he remember.
Corv. Has he children?
Mos. Bastards,
Some dozen, or more, that he begot on beggars,
Gypsies, and Jews, and black-moors, when he was drunk.
Knew you not that, sir? 'tis the common fable.
The dwarf, the fool, the eunuch, are all his;

He's the true father of his family.
In all, save me:—but he has given them nothing.

Corv. That's well, that's well! Art sure he does not hear us?

Mos. Sure, sir! why, look you, credit your own sense.

Shouts in VOLPONE'S *ear*

The pox approach, and add to your diseases,
If it would send you hence the sooner, sir,
For your incontinence, it hath deserv'd it
Thoroughly, and thoroughly, and the plague to boot!—
You may come near, sir.—Would you would once close
Those filthy eyes of yours, that flow with slime,
Like two frog-pits; and those same hanging cheeks,
Cover'd with hide instead of skin—Nay, help, sir—
That look like frozen dish-clouts set on end!

Corv. [*Aloud*] Or like an old smoked wall, on which the rain
Ran down in streaks!

Mos. Excellent, sir! speak out:
You may be louder yet; a culverin
Discharged in his ear would hardly bore it.

Corv. His nose is like a common sewer, still running.

Mos. 'Tis good! And what his mouth?

Corv. A very draught.

Mos. O, stop it up—

Corv. By no means.

Mos. 'Pray you, let me:
Faith I could stifle him rarely with a pillow,
As well as any woman that should keep him.

Corv. Do as you will; but I'll begone.

Mos. Be so:
It is your presence makes him last so long.

Corv. I pray you, use no violence.

Mos. No, sir! why?
Why should you be thus scrupulous, pray you, sir?

Corv. Nay, at your discretion.

Mos. Well, good sir, begone.
Corv. I will not trouble him now, to take my pearl.
Mos. Puh! nor your diamond. What a needless care
Is this afflicts you? Is not all here yours?
Am not I here, whom you have made your creature?
That owe my being to you?
Corv. Grateful Mosca!
Thou art my friend, my fellow, my companion,
My partner, and shalt share in all my fortunes.
Mos. Excepting one.
Corv. What's that?
Mos. Your gallant wife, sir,— *Exit* CORVINO
Now is he gone: we had no other means
To shoot him hence, but this.
Volp. My divine Mosca!
Thou hast to-day outgone thyself. [*Knocking within*]—
Who's there?
I will be troubled with no more. Prepare
Me music, dances, banquets, all delights;
The Turk is not more sensual in his pleasures,
Than will Volpone. [*Exit* MOSCA] Let me see; a pearl!
A diamond! plate! chequines! Good morning's purchase.
Why, this is better than rob churches, yet;
Or fat, by eating, once a month, a man—

Re-enter MOSCA

Who is't?
Mos. The beauteous lady Would-be, sir,
Wife to the English knight, sir Politick Would-be,
(This is the style, sir, is directed me,)
Hath sent to know how you have slept to-night,
And if you would be visited?
Volp. Not now:
Some three hours hence—
Mos. I told the squire so much.

Volp. When I am high with mirth and wine; then, then:
'Fore heaven, I wonder at the desperate valour
Of the bold English, that they dare let loose
Their wives to all encounters!
Mos. Sir, this knight
Had not his name for nothing, he is *politick,*
And knows, howe'er his wife affect strange airs,
She hath not yet the face to be dishonest:
But had she signior Corvino's wife's face—
Volp. Has she so rare a face?
Mos. O, sir, the wonder,
The blazing star of Italy! a wench
Of the first year! a beauty ripe as harvest!
Whose skin is whiter than a swan all over,
Than silver, snow, or lilies! a soft lip,
Would tempt you to eternity of kissing!
And flesh that melteth in the touch to blood!
Bright as your gold, and lovely as your gold!
Volp. Why had not I known this before?
Mos. Alas, sir,
Myself but yesterday discover'd it.
Volp. How might I see her?
Mos. O, not possible;
She's kept as warily as is your gold;
Never does come abroad, never takes air,
But at a window. All her looks are sweet,
As the first grapes or cherries, and are watch'd
As near as they are.
Volp. I must see her.
Mos. Sir,
There is a guard of spies ten thick upon her,
All his whole household; each of which is set
Upon his fellow, and have all their charge,
When he goes out, when he comes in, examined.
Volp. I will go see her, though but at her window.
Mos. In some disguise, then.

Volp. That is true; I must
Maintain mine own shape still the same: we'll think.
Exeunt

[ACT II, SCENE I]

[*St. Mark's Place; a retired corner before Corvino's House*]

Enter Sir Politick Would-be, *and* Peregrine

Sir P. Sir, to a wise man, all the world's his soil:
It is not Italy, nor France, nor Europe,
That must bound me, if my fates call me forth.
Yet, I protest, it is no salt desire
Of seeing countries, shifting a religion,
Nor any disaffection to the state
Where I was bred, and unto which I owe
My dearest plots, hath brought me out; much less,
That idle, antique, stale, gray-headed project
Of knowing men's minds and manners, with Ulysses!
But a peculiar humour of my wife's
Laid for this height of Venice, to observe,
To quote, to learn the language, and so forth—
I hope you travel, sir, with license?
Per. Yes.
Sir P. I dare the safelier converse——How long, sir,
Since you left England?
Per. Seven weeks.
Sir P. So lately!
You have not been with my lord ambassador?
Per. Not yet, sir.
Sir P. Pray you, what news, sir, vents our climate?
I heard last night a most strange thing reported
By some of my lord's followers, and I long
To hear how 'twill be seconded.
Per. What was't, sir?
Sir P. Marry, sir, of a raven that should build

In a ship royal of the king's.

Per. This fellow,

Does he gull me, trow? or is gull'd? [*Aside*] Your name, sir.

Sir P. My name is Politick Would-be.

Per. [*Aside*] O, that speaks him.—

A knight, sir?

Sir P. A poor knight, sir.

Per. Your lady

Lies here in Venice, for intelligence

Of tires, and fashions, and behaviour,

Among the courtezans? the fine lady Would-be?

Sir P. Yes, sir; the spider and the bee, ofttimes,

Suck from one flower.

Per. Good sir Politick,

I cry you mercy; I have heard much of you:

'Tis true, sir, of your raven.

Sir P. On your knowledge?

Per. Yes, and your lion's whelping in the Tower.

Sir P. Another whelp!

Per. Another, sir.

Sir P. Now heaven!

What prodigies be these? The fires at Berwick!

And the new star! these things concurring, strange,

And full of omen! Saw you those meteors?

Per. I did, sir.

Sir P. Fearful! Pray you, sir, confirm me,

Were there three porpoises seen above the bridge,

As they give out?

Per. Six, and a sturgeon, sir.

Sir P. I am astonish'd.

Per. Nay, sir, be not so;

I'll tell you a greater prodigy than these.

Sir P. What should these things portend?

Per. The very day

(Let me be sure) that I put forth from London,

There was a whale discover'd in the river,
As high as Woolwich, that had waited there,
Few know how many months, for the subversion
Of the Stode fleet.

Sir P. Is't possible? believe it,
'Twas either sent from Spain, or the archdukes:
Spinola's whale, upon my life, my credit!
Will they not leave these projects? Worthy sir,
Some other news.

Per. Faith, Stone the fool is dead,
And they do lack a tavern fool extremely.

Sir P. Is Mass Stone dead?

Per. He's dead, sir; why, I hope
You thought him not immortal?—[*Aside*] O, this knight,
Were he well known, would be a precious thing
To fit our English stage: he that should write
But such a fellow, should be thought to feign
Extremely, if not maliciously.

Sir P. Stone dead!

Per. Dead.—Lord! how deeply, sir, you apprehend it?
He was no kinsman to you?

Sir P. That I know of.
Well! the same fellow was an unknown fool.

Per. And yet you knew him, it seems?

Sir P. I did so. Sir,
I knew him one of the most dangerous heads
Living within the state, and so I held him.

Per. Indeed, sir?

Sir P. While he lived, in action.
He has received weekly intelligence,
Upon my knowledge, out of the Low Countries,
For all parts of the world, in cabbages;
And those dispensed again to ambassadors,
In oranges, musk-melons, apricocks,
Lemons, pome-citrons, and such-like; sometimes
In Colchester oysters, and your Selsey cockles.

Per. You make me wonder.
Sir P. Sir, upon my knowledge.
Nay, I've observed him, at your public ordinary,
Take his advertisement from a traveller,
A conceal'd statesman, in a trencher of meat;
And instantly, before the meal was done,
Convey an answer in a tooth-pick.
Per. Strange!
How could this be, sir?
Sir P. Why, the meat was cut
So like his character, and so laid, as he
Must easily read the cipher.
Per. I have heard,
He could not read, sir.
Sir P. So 'twas given out,
In policy, by those that did employ him:
But he could read, and had your languages,
And to't, as sound a noddle—
Per. I have heard, sir,
That your baboons were spies, and that they were
A kind of subtle nation near to China.
Sir P. Ay, ay, your Mamaluchi. Faith, they had
Their hand in a French plot or two; but they
Were so extremely given to women, as
They made discovery of all: yet I
Had my advices here, on Wednesday last.
From one of their own coat, they were return'd,
Made their relations, as the fashion is,
And now stand fair for fresh employment.
Per. [*Aside*] 'Heart!
This sir Pol will be ignorant of nothing.
It seems, sir, you know all.
Sir P. Not all, sir, but
I have some general notions. I do love
To note and to observe: though I live out,
Free from the active torrent, yet I'd mark

The currents and the passages of things,
For mine own private use; and know the ebbs
And flows of state.

Per. Believe it, sir, I hold
Myself in no small tie unto my fortunes,
For casting me thus luckily upon you,
Whose knowledge, if your bounty equal it,
May do me great assistance, in instruction
For my behaviour, and my bearing, which
Is yet so rude and raw.

Sir P. Why, came you forth
Empty of rules for travel?

Per. Faith, I had
Some common ones, from out that vulgar grammar,
Which he that cried Italian to me, taught me.

Sir P. Why this it is that spoils all our brave bloods,
Trusting our hopeful gentry unto pedants,
Fellows of outside, and mere bark. You seem
To be a gentleman, of ingenuous race:—
I not profess it, but my fate hath been
To be, where I have been consulted with,
In this high kind, touching some great men's sons,
Persons of blood and honour.—

Enter MOSCA *and* NANO *disguised, followed by persons with materials for erecting a Stage*

Per. Who be these, sir?

Mos. Under that window, there 't must be. The same.

Sir P. Fellows, to mount a bank. Did your instructor
In the dear tongues, never discourse to you
Of the Italian mountebanks?

Per. Yes, sir.

Sir P. Why,
Here you shall see one.

Per. They are quacksalvers;

Fellows, that live by venting oils and rugs.
Sir P. Was that the character he gave you of them?
Per. As I remember.
Sir P. Pity his ignorance.
They are the only knowing men of Europe!
Great general scholars, excellent physicians,
Most admired statesmen, profest favourites,
And cabinet counsellors to the greatest princes;
The only languaged men of all the world!
Per. And, I have heard, they are most lewd impostors;
Made all of terms and shreds; no less beliers
Of great men's favours, than their own vile med'cines;
Which they will utter upon monstrous oaths:
Selling that drug for two-pence, ere they part,
Which they have valued at twelve crowns before.
Sir P. Sir, calumnies are answer'd best with silence.
Yourself shall judge.—Who is it mounts, my friends?
Mos. Scoto of Mantua, sir.
Sir P. Is't he? Nay, then
I'll proudly promise, sir, you shall behold
Another man than has been phant'sied to you.
I wonder yet, that he should mount his bank,
Here in this nook, that has been wont t'appear
In face of the Piazza!—Here he comes.

Enter VOLPONE, *disguised as a mountebank Doctor, and followed by a crowd of people*

Volp. Mount, zany. [*to* NANO]
Mob. Follow, follow, follow, follow!
Sir P. See how the people follow him! he's a man
May write ten thousand crowns in bank here. Note,
VOLPONE *mounts the Stage*
Mark but his gesture:—I do use to observe
The state he keeps in getting up.
Per. 'Tis worth it, sir.

Volp. Most noble gentlemen, and my worthy patrons! It may seem strange, that I, your Scoto Mantuano, who was ever wont to fix my bank in face of the public Piazza, near the shelter of the Portico to the Procuratia, should now, after eight months' absence from this illustrious city of Venice, humbly retire myself into an obscure nook of the Piazza.

Sir P. Did not I now object the same?

Per. Peace, sir.

Volp. Let me tell you: I am not, as your Lombard proverb saith, cold on my feet; or content to part with my commodities at a cheaper rate, than I accustomed: look not for it. Nor that the calumnious reports of that impudent detractor, and shame to our profession, (Alessandro Buttone, I mean,) who gave out, in public, I was condemned a sforzato to the galleys, for poisoning the cardinal Bembo's —— cook, hath at all attached, much less dejected me. No, no, worthy gentlemen; to tell you true, I cannot endure to see the rabble of these ground ciarlitani, that spread their cloaks on the pavement, as if they meant to do feats of activity, and then come in lamely, with their mouldy tales out of Boccacio, like stale Tabarine, the fabulist: some of them discoursing their travels, and of their tedious captivity in the Turks' gallies, when, indeed, were the truth known, they were the Christians' gallies, where very temperately they eat bread, and drunk water, as a wholesome penance, enjoined them by their confessors, for base pilferies.

Sir P. Note but his bearing, and contempt of these.

Volp. These turdy-facy-nasty-paty-lousy-fartical rogues, with one poor groat's-worth of unprepared antimony, finely wrapt up in several scartoccios, are able, very well, to kill their twenty a week, and play; yet, these meagre, starved spirits, who have half stopt the organs of their minds with earthy oppilations, want not their favourers among your shrivell'd sallad-eating artizans, who are overjoyed that they may have their half-pe'rth of physic; though it purge them into another world, it makes no matter.

Sir P. Excellent! have you heard better language, sir?

Volp. Well, let them go. And, gentlemen, honourable gentlemen, know, that for this time, our bank, being thus removed from the clamours of the canaglia, shall be the scene of pleasure and delight; for I have nothing to sell, little or nothing to sell.

Sir P. I told you, sir, his end.

Per. You did so, sir.

Volp. I protest, I, and my six servants, are not able to make of this precious liquor, so fast as it is fetch'd away from my lodging by gentlemen of your city; strangers of the Terra-firma; worshipful merchants; ay, and senators too: who, ever since my arrival, have detained me to their uses, by their splendidous liberalities. And worthily; for, what avails your rich man to have his magazines stuft with moscadelli, or of the purest grape, when his physicians prescribe him, on pain of death, to drink nothing but water cocted with aniseeds? O, health! health! the blessing of the rich! the riches of the poor! who can buy thee at too dear a rate, since there is no enjoying this world without thee? Be not then so sparing of your purses, honourable gentlemen, as to abridge the natural course of life—

Per. You see his end.

Sir P. Ay, is't not good?

Volp. For, when a humid flux, or catarrh, by the mutability of air, falls from your head into an arm or shoulder, or any other part; take you a ducket, or your chequin of gold, and apply to the place affected: see what good effect it can work. No, no, 'tis this blessed unguento, this rare extraction, that hath only power to disperse all malignant humours, that proceed either of hot, cold, moist, or windy causes—

Per. I would he had put in dry too.

Sir P. 'Pray you, observe.

Volp. To fortify the most indigest and crude stomach, ay, were it of one that, through extreme weakness, vomited blood, applying only a warm napkin to the place, after the unction and fricace;—for the vertigine in the head, putting but a drop into your nostrils, likewise behind the ears; a most sovereign and approved remedy: the mal caduco, cramps, convulsions, paralysies, epilepsies, tremor-cordia, retired nerves, ill vapours of the spleen, stopping of the liver, the stone, the strangury, hernia ventosa, iliaca passio; stops a dysenteria immediately; easeth the torsion of the small guts; and cures melancholia hypondriaca, being taken and applied according to my printed receipt. [*Pointing to his bill and his vial*] For, this is the physician, this the medicine; this counsels, this cures; this gives the direction, this works the effect; and, in sum, both together may be termed an abstract of the theorick and practick in the Æsculapian art. 'Twill cost you eight crowns. And,—Zan Fritada, prithee sing a verse extempore in honour of it.

Sir P. How do you like him, sir?

Per. Most strangely, I!

Sir P. Is not his language rare?

Per. But alchemy,
I never heard the like; or Broughton's books.

NANO *sings*

Had old Hippocrates, or Galen,
That to their books put med'cines all in,
But known this secret, they had never
(Of which they will be guilty ever)
Been murderers of so much paper,
Or wasted many a hurtless taper;
No Indian drug had e'er been famed,
Tobacco, sassafras not named;
Ne yet, of guacum one small stick, sir,
Nor Raymund Lully's great elixir.
Ne had been known the Danish Gonswart,
Or Paracelsus, with his long sword.

Per. All this, yet, will not do; eight crowns is high.

Volp. No more.—Gentlemen, if I had but time to discourse

to you the miraculous effects of this my oil, surnamed Oglio del Scoto; with the countless catalogue of those I have cured of the aforesaid, and many more diseases; the patents and privileges of all the princes and commonwealths of Christendom; or but the depositions of those that appeared on my part, before the signiory of the Sanita and most learned College of Physicians; where I was authorised, upon notice taken of the admirable virtues of my medicaments, and mine own excellency in matter of rare and unknown secrets, not only to disperse them publicly in this famous city, but in all the territories, that happily joy under the government of the most pious and magnificent states of Italy. But may some other gallant fellow say, O, there be divers that make professions to have as good, and as experimented receipts as yours: indeed, very many have assayed, like apes, in imitation of that, which is really and essentially in me, to make of this oil; bestowed great cost in furnaces, stills, alembecks, continual fires, and preparation of the ingredients, (as indeed there goes to it six hundred several simples, besides some quantity of human fat, for the conglutination, which we buy of the anatomists,) but, when these practitioners come to the last decoction, blow, blow, puff, puff, and all flies in fumo: ha, ha, ha! Poor wretches! I rather pity their folly and indiscretion, than their loss of time and money; for these may be recovered by industry: but to be a fool born, is a disease incurable.

For myself, I always from my youth have endeavoured to get the rarest secrets, and book them, either in exchange, or for money: I spared nor cost nor labour, where any thing was worthy to be learned. And, gentlemen, honourable gentlemen, I will undertake, by virtue of chemical art, out of the honourable hat that covers your head, to extract the four elements; that is to say, the fire, air, water, and earth, and return you your felt without burn or stain. For, whilst others have been at the Balloo, I have been at my book; and am now past the craggy paths of study, and come to the flowery plains of honour and reputation.

Sir P. I do assure you, sir, that is his aim.

Volp. But to our price—

Per. And that withal, sir Pol.

Volp. You all know, honourable gentlemen, I never valued this ampulla, or vial, at less than eight crowns; but for this time, I am content to be deprived of it for six: six crowns is the price, and less in courtesy I know you cannot offer me; take it or leave it, howsoever, both it and I am at your service. I ask you not as the value of the thing, for then I should demand of you a thousand crowns, so the cardinals Montalto, Fernese, the great Duke of Tuscany, my gossip, with divers other princes, have given me; but I despise money. Only to shew my affection to you, honourable gentlemen, and your illustrious State here, I have neglected the messages of these princes, mine own offices, framed my journey hither, only to present you with the fruits of my travels.—Tune your voices once more to the touch of your instruments, and give the honourable assembly some delightful recreation.

Per. What monstrous and most painful circumstance
Is here, to get some three or four gazettes,
Some three-pence in the whole! for that 'twill come to.

NANO *sings*

You that would last long, list to my song,
Make no more coil, but buy of this oil.
Would you be ever fair and young?
Stout of teeth, and strong of tongue?
Tart of palate? quick of ear?
Sharp of sight? of nostril clear?
Moist of hand? and light of foot?
Or, I will come nearer to't,
Would you live free from all diseases?
Do the act your mistress pleases,

Yet fright all aches from your bones?
Here's a medicine for the nones.

Volp. Well, I am in a humour at this time to make a present of the small quantity my coffer contains; to the rich in courtesy, and to the poor for God's sake. Wherefore now mark: I ask'd you six crowns; and six crowns, at other times, you have paid me; you shall not give me six crowns, nor five, not four, nor three, nor two, nor one; nor half a ducat; no, nor a moccinigo. Sixpence it will cost you, or six hundred pound —expect no lower price, for, by the banner of my front, I will not bate a bagatine,—that I will have, only, a pledge of your loves, to carry something from amongst you, to shew I am not contemn'd by you. Therefore, now, toss your handkerchiefs, cheerfully, cheerfully; and be advertised, that the first heroic spirit that deigns to grace me with a handkerchief, I will give it a little remembrance of something, beside, shall please it better, than if I had presented it with a double pistolet.

Per. Will you be that *heroic spark,* sir Pol?

Celia at a window above, throws down her handkerchief

O, see! the window has prevented you.

Volp. Lady, I kiss your bounty; and for this timely grace you have done your poor Scoto of Mantua, I will return you, over and above my oil, a secret of that high and inestimable nature, shall make you for ever enamour'd on that minute, wherein your eye first descended on so mean, yet not altogether to be despised, an object. Here is a powder conceal'd in this paper, of which, if I should speak to the worth, nine thousand volumes were but as one page, that page as a line, that line as a word; so short is this pilgrimage of man (which some call life) to the expressing of it. Would I reflect on the price? why, the whole world is but as an empire, that empire as a province, that province as a bank, that bank as a private purse to the purchase of it. I will only tell you; it is the powder that made Venus a goddess (given her by Apollo,) that kept her perpetually young, clear'd her wrinkles, firm'd her gums, fill'd her skin, colour'd her hair; from her derived to Helen, and at the sack of Troy unfortunately lost: till now, in this our age, it was as happily recovered, by a studious antiquary, out of some ruins of Asia, who sent a moiety of it to the court of France, (but much sophisticated,) wherewith the ladies there, now, colour their hair. The rest, of this present, remains with me; extracted to a quintessence: so that, wherever it but touches, in youth it perpetually preserves, in age restores the complexion; seats your teeth, did they dance like virginal jacks, firm as a wall; makes them white as ivory, that were black as—

Enter CORVINO

Cor. Spight o' the devil, and my shame! come down here;
Come down;—No house but mine to make your scene?
Signior Flaminio, will you down, sir? down?
What, is my wife your Franciscina, sir?
No windows on the whole Piazza, here,
To make your properties, but mine? but mine?
Beats away VOLPONE, NANO, *etc.*
Heart! ere to-morrow I shall be new-christen'd,
And call'd the Pantalone di Besogniosi,
About the town.
Per. What should this mean, sir Pol?
Sir P. Some trick of state, believe it; I will home.
Per. It may be some design on you.
Sir P. I know not,
I'll stand upon my guard.
Per. It is your best, sir.
Sir P. This three weeks, all my advices, all my letters,
They have been intercepted.
Per. Indeed, sir!
Best have a care.

Sir P. Nay, so I will.
Per. This knight,
I may not lose him, for my mirth, till night. *Exeunt*

[SCENE II]

[*A Room in Volpone's House*]

Enter VOLPONE *and* MOSCA

Volp. O, I am wounded!
Mos. Where, sir?
Volp. Not without;
Those blows were nothing: I could bear them ever.
But angry Cupid, bolting from her eyes,
Hath shot himself into me like a flame;
Where, now, he flings about his burning heat,
As in a furnace an ambitious fire,
Whose vent is stopt. The fight is all within me.
I cannot live, except thou help me, Mosca;
My liver melts, and I, without the hope
Of some soft air, from her refreshing breath,
Am but a heap of cinders.
Mos. 'Las, good sir,
Would you had never seen her!
Volp. Nay, would thou
Had'st never told me of her!
Mos. Sir, 'tis true;
I do confess I was unfortunate,
And you unhappy: but I'm bound in conscience,
No less than duty, to effect my best
To your release of torment, and I will, sir.
Volp. Dear Mosca, shall I hope?
Mos. Sir, more than dear,
I will not bid you to despair of aught
Within a human compass.
Volp. O, there spoke

My better angel. Mosca, take my keys,
Gold, plate, and jewels, all's at thy devotion;
Employ them how thou wilt; nay, coin me too:
So thou, in this, but crown my longings, Mosca.
Mos. Use but your patience.
Volp. So I have.
Mos. I doubt not.
To bring success to your desires.
Volp. Nay, then,
I not repent me of my late disguise.
Mos. If you can horn him, sir, you need not.
Volp. True:
Besides, I never meant him for my heir.—
Is not the colour of my beard and eyebrows
To make me known?
Mos. No jot.
Volp. I did it well.
Mos. So well, would I could follow you in mine,
With half the happiness!—[*Aside*] and yet I would
Escape your epilogue.
Volp. But were they gull'd
With a belief that I was Scoto?
Mos. Sir,
Scoto himself could hardly have distinguish'd!
I have not time to flatter you now; we'll part;
And as I prosper, so applaud my art. *Exeunt*

[SCENE III]

[*A Room in Corvino's House*]

Enter CORVINO, *with his sword in his hand, dragging in* CELIA

Corv. Death of mine honour, with the city's fool!
A juggling, tooth-drawing, prating mountebank!
And at a public window! where, whilst he,
With his strain'd action, and his dole of faces,

To his drug-lecture draws your itching ears,
A crew of old, unmarried, noted letchers,
Stood leering up like satyrs; and you smile
Most graciously, and fan your favours forth,
To give your hot spectators satisfaction!
What, was your mountebank their call? their whistle?
Or were you enamour'd on his copper rings,
His saffron jewel. with the toad-stone in't,
Or his embroider'd suit, with the cope-stitch,
Made of a herse cloth? or his old tilt-feather?
Or his starch'd beard? Well, you shall have him, yes!
He shall come home, and minister unto you
The fricace for the mother. Or, let me see,
I think you'd rather mount; would you not mount?
Why, if you'll mount, you may; yes, truly, you may:
And so you may be seen, down to the foot.
Get you a cittern, lady Vanity,
And be a dealer with the virtuous man;
Make one: I'll but protest myself a cuckold,
And save your dowry. I'm a Dutchman, I!
For, if you thought me an Italian,
You would be damn'd, ere you did this, you whore!
Thou'dst tremble, to imagine, that the murder
Of father, mother, brother, all thy race,
Should follow, as the subject of my justice.

Cel. Good sir, have patience.

Corv. What couldst thou propose
Less to thyself, than in this heat of wrath.
And stung with my dishonour, I should strike
This steel into thee, with as many stabs,
As thou wert gaz'd upon with goatish eyes?

Cel. Alas, sir, be appeased! I could not think
My being at the window should more now
Move your impatience, than at other times.

Corv. No! not to seek and entertain a parley
With a known knave, before a multitude!

You were an actor with your handkerchief,
Which he most sweetly kist in the receipt,
And might, no doubt, return it with a letter,
And point the place where you might meet; your sister's,
Your mother's, or your aunt's might serve the turn.
Cel. Why, dear sir, when do I make these excuses,
Or ever stir abroad, but to the church?
And that so seldom—
Corv. Well, it shall be less;
And thy restraint before was liberty,
To what I now decree: and therefore mark me.
First, I will have this bawdy light damm'd up;
And till't be done, some two or three yards off,
I'll chalk a line: o'er which if thou but chance
To set thy desperate foot, more hell, more horror,
More wild remorseless rage shall seize on thee,
Than on a conjuror, that had needless left
His circle's safety ere his devil was laid.
Then here's a lock which I will hang upon thee,
And, now I think on't, I will keep thee backwards;
Thy lodging shall be backwards; thy walks backwards;
Thy prospect, all be backwards; and no pleasure,
That thou shalt know but backwards: nay, since you force
My honest nature, know, it is your own,
Being too open, makes me use you thus:
Since you will not contain your subtle nostrils
In a sweet room, but they must snuff the air
Of rank and sweaty passengers. [*Knocking within*]—One knocks.
Away, and be not seen, pain of thy life;
Nor look toward the window: if thou dost—
Nay, stay, hear this—let me not prosper, whore,
But I will make thee an anatomy,
Dissect thee mine own self, and read a lecture
Upon thee to the city, and in public.
Away!— *Exit* CELIA

Enter Servant

Who's there?

Serv. 'Tis signior Mosca, sir.

Corv. Let him come in. [*Exit* Servant] His master's dead: there's yet
Some good to help the bad.—

Enter Mosca

My Mosca, welcome!
I guess your news.

Mos. I fear you cannot, sir.

Corv. Is't not his death?

Mos. Rather the contrary.

Corv. Not his recovery?

Mos. Yes, sir.

Corv. I am curs'd,
I am bewitch'd, my crosses meet to vex me.
How? how? how? how?

Mos. Why, sir, with Scoto's oil;
Corbaccio and Voltore brought of it,
Whilst I was busy in an inner room—

Corv. Death! that damn'd mountebank; but for the law
Now, I could kill the rascal: it cannot be,
His oil should have that virtue. Have not I
Known him a common rogue, come fidling in
To the osteria, with a tumbling whore,
And, when he has done all his forced tricks, been glad
Of a poor spoonful of dead wine, with flies in't?
It cannot be. All his ingredients
Are a sheep's gall, a roasted bitch's marrow,
Some few sod earwigs, pounded caterpillars,
A little capon's grease, and fasting spittle:
I know them to a dram.

Mos. I know not, sir;
But some on't, there, they pour'd into his ears,

Some in his nostrils, and recover'd him;
Applying but the fricace.
Corv. Pox o' that fricace!
Mos. And since, to seem the more officious
And flatt'ring of his health, there, they have had,
At extreme fees, the college of physicians
Consulting on him, how they might restore him;
Where one would have a cataplasm of spices,
Another a flay'd ape clapp'd to his breast,
A third would have it a dog, a fourth an oil,
With wild cats' skins: at last, they all resolved
That, to preserve him, was no other means,
But some young woman must be straight sought out,
Lusty, and full of juice, to sleep by him;
And to this service, most unhappily,
And most unwillingly, am I now employ'd,
Which here I thought to pre-acquaint you with,
For your advice, since it concerns you most;
Because, I would not do that thing might cross
Your ends, on whom I have my whole dependance, sir:
Yet, if I do it not, they may delate
My slackness to my patron, work me out
Of his opinion; and there all your hopes,
Ventures, or whatsoever, are all frustrate!
I do but tell you, sir. Besides, they are all
Now striving, who shall first present him; therefore—
I could entreat you, briefly conclude somewhat;
Prevent them if you can.
Corv. Death to my hopes,
This is my villainous fortune! Best to hire
Some common courtezan.
Mos. Ay, I thought on that, sir;
But they are all so subtle, full of art—
And age again doting and flexible,
So as—I cannot tell—we may, perchance,
Light on a quean may cheat us all.

Corv. 'Tis true.

Mos. No, no: it must be one that has no tricks, sir,
Some simple thing, a creature made unto it;
Some wench you may command. Have you no kinswoman?
Odso—Think, think, think, think, think, think, think, sir.
One o' the doctors offer'd there his daughter.

Corv. How!

Mos. Yes, signior Lupo, the physician.

Corv. His daughter!

Mos. And a virgin, sir. Why, alas,
He knows the state of's body, what it is;
That nought can warm his blood, sir, but a fever;
Nor any incantation raise his spirit:
A long forgetfulness hath seized that part.
Besides sir, who shall know it? some one or two—

Corv. I pray thee give me leave. [*Walks aside*]. If any man
But I had had this luck—The thing in't self,
I know, is nothing—Wherefore should not I
As well command my blood and my affections,
As this dull doctor? In the point of honour,
The cases are all one of wife and daughter.

Mos. [*Aside*] I hear him coming.

Corv. She shall do't: 'tis done.
Slight! if this doctor, who is not engaged,
Unless 't be for his counsel, which is nothing,
Offer his daughter, what should I, that am
So deeply in? I will prevent him: Wretch!
Covetous wretch!—Mosca, I have determined.

Mos. How, sir?

Corv. We'll make all sure. The party you wot of
Shall be mine own wife, Mosca.

Mos. Sir, the thing,
But that I would not seem to counsel you,
I should have motion'd to you, at the first:
And make your count, you have cut all their throats.

Why, 'tis directly taking a possession!
And in his next fit, we may let him go.
'Tis but to pull the pillow from his head,
And he is throttled: it had been done before,
But for your scrupulous doubts.
Corv. Ay, a plague on't,
My conscience fools my wit! Well, I'll be brief,
And so be thou, lest they should be before us:
Go home, prepare him, tell him with what zeal
And willingness I do it; swear it was
On the first hearing, as thou may'st do, truly,
Mine own free motion.
Mos. Sir, I warrant you,
I'll so possess him with it, that the rest
Of his starv'd clients shall be banish'd all;
And only you received. But come not, sir,
Until I send, for I have something else
To ripen for your good, you must not know't.
Corv. But do not you forget to send now.
Mos. Fear not. *Exit*
Corv. Where are you, wife? my Celia! wife!

Re-enter Celia

—What, blubbering?
Come, dry those tears. I think thou thought'st me in earnest;
Ha! by this light I talk'd so but to try thee:
Methinks the lightness of the occasion
Should have confirm'd thee. Come, I am not jealous.
Cel. No!
Corv. Faith I am not, I, nor never was;
It is a poor unprofitable humour.
Do not I know, if women have a will,
They'll do 'gainst all the watches of the world,
And that the fiercest spies are tamed with gold?
Tut, I am confident in thee, thou shalt see't;

And see I'll give thee cause too, to believe it.
Come kiss me. Go, and make thee ready, straight,
In all thy best attire, thy choicest jewels,
Put them all on, and, with them, thy best looks:
We are invited to a solemn feast,
At old Volpone's, where it shall appear
How far I am free from jealousy or fear. *Exeunt*

[ACT III, SCENE I]

[*A Street*]

Enter MOSCA

Mos. I fear, I shall begin to grow in love
With my dear self, and my most properous parts,
They do so spring and burgeon; I can feel
A whimsy in my blood: I know not how,
Success hath made me wanton. I could skip
Out of my skin, now, like a subtle snake,
I am so limber. O! your parasite
Is a most precious thing, dropt from above,
Not bred 'mongst clods and clodpoles, here on earth.
I muse, the mystery was not made a science,
It is so liberally profest! almost
All the wise world is little else, in nature,
But parasites or sub-parasites.—And yet,
I mean not those that have your bare town-art,
To know who's fit to feed them; have no house,
No family, no care, and therefore mould
Tales for men's ears, to bait that sense; or get
Kitchen-invention, and some stale receipts
To please the belly, and the groin; nor those,
With their court dog-tricks, that can fawn and fleer,
Make their revenue out of legs and faces,
Echo my lord, and lick away a moth:

But your fine elegant rascal, that can rise,
And stoop, almost together, like an arrow;
Shoot through the air as nimbly as a star;
Turn short as doth a swallow; and be here,
And there, and here, and yonder, all at once;
Present to any humour, all occasion;
And change a visor, swifter than a thought!
This is the creature had the art born with him;
Toils not to learn it, but doth practise it
Out of most excellent nature: and such sparks
Are the true parasites, others but their zanis.

Enter BONARIO

Who's this? Bonario, old Corbaccio's son?
The person I was bound to seek.—Fair sir,
You are happily met.
Bon. That cannot be by thee.
Mos. Why, sir?
Bon. Nay, pray thee, know thy way, and leave me:
I would be loth to interchange discourse
With such a mate as thou art.
Mos. Courteous sir,
Scorn not my poverty.
Bon. Not I, by heaven;
But thou shalt give me leave to hate thy baseness.
Mos. Baseness!
Bon. Ay; answer me, is not thy sloth
Sufficient argument? thy flattery?
Thy means of feeding?
Mos. Heaven be good to me!
These imputations are too common, sir,
And easily stuck on virtue when she's poor.
You are unequal to me, and however
Your sentence may be righteous, yet you are not
That, ere you know me, thus proceed in censure:

St. Mark bear witness 'gainst you, 'tis inhuman. *Weeps*
Bon. [*Aside*] What! does he weep? the sign is soft and good:
I do repent me that I was so harsh.
Mos. 'Tis true, that, sway'd by strong necessity,
I am enforced to eat my careful bread
With too much obsequy; 'tis true, beside,
That I am fain to spin mine own poor raiment
Out of my mere observance, being not born
To a free fortune: but that I have done
Base offices, in rending friends asunder,
Dividing families, betraying counsels,
Whispering false lies, or mining men with praises,
Train'd their credulity with perjuries,
Corrupted chastity, or am in love
With mine own tender ease, but would not rather
Prove the most rugged, and laborious course,
That might redeem my present estimation,
Let me here perish, in all hope of goodness.
Bon. [*Aside*] This cannot be a personated passion.—
I was to blame, so to mistake thy nature;
Prithee, forgive me: and speak out thy business.
Mos. Sir, it concerns you; and though I may seem,
At first to make a main offence in manners,
And in my gratitude unto my master;
Yet, for the pure love, which I bear all right,
And hatred of the wrong, I must reveal it.
This very hour your father is in purpose
To disinherit you—
Bon. How!
Mos. And thrust you forth,
As a mere stranger to his blood; 'tis true, sir,
The work no way engageth me, but, as
I claim an interest in the general state
Of goodness and true virtue, which I hear
To abound in you: and, for which mere respect,

Without a second aim, sir, I have done it.
Bon. This tale hath lost thee much of the late trust
Thou hadst with me; it is impossible:
I know not how to lend it any thought,
My father should be so unnatural.
Mos. It is a confidence that well becomes,
Your piety; and form'd, no doubt, it is
From your own simple innocence: which makes
Your wrong more monstrous and abhorr'd. But, sir,
I now will tell you more. This very minute,
It is, or will be doing; and, if you
Shall be but pleased to go with me, I'll bring you,
I dare not say where you shall see, but where
Your ear shall be a witness of the deed;
Hear yourself written bastard, and profest
The common issue of the earth.
Bon. I am amazed!
Mos. Sir, if I do it not, draw your just sword,
And score your vengeance on my front and face:
Mark me your villain: you have too much wrong,
And I do suffer for you, sir. My heart
Weeps blood in anguish—
Bon. Lead; I follow thee. *Exeunt*

[SCENE II]

[*A Room in Volpone's House*]

Enter VOLPONE

Volp. Mosca stays long, methinks.—Bring forth youı sports,
And help to make the wretched time more sweet.

Enter NANO, ANDROGYNO, *and* CASTRONE

Nan. Dwarf, fool, and eunuch, well met here we be.

A question it were now, whether of us three,
Being all the known delicates of a rich man,
In pleasing him, claim the precedency can?

Cas. I claim for myself.

And. And so doth the fool.

Nan. 'Tis foolish indeed: let me set you both to school.
First for your dwarf, he's little and witty,
And every thing, as it is little, is pretty;
Else why do men say to a creature of my shape,
So soon as they see him, It's a pretty little ape?
And why a pretty ape, but for pleasing imitation
Of greater men's actions, in a ridiculous fashion?
Beside, this feat body of mine doth not crave
Half the meat, drink, and cloth, one of your bulks will have.
Admit your fool's face be the mother of laughter,
Yet, for his brain, it must always come after:
And though that do feed him, it's a pitiful case,
His body is beholding to such a bad face. [*Knocking within*

Volp. Who's there? my couch; away! look! Nano, see:
Exeunt ANDROGYNO *and* CASTRONE
Give me my caps, first——go, enquire. [*Exit* NANO]—Now, Cupid
Send it be Mosca, and with fair return!

Nan. [*Within*] It is the beauteous madam—

Volp. Would-be—is it?

Nan. The same.

Volp. Now torment on me! Squire her in;
For she will enter, or dwell here for ever:
Nay, quickly. [*Retires to his couch*]—That my fit were past! I fear
A second hell too, that my lothing this
Will quite expel my appetite to the other:
Would she were taking now her tedious leave.
Lord, how it threats me what I am to suffer!

Re-enter NANO, *with* Lady POLITICK WOULD-BE

Lady P. I thank you, good sir. 'Pray you signify
Unto your patron, I am here.—This band
Shews not my neck enough.—I trouble you, sir;
Let me request you, bid one of my women
Come hither to me.—In good faith, I am drest
Most favourably to-day! It is no matter:
'Tis well enough.—

Enter 1 Waiting-woman

Look, see, these petulant things,
How they have done this!
Volp. [*Aside*] I do feel the fever
Entering in at mine ears; O, for a charm,
To fright it hence!
Lady P. Come nearer: is this curl
In his right place, or this? Why is this higher
Than all the rest? You have not wash'd your eyes, yet!
Or do they not stand even in your head?
Where is your fellow? call her. *Exit* 1 Woman
Nan. Now, St. Mark
Deliver us! anon, she'll beat her women,
Because her nose is red.

Re-enter 1 *with* 2 Woman

Lady P. I pray you, view
This tire, forsooth: are all things apt, or no?
1 *Wom.* One hair a little, here, sticks out, forsooth.
Lady P. Does't so, forsooth! and where was your dear sight,
When it did so, forsooth! What now! bird-eyed?
And you, too? 'Pray you, both approach and mend it.
Now, by that light, I muse you are not ashamed!
I, that have preach'd these things so oft unto you,
Read you the principles, argued all the grounds,
Disputed every fitness, every grace,

Call'd you to counsel of so frequent dressings—

Nan. [*Aside*] More carefully than of your fame or honour.

Lady P. Made you acquainted, what an ample dowry
The knowledge of these things would be unto you,
Able, alone, to get you noble husbands
At your return: and you thus to neglect it!
Besides you seeing what a curious nation
The Italians are, what will they say of me?
The English lady cannot dress herself.
Here's a fine imputation to our country!
Well, go your ways, and stay in the next room.
This fucus was too coarse too; it's no matter.—
Good sir, you'll give them entertainment?

Exeunt NANO *and* Waiting-women

Volp. The storm comes toward me.

Lady P. [*Goes to the couch*] How does my Volpone?

Volp. Troubled with noise, I cannot sleep; I dreamt
That a strange fury enter'd, now, my house,
And, with the dreadful tempest of her breath,
Did cleave my roof asunder.

Lady P. Believe me, and I
Had the most fearful dream, could I remember't—

Volp. [*Aside*] Out of my fate! I have given her the occasion
How to torment me: she will tell me her's.

Lady P. Me thought, the golden mediocrity,
Polite and delicate—

Volp. O, if you do love me,
No more: I sweat, and suffer, at the mention
Of any dream; feel how I tremble yet.

Lady P. Alas, good soul! the passion of the heart.
Seed-pearl were good now, boil'd with syrup of apples,
Tincture of gold, and coral, citron-pills,
Your elicampane root, myrobalanes—

Volp. [*Aside*] Ah me, I have ta'en a grass-hopper by the wing!

Lady P. Burnt silk, and amber: You have muscadel
Good in the house—
Volp. You will not drink, and part?
Lady P. No, fear not that. I doubt, we shall not get
Some English saffron, half a dram would serve;
Your sixteen cloves, a little musk, dried mints,
Bugloss, and barley-meal—
Volp. [*Aside*] She's in again!
Before I feign'd diseases, now I have one.
Lady P. And these applied with a right scarlet cloth.
Volp. [*Aside*] Another flood of words! a very torrent!
Lady P. Shall I, sir, make you a poultice?
Volp. No, no, no,
I'm very well, you need prescribe no more.
Lady P. I have a little studied physic; but now,
I'm all for music, save, in the forenoons,
An hour or two for painting. I would have
A lady, indeed, to have all, letters and arts,
Be able to discourse, to write, to paint,
But principal, as Plato holds, your music,
And so does wise Pythagoras, I take it,
Is your true rapture: when there is concent
In face, in voice, and clothes: and is, indeed,
Our sex's chiefest ornament.
Volp. The poet
As old in time as Plato, and as knowing,
Says, that your highest female grace is silence.
Lady P. Which of your poets? Petrarch, or Tasso, or
Dante?
Guarini? Ariosto? Aretine?
Cieco di Hadria? I have read them all.
Volp. [*Aside*] Is every thing a cause to my destruction?
Lady P. I think I have two or three of them about me.
Volp. [*Aside*] The sun, the sea, will sooner both stand
still
Than her eternal tongue! nothing can 'scape it.

Lady P. Here's Pastor Fido—

Volp. [*Aside*] Profess obstinate silence;
That's now my safest.

Lady P. All our English writers,
I mean such as are happy in the Italian,
Will deign to steal out of this author, mainly:
Almost as much as from Montagnié:
He has so modern and facile a vein,
Fitting the time, and catching the court-ear!
Your Petrarch is more passionate, yet he,
In days of sonnetting, trusted them with much:
Dante is hard, and few can understand him.
But, for a desperate wit, there's Aretine;
Only, his pictures are a little obscene—
You mark me not.

Volp. Alas, my mind's perturb'd.

Lady P. Why, in such cases, we must cure ourselves,
Make use of our philosophy—

Volp. Oh me!

Lady P. And as we find our passions do rebel,
Encounter them with reason, or divert them,
By giving scope unto some other humour
Of lesser danger: as, in politic bodies,
There's nothing more doth overwhelm the judgment,
And cloud the understanding, than too much
Settling and fixing, and, as 'twere, subsiding
Upon one object. For the incorporating
Of these same outward things, into that part,
Which we call mental, leaves some certain fæces
That stop the organs, and as Plato says,
Assassinate our knowledge.

Volp. [*Aside*] Now, the spirit
Of patience help me!

Lady P. Come, in faith, I must
Visit you more a days; and make you well:
Laugh and be lusty.

Volp. [*Aside*] My good angel save me!
Lady P. There was but one sole man in all the world,
With whom I e'er could sympathise; and he
Would lie you, often, three, four hours together
To hear me speak; and be sometimes so rapt,
As he would answer me quite from the purpose,
Like you, and you are like him, just. I'll discourse,
An't be but only, sir, to bring you asleep,
How we did spend our time and loves together,
For some six years.
Volp. Oh, oh, oh, oh, oh, oh!
Lady P. For we were coætanei, and brought up—
Volp. Some power, some fate, some fortunes rescue me!

Enter Mosca

Mos. God save you, madam!
Lady P. Good sir.
Volp. Mosca! welcome,
Welcome to my redemption.
Mos. Why, sir?
Volp. Oh,
Rid me of this my torture, quickly, there;
My madam, with the everlasting voice:
The bells, in time of pestilence, ne'er made
Like noise, or were in that perpetual motion!
The Cock-pit comes not near it. All my house,
But now, steam'd like a bath with her thick breath,
A lawyer could not have been heard; nor scarce
Another woman, such a hail of words
She has let fall. For hell's sake, rid her hence.
Mos. Has she presented?
Volp. O, I do not care;
I'll take her absence, upon any price,
With any loss.
Mos. Madam—

Lady P. I have brought your patron
A toy, a cap here, of mine own work.
Mos. 'Tis well.
I had forgot to tell you, I saw your knight.
Where you would little think it.—
Lady P. Where?
Mos. Marry,
Where yet, if you make haste, you may apprehend
Rowing upon the water in a gondole
With the most cunning courtezan of Venice.
Lady P. Is't true?
Mos. Pursue them, and believe your eyes:
Leave me, to make your gift. [*Exit* Lady P. *hastily*]—I knew 'twould take:
For, lightly, they that use themselves most license,
Are still most jealous.
Volp. Mosca, hearty thanks,
For thy quick fiction, and delivery of me.
Now to my hopes, what say'st thou?

Re-enter Lady Politick Would-be

Lady P. But do you hear, sir?—
Volp. Again! I fear a paroxysm.
Lady P. Which way
Row'd they together?
Mos. Toward the Rialto.
Lady P. I pray you lend me your dwarf.
Mos. I pray you take him.— *Exit* Lady P.
Your hopes, sir, are like happy blossoms, fair,
And promise timely fruit, if you will stay
But the maturing; keep you at your couch,
Corbaccio will arrive straight, with the Will;
When he is gone, I'll tell you more. *Exit*
Volp. My blood,
My spirits are return'd; I am alive:

And like your wanton gamester at primero,
Whose thought had whisper'd to him, not go less,
Methinks I lie, and draw—for an encounter.

The scene closes upon VOLPONE

[SCENE III]

[*The Passage leading to Volpone's Chamber.*]

Enter MOSCA *and* BONARIO

Mos. Sir, here conceal'd, [*shews him a closet*] you may hear all. But, pray you,
Have patience, sir; [*knocking within*]—the same's your father knocks:
I am compell'd to leave you. *Exit*

Bon. Do so.—Yet
Cannot my thought imagine this a truth.

Goes into the closet

[SCENE IV]

[*Another Part of the same*]

Enter MOSCA *and* CORVINO, CELIA *following*

Mos. Death on me! you are come too soon, what meant you?
Did not I say, I would send?

Corv. Yes, but I fear'd
You might forget it, and then they prevent us.

Mos. [*Aside*] Prevent! did e'er man haste so, for his horns?
A courtier would not ply it so, for a place.
Well, now there is no helping it, stay here;
I'll presently return. *Exit*

Corv. Where are you, Celia?
You know not wherefore I have brought you hither?

Cel. Not well, except you told me.

Corv. Now, I will:
Hark hither. *Exeunt*

[SCENE V]

[*A Closet opening into a Gallery*]

Enter MOSCA *and* BONARIO

Mos. Sir, your father hath sent word,
It will be half an hour ere he come;
And therefore, if you please to walk the while
Into that gallery—at the upper end,
There are some books to entertain the time:
And I'll take care no man shall come unto you, sir.
Bon. Yes, I will stay there.—I do doubt this fellow.
Aside, and Exit

Mos. [*Looking after him*] There; he is far enough; he can hear nothing:
And, for his father, I can keep him off. *Exit*

[SCENE VI]

[*Volpone's Chamber.—Volpone on his couch. Mosca sitting by him*]

Enter CORVINO, *forcing in* CELIA

Corv. Nay, now, there is no starting back, and therefore,
Resolve upon it: I have so decreed.
It must be done. Nor would I move't afore,
Because I would avoid all shifts and tricks,
That might deny me.
Cel. Sir, let me beseech you,
Affect not these strange trials; if you doubt
My chastity, why, lock me up for ever;
Make me the heir of darkness. Let me live,
Where I may please your fears, if not your trust.
Corv. Believe it, I have no huch humour, I.

All that I speak I mean; yet I 'm not mad;
Nor horn-mad, see you? Go to, shew yourself
Obedient, and a wife.

Cel. O heaven!

Corv. I say it,
Do so.

Cel. Was this the train?

Corv. I've told you reasons;
What the physicians have set down: how much
It may concern me; what my engagements are;
My means; and the necessity of those means,
For my recovery: wherefore, if you be
Loyal, and mine, be won, respect my venture.

Cel. Before your honour?

Corv. Honour! tut, a breath:
There's no such thing in nature: a mere term
Invented to awe fools. What is my gold
The worse for touching, clothes for being look'd on?
Why, this is no more. An old decrepit wretch,
That has no sense, no sinew; takes his meat
With others' fingers; only knows to gape,
When you do scald his gums; a voice, a shadow;
And, what can this man hurt you?

Cel. [*Aside*] Lord! what spirit
Is this hath enter'd him?

Corv. And for your fame,
That's such a jig; as if I would go tell it,
Cry it on the Piazza! who shall know it,
But he that cannot speak it, and this fellow,
Whose lips are in my pocket? save yourself,
(If you'll proclaim't, you may,) I know no other
Shall come to know it.

Cel. Are heaven and saints then nothing?
Will they be blind or stupid?

Corv. How!

Cel. Good sir,

Be jealous still, emulate them; and think
What hate they burn with toward every sin.
Corv. I grant you: if I thought it were a sin,
I would not urge you. Should I offer this
To some young Frenchman, or hot Tuscan blood
That had read Aretine, conn'd all his prints,
Knew every quirk within lust's labyrinth,
And were professed critic in lechery;
And I would look upon him, and applaud him,
This were a sin: but here, 'tis contrary,
A pious work, mere charity for physic,
And honest polity, to assure mine own.
Cel. O heaven! canst thou suffer such a change?
Volp. Thou art mine honour, Mosca, and my pride,
My joy, my tickling, my delight! Go bring them.
Mos. [*Advancing*] Please you draw near, sir.
Corv. Come on, what—
You will not be rebellious? by that light—
Mos. Sir,
Signior Corvino, here, is come to see you.
Volp. Oh!
Mos. And hearing of the consultation had,
So lately, for your health, is come to offer,
Or rather, sir, to prostitute—
Corv. Thanks, sweet Mosca.
Mos. Freely, unask'd, or unintreated—
Corv. Well.
Mos. As the true fervent instance of his love,
His own most fair and proper wife; the beauty,
Only of price in Venice—
Corv. 'Tis well urged.
Mos. To be your comfortress, and to preserve you.
Volp. Alas, I am past, already! Pray you, thank him
For his good care and promptness; but for that,
'Tis a vain labour e'en to fight 'gainst heaven;
Applying fire to stone—uh, uh, uh, uh! [*Coughing*]

Making a dead leaf grow again. I take
His wishes gently, though; and you may tell him,
What I have done for him: marry, my state is hopeless.
Will him to pray for me; and to use his fortune
With reverence, when he comes to't.

Mos. Do you hear, sir?
Go to him with your wife.

Corv. Heart of my father!
Wilt thou persist thus? come, I pray thee, come.
Thou seest 'tis nothing, Celia. By this hand,
I shall grow violent. Come, do't, I say.

Cel. Sir, kill me, rather: I will take down poison,
Eat burning coals, do any thing.—

Corv. Be damn'd!
Heart, I will drag thee hence, home, by the hair;
Cry thee a strumpet through the streets; rip up
Thy mouth unto thine ears; and slit thy nose,
Like a raw rochet!—Do not tempt me; come,
Yield, I am loth—Death! I will buy some slave
Whom I will kill, and bind thee to him, alive;
And at my window hang you forth, devising
Some monstrous crime, which I, in capital letters,
Will eat into thy flesh with aquafortis,
And burning corsives, on this stubborn breast.
Now, by the blood thou hast incensed, I'll do it!

Cel. Sir, what you please, you may, I am your martyr.

Corv. Be not thus obstinate, I have not deserved it:
Think who it is intreats you. 'Prithee, sweet;—
Good faith, thou shalt have jewels, gowns, attires,
What thou wilt think, and ask. Do but go kiss him.
Or touch him, but. For my sake.—At my suit.—
This once.—No! not! I shall remember this.
Will you disgrace me thus? Do you thirst my undoing?

Mos. Nay, gentle lady, be advised.

Corv. No, no.
She has watch'd her time. Ods precious, this is scurvy,
'Tis very scurvy; and you are—

Mos. Nay, good sir.

Corv. An arrant locust, by heaven, a locust!
Whore, crocodile, that hast thy tears prepared,
Expecting how thou'lt bid them flow—

Mos. Nay, 'pray you, sir!
She will consider.

Cel. Would my life would serve
To satisfy—

Corv. S'death! if she would but speak to him,
And save my reputation, it were somewhat;
But spightfully to affect my utter ruin!

Mos. Ay, now you have put your fortune in her hands.
Why i'faith, it is her modesty, I must quit her.
If you were absent, she would be more cunning;
I know it: and dare undertake for her.
What woman can before her husband? 'pray you,
Let us depart, and leave her here.

Corv. Sweet Celia,
Thou may'st redeem all, yet; I'll say no more:
If not, esteem yourself as lost. Nay, stay there.

Shuts the door, and exit with Mosca

Cel. O God, and his good angels! whither, whither,
Is shame fled human breasts? that with such ease,
Men dare put off your honours, and their own?
Is that, which ever was a cause of life,
Now placed beneath the basest circumstance,
And modesty an exile made, for money?

Volp. Ay, in Corvino, and such earth-fed minds,

Leaping from his couch

That never tasted the true heaven of love.
Assure thee, Celia, he that would sell thee,
Only for hope of gain, and that uncertain,
He would have sold his part of Paradise

For ready money, had he met a cope-man.
Why art thou mazed to see me thus revived?
Rather applaud thy beauty's miracle;
'Tis thy great work: that hath, not now alone,
But sundry times raised me, in several shapes,
And, but this morning, like a mountebank,
To see thee at thy window: ay, before
I would have left my practice, for thy love,
In varying figures, I would have contended
With the blue Porteus, or the horned flood.
Now art thou welcome.
Cel. Sir!
Volp. Nay, fly me not.
Nor let thy false imagination
That I was bed-rid, make thee think I am so:
Thou shalt not find it. I am, now, as fresh,
As hot, as high, and in as jovial plight,
As when, in that so celebrated scene,
At recitation of our comedy,
For entertainment of the great Valois,
I acted young Antinous; and attracted
The eyes and ears of all the ladies present,
To admire each graceful gesture, note, and footing. *Sings*

Come, my Celia, let us prove,
While we can, the sports of love,
Time will not be ours for ever,
He, at length, our good will sever;
Spend not then his gifts in vain;
Suns, that set, may rise again;
But if once we lose this light,
'Tis with us perpetual night.
Why should we defer our joys?
Fame and rumour are but toys.
Cannot we delude the eyes

Of a few poor household spies?
Or his easier ears beguile,
Thus removed by our wile?—
'Tis no sin love's fruits to steal:
But the sweet thefts to reveal;
To be taken, to be seen,
These have crimes accounted been.

Cel. Some serene blast me, or dire lightning strike
This my offending face!
Volp. Why droops my Celia?
Thou hast, in place of a base husband, found
A worthy lover: use thy fortune well,
With secrecy and pleasure. See, behold,
What thou art queen of; not in expectation,
As I feed others: but possess'd and crown'd.
See, here, a rope of pearl; and each, more orient
Than that the brave Ægyptian queen caroused:
Dissolve and drink them. See, a carbuncle,
May put out both the eyes of our St. Mark;
A diamond, would have bought Lollia Paulina,
When she came in like star-light, hid with jewels,
That were the spoils of provinces; take these,
And wear, and lose them: yet remains an ear-ring
To purchase them again, and this whole state.
A gem but worth a private patrimony,
Is nothing: we will eat such at a meal.
The heads of parrots, tongues of nightingales,
The brains of peacocks, and of estriches,
Shall be our food: and, could we get the phœnix,
Though nature lost her kind, she were our dish.
Cel. Good sir, these things might move a mind affected
With such delights; but I, whose innocence
Is all I can think wealthy, or worth th' enjoying,
And which, once lost, I have nought to lose beyond it,

Cannot be taken with these sensual baits:
If you have conscience—
Volp. 'Tis the beggar's virtue;
If thou hast wisdom, hear me, Celia.
Thy baths shall be the juice of July-flowers,
Spirit of roses, and of violets,
The milk of unicorns, and panthers' breath
Gather'd in bags, and mixt with Cretan wines.
Our drink shall be prepared gold and amber;
Which we will take, until my roof whirl round
With the vertigo: and my dwarf shall dance,
My eunuch sing, my fool make up the antic,
Whilst we, in changed shapes, act Ovid's tales,
Thou, like Europa now, and I like Jove,
Then I like Mars, and thou like Erycine:
So, of the rest, till we have quite run through,
And wearied all the fables of the gods.
Then will I have thee in more modern forms,
Attired like some sprightly dame of France,
Brave Tuscan lady, or proud Spanish beauty;
Sometimes, unto the Persian sophy's wife;
Or the grand signior's mistress; and, for change,
To one of our most artful courtezans,
Or some quick Negro, or cold Russian;
And I will meet thee in as many shapes:
Where we may so transfuse our wandering souls
Out at our lips, and score up sums of pleasures, *Sings*

That the curious shall not know
How to tell them as they flow;
And the envious, when they find
What their number is, be pined.

Cel. If you have ears that will be pierced—or eyes
That can be open'd—a heart that may be touch'd—

Or any part that yet sounds man about you—
If you have touch of holy saints—or heaven—
Do me the grace to let me 'scape—if not,
Be bountiful and kill me. You do know,
I am a creature, hither ill betray'd,
By one, whose shame I would forget it were:
If you will deign me neither of these graces,
Yet feed your wrath, sir, rather than your lust,
(It is a vice comes nearer manliness,)
And punish that unhappy crime of nature,
Which you miscall my beauty: flay my face,
Or poison it with ointments, for seducing
Your blood to this rebellion. Rub these hands,
With what may cause an eating leprosy,
E'en to my bones and marrow: any thing,
That may disfavour me, save in my honour—
And I will kneel to you, pray for you, pay down
A thousand hourly vows, sir, for your health;
Report, and think you virtuous—

Volp. Think me cold,
Frozen and impotent, and so report me?
That I had Nestor's hernia, thou wouldst think.
I do degenerate, and abuse my nation,
To play with opportunity thus long;
I should have done the act, and then have parley'd.
Yield, or I'll force thee. *Seizes her*

Cel. O! just God!

Volp. In vain—

Bon. [*Rushing in*] Forbear, foul ravisher, libidinous swine!
Free the forced lady, or thou diest, impostor.
But that I'm loth to snatch thy punishment
Out of the hand of justice, thou shouldst, yet,
Be made the timely sacrifice of vengeance,
Before this altar, and this dross, thy idol.—
Lady, let's quit the place, it is the den

Of villainy; fear nought, you have a guard:
And he, ere long, shall meet his just reward.

Exeunt BONARIO *and* CELIA

Volp. Fall on me, roof, and bury me in ruin!
Become my grave, that wert my shelter! O!
I am unmask'd, unspirited, undone,
Betray'd to beggary, to infamy—

Enter MOSCA, *wounded and bleeding*

Mos. Where shall I run, most wretched shame of men,
To beat out my unlucky brains?
Volp. Here, here.
What! dost thou bleed?
Mos. O that his well-driv'n sword
Had been so courteous to have cleft me down
Unto the navel, ere I lived to see
My life, my hopes, my spirits, my patron, all
Thus desperately engaged, by my error!
Volp. Woe on thy fortune!
Mos. And my follies, sir.
Volp. Thou hast made me miserable.
Mos. And myself, sir.
Who would have thought he would have hearken'd so?
Volp. What shall we do?
Mos. I know not; if my heart
Could expiate the mischance, I'd pluck it out.
Will you be pleased to hang me, or cut my throat?
And I'll requite you, sir. Let's die like Romans,
Since we have lived like Grecians. *Knocking within*
Volp. Hark! who's there?
I hear some footing; officers, the saffi,
Come to apprehend us! I do feel the brand
Hissing already at my forehead; now,
Mine ears are boring.
Mos. To your couch, sir, you,

Make that place good, however.

VOLPONE *lies down, as before*

Guilty men
Suspect what they deserve still.

Enter CORBACCIO

Signior Corbaccio!

Corb. Why, how now, Mosca?

Mos. O, undone, amazed, sir.
Your son, I know not by what accident,
Acquainted with your purpose to my patron,
Touching your Will, and making him your heir,
Enter'd our house with violence, his sword drawn
Sought for you, call'd you wretch, unnatural,
Vow'd he would kill you.

Corb. Me!

Mos. Yes, and my patron.

Corb. This act shall disinherit him indeed;
Here is the Will.

Mos. 'Tis well, sir.

Corb. Right and well:
Be you as careful now for me.

Enter VOLTORE, *behind*

Mos. My life, sir,
Is not more tender'd; I am only yours.

Corb. How does he? will he die shortly, think'st thou?

Mos. I fear
He'll outlast May.

Corb. To-day?

Mos. No, last out May, sir.

Corb. Could'st thou not give him a dram?

Mos. O, by no means, sir.

Corb. Nay, I'll not bid you.

Volt. [*Coming forward*] This is a knave, I see.

Mos. [*Seeing* VOLTORE. *Aside*] How, signior Voltore! did he hear me?

Volt. Parasite!

Mos. Who's that?—O, sir, most timely welcome—

Volt. Scarce,
To the discovery of your tricks, I fear.
You are his, *only?* and mine also, are you not?

Mos. Who? I, sir?

Volt. You, sir. What device is this
About a Will?

Mos. A plot for you, sir.

Volt. Come,
Put not your foists upon me; I shall scent them.

Mos. Did you not hear it?

Volt. Yes, I hear Corbaccio
Hath made your patron there his heir.

Mos. 'Tis true,
By my device, drawn to it by my plot,
With hope—

Volt. Your patron should reciprocate?
And you have promised?

Mos. For your good, I did, sir.
Nay, more, I told his son, brought, hid him here,
Where he might hear his father pass the deed:
Being persuaded to it by this thought, sir,
That the unnaturalness, first, of the act,
And then his father's oft disclaiming in him,
(Which I did mean t'help on,) would sure enrage him
To do some violence upon his parent,
On which the law should take sufficient hold,
And you be stated in a double hope:
Truth be my comfort, and my conscience,
My only aim was to dig you a fortune
Out of these two old rotten sepulchres—

Volt. I cry thee mercy, Mosca.

Mos. Worth your patience,

And your great merit, sir. And see the change!

Volt. Why, what success?

Mos. Most hapless! you must help, sir.
Whilst we expected the old raven, in comes
Corvino's wife, sent hither by her husband—

Volt. What, with a present?

Mos. No, sir, on visitation;
(I'll tell you how anon;) and staying long,
The youth he grows impatient, rushes forth,
Seizeth the lady, wounds me, makes her swear
(Or he would murder her, that was his vow)
To affirm my patron to have done her rape:
Which how unlike it is, you see! and hence,
With that pretext he's gone, to accuse his father,
Defame my patron, defeat you—

Volt. Where is her husband?
Let him be sent for straight.

Mos. Sir, I'll go fetch him.

Volt. Bring him to the Scrutineo.

Mos. Sir, I will.

Volt. This must be stopt.

Mos. O you do nobly, sir.
Alas, 'twas labour'd all, sir, for your good;
Nor was there want of counsel in the plot:
But fortune can, at any time, o'erthrow
The projects of a hundred learned clerks, sir.

Corb. [*Listening*] What's that?

Volt. Will't please you, sir, to go along?

Exit CORBACCIO, *followed by* VOLTORE

Mos. Patron, go in, and pray for our success.

Volp. [*Rising from his couch*] Need makes devotion: heaven your labour bless! *Exeunt*

[ACT IV, SCENE I]

[*A Street*]

Enter Sir Politick Would-be *and* Peregrine

Sir P. I told you, sir, it was a plot; you see
What observation is! You mention'd me
For some instructions: I will tell you, sir,
(Since we are met here in the height of Venice,)
Some few particulars I have set down,
Only for this meridian, fit to be known
Of your crude traveller; and they are these.
I will not touch, sir, at your phrase, or clothes,
For they are old.

Per. Sir, I have better.

Sir P. Pardon,
I meant, as they are themes.

Per. O, sir, proceed:
I'll slander you no more of wit, good sir.

Sir P. First, for your garb, it must be grave and serious,
Very reserv'd and lock'd; not tell a secret
On any terms, not to your father; scarce
A fable, but with caution: made sure choice
Both of your company, and discourse; beware
You never speak a truth—

Per. How!

Sir P. Not to strangers,
For those be they you must converse with most;
Others I would not know, sir, but at distance,
So as I still might be a saver in them:
You shall have tricks else past upon you hourly.
And then, for your religion, profess none,
But wonder at the diversity, of all:
And, for your part, protest, were there no other
But simply the laws o' the land, you could content you
Nic. Machiavel, and Monsieur Bodin, both

Were of this mind. Then must you learn the use
And handling of your silver fork at meals,
The metal of your glass; (these are main matters
With your Italian;) and to know the hour
When you must eat your melons, and your figs.

Per. Is that a point of state too?

Sir P. Here it is:
For your Venetian, if he see a man
Preposterous in the least, he has him straight;
He has; he strips him. I'll acquaint you, sir,
I now have lived here, 'tis some fourteen months
Within the first week of my landing here,
All took me for a citizen of Venice,
I knew the forms so well—

Per. [*Aside*] And nothing else.

Sir P. I had read Contarene, took me a house,
Dealt with my Jews to furnish it with moveables—
Well, if I could but find one man, one man
To mine own heart, whom I durst trust, I would—

Per. What, what, sir?

Sir P. Make him rich; make him a fortune:
He should not think again. I would command it.

Per. As how?

Sir P. With certain projects that I have;
Which I may not discover.

Per. [*Aside*] If I had
But one to wager with, I would lay odds now,
He tells me instantly.

Sir P. One is, and that
I care not greatly who knows, to serve the state
Of Venice with red herrings for three years,
And at a certain rate, from Rotterdam,
Where I have correspondence. There's a letter,
Sent me from one o' the states, and to that purpose:
He cannot write his name, but that's his mark.

Per. He is a chandler?

Sir P. No, a cheesemonger.
There are some others too with whom I treat
About the same negociation;
And I will undertake it: for, 'tis thus.
I'll do't with ease, I have cast it all: Your hoy
Carries but three men in her, and a boy;
And she shall make me three returns a year:
So, if there come but one of three, I save;
If two, I can defalk:—but this is now,
If my main project fail.
Per. Then you have others?
Sir P. I should be loth to draw the subtle air
Of such a place, without my thousand aims.
I'll not dissemble, sir: where'er I come,
I love to be considerative; and 'tis true,
I have at my free hours thought upon
Some certain goods unto the state of Venice,
Which I do call *my Cautions;* and, sir, which
I mean, in hope of pension, to propound
To the Great Council, then unto the Forty,
So to the Ten. My means are made already—
Per. By whom?
Sir P. Sir, one that, though his place be obscure,
Yet he can sway, and they will hear him. He's
A commandador.
Per. What! a common serjeant?
Sir P. Sir, such as they are, put it in their mouths,
What they should say, sometimes as well as greater:
I think I have my notes to shew you— [*Searching his pockets*
Per. Good sir.
Sir P. But you shall swear unto me, on your gentry,
Not to anticipate—
Per. I, sir!
Sir P. Nor reveal
A circumstance——My paper is not with me.
Per. O, but you can remember, sir.

Sir P. My first is
Concerning tinder-boxes. You must know,
No family is here without its box.
Now, sir, it being so portable a thing,
Put case, that you or I were ill affected
Unto the state, sir; with it in our pockets,
Might not I go into the Arsenal,
Or you, come out again, and none the wiser?
Per. Except yourself, sir.
Sir P. Go to, then. I therefore
Advertise to the state, how fit it were,
That none but such as were known patriots,
Sound lovers of their country, should be suffer'd
To enjoy them in their houses; and even those
Seal'd at some office, and at such a bigness
As might not lurk in pockets.
Per. Admirable!
Sir P. My next is, how to enquire, and be resolv'd,
By present demonstration, whether a ship,
Newly arrived from Soria, or from
Any suspected part of all the Levant,
Be guilty of the plague: and where they use
To lie out forty, fifty days, sometimes,
About the Lazaretto, for their trial;
I'll save that charge and loss unto the merchant,
And in an hour clear the doubt.
Per. Indeed, sir!
Sir P. Or—I will lose my labour.
Per. 'My faith, that's much.
Sir P. Nay, sir, conceive me. It will cost me in onions,
Some thirty livres—
Per. Which is one pound sterling.
Sir P. Beside my water-works: for this I do, sir.
First, I bring in your ship 'twixt two brick walls;
But those the state shall venture: On the one
I strain me a fair tarpauling, and in that

I stick my onions, cut in halves: the other
Is full of loop-holes, out at which I thrust
The noses of my bellows; and those bellows
I keep, with water-works, in perpetual motion,
Which is the easiest matter of a hundred.
Now, sir, your onion, which doth naturally
Attract the infection, and your bellows blowing
The air upon him, will show, instantly,
By his changed colour, if there be contagion;
Or else remain as fair as at the first.
—Now it is known, 'tis nothing.

Per. You are right, sir.

Sir P. I would I had my note.

Per. 'Faith, so would I:
But you have done well for once, sir.

Sir P. Were I false,
Or would be made so, I could shew you reasons
How I could sell this state now to the Turk,
Spite of their gallies or their— *Examining his papers*

Per. Pray you, sir Pol.

Sir P. I have them not about me.

Per. That I fear'd:
They are there, sir.

Sir P. No, this is my diary,
Wherein I note my actions of the day.

Per. Pray you, let's see, sir. What is here? [*Reads*] Notandum,
A rat had knawn my spur-leathers; notwithstanding,
I put on new, and did go forth: but first
I threw three beans over the threshold. Item,
I went and bought two tooth-picks, whereof one
I burst immediately, in a discourse
With a Dutch merchant, 'bout ragion del stato.
From him I went and paid a moccinigo
For piecing my silk stockings; by the way

I cheapen'd sprats; and at St. Mark's I urined.
'Faith these are politic notes!

Sir P. Sir, I do slip
No action of my life, but thus I quote it.

Per. Believe me, it is wise!

Sir P. Nay, sir, read forth.

Enter, at a distance, Lady POLITICK WOULD-BE, NANO, *and two* Waiting-women.

Lady P. Where should this loose knight be, trow? sure he's housed.

Nan. Why, then he's fast.

Lady P. Ay, he plays both with me.
I pray you stay. This heat will do more harm
To my complexion, than his heart is worth.
(I do not care to hinder, but to take him.)
How it comes off! *Rubbing her cheeks*

1 *Wom.* My master's yonder.

Lady P. Where?

2 *Wom.* With a young gentleman.

Lady P. That same's the party;
In man's apparel! 'Pray you, sir, jog my knight:
I will be tender to his reputation,
However he demerit.

Sir P. [*Seeing her*] My lady!

Per. Where?

Sir P. 'Tis she indeed, sir; you shall know her. She is,
Were she not mine, a lady of that merit,
For fashion and behaviour; and for beauty
I durst compare—

Per. It seems you are not jealous,
That dare commend her.

Sir P. Nay, and for discourse—

Per. Being your wife, she cannot miss that.

Sir P. [*Introducing* PEREGRINE] Madam,
Here is a gentleman, pray you, use him fairly;
He seems a youth, but he is—
Lady P. None.
Sir P. Yes, one
Has put his face as soon into the world—
Lady P. You mean, as early? but to-day?
Sir P. How's this?
Lady P. Why, in this habit, sir; you apprehend me:—
Well, master Would-be, this doth not become you;
I had thought the odour, sir, of your good name
Had been more precious to you; that you would not
Have done this dire massacre on your honour;
One of your gravity and rank besides!
But knights, I see, care little for the oath
They make to ladies; chiefly, their own ladies.
Sir P. Now, by my spurs, the symbol of my knighthood,—
Per. [*Aside*] Lord, how his brain is humbled for an oath!
Sir P. I reach you not.
Lady P. Right, sir, your policy
May bear it through thus.—Sir, a word with you.
To PEREGRINE
I would be loth to contest publicly
With any gentlewoman, or to seem
Forward, or violent, as the courtier says;
It comes too near rusticity in a lady,
Which I would shun by all means: and however
I may deserve from master Would-be, yet
T'have one fair gentlewoman thus be made
The unkind instrument to wrong another,
And one she knows not, ay, and to perséver;
In my poor judgment, is not warranted
From being a solecism in our sex,
If not in manners.
Per. How is this!
Sir P. Sweet madam,

Come nearer to your aim.
Lady P. Marry, and will, sir.
Since you provoke me with your impudence,
And laughter of your light land-syren here,
Your Sporus, your hermaphrodite—
Per. What's here?
Poetic fury, and historic storms!
Sir P. The gentleman, believe it, is of worth,
And of our nation.
Lady P. Ay, your White-friars nation.
Come, I blush for you, master Would-be, I;
And am asham'd you should have no more forehead,
Than thus to be the patron, or St. George,
To a lewd harlot, a base fricatrice,
A female devil, in a male outside.
Sir P. Nay,
An you be such a one, I must bid adieu
To your delights. The case appears too liquid. *Exit*
Lady P. Ay, you may carry't clear, with your state-face!—
But for your carnival concupiscence,
Who here is fled for liberty of conscience,
From furious persecution of the marshal,
Her will I dis'ple.
Per. This is fine, i'faith!
And do you use this often? Is this part
Of your wit's exercise, 'gainst you have occasion?
Madam—
Lady P. Go to, sir.
Per. Do you hear me, lady?
Why, if your knight have set you to beg shirts,
Or to invite me home, you might have done it
A nearer way, by far.
Lady P. This cannot work you
Out of my snare.
Per. Why, am I in it, then?
Indeed your husband told me you were fair.

And so you are; only your nose inclines,
That side that's next the sun, to the queen-apple.

Lady P. This cannot be endur'd by any patience.

Enter MOSCA

Mos. What is the matter, madam?

Lady P. If the senate
Right not my quest in this, I will protest them
To all the world, no aristocracy.

Mos. What is the injury, lady?

Lady P. Why, the callet
You told me of, here I have ta'en disguised.

Mos. Who? this! what means your ladyship? the creature
I mention'd to you is apprehended now,
Before the senate; you shall see her—

Lady P. Where?

Mos. I'll bring you to her. This young gentleman,
I saw him land this morning at the port.

Lady P. Is't possible! how has my judgment wander'd?
Sir, I must, blushing, say to you, I have err'd;
And plead your pardon.

Per. What, more changes yet!

Lady P. I hope you have not the malice to remember
A gentlewoman's passion. If you stay
In Venice here, please you to use me, sir—

Mos. Will you go, madam?

Lady P. 'Pray you, sir, use me; in faith,
The more you see me, the more I shall conceive
You have forgot our quarrel.

Exeunt Lady WOULD-BE, MOSCA, NANO, *and* Waiting-women

Per. This is rare!
Sir Politick Would-be? no; sir Politick Bawd,
To bring me thus acquainted with his wife!
Well, wise sir Pol, since you have practised thus

Upon my freshman-ship, I'll try your salt-head,
What proof it is against a counter-plot. *Exit*

[SCENE II]

[*The Scrutineo, or Senate-House*]

Enter VOLTORE, CORBACCIO, CORVINO, *and* MOSCA

Volt. Well, now you know the carriage of the business,
Your constancy is all that is required
Unto the safety of it.
Mos. Is the lie
Safely convey'd amongst us? is that sure?
Knows every man his burden?
Corv. Yes.
Mos. Then shrink not.
Corv. But knows the advocate the truth?
Mos. O, sir,
By no means; I devised a formal tale,
That salv'd your reputation. But be valiant, sir.
Corv. I fear no one but him, that this his pleading
Should make him stand for a co-heir—
Mos. Co-halter!
Hang him; we will but use his tongue, his noise,
As we do croakers here.
Corv. Ay, what shall he do?
Mos. When we have done, you mean?
Corv. Yes.
Mos. Why, we'll think:
Sell him for mummia; he's half dust already.
Do you not smile, [*to Voltore*] to see this buffalo,
How he doth sport it with his head?—I should,
If all were well and past. [*Aside*]—Sir, [*To* CORBACCIO] only you
Are he that shall enjoy the crop of all,
And these not know for whom they toil.

Corb. Ay, peace.

Mos. [*Turning to* CORVINO] But you shall eat it. Much!
[*Aside*]—Worshipful sir, [*To* VOLTORE]
Mercury sit upon your thundering tongue,
Or the French Hercules, and make your language
As conquering as his club, to beat along,
As with a tempest, flat, our adversaries;
But much more yours, sir.

Volt. Here they come, have done.

Mos. I have another witness, if you need, sir,
I can produce.

Volt. Who is it?

Mos. Sir, I have her.

Enter Avocatori *and take their seats,* BONARIO, CELIA, Notario, Commandadori, Saffi, *and other* Officers *of justice*

1 *Avoc.* The like of this the senate never heard of.

2 *Avoc.* 'Twill come most strange to them when we report it.

4 *Avoc.* The gentlewoman has been ever held
Of unreproved name.

3 *Avoc.* So has the youth.

4 *Avoc.* The more unnatural part that of his father.

2 *Avoc.* More of the husband.

1 *Avoc.* I not know to give
His act a name, it is so monstrous!

4 *Avoc.* But the impostor, he's a thing created
To exceed example!

1 *Avoc.* And all after-times!

2 *Avoc.* I never heard a true voluptuary
Described, but him.

3 *Avoc.* Appear yet those were cited?

Not. All but the old magnifico, Volpone.

1 *Avoc.* Why is not he here?

Mos. Please your fatherhoods,

Here is his advocate: himself's so weak,
So feeble—
4 *Avoc.* What are you?
Bon. His parasite,
His knave, his pandar: I beseech the court,
He may be forced to come, that your grave eyes
May bear strong witness of his strange impostures.
Volt. Upon my faith and credit with your virtues,
He is not able to endure the air.
2 *Avoc.* Bring him, however.
3 *Avoc.* We will see him.
4 *Avoc.* Fetch him.
Volt. Your fatherhoods' fit pleasures be obey'd;
Exeunt Officers
But sure, the sight will rather move your pities,
Than indignation. May it please the court,
In the mean time, he may be heard in me;
I know this place most void of prejudice,
And therefore crave it, since we have no reason
To fear our truth should hurt our cause.
3 *Avoc.* Speak free.
Volt. Then know, most honour'd fathers, I must now
Discover to your strangely abused ears,
The most prodigious and most frontless piece
Of solid impudence, and treachery,
That ever vicious nature yet brought forth
To shame the state of Venice. This lewd woman,
That wants no artificial looks or tears
To help the vizor she has now put on,
Hath long been known a close adulteress
To that lascivious youth there; not suspected,
I say, but known, and taken in the act
With him; and by this man, the easy husband,
Pardon'd; whose timeless bounty makes him now
Stand here, the most unhappy, innocent person,
That ever man's own goodness made accused.

For these not knowing how to owe a gift
Of that dear grace, but with their shame; being placed
So above all powers of their gratitude,
Began to hate the benefit; and, in place
Of thanks, devise to extirpe the memory
Of such an act: wherein I pray your fatherhoods
To observe the malice, yea, the rage of creatures
Discover'd in their evils; and what heart
Such take, even from their crimes:—but that anon
Will more appear.—This gentleman, the father,
Hearing of this foul fact, with many others,
Which daily struck at his too tender ears,
And grieved in nothing more than that he could not
Preserve himself a parent, (his son's ills
Growing to that strange flood,) at last decreed
To disinherit him.

1 *Avoc.* These be strange turns!

2 *Avoc.* The young man's fame was ever fair and honest.

Volt. So much more full of danger is his vice,
That can beguile so under shade of virtue.
But, as I said, my honour'd sires, his father
Having this settled purpose, by what means
To him betray'd, we know not, and this day
Appointed for the deed; that parricide,
I cannot style him better, by confederacy
Preparing this his paramour to be there,
Enter'd Volpone's house, (who was the man,
Your fatherhoods must understand, design'd
For the inheritance,) there sought his father:—
But with what purpose sought he him, my lords?
I tremble to pronounce it, that a son
Unto a father, and to such a father,
Should have so foul, felonious intent!
It was to murder him: when being prevented
By his more happy absence, what then did he?
Not check his wicked thoughts; no, now new deeds,

(Mischief doth never end where it begins)
An act of horror, fathers! he dragg'd forth
The aged gentleman that had there lain bed-rid
Three years and more, out of his innocent couch,
Naked upon the floor, there left him; wounded
His servant in the face: and, with this strumpet
The stale to his forged practice, who was glad
To be so active,—(I shall here desire
Your fatherhoods to note but my collections,
As most remarkable,—) thought at once to stop
His father's ends, discredit his free choice
In the old gentleman, redeem themselves,
By laying infamy upon this man,
To whom, with blushing, they should owe their lives.

1 *Avoc.* What proofs have you of this?

Bon. Most honoured fathers,
I humbly crave there be no credit given
To this man's mercenary tongue.

2 *Avoc.* Forbear.

Bon. His soul moves in his fee.

3 *Avoc.* O sir.

Bon. This fellow,
For six sols more, would plead against his Maker.

1 *Avoc.* You do forget yourself.

Volt. Nay, nay, grave fathers,
Let him have scope: can any man imagine
That he will spare his accuser, that would not
Have spared his parent?

1 *Avoc.* Well, produce your proofs.

Cel. I would I could forget I were a creature.

Volt. Signior Corbaccio! CORBACCIO *comes forward*

4 *Avoc.* What is he?

Volt. The father.

2 *Avoc.* Has he had an oath?

Not. Yes.

Corb. What must I do now?

Not. Your testimony's craved.

Corb. Speak to the knave?
I'll have my mouth first stopt with earth; my heart
Abhors his knowledge: I disclaim in him.

1 *Avoc.* But for what cause?

Corb. The mere portent of nature!
He is an utter stranger to my loins.

Bon. Have they made you to this?

Corb. I will not hear thee,
Monster of men, swine, goat, wolf, parricide!
Speak not, thou viper.

Bon. Sir, I will sit down,
And rather wish my innocence should suffer,
Than I resist the authority of a father.

Volt. Signior Corvino! CORVINO *comes forward*

2 *Avoc.* This is strange.

1 *Avoc.* Who's this?

Not. The husband.

4 *Avoc.* Is he sworn?

Not. He is.

3 *Avoc.* Speak, then.

Corv. This woman, please your fatherhoods, is a whore,
Of most hot exercise, more than a partrich,
Upon record—

1 *Avoc.* No more.

Corv. Neighs like a jennet.

Not. Preserve the honour of the court.

Corv. I shall,
And modesty of your most reverend ears.
And yet I hope that I may say, these eyes
Have seen her glued unto that piece of cedar,
That fine well-timber'd gallant; and that here
The letters may be read, thorough the horn,
That makes the story perfect.

Mos. Excellent! sir.

Corv. [*Aside to* MOSCA] There is no shame in this now, is there?

Mos. None.

Corv. Or if I said, I hoped that she were onward
To her damnation, if there be a hell
Greater than whore and woman; a good catholic
May make the doubt.

3 *Avoc.* His grief hath made him frantic.

1 *Avoc.* Remove him hence.

2 *Avoc.* Look to the woman. CELIA *swoons*

Corv. Rare!
Prettily feign'd, again!

4 *Avoc.* Stand from about her.

1 *Avoc.* Give her the air.

3 *Avoc.* [*To* MOSCA] What can you say?

Mos. My wound,
May it please your wisdoms, speaks for me, received
In aid of my good patron, when he mist
His sought-for father, when that well-taught dame
Had her cue given her, to cry out, A rape!

Bon. O most laid impudence! Fathers—

3 *Avoc.* Sir, be silent;
You had your hearing free, so must they theirs.

2 *Avoc.* I do begin to doubt the imposture here.

4 *Avoc.* This woman has too many moods.

Volt. Grave fathers,
She is a creature of a most profest
And prostituted lewdness.

Corv. Most impetuous,
Unsatisfied, grave fathers!

Volt. May her feignings
Not take your wisdoms: but this day she baited
A stranger, a grave knight, with her loose eyes,
And more lascivious kisses. This man saw them
Together on the water, in a gondola.

Mos. Here is the lady herself, that saw them too;

Without; who then had in the open streets
Pursued them, but for saving her knight's honour.

1 *Avoc.* Produce that lady.

2 *Avoc.* Let her come. *Exit* MOSCA

4 *Avoc.* These things,
They strike with wonder.

3 *Avoc.* I am turn'd a stone.

Re-enter MOSCA *with* Lady WOULD-BE

Mos. Be resolute, madam.

Lady P. Ay, this same is she. *Pointing to* CELIA
Out, thou camelion harlot! now thine eyes
Vie tears with the hyæna. Dar'st thou look
Upon my wronged face?—I cry your pardons,
I fear I have forgettingly transgrest
Against the dignity of the court—

2 *Avoc.* No, madam.

Lady P. And been exorbitant—

2 *Avoc.* You have not, lady.

4 *Avoc.* These proofs are strong.

Lady P. Surely, I had no purpose
To scandalise your honours, or my sex's.

3 *Avoc.* We do believe it.

Lady P. Surely, you may believe it.

2 *Avoc.* Madam, we do.

Lady P. Indeed you may; my breeding
Is not so coarse—

4 *Avoc.* We know it.

Lady P. To offend
With pertinacy—

3 *Avoc.* Lady—

Lady P. Such a presence!
No surely.

1 *Avoc.* We well think it.

Lady P. You may think it.

1 *Avoc.* Let her o'ercome. What witnesses have you

To make good your report?

Bon. Our consciences.

Cel. And heaven, that never fails the innocent.

4 *Avoc.* These are no testimonies.

Bon. Not in your courts,
Where multitude, and clamour overcomes.

1 *Avoc.* Nay, then you do wax insolent.

Re-enter Officers, *bearing* VOLPONE *on a couch*

Volt. Here, here,
The testimony comes, that will convince,
And put to utter dumbness their bold tongues:
See here, grave fathers, here's the ravisher,
The rider on men's wives, the great impostor,
The grand voluptuary! Do you not think
These limbs should affect venery? or these eyes
Covet a concubine? pray you mark these hands;
Are they not fit to stroke a lady's breasts?—
Perhaps he doth dissemble!

Bon. So he does.

Volt. Would you have him tortured?

Bon. I would have him proved.

Volt. Best try him then with goads, or burning irons;
Put him to the strappado: I have heard
The rack hath cured the gout; 'faith, give it him,
And help him of a malady; be courteous.
I'll undertake, before these honour'd fathers,
He shall have yet as many left diseases,
As she has known adulterers, or thou strumpets.—
O, my most equal hearers, if these deeds,
Acts of this bold and most exorbitant strain,
May pass with sufferance, what one citizen
But owes the forfeit of his life, yea, fame,
To him that dares traduce him? which of you
Are safe, my honour'd fathers? I would ask,
With leave of your grave fatherhoods, if their plot

Have any face or colour like to truth?
Or if, unto the dullest nostril here,
It smell not rank, and most abhorred slander?
I crave your care of this good gentleman,
Whose life is much endanger'd by their fable;
And as for them, I will conclude with this,
That vicious persons, when they're hot and flesh'd
In impious acts, their constancy abounds:
Damn'd deeds are done with greatest confidence.

1 *Avoc.* Take them to custody, and sever them.

2 *Avoc.* 'Tis pity two such prodigies should live.

1 *Avoc.* Let the old gentleman be return'd with care.

Exeunt Officers *with* VOLPONE

I'm sorry your credulity hath wrong'd him.

4 *Avoc.* These are two creatures!

3 *Avoc.* I've an earthquake in me.

2 *Avoc.* Their shame, even in their cradles, fled their faces.

4 *Avoc.* [*To* VOLTORE] You have done a worthy service to the state, sir,
In their discovery.

1 *Avoc.* You shall hear, ere night,
What punishment the court decrees upon them.

Exeunt Avocatori, Notario, *and* Officers *with* BONARIO *and* CELIA

Volt. We thank your fatherhoods.—How like you it?

Mos. Rare.
I'd have your tongue, sir, tipt with gold for this;
I'd have you be the heir to the whole city;
The earth I'd have want men, ere you want living:
They're bound to erect your statue in St. Mark's.
Signior Corvino, I would have you go
And shew yourself, that you have conquer'd.

Corv. Yes.

Mos. It was much better that you should profess
Yourself a cuckold thus, than that the other

Should have been proved.

Corv. Nay, I consider'd that:
Now it is her fault.

Mos. Then it had been yours.

Corv. True; I do doubt this advocate still.

Mos. I'faith
You need not, I dare ease you of that care.

Corv. I trust thee, Mosca. *Exit*

Mos. As your own soul, sir.

Corb. Mosca!

Mos. Now for your business, sir.

Corb. How! have you business?

Mos. Yes, your's, sir.

Corb. O, none else?

Mos. None else, not I.

Corb. Be careful, then.

Mos. Rest you with both your eyes, sir.

Corb. Dispatch it.

Mos. Instantly.

Corb. And look that all,
Whatever, be put in, jewels, plate, moneys,
Household stuff, bedding, curtains.

Mos. Curtain-rings, sir:
Only the advocate's fee must be deducted.

Corb. I'll pay him now; you'll be too prodigal.

Mos. Sir, I must tender it.

Corb. Two chequines is well.

Mos. No, six, sir.

Corb. 'Tis too much.

Mos. He talk'd a great while;
You must consider that, sir.

Corb. Well, there's three—

Mos. I'll give it him.

Corb. Do so, and there's for thee. *Exit*

Mos. Bountiful bones! What horrid strange offence
Did he commit 'gainst nature, in his youth,

Worthy this age? [*Aside*]—You see, sir, [*To* VOLTORE] how I work
Unto your ends: take you no notice.
Volt. No,
I'll leave you. *Exit*
Mos. All is yours, the devil and all:
Good advocate!—Madam, I'll bring you home.
Lady P. No, I'll go see your patron.
Mos. That you shall not:
I'll tell you why. My purpose is to urge
My patron to reform his Will; and for
The zeal you have shewn to-day, whereas before
You were but third or fourth, you shall be now
Put in the first: which would appear as begg'd,
If you were present. Therefore—
Lady P. You shall sway me. *Exeunt*

[ACT V, SCENE I]

[*A Room in Volpone's House*]

Enter VOLPONE

Volp. Well, I am here, and all this brunt is past.
I ne'er was in dislike with my disguise
'Till this fled moment: here 'twas good, in private;
But in your public,—*cave* whilst I breathe.
'Fore God, my left leg 'gan to have the cramp,
And I apprehended straight some power had struck me
With a dead palsy: Well! I must be merry,
And shake it off. A many of these fears
Would put me into some villainous disease,
Should they come thick upon me: I'll prevent 'em.
Give me a bowl of lusty wine, to fright
This humour from my heart. [*Drinks*]—Hum, hum, hum!
'Tis almost gone already; I shall conquer.
Any device, now, of rare ingenious knavery,
That would possess me with a violent laughter,

Would make me up again. [*Drinks again*]—So, so, so, so!
This heat is life; 'tis blood by this time:—Mosca!

Enter MOSCA

Mos. How now, sir? does the day look clear again?
Are we recover'd, and wrought out of error,
Into our way, to see our path before us?
Is our trade free once more?
Volp. Exquisite Mosca!
Mos. Was it not carried learnedly?
Volp. And stoutly:
Good wits are greatest in extremities.
Mos. It were a folly beyond thought, to trust
Any grand act unto a cowardly spirit:
You are not taken with it enough, methinks.
Volp. O, more than if I had enjoy'd the wench:
The pleasure of all woman-kind's not like it.
Mos. Why now you speak, sir. We must here be fix'd;
Here we must rest; this is our master-piece;
We cannot think to go beyond this.
Volp. True,
Thou hast play'd thy prize, my precious Mosca.
Mos. Nay, sir,
To gull the court—
Volp. And quite divert the torrent
Upon the innocent.
Mos. Yes, and to make
So rare a music out of discords—
Volp. Right.
That yet to me's the strangest, how thou hast borne it!
That these, being so divided 'mongst themselves,
Should not scent somewhat, or in me or thee,
Or doubt their own side.
Mos. True, they will not see't.
Too much light blinds them, I think. Each of them
Is so possest and stuft with his own hopes,

That any thing unto the contrary,
Never so true, or never so apparent,
Never so palpable, they will resist it—
Volp. Like a temptation of the devil.
Mos. Right, sir.
Merchants may talk of trade, and your great signiors
Of land that yields well; but if Italy
Have any glebe more fruitful than these fellows,
I am deceiv'd. Did not your advocate rare?
Volp. O—*My most honour'd fathers, my grave fathers,*
Under correction of your fatherhoods,
What face of truth is here? If these strange deeds
May pass, most honour'd fathers—I had much ado
To forbear laughing.
Mos. It seem'd to me, you sweat, sir.
Volp. In troth, I did a little.
Mos. But confess, sir,
Were you not daunted?
Volp. In good faith, I was
A little in a mist, but not dejected;
Never, but still my self.
Mos. I think it, sir.
Now, so truth help me, I must needs say this, sir,
And out of conscience for your advocate,
He has taken pains, in faith, sir, and deserv'd,
In my poor judgment, I speak it under favour,
Not to contrary you, sir, very richly—
Well—to be cozen'd.
Volp. Troth, and I think so too,
By that I heard him, in the latter end.
Mos. O, but before, sir: had you heard him first
Draw it to certain heads, then aggravate,
Then use his vehement figures—I look'd still
When he would shift a shirt: and, doing this
Out of pure love, no hope of gain—
Volp. 'Tis right.

I cannot answer him, Mosca, as I would,
Not yet; but for thy sake, at thy entreaty,
I will begin, even now—to vex them all,
This very instant.
  Mos. Good sir.
  Volp. Call the dwarf
And eunuch forth.
  Mos. Castrone, Nano!

Enter CASTRONE *and* NANO

  Nano. Here.
  Volp. Shall we have a jig now?
  Mos. What you please, sir.
  Volp. Go.
Straight give out about the streets, you two,
That I am dead; do it with constancy,
Sadly, do you hear? impute it to the grief
Of this late slander. *Exeunt* CASTRONE *and* NANO
  Mos. What do you mean, sir?
  Volp. O,
I shall have instantly my Vulture, Crow,
Raven, come flying hither, on the news,
To peck for carrion, my she-wolf, and all,
Greedy, and full of expectation—
  Mos. And then to have it ravish'd from their mouths!
  Volp. 'Tis true. I will have thee put on a gown,
And take upon thee, as thou wert mine heir:
Shew them a will: Open that chest, and reach
Forth one of those that has the blanks; I'll straight
Put in thy name.
  Mos. It will be rare, sir. *Gives him a paper*
  Volp. Ay,
When they ev'n gape, and find themselves deluded—
  Mos. Yes.
  Volp. And thou use them scurvily!
Dispatch, get on thy gown.

Mos. [*Putting on a gown*] But what, sir, if they ask
After the body?
Volp. Say, it was corrupted.
Mos. I'll say, it stunk, sir; and was fain to have it
Coffin'd up instantly, and sent away.
Volp. Any thing; what thou wilt. Hold, here's my will.
Get thee a cap, a count-book, pen and ink,
Papers afore thee; sit as thou wert taking
An inventory of parcels: I'll get up
Behind the curtain, on a stool, and hearken;
Sometime peep over, see how they do look,
With what degrees their blood doth leave their faces,
O, 'twill afford me a rare meal of laughter!
Mos. [*Putting on a cap, and setting out the table, etc.*]
Your advocate will turn stark dull upon it.
Volp. It will take off his oratory's edge.
Mos. But your clarissimo, old round-back, he
Will crump you like a hog-louse, with the touch.
Volp. And what Corvino?
Mos. O, sir, look for him,
To-morrow morning, with a rope and dagger,
To visit all the streets; he must run mad.
My lady too, that came into the court,
To bear false witness for your worship—
Volp. Yes,
And kiss'd me 'fore the fathers, when my face
Flow'd all with oils.
Mos. And sweat, sir. Why, your gold
Is such another med'cine, it dries up
All those offensive savours: it transforms
The most deformed, and restores them lovely,
As 'twere the strange poetical girdle. Jove
Could not invent t' himself a shroud more subtle
To pass Acrisius' guards. It is the thing
Makes all the world her grace, her youth, her beauty.
Volp. I think she loves me.

Mos. Who? the lady, sir?
She's jealous of you.
Volp. Dost thou say so? *Knocking within*
Mos. Hark,
There's some already.
Volp. Look.
Mos. It is the Vulture;
He has the quickest scent.
Volp. I'll to my place,
Thou to thy posture. *Goes behind the curtain*
Mos. I am set.
Volp. But, Mosca,
Play the artificer now, torture them rarely.

Enter VOLTORE

Volt. How now, my Mosca?
Mos. [*Writing*] Turkey carpets, nine—
Volt. Taking an inventory! that is well.
Mos. Two suits of bedding, tissue—
Volt. Where's the Will?
Let me read that the while.

Enter Servants, *with* CORBACCIO *in a chair*

Corb. So, set me down,
And get you home. *Exeunt* Servants
Volt. Is he come now, to trouble us!
Mos. Of cloth of gold, two more—
Corb. Is it done, Mosca?
Mos. Of several velvets eight—
Volt. I like his care.
Corb. Dost thou not hear?

Enter CORVINO

Corb. Ha! is the hour come, Mosca?
Volp. [*Peeping over the curtain*] Ay, now they muster.

Corv. What does the advocate here,
Or this Corbaccio?
Corb. What do these here?

Enter Lady POLITICK WOULD-BE

Lady P. Mosca!
Is his thread spun?
Mos. Eight chests of linen—
Volp. O,
My fine dame Would-be, too!
Corv. Mosca, the Will,
That I may shew it these, and rid them hence.
Mos. Six chests of diaper, four of damask.—There.
Gives them the Will carelessly, over his shoulder
Corb. Is that the Will?
Mos. Down-beds and bolsters—
Volp. Rare!
Be busy still. Now they begin to flutter:
They never think of me. Look, see, see, see!
How their swift eyes run over the long deed,
Unto the name, and to the legacies,
What is bequeathed them there—
Mos. Ten suits of hangings—
Volp. Ay, in their garters, Mosca. Now their hopes
Are at the gasp.
Volt. Mosca the heir!
Corb. What's that?
Volp. My advocate is dumb; look to my merchant,
He has heard of some strange storm, a ship is lost,
He faints; my lady will swoon. Old glazen eyes,
He hath not reach'd his despair yet.
Corb. All these
Are out of hope; I am, sure, the man. *Takes the Will*
Corv. But, Mosca—
Mos. Two cabinets.

Corv. Is this in earnest?
Mos. One
Of ebony—
Corv. Or do you but delude me?
Mos. The other, mother of pearl—I am very busy.
Good faith, it is a fortune thrown upon me—
Item, one salt of agate—not my seeking.
Lady P. Do you hear, sir?
Mos. A perfumed box—'Pray you forbear,
You see I'm troubled—made of an onyx—
Lady P. How!
Mos. To-morrow or next day, I shall be at leisure
To talk with you all.
Corv. Is this my large hope's issue?
Lady P. Sir, I must have a fairer answer.
Mos. Madam!
Marry, and shall: 'pray you, fairly quit my house.
Nay, raise no tempest with your looks; but hark you,
Remember what your ladyship offer'd me
To put you in an heir; go to, think on it:
And what you said e'en your best madams did
For maintenance; and why not you? Enough.
Go home, and use the poor sir Pol, your knight, well,
For fear I tell some riddles; go, be melancholy.
Exit Lady WOULD-BE
Volp. O, my fine devil!
Corv. Mosca, 'pray you a word.
Mos. Lord! will you not take your dispatch hence yet?
Methinks, of all, you should have been the example.
Why should you stay here? with what thoughts, what promise?
Hear you; do you not know, I know you an ass,
And that you would most fain have been a wittol,
If fortune would have let you? that you are
A declared cuckold, on good terms? This pearl,
You'll say, was yours? right: this diamond?

I'll not deny't, but thank you. Much here else?
It may be so. Why, think that these good works
May help to hide your bad. I'll not betray you;
Although you be but extraordinary,
And have it only in title, it sufficeth:
Go home, be melancholy too, or mad. *Exit* CORVINO

Volp. Rare Mosca! how his villainy becomes him!

Volt. Certain he doth delude all these for me.

Corb. Mosca the heir!

Volp. O, his four eyes have found it.

Corb. I am cozen'd, cheated, by a parasite slave;
Harlot, thou hast gull'd me.

Mos. Yes, sir. Stop your mouth,
Or I shall draw the only tooth is left.
Are not you he, that filthy covetous wretch,
With the three legs, that here, in hope of prey,
Have, any time this three years, snuff'd about,
With your most grovelling nose, and would have hired
Me to the poisoning of my patron, sir?
Are not you he that have to-day in court
Profess'd the disinheriting of your son?
Perjured yourself? Go home, and die, and stink.
If you but croak a syllable, all comes out:
Away, and call your porters! [*Exit* CORBACCIO] Go, go, stink.

Volp. Excellent varlet!

Volt. Now, my faithful Mosca,
I find thy constancy.

Mos. Sir!

Volt. Sincere.

Mos. [*Writing*] A table
Of porphyry—I marle you'll be thus troublesome.

Volt. Nay, leave off now, they are gone.

Mos. Why, who are you?
What! who did send for you? O, cry you mercy,
Reverend sir! Good faith, I am grieved for you,

That any chance of mine should thus defeat
Your (I must needs say) most deserving travails:
But I protest, sir, it was cast upon me,
And I could almost wish to be without it,
But that the will o' the dead must be observ'd.
Marry, my joy is that you need it not;
You have a gift, sir, (thank your education,)
Will never let you want, while there are men,
And malice, to breed causes. Would I had
But half the like, for all my fortune, sir!
If I have any suits, as I do hope,
Things being so easy and direct, I shall not,
I will make bold with your obstreperous aid,
Conceive me,—for your fee, sir. In mean time,
You that have so much law, I know have the conscience
Not to be covetous of what is mine.
Good sir, I thank you for my plate; 'twill help
To set up a young man. Good faith, you look
As you were costive; best go home and purge, sir.

Exit VOLTORE

Volp. [*Comes from behind the curtain*] Bid him eat lettuce well. My witty mischief,
Let me embrace thee. O that I could now
Transform thee to a Venus!—Mosca, go,
Straight take my habit of clarissimo,
And walk the streets; be seen, torment them more:
We must pursue, as well as plot. Who would
Have lost this feast?

Mos. I doubt it will lose them.

Volp. O, my recovery shall recover all.
That I could now but think on some disguise
To meet them in, and ask them questions:
How I would vex them still at every turn!

Mos. Sir, I can fit you.

Volp. Canst thou?

Mos. Yes, I know
One o' the commandadori, sir, so like you;
Him will I straight make drunk, and bring you his habit.
Volp. A rare disguise, and answering thy brain!
O, I will be a sharp disease unto them.
Mos. Sir, you must look for curses—
Volp. Till they burst;
The Fox fares ever best when he is curst. *Exeunt*

[SCENE II]

[*A Hall in Sir Politick's House*]

Enter PEREGRINE *disguised, and three* Merchants

Per. Am I enough disguised?
1 *Mer.* I warrant you.
Per. All my ambition is to fright him only.
2 *Mer.* If you could ship him away, 'twere excellent.
3 *Mer.* To Zant, or to Aleppo?
Per. Yes, and have his
Adventures put i' the Book of Voyages,
And his gull'd story register'd for truth.
Well, gentlemen, when I am in a while,
And that you think us warm in our discourse,
Know your approaches.
1 *Mer.* Trust it to our care. *Exeunt* Merchants

Enter Waiting-woman.

Per. Save you, fair lady! Is sir Pol within?
Wom. I do not know, sir.
Per. Pray you say unto him,
Here is a merchant, upon earnest business,
Desires to speak with him.
Wom. I will see, sir. *Exit*
Per. I pray you.—
I see the family is all female here.

Re-enter Waiting-woman

Wom. He says, sir, he has weighty affairs of state,
That now require him whole; some other time
You may possess him.
Per. Pray you say again,
If those require him whole, these will exact him,
Whereof I bring him tidings. [*Exit* Woman]—What might be
His grave affair of state now; how to make
Bolognian sausages here in Venice, sparing
One o' the ingredients?

Re-enter Waiting-woman

Wom. Sir, he says, he knows
By your word *tidings,* that you are no statesman,
And therefore wills you stay.
Per. Sweet, pray you return him;
I have not read so many proclamations,
And studied them for words, as he has done—
But—here he deigns to come. *Exit* Woman

Enter Sir Politick

Sir P. Sir, I must crave
Your courteous pardon. There hath chanced to-day,
Unkind disaster 'twixt my lady and me;
And I was penning my apology,
To give her satisfaction, as you came now.
Per. Sir, I am grieved I bring you worse disaster:
The gentleman you met at the port to-day,
That told you, he was newly arrived—
Sir P. Ay, was
A fugitive punk?
Per No, sir, a spy set on you;
And he has made relation to the senate,
That you profest to him to have a plot

To sell the State of Venice to the Turk.

Sir P. O me!

Per. For which, warrants are sign'd by this time,
To apprehend you, and to search your study
For papers—

Sir P. Alas, sir, I have none, but notes
Drawn out of play-books—

Per. All the better, sir.

Sir P. And some essays. What shall I do?

Per. Sir, best
Convey yourself into a sugar-chest;
Or, if you could lie round, a frail were rare,
And I could send you aboard.

Sir P. Sir, I but talk'd so,
For discourse sake merely. *Knocking within*

Per. Hark! they are there.

Sir P. I am a wretch, a wretch!

Per. What will you do, sir?
Have you ne'er a currant-butt to leap into?
They'll put you to the rack; you must be sudden.

Sir P. Sir, I have an ingine—

3 *Mer.* [*Within*] Sir Politick Would-be!

2 *Mer.* [*Within*] Where is he?

Sir P. That I have thought upon before time.

Per. What is it?

Sir P. I shall ne'er endure the torture.
Marry, it is, sir, of a tortoise-shell,
Fitted for these extremities: pray you, sir, help me.
Here I've a place, sir, to put back my legs,
Please you to lay it on, sir [*Lies down while Peregrine places the shell upon him*]—with this cap,
And my black gloves. I'll lie, sir, like a tortoise,
'Till they are gone.

Per. And call you this an ingine?

Sir P. Mine own device——Good sir, bid my wife's women
To burn my papers. *Exit* PEREGRINE

The three Merchants *rush in*

1 *Mer.* Where is he hid?
3 *Mer.* We must,
And will sure find him.
2 *Mer.* Which is his study?

Re-enter PEREGRINE

1 *Mer.* What
Are you, sir?
Per. I am a merchant, that came here
To look upon this tortoise.
3 *Mer.* How!
1 *Mer.* St. Mark!
What beast is this!
Per. It is a fish.
2 *Mer.* Come out here!
Per. Nay, you may strike him, sir, and tread upon him;
He'll bear a cart.
1 *Mer.* What, to run over him?
Per. Yes, sir.
3 *Mer.* Let's jump upon him.
2 *Mer.* Can he not go?
Per. He creeps, sir.
1 *Mer.* Let's see him creep.
Per. No, good sir, you will hurt him.
2 *Mer.* Heart, I will see him creep, or prick his guts.
3 *Mer.* Come out here!
Per. [*Aside to* SIR POLITICK] Pray you, sir!—Creep a little.
1 *Mer.* Forth.
2 *Mer.* Yet farther.
Per. Good sir!—Creep.

2 *Mer.* We'll see his legs.

They pull off the shell and discover him

3 *Mer.* Ods so, he has garters!

1 *Mer.* Ay, and gloves!

2 *Mer.* Is this
Your fearful tortoise?

Per. [*Discovering himself*] Now, sir Pol, we are even;
For your next project I shall be prepared:
I am sorry for the funeral of your notes, sir.

1 *Mer.* 'Twere a rare motion to be seen in Fleet-street.

2 *Mer.* Ay, in the Term.

1 *Mer.* Or Smithfield, in the fair.

3 *Mer.* Methinks 'tis but a melancholy sight.

Per. Farewell, most politic tortoise!

Exeunt PEREGRINE *and* Merchants

Re-enter Waiting-woman

Sir P. Where's my lady?
Knows she of this?

Wom. I know not, sir.

Sir P. Enquire.—
O, I shall be the fable of all feasts,
The freight of the gazetti, ship-boy's tale;
And, which is worst, even talk for ordinaries.

Wom. My lady's come most melancholy home,
And says, sir, she will straight to sea for physic.

Sir P. And I to shun this place and clime for ever,
Creeping with house on back, and think it well
To shrink my poor head in my politic shell. *Exeunt*

[SCENE III]

[*A Room in Volpone's House*]

Enter MOSCA *in the habit of a Clarissimo, and* VOLPONE *in that of a Commandadore*

Volp. Am I then like him?

Mos. O, sir, you are he:
No man can sever you.
Volp. Good.
Mos. But what am I?
Volp. 'Fore heaven, a brave clarissimo; thou becom'st it!
Pity thou wert not born one.
Mos. [*Aside*] If I hold
My made one, 'twill be well.
Volp. I'll go and see
What news first at the court. *Exit*
Mos. Do so. My Fox
Is out of his hole, and ere he shall re-enter,
I'll make him languish in his borrow'd case,
Except he come to composition with me.—
Androgyno, Castrone, Nano!

Enter ANDROGYNO, CASTRONE, *and* NANO

All. Here.
Mos. Go, recreate yourselves abroad; go sport.— *Exeunt*
So, now I have the keys, and am possest.
Since he will needs be dead afore his time,
I'll bury him, or gain by him: I am his heir,
And so will keep me, till he share at least.
To cozen him of all, were but a cheat
Well placed; no man would construe it a sin:
Let his sport pay for't. This is call'd the Fox-trap. *Exit*

[SCENE IV]

[*A Street*]

Enter CORBACCIO *and* CORVINO

Corb. They say, the court is set.

Corv. We must maintain
Our first tale good, for both our reputations.
Corb. Why, mine's no tale: my son would there have kill'd me.
Corv. That's true, I had forgot:—[*Aside*] mine is, I'm sure.
But for your Will, sir.
Corb. Ay, I'll come upon him
For that hereafter, now his patron's dead.

Enter VOLPONE

Volp. Signior Corvino! and Corbaccio! sir,
Much joy unto you.
Corv. Of what?
Volp. The sudden good
Dropt down upon you—
Corb. Where?
Volp. And none knows how,
From old Volpone, sir.
Corb. Out, arrant knave!
Volp. Let not your too much wealth, sir, make you furious.
Corb. Away, thou varlet!
Volp. Why, sir?
Corb. Dost thou mock me?
Volp. You mock the world, sir; did you not change Wills?
Corb. Out, harlot!
Volp. O! belike you are the man,
Signior Corvino? 'faith, you carry it well;
You grow not mad withal; I love your spirit:
You are not over-leaven'd with your fortune.
You should have some would swell now, like a wine-fat,
With such an autumn——Did he give you all, sir?
Corv Avoid, you rascal!
Volp. Troth, your wife has shewn
Herself a very woman; but you are well,

You need not care, you have a good estate,
To bear it out, sir, better by this chance:
Except Corbaccio have a share.

Corb. Hence, varlet.

Volp. You will not be acknown, sir; why, 'tis wise.
Thus do all gamesters, at all games, dissemble:
No man will seem to win. [*Exeunt* CORVINO *and* CORBACCIO]
—Here comes my vulture,
Heaving his beak up in the air, and snuffing.

Enter VOLTORE

Volt. Outstript thus, by a parasite! a slave,
Would run on errands, and make legs for crumbs!
Well, what I'll do—

Volp. The court stays for your worship.
I e'en rejoice, sir, at your worship's happiness,
And that it fell into so learned hands,
That understand the fingering—

Volt. What do you mean?

Volp. I mean to be a suitor to your worship,
For the small tenement, out of reparations,
That, to the end of your long row of houses,
By the Piscaria: it was, in Volpone's time,
Your predecessor, ere he grew diseased,
A handsome, pretty, custom'd bawdy-house
As any was in Venice, none dispraised;
But fell with him: his body and that house
Decay'd together.

Volt. Come, sir, leave your prating.

Volp. Why, if your worship give me but your hand,
That I may have the refusal, I have done.
'Tis a mere toy to you, sir; candle-rents;
As your learn'd worship knows—

Volt. What do I know?

Volp. Marry, no end of your wealth, sir; God decrease it!

Volt. Mistaking knave! what, mock'st thou my misfortune? *Exit*

Volp. His blessing on your heart, sir; would 'twere more!—
Now to my first again, at the next corner. *Exit*

[SCENE V]

[*Another part of the Street*]

Enter CORBACCIO *and* CORVINO;—MOSCA *passes over the Stage, before them*

Corb. See, in our habit! see the impudent varlet!

Corv. That I could shoot mine eyes at him like gunstones!

Enter VOLPONE

Volp. But is this true, sir, of the parasite?

Corb. Again, to afflict us! monster!

Volp. In good faith, sir,
I'm heartily grieved, a beard of your grave length
Should be so over-reach'd. I never brook'd
That parasite's hair; methought his nose should cozen:
There still was somewhat in his look, did promise
The bane of a clarissimo.

Corb. Knave—

Volp. Methinks
Yet you, that are so traded in the world,
A witty merchant, the fine bird, Corvino,
That have such moral emblems on your name,
Should not have sung your shame, and dropt your cheese,
To let the Fox laugh at your emptiness.

Corv. Sirrah, you think the privilege of the place,
And your red saucy cap, that seems to me
Nail'd to your jolt-head with those two chequines,
Can warrant your abuses; come you hither:

You shall perceive, sir, I dare beat you; approach.

Volp. No haste, sir, I do know your valour well,
Since you durst publish what you are, sir.

Corv. Tarry,
I'd speak with you.

Volp. Sir, sir, another time—

Corv. Nay, now.

Volp. O lord, sir! I were a wise man,
Would stand the fury of a distracted cuckold.

As he is running off, re-enter MOSCA

Corb. What, come again!

Volp. Upon 'em, Mosca; save me.

Corb. The air's infected where he breathes.

Corv. Let's fly him. *Exeunt* CORVINO *and* CORBACCIO

Volp. Excellent basilisk! turn upon the vulture.

Enter VOLTORE

Volt. Well, flesh-fly, it is summer with you now;
Your winter will come on.

Mos. Good advocate,
Prithee not rail, nor threaten out of place thus;
Thou'lt make a solecism, as madam says.
Get you a biggin more, your brain breaks loose. *Exit*

Volt. Well, sir.

Volp. Would you have me beat the insolent slave,
Throw dirt upon his first good clothes?

Volt. This same
Is doubtless some familiar.

Volp. Sir, the court,
In troth, stays for you. I am mad, a mule
That never read Justinian, should get up,
And ride an advocate. Had you no quirk
To avoid gullage, sir, by such a creature?
I hope you do but jest; he has not done it,
'Tis but confederacy, to blind the rest.

You are the heir.

Volt. A strange, officious,
Troublesome knave! thou dost torment me.

Volp. I know—
It cannot be, sir, that you should be cozen'd;
'Tis not within with the wit of man to do it;
You are so wise, so prudent; and 'tis fit
That wealth and wisdom still should go together. *Exeunt*

[SCENE VI]

[*The Scrutineo or Senate-House*]

Enter Avocatori, Notario, Bonario, Celia, Corbaccio, Corvino, Commandadori, Saffi, *etc.*

1 *Avoc.* Are all the parties here?

Not. All but the advocate.

2 *Avoc.* And here he comes.

Enter Voltore *and* Volpone

1 *Avoc.* Then bring them forth to sentence.

Volt. O, my most honour'd fathers, let your mercy
Once win upon your justice, to forgive—
I am distracted—

Volp. [*Aside*] What will he do now?

Volt. O,
I know not which to address myself to first;
Whether your fatherhoods, or these innocents—

Corv. [*Aside*] Will he betray himself?

Volt. Whom equally
I have abused, out of most covetous ends—

Corv. The man is mad!

Corb. What's that?

Corv. He is possest.

Volt. For which, now struck in conscience, here, I prostrate

Myself at your offended feet, for pardon.

1, 2 *Avoc.* Arise.

Cel. O heaven, how just thou art!

Volp. [*Aside*] I am caught
In mine own noose—

Corv. [*To* CORBACCIO] Be constant, sir: nought now
Can help, but impudence.

1 *Avoc.* Speak forward.

Com. Silence!

Volt. It is not passion in me, reverend fathers,
But only conscience, conscience, my good sires,
That makes me now tell truth. That parasite,
That knave, hath been the instrument of all.

1 *Avoc.* Where is that knave? fetch him.

Volp. I go. *Exit*

Corv. Grave fathers,
This man's distracted; he confest it now:
For, hoping to be old Volpone's heir,
Who now is dead—

3 *Avoc.* How!

2 *Avoc.* Is Volpone dead?

Corv. Dead since, grave fathers.

Bon. O sure vengeance!

1 *Avoc.* Stay,
Then he was no deceiver.

Volt. O no, none:
The parasite, grave fathers.

Corv. He does speak
Out of mere envy, 'cause the servant's made
The thing he gaped for: please your fatherhoods,
This is the truth, though I'll not justify
The other, but he may be some-deal faulty.

Volt. Ay, to your hopes, as well as mine, Corvino:
But I'll use modesty. Pleaseth your wisdoms,
To view these certain notes, and but confer them;
As I hope favour, they shall speak clear truth.

Corv. The devil has enter'd him!

Bon. Or bides in you.

4 *Avoc.* We have done ill, by a public officer
To send for him, if he be heir.

2 *Avoc.* For whom?

4 *Avoc.* Him that they call the parasite.

3 *Avoc.* 'Tis true,
He is a man of great estate, now left.

4 *Avoc.* Go you, and learn his name, and say, the court
Entreats his presence here, but to the clearing
Of some few doubts. [*Exit* Notary

2 *Avoc.* This same's a labyrinth!

1 *Avoc.* Stand you unto your first report?

Corv. My state,
My life, my fame—

Bon. Where is it?

Corv. Are at the stake.

1 *Avoc.* Is yours so too?

Corb. The advocate's a knave,
And has a forked tongue—

2 *Avoc.* Speak to the point.

Corb. So is the parasite too.

1 *Avoc.* This is confusion.

Volt. I do beseech your fatherhoods, read but those—
Giving them papers

Corv. And credit nothing the false spirit hath writ:
It cannot be, but he's possest, grave fathers.
The scene closes

[SCENE VII]

[*A Street*]

Enter VOLPONE

Volp. To make a snare for mine own neck! and run
My head into it, wilfully! with laughter!

When I had newly 'scaped, was free, and clear,
Out of mere wantonness! O, the dull devil
Was in this brain of mine, when I devised it,
And Mosca gave it second; he must now
Help to sear up this vein, or we bleed dead.—

Enter NANO, ANDROGYNO, *and* CASTRONE

How now! who let you loose? whither go you now?
What, to buy gingerbread, or to drown kitlings?
Nan. Sir, master Mosca call'd us out of doors,
And bid us all go play, and took the keys.
And. Yes.
Volp. Did master Mosca take the keys? why so!
I'm farther in. These are my fine conceits!
I must be merry, with a mischief to me!
What a vile wretch was I, that could not bear
My fortune soberly? I must have my crotchets,
And my conundrums! Well, go you, and seek him:
His meaning may be truer than my fear.
Bid him, he straight come to me to the court;
Thither will I, and, if't be possible,
Unscrew my advocate, upon new hopes:
When I provoked him, then I lost myself. *Exeunt*

[SCENE VIII]

[*The Scrutineo, or Senate-House*]

Avocatori, BONARIO, CELIA, CORBACCIO, CORVINO, Commandadori, Saffi, *etc., as before*

1 *Avoc.* These things can ne'er be reconciled. He, here, [*Shewing the papers*
Professeth, that the gentleman was wrong'd,
And that the gentlewoman was brought thither,
Forced by her husband, and there left.

Volt. Most true.

Cel. How ready is heaven to those that pray!

1 *Avoc.* But that
Volpone would have ravish'd her, he holds
Utterly false, knowing his impotence.

Corv. Grave fathers, he's possest; again, I say,
Possest: nay, if there be possession, and
Obsession, he has both.

3 *Avoc.* Here comes our officer.

Enter VOLPONE

Volp. The parasite will straight be here, grave fathers.

4 *Avoc.* You might invent some other name, sir varlet.

3 *Avoc.* Did not the notary meet him?

Volp. Not that I know.

4 *Avoc.* His coming will clear all.

2 *Avoc.* Yet, it is misty.

Volt. May't please your fatherhoods—

Volp. [*Whispers* VOLTORE] Sir, the parasite
Will'd me to tell you, that his master lives;
That you are still the man; your hopes the same;
And this was only a jest—

Volt. How?

Volp. Sir, to try
If you were firm, and how you stood affected.

Volt. Art sure he lives?

Volp. Do I live, sir?

Volt. O me!
I was too violent.

Volp. Sir, you may redeem it.
They said, you were possest; fall down, and seem so:
I'll help to make it good. [VOLTORE *falls*]—God bless the man!—
Stop your wind hard, and swell—See, see, see, see!
He vomits crooked pins! his eyes are set,

Like a dead hare's hung in a poulter's shop!
His mouth's running away! Do you see, signior?
Now it is in his belly.

Corv. Ay, the devil!

Volp. Now in his throat.

Corv. Ay, I perceive it plain.

Volp. 'Twill out, 'twill out! stand clear. See where it flies,
In shape of a blue toad, with a bat's wings!
Do you not see it, sir?

Corb. What? I think I do.

Corv. 'Tis too manifest.

Volp. Look! he comes to himself!

Volt. Where am I?

Volp. Take good heart, the worst is past, sir.
You are dispossest.

1 *Avoc.* What accident is this!

2 *Avoc.* Sudden, and full of wonder!

3 *Avoc.* If he were
Possest, as it appears, all this is nothing.

Corv. He has been often subject to these fits.

1 *Avoc.* Shew him that writing:—do you know it, sir?

Volp. [*Whispers* VOLTORE] Deny it, sir, forswear it; know it not.

Volt. Yes, I do know it well, it is my hand;
But all that it contains is false.

Bon. O practice!

2 *Avoc.* What maze is this!

1 *Avoc.* Is he not guilty then,
Whom you there name the parasite?

Volt. Grave fathers,
No more than his good patron, old Volpone.

4 *Avoc.* Why, he is dead.

Volt. O no, my honour'd fathers,
He lives—

1 *Avoc.* How! lives?

Volt. Lives.

2 *Avoc.* This is subtler yet!

3 *Avoc.* You said he was dead.

Volt. Never.

3 *Avoc.* You said so.

Corv. I heard so.

4 *Avoc.* Here comes the gentleman; make him way.

Enter Mosca

3 *Avoc.* A stool.

4 *Avoc.* [*Aside*] A proper man; and, were Volpone dead,
A fit match for my daughter.

3 *Avoc.* Give him way.

Volp. [*Aside to* Mosca] Mosca, I was almost lost; the advocate
Had betrayed all; but now it is recovered;
All's on the hinge again——Say, I am living.

Mos. What busy knave is this!—Most reverend fathers,
I sooner had attended your grave pleasures,
But that my order for the funeral
Of my dear patron, did require me—

Volp. [*Aside*] Mosca!

Mos. Whom I intend to bury like a gentleman.

Volp. [*Aside*] Ay, quick, and cozen me of all.

2 *Avoc.* Still stranger!
More intricate!

1 *Avoc.* And come about again!

4 *Avoc.* [*Aside*] It is a match, my daughter is bestow'd.

Mos. [*Aside to* Volpone] Will you give me half?

Volp. First, I'll be hang'd.

Mos. I know
Your voice is good, cry not so loud.

1 *Avoc.* Demand
The advocate.—Sir, did you not affirm
Volpone was alive?

Volp. Yes, and he is;

This gentleman told me so. [*Aside to* MOSCA]—Thou shalt have half.—

Mos. Whose drunkard is this same? speak, some that know him:
I never saw his face. [*Aside to* VOLPONE]—I cannot now
Afford it you so cheap.

Volp. No!

1 *Avoc.* What say you?

Volt. The officer told me.

Volp. I did, grave fathers,
And will maintain he lives, with mine own life,
And that this creature [*Points to* MOSCA] told me. [*Aside*] —I was born
With all good stars my enemies.

Mos. Most grave fathers,
If such an insolence as this must pass
Upon me, I am silent: 'twas not this
For which you sent, I hope.

2 *Avoc.* Take him away.

Volp. Mosca!

3 *Avoc.* Let him be whipt.

Volp. Wilt thou betray me?
Cozen me?

3 *Avoc.* And taught to bear himself
Toward a person of his rank.

4 *Avoc.* Away. *The Officers seize* VOLPONE

Mos. I humbly thank your fatherhoods.

Volp. [*Aside*] Soft, soft: Whipt!
And lose all that I have! If I confess,
It cannot be much more.

4 *Avoc.* Sir, are you married?

Volp. They'll be allied anon; I must be resolute:
The Fox shall here uncase. *Throws off his disguise*

Mos. Patron!

Volp. Nay, now
My ruins shall not come alone: your match

I'll hinder sure: my substance shall not glue you,
Nor screw you into a family.

Mos. Why, patron!

Volp. I am Volpone, and this is my knave;

Pointing to MOSCA

This, [*To* VOLTORE] his own knave; this, [*To* CORBACCIO] avarice's fool;
This, [*To* CORVINO] a chimera of wittol, fool, and knave:
And, reverend fathers, since we all can hope
Nought but a sentence, let's not now despair it.
You hear me brief.

Corv. May it please your fatherhoods—

Com. Silence.

1 *Avoc.* The knot is now undone by miracle.

2 *Avoc.* Nothing can be more clear.

3 *Avoc.* Or can more prove
These innocent.

1 *Avoc.* Give them their liberty.

Bon. Heaven could not long let such gross crimes be hid.

2 *Avoc.* If this be held the high-way to get riches,
May I be poor!

3 *Avoc.* This is not the gain, but torment.

1 *Avoc.* These possess wealth, as sick men possess fevers,
Which trulier may be said to possess them.

2 *Avoc.* Disrobe that parasite.

Corv. Mos. Most honour'd fathers!—

1 *Avoc.* Can you plead aught to stay the course of justice?
If you can, speak.

Corv. Volt. We beg favour.

Cel. And mercy.

1 *Avoc.* You hurt your innocence, suing for the guilty.
Stand forth; and first the parasite: You appear
T'have been the chiefest minister, if not plotter,
In all these lewd impostures; and now, lastly,
Have with your impudence abused the court,

And habit of a gentleman of Venice,
Being a fellow of no birth or blood:
For which our sentence is, first, thou be whipt;
Then live perpetual prisoner in our gallies.

Volp. I thank you for him.

Mos. Bane to thy wolvish nature!

1 *Avoc.* Deliver him to the saffi. [MOSCA *is carried out*]
—Thou, Volpone,
By blood and rank a gentleman, canst not fall
Under like censure; but our judgment on thee
Is, that thy substance all be straight confiscate
To the hospital of the Incurabili:
And, since the most was gotten by imposture,
By feigning lame, gout, palsy, and such diseases,
Thou art to lie in prison, cramp'd with irons,
Till thou be'st sick and lame indeed.—Remove him.

He is taken from the Bar.

Volp. This is call'd mortifying of a Fox.

1 *Avoc.* Thou, Voltore, to take away the scandal
Thou hast given all worthy men of thy profession,
Art banish'd from their fellowship, and our state.
Corbaccio!—bring him near—We here possess
Thy son of all thy state, and confine thee
To the monastery of San Spirito;
Where, since thou knewest not how to live well here,
Thou shalt be learn'd to die well.

Corb. Ah! what said he?

Com. You shall know anon, sir.

1 *Avoc.* Thou, Corvino, shalt
Be straight embark'd from thine own house, and row'd
Round about Venice, through the grand canale,
Wearing a cap, with fair long ass's ears,
Instead of horns; and so to mount, a paper
Pinn'd on thy breast, to the Berlina—

Corv. Yes,
And have mine eyes beat out with stinking fish,

Bruised fruit, and rotten eggs—'Tis well. I am glad
I shall not see my shame yet.

1 *Avoc.* And to expiate
Thy wrongs done to thy wife, thou art to send her
Home to her father, with her dowry trebled:
And these are all your judgments.

All. Honour'd fathers.—

1 *Avoc.* Which may not be revoked. Now you begin,
When crimes are done, and past, and to be punish'd,
To think what your crimes are: away with them.
Let all that see these vices thus rewarded,
Take heart and love to study 'em! Mischiefs feed
Like beasts, till they be fat, and then they bleed. *Exeunt*

VOLPONE *comes forward*

The seasoning of a play, is the applause.
Now, though the Fox be punish'd by the laws,
He yet doth hope, there is no suffering due,
For any fact which he hath done 'gainst you;
If there be, censure him; here he doubtful stands:
If not, fare jovially, and clap your hands. *Exit*

THE MAID'S TRAGEDY

by

FRANCIS BEAUMONT AND JOHN FLETCHER

THE MAID'S TRAGEDY

[ACT I, SCENE I]

[*An Apartment in the Palace*]

Enter CLEON, STRATO, LYSIPPUS, DIPHILUS

Cle. The rest are making ready, sir.
Lys. So let them;
There's time enough.
Diph. You are the brother to the King, my lord;
We'll take your word.
Lys. Strato, thou has some skill in poetry;
What think'st thou of a masque? will it be well?
Stra. As well as masques can be.
Lys. As masques can be!
Stra. Yes; they must commend their king, and speak in praise
Of the assembly, bless the bride and bridegroom
In person of some god; they're tied to rules
Of flattery.
Cle. See, good my lord, who is returned!

Enter MELANTIUS

Lys. Noble Melantius!
The land by me welcomes thy virtues home;
Thou that with blood abroad buy'st us our peace!
The breath of kings is like the breath of gods;
My brother wished thee here, and thou art here:
He will be too-too kind, and weary thee
With often welcomes; but the time doth give thee

A welcome above his or all the world's.

Mel. My lord, my thanks; but these scratched limbs of mine
Have spoke my love and truth unto my friends,
More than my tongue e'er could. My mind's the same
It ever was to you: where I find worth,
I love the keeper till he let it go,
And then I follow it.

Diph. Hail, worthy brother!
He that rejoices not at your return
In safety is mine enemy for ever.

Mel. I thank thee, Diphilus. But thou art faulty:
I sent for thee to exercise thine arms
With me at Patria; thou cam'st not, Diphilus;
'Twas ill.

Diph. My noble brother, my excuse
Is my King's strict command,—which you, my lord,
Can witness with me.

Lys. 'Tis most true, Melantius;
He might not come till the solemnities
Of this great match were past.

Diph. Have you heard of it?

Mel. Yes, and have given cause to those that here
Envy my deeds abroad to call me gamesome;
I have no other business here at Rhodes.

Lys. We have a masque to-night, and you must tread
A soldier's measure.[1]

Mel. Those soft and silken wars are not for me:
The music must be shrill and all confused
That stirs my blood; and then I dance with arms.
But is Amintor wed?

Diph. This day.

Mel. All joys upon him! for he is my friend.
Wonder not that I call a man so young my friend:
His worth is great; valiant he is and temperate;

[1] A stately dance.

And one that never thinks his life his own,
If his friend need it. When he was a boy,
As oft as I returned (as, without boast,
I brought home conquest), he would gaze upon me
And view me round, to find in what one limb
The virtue lay to do those things he heard;
Then would he wish to see my sword, and feel
The quickness of the edge, and in his hand
Weigh it: he oft would make me smile at this.
His youth did promise much, and his ripe years
Will see it all performed.—

Enter ASPATIA, *passing by*

Hail, maid and wife!
Thou fair Aspatia, may the holy knot,
That thou hast tied to-day, last till the hand
Of age undo it! may'st thou bring a race
Unto Amintor, that may fill the world
Successively with soldiers!

Asp. My hard fortunes
Deserve not scorn, for I was never proud
When they were good. *Exit* ASPATIA

Mel. How's this?

Lys. You are mistaken, sir; she is not married.

Mel. You said Amintor was.

Diph. 'Tis true; but—

Mel. Pardon me; I did receive
Letters at Patria from my Amintor,
That he should marry her.

Diph. And so it stood
In all opinion long; but your arrival
Made me imagine you had heard the change.

Mel. Who hath he taken then?

Lys. A lady, sir,
That bears the light above her,[1] and strikes dead

[1] Excels her.

With flashes of her eye; the fair Evadne,
Your virtuous sister.
Mel. Peace of heart betwixt them!
But this is strange.
Lys. The King, my brother, did it
To honor you; and these solemnities
Are at his charge.
Mel. 'Tis royal, like himself. But I am sad
My speech bears so unfortunate a sound
To beautiful Aspatia. There is rage
Hid in her father's breast, Calianax,
Bent long against me; and he should not think,
Could I but call it back, that I would take
So base revenges, as to scorn the state
Of his neglected daughter. Holds he still
His greatness with the King?
Lys. Yes. But this lady
Walks discontented, with her watery eyes
Bent on the earth. The unfrequented woods
Are her delight; where, when she sees a bank
Stuck full of flowers, she with a sigh will tell
Her servants what a pretty place it were
To bury lovers in; and make her maids
Pluck 'em, and strow her over like a corse.[1]
She carries with her an infectious grief,
That strikes all her beholders: she will sing
The mournful'st things that ever ear hath heard,
And sigh, and sing again; and when the rest
Of our young ladies, in their wanton blood,
Tell mirthful tales in course,[2] that fill the room
With laughter, she will, with so sad a look,
Bring forth a story of the silent death
Of some forsaken virgin, which her grief
Will put in such a phrase, that, ere she end,
She'll send them weeping one by one away.

[1] Corpse. [2] In turn.

Mel. She has a brother under my command,
Like her; a face as womanish as hers;
But with a spirit that hath much outgrown
The number of his years.

Enter AMINTOR

Cle. My lord the bridegroom!
Mel. I might run fiercely, not more hastily,
Upon my foe. I love thee well, Amintor;
My mouth is much too narrow for my heart;
I joy to look upon those eyes of thine;
Thou art my friend, but my disordered speech
Cuts off my love.
Amin. Thou art Melantius;
All love is spoke in that. A sacrifice,
To thank the gods Melantius is returned
In safety! Victory sits on his sword,
As she was wont: may she build there and dwell;
And may thy armor be, as it hath been,
Only thy valor and thine innocence!
What endless treasures would our enemies give,
That I might hold thee still thus!
Mel. I am poor
In words; but credit me, young man, thy mother
Could do no more but weep for joy to see thee
After long absence: all the wounds I gave
Fetched not so much away, nor all the cries
Of widowèd mothers. But this is peace,
And that was war.
Amin. Pardon, thou holy god
Of marriage-bed, and frown not, I am forced,
In answer of such noble tears as those,
To weep upon my wedding-day!
Mel. I fear thou art grown too fickle; for I hear
A lady mourns for thee; men say, to death;
Forsaken of thee; on what terms I know not.

Amin. She had my promise; but the King forbade it,
And made me make this worthy change, thy sister,
Accompanied with graces [far] above her;
With whom I long to lose my lusty youth,
And grow old in her arms.

Mel. Be prosperous!

Enter Messenger

Mess. My lord, the masquers rage for you.

Lys. We are gone.—
Cleon, Strato, Diphilus!

Amin. We'll all attend you.—

Exeunt LYSIPPUS, CLEON, STRATO, DIPHILUS

We shall trouble you
With our solemnities.

Mel. Not so, Amintor:
But if you laugh at my rude carriage
In peace, I'll do as much for you in war,
When you come thither. Yet I have a mistress
To bring to your delights; rough though I am,
I have a mistress, and she has a heart
She says; but, trust me, it is stone, no better;
There is no place that I can challenge in't.
But you stand still, and here my way lies. *Exeunt*

[SCENE II]

[*A Hall in the Palace, with a Gallery full of Spectators*]

Enter CALIANAX *with* DIAGORAS

Cal. Diagoras, look to the doors better, for shame! you let in all the world, and anon the King will rail at me. Why, very well said. By Jove, the King will have the show i' th' court.

Diag. Why do you swear so, my lord? you know he'll have it here.

Cal. By this light, if he be wise, he will not.

Diag. And if he will not be wise, you are forsworn.

Cal. One must sweat his heart out with swearing, and get thanks on no side. I'll be gone, look to't who will.

Diag. My lord, I shall never keep them out. Pray, stay; your looks will terrify them.

Cal. My looks terrify them, you coxcombly ass, you! I'll be judged by all the company whether thou hast not a worse face than I.

Diag. I mean, because they know you and your office.

Cal. Office! I would I could put it off! I am sure I sweat quite through my office. I might have made room at my daughter's wedding: they ha' near killed her amongst them; and now I must do service for him that hath forsaken her. Serve that will! *Exit* CALIANAX

Diag. He's so humorous [1] since his daughter was forsaken! [*Knock within*] Hark, hark! there, there! so, so! codes, codes! [2] What now?

Mel. [*Within*] Open the door.

Diag. Who's there?

Mel. [*Within*] Melantius.

Diag. I hope your lordship brings no troop with you; for, if you do, I must return them.[3] *Opens the door*

Enter MELANTIUS *and a* Lady

Mel. None but this lady, sir.

Diag. The ladies are all placed above, save those that come in the King's troop: the best of Rhodes sit there, and there's room.

Mel. I thank you, sir.—When I have seen you placed, madam, I must attend the King; but, the masque done, I'll wait on you again.

Diag. [*Opening another door*] Stand back there!—Room

[1] Testy.
[2] Perhaps an attenuated oath, *gods*.
[3] Turn them back.

for my lord Melantius! [*Exeunt* MELANTIUS, Lady, *other door*]—Pray, bear back—this is no place for such youths and their trulls—let the doors shut again.—No!—do your heads itch? I'll scratch them for you. [*Shuts the door*]—So, now thrust and hang. [*Knocking within*]—Again! who is't now? —I cannot blame my lord Calianax for going away: would he were here! he would run raging among them, and break a dozen wiser heads than his own in the twinkling of an eye. —What's the news now?

[*Within*] I pray you, can you help me to the speech of the master-cook?

Diag. If I open the door, I'll cook some of your calves-heads. Peace, rogues! [*Knocking within*]—Again! who is't?

Mel. [*Within*] Melantius.

Enter CALIANAX *to* MELANTIUS

Cal. Let him not in.

Diag. O, my lord, a' must.—Make room there for my lord!

Is your lady placed?

Mel. Yes, sir; I thank you.—
My lord Calianax, well met:
Your causeless hate to me I hope is burièd.

Cal. Yes, I do service for your sister here,
That brings my own poor child to timeless death:
She loves your friend Amintor; such another
False-hearted lord as you.

Mel. You do me wrong,
A most unmanly one, and I am slow
In taking vengeance; but be well advised.

Cal. It may be so.—Who placed the lady there,
So near the presence of the King?

Mel. I did.

Cal. My lord, she must not sit there.

Mel. Why?

Cal. The place
Is kept for women of more worth.
Mel. More morth than she! It misbecomes your age
And place to be thus womanish: forbear!
What you have spoke, I am content to think
The palsy shook your tongue to.
Cal. Why, 'tis well:
If I stand here to place men's wenches—
Mel. I
Shall quite forget this place, thy age, my safety,
And, through all, cut that poor sickly week
Thou hast to live away from thee!
Cal. Nay, I know you can fight for your whore.
Mel. Bate me the King,[1] and, be he flesh and blood,
A' lies that says it! Thy mother at fifteen
Was black and sinful to her.
Diag. Good my lord—
Mel. Some god pluck threescore years from that fond[2] man,
That I may kill him, and not stain mine honor!
It is the curse of soldiers, that in peace
They shall be braved by such ignoble men,
As, if the land were troubled, would with tears
And knees beg succor from 'em. Would the blood,
That sea of blood, that I have lost in fight,
Were running in thy veins, that it might make thee
Apt to say less, or able to maintain,
Should'st thou say more! This Rhodes, I see, is nought
But a place privileged to do men wrong.
Cal. Ay, you may say your pleasure.

Enter AMINTOR

Amin. What vild[3] injury
Has stirred my worthy friend, who is as slow

[1] Excepting the King.
[2] Foolish.
[3] Vile.

To fight with words as he is quick of hand?

Mel. That heap of age, which I should reverence
If it were temperate; but testy years
Are most contemptible.

Amin. Good sir, forbear.

Cal. There is just such another as yourself.

Amin. He will wrong you, or me, or any man,
And talk as if he had no life to lose,
Since this our match. The King is coming in;
I would not for more wealth than I enjoy
He should perceive you raging: he did hear
You were at difference now, which hastened him.

Cal. Make room there! *Hautboys play within*

Enter KING, EVADNE, ASPATIA, Lords *and* Ladies

King. Melantius, thou art welcome, and my love
Is with thee still: but this is not a place
To brabble [1] in.—Calianax, join hands.

Cal. He shall not have mine hand.

King. This is no time
To force you to 't. I do love you both:—
Calianax, you look well to your office;—
And you, Melantius, are welcome home.—
Begin the masque.

Mel. Sister, I joy to see you and your choice;
You looked with my eyes when you took that man:
Be happy in him! *Recorders* [2] [*play*]

Evad. O, my dearest brother,
Your presence is more joyful than this day
Can be unto me!

THE MASQUE

NIGHT *rises in mists*

Night. Our reign is come; for in the quenching sea

[1] Squabble. [2] Flageolets.

'The sun is drowned, and with him fell the Day.
Bright Cynthia, hear my voice! I am the Night,
For whom thou bear'st about thy borrowed light:
Appear! no longer thy pale visage shroud,
But strike thy silver horns quite through a cloud,
And send a beam upon my swarthy face,
By which I may discover all the place
And persons, and how many longing eyes
Are come to wait on our solemnities.

Enter CYNTHIA

How dull and black am I! I could not find
This beauty without thee, I am so blind:
Methinks they show like to those eastern streaks,
That warn us hence before the morning breaks.
Back, my pale servant! for these eyes know how
To shoot far more and quicker rays than thou.
Cynth. Great queen, they be a troop for whom alone
One of my clearest moons I have put on;
A troop, that looks as if thyself and I
Had plucked our reins in and our whips laid by,
To gaze upon these mortals, that appear
Brighter than we.
Night. Then let us keep 'em here;
And never more our chariots drive away,
But hold our places and outshine the Day.
Cynth. Great queen of shadows, you are pleased to speak
Of more than may be done: we may not break
The gods' decrees; but, when our time is come,
Must drive away, and give the Day our room.
Yet, whilst our reign lasts, let us stretch our power
To give our servants one contented hour,
With such unwonted solemn grace and state,
As may for ever after force them hate
Our brother's glorious beams, and wish the Night
Crowned with a thousand stars and our cold light:

For almost all the world their service bend
To Phœbus, and in vain my light I lend,
Gazed on unto my setting from my rise
Almost of none but of unquiet eyes.

Night. Then shine at full, fair queen, and by thy power
Produce a birth, to crown this happy hour,
Of nymphs and shepherds; let their songs discover,
Easy and sweet, who is a happy lover;
Or, if thou woo't, thine own Endymion
From the sweet flowery bank he lies upon,
On Latmus' brow, thy pale beams drawn away,
And of his long night let him make this day.

Cynth. Thou dream'st, dark queen; that fair boy was not mine,
Nor went I down to kiss him. Ease and wine
Have bred these bold tales: poets, when they rage,
Turn gods to men, and make an hour an age.
But I will give a greater state and glory,
And raise to time a nobler memory
Of what these lovers are.—Rise, rise, I say,
Thou power of deeps, thy surges laid away,
Neptune, great king of waters, and by me
Be proud to be commanded!

NEPTUNE *rises*

Nept. Cynthia, see,
Thy word hath fetched me hither: let me know
Why I ascend.

Cynth. Doth this majestic show
Give thee no knowledge yet?

Nept. Yes, now I see
Something intended, Cynthia, worthy thee.
Go on; I'll be a helper.

Cynth. Hie thee, then,
And charge the Wind fly from his rocky den,
Let loose his subjects; only Boreas,

Too foul for our intention, as he was,
Still keep him fast chained: we must have none here
But vernal blasts and gentle winds appear,
Such as blow flowers, and through the glad boughs sing
Many soft welcomes to the lusty spring;
These are our music; next, thy watery race
Bring on in couples; we are pleased to grace
This noble night, each in their richest things
Your own deeps or the broken vessel brings:
Be prodigal, and I shall be as kind
And shine at full upon you.

Nept. Ho, the wind-
Commanding Æolus!

Enter ÆOLUS *out of a Rock*

Æol. Great Neptune!

Nept. He.

Æol. What is thy will?

Nept. We do command thee free
Favonius and thy milder winds, to wait
Upon our Cynthia; but tie Boreas strait,[1]
He's too rebellious.

Æol. I shall do it.

Nept. Do. [*Exit* ÆOLUS

Æol. [*Within*] Great master of the flood and all below,
Thy full command has taken. Ho, the Main!
Neptune!

Re-enter ÆOLUS, *followed by* FAVONIUS *and other Winds*

Nept. Here.

Æol. Boreas has broke his chain,
And, struggling with the rest, has got away.

Nept. Let him alone, I'll take him up at sea;
I will not long be thence. Go once again,

[1] At once.

And call out of the bottoms of the main
Blue Proteus and the rest; charge them put on
Their greatest pearls, and the most sparkling stone
The beaten [1] rock breeds; tell this night is done
By me a solemn honor to the Moon:
Fly, like a full sail.

Æol. I am gone. *Exit*

Cynth. Dark Night,
Strike a full silence, do a thorough right
To this great chorus, that our music may
Touch high as heaven, and make the east break day
At midnight. *Music*

FIRST SONG

During which PROTEUS *and other* Sea-deities *enter*

Cynthia, to thy power and thee
We obey.
Joy to this great company!
And no day
Come to steal this night away,
Till the rites of love are ended,
And the lusty bridegroom say,
Welcome, light, of all befriended!

Pace out, you watery powers below,
Let your feet,
Like the galleys when they row,
Even beat:
Let your unknown measures, set
To the still winds, tell to all,
That gods are come, immortal, great,
To honor this great nuptial.

The Measure

[1] Beaten by the waves. Bullen explains, overlaid, embossed with gold.

SECOND SONG

Hold back thy hours, dark Night, till we have done;
The Day will come too soon:
Young maids will curse thee, if thou steal'st away,
And leav'st their losses open to the day:
Stay, stay, and hide
The blushes of the bride.

Stay, gentle Night, and with thy darkness cover
The kisses of her lover;
Stay, and confound her tears and her shrill cryings,
Her weak denials, vows, and often-dyings;
Stay, and hide all:
But help not, though she call.

Another Measure

Nept. Great queen of us and heaven, hear what I bring
To make this hour a full one.

Cynth. Speak, sea's king.

Nept. The tunes my Amphitrite joys to have,
When she will dance upon the rising wave,
And court me as she sails. My Tritons, play
Music to lay a storm! I'll lead the way.

Measure

The Masquers dance which Neptune leads

THIRD SONG

To bed, to bed! Come, Hymen, lead the bride,
And lay her by her husband's side;
Bring in the virgins every one,
That grieve to lie alone;
That they may kiss while they may say a maid;
To-morrow 'twill be other kissed and said.
Hesperus, be long a-shining,
Whilst these lovers are a-twining.

Æol. [*Within*] Ho, Neptune!

Nept. Æolus!

Re-enter ÆOLUS

Æol. The sea goes high,
Boreas hath raised a storm: go and apply
Thy trident; else, I prophesy, ere day
Many a tall ship will be cast away.
Descend with all the gods and all their power,
To strike a calm. *Exit*

Cynth. We thank you for this hour:
My favor to you all. To gradulate
So great a service, done at my desire,
Ye shall have many floods, fuller and higher
Than you have wished for; and no ebb shall dare
To let the Day see where your dwellings are.
Now back unto your governments in haste,
Lest your proud charge should swell above the waste,
And win upon the island.

Nept. We obey.

NEPTUNE *descends and the* Sea-gods

Cynth. Hold up thy head, dead Night; see'st thou not Day?
The east begins to lighten: I must down,
And give my brother place.

Night. O, I could frown
To see the Day, the Day that flings his light
Upon my kingdom and contemns old Night!
Let him go on and flame! I hope to see
Another wild-fire in his axle-tree,[1]
And all fall drenched. But I forget; speak, queen:
The Day grows on; I must no more be seen.

Cynth. Heave up thy drowsy head again, and see
A greater light, a greater majesty,

[1] The allusion is to Phaeton and his mad driving of the horses of the Sun.

Between our sect and us! whip up thy team:
The Day breaks here, and yon sun-flaring stream
Shot from the south.[1] Which way wilt thou go? say.

Night. I'll vanish into mists.

Cynth. I into Day.

Exeunt

Finis Masque

King. Take lights there!—Ladies, get the bride to bed.—
We will not see you laid; good night, Amintor;
We'll ease you of that tedious ceremony:
Were it my case, I should think time run slow.
If thou be'st noble, youth, get me a boy,
That may defend my kingdom from my foes.

Amin. All happiness to you!

King. Good night, Melantius. [*Exeunt*

[ACT II, SCENE I]

[*Ante-room to Evadne's Bedchamber*]

Enter EVADNE, ASPATIA, DULA, *and other* Ladies

Dula. Madam, shall we undress you for this fight?
The wars are nak'd that you must make to-night.

Evad. You are very merry, Dula.

Dula. I should be
Far merrier, madam, if it were with me
As it is with you.

Evad. How's that?

Dula. That I might go
To bed with him wi' th' credit that you do.

Evad. Why, how now, wench?

Dula. Come, ladies, will you help?

Evad. I am soon undone.

Dula. And as soon done:

[1] There seems an incurable corruption here.

Good store of clothes will trouble you at both.
Evad. Art thou drunk, Dula?
Dula. Why, here's none but we.
Evad. Thou think'st belike there is no modesty
When we're alone.
Dula. Ay, by my troth, you hit my thoughts aright.
Evad. You prick me, lady.
1 *Lady.* 'Tis against my will.
Dula. Anon you must endure more and lie still;
You're best to practise.
Evad. Sure, this wench is mad.
Dula. No, faith, this is a trick that I have had
Since I was fourteen.
Evad. 'Tis high time to leave it.
Dula. Nay, now I'll keep it till the trick leave me.
A dozen wanton words, put in your head,
Will make you livelier in your husband's bed.
Evad. Nay, faith, then take it.[1]
Dula. Take it, madam! where?
We all, I hope, will take it that are here.
Evad. Nay, then, I'll give you o'er.
Dula. So I will make
The ablest man in Rhodes, or his heart ache.
Evad. Wilt take my place to-night?
Dula. I'll hold your cards against any two I know.
Evad. What wilt thou do?
Dula. Madam, we'll do't, and make 'em leave play too.
Evad. Aspatia, take her part.
Dula. I will refuse it:
She will pluck down a side;[2] she does not use it.
Evad. Why, do, I prithee.
Dula. You will find the play
Quickly, because your head lies well that way.

[1] This passage is made up of a series of plays upon words connected with games of cards.
[2] Lose the game.

Evad. I thank thee, Dula. Would thou couldst instil
Some of thy mirth into Aspatia!
Nothing but sad thoughts in her breast do dwell:
Methinks, a mean betwixt you would do well.
Dula. She is in love: hang me, if I were so,
But I could run my country. I love too
To do those things that people in love do.
Asp. It was a timeless [1] smile should prove my cheek;
It were a fitter hour for me to laugh,
When at the altar the religious priest
Were pacifying the offended powers
With sacrifice, than now. This should have been
My rite; and all your hands have been employed
In giving me a spotless offering
To young Amintor's bed, as we are now
For you. Pardon, Evadne: would my worth
Were great as yours, or that the King, or he,
Or both, thought so! Perhaps he found me worthless:
But till he did so, in these ears of mine,
These credulous ears, he poured the sweetest words
That art or love could frame. If he were false,
Pardon it, heaven! and, if I did want
Virtue, you safely may forgive that too;
For I have lost none that I had from you
Evad. Nay, leave this sad talk, madam.
Asp. Would I could!
Then should I leave the cause.
Evad. See, if you have not spoiled all Dula's mirth!
Asp. Thou think'st thy heart hard; but, if thou be'st caught,
Remember me; thou shalt perceive a fire
Shot suddenly into thee.
Dula. That's not so good; let 'em shoot anything but fire,
I fear 'em not.
Asp. Well, wench, thou may'st be taken.

[1] Untimely.

Evad. Ladies, good night: I'll do the rest myself.
Dula. Nay, let your lord do some.
Asp. [*Singing*] Lay a garland on my hearse
Of the dismal yew—
Evad. That's one of your sad songs, madam.
Asp. Believe me, 'tis a very pretty one.
Evad. How is it, madam?
Asp. [*Singing*]

Lay a garland on my hearse
Of the dismal yew;
Maidens, willow-branches bear;
Say I died true.
My love was false, but I was firm
From my hour of birth:
Upon my buried body lie
Lightly, gentle earth!

Evad. Fie on't, madam! the words are so strange, they are able to make one dream of hobgoblins.—
I could never have the power—sing that, Dula.
Dula. [*Singing*]

I could never have the power
To love one above an hour,
But my heart would prompt mine eye
On some other man to fly.
Venus, fix mine eyes fast,
Or, if not, give me all that I shall see at last!

Evad. So, leave me now.
Dula. Nay, we must see you laid.
Asp. Madam, good night. May all the marriage-joys
That longing maids imagine in their beds
Prove so unto you! May no discontent
Grow 'twixt your love and you! but, if there do,

Inquire of me, and I will guide your moan;
Teach you an artificial [1] way to grieve,
To keep your sorrow waking. Love your lord
No worse than I: but, if you love so well,
Alas, you may displease him! so did I.
This is the last time you shall look on me.—
Ladies, farewell. As soon as I am dead,
Come all and watch one night about my hearse;
Bring each a mournful story and a tear,
To offer at it when I go to earth;
With flattering ivy clasp my coffin round;
Write on my brow my fortune; let my bier
Be borne by virgins, that shall sing by course [2]
The truth of maids and perjuries of men.

Evad. Alas, I pity thee. *Exit* EVADNE

All. Madam, good night.

1 *Lady.* Come, we'll let in the bridegroom.

Dula. Where's my lord?

Enter AMINTOR

1 *Lady.* Here, take this light:

Dula. You'll find her in the dark.

1 *Lady.* Your lady's scarce a-bed yet; you must help her.

Asp. Go, and be happy in your lady's love.
May all the wrongs that you have done to me
Be utterly forgotten in my death!
I'll trouble you no more; yet I will take
A parting kiss, and will not be denied.—

Kisses AMINTOR

You'll come, my lord, and see the virgins weep
When I am laid in earth, though you yourself
Can know no pity. Thus I wind myself
Into this willow-garland,[3] and am prouder

[1] Artful.
[2] In turn.
[3] Emblem of the deserted lover.

That I was once your love, though now refused,
Than to have had another true to me.
So with my prayers I leave you, and must try
Some yet unpractised way to grieve and die. *Exit* ASPATIA

Dula. Come, ladies, will you go?

All. Good night, my lord.

Amin. Much happiness unto you all! *Ladies exeunt*
I did that lady wrong. Methinks, I feel
A grief shoot suddenly through all my veins;
Mine eyes rain: this is strange at such a time.
It was the King first moved me to't; but he
Has not my will in keeping. Why do I
Perplex myself thus? Something whispers me,
Go not to bed. My guilt is not so great
As mine own conscience too sensible [1]
Would make me think; I only brake a promise,
And 'twas the King that forced me. Timorous flesh,
Why shak'st thou so? Away, my idle fears!

Enter EVADNE

Yonder she is, the luster of whose eye
Can blot away the sad remembrance
Of all these things.—O, my Evadne, spare
That tender body; let it not take cold!
The vapors of the night shall not fall here.
To bed, my love: Hymen will punish us
For being slack performers of his rites.
Camest thou to call me?

Evad. No.

Amin. Come, come, my love,
And let us lose ourselves to one another.
Why art thou up so long?

Evad. I am not well.

Amin. To bed then; let me wind thee in these arms
Till I have banished sickness.

[1] Sensitive.

Evad. Good my lord,
I cannot sleep.
Amin. Evadne, we will watch; [1]
I mean no sleeping.
Evad. I'll not go to bed.
Amin. I prithee, do.
Evad. I will not for the world.
Amin. Why, my dear love?
Evad. Why! I have sworn I will not.
Amin. Sworn!
Evad. Ay,
Amin. How? sworn, Evadne!
Evad. Yes, sworn, Amintor; and will swear again,
If you will wish to hear me.
Amin. To whom have you sworn this?
Evad. If I should name him, the matter were not great.
Amin. Come, this is but the coyness of a bride.
Evad. The coyness of a bride!
Amin. How prettily
That frown becomes thee!
Evad. Do you like it so?
Amin. Thou canst not dress thy face in such a look
But I shall like it.
Evad. What look likes you best?
Amin. Why do you ask?
Evad. That I may show you one less pleasing to you.
Amin. How's that?
Evad. That I may show you one less pleasing to you.
Amin. I prithee, put thy jests in milder looks;
It shows as thou wert angry.
Evad. So perhaps
I am indeed.
Amin. Why, who has done thee wrong?
Name me the man, and by thyself I swear,
Thy yet-unconquered self, I will revenge thee!

[1] Wake.

Evad. Now I shall try thy truth. If thou dost love me,
Thou weigh'st not any thing compared with me:
Life, honor, joys eternal, all delights
This world can yield, or hopeful people feign,
Or in the life to come, are light as air
To a true lover when his lady frowns,
And bids him *do this.* Wilt thou kill this man?
Swear, my Amintor, and I'll kiss the sin
Off from thy lips.

Amin. I wo' not swear, sweet love,
Till I do know the cause.

Evad. I would thou wouldst.
Why, it is thou that wrong'st me; I hate thee;
Thou should'st have killed thyself.

Amin. If I should know that, I should quickly kill
The man you hated.

Evad. Know it, then, and do't.

Amin. O, no! what look soe'er thou shalt put on
To try my faith, I shall not think thee false;
I cannot find one blemish in thy face,
Where falsehood should abide. Leave, and to bed.
If you have sworn to any of the virgins
That were your old companions to preserve
Your maidenhead a night, it may be done
Without this means.

Evad. A maidenhead, Amintor,
At my years!

Amin. Sure she raves; this cannot be
Her natural temper.—Shall I call thy maids?
Either thy healthful sleep hath left thee long,
Or else some fever rages in thy blood.

Evad. Neither, Amintor: think you I am mad,
Because I speak the truth?

Amin. Is this the truth?
Will you not lie with me to-night?

Evad. To-night!

You talk as if you thought I would hereafter.

Amin. Hereafter! yes, I do.

Evad. You are deceived.
Put off amazement, and with patience mark
What I shall utter, for the oracle
Knows nothing truer: 'tis not for a night
Or two that I forbear thy bed, but ever.

Amin. I dream. Awake, Amintor!

Evad. You hear right:
I sooner will find out the beds of snakes,
And with my youthful blood warm their cold flesh,
Letting them curl themselves about my limbs,
Than sleep one night with thee. This is not feigned,
Nor sounds it like the coyness of a bride.

Amin. Is flesh so earthly to endure all this?
Are these the joys of marriage?—Hymen, keep
This story (that will make succeeding youth
Neglect thy ceremonies) from all ears;
Let it not rise up, for thy shame and mine
To after-ages: we will scorn thy laws,
If thou no better bless them. Touch the heart
Of her that thou hast sent me, or the world
Shall know this: not an altar then will smoke
In praise of thee; we will adopt us sons;
Then virtue shall inherit, and not blood.
If we do lust, we'll take the next we meet,
Serving ourselves as other creatures do;
And never take note of the female more,
Nor of her issue. I do rage in vain;
She can but jest.—O, pardon me, my love!
So dear the thoughts are that I hold of thee,
That I must break forth. Satisfy my fear;
It is a pain, beyond the hand of death,
To be in doubt: confirm it with an oath,
If this be true.

Evad. Do you invent the form:

Let there be in it all the binding words
Devils and conjurers can put together,
And I will take it. I have sworn before,
And here by all things holy do again,
Never to be acquainted with thy bed!
Is your doubt over now?

Amin. I know too much; would I had doubted still!
Was ever such a marriage-night as this!
You powers above, if you did ever mean
Man should be used thus, you have thought a way
How he may bear himself, and save his honor:
Instruct me in it; for to my dull eyes
There is no mean, no moderate course to run;
I must live scorned, or be a murderer:
Is there a third? Why is this night so calm?
Why does not heaven speak in thunder to us,
And drown her voice?

Evad. This rage will do no good.

Amin. Evadne, hear me. Thou hast ta'en an oath,
But such a rash one, that to keep it were
Worse than to swear it: call it back to thee;
Such vows as that never ascend the heaven;
A tear or two will wash it quite away.
Have mercy on my youth, my hopeful youth,
If thou be pitiful! for, without boast,
This land was proud of me: what lady was there,
That men called fair and virtuous in this isle,
That would have shunned my love? It is in thee
To make me hold this worth.—O, we vain men,
That trust out all our reputation
To rest upon the weak and yielding hand
Of feeble woman! But thou art not stone;
Thy flesh is soft, and in thine eyes doth dwell
The spirit of love; thy heart cannot be hard.
Come, lead me from the bottom of despair
To all the joys thou hast; I know thou wilt;

And make me careful lest the sudden change
O'ercome my spirits.

Evad. When I call back this oath,
The pains of hell environ me!

Amin. I sleep, and am too temperate. Come to bed!
Or by those hairs, which, if thou hadst a soul
Like to thy locks, were threads for kings to wear
About their arms—

Evad. Why, so perhaps they are.

Amin. I'll drag thee to my bed, and make thy tongue
Undo this wicked oath, or on thy flesh
I'll print a thousand wounds to let out life!

Evad. I fear thee not: do what thou darest to me!
Every ill-sounding word or threatening look
Thou showest to me will be revenged at full.

Amin. It will not sure, Evadne?

Evad. Do not you hazard that.

Amin. Ha' ye your champions?

Evad. Alas, Amintor, think'st thou I forbear
To sleep with thee, because I have put on
A maiden's strictness? Look upon these cheeks,
And thou shalt find the hot and rising blood
Unapt for such a vow. No; in this heart
There dwells as much desire and as much will
To put that wished act in practice as ever yet
Was known to woman; and they have been shown
Both. But it was the folly of thy youth
To think this beauty, to what hand soe'er
It shall be called, shall stoop [1] to any second.
I do enjoy the best, and in that height
Have sworn to stand or die: you guess the man.

Amin. No; let me know the man that wrongs me so,
That I may cut his body into motes,
And scatter it before the northern wind.

Evad. You dare not strike him.

[1] As a hawk.

Amin. Do not wrong me so:
Yes, if his body were a poisonous plant
That it were death to touch, I have a soul
Will throw me on him.
Evad. Why, 'tis the King.
Amin. The King!
Evad. What will you do now?
Amin. It is not the King!
Evad. What did he make this match for, dull Amintor?
Amin. O, thou hast named a word that wipes away
All thoughts revengeful! In that sacred name,
'The King,' there lies a terror: what frail man
Dares lift his hand against it? Let the gods
Speak to him when they please: till when, let us
Suffer and wait.
Evad. Why should you fill yourself so full of heat,
And haste so to my bed? I am no virgin.
Amin. What devil put it in thy fancy, then,
To marry me?
Evad. Alas, I must have one
To father children, and to bear the name
Of husband to me, that my sin may be
More honorable!
Amin. What strange thing am I!
Evad. A miserable one; one that myself
Am sorry for.
Amin. Why, show it then in this:
If thou hast pity, though thy love be none,
Kill me; and all true lovers, that shall live
In after ages crossed in their desires,
Shall bless thy memory, and call thee good,
Because such mercy in thy heart was found,
To rid [1] a lingering wretch.
Evad. I must have one
To fill thy room again, if thou wert dead;

[1] Slay.

Else, by this night, I would! I pity thee.
Amin. These strange and sudden injuries have fallen
So thick upon me, that I lose all sense
Of what they are. Methinks, I am not wronged;
Nor is it aught, if from the censuring world
I can but hide it. Reputation,
Thou art a word, no more!—But thou hast shown
An impudence so high, that to the world
I fear thou wilt betray or shame thyself.
Evad. To cover shame, I took thee; never fear
That I would blaze [1] myself.
Amin. Nor let the King
Know I conceive he wrongs me; then mine honor
Will thrust me into action: that my flesh
Could bear with patience. And it is some ease
To me in these extremes, that I knew this
Before I touched thee; else, had all the sins
Of mankind stood betwixt me and the King,
I had gone through 'em to his heart and thine.
I have left one desire: 'tis not his crown
Shall buy me to thy bed, now I resolve
He has dishonored thee. Give me thy hand:
Be careful of thy credit, and sin close; [2]
'Tis all I wish. Upon thy chamber-floor
I'll rest to-night, that morning visitors
May think we did as married people use:
And, prithee, smile upon me when they come,
And seem to toy, as if thou hadst been pleased
With what we did.
Evad. Fear not; I will do this
Amin. Come, let us practise; and, as wantonly
As ever longing bride and bridegroom met,
Let's laugh and enter here.
Evad. I am content.

[1] Declare.
[2] Secretly.

Amin. Down all the swellings of my troubled heart!
When we walk thus intwined, let all eyes see
If ever lovers better did agree. *Exeunt*

[SCENE II]

[*An Apartment in the House of Calianax*]

Enter ASPATIA, ANTIPHILA, *and* OLYMPIAS

Asp. Away, you are not sad! force it no further.
Good gods, how well you look! Such a full color
Young bashful brides put on: sure, you are new married!
Ant. Yes, madam, to your grief.
Asp. Alas, poor wenches!
Go learn to love first; learn to lose yourselves;
Learn to be flattered, and believe and bless
The double tongue that did it; make a faith
Out of the miracles of ancient lovers,
Such as spake truth, and died in't; and, like me,
Believe all faithful, and be miserable.
Did you ne'er love yet, wenches ? Speak, Olympias;
Thou hast an easy temper, fit for stamp.
Olym. Never.
Asp. Nor you, Antiphila?
Ant. Nor I.
Asp. Then, my good girls, be more than women, wise;
At least be more than I was; and be sure
You credit any thing the light gives life to,
Before a man. Rather believe the sea
Weeps for the ruined merchant, when he roars;
Rather, the wind courts but the pregnant sails,
When the strong cordage cracks; rather, the sun
Comes but to kiss the fruit in wealthy autumn,
When all falls blasted. If you needs must love,
(Forced by ill fate,) take to your maiden-bosoms

Two dead-cold aspics,[1] and of them make lovers:
They cannot flatter nor forswear; one kiss
Makes a long peace for all. But man.—
O, that beast man! Come, let's be sad, my girls:
That down-cast of thine eyes, Olympias,
Shows a fine sorrow.—Mark, Antiphila;
Just such another was the nymph Œnone's,
When Paris brought home Helen.—Now, a tear;
And then thou art a piece expressing fully
The Carthage-queen, when from a cold sea-rock,
Full with her sorrow, she tied fast her eyes
To the fair Trojan ships; and, having lost them,
Just as thine eyes do, down stole a tear.—Antiphila,
What would this wench do, if she were Aspatia?
Here she would stand, till some more pitying god
Turned her to marble.—'Tis enough, my wench.—
Show me the piece of needlework you wrought.

Ant. Of Ariadne,[2] madam?

Asp. Yes, that piece.—
This should be Theseus; h'as a cozening[3] face.—
You meant him for a man?

Ant. He was so, madam.

Asp. Why, then, 'tis well enough.—Never look back;
You have a full wind and a false heart, Theseus.—
Does not the story say, his keel was split,
Or his masts spent, or some kind rock or other
Met with his vessel?

Ant. Not as I remember.

Asp. It should ha' been so. Could the gods know this,
And not, of all their number, raise a storm?
But they are all as evil. This false smile
Was well expressed; just such another caught me.—
You shall not go so.[4]—

[1] Asps.
[2] Deserted by Theseus. [3] Deceiving.
[4] Addressing the embroidered image of Theseus.

Antiphila, in this place work a quicksand,
And over it a shallow smiling water,
And his ship ploughing it; and then a Fear;
Do that Fear to the life, wench.

Ant. 'Twill wrong the story.

Asp. 'Twill make the story, wronged by wanton poets,
Live long and be believed. But where's the lady?

Ant. There, madam.

Asp. Fie, you have missed it here, Antiphila;
You are much mistaken, wench:
These colors are not dull and pale enough
To show a soul so full of misery
As this sad lady's was. Do it by me,
Do it again by me, the lost Aspatia;
And you shall find all true but the wild island.
Suppose I stand upon the sea-beach now,
Mine arms thus, and mine hair blown with the wind,
Wild as that desert; and let all about me
Tell that I am forsaken. Do my face
(If thou hadst ever feeling of a sorrow)
Thus, thus, Antiphila: strive to make me look
Like Sorrow's monument; and the trees about me,
Let them be dry and leafless; let the rocks
Groan with continual surges; and behind me,
Make all a desolation. See, see, wenches,
A miserable life [1] of this poor picture!

Olym. Dear madam!

Asp. I have done. Sit down; and let us
Upon that point fix all our eyes, that point there.
Make a dull silence, till you feel a sudden sadness
Give us new souls.

Enter CALIANAX

Cal. The King may do this, and he may not do it:
My child is wronged, disgraced.—Well, how now, huswives?

[1] A miserable example of life.

What, at your ease! is this a time to sit still?
Up, you young lazy whores, up, or I'll swinge you!

Olym. Nay, good my lord—

Cal. You'll lie down shortly. Get you in, and work!
What, are you grown so resty [1] you want heats?
We shall have some of the court-boys heat you shortly.

Ant. My lord, we do no more than we are charged:
It is the lady's pleasure we be thus;
In grief she is forsaken.

Cal. There's a rogue too.
A young dissembling slave!—Well, get you in.—
I'll have a bout with that boy. 'Tis high time
Now to be valiant: I confess my youth
Was never prone that way. What, made an ass!
A court-stale! [2] Well, I will be valiant,
And beat some dozen of these whelps; I will!
And there's another of 'em, a trim cheating soldier,[3]
I'll maul that rascal; h'as out-braved me twice:
But now, I thank the gods, I am valiant.—
Go, get you in.—I'll take a course with all.

Exeunt omnes

[ACT III, SCENE I]

[*Ante-room to Evadne's Bedchamber*]

Enter CLEON, STRATO, *and* DIPHILUS

Cle. Your sister is not up yet.

Diph. O, brides must take their morning's rest; the night is troublesome.

Stra. But not tedious.

Diph. What odds, he has not my sister's maidenhead to-night?

[1] Restless.
[2] A laughing-stock.
[3] Melantius.

Stra. None; it's odds against any bridegroom living, he ne'er gets it while he lives.

Diph. Y'are merry with my sister; you'll please to allow me the same freedom with your mother.

Stra. She's at your service.

Diph. Then she's merry enough of herself; she needs no tickling. Knock at the door.

Stra. We shall interrupt them.

Diph. No matter; they have the year before them.—Goor morrow, sister. Spare yourself to-day; the night will come again.

Enter AMINTOR

Amin. Who's there? my brother! I'm no readier yet.
Your sister is but now up.

Diph. You look as you had lost your eyes to-night: I think you ha' not slept.

Amin. I'faith I have not.

Diph. You have done better, then.

Amin. We ventured for a boy; when he is twelve,
'A shall command against the foes of Rhodes.
Shall we be merry?

Stra. You cannot; you want sleep.

Amin. 'Tis true;—[*Aside*] but she,
As if she had drunk Lethe, or had made
Even with heaven, did fetch so still a sleep,
So sweet and sound—

Diph. What's that?

Amin. Your sister frets
This morning, and does turn her eyes upon me,
As people on their headsman. She does chafe,
And kiss, and chafe again, and clap my cheeks!
She's in another world.

Diph. Then I had lost: I was about to lay
You had not got her maidenhead to-night.

Amin. [*Aside*] Ha! does he not mock me?—Y'ad lost indeed;
I do not use to bungle.

Cle. You do deserve her.

Amin. [*Aside*] I laid my lips to hers, and that wild breath,
That was so rude and rough to me last night,
Was sweet as April. I'll be guilty too,
If these be the effects.—

Enter MELANTIUS

Mel. Good day, Amintor; for to me the name
Of brother is too distant: we are friends,
And that is nearer.

Amin. Dear Melantius!
Let me behold thee.—Is it possible?

Mel. What sudden gaze is this?

Amin. 'Tis wondrous strange!

Mel. Why does thine eye desire so strict a view
Of that it knows so well? There's nothing here
That is not thine.

Amin. I wonder much, Melantius,
To see those noble looks, that make me think
How virtuous thou art: and, on the sudden,
'Tis strange to me thou shouldst have worth and honor;
Or not be base, and false, and treacherous,
And every ill. But—

Mel. Stay, stay, my friend;
I fear this sound will not become our loves:
No more embrace me.

Amin. O, mistake me not!
I know thee to be full of all those deeds
That we frail men call good; but by the course
Of nature thou shouldst be as quickly changed
As are the winds; dissembling as the sea,
That now wears brows as smooth as virgins' be,
Tempting the merchant to invade his face,

And in an hour calls his billows up,
And shoots 'em at the sun, destroying all
'A carries on him.—[*Aside*] O, how near am I
To utter my sick thoughts!—

Mel. But why, my friend, should I be so by nature?

Amin. I have wed thy sister, who hath virtuous thoughts
Enough for one whole family; and it is strange
That you should feel no want.

Mel. Believe me, this is compliment too cunning for me.

Diph. What should I be then by the course of nature,
They having both robbed me of so much virtue?

Stra. O, call the bride, my lord Amintor,
That we may see her blush, and turn her eyes down:
It is the prettiest sport!

Amin. Evadne!

Evad. [*Within*] My lord?

Amin. Come forth, my love:
Your brothers do attend to wish you joy.

Evad. I am not ready yet.

Amin. Enough, enough.

Evad. They'll mock me.

Amin. Faith, thou shalt come in

Enter EVADNE

Mel. Good morrow, sister. He that understands
Whom you have wed, need not to wish you joy;
You have enough: take heed you be not proud.

Diph. O, sister, what have you done?

Evad. I done! why, what have I done?

Stra. My lord Amintor swears you are no maid now.

Evad. Pish!

Stra. I'faith, he does.

Evad. I knew I should be mocked.

Diph. With a truth.

Evad. If 'twere to do again, in faith I would not marry.

Amin. [*Aside*] Nor I, by heaven!—

Diph. Sister, Dula swears she heard you cry two rooms off.

Evad. Fie, how you talk!

Diph. Let's see you walk, Evadne. By my troth y'are spoiled.

Mel. Amintor—

Amin. Ha!

Mel. Thou art sad.

Amin. Who, I? I thank you for that.
Shall Diphilus, thou, and I, sing a catch?

Mel. How!

Amin. Prithee, let's.

Mel. Nay, that's too much the other way.

Amin. I'm so lightened with my happiness!—
How dost thou, love? kiss me.

Evad. I cannot love you, you tell tales of me.

Amin. Nothing but what becomes us.—Gentlemen,
Would you had all such wives, and all the world,
That I might be no wonder! Y'are all sad:
What, do you envy me? I walk, methinks,
On water, and ne'er sink, I am so light.

Mel. 'Tis well you are so.

Amin. Well! how can I be other, when she looks thus?
Is there no music there? Let's dance.

Mel. Why, this is strange, Amintor!

Amin. I do not know myself; yet I could wish
My joy were less.

Diph. I'll marry too, if it will make one thus.

Evad. [*Aside*] Amintor, hark.

Amin. What says my love? I must obey.—

Evad. You do it scurvily, 'twill be perceived.

Cle. My lord, the King is here.

Enter King *and* Lysippus

Amin. Where?

Stra. And his brother.

King. Good morrow, all!—
Amintor, joy on joy fall thick upon thee!—
And, madam, you are altered since I saw you;
(I must salute you) you are now another's.
How liked you your night's rest?

Evad. Ill, sir.

Amin. Indeed she took but little.

Lys. You'll let her take more, and thank her too, shortly.

King. Amintor, wert thou truly honest till thou wert married?

Amin. Yes, sir.

King. Tell me, then, how shows the sport unto thee?

Amin. Why, well.

King. What did you do?

Amin. No more, nor less, than other couples use;
You know what 'tis; it has but a coarse name.

King. But prithee, I should think, by her black eye,
And her red cheek, she would be quick and stirring
In this same business; ha?

Amin. I cannot tell;
I ne'er tried other, sir; but I perceive
She is as quick as you delivered.[1]

King. Well, you'll trust me then, Amintor,
To choose a wife for you again?

Amin. No, never, sir.

King. Why, like you this so ill?

Amin. So well I like her.
For this I bow my knee in thanks to you,
And unto heaven will pay my grateful tribute
Hourly; and do hope we shall draw out
A long contented life together here,
And die, both, full of grey hairs, in one day:
For which the thanks is yours. But if the powers
That rule us please to call her first away,
Without pride spoke, this world holds not a wife

[1] As alive as you have said.

Worthy to take her room.

King. [*Aside*] I do not like this.
All forbear the room, but you, Amintor,
And your lady. [*Exeunt all but the* KING, AMINTOR, *and* EVADNE] I have some speech with you,
That may concern your after living well.

Amin. [*Aside*] 'A will not tell me that he lies with her?
If he do, something heavenly stay my heart,
For I shall be apt to thrust this arm of mine
To acts unlawful!—

King. You will suffer me
To talk with her, Amintor, and not have
A jealous pang?

Amin. Sir, I dare trust my wife
With whom she dares to talk, and not be jealous. [*Retires*

King. How do you like Amintor?

Evad. As I did, sir.

King. How's that?

Evad. As one that, to fulfil your will and pleasure,
I have given leave to call me wife and love.

King. I see there is no lasting faith in sin;
They that break word with heaven will break again
With all the world, and so dost thou with me.

Evad. How, sir?

King. This subtle woman's ignorance
Will not excuse you: thou hast taken oaths,
So great, methought they did not well become
A woman's mouth, that thou wouldst ne'er enjoy
A man but me.

Evad. I never did swear so;
You do me wrong.

King. Day and night have heard it.

Evad. I swore indeed that I would never love
A man of lower place; but, if your fortune
Should throw you from this height, I bade you trust
I would forsake you, and would bend to him

That won your throne: I love with my ambition,
Not with my eyes. But, if I ever yet
Touched any other, leprosy light here
Upon my face! which for your royalty
I would not stain!

King. Why, thou dissemblest, and it is in me
To punish thee.

Evad. Why, it is in me, then,
Not to love you, which will more afflict
Your body than your punishment can mine.

King. But thou hast let Amintor lie with thee.

Evad. I ha' not.

King. Impudence! he says himself so.

Evad. 'A lies.

King. 'A does not.

Evad. By this light, he does,
Strangely and basely! and I'll prove it so:
I did not only shun him for a night,
But told him I would never close with him.

King. Speak lower; 'tis false.

Evad. I am no man
To answer with a blow; or, if I were,
You are the King. But urge me not; 'tis most true.

King. Do not I know the uncontrollèd thoughts
That youth brings with him, when his blood is high
With expectation and desire of that
He long hath waited for? Is not his spirit,
Though he be temperate, of a valiant strain
As this our age hath known? What could he do,
If such a sudden speech had met his blood,
But ruin thee for ever, if he had not killed thee?
He could not bear it thus: he is as we,
Or any other wronged man.

Evad. It is dissembling.

King. Take him! farewell: henceforth I am thy foe;
And what disgraces I can blot thee with look for.

Evad. Stay, sir!—Amintor!—You shall hear.—Amintor!
Amin. What, my love?
Evad. Amintor, thou hast an ingenious [1] look,
And shouldst be virtuous: it amazeth me
That thou canst make such base malicious lies!
Amin. What, my dear wife?
Evad. 'Dear wife!' I do despise thee.
Why, nothing can be baser than to sow
Dissension amongst lovers.
Amin. Lovers! who?
Evad. The King and me—
Amin. O, God!
Evad. Who should live long, and love without distaste,
Were it not for such pickthanks [2] as thyself.
Did you lie with me? swear now, and be punished
In hell for this!
Amin. The faithless sin I made
To fair Aspatia is not yet revenged;
It follows me.—I will not lose a word
To this vild [3] woman: but to you, my King,
The anguish of my soul thrusts out this truth,
Y' are a tyrant! and not so much to wrong
An honest man thus, as to take a pride
In talking with him of it.
Evad. Now, sir, see
How loud this fellow lied!
Amin. You that can know to wrong, should know how men
Must right themselves. What punishment is due
From me to him that shall abuse my bed?
Is it not death? nor can that satisfy,
Unless I show how nobly I have freed myself.
King. Draw not thy sword; thou knowest I cannot fear
A subject's hand; but thou shalt feel the weight
Of this, if thou dost rage.

[1] Ingenuous. [2] Tale-bearers. [3] Vile.

Amin. The weight of that!
If you have any worth, for heaven's sake, think
I fear not swords; for, as you are mere man,
I dare as easily kill you for this deed,
As you dare think to do it. But there is
Divinity about you, that strikes dead
My rising passions: as you are my king,
I fall before you, and present my sword
To cut mine own flesh, if it be your will.
Alas, I am nothing but a multitude
Of walking griefs! Yet, should I murder you,
I might before the world take the excuse
Of madness: for, compare my injuries,
And they will well appear too sad a weight
For reason to endure: but, fall I first
Amongst my sorrows, ere my treacherous hand
Touch holy things! But why (I know not what
I have to say), why did you choose out me
To make thus wretched? there were thousands, fools
Easy to work on, and of state enough,
Within the island.

Evad. I would not have a fool;
It were no credit for me.

Amin. Worse and worse!
Thou, that darest talk unto thy husband thus,
Profess thyself a whore, and, more than so,
Resolve to be so still!—It is my fate
To bear and bow beneath a thousand griefs,
To keep that little credit with the world.—
But there were wise ones too; you might have ta'en
Another.

King. No: for I believed thee honest,
As thou wert valiant.

Amin. All the happiness
Bestowed upon me turns into disgrace.
Gods, take your honesty again, for I

Am loaden with it!—Good my lord the King,
Be private in it.
King. Thou mayst live, Amintor,
Free as thy king, if thou wilt wink at this,
And be a means that we may meet in secret.
Amin. A bawd! Hold, hold, my breast! A bitter curse
Seize me, if I forget not all respects
That are religious, on another word
Sounded like that; and through a sea of sins
Will wade to my revenge, though I should call
Pains here and after life upon my soul!
King. Well, I am resolute you lay not with her;
And so I leave you. *Exit* KING
Evad. You must needs be prating;
And see what follows!
Amin. Prithee, vex me not:
Leave me; I am afraid some sudden start
Will pull a murther on me.
Evad. I am gone;
I love my life well. *Exit* EVADNE
Amin. I hate mine as much.
This 'tis to break a troth! I should be glad,
If all this tide of grief would make me mad. *Exit*

[SCENE II]

[*A Room in the Palace*]

Enter MELANTIUS

Mel. I'll know the cause of all Amintor's griefs,
Or friendship shall be idle.

Enter CALIANAX

Cal. O Melantius,
My daughter will die!
Mel. Trust me, I am sorry:

Would thou hadst ta'en her room! [1]

Cal. Thou art a slave,
A cut-throat slave, a bloody treacherous slave!

Mel. Take heed, old man; thou wilt be heard to rave,
And lose thine offices.

Cal. I am valiant grown
At all these years, and thou art but a slave!

Mel. Leave!
Some company will come, and I respect
Thy years, not thee, so much, that I could wish
To laugh at thee alone.

Cal. I'll spoil your mirth:
I mean to fight with thee. There lie, my cloak.
This was my father's sword, and he durst fight.
Are you prepared?

Mel. Why wilt thou dote thyself
Out of thy life? Hence, get thee to bed;
Have careful looking-to, and eat warm things,
And trouble not me: my head is full of thoughts
More weighty than thy life or death can be.

Cal. You have a name in war, where you stand safe
Amongst a multitude; but I will try
What you dare do unto a weak old man
In single fight. You'll give ground, I fear.
Come draw.

Mel. I will not draw, unless thou pull'st thy death
Upon thee with a stroke. There's no one blow,
That thou canst give hath strength enough to kill me.
Tempt me not so far, then: the power of earth
Shall not redeem thee.—

Cal. [*Aside*] I must let him alone;
He's stout and able; and, to say the truth,
However I may set a face and talk,
I am not valiant. When I was a youth,
I kept my credit with a testy trick [2]

[1] Taken her place. [2] Trick of testiness.

I had 'mongst cowards, but durst never fight.—

Mel. I will not promise to preserve your life,
If you do stay.—

Cal. [*Aside*] I would give half my land
That I durst fight with that proud man a little:
If I had men to hold him, I would beat him
Till he asked me mercy.—

Mel. Sir, will you be gone?—

Cal. [*Aside*] I dare not stay; but I will go home, and beat
My servants all over for this. *Exit*

Mel. This old fellow haunts me.
But the distracted carriage of mine Amintor
Takes deeply on me.[1] I will find the cause:
I fear his conscience cries, he wronged Aspatia.

Enter AMINTOR

Amin. [*Aside*] Men's eyes are not so subtle to perceive
My inward misery: I bear my grief
Hid from the world. How art thou wretched then?
For aught I know, all husbands are like me;
And every one I talk with of his wife
Is but a well dissembler of his woes,
As I am. Would I knew it! for the rareness
Afflicts me now.

Mel. Amintor, we have not enjoyed our friendship of late; for we were wont to change our souls in talk.

Amin. Melantius, I can tell thee a good jest of Strato and a lady the last day.

Mel. How was't?

Amin. Why, such an odd one!

Mel. I have longed to speak with you; not of an idle jest, that's forced, but of matter you are bound to utter to me.

Amin. What is that, my friend?

Mel. I have observed your words fall from your tongue

[1] Deeply affects me.

Wildly; and all your carriage
Like one that strove to show his merry mood,
When he were ill-disposed: you were not wont
To put such scorn into your speech, or wear
Upon your face ridiculous jollity.
Some sadness sits here, which your cunning would
Cover o'er with smiles, and 'twill not be. What is it?

Amin. A sadness here, [Melantius!] what cause
Can fate provide for me to make me so?
Am I not loved through all this isle? The King
Rains greatness on me. Have I not received
A lady to my bed, that in her eye
Keeps mounting fire, and on her tender cheeks
Inevitable color,[1] in her heart
A prison for all virtue? Are not you,
Which is above all joys, my constant friend?
What sadness can I have? No; I am light,
And feel the courses of my blood more warm
And stirring than they were. Faith, marry too;
And you will feel so unexpressed a joy
In chaste embraces, that you will indeed
Appear another.

Mel. You may shape, Amintor,
Causes to cozen [2] the whole world withal,
And yourself too; but 'tis not like a friend
To hide your soul from me. 'Tis not your nature
To be thus idle: I have seen you stand
As you were blasted 'midst of all your mirth;
Call thrice aloud, and then start, feigning joy
So coldly!—World, what do I here? a friend
Is nothing. Heaven, I would ha' told that man
My secret sins! I'll search an unknown land,
And there plant friendship; all is withered here.
Come with a compliment! I would have fought,

[1] Irresistible.
[2] Deceive.

Or told my friend 'a lied, ere soothed [1] him so.
Out of my bosom!

Amin. But there is nothing.

Mel. Worse and worse! farewell:
From this time have acquaintance, but no friend.

Amin. Melantius, stay: you shall know what that is.

Mel. See, how you played with friendship! be advised
How you give cause unto yourself to say
You ha' lost a friend.

Amin. Forgive what I ha' done;
For I am so o'ergone with injuries
Unheard of, that I lose consideration
Of what I ought to do,—O!—O!

Mel. Do not weep. What is't?
May I once but know the man
Hath turned my friend thus!

Amin. I had spoke at first,
But that —

Mel. But what?

Amin. I held it most unfit
For you to know. Faith, do not know it yet.

Mel. Thou see'st my love, that will keep company
With thee in tears; hide nothing, then, from me;
For when I know the cause of thy distemper,
With mine old armor I'll adorn myself,
My resolution, and cut through thy foes,
Unto thy quiet, till I place thy heart
As peaceable as spotless innocence.
What is it?

Amin. Why, 'tis this—it is too big
To get out—let my tears make way awhile.

Mel. Punish me strangely, heaven, if he scape
Of life or fame, that brought this youth to this!

Amin. Your sister—

Mel. Well said.

[1] Deceived.

Amin. You'll wish't unknown, when you have heard it.
Mel. No.
Amin. Is much to blame,
And to the King has given her honor up,
And lives in whoredom with him.
Mel. How is this?
Thou art run mad with injury indeed;
Thou couldst not utter this else. Speak again;
For I forgive it freely; tell thy griefs.
Amin. She's wanton: I am loath to say, a whore,
Though it be true.
Mel. Speak yet again, before mine anger grow
Up beyond throwing down: what are thy griefs?
Amin. By all our friendship, these.
Mel. What, am I tame?
After mine actions, shall the name of friend
Blot all our family, and strike the brand
Of whore upon my sister, unrevenged?
My shaking flesh, be thou a witness for me,
With what unwillingness I go to scourge
This railer, whom my folly hath called friend!—
I will not take thee basely: thy sword [*Draws his sword*
Hangs near thy hand; draw it, that I may whip
Thy rashness to repentance; draw thy sword!
Amin. Not on thee, did thine anger swell as high
As the wild surges. Thou shouldst do me ease
Here and eternally, if thy noble hand
Would cut me from my sorrows.
Mel. This is base
And fearful. They that use to utter lies
Provide not blows but words to qualify [1]
The men they wronged. Thou hast a guilty cause.
Amin. Thou pleasest me; for so much more like this
Will raise my anger up above my griefs,
(Which is a passion easier to be borne,)

[1] Mollify.

And I shall then be happy.
Mel. Take, then, more
To raise thine anger: 'tis mere cowardice
Makes thee not draw; and I will leave thee dead,
However. But if thou art so much pressed
With guilt and fear as not to dare to fight,
I'll make thy memory loathed, and fix a scandal
Upon thy name for ever.
Amin. [*Drawing his sword*] Then I draw,
As justly as our magistrates their swords
To cut offenders off. I knew before
'Twould grate your ears; but it was base in you
To urge a weighty secret from your friend,
And then rage at it. I shall be at ease,
If I be killed; and, if you fall by me,
I shall not long outlive you.
Mel. Stay awhile.—
The name of friend is more than family,
Or all the world besides: I was a fool.
Thou searching human nature, that didst wake
To do me wrong, thou art inquisitive,
And thrusts me upon questions that will take
My sleep away! Would I had died, ere known
This sad dishonor!—Pardon me, my friend.
Sheathes his sword
If thou wilt strike, here is a faithful heart;
Pierce it, for I will never heave my hand
To thine. Behold the power thou hast in me!
I do believe my sister is a whore,
A leprous one. Put up thy sword, young man.
Amin. How should I bear it, then, she being so?
I fear, my friend, that you will lose me shortly;
Sheathes his sword
And I shall do a foul act on myself
Through these disgraces.
Mel. Better half the land

Were buried quick [1] together. No, Amintor;
Thou shalt have ease. O, this adulterous king,
That drew her to't; where got he the spirit
To wrong me so?

Amin. What is it, then, to me,
If it be wrong to you?

Mel. Why, not so much:
The credit of our house is thrown away.
But from his iron den I'll waken Death,
And hurl him on this king: my honesty
Shall steel my sword; and on its horrid point
I'll wear my cause, that shall amaze the eyes
Of this proud man, and be too glittering
For him to look on.

Amin. I have quite undone my fame.

Mel. Dry up thy watery eyes,
And cast a manly look upon my face;
For nothing is so wild as I thy friend
Till I have freed thee: still this swelling breast.
I go thus from thee, and will never cease
My vengeance till I find thy heart at peace.

Amin. It must not be so. Stay. Mine eyes would tell
How loath I am to this; but, love and tears,
Leave me awhile! for I have hazarded
All that this world calls happy.—Thou hast wrought
A secret from me, under name of friend,
Which art could ne'er have found, nor torture wrung
From out my bosom. Give it me again;
For I will find it, wheresoe'er it lies,
Hid in the mortal'st part: invent a way
To give it back.

Mel. Why would you have it back?
I will to death pursue him with revenge.

Amin. Therefore I call it back from thee; for I know

[1] Alive.

Thy blood so high, that thou wilt stir in this,
And shame me to posterity. Take to thy weapon.
Draws

Mel. Hear thy friend, that bears more years than thou.

Amin. I will not hear: but draw, or I—

Mel. Amintor!

Amin. Draw, then; for I am full as resolute
As fame and honor can enforce me be:
I cannot linger. Draw!

Mel. I do. [*Draws*] But is not
My share of credit equal with thine,
If I do stir?

Amin. No; for it will be called
Honor in thee to spill thy sister's blood,
If she her birth abuse, and on the King
A brave revenge; but on me, that have walked
With patience in it, it will fix the name
Of fearful cuckold. O, that word! Be quick.

Mel. Then, join with me.

Amin. I dare not do a sin, or else I would.
Be speedy.

Mel. Then, dare not fight with me; for that's a sin.—
His grief distracts him.—Call thy thoughts again,
And to thy self pronounce the name of friend,
And see what that will work. I will not fight.

Amin. You must.

Mel. [*Sheathing*] I will be killed first. Though my passions
Offered the like to you, 'tis not this earth
Shall buy my reason to it. Think awhile,
For you are (I must weep when I speak that)
Almost beside yourself.

Amin. [*Sheathing*] O, my soft temper!
So many sweet words from thy sister's mouth,
I am afraid would make me take her to
Embrace, and pardon her. I am mad indeed,

And know not what I do. Yet have a care
Of me in what thou dost.

Mel. Why, thinks my friend
I will forget his honor? or, to save
The bravery of our house, will lose his fame,
And fear to touch the throne of majesty?

Amin. A curse will follow that; but rather live
And suffer with me.

Mel. I will do what worth
Shall bid me, and no more.

Amin. Faith, I am sick,
And desperately, I hope; yet, leaning thus,
I feel a kind of ease.

Mel. Come, take again
Your mirth about you.

Amin. I shall never do't.

Mel. I warrant you; look up; we'll walk together;
Put thine arm here; all shall be well again.

Amin. Thy love (O, wretched!) ay, thy love, Melantius;
Why, I have nothing else.

Mel. Be merry, then.

Exeunt

Enter MELANTIUS *again*

Mel. This worthy young man may do violence
Upon himself; but I have cherished him
To my best power, and sent him smiling from me,
To counterfeit again. Sword, hold thine edge;
My heart will never fail me.—

Enter DIPHILUS

Diphilus!
Thou com'st as sent.

Diph. Yonder has been such laughing.

Mel. Betwixt whom?

Diph. Why, our sister and the King;

I thought their spleens would break; they laughed us all
Out of the room.
Mel. They must weep, Diphilus.
Diph. Must they?
Mel. They must.
Thou art my brother; and, if I did believe
Thou hadst a base thought, I would rip it out,
Lie where it durst.
Diph. You should not; I would first
Mangle myself and find it.
Mel. That was spoke
According to our strain. Come, join thy hands,
And swear a firmness to what project I
Shall lay before thee.
Diph. You do wrong us both;
People hereafter shall not say, there passed
A bond, more than our loves, to tie our lives
And deaths together.
Mel. It is as nobly said as I would wish.
Anon I'll tell you wonders: we are wronged.
Diph. But I will tell you now, we'll right ourselves.
Mel. Stay not: prepare the armor in my house;
And what friends you can draw unto our side,
Not knowing of the cause, make ready too.
Haste, Diphilus, the time requires it, haste!
Exit DIPHILUS
I hope my cause is just; I know my blood
Tells me it is; and I will credit it.
To take revenge, and lose myself withal,
Were idle; and to scape impossible,
Without I had the fort, which (misery!)
Remaining in the hands of my old enemy
Calianax—but I must have it. See,

Enter CALIANAX

Where he comes shaking by me!—Good my lord,

Forget your spleen to me; I never wronged you,
But would have peace with every man.

Cal. 'Tis well;
If I durst fight, your tongue would lie at quiet.

Mel. Y'are touchy without all cause.

Cal. Do, mock me.

Mel. By mine honor, I speak truth.

Cal. Honor! where is't?

Mel. See, what starts you make
Into your idle hatred to my love
And freedom to you.
I come with resolution to obtain
A suit of you.

Cal. A suit of me!
'Tis very like it should be granted, sir.

Mel. Nay, go not hence:
'Tis this; you have the keeping of the fort,
And I would wish you, by the love you ought
To bear unto me, to deliver it
Into my hands.

Cal. I am in hope thou art mad to talk to me thus.

Mel. But there is a reason to move you to it:
I would kill the King, that wronged you and your daughter.

Cal. Out, traitor!

Mel. Nay, but stay: I cannot scape,
The deed once done, without I have this fort.

Cal. And should I help thee?
Now thy treacherous mind betrays itself.

Mel. Come, delay me not;
Give me a sudden answer, or already
Thy last is spoke! refuse not offered love,
When it comes clad in secrets.

Cal. [*Aside*] If I say
I will not, he will kill me; I do see't
Writ in his looks; and should I say I will,
He'll run and tell the King.—I do not shun

Your friendship, dear Melantius; but this cause
Is weighty: give me but an hour to think.

Mel. Take it.—[*Aside*] I know this goes unto the King;
But I am armed.— *Exit* MELANTIUS

Cal. Methinks I feel myself
But twenty now again. This fighting fool
Wants policy: I shall revenge my girl,
And make her red again. I pray my legs
Will last that pace that I will carry them:
I shall want breath before I find the King. *Exit*

[ACT IV, SCENE I]

[*An Apartment of Evadne*]

Enter MELANTIUS, EVADNE *and* Ladies

Mel. Save you!

Evad. Save you, sweet brother!

Mel. In my blunt eye, methinks, you look, Evadne—

Evad. Come, you would make me blush.

Mel. I would, Evadne;
I shall displease my ends else.

Evad. You shall, if you command me; I am bashful.
Come, sir, how do I look?

Mel. I would not have your women hear me
Break into commendation of you; 'tis not seemly.

Evad. Go wait me in the gallery.— [*Exeunt* Ladies
Now speak.

Mel. I'll lock your doors first.

Evad. Why?

Mel. I will not have your gilded things, that dance
In visitation with their Milan skins,[1]
Choke up my business.

Evad. You are strangely disposed, sir.

[1] Nares explains this as fine gloves made in Milan.

Mel. Good madam, not to make you merry.
Evad. No; if you praise me, 'twill make me sad.
Mel. Such a sad commendation I have for you.
Evad. Brother, the court hath made you witty,
And learn to riddle.
Mel. I praise the court for't: has it learned you nothing?
Evad. Me!
Mel. Ay, Evadne; thou art young and handsome,
A lady of a sweet complexion,
And such a flowing carriage,[1] that it cannot
Choose but inflame a kingdom.
Evad. Gentle brother!
Mel. 'Tis yet in thy repentance, foolish woman,
To make me gentle.
Evad. How is this?
Mel. 'Tis base;
And I could blush, at these years, thorough all
My honored scars, to come to such a parley.
Evad. I understand ye not.
Mel. Ye dare not, fool!
They that commit thy faults fly the remembrance.
Evad. My faults, sir! I would have you know, I care not
If they were written here, here in my forehead.
Mel. Thy body is too little for the story,
The lusts of which would fill another woman,
Though she had twins within her.
Evad. This is saucy:
Look you intrude no more; there lies your way.
Mel. Thou art my way, and I will tread upon thee,
Till I find truth out.
Evad. What truth is that you look for?
Mel. Thy long-lost honor. Would the gods had set me
Rather to grapple with the plague, or stand
One of their loudest bolts! Come, tell me quickly,

[1] Graceful bearing.

Do it without enforcement, and take heed
You swell me not above my temper.
Evad. How, sir!
Where got you this report?
Mel. Where there was people,
In every place.
Evad. They and the seconds of it are base people:
Believe them not, they lied.
Mel. Do not play with mine anger, do not, wretch!
I come to know that desperate fool that drew thee
From thy fair life: be wise, and lay him open.
Evad. Unhand me, and learn manners! such another
Forgetfulness forfeits your life.
Mel. Quench me this mighty humor, and then tell me
Whose whore you are; for you are one, I know it.
Let all mine honors perish but I'll find him,
Though he lie locked up in thy blood! Be sudden;
There is no facing it; and be not flattered;
The burnt air, when the Dog reigns,[1] is not fouler
Than thy contagious name, till thy repentance
(If the gods grant thee any) purge thy sickness.
Evad. Begone! you are my brother; that's your safety.
Mel. I'll be a wolf first: 'tis, to be thy brother,
An infamy below the sin of coward.
I am as far from being part of thee
As thou art from thy virtue: seek a kindred
'Mongst sensual beasts, and make a goat thy brother;
A goat is cooler. Will you tell me yet?
Evad. If you stay here and rail thus, I shall tell you
I'll ha' you whipped. Get you to your command,
And there preach to your sentinels, and tell them
What a brave man you are: I shall laugh at you.
Mel. Y'are grown a glorious whore! Where be your fighters?
What mortal fool durst raise thee to this daring,

[1] The dog-star, Sirius.

And I alive! By my just sword, h'ad safer
Bestrid a billow when the angry north
Ploughs up the sea, or made heaven's fire his foe!
Work me no higher. Will you discover yet?

Evad. The fellow's mad. Sleep, and speak sense.

Mel. Force my swoln heart no further: I would save thee.
Your great maintainers are not here, they dare not:
Would they were all, and armed! I would speak loud;
Here's one should thunder to 'em! Will you tell me?—
Thou hast no hope to scape: he that dares most,
And damns away his soul to do thee service,
Will sooner snatch meat from a hungry lion
Than come to rescue thee; thou hast death about thee;—
He has undone thine honor, poisoned thy virtue,
And, of a lovely rose, left thee a canker.

Evad. Let me consider.

Mel. Do, whose child thou wert,
Whose honor thou hast murdered, whose grave opened
And so pulled on the gods, that in their justice
They must restore him flesh again and life,
And raise his dry bones to revenge this scandal.

Evad. The gods are not of my mind; they had better
Let 'em lie sweet still in the earth; they'll stink here.

Mel. Do you raise mirth out of my easiness?
Forsake me, then, all weaknesses of nature,
Draws his sword
That make men women! Speak, you whore, speak truth,
Or, by the dear soul of thy sleeping father,
This sword shall be thy lover! tell, or I'll kill thee;
And, when thou hast told all, thou wilt deserve it.

Evad. You will not murder me?

Mel. No; 'tis a justice, and a noble one,
To put the light out of such base offenders.

Evad. Help!

Mel. By thy foul self, no human help shall help thee,

If thou criest! When I have killed thee, as I
Have vowed to do if thou confess not, naked,
As thou hast left thine honor, will I leave thee;
That on thy branded flesh the world may read
Thy black shame and my justice. Wilt thou bend yet?

Evad. Yes.

Mel. Up, and begin your story.

Evad. O, I
Am miserable!

Mel. 'Tis true, thou art. Speak truth still.

Evad. I have offended: noble sir, forgive me!

Mel. With what secure slave?

Evad. Do not ask me, sir;
Mine own remembrance is a misery
Too mighty for me.

Mel. Do not fall back again; my sword's unsheathèd yet.

Evad. What shall I do?

Mel. Be true, and make your fault less.

Evad. I dare not tell.

Mel. Tell, or I'll be this day a-killing thee.

Evad. Will you forgive me, then?

Mel. Stay; I must ask mine honor first.
I have too much foolish nature in me: speak.

Evad. Is there none else here?

Mel. None but a fearful [1] conscience; that's too many. Who is't?

Evad. O, hear me gently! It was the King.

Mel. No more. My worthy father's and my services
Are liberally rewarded! King, I thank thee!
For all my dangers and my wounds thou hast paid me
In my own metal: these are soldiers' thanks!—
How long have you lived thus, Evadne?

Evad. Too long.

Mel. Too late you find it. Can you be sorry?

[1] Cowardly.

Evad. Would I were half as blameless!
Mel. Evadne, thou wilt to thy trade again.
Evad. First to my grave.
Mel. Would gods thou hadst been so blest!
Dost thou not hate this King now? prithee hate him:
Couldst thou not curse him? I command thee, curse him;
Curse till the gods hear, and deliver him
To thy just wishes. Yet I fear, Evadne,
You had rather play your game out.
Evad. No; I feel
Too many sad confusions here, to let in
Any loose flame hereafter.
Mel. Dost thou not feel, amongst all those, one brave anger,
That breaks out nobly, and directs thine arm
To kill this base King?
Evad. All the gods forbid it!
Mel. No, all the gods require it; they are
Dishonored in him.
Evad. 'Tis too fearful.
Mel. Y'are valiant in his bed, and bold enough
To be a stale whore, and have your madam's name
Discourse for grooms and pages; and hereafter,
When his cool majesty hath laid you by,
To be at pension with some needy sir
For meat and coarser clothes: thus far you know
No fear. Come, you shall kill him.
Evad. Good sir!
Mel. An 'twere to kiss him dead, thou'dst smother him:
Be wise, and kill him. Canst thou live, and know
What noble minds shall make thee, see thyself
Found out with every finger, made the shame
Of all successions, and in this great ruin
Thy brother and thy noble husband broken?
Thou shalt not live thus. Kneel, and swear to help me,

When I shall call thee to it; or, by all
Holy in heaven and earth, thou shalt not live
To breathe a full hour longer; not a thought!
Come, 'tis a righteous oath. Give me thy hands,
And, both to heaven held up, swear, by that wealth
This lustful thief stole from thee, when I say it,
To let his foul soul out.

Evad. Here I swear it; *Kneels*
And, all you spirits of abusèd ladies,
Help me in this performance!

Mel. [*Raising her*] Enough. This must be known to none
But you and I, Evadne; not to your lord,
Though he be wise and noble, and a fellow
Dares step as far into a worthy action
As the most daring, ay, as far as justice.
Ask me not why. Farewell. *Exit*

Evad. Would I could say so to my black disgrace!
O, where have I been all this time? how friended,
That I should lose myself thus desperately,
And none for pity show me how I wandered?
There is not in the compass of the light
A more unhappy creature: sure, I am monstrous;
For I have done those follies, those mad mischiefs,
Would dare[1] a woman. O, my loaded soul,
Be not so cruel to me; choke not up
The way to my repentance!

Enter AMINTOR

O, my lord!

Amin. How now?

Evad. My much-abusèd lord! *Kneels*

Amin. This cannot be!

Evad. I do not kneel to live; I dare not hope it;
The wrongs I did are greater. Look upon me,

[1] Daunt.

Though I appear with all my faults.
Amin. Stand up.
This is a new way to beget more sorrow:
Heaven knows I have too many. Do not mock me:
Though I am tame, and bred up with my wrongs,
Which are my foster-brothers, I may leap,
Like a hand-wolf,[1] into my natural wildness,
And do an outrage: prithee, do not mock me.
Evad. My whole life is so leprous, it infects
All my repentance. I would buy your pardon,
Though at the highest set,[2] even with my life:
That slight contrition, that's no sacrifice
For what I have committed.
Amin. Sure, I dazzle:
There cannot be a faith in that foul woman,
That knows no god more mighty than her mischiefs.
Thou dost still worse, still number on thy faults,
To press my poor heart thus. Can I believe
There's any seed of virtue in that woman
Left to shoot up, that dares go on in sin
Known, and so known as thine is? O Evadne,
Would there were any safety in thy sex,
That I might put a thousand sorrows off,
And credit thy repentance! but I must not:
Thou hast brought me to that dull calamity,
To that strange misbelief of all the world
And all things that are in it, that I fear
I shall fall like a tree, and find my grave,
Only remembering that I grieve.
Evad. My lord,
Give me your griefs: you are an innocent,
A soul as white as heaven; let not my sins
Perish your noble youth. I do not fall here
To shadow by dissembling with my tears,

[1] Tame wolf.
[2] Stake.

(As all say women can,) or to make less
What my hot will hath done, which heaven and you
Know to be tougher than the hand of time
Can cut from man's remembrance; no, I do not;
I do appear the same, the same Evadne,
Dressed in the shames I lived in, the same monster.
But these are names of honor to what I am;
I do present myself the foulest creature,
Most poisonous, dangerous, and despised of men,
Lerna [1] e'er bred or Nilus. I am hell,
Till you, my dear lord, shoot your light into me,
The beams of your forgiveness; I am soulsick,
And wither with the fear of one condemned,
Till I have got your pardon.

Amin. Rise, Evadne.
Those heavenly powers that put this good into thee
Grant a continuance of it! I forgive thee:
Make thyself worthy of it; and take heed,
Take heed, Evadne, this be serious.
Mock not the powers above, that can and dare
Give thee a great example of their justice
To all ensuing eyes,[2] if thou play'st
With thy repentance, the best sacrifice.[3]

Evad. I have done nothing good to win belief,
My life hath been so faithless. All the creatures,
Made for heaven's honors, have their ends, and good ones
All but the cozening crocodiles, false women:
They reign here like those plagues, those killing sores,
Men pray against; and when they die, like tales
Ill told and unbelieved, they pass away,
And go to dust forgotten. But, my lord,
Those short days I shall number to my rest

[1] A marsh, the haunt of Hydra, the monster slain by Hercules.
[2] Eyes which follow thee; some emend *ages*.
[3] If you palter with repentance which is the best sacrifice you can make.

(As many must not see me) shall, though too late,
Though in my evening, yet perceive a will,
Since I can do no good, because a woman,
Reach constantly at something that is near it:
I will redeem one minute of my age,
Or, like another Niobe, I'll weep,
Till I am water.

Amin. I am now dissolved;
My frozen soul melts. May each sin thou hast,
Find a new mercy! Rise; I am at peace.
Hadst thou been thus, thus excellently good,
Before that devil-king tempted thy frailty,
Sure thou hadst made a star. Give me thy hand:
From this time I will know thee; and, as far
As honor gives me leave, by thy Amintor.
When we meet next, I will salute thee fairly,
And pray the gods to give thee happy days:
My charity shall go along with thee,
Though my embraces must be far from thee.
I should ha' killed thee, but this sweet repentance
Locks up my vengeance; for which thus I kiss thee—
The last kiss we must take: and would to heaven
The holy priest that gave our hands together
Had given us equal virtues! Go, Evadne;
The gods thus part our bodies. Have a care
My honor falls no farther: I am well, then.

Evad. All the dear joys here, and above hereafter,
Crown thy fair soul! Thus I take leave, my lord;
And never shall you see the foul Evadne,
Till she have tried all honored means, that may
Set her in rest and wash her stains away. *Exeunt* [*severally*]

[SCENE II]

[*A Hall in the Palace*]

Banquet [*spread*]. *Enter* KING *and* CALIANAX. Hautboys *play within*

King. I cannot tell how I should credit this
From you, that are his enemy.
Cal. I am sure
He said it to me; and I'll justify it
What way he dares oppose—but with my sword.
King. But did he break, without all circumstance,
To you, his foe, that he would have the fort,
To kill me, and then scape?
Cal. If he deny it,
I'll make him blush.
King. It sounds incredibly.
Cal. Ay, so does every thing I say of late.
King. Not so, Calianax.
Cal. Yes, I should sit
Mute whilst a rogue with strong arms cuts your throat.
King. Well, I will try him; and, if this be true,
I'll pawn my life I'll find it; if 't be false,
And that you clothe your hate in such a lie,
You shall hereafter dote in your own house,
Not in the court.
Cal. Why, if it be a lie,
Mine ears are false, for I'll be sworn I heard it.
Old men are good for nothing: you were best
Put me to death for hearing, and free him
For meaning it. You would a trusted me
Once, but the time is altered.
King. And will still,
Where I may do with justice to the world:
You have no witness.
Cal. Yes, myself.

King. No more,
I mean, there were that heard it.

Cal. How? no more!
Would you have more? why, am not I enough
To hang a thousand rogues?

King. But so you may
Hang honest men too, if you please.

Cal. I may!
'Tis like I will do so: there are a hundred
Will swear it for a need too, if I say it—

King. Such witnesses we need not.

Cal. And 'tis hard
If my word cannot hang a boisterous knave.

King. Enough.—Where's Strato?

Enter STRATO

Stra. Sir?

King. Why, where's all the company? Call Amintor in;
Evadne. Where's my brother, and Melantius?
Bid him come too; and Diphilus. Call all
That are without there.— *Exit* STRATO

If he should desire
The combat of you, 'tis not in the power
Of all our laws to hinder it, unless
We mean to quit 'em.

Cal. Why, if you do think
'Tis fit an old man and a councillor
To fight for what he says, then you may grant it.

Enter AMINTOR, EVADNE, MELANTIUS, DIPHILUS, [LYSIPPUS], CLEON, STRATO, *and* DIAGORAS

King. Come, sirs!—Amintor, thou art yet a bridegroom,
And I will use thee so; thou shalt sit down.—
Evadne, sit;—and you, Amintor, too;
This banquet is for you, sir.—Who has brought

A merry tale about him, to raise laughter
Amongst our wine? Why, Strato, where art thou?
Thou wilt chop out with them unseasonably,
When I desire 'em not.

Stra. 'Tis my ill luck, sir, so to spend them, then.

King. Reach me a bowl of wine.—Melantius, thou
Art sad.

Mel. I should be, sir, the merriest here,
But I ha' ne'er a story of mine own
Worth telling at this time.

King. Give me the wine.—
Melantius, I am now considering
How easy 'twere for any man we trust
To poison one of us in such a bowl.

Mel. I think it were not hard, sir, for a knave.

Cal. [*Aside*] Such as you are.

King. I' faith, 'twere easy. It becomes us well
To get plain-dealing men about ourselves,
Such as you all are here.—Amintor, to thee;
And to thy fair Evadne! *Drinks*

Mel. [*Apart to* CALIANAX] Have you thought
Of this, Calianax?

Cal. Yes, marry, have I.

Mel. And what's your resolution?

Cal. We shall have it,
Soundly, I warrant you.

King. Reach to Amintor, Strato.

Amin. Here, my love;

Drinks, and then hands the cup to EVADNE

This wine will do thee wrong, for it will set
Blushes upon thy cheeks; and, till thou dost
A fault, 'twere pity.

King. Yet I wonder much
Of the strange desperation of these men,
That dare attempt such acts here in our state:
He could not scape that did it.

Mel. Were he known, unpossible.
King. It would be known, Melantius.
Mel. It ought to be. If he got then away,
He must wear all our lives upon his sword:
He need not fly the island; he must leave
No one alive.
King. No; I should think no man
Could kill me, and scape clear, but that old man.
Cal. But I! heaven bless me! I! should I, my liege?
King. I do not think thou wouldst; but yet thou mightst,
For thou hast in thy hands the means to scape,
By keeping of the fort.—He has, Melantius,
And he has kept it well.
Mel. From cobwebs, sir,
'Tis clean swept: I can find no other art
In keeping of it now: 'twas ne'er besieged
Since he commanded.
Cal. I shall be sure
Of your good word: but I have kept it safe
From such as you.
Mel. Keep your ill temper in:
I speak no malice; had my brother kept it,
I should ha' said as much.
King. You are not merry.
Brother, drink wine. Sit you all still.—Calianax, *Aside*
I cannot trust this: I have thrown out words,
That would have fetched warm blood upon the cheeks
Of guilty men, and he is never moved;
He knows no such thing.
Cal. Impudence may scape,
When feeble virtue is accused.
King. 'A must,
If he were guilty, feel an alteration
At this our whisper, whilst we point at him:
You see he does not.
Cal. Let him hang himself:

What care I what he does? this he did say.
King. Melantius, you can easily conceive
What I have meant; for men that are in fault
Can subtly apprehend when others aim
At what they do amiss: but I forgive
Freely before this man: heaven do so too!
I will not touch thee, so much as with shame
Of telling it. Let it be so no more.
Cal. Why, this is very fine!
Mel. I cannot tell
What 'tis you mean; but I am apt enough
Rudely to thrust into an ignorant fault.
But let me know it: happily 'tis nought
But misconstruction; and, where I am clear,
I will not take forgiveness of the gods,
Much less of you.
King. Nay, if you stand so stiff,
I shall call back my mercy.
Mel. I want smoothness
To thank a man for pardoning of a crime
I never knew.
King. Not to instruct your knowledge, but to show you
My ears are every where; you meant to kill me,
And get the fort to scape.
Mel. Pardon me, sir;
My bluntness will be pardoned. You preserve
A race of idle people here about you,
Facers [1] and talkers, to defame the worth
Of those that do things worthy. The man that uttered this
Had perished without food, be't who it will,
But for this arm, that fenced him from the foe:
And if I thought you gave a faith to this,
The plainness of my nature would speak more.
Give me a pardon (for you ought to do't)
To kill him that spake this.

[1] Braggart.

Cal. [*Aside*] Ay, that will be
The end of all: then I am fairly paid
For all my care and service.—

Mel. That old man,
Who calls me enemy, and of whom I
(Though I will never match my hate so low)
Have no good thought, would yet, I think, excuse me,
And swear he thought me wronged in this.

Cal. Who, I?
Thou shameless fellow! didst thou not speak to me
Of it thyself?

Mel. O, then, it came from him!

Cal. From me! who should it come from but from me?

Mel. Nay, I believe your malice is enough:
But I ha' lost my anger.—Sir, I hope
You are well satisfied.

King. Lysippus, cheer
Amintor and his lady: there's no sound
Comes from you; I will come and do't myself.

Amin. You have done already, sir, for me, I thank you.

King. Melantius, I do credit this from him,
How slight soe'er you make't.

Mel. 'Tis strange you should.

Cal. 'Tis strange 'a should believe an old man's word,
That never lied in's life!

Mel. I talk not to thee.—
Shall the wild words of this distempered man,
Frantic with age and sorrow, make a breach
Betwixt your majesty and me? 'Twas wrong
To hearken to him; but to credit him,
As much at least as I have power to bear.
But pardon me—whilst I speak only truth,
I may commend myself—I have bestowed
My careless blood [1] with you, and should be loath
To think an action that would make me lose

[1] Blood in the shedding of which I have been careless.

That and my thanks too. When I was a boy,
I thrust myself into my country's cause,
And did a deed that plucked five years from time,
And styled me man then. And for you, my King,
Your subjects all have fed by virtue of
My arm: this sword of mine hath ploughed the ground,
And reaped the fruit in peace;
And you yourself have lived at home in ease.
So terrible I grew, that without swords
My name hath fetched you conquest: and my heart
And limbs are still the same; my will as great
To do you service. Let me not be paid
With such a strange distrust.

King. Melantius,
I held it great injustice to believe
Thine enemy, and did not; if I did,
I do not; let that satisfy.—What, struck
With sadness all? More wine!

Cal. A few fine words
Have overthrown my truth. Ah, th'art a villain!

Mel. Why, thou wert better let me have the fort:

Aside

Dotard, I will disgrace thee thus for ever;
There shall no credit lie upon thy words:
Think better, and deliver it.

Cal. My liege,
He's at me now again to do it.—Speak;
Deny it, if thou canst.—Examine him
Whilst he is hot, for, if he cool again,
He will forswear it.

King. This is lunacy,
I hope, Melantius.

Mel. He hath lost himself
Much, since his daughter missed the happiness
My sister gained; and, though he call me foe,
I pity him.

Cal. Pity! a pox upon you!
Mel. Mark his disordered words: and at the masque
Diagoras knows he raged and railed at me,
And called a lady 'whore,' so innocent
She understood him not. But it becomes
Both you and me too to forgive distraction:
Pardon him, as I do.
Cal. I'll not speak for thee,
For all thy cunning.—If you will be safe,
Chop off his head; for there was never known
So impudent a rascal.
King. Some, that love him,
Get him to bed. Why, pity should not let
Age make itself contemptible; we must be
All old. Have him away.
Mel. Calianax,
The King believes you: come, you shall go home,
And rest; you ha' done well. [*Aside*]—You'll give it up,
When I have used you thus a month, I hope.—
Cal. Now, now, 'tis plain, sir: he does move me still:
He says, he knows I'll give him up the fort,
When he has used me thus a month. I am mad,
Am I not, still?
All. Ha, ha, ha!
Cal. I shall be mad indeed, if you do thus.
Why should you trust a sturdy fellow there,
That has no virtue in him, (all's in his sword)
Before me? Do but take his weapons from him,
And he's an ass; and I am a very fool,
Both with him and without him, as you use me.
All. Ha, ha, ha!
King. 'Tis well, Calianax: but if you use
This once again, I shall entreat some other
To see your offices be well discharged.—
Be merry, gentlemen.—It grows somewhat late.—
Amintor, thou wouldst be a-bed again.

Amin. Yes, sir.
King. And you, Evadne.—Let me take
Thee in my arms, Melantius, and believe
Thou art, as thou deservest to be, my friend
Still and for ever.—Good Calianax,
Sleep soundly; it will bring thee to thyself.
Exeunt omnes. Manent MELANTIUS *and* CALIANAX
Cal. Sleep soundly! I sleep soundly now, I hope;
I could not be thus else.—How darest thou stay
Alone with me, knowing how thou hast used me?
Mel. You cannot blast me with your tongue, and that's
The strongest part you have about you.
Cal. I
Do look for some great punishment for this;
For I begin to forget all my hate,
And take't unkindly that mine enemy
Should use me so extraordinarily scurvily.
Mel. I shall melt too, if you begin to take
Unkindnesses: I never meant you hurt.
Cal. Thou'lt anger me again. Thou wretched rogue,
Meant me no hurt! disgrace me with the King!
Lose all my offices! This is no hurt,
Is it? I prithee, what dost thou call hurt?
Mel. To poison men, because they love me not;
To call the credit of men's wives in question;
To murder children betwixt me and land;[1]
This is all hurt.
Cal. All this thou think'st is sport;
For mine is worse: but use thy will with me;
For betwixt grief and anger I could cry.
Mel. Be wise, then, and be safe; thou may'st revenge.
Cal. Ay, o' the King: I would revenge of thee.
Mel. That you must plot yourself.
Cal. I am a fine plotter.
Mel. The short is, I will hold thee with the King

[1] Who stand as heirs.

In this perplexity, till peevishness
And thy disgrace have laid thee in thy grave:
But if thou wilt deliver up the fort,
I'll take thy trembling body in my arms,
And bear thee over dangers: thou shalt hold
Thy wonted state.

Cal. If I should tell the King,
Canst thou deny't again?

Mel. Try, and believe.

Cal. Nay, then, thou canst bring any thing about.
Melantius, thou shalt have the fort.

Mel. Why, well.
Here let our hate be buried; and this hand
Shall right us both. Give me thy agèd breast
To compass.

Cal. Nay, I do not love thee yet;
I cannot well endure to look on thee;
And if I thought it were a courtesy,
Thou shouldst not have it. But I am disgraced;
My offices are to be ta'en away;
And, if I did but hold this fort a day,
I do believe the King would take it from me,
And give it thee, things are so strangely carried.
Ne'er thank me for't; but yet the King shall know
There was some such thing in't I told him of,
And that I was an honest man.

Mel. He'll buy
That knowledge very dearly.—

Enter DIPHILUS

Diphilus,
What news with thee?

Diph. This were a night indeed
To do it in: the King hath sent for her.

Mel. She shall perform it, then.—Go, Diphilus,
And take from this good man, my worthy friend,

The fort, he'll give it thee.

Diph. Ha' you got that?

Cal. Art thou of the same breed? canst thou deny
This to the King too?

Diph. With a confidence
As great as his.

Cal. Faith, like enough.

Mel. Away, and use him kindly.

Cal. Touch not me;
I hate the whole strain.[1] If thou follow me
A great way off, I'll give thee up the fort;
And hang yourselves.

Mel. Begone.

Diph. He's finely wrought.

Exeunt CALIANAX *and* DIPHILUS

Mel. This is a night, spite of astronomers,[2]
To do the deed in. I will wash the stain
That rests upon our house off with his blood.

Enter AMINTOR

Amin. Melantius, now assist me: if thou be'st
That which thou say'st, assist me. I have lost
All my distempers, and have found a rage
So pleasing! Help me.

Mel. [*Aside*] Who can see him thus,
And not swear vengeance?—What's the matter, friend?

Amin. Out with thy sword; and, hand in hand with me,
Rush to the chamber of this hated King,
And sink him with the weight of all his sins
To hell for ever.

Mel. 'Twere a rash attempt,
Not to be done with safety. Let your reason
Plot your revenge, and not your passion.

Amin. If thou refusest me in these extremes,

[1] Family.
[2] Astrologers.

Thou art no friend. He sent for her to me;
By heaven, to me, myself! and I must tell ye,
I love her as a stranger: there is worth
In that vild[1] woman, worthy things, Melantius;
And she repents. I'll do't myself alone,
Though I be slain. Farewell.

Mel. He'll overthrow
My whole design with madness.—Amintor,
Think what thou dost: I dare as much as valor;
But 'tis the King, the King, the King, Amintor,
With whom thou fightest!—[*Aside*] I know he's honest,
And this will work with him.—

Amin. I cannot tell
What thou hast said; but thou hast charmed my sword
Out of my hand, and left me shaking here,
Defenceless.

Mel. I will take it up for thee.

Amin. What wild beast is uncollected[2] man!
The thing that we call honor bears us all
Headlong unto sin, and yet itself is nothing.

Mel. Alas, how variable are thy thoughts!

Amin. Just like my fortunes. I was run to that
I purposed to have chid thee for. Some plot,
I did distrust, thou hadst against the King,
By that old fellow's carriage. But take heed;
There's not the least limb growing to a king
But carries thunder in it.

Mel. I have none
Against him.

Amin. Why, come, then; and still remember
We may not think revenge.

Mel. I will remember. *Exeunt*

[1] Vile.
[2] Uncontrolled.

[ACT V, SCENE I]

[*A Room in the Palace*]

Enter EVADNE *and a* Gentleman

Evad. Sir, is the King a-bed?
Gent. Madam, an hour ago.
Evad. Give me the key, then; and let none be near;
'Tis the King's pleasure.
Gent. I understand you, madam; would 'twere mine!
I must not wish good rest unto your ladyship.
Evad. You talk, you talk.
Gent. 'Tis all I dare do, madam; but the King
Will wake, and then, methinks—
Evad. Saving your imagination, pray, good night, sir.
Gent. A good night be it, then, and a long one, madam.
I am gone. *Exit*
Evad. The night grows horrible; and all about me
Like my black purpose. [*Draws a curtain disclosing the* KING *abed*] O, the conscience
Of a lost virtue, whither wilt thou pull me?
To what things dismal as the depth of hell
Wilt thou provoke me? Let no woman dare
From this hour be disloyal, if her heart be flesh,
If she have blood, and can fear. 'Tis a daring
Above that desperate fool's that left his peace,
And went to sea to fight: 'tis so many sins
An age cannot repent 'em; and so great,
The gods want mercy for. Yet I must through 'em:
I have begun a slaughter on my honor,
And I must end it there.—'A sleeps. O God,
Why give you peace to this untemperate beast,
That hath so long transgressed you? I must kill him,
And I will do it bravely: the mere joy
Tells me, I merit in it. Yet I must not
Thus tamely do it, as he sleeps—that were

To rock him to another world; my vengeance
Shall take him waking, and then lay before him
The number of his wrongs and punishments:
I'll shape his sins like Furies, till I waken
His evil angel, his sick conscience,
And then I'll strike him dead. King, by your leave;
Ties his arms to the bed
I dare not trust your strength; your grace and I
Must grapple upon even terms no more.
So, if he rail me not from my resolution,
I shall be strong enough.—
My lord the King!—My lord!—'A sleeps,
As if he meant to wake no more.—My lord!—
Is he not dead already? Sir! my lord!

King. Who's that?

Evad. O, you sleep soundly, sir!

King. My dear Evadne,
I have been dreaming of thee: come to bed.

Evad. I am come at length, sir; but how welcome?

King. What pretty new device is this, Evadne?
What, do you tie me to you? By my love,
This is a quaint one. Come, my dear, and kiss me;
I'll be thy Mars; to bed, my queen of love:
Let us be caught together, that the gods may see
And envy our embraces.

Evad. Stay, sir, stay;
You are too hot, and I have brought you physic
To temper your high veins.

King. Prithee, to bed, then; let me take it warm;
There thou shalt know the state of my body better.

Evad. I know you have a surfeited foul body;
And you must bleed. *Draws a dagger*

King. Bleed!

Evad. Ay, you shall bleed. Lie still; and, if the devil,
Your lust, will give you leave, repent. This steel
Comes to redeem the honor that you stole,

King, my fair name; which nothing but thy death
Can answer to the world.

King. How's this, Evadne?

Evad. I am not she; nor bear I in this breast
So much cold spirit to be called a woman:
I am a tiger; I am any thing
That knows not pity. Stir not: if thou dost,
I'll take thee unprepared, thy fears upon thee,
That make thy sins look double, and so send thee
(By my revenge, I will!) to look those torments
Prepared for such black souls.

King. Thou dost not mean this; 'tis impossible;
Thou art too sweet and gentle.

Evad. No, I am not:
I am as foul as thou art, and can number
As many such hells here. I was once fair,
Once I was lovely; not a blowing rose
More chastely sweet, till thou, thou, thou, foul canker,
(Stir not) didst poison me. I was a world of virtue,
Till your cursed court and you (hell bless you for't)
With your temptations on temptations
Made me give up mine honor; for which, King,
I am come to kill thee.

King. No!

Evad. I am.

King. Thou art not!
I prithee speak not these things: thou art gentle,
And wert not meant thus rugged.

Evad. Peace, and hear me.
Stir nothing but your tongue, and that for mercy
To those above us; by whose lights I vow
Those blessèd fires [1] that shot to see our sin,
If thy hot soul had substance with thy blood,
I would kill that too; which, being past my steel,
My tongue shall reach. Thou art a shameless villain;

[1] Shooting stars.

A thing out of the overcharge of nature,
Sent, like a thick cloud, to disperse a plague
Upon weak catching [1] women; such a tyrant,
That for his lust would sell away his subjects,
Ay, all his heaven hereafter!

King. Hear, Evadne,
Thou soul of sweetness, hear! I am thy King.

Evad. Thou art my shame! Lie still; there's none about you,
Within your cries; all promises of safety
Are but deluding dreams. Thus, thus, thou foul man,
Thus I begin my vengeance! *Stabs him*

King. Hold, Evadne!
I do command thee hold!

Evad. I do not mean, sir,
To part so fairly with you; we must change
More of these love-tricks yet.

King. What bloody villain
Provoked thee to this murder?

Evad. Thou, thou monster!

King. O!

Evad. Thou kept'st me brave [2] at court, and whored me, King;
Then married me to a young noble gentleman,
And whored me still.

King. Evadne, pity me!

Evad. Hell take me, then! This for my lord Amintor.
This for my noble brother! and this stroke
For the most wronged of women! *Kills him*

King. O! I die.

Evad. Die all our faults together! I forgive thee. *Exit*

Enter two of the Bedchamber

1 *Gent.* Come, now she's gone, let's enter; the King expects it, and will be angry.

[1] Susceptible.

[2] Handsomely dressed and attended.

2 *Gent.* 'Tis a fine wench; we'll have a snap at her one of these nights, as she goes from him.

1 *Gent.* Content. How quickly he had done with her! I see kings can do no more that way than other mortal people.

2 *Gent.* How fast he is! I cannot hear him breathe.

1 *Gent.* Either the tapers give a feeble light,
Or he looks very pale.

2 *Gent.* And so he does:
Pray heaven he be well! let's look.—Alas!
He's stiff, wounded, and dead! Treason, treason!

1 *Gent.* Run forth and call.

2 *Gent.* Treason, treason! *Exit*

1 *Gent.* This will be laid on us: who can believe
A woman could do this?

Enter CLEON *and* LYSIPPUS

Cle. How now! where's the traitor?

1 *Gent.* Fled, fled away; but there her woeful act
Lies still.

Cle. Her act! a woman!

Lys. Where's the body?

1 *Gent.* There.

Lys. Farewell, thou worthy man! There were two bonds
That tied our loves, a brother and a king,
The least of which might fetch a flood of tears;
But such the misery of greatness is,
They have no time to mourn; then, pardon me!

Enter STRATO

Sirs, which way went she?

Stra. Never follow her;
For she, alas! was but the instrument.
News is now brought in, that Melantius
Has got the fort, and stands upon the wall,
And with a loud voice calls those few that pass

At this dead time of night, delivering
The innocence of this act.

Lys. Gentlemen, I am your King.

Stra. We do acknowledge it.

Lys. I would I were not! Follow, all; for this
Must have a sudden stop. *Exeunt*

[SCENE II]

[*Before the Citadel*]

Enter MELANTIUS, DIPHILUS, *and* CALIANAX, *on the wall*

Mel. If the dull people can believe I am armed,
(Be constant, Diphilus,) now we have time
Either to bring our banished honors home,
Or create new ones in our ends.

Diph. I fear not;
My spirit lies not that way.—Courage, Calianax!

Cal. Would I had any! you should quickly know it.

Mel. Speak to the people; thou art eloquent.

Cal. 'Tis a fine eloquence to come to the gallows:
You were born to be my end; the devil take you!
Now must I hang for company. 'Tis strange,
I should be old, and neither wise nor valiant.

Enter LYSIPPUS, DIAGORAS, CLEON, STRATO, *and* Guard

Lys. See where he stands, as boldly confident
As if he had his full command about him!

Stra. He looks as if he had the better cause, sir;
Under your gracious pardon, let me speak it.
Though he be mighty-spirited, and forward
To all great things, to all things of that danger
Worse men shake at the telling of, yet certainly
I do believe him noble, and this action
Rather pulled on than sought: his mind was ever
As worthy as his hand.

Lys. 'Tis my fear too.
Heaven forgive all!—Summon him, lord Cleon.
Cle. Ho, from the walls there!
Mel. Worthy Cleon, welcome:
We could a wished you here, lord: you are honest.
Cal. [*Aside*] Well, thou art as flattering a knave, though I dare not tell thee so—
Lys. Melantius!
Mel. Sir?
Lys. I am sorry that we meet thus; our old love
Never required such distance. Pray to heaven,
You have not left yourself, and sought this safety
More out of fear than honor! You have lost
A noble master; which your faith, Melantius,
Some think might have preserved: yet you know best.
Cal. [*Aside*] When time was I was mad! Some that dares fight,
I hope will pay this rascal.
Mel. Royal young man, those tears look lovely on thee:
Had they been shed for a deserving one,
They had been lasting monuments. Thy brother,
Whilst he was good, I called him King, and served him
With that strong faith, that most unwearied valor,
Pulled people from the farthest sun to seek him,
And beg his friendship. I was then his soldier.
But since his hot pride drew him to disgrace me,
And brand my noble actions with his lust,
(That never-cured dishonor of my sister,
Base stain of whore, and, which is worse,
The joy to make it still so,) like myself,
Thus I have flung him off with my allegiance;
And stand here mine own justice, to revenge
What I have suffered in him, and this old man
Wronged almost to lunacy.
Cal. Who, I?
You would draw me in. I have had no wrong;

I do disclaim ye all.

Mel. The short is this.
'Tis no ambition to lift up myself
Urgeth me thus; I do desire again
To be a subject, so I may be free:
If not, I know my strength, and will unbuild
This goodly town. Be speedy, and be wise,
In a reply.

Stra. Be sudden, sir, to tie
All up again. What's done is past recall,
And past you to revenge; and there are thousands
That wait for such a troubled hour as this.
Throw him the blank.[1]

Lys. Melantius, write in that thy choice:
My seal is at it. *Throws* MELANTIUS *the paper*

Mel. It was our honors drew us to this act,
Not gain; and we will only work our pardons.

Cal. Put my name in too.

Diph. You disclaimed us all, but now, Calianax.

Cal. That is all one;
I'll not be hanged hereafter by a trick:
I'll have it in.

Mel. You shall, you shall.—
Come to the back gate, and we'll call you King,
And give you up the fort.

Lys. Away, away! *Exeunt omnes*

[SCENE III]

[*Ante-room to* AMINTOR'S *Apartments*]

Enter ASPATIA, *in man's apparel and with artificial scars on her face*

Asp. This is my fatal hour. Heaven may forgive
My rash attempt, that causelessly hath laid

[1] Carte blanche.

Griefs on me that will never let me rest,
And put a woman's heart into my breast.
It is more honor for you that I die;
For she that can endure the misery
That I have on me, and be patient too,
May live and laugh at all that you can do.

Enter Servant

God save you, sir!
Ser. And you, sir! What's your business?
Asp. With you, sir, now; to do me the fair office
To help me to your lord.
Ser. What, would you serve him?
Asp. I'll do him any service; but, to haste,
For my affairs are earnest, I desire
To speak with him.
Ser. Sir, because you are in such haste, I would be loath
Delay you longer: you can not.
Asp. It shall become you, though, to tell your lord.
Ser. Sir, he will speak with nobody;
But in particular, I have in charge,[1]
About no weighty matters.
Asp. This is most strange.
Art thou gold-proof? there's for thee; help me to him.
Gives money
Ser. Pray be not angry, sir: I'll do my best. *Exit*
Asp. How stubbornly this fellow answered me!
There is a vild dishonest trick in man,
More than in woman. All the men I meet
Appear thus to me, are harsh and rude,
And have a subtilty in every thing,
Which love could never know; but we fond[2] women
Harbor the easiest and the smoothest thoughts,
And think all shall go so. It is unjust

[1] I have been charged.
[2] Foolish.

That men and women should be matched together.

Enter AMINTOR *and his* Man

Amin. Where is he?
Ser. There, my lord.
Amin. What would you, sir?
Asp. Please it your lordship to command your man
Out of the room, I shall deliver things
Worthy your hearing.
Amin. Leave us. *Exit* Servant
Asp. [*Aside*] O, that that shape
Should bury falsehood in it!—
Amin. Now your will, sir.
Asp. When you know me, my lord, you needs must guess
My business; and I am not hard to know;
For, till the chance of war marked this smooth face
With these few blemishes, people would call me
My sister's picture, and her mine. In short,
I am brother to the wronged Aspatia.
Amin. The wronged Aspatia! would thou wert so too
Unto the wronged Amintor! Let me kiss
Kisses her hand
That hand of thine, in honor that I bear
Unto the wronged Aspatia. Here I stand
That did it. Would he could not! Gentle youth,
Leave me; for there is something in thy looks
That calls my sins in a most hideous form
Into my mind; and I have grief enough
Without thy help.
Asp. I would I could with credit!
Since I was twelve years old, I had not seen
My sister till this hour I now arrived:
She sent for me to see her marriage;
A woeful one! but they that are above
Have ends in every thing. She used few words,
But yet enough to make me understand

The baseness of the injuries you did her.
That little training I have had is war:
I may behave myself rudely in peace;
I would not, though. I shall not need to tell you,
I am but young, and would be loath to lose
Honor, that is not easily gained again.
Fairly I mean to deal: the age is strict
For single combats; and we shall be stopped,
If it be published. If you like your sword,
Use it; if mine appear a better to you,
Change; for the ground is this, and this the time,
To end our difference. *Draws*

Amin. Charitable youth,
If thou be'st such, think not I will maintain
So strange a wrong: and, for thy sister's sake,
Know, that I could not think that desperate thing
I durst not do; yet, to enjoy this world,
I would not see her; for, beholding thee,
I am I know not what. If I have aught
That may content thee, take it, and begone,
For death is not so terrible as thou;
Thine eyes shoot guilt into me.

Asp. Thus, she swore,
Thou wouldst behave thyself, and give me words
That would fetch tears into mine eyes; and so
Thou dost indeed. But yet she bade me watch,
Lest I were cozened, and be sure to fight
Ere I returned.

Amin. That must not be with me.
For her I'll die directly; but against her
Will never hazard it.

Asp. You must be urged:
I do not deal uncivilly with those
That dare to fight; but such a one as you
Must be used thus. *She strikes him*

Amin. I prithee, youth, take heed.

Thy sister is a thing to me so much
Above mine honor, that I can endure
All this—Good gods! a blow I can endure;
But stay not, lest thou draw a timeless death
Upon thyself.

Asp. Thou art some prating fellow;
One that hath studied out a trick to talk,
And move soft-hearted people; to be kicked,
She kicks him
Thus to be kicked.—[*Aside*] Why should he be so slow
In giving me my death?

Amin. A man can bear
No more, and keep his flesh. Forgive me, then?
I would endure yet, if I could. Now show *Draws*
The spirit thou pretendest, and understand
Thou hast no hour to live.
They fight, ASPATIA *is wounded*
What dost thou mean?
Thou canst not fight: the blows thou mak'st at me
Are quite besides; and those I offer at thee,
Thou spread'st thine arms, and tak'st upon thy breast,
Alas, defenceless!

Asp. I have got enough,
And my desire. There is no place so fit
For me to die as here. *Falls*

Enter EVADNE, *her hands bloody, with a knife*

Evad. Amintor, I am loaden with events,
That fly to make thee happy; I have joys,
That in a moment can call back thy wrongs,
And settle thee in thy free state again.
It is Evadne still that follows thee,
But not her mischiefs.

Amin. Thou canst not fool me to believe again;
But thou hast looks and things so full of news,
That I am stayed.

Evad. Noble Amintor, put off thy amaze;
Let thine eyes loose, and speak. Am I not fair?
Looks not Evadne beauteous with these rites now?
Were those hours half so lovely in thine eyes
When our hands met before the holy man?
I was too foul within to look fair then:
Since I knew ill, I was not free till now.

Amin. There is presage of some important thing
About thee, which, it seems, thy tongue hath lost:
Thy hands are bloody, and thou hast a knife.

Evad. In this consists thy happiness and mine:
Joy to Amintor! for the King is dead.

Amin. Those have most power to hurt us, that we love;
We lay our sleeping lives within their arms.
Why, thou hast raised up mischief to his height,
And found one to out-name[1] thy other faults;
Thou hast no intermission of thy sins
But all thy life is a continued ill:
Black is thy color now, disease thy nature.
'Joy to Amintor!' Thou hast touched a life,
The very name of which had power to chain
Up all my rage, and calm my wildest wrongs.

Evad. 'Tis done; and, since I could not find a way
To meet thy love so clear as through this life,
I cannot now repent it.

Amin. Couldst thou procure the gods to speak to me,
To bid me love this woman and forgive,
I think I should fall out with them. Behold,
Here lies a youth whose wounds bleed in my breast,
Sent by a violent fate to fetch his death
From my slow hand! And, to augment my woe,
You now are present, stained with a king's blood
Violently shed. This keeps night here,
And throws an unknown wilderness about me.

Asp. O, O, O!

[1] Surpass.

Amin. No more; pursue me not.
Evad. Forgive me, then,
And take me to thy bed: we may not part.
Amin. Forbear, be wise, and let my rage go this way.
Evad. 'Tis you that I would stay, not it.
Amin. Take heed;
It will return with me.
Evad. If it must be,
I shall not fear to meet it: take me home.
Amin. Thou monster of cruelty, forbear!
Evad. For heaven's sake, look more calm: thine eyes are sharper
Than thou canst make thy sword. *Kneels*
Amin. Away, away!
Thy knees are more to me than violence;
I am worse than sick to see knees follow me
For that I must not grant. For heaven's sake, stand.
Evad. Receive me, then.
Amin. I dare not stay thy language:
In midst of all my anger and my grief,
Thou dost awake something that troubles me,
And says, I loved thee once. I dare not stay;
There is no end of woman's reasoning. *Leaves her*
Evad. [*Rising*] Amintor, thou shalt love me now again:
Go; I am calm. Farewell, and peace for ever!
Evadne, whom thou hatest, will die for thee. *Kills herself*
Amin. I have a little human nature yet,
That's left for thee, that bids me stay thy hand. *Returns*
Evad. Thy hand was welcome, but it came too late.
O, I am lost! the heavy sleep makes haste. *She dies*
Asp. O, O, O!
Amin. This earth of mine doth tremble, and I feel
A stark affrighted motion in my blood;
My soul grows weary of her house, and I
All over am a trouble to myself.
There is some hidden power in these dead things,

That calls my flesh unto 'em; I am cold:
Be resolute, and bear 'em company.
There's something yet, which I am loath to leave:
There's man enough in me to meet the fears
That death can bring; and yet would it were done!
I can find nothing in the whole discourse
Of death, I durst not meet the boldest way;
Yet still, betwixt the reason and the act,
The wrong I to Aspatia did stands up;
I have not such another fault to answer:
Though she may justly arm herself with scorn
And hate of me, my soul will part less troubled,
When I have paid to her in tears my sorrow:
I will not leave this act unsatisfied,
If all that's left in me can answer it.

Asp. Was it a dream? there stands Amintor still;
Or I dream still.

Amin. How dost thou? speak; receive my love and help.
Thy blood climbs up to his old place again;
There's hope of thy recovery.

Asp. Did you not name Aspatia?

Amin. I did.

Asp. And talked of tears and sorrow unto her?

Amin. 'Tis true; and, till these happy signs in thee
Did stay my course, 'twas thither I was going.

Asp. Thou art there already, and these wounds are hers:
Those threats I brought with me sought not revenge,
But came to fetch this blessing from thy hand:
I am Aspatia yet.

Amin. Dare my soul ever look abroad again?

Asp. I shall sure live, Amintor; I am well;
A kind of healthful joy wanders within me.

Amin. The world wants lines to excuse thy loss;
Come, let me bear thee to some place of help.

Asp. Amintor, thou must stay; I must rest here;
My strength begins to disobey my will.

How dost thou, my best soul? I would fain live
Now, if I could: wouldst thou have loved me, then?

Amin. Alas,
All that I am's not worth a hair from thee!

Asp. Give me thine hand; mine hands grope up and down,
And cannot find thee; I am wondrous sick:
Have I thy hand, Amintor?

Amin. Thou greatest blessing of the world, thou hast.

Asp. I do believe thee better than my sense.
O, I must go! farewell! *Dies*

Amin. She swounds.[1]—Aspatia!—Help! for God's sake, water,
Such as may chain life ever to this frame!—
Aspatia, speak!—What, no help yet? I fool;
I'll chafe her temples. Yet there's nothing stirs:
Some hidden power tell her, Amintor calls,
And let her answer me!—Aspatia, speak!—
I have heard, if there be any life, but bow
The body thus, and it will show itself.
O, she is gone! I will not leave her yet.
Since out of justice we must challenge nothing,
I'll call it mercy, if you'll pity me,
You heavenly powers, and lend forth some few years
The blessèd soul to this fair seat again!
No comfort comes; the gods deny me too.
I'll bow the body once again.—Aspatia!—
The soul is fled for ever; and I wrong
Myself, so long to lose her company.
Must I talk now? Here's to be with thee, love!
Wounds himself

Enter Servant

Ser. This is a great grace to my lord, to have the new king come to him: I must tell him he is entering.—O God!—Help, help!

[1] Swoons.

Enter Lysippus, Melantius, Calianax, Cleon, Diphilus, *and* Strato

Lys. Where's Amintor?
Ser. O, there, there!
Lys. How strange is this!
Cal. What should we do here?
Mel. These deaths are such acquainted things with me,
That yet my heart dissolves not. May I stand
Stiff here for ever! Eyes, call up your tears!
This is Amintor: heart, he was my friend;
Melt! now it flows.—Amintor, give a word
To call me to thee.
Amin. O!
Mel. Melantius calls his friend Amintor, O,
Thy arms are kinder to me than thy tongue!
Speak, speak!
Amin. What?
Mel. That little word was worth all the sounds
That ever I shall hear again.
Diph. O, brother,
Here lies your sister slain! you lose yourself
In sorrow there.
Mel. Why, Diphilus, it is
A thing to laugh at, in respect of this:
Here was my sister, father, brother, son;
All that I had.—Speak once again; what youth
Lies slain there by thee?
Amin. 'Tis Aspatia.
My last is said. Let me give up my soul
Into thy bosom. *Dies*
Cal. What's that? what's that? Aspatia!
Mel. I never did
Repent the greatness of my heart till now;
It will not burst at need.
Cal. My daughter dead here too! And you have all fine

new tricks to grieve; but I ne'er knew any but direct crying.

Mel. I am a prattler: but no more. *Offers to stab himself*

Diph. Hold, brother!

Lys. Stop him.

Diph. Fie, how unmanly was this offer in you!
Does this become our strain? [1]

Cal. I know not what the matter is, but I am grown very kind, and am friends with you all now. You have given me that among you will kill me quickly; but I'll go home, and live as long as I can. *Exit*

Mel. His spirit is but poor that can be kept
From death for want of weapons.
Is not my hands a weapon good enough
To stop my breath? or, if you tie down those,
I vow, Amintor, I will never eat,
Or drink, or sleep, or have to do with that
That may preserve life! This I swear to keep.

Lys. Look to him, though, and bear those bodies in.
May this a fair example be to me,
To rule with temper; for on lustful kings
Unlooked-for sudden deaths from God are sent;
But cursed is he that is their instrument.

Exeunt

[1] Stock.

THE DUCHESS OF MALFI

by

JOHN WEBSTER

DRAMATIS PERSONÆ

FERDINAND, *Duke of Calabria*
THE CARDINAL, *his Brother*
ANTONIO BOLOGNA, *Steward of the household to the Duchess*
DELIO, *his Friend*
DANIEL DE BOSOLA, *Gentleman of the horse to the Duchess*
CASTRUCHIO [1]
MARQUIS OF PESCARA
COUNT MALATESTE

SILVIO, *a Lord, of Milan* } *Gentlemen attending on the Duchess*
RODERIGO }

GRISOLAN
DOCTOR
Several Madmen, Pilgrims, Executioners, Officers, Attendants, &c.

DUCHESS OF MALFI, *sister of Ferdinand and the Cardinal*
CARIOLA, *her Woman*
JULIA, *Castruchio's Wife, and the Cardinal's Mistress*
Old Lady, Ladies and Children

SCENE—Amalfi, Rome, and Milan

[1] In Italian, Castruccio.

THE DUCHESS OF MALFI

ACT THE FIRST

[SCENE I]

[*Amalfi. The Presence-chamber in the Duchess's Palace.*]

Enter ANTONIO *and* DELIO

Del. You are welcome to your country, dear Antonio;
You have been long in France, and you return
A very formal Frenchman in your habit:
How do you like the French court?
Ant. I admire it:
In seeking to reduce both state and people
To a fix'd order, their judicious king
Begins at home; quits [1] first his royal palace
Of flattering sycophants, of dissolute
And infamous persons,—which [2] he sweetly terms
His master's masterpiece, the work of Heaven;
Considering duly that a prince's court
Is like a common fountain, whence should flow
Pure silver drops in general, but if't chance
Some curs'd example poison't near the head,
Death and diseases through the whole land spread.
And what is't makes this blessed government
But a most provident council, who dare freely
Inform him the corruption of the times?
Though some o' th' court hold it presumption

[1] Frees.
[2] i. e. which action; but Professor Vaughan takes the antecedent to be 'palace', and Professor Sampson 'persons'.

To instruct princes what they ought to do,
It is a noble duty to inform them
What they ought to foresee.—Here comes Bosola,
The only court-gall; yet I observe his railing
Is not for simple love of piety:
Indeed, he rails at those things which he wants;
Would be as lecherous, covetous, or proud,
Bloody, or envious, as any man,
If he had means to be so.—Here's the Cardinal.

Enter the CARDINAL *and* BOSOLA

Bos. I do haunt you still.

Card. So.

Bos. I have done you better service than to be slighted thus. Miserable age, where only the reward of doing well is the doing of it!

Card. You enforce your merit too much.

Bos. I fell into the galleys in your service; where, for two years together, I wore two towels instead of a shirt, with a knot on the shoulder, after the fashion of a Roman mantle. Slighted thus? I will thrive some way: blackbirds fatten best in hard weather; why not I in these dog-days?

Card. Would you could become honest!

Bos. With all your divinity do but direct me the way to it. I have known many travel far for it, and yet return as arrant knaves as they went forth, because they carried themselves always along with them. [*Exit* CARDINAL] Are you gone? Some fellows, they say, are possessed with the devil, but this great fellow were able to possess the greatest devil, and make him worse.

Ant. He hath denied thee some suit?

Bos. He and his brother are like plum-trees that grow crooked over standing-pools; they are rich and o'er-laden with fruit, but none but crows, pies, and caterpillars feed on them. Could I be one of their flattering panders, I would hang on their ears like a horseleech, till I were full, and then drop off. I pray, leave me. Who would rely upon these miserable dependencies, in expectation to be advanc'd to-morrow? what creature ever fed worse than hoping Tantalus? nor ever died any man more fearfully than he that hop'd for a pardon. There are rewards for hawks and dogs when they have done us service; but for a soldier that hazards his limbs in a battle, nothing but a kind of geometry in his last supportation.

Del. Geometry?

Bos. Aye, to hang in a fair pair of slings, take his latter swing in the world upon an honourable pair of crutches, from hospital to hospital. Fare ye well, sir: and yet do not you scorn us; for places in the court are but like beds in the hospital, where this man's head lies at that man's foot, and so lower and lower. *Exit*

Del. I knew this fellow seven years in the galleys
For a notorious murder; and 'twas thought
The Cardinal suborn'd it: he was releas'd
By the French general, Gaston de Foix,
When he recover'd Naples.

Ant. 'Tis great pity
He should be thus neglected: I have heard
He 's very valiant. This foul melancholy
Will poison all his goodness; for, I'll tell you,
If too immoderate sleep be truly said
To be an inward rust unto the soul,
It then doth follow want of action
Breeds all black malcontents; and their close rearing,
Like moths in cloth, do hurt for want of wearing.

Del.[1] The presence 'gins to fill: you promis'd me
To make me the partaker of the natures
Of some of your great courtiers.

Ant. The lord Cardinal's,
And other strangers' that are now in court?
I shall.—Here comes the great Calabrian duke.

[1] The early quartos mark Scene ii as beginning here.

Enter FERDINAND, CASTRUCHIO, SILVIO, RODERIGO, GRISOLAN, *and* Attendants

Ferd. Who took the ring oftenest? [1]

Silv. Antonio Bologna, my lord.

Ferd. Our sister duchess's great-master of her household? give him the jewel.—When shall we leave this sportive action, and fall to action indeed?

Cas. Methinks, my lord, you should not desire to go to war in person.

Ferd. Now for some gravity:—why, my lord?

Cas. It is fitting a soldier arise to be a prince, but not necessary a prince descend to be a captain.

Ferd. No?

Cas. No, my lord; he were far better do it by a deputy.

Ferd. Why should he not as well sleep or eat by a deputy? this might take idle, offensive, and base office from him, whereas the other deprives him of honour.

Cas. Believe my experience, that realm is never long in quiet where the ruler is a soldier.

Ferd. Thou told'st me thy wife could not endure fighting.

Cas. True, my lord.

Ferd. And of a jest she broke of a captain she met full of wounds: I have forgot it.

Cas. She told him, my lord, he was a pitiful fellow, to lie, like the children of Ismael, all in tents.[2]

Ferd. Why, there's a wit were able to undo all the chirurgeons o' the city; for although gallants should quarrel, and had drawn their weapons, and were ready to go to it, yet her persuasions would make them put up.

Cas. That she would, my lord.

[1] In tilting at the ring.

[2] In surgery, *tent* is a roll of lint or other material placed in a wound.

Ferd.[1] How do you like my Spanish gennet?

Rod. He is all fire.

Ferd. I am of Pliny's opinion, I think he was begot by the wind; he runs as if he were ballass'd [2] with quick-silver.

Silv. True, my lord, he reels from the tilt often.

Rod. and Gris. Ha, ha, ha!

Ferd. Why do you laugh? methinks you that are courtiers should be my touchwood, take fire when I give fire; that is, laugh [but] when I laugh, were the subject never so witty.

Cas. True, my lord: I myself have heard a very good jest, and have scorn'd to seem to have so silly a wit as to understand it.

Ferd. But I can laugh at your fool, my lord.

Cas. He cannot speak, you know, but he makes faces: my lady cannot abide him.

Ferd. No?

Cas. Nor endure to be in merry company; for she says too much laughing, and too much company, fills her too full of the wrinkle.

Ferd. I would, then, have a mathematical instrument made for her face, that she might not laugh out of compass. —I shall shortly visit you at Milan, Lord Silvio.

Silv. Your grace shall arrive most welcome.

Ferd. You are a good horseman, Antonio: you have excellent riders in France: what do you think of good horsemanship?

Ant. Nobly, my lord: as out of the Grecian horse issued many famous princes, so out of brave horsemanship arise the first sparks of growing resolution, that raise the mind to noble action.

Ferd. You have bespoke it worthily.

Silv. Your brother, the lord Cardinal, and sister duchess.

[1] An emendation of Professor Sampson's; all previous editions give the speech to Castruchio.
[2] Ballasted or freighted.

Re-enter CARDINAL, *with* DUCHESS, CARIOLA, *and* JULIA

Card. Are the galleys come about?
Gris. They are, my lord.
Ferd. Here's the Lord Silvio is come to take his leave.
Del. [*Aside to* ANTONIO] Now, sir, your promise; what's that Cardinal?
I mean his temper? they say he's a brave fellow,
Will play his five thousand crowns at tennis, dance,
Court ladies, and one that hath fought single combats.

Ant. Some such flashes superficially hang on him for form; but observe his inward character: he is a melancholy churchman; the spring in his face is nothing but the engendering of toads; where he is jealous of any man, he lays worse plots for them than ever was impos'd on Hercules, for he strews in his way flatter[er]s, panders, intelligencers,[1] atheists, and a thousand such political monsters. He should have been Pope; but instead of coming to it by the primitive decency of the Church, he did bestow bribes so largely and so impudently as if he would have carried it away without Heaven's knowledge. Some good he hath done——

Del. You have given too much of him. What's his brother?
Ant. The duke there? a most perverse and turbulent nature:
What appears in him mirth is merely outside;
If he laughs heartily, it is to laugh
All honesty out of fashion.
Del. Twins?
Ant. In quality.
He speaks with others' tongues, and hears men's suits
With others' ears; will seem to sleep o' th' bench
Only to entrap offenders in their answers;
Dooms men to death by information;
Rewards by hearsay.

[1] Informers.

Del. Then the law to him
Is like a foul black cobweb to a spider,—
He makes [of] it his dwelling and a prison
To entangle those shall feed him.

Ant. Most true:
He never pays debts unless they be shrewd turns,
And those he will confess that he doth owe.
Last, for his brother there, the Cardinal,
They that do flatter him most say oracles
Hang at his lips; and verily I believe them,
For the devil speaks in them.
But for their sister, the right noble duchess,
You never fixed your eye on three fair medals
Cast in one figure, of so different temper.
For her discourse, it is so full of rapture,
You only will begin then to be sorry
When she doth end her speech, and wish, in wonder,
She held it less vain-glory to talk much,
Than your penance to hear her: whilst she speaks,
She throws upon a man so sweet a look,
That it were able [to] [1] raise one to a galliard [2]
That lay in a dead palsy, and to dote
On that sweet countenance; but in that look
There speaketh so divine a continence
As cuts off all lascivious and vain hope.
Her days are practis'd in such noble virtue,
That sure her nights, nay, more, her very sleeps,
Are more in heaven than other ladies' shrifts.
Let all sweet ladies break their flattering glasses,
And dress themselves in her.

Del. Fie, Antonio,
You play the wire-drawer [3] with her commendations.

Ant. I'll case the picture up: only thus much;

[1] From the 1678 quarto.
[2] A lively dance in triple time.
[3] i. e. spin out at tedious length.

All her particular worth grows to this sum,—
She stains the time past, lights the time to come.

Car. You must attend my lady in the gallery,
Some half an hour hence.

Ant. I shall.

Exeunt ANTONIO *and* DELIO

Ferd. Sister, I have a suit to you.

Duch. To me, sir?

Ferd. A gentleman here, Daniel de Bosola,
One that was in the galleys—

Duch. Yes, I know him.

Ferd. A worthy fellow he is: pray, let me entreat for
The provisorship of your horse.

Duch. Your knowledge of him
Commends him and prefers him.

Ferd. Call him hither.

Exit Attendant

We [are] now upon parting. Good Lord Silvio,
Do us commend to all our noble friends
At the leaguer.

Silv. Sir, I shall.

Duch.[1] You are for Milan?

Silv. I am.

Duch. Bring the caroches.[2] We'll bring you down
To the haven.

Exeunt all but FFRDINAND *and the* CARDINAL

Card. Be sure you entertain[3] that Bosola
For your intelligence: I would not be seen in 't;
And therefore many times I have slighted him
When he did court our furtherance, as this morning.

Ferd. Antonio, the great-master of her household,
Had been far fitter.

Card. You are deceiv'd in him:

[1] Professor Sampson's correction for the 'Ferd.' of the quartos.
[2] Coaches.
[3] Make use of.

His nature is too honest for such business.—
He comes: I'll leave you. *Exit*

Re-enter BOSOLA

Bos. I was lur'd to you.
Ferd. My brother, here, the Cardinal could never
Abide you.
Bos. Never since he was in my debt.
Ferd. Maybe some oblique character in your face
Made him suspect you.
Bos. Doth he study physiognomy?
There's no more credit to be given to th' face
Than to a sick man's urine, which some call
The physician's whore because she cozens him.
He did suspect me wrongfully.
Ferd. For that
You must give great men leave to take their times.
Distrust doth cause us seldom be deceiv'd:
You see the oft shaking of the cedar-tree
Fastens it more at root.
Bos. Yet, take heed;
For to suspect a friend unworthily
Instructs him the next way to suspect you,
And prompts him to deceive you.
Ferd. [*Giving him money*] There's gold.
Bos. So:
What follows? never rained such showers as these
Without thunderbolts i' th' tail of them: whose throat must
I cut?
Ferd. Your inclination to shed blood rides post
Before my occasion to use you. I give you that
To live i' th' court here, and observe the duchess;
To note all the particulars of her haviour,
What suitors do solicit her for marriage,
And whom she best affects. She's a young widow:
I would not have her marry again.

Bos. No, sir?

Ferd. Do not you ask the reason; but be satisfied
I say I would not.

Bos. It seems you would create me
One of your familiars.

Ferd. Familiar? what's that?

Bos. Why, a very quaint invisible devil in flesh,
An intelligencer.

Ferd. Such a kind of thriving thing
I would wish thee; and ere long thou may'st arrive
At a higher place by 't.

Bos. Take your devils,
Which hell calls angels; these curs'd gifts would make
You a corrupter, me an impudent traitor;
And should I take these, they'd take me [to] hell.

Ferd. Sir, I'll take nothing from you that I have given:
There is a place that I procur'd for you
This morning, the provisorship o' th' horse;
Have you heard on 't?

Bos. No.

Ferd. 'Tis yours: is't not worth thanks?

Bos. I would have you curse yourself now, that your bounty,
Which makes men truly noble, e'er should make me
A villain. Oh, that to avoid ingratitude
For the good deed you have done me, I must do
All the ill man can invent! Thus the devil
Candies all sins o'er; and what heaven terms vile,
That names he complimental.[1]

Ferd. Be yourself;
Keep your old garb of melancholy; 'twill express
You envy those that stand above your reach,
Yet strive not to come near 'em: this will gain
Access to private lodgings, where yourself
May, like a politic dormouse—

[1] Required by courtesy.

Bos. As I have seen some
Feed in a lord's dish, half asleep, not seeming
To listen to any talk; and yet these rogues
Have cut his throat in a dream. What's my place?
The provisorship o' th' horse? say, then, my corruption
Grew out of horse-dung: I am your creature.

Ferd. Away! *Exit*

Bos. Let good men, for good deeds, covet good fame,
Since place and riches oft are bribes of shame:
Sometimes the devil doth preach. *Exit*

[SCENE II]

[*A Gallery in the Duchess's Palace*]

Enter FERDINAND, DUCHESS, CARDINAL, *and* CARIOLA

Card. We are to part from you; and your own discretion
Must now be your director.

Ferd. You are a widow:
You know already what man is; and therefore
Let not youth, high promotion, eloquence—

Card. No,
Nor any thing without the addition, honour,
Sway your high blood.

Ferd. Marry! they are most luxurious [1]
Will wed twice.

Card. Oh, fie!

Ferd. Their livers are more spotted
Than Laban's sheep.

Duchess. Diamonds are of most value,
They say, that have passed through most jewellers' hands.

Ferd. Whores by that rule are precious.

Duch. Will you hear me?
I'll never marry.

Card. So most widows say;

[1] Lascivious.

But commonly that motion lasts no longer
Than the turning of an hour-glass: the funeral sermon
And it end both together.

Ferd. Now hear me:
You live in a rank pasture, here, i' th' court;
There is a kind of honey-dew that's deadly;
'Twill poison your fame; look to't: be not cunning;
For they whose faces do belie their hearts
Are witches ere they arrive at twenty years,
Aye, and give the devil suck.

Duch. This is terrible good counsel.

Ferd. Hypocrisy is woven of a fine small thread,
Subtler than Vulcan's engine: [1] yet, believe't,
Your darkest actions, nay, your privat'st thoughts,
Will come to light.

Card. You may flatter yourself,
And take your own choice; privately be married
Under the eaves of night—

Ferd. Think'st the best voyage
That e'er you made; like the irregular crab,
Which, though't goes backward, thinks that it goes right
Because it goes its own way; but observe,
Such weddings may more properly be said
To be executed than celebrated.

Card. The marriage night
Is the entrance into some prison.

Ferd. And those joys,
Those lustful pleasures, are like heavy sleeps
Which do forerun man's mischief.

Card. Fare you well.
Wisdom begins at the end: remember it. *Exit*

Duchess. I think this speech between you both was studied,
It came so roundly off.

Ferd. You are my sister;

[1] The net in which he caught Mars and Venus.

This was my father's poniard, do you see?
I'd be loth to see 't look rusty, 'cause 'twas his.
I would have you to give o'er these chargeable revels:
A visor and a mask are whispering-rooms
That were never built for goodness;—fare ye well;—
And women like that part which, like the lamprey,
Hath never a bone in 't.

Duch. Fie, sir!

Ferd. Nay,
I mean the tongue; variety of courtship:
What cannot a neat knave with a smooth tale
Make a woman believe? Farewell, lusty widow. *Exit*

Duch. Shall this move me? If all my royal kindred
Lay in my way unto this marriage,
I'd make them my low footsteps: and even now,
Even in this hate, as men in some great battles,
By apprehending danger, have achiev'd
Almost impossible actions (I have heard soldiers say so),
So I through frights and threatenings will assay
This dangerous venture. Let old wives report
I wink'd and chose a husband.—Cariola,
To thy known secrecy I have given up
More than my life—my fame.

Car. Both shall be safe;
For I'll conceal this secret from the world
As warily as those that trade in poison
Keep poison from their children.

Duch. Thy protestation
Is ingenious [1] and hearty: I believe it.
Is Antonio come?

Car. He attends you.

Duch. Good dear soul,
Leave me; but place thyself behind the arras,
Where thou mayst overhear us. Wish me good speed;
For I am going into a wilderness

[1] Ingenuous.

Where I shall find nor path nor friendly clue
To be my guide. CARIOLA *goes behind the arras.*

Enter ANTONIO

I sent for you: sit down;
Take pen and ink, and write: are you ready?
Ant. Yes.
Duch. What did I say?
Ant. That I should write somewhat.
Duch. Oh, I remember.
After these triumphs and this large expense,
It's fit, like thrifty husbands, we inquire
What's laid up for to-morrow.
Ant. So please your beauteous excellence.
Duch. Beauteous?
Indeed, I thank you: I look young for your sake;
You have ta'en my cares upon you.
Ant. I'll fetch your grace
The particulars of your revenue and expense.
Duch. Oh, you are an upright treasurer: but you mistook;
For when I said I meant to make inquiry
What's laid up for to-morrow, I did mean
What's laid up yonder for me.
Ant. Where?
Duch. In heaven.
I am making my will (as 'tis fit princes should,
In perfect memory), and, I pray, sir, tell me,
Were not one better make it smiling, thus,
Than in deep groans and terrible ghastly looks,
As if the gifts we parted with procur'd
That violent distraction? [1]
Ant. Oh, much better.
Duch. If I had a husband now, this care were quit:

[1] Destruction, in the first two quartos.

But I intend to make you overseer.
What good deed shall we first remember? say.

Ant. Begin with that first good deed began i' th' world
After man's creation, the sacrament of marriage:
I'd have you first provide for a good husband;
Give him all.

Duch. All?

Ant. Yes, your excellent self.

Duch. In a winding-sheet?

Ant. In a couple.

Duch. Saint Winfred,
That were a strange will!

Ant. 'Twere strange[r] if there were no will in you
To marry again.

Duch. What do you think of marriage?

Ant. I take't, as those that deny purgatory;
It locally contains or Heaven or hell;
There's no third place in 't.

Duch. How do you affect it?

Ant. My banishment, feeling my melancholy,
Would often reason thus.

Duch. Pray, let's hear it.

Ant. Say a man never marry, nor have children,
What takes that from him? only the bare name
Of being a father, or the weak delight
To see the little wanton ride a-cock-horse
Upon a painted stick, or hear him chatter
Like a taught starling.

Duch. Fie, fie, what's all this?
One of your eyes is blood-shot; use my ring to 't,
They say 'tis very sovereign: 'twas my wedding-ring,
And I did vow never to part with it
But to my second husband.

Ant. You have parted with it now.

Duch. Yes, to help your eyesight.

Ant. You have made me stark blind.

Duch. How?

Ant. There is a saucy and ambitious devil
Is dancing in this circle.

Duch. Remove him.

Ant. How?

Duch. There needs small conjuration, when your finger
May do it: this; is it fit?

She puts the ring upon his finger: he kneels

Ant. What said you?

Duch. Sir,
This goodly roof of yours is too low built;
I cannot stand upright in 't nor discourse,
Without I raise it higher: raise yourself;
Or, if you please, my hand to help you: so. *Raises him*

Ant. Ambition, madam, is a great man's madness,
That is not kept in chains and close-pent rooms,
But in fair lightsome lodgings, and is girt
With the wild noise of prattling visitants,
Which makes it lunatic beyond all cure.
Conceive not I am so stupid but I aim [1]
Whereto your favours tend: but he's a fool
That, being a-cold, would thrust his hands i' th' fire
To warm them.

Duch. So, now the ground's broke,
You may discover what a wealthy mine
I make you lord of.

Ant. O my unworthiness!

Duch. You were ill to sell yourself:
This darkening of your worth is not like that
Which tradesmen use i' th' city, their false lights
Are to rid bad wares off: and I must tell you,
If you will know where breathes a complete man
(I speak it without flattery), turn your eyes,
And progress through yourself.

Ant. Were there nor heaven

[1] Guess.

Nor hell, I should be honest: I have long serv'd virtue,
And ne'er ta'en wages of her.

Duch. Now she pays it.
The misery of us that are born great!
We are forc'd to woo, because none dare woo us;
And as a tyrant doubles with his words,
And fearfully equivocates, so we
Are forc'd to express our violent passions
In riddles and in dreams, and leave the path
Of simple virtue, which was never made
To seem the thing it is not. Go, go brag
You have left me heartless; mine is in your bosom:
I hope 'twill multiply love there. You do tremble:
Make not your heart so dead a piece of flesh,
To fear more than to love me. Sir, be confident:
What is 't distracts you? This is flesh and blood, sir;
'Tis not the figure cut in alabaster
Kneels at my husband's tomb. Awake, awake, man!
I do here put off all vain ceremony,
And only do appear to you a young widow
That claims you for her husband, and, like a widow,
I use but half a blush in 't.

Ant. Truth speak for me;
I will remain the constant sanctuary
Of your good name.

Duch. I thank you, gentle love:
And 'cause you shall not come to me in debt,
Being now my steward, here upon your lips
I sign your Quietus est.[1] This you should have begg'd now:
I have seen children oft eat sweetmeats thus,
As fearful to devour them too soon.

Ant. But for your brothers?

Duch. Do not think of them:
All discord without this circumference
Is only to be pitied, and not fear'd:

[1] Acquittance.

Yet, should they know it, time will easily
Scatter the tempest.

Ant. These words should be mine,
And all the parts you have spoke, if some part of it
Would not have savour'd flattery.

Duch. Kneel.

CARIOLA *comes from behind the arras*

Ant. Ha!

Duch. Be not amazed; this woman's of my counsel:
I have heard lawyers say, a contract in a chamber
Per verba [de] presenti is absolute marriage.

She and ANTONIO *kneel*

Bless, heaven, this sacred gordian, which let violence [1]
Never untwine!

Ant. And may our sweet affections, like the spheres,
Be still in motion!

Duch. Quickening, and make
The like soft music!

Ant. That we may imitate the loving palms,
Best emblem of a peaceful marriage, that ne'er
Bore fruit, divided!

Duch. What can the Church force more?

Ant. That fortune may not know an accident,
Either of joy or sorrow, to divide
Our fixèd wishes!

Duch. How can the Church build faster?
We now are man and wife, and 'tis the Church
That must but echo this.—Maid, stand apart:
I now am blind.

Ant. What's your conceit in this?

Duch. I would have you lead your fortune by the hand
Unto your marriage bed:
(You speak in me this, for we now are one:)
We'll only lie, and talk together, and plot
To appease my humorous kindred; and if you please,

[1] The arrangement of these lines is very questionable.

Like the old tale in 'Alexander and Lodowick',[1]
Lay a naked sword between us, keep us chaste.
Oh, let me shroud my blushes in your bosom,
Since 'tis the treasury of all my secrets!

Exeunt DUCHESS *and* ANTONIO

Car. Whether the spirit of greatness or of woman
Reign most in her, I know not; but it shows
A fearful madness: I owe her much of pity. *Exit*

ACT THE SECOND

[SCENE I]

[*A Room in the Palace of the Duchess*]

Enter BOSOLA *and* CASTRUCHIO

Bos. You say you would fain be taken for an eminent courtier?

Cas. 'Tis the very main of my ambition.

Bos. Let me see: you have a reasonable good face for 't already, and your nightcap expresses your ears sufficient largely. I would have you learn to twirl the strings of your band with a good grace, and in a set speech, at th' end of every sentence, to hum three or four times, or blow your nose till it smart again, to recover your memory. When you come to be a president in criminal causes, if you smile upon a prisoner, hang him, but if you frown upon him and threaten him, let him be sure to scape the gallows.

Cas. I would be a very merry president.

Bos. Do not sup o' night; 'twill beget you an admirable wit.

Cas. Rather it would make me have a good stomach to quarrel; for they say, your roaring boys eat meat seldom,

[1] *The Two Faithful Friends, the pleasant History of Alexander and Lodwicke,* is reprinted from the Pepys collection in Evans's *Old Ballads.—Dyce*

and that makes them so valiant. But how shall I know whether the people take me for an eminent fellow?

Bos. I will teach a trick to know it: give out you lie a-dying, and if you hear the common people curse you, be sure you are taken for one of the prime nightcaps.[1]

Enter an Old Lady

You come from painting now.

Old L. From what?

Bos. Why, from your scurvy face-physic. To behold thee not painted inclines somewhat near a miracle; these in thy face here were deep ruts and foul sloughs the last progress.[2] There was a lady in France that, having had the small-pox, flayed the skin off her face to make it more level; and whereas before she look'd like a nutmeg-grater, after she resembled an abortive hedgehog.

Old L. Do you call this painting?

Bos. No, no, but you call [it] careening of an old morphewed[3] lady, to make her disembogue[4] again: there's rough-cast phrase to your plastic.[5]

Old L. It seems you are well acquainted with my closet.

Bos. One would suspect it for a shop of witchcraft, to find in it the fat of serpents, spawn of snakes, Jews' spittle, and their young children's ordure; and all these for the face. I would sooner eat a dead pigeon taken from the soles of the feet of one sick of the plague than kiss one of you fasting. Here are two of you, whose sin of your youth is the very patrimony of the physician; makes him renew his foot-cloth with the spring, and change his high-priced courtezan with the fall of the leaf. I do wonder you do not loathe yourselves. Observe my meditation now.

What thing is in this outward form of man

[1] A cant name for the Mohocks of the time.
[2] State procession.
[3] Leprous.
[4] Discharge herself.
[5] i. e. plain language instead of your fine phrases.

To be belov'd? We account it ominous,
If nature do produce a colt, or lamb,
A fawn, or goat, in any limb resembling
A man, and fly from 't as a prodigy:
Man stands amaz'd to see his deformity
In any other creature but himself.
But in our own flesh, though we bear diseases
Which have their true names only ta'en from beasts,—
As the most ulcerous wolf and swinish measle,[1]—
Though we are eaten up of lice and worms,
And though continually we bear about us
A rotten and dead body, we delight
To hide it in rich tissue: all our fear,
Nay, all our terror, is lest our physician
Should put us in the ground to be made sweet.—
Your wife's gone to Rome: you two couple, and get you
To the wells at Lucca to recover your aches.
I have other work on foot.

Exeunt CASTRUCHIO *and* Old Lady

I observe our duchess
Is sick a-days, she pukes, her stomach seethes,
The fins of her eye-lids look most teeming blue,
She wanes i' th' cheek, and waxes fat i' th' flank,
And, contrary to our Italian fashion,
Wears a loose-bodied gown: there's somewhat in 't.
I have a trick may chance discover it,
A pretty one; I have brought some apricocks,
The first our spring yields.

Enter ANTONIO *and* DELIO, *talking together apart.*

Del. And so long since married?
You amaze me.
Ant. Let me seal your lips for ever:

[1] A disease to which swine are subject, not the same as the human ailment.

For, did I think that anything but th' air
Could carry these words from you, I should wish
You had no breath at all.—Now, sir, in your contemplation?
You are studying to become a great wise fellow?

Bos. Oh, sir, the opinion of wisdom is a foul tetter [1] that runs all over a man's body: if simplicity direct us to have no evil, it directs us to a happy being; for the subtlest folly proceeds from the subtlest wisdom: let me be simply honest.

Ant. I do understand your inside.

Bos. Do you so?

Ant. Because you would not seem to appear to th' world
Puff'd up with your preferment, you continue
This out-of-fashion melancholy: leave it, leave it.

Bos. Give me leave to be honest in any phrase, in any compliment whatsoever. Shall I confess myself to you? I look no higher than I can reach: they are the gods that must ride on winged horses. A lawyer's mule of a slow pace will both suit my disposition and business; for, mark me, when a man's mind rides faster than his horse can gallop, they quickly both tire.

Ant. You would look up to heaven, but I think
The devil, that rules i' th' air, stands in your light.

Bos. Oh, sir, you are lord of the ascendant, chief man with the duchess; a duke was your cousin-german remov'd. Say you were lineally descended from King Pepin, or he himself, what of this? search the heads of the greatest rivers in the world, you shall find them but bubbles of water. Some would think the souls of princes were brought forth by some more weighty cause than those of meaner persons: they are deceiv'd, there's the same hand to them; the like passions sway them; the same reason that makes a vicar go to law for a tithe-pig, and undo his neighbours, makes them spoil a whole province, and batter down goodly cities with the cannon.

[1] Skin disease.

Enter DUCHESS *and* Ladies

Duch. Your arm, Antonio: do I not grow fat?
I am exceeding short-winded.—Bosola,
I would have you, sir, provide for me a litter;
Such a one as the Duchess of Florence rode in.

Bos. The duchess used one when she was great with child.

Duch. I think she did.—Come hither, mend my ruff;
Here, when? [1]
Thou art such a tedious lady; and thy breath smells
Of lemon-peels; would thou hadst done! Shall I swoon
Under thy fingers! I am so troubled
With the mother! [2]

Bos. [*Aside*] I fear too much.

Duch. I have heard you say
That the French courtiers wear their hats on 'fore
The king.

Ant. I have seen it.

Duch. In the presence?

Ant. Yes.

Duch. Why should not we bring up that fashion? 'Tis
Ceremony more than duty that consists
In the removing of a piece of felt:
Be you the example to the rest o' th' court;
Put on your hat first.

Ant. You must pardon me:
I have seen, in colder countries than in France,
Nobles stand bare to th' prince; and the distinction
Methought show'd reverently.

Bos. I have a present for your grace.

Duch. For me, sir?

Bos. Apricocks, madam.

Duch. O, sir, where are they?
I have heard of none to-year.

[1] A common exclamation of impatience.
[2] Hysteria.

Bos. [*Aside*] Good; her colour rises.
Duch. Indeed, I thank you: they are wondrous fair ones.
What an unskilful fellow is our gardener!
We shall have none this month.
Bos. Will not your grace pare them?
Duch. No: they taste of musk, methinks; indeed they do.
Bos. I know not: yet I wish your grace had pared 'em.
Duch. Why?
Bos. I forgot to tell you, the knave gardener,
Only to raise his profit by them the sooner,
Did ripen them in horse-dung.
Duch. O, you jest.—
You shall judge: pray taste one.
Ant. Indeed, madam,
I do not love the fruit.
Duch. Sir, you are loath
To rob us of our dainties: 'tis a delicate fruit;
They say they are restorative.
Bos. 'Tis a pretty art,
This grafting.
Duch. 'Tis so; a bettering of nature.
Bos. To make a pippin grow upon a crab,
A damson on a blackthorn.—[*Aside*] How greedily she eats them!
A whirlwind strike off these bawd farthingales!
For, but for that and the loose-bodied gown,
I should have discovered apparently
The young springal[1] cutting a caper in her belly.
Duch. I thank you, Bosola: they were right good ones,
If they do not make me sick.
Ant. How now, madam?
Duch. This green fruit and my stomach are not friends:
How they swell me!
Bos. [*Aside*] Nay, you are too much swelled already.
Duch. Oh, I am in an extreme cold sweat!

[1] Stripling.

Bos. I am very sorry.

Duch. Lights to my chamber!—O good Antonio,
I fear I am undone!

Del. Lights there, lights!

Exeunt DUCHESS *and* Ladies.—*Exit, on the other side,* BOSOLA

Ant. O my most trusty Delio, we are lost!
I fear she's fall'n in labour; and there's left
No time for her remove.

Del. Have you prepar'd
Those ladies to attend her? and procur'd
That politic safe conveyance for the midwife
Your duchess plotted?

Ant. I have.

Del. Make use, then, of this forc'd occasion:
Give out that Bosola hath poison'd her
With these apricocks; that will give some colour
For her keeping close.

Ant. Fie, fie, the physicians
Will then flock to her.

Del. For that you may pretend
She'll use some prepar'd antidote of her own,
Lest the physicians should re-poison her.

Ant. I am lost in amazement: I know not what to think on 't. *Exeunt*

[SCENE II]

[*A Hall in the same Palace*]

Enter BOSOLA

Bos. So, so, there's no question but her tetchiness and most vulturous eating of the apricocks are apparent signs of breeding.

Enter an Old Lady

Now?

Old L. I am in haste, sir.

Bos. There was a young waiting-woman had a monstrous desire to see the glass-house——

Old L. Nay, pray let me go.

Bos. And it was only to know what strange instrument it was should swell up a glass to the fashion of a woman's belly.

Old L. I will hear no more of the glass-house. You are still abusing women?

Bos. Who, I? no; only, by the way now and then, mention your frailties. The orange-tree bear[s] ripe and green fruit and blossoms all together; and some of you give entertainment for pure love, but more for more precious reward. The lusty spring smells well; but drooping autumn tastes well. If we have the same golden showers that rained in the time of Jupiter the thunderer, you have the same Danaës still, to hold up their laps to receive them. Didst thou never study the mathematics?

Old L. What's that, sir?

Bos. Why, to know the trick how to make a many lines meet in one centre. Go, go, give your foster-daughters good counsel: tell them, that the devil takes delight to hang at a woman's girdle, like a false rusty watch, that she cannot discern how the time passes. *Exit* Old Lady

Enter Antonio, Delio, Roderigo, *and* Grisolan

Ant. Shut up the court-gates.

Rod. Why, sir? what's the danger?

Ant. Shut up the posterns presently, and call
All the officers o' th' court.

Gris. I shall instantly. *Exit*

Ant. Who keeps the key o' th' park gate?

Rod. Forobosco.[1]

Ant. Let him bring 't presently.

[1] This character is included in the quarto dramatis personæ and assigned to an actor, but he is not mentioned elsewhere in the play.

Re-enter GRISOLAN *with* Servants

1 *Serv.* O, gentlemen o' the court, the foulest treason!
Bos. [*Aside*] If that these apricocks should be poison'd now,
Without my knowledge!
1 *Serv.* There was taken even now
A Switzer in the duchess' bed chamber—
2 *Serv.* A Switzer?
1 *Serv.* With a pistol in his great cod-piece.
Bos. Ha, ha, ha!
1 *Serv.* The cod-piece was the case for 't.
2 *Serv.* There was
A cunning traitor: who would have search'd his cod-piece?
1 *Serv.* True, if he had kept out of the ladies' chambers:
And all the moulds of his buttons were leaden bullets.
2 *Serv.* O wicked cannibal!
A fire-lock in 's cod-piece!
1 *Serv.* 'Twas a French plot,
Upon my life.
2 *Serv.* To see what the devil can do!
Ant. [Are] all the officers here?
Servants. We are.
Ant. Gentlemen,
We have lost much plate you know; and but this evening
Jewels, to the value of four thousand ducats,
Are missing in the duchess' cabinet.
Are the gates shut?
Serv. Yes.
Ant. 'Tis the duchess' pleasure
Each officer be lock'd into his chamber
Till the sun-rising; and to send the keys
Of all their chests and of their outward doors
Into her bed-chamber. She is very sick.
Rod. At her pleasure.
Ant. She entreats you take 't not ill:

The innocent shall be the more approv'd by it.

Bos. Gentleman o' th' wood-yard, where's your Switzer now?

1 *Serv.* By this hand, 'twas credibly reported by one o' th' black guard. *Exeunt all except* ANTONIO *and* DELIO

Del. How fares it with the duchess?

Ant. She's expos'd
Unto the worst of torture, pain and fear.

Del. Speak to her all happy comfort.

Ant. How I do play the fool with mine own danger!
You are this night, dear friend, to post to Rome:
My life lies in your service.

Del. Do not doubt me.

Ant. Oh, 'tis far from me: and yet fear presents me
Somewhat that looks like danger.

Del. Believe it,
'Tis but the shadow of your fear, no more;
How superstitiously we mind our evils!
The throwing down salt, or crossing of a hare,
Bleeding at nose, the stumbling of a horse,
Or singing of a cricket, are of power
To daunt whole man in us. Sir, fare you well:
I wish you all the joys of a bless'd father:
And, for my faith, lay this unto your breast,—
Old friends, like old swords, still are trusted best. *Exit*

Enter CARIOLA

Car. Sir, you are the happy father of a son:
Your wife commends him to you.

Ant. Blessèd comfort!—
For Heaven's sake tend her well: I'll presently
Go set a figure for 's nativity. *Exeunt*

[SCENE III]

[*The Courtyard of the same Palace*]

Enter BOSOLA, *with a dark lantern*

Bos. Sure I did hear a woman shriek: list, ha!
And the sound came, if I receiv'd it right,
From the duchess' lodgings. There's some stratagem
In the confining all our courtiers
To their several wards: I must have part of it;
My intelligence will freeze else. List, again!
It may be 'twas the melancholy bird,
Best friend of silence and of solitariness,
The owl, that scream'd so.—Ha! Antonio?

Enter ANTONIO *with a Candle, his Sword drawn*

Ant. I heard some noise.—Who's there? what art thou? speak.

Bos. Antonio? put not your face nor body
To such a forc'd expression of fear:
I am Bosola, your friend.

Ant. Bosola!—
[*Aside*] This mole does undermine me.—Heard you not
A noise even now?

Bos. From whence?

Ant. From the duchess' lodging.

Bos. Not I: did you?

Ant. I did, or else I dream'd.

Bos. Let's walk towards it.

Ant. No: it may be 'twas
But the rising of the wind.

Bos. Very likely.
Methinks 'tis very cold, and yet you sweat:
You look wildly.

Ant. I have been setting a figure

For the duchess' jewels.

Bos. Ah, and how falls your question?
Do you find it radical? [1]

Ant. What's that to you?
'Tis rather to be questioned what design,
When all men were commanded to their lodgings,
Makes you a night-walker.

Bos. In sooth, I'll tell you:
Now all the court's asleep, I thought the devil
Had least to do here; I came to say my prayers;
And if it do offend you I do so,
You are a fine courtier.

Ant. [*Aside*] This fellow will undo me.—
You gave the duchess apricocks to-day:
Pray Heaven they were not poison'd!

Bos. Poison'd? [2] A Spanish fig
For the imputation!

Ant. Traitors are ever confident
Till they are discover'd. There were jewels stol'n too:
In my conceit, none are to be suspected
More than yourself.

Bos. You are a false steward.

Ant. Saucy slave, I'll pull thee up by the roots.

Bos. Maybe the ruin will crush you to pieces.

Ant. You are an impudent snake indeed, sir:
Are you scarce warm, and do you show your sting?
You libel well, sir.

Bos. No, sir: copy it out,
And I will set my hand to't.

Ant. [*Aside*] My nose bleeds.
One that were superstitious would count
This ominous, when it merely comes by chance:
Two letters, that are wrought here for my name,
Are drown'd in blood!

[1] i. e. capable of solution.
[2] Query, omit this word.

Mere accident.—For you, sir, I'll take order
I' th' morn you shall be safe:—[*Aside*] 'tis that must colour
Her lying-in: —sir, this door you pass not:
I do not hold it fit that you come near
The duchess' lodgings, till you have quit yourself.—
[*Aside*] The great are like the base, nay, they are the same,
When they seek shameful ways to avoid shame. *Exit*

Bos. Antonio hereabout did drop a paper:—
Some of your help, false friend: [*Opening his lantern*] —Oh,
here it is.
What's here? a child's nativity calculated? *Reads*

'The duchess was deliver'd of a son, 'tween the hours twelve and one in the night, Anno Dom. 1504,'—that's this year—'decimo nono Decembris,'—that's this night,—'taken according to the meridian of Malfi,'—that's our duchess: happy discovery!—'The lord of the first house being combust in the ascendant, signifies short life; and Mars being in a human sign, join'd to the tail of the Dragon, in the eighth house, doth threaten a violent death. Caetera non scrutantur.'

Why, now 'tis most apparent: this precise fellow
Is the duchess' bawd:—I have it to my wish!
This is a parcel of intelligency
Our courtiers were cas'd up for: it needs must follow
That I must be committed on pretence
Of poisoning her; which I'll endure, and laugh at.
If one could find the father now! but that
Time will discover. Old Castruchio
I' th' morning posts to Rome: by him I'll send
A letter that shall make her brothers' galls
O'erflow their livers. This was a thrifty way.
Though lust do mask in ne'er so strange disguise,
She's oft found witty, but is never wise. *Exit*

[SCENE IV]

[*A Room in the Palace of the Cardinal at Rome*]

Enter CARDINAL *and* JULIA

Card. Sit: thou art my best of wishes. Prithee, tell me
What trick didst thou invent to come to Rome
Without thy husband.
Jul. Why, my lord, I told him
I came to visit an old anchorite
Here for devotion.
Card. Thou art a witty false one,—
I mean, to him.
Jul. You have prevailed with me
Beyond my strongest thoughts! I would not now
Find you inconstant.
Card. Do not put thyself
To such a voluntary torture, which proceeds
Out of your own guilt.
Jul. How, my lord?
Card. You fear
My constancy, because you have approved
Those giddy and wild turning[s] in yourself.
Jul. Did you e'er find them?
Card. Sooth, generally for women;
A man might strive to make glass malleable,
Ere he should make them fixed.
Jul. So, my lord.
Card. We had need go borrow that fantastic glass
Invented by Galileo the Florentine
To view another spacious world i' th' moon,
And look to find a constant woman there.
Jul. This is very well, my lord.
Card. Why do you weep?
Are tears your justification? the self-same tears

Will fall into your husband's bosom, lady,
With a loud protestation that you love him
Above the world. Come, I'll love you wisely,
That's jealously; since I am very certain
You cannot make me cuckold.

Jul. I'll go home
To my husband.

Card. You may thank me, lady,
I have taken you off your melancholy perch,
Bore you upon my fist, and show'd you game,
And let you fly at it.—I pray thee, kiss me.—
When thou wast with thy husband, thou wast watch'd
Like a tame elephant:—still you are to thank me:—
Thou hadst only kisses from him and high feeding;
But what delight was that? 'twas just like one
That hath a little fingering on the lute,
Yet cannot tune it:—still you are to thank me.

Jul. You told me of a piteous wound i' th' heart
And a sick liver, when you wooed me first,
And spake like one in physic.

Card. Who's that?—

Enter Servant

Rest firm, for my affection to thee,
Lightning moves slow to 't.

Serv. Madam, a gentleman,
That's come post from Malfi, desires to see you.

Card. Let him enter: I'll withdraw. *Exit*

Serv. He says
Your husband, old Castruchio, is come to Rome,
Most pitifully tir'd with riding post. *Exit*

Enter Delio

Jul. Signior Delio! [*Aside*] 'tis one of my old suitors.

Del. I was bold to come and see you.

Jul. Sir, you are welcome.

Del. Do you lie here?

Jul. Sure, your own experience
Will satisfy you no: our Roman prelates
Do not keep lodging for ladies.

Del. Very well:
I have brought you no commendations from your husband,
For I know none by him.

Jul. I hear he's come to Rome.

Del. I never knew man and beast, of a horse and a knight,
So weary of each other: if he had had a good back,
He would have undertook to have borne his horse,
His breech was so pitifully sore.

Jul. Your laughter
Is my pity.

Del. Lady, I know not whether
You want money, but I have brought you some.

Jul. From my husband?

Del. No, from mine own allowance.

Julia. I must hear the condition, ere I be bound to take it.

Del. Look on't, 'tis gold: hath it not a fine colour?

Jul. I have a bird more beautiful.

Del. Try the sound on 't.

Julia. A lute-string far exceeds it:
It hath no smell, like cassia or civet;
Nor is it physical, though some fond doctors
Persuade us seethe 't in cullises. I'll tell you,
This is a creature bred by——

Re-enter Servant

Serv. Your husband's come,
Hath deliver'd a letter to the Duke of Calabria
That, to my thinking, hath put him out of his wits. *Exit*

Jul. Sir, you hear:
Pray, let me know your business and your suit

As briefly as can be.

Del. With good speed: I would wish you,
At such time as you are non-resident
With your husband, my mistress.

Julia. Sir, I'll go ask my husband if I shall,
And straight return your answer. *Exit*

Del. Very fine!
Is this her wit, or honesty, that speaks thus?
I heard one say the duke was highly mov'd
With a letter sent from Malfi. I do fear
Antonio is betray'd: how fearfully
Shows his ambition now! unfortunate fortune!
They pass through whirlpools, and deep woes do shun,
Who the event weigh ere the action's done. *Exit*

[SCENE V]

[*Another Room in the same Palace*]

Enter CARDINAL, *and* FERDINAND *with a letter*

Ferd. I have this night digged up a mandrake.

Card. Say you?

Ferd. And I am grown mad with 't.

Card. What's the prodigy?

Ferd. Read there,—a sister damn'd: she's loose i' th' hilts;
Grown a notorious strumpet.

Card. Speak lower.

Ferd. Lower?
Rogues do not whisper 't now, but seek to publish 't
(As servants do the bounty of their lords)
Aloud; and with a covetous searching eye,
To mark who note them. O, confusion seize her!
She hath had most cunning bawds to serve her turn,
And more secure conveyances for lust
Than towns of garrison for service.

Card. Is 't possible?
Can this be certain?
Ferd. Rhubarb, oh, for rhubarb
To purge this choler! here's the cursèd day
To prompt my memory; and here 't shall stick
Till of her bleeding heart I make a sponge
To wipe it out.
Card. Why do you make yourself
So wild a tempest?
Ferd. Would I could be one,
That I might toss her palace 'bout her ears,
Root up her goodly forests, blast her meads,
And lay her general territory as waste
As she hath done her honours.
Card. Shall our blood,
The royal blood of Arragon and Castile,
Be thus attainted?
Ferd. Apply desperate physic:
We must not now use balsamum, but fire,
The smarting cupping-glass, for that 's the mean
To purge infected blood, such blood as hers.
There is a kind of pity in mine eye,—
I'll give it to my handkercher; and now 'tis here,
I'll bequeath this to her bastard.
Card. What to do?
Ferd. Why, to make soft lint for his mother's wounds,
When I have hewed her to pieces.
Card. Curs'd creature!
Unequal nature, to place women's hearts
So far upon the left side!
Ferd. Foolish men,
That e'er will trust their honour in a bark
Made of so slight weak bulrush as is woman,
Apt every minute to sink it!
Card. Thus ignorance, when it hath purchas'd honour,
It cannot wield it.

Ferd. Methinks I see her laughing—
Excellent hyena! Talk to me somewhat, quickly,
Or my imagination will carry me
To see her in the shameful act of sin.

Card. With whom?

Ferd. Happily [1] with some strong-thigh'd bargeman,
Or one [o'] the woodyard that can quoit the sledge [2]
Or toss the bar, or else some lovely squire
That carries coals up to her privy lodgings.

Card. You fly beyond your reason.

Ferd. Go to, mistress!
'Tis not your whore's milk that shall quench my wild fire,
But your whore's blood.

Card. How idly shows this rage, which carries you,
As men convey'd by witches through the air,
On violent whirlwinds! this intemperate noise
Fitly resembles deaf men's shrill discourse,
Who talk aloud, thinking all other men
To have their imperfection.

Ferd. Have not you
My palsy?

Card. Yes, I can be angry, [but]
Without this rupture:[3] there is not in nature
A thing that makes man so deform'd, so beastly,
As doth intemperate anger. Chide yourself.
You have divers men who never yet express'd
Their strong desire of rest but by unrest,
By vexing of themselves. Come, put yourself
In tune.

Ferd. So; I will only study to seem
The thing I am not. I could kill her now,
In you, or in myself; for I do think
It is some sin in us heaven doth revenge

[1] Often used for 'haply'
[2] Throw the hammer.
[3] Outburst.

By her.

Card. Are you stark mad?

Ferd. I would have their bodies
Burnt in a coal-pit with the ventage stopp'd,
That their curs'd smoke might not ascend to heaven;
Or dip the sheets they lie in in pitch or sulphur,
Wrap them in 't, and then light them like a match;
Or else to boil their bastard to a cullis,
And give 't his lecherous father to renew
The sin of his back.

Card. I'll leave you.

Ferd. Nay, I have done.
I am confident, had I been damn'd in hell,
And should have heard of this, it would have put me
Into a cold sweat. In, in; I'll go sleep.
Till I know who leaps my sister, I'll not stir:
That known, I'll find scorpions to string my whips,
And fix her in a general eclipse. *Exeunt*

Act The Third

[SCENE I]

[*A Room in the Palace of the Duchess*]

Enter Antonio *and* Delio

Ant. Our noble friend, my most beloved Delio!
Oh, you have been a stranger long at court;
Came you along with the Lord Ferdinand?

Del. I did, sir: and how fares your noble duchess?

Ant. Right fortunately well: she 's an excellent
Feeder of pedigrees; since you last saw her,
She hath had two children more, a son and daughter.

Del. Methinks 'twas yesterday: let me but wink,
And not behold your face, which to mine eye
Is somewhat leaner, verily I should dream

It were within this half-hour.

Ant. You have not been in law, friend Delio,
Nor in prison, nor a suitor at the court,
Nor begged the reversion of some great man's place,
Nor troubled with an old wife, which doth make
Your time so insensibly hasten.

Del. Pray, sir, tell me,
Hath not this news arriv'd yet to the ear
Of the lord cardinal?

Ant. I fear it hath:
The Lord Ferdinand, that 's newly come to court,
Doth bear himself right dangerously.

Del. Pray, why?

Ant. He is so quiet that he seems to sleep
The tempest out, as dormice do in winter:
Those houses that are haunted are most still
Till the devil be up.

Del. What say the common people?

Ant. The common rabble do directly say
She is a strumpet.

Del. And your graver heads
Which would be politic, what censure [1] they?

Ant. They do observe I grow to infinite purchase,[2]
The left hand way, and all suppose the duchess
Would amend it, if she could; for, say they,
Great princes, though they grudge their officers
Should have such large and unconfinèd means
To get wealth under them, will not complain,
Lest thereby they should make them odious
Unto the people; for other obligation
Of love or marriage between her and me
They never dream of.

Del. The Lord Ferdinand
Is going to bed.

[1] Think.
[2] Acquired property, wealth.

Enter DUCHESS, FERDINAND, *and* BOSOLA

Ferd. I'll instantly to bed,
For I am weary.—I am to bespeak
A husband for you.
Duch. For me, sir? pray, who is 't?
Ferd. The great Count Malateste.
Duch. Fie upon him!
A count? he 's a mere stick of sugar-candy;
You may look quite thorough him. When I choose
A husband, I will marry for your honour.
Ferd. You shall do well in 't.—How is 't, worthy Antonio?
Duch. But, sir, I am to have private conference with you
About a scandalous report is spread
Touching mine honour.
Ferd. Let me be ever deaf to 't:
One of Pasquil's [1] paper bullets, court-calumny,
A pestilent air, which princes' palaces
Are seldom purged of. Yet, say that it were true,
I pour it in your bosom, my fix'd love
Would strongly excuse, extenuate, nay, deny
Faults, were they apparent in you. Go, be safe
In your own innocency.
Duch. [*Aside*] O bless'd comfort!
This deadly air is purg'd.
Exeunt DUCHESS, ANTONIO, *and* DELIO
Ferd. Her guilt treads on
Hot-burning coulters.—Now, Bosola,
How thrives our intelligence?
Bos. Sir, uncertainly
'Tis rumour'd she hath had three bastards, but
By whom we may go read i' th' stars.
Ferd. Why, some
Hold opinion all things are written there.
Bos. Yes, if we could find spectacles to read them.

[1] Or Pasquin's.

I do suspect there hath been some sorcery
Us'd on the duchess.
  Ferd. Sorcery? to what purpose?
  Bos. To make her dote on some desertless fellow
She shames to acknowledge.
  Ferd. Can your faith give way
To think there 's power in potions or in charms,
To make us love whether we will or no?
  Bos. Most certainly.
  Ferd. Away! these are mere gulleries, horrid things,
Invented by some cheating mountebanks
To abuse us. Do you think that herbs or charms
Can force the will? Some trials have been made
In this foolish practice, but the ingredients
Were lenitive poisons, such as are of force
To make the patient mad; and straight the witch
Swears by equivocation they are in love.
The witchcraft lies in her rank blood. This night
I will force confession from her. You told me
You had got, within these two days, a false key
Into her bed-chamber.
  Bos. I have.
  Ferd. As I would wish.
  Bos. What do you intend to do?
  Ferd. Can you guess?
  Bos. No.
  Ferd. Do not ask, then:
He that can compass me, and know my drifts,
May say he hath put a girdle 'bout the world,
And sounded all her quicksands.
  Bos. I do not
Think so.
  Ferd. What do you think, then, pray?
  Bos. That you
Are your own chronicle too much, and grossly
Flatter yourself.

Ferd. Give me thy hand; I thank thee:
I never gave pension but to flatterers,
Till I entertained thee. Farewell.
That friend a great man's ruin strongly checks,
Who rails into his belief all his defects. *Exeunt*

[SCENE II]

[*The Bedchamber of the Duchess*]

Enter DUCHESS, ANTONIO, *and* CARIOLA

Duch. Bring me the casket hither, and the glass.—
You get no lodging here to-night, my lord.
Ant. Indeed, I must persuade one.
Duch. Very good:
I hope in time 'twill grow into a custom,
That noblemen shall come with cap and knee
To purchase a night's lodging of their wives.
Ant. I must lie here.
Duch. Must! you are a lord of misrule.
Ant. Indeed, my rule is only in the night.
Duch. To what use will you put me?
Ant. We'll sleep together.
Duch. Alas,
What pleasure can two lovers find in sleep!
Car. My lord, I lie with her often; and I know
She'll much disquiet you.
Ant. See, you are complain'd of.
Car. For she 's the sprawling'st bedfellow.
Ant. I shall like her
The better for that.
Car. Sir, shall I ask you a question?
Ant. Oh, I pray thee, Cariola.
Car. Wherefore still, when you lie
With my lady, do you rise so early?
Ant. Labouring men

Count the clock oftenest, Cariola, are glad
When their task 's ended.
Duch. I'll stop your mouth. *Kisses him*
Ant. Nay, that 's but one; Venus had two soft doves
To draw her chariot; I must have another—
She kisses him again
When wilt thou marry, Cariola?
Car. Never, my lord.
Ant. Oh, fie upon this single life! forgo it.
We read how Daphne, for her peevish [1] flight,
Became a fruitless bay-tree; Syrinx turn'd
To the pale empty reed; Anaxarete
Was frozen into marble: whereas those
Which married, or prov'd kind unto their friends,
Were by a gracious influence transhap'd
Into the olive, pomegranate, mulberry,
Became flowers, precious stones, or eminent stars.
Car. This is a vain poetry: but I pray you tell me,
If there were propos'd me, wisdom, riches, and beauty,
In three several young men, which should I choose?
Ant. 'Tis a hard question: this was Paris' case,
And he was blind in 't, and there was great cause;
For how was 't possible he could judge right,
Having three amorous goddesses in view,
And they stark naked? 'twas a motion
Were able to benight the apprehension
Of the severest counsellor of Europe.
Now I look on both your faces so well form'd,
It puts me in mind of a question I would ask.
Car. What is 't?
Ant. I do wonder why hard-favour'd ladies,
For the most part, keep worse-favour'd waiting-women
To attend them, and cannot endure fair ones.
Duch. Oh, that's soon answer'd.
Did you ever in your life know an ill painter

[1] Foolish

Desire to have his dwelling next door to the shop
Of an excellent picture-maker? 'twould disgrace
His face-making, and undo him. I prithee,
When were we so merry?—My hair tangles.

Ant. Pray thee, Cariola, let 's steal forth the room,
And let her talk to herself: I have divers times
Serv'd her the like, when she hath chaf'd extremely.
I love to see her angry. Softly, Cariola.

Exeunt ANTONIO *and* CARIOLA

Duch. Doth not the colour of my hair 'gin to change?
When I wax grey, I shall have all the court
Powder their hair with arras,[1] to be like me.
You have cause to love me; I enter'd you into my heart
Before you would vouchsafe to call for the keys.

Enter FERDINAND *behind*

We shall one day have my brothers take you napping;
Methinks his presence, being now in court,
Should make you keep your own bed; but you'll say
Love mix'd with fear is sweetest. I'll assure you,
You shall get no more children till my brothers
Consent to be your gossips. Have you lost your tongue?
'Tis welcome:
For know, whether I am doom'd to live or die,
I can do both like a prince.

Ferd. Die, then, quickly!

Giving her a poniard

Virtue, where art thou hid? what hideous thing
Is it that doth eclipse thee?

Duch. Pray, sir, hear me.

Ferd. Or is it true thou art but a bare name,
And no essential thing?

Duch. Sir,—

Ferd. Do not speak.

[1] Orris powder, which was the colour of flour.

Duch. No, sir: I will plant my soul in mine ears, to hear you.

Ferd. O most imperfect light of human reason,
That mak'st [us] so unhappy to foresee
What we can least prevent! Pursue thy wishes,
And glory in them: there 's in shame no comfort
But to be past all bounds and sense of shame.

Duch. I pray, sir, hear me: I am married.

Ferd. So!

Duch. Happily, not to your liking: but for that,
Alas, your shears do come untimely now
To clip the bird's wings that 's already flown!
Will you see my husband?

Ferd. Yes, if I could change
Eyes with a basilisk.

Duch. Sure, you came hither
By his confederacy.

Ferd. The howling of a wolf
Is music to thee, screech-owl: prithee, peace.—
Whate'er thou art that hast enjoy'd my sister,
For I am sure thou hear'st me, for thine own sake
Let me not know thee. I came hither prepar'd
To work thy discovery; yet am now persuaded
It would beget such violent effects
As would damn us both. I would not for ten millions
I had beheld thee: therefore use all means
I never may have knowledge of thy name;
Enjoy thy lust still, and a wretched life,
On that condition.—And for thee, vile woman,
If thou do wish thy lecher may grow old
In thy embracements, I would have thee build
Such a room for him as our anchorites
To holier use inhabit. Let not the sun
Shine on him till he 's dead; let dogs and monkeys
Only converse with him, and such dumb things
To whom nature denies use to sound his name;

Do not keep a paraquito, lest she learn it;
If thou do love him, cut out thine own tongue,
Lest it bewray him.

Duch. Why might not I marry?
I have not gone about in this to create
Any new world or custom.

Ferd. Thou art undone;
And thou hast ta'en that massy sheet of lead
That hid thy husband's bones, and folded it
About my heart.

Duch. Mine bleeds for 't.

Ferd. Thine? thy heart?
What should I name 't unless a hollow bullet
Fill'd with unquenchable wild-fire?

Duch. You are in this
Too strict; and were you not my princely brother,
I would say, too wilful: my reputation
Is safe.

Ferd. Dost thou know what reputation is?
I'll tell thee,—to small purpose, since the instruction
Comes now too late.
Upon a time Reputation, Love, and Death,
Would travel o'er the world; and it was concluded
That they should part, and take three several ways.
Death told them, they should find him in great battles,
Or cities plagu'd with plagues: Love gives them counsel
To inquire for him 'mongst unambitious shepherds,
Where dowries were not talk'd of, and sometimes
'Mongst quiet kindred that had nothing left
By their dead parents: 'Stay,' quoth Reputation,
'Do not forsake me; for it is my nature,
If once I part from any man I meet,
I am never found again.' And so for you:
You have shook hands with Reputation,
And made him invisible. So, fare you well:
I will never see you more.

Duch. Why should only I,
Of all the other princes of the world,
Be cas'd up, like a holy relic? I have youth
And a little beauty.
Ferd. So you have some virgins
That are witches. I will never see thee more. *Exit*

Re-enter ANTONIO *with a Pistol, and* CARIOLA

Duch. You saw this apparition?
Ant. Yes: we are
Betray'd. How came he hither?—I should turn
This to thee, for that. *Pointing the pistol at* CARIOLA
Car. Pray, sir, do; and when
That you have cleft my heart, you shall read there
Mine innocence.
Duch. That gallery gave him entrance.
Ant. I would this terrible thing would come again,
That, standing on my guard, I might relate
My warrantable love.— *She shows the poniard*
Ha! what means this?
Duch. He left this with me.
Ant. And it seems did wish
You would use it on yourself.
Duch. His action seem'd
To intend so much.
Ant. This hath a handle to 't.
As well as a point: turn it towards him, and
So fasten the keen edge in his rank gall. *Knocking within*
How now! who knocks? more earthquakes?
Duch. I stand
As if a mine beneath my feet were ready
To be blown up.
Car. 'Tis Bosola.
Duch. Away!
O misery! methinks unjust actions
Should wear these masks and curtains, and not we.

You must instantly part hence: I have fashion'd it
Already. *Exit* ANTONIO

Enter BOSOLA

Bos. The duke your brother is ta'en up in a whirlwind,
Hath took horse, and 's rid post to Rome.

Duch. So late?

Bos. He told me, as he mounted into th' saddle,
You were undone.

Duch. Indeed, I am very near it.

Bos. What 's the matter?

Duch. Antonio, the master of our household,
Hath dealt so falsely with me in 's accounts:
My brother stood engag'd with me for money
Ta'en up of certain Neapolitan Jews,
And Antonio lets the bonds be forfeit.

Bos. Strange!—[*Aside*] This is cunning.

Duch. And hereupon
My brother's bills at Naples are protested
Against.—Call up our officers.

Bos. I shall. *Exit*

Re-enter ANTONIO

Duch. The place that you must fly to is Ancona:
Hire a house there; I'll send after you
My treasure and my jewels. Our weak safety
Runs upon enginous wheels: [1] short syllables
Must stand for periods. I must now accuse you
Of such a feignèd crime as Tasso calls
Magnanima menzogna, a noble lie,
'Cause it must shield our honours.—Hark! they are coming.

Re-enter BOSOLA *and* Officers

Ant. Will your grace hear me?

Duch. I have got well by you; you have yielded me

[1] i. e. is rapidly leaving us.

A million of loss: I am like to inherit
The people's curses for your stewardship.
You had the trick in audit-time to be sick,
Till I had sign'd your quietus; and that cur'd you
Without help of a doctor.—Gentlemen,
I would have this man be an example to you all;
So shall you hold my favour; I pray, let him;
For h'as done that, alas, you would not think of,
And, because I intend to be rid of him,
I mean not to publish.—Use your fortune elsewhere.

Ant. I am strongly arm'd to brook my overthrow;
As commonly men bear with a hard year,
I will not blame the cause on 't; but do think
The necessity of my malevolent star
Procures this, not her humour. Oh, the inconstant
And rotten ground of service! you may see,
'Tis even like him, that in a winter night,
Takes a long slumber o'er a dying fire,
A-loth to part from 't; yet parts thence as cold
As when he first sat down.

Duch. We do confiscate,
Towards the satisfying of your accounts,
All that you have.

Ant. I am all yours; and 'tis very fit
All mine should be so.

Duch. So, sir, you have your pass.

Ant. You may see, gentlemen, what 'tis to serve
A prince with body and soul. *Exit*

Bos. [1] Here's an example for extortion: what moisture is drawn out of the sea, when foul weather comes, pours down, and runs into the sea again.

Duch. I would know what are your opinions of this Antonio.

[1] The next sixty or seventy lines may be read as a kind of galloping blank verse, but they read more easily as prose.

2 *Off.* He could not abide to see a pig's head gaping: I thought your grace would find him a Jew.

3 *Off.* I would you had been his officer, for your own sake.

4 *Off.* You would have had more money.

1 *Off.* He stopped his ears with black wool, and to those came to him for money said he was thick of hearing.

2 *Off.* Some said he was an hermaphrodite, for he could not abide a woman.

4 *Off.* How scurvy proud he would look when the treasury was full! Well, let him go!

1 *Off.* Yes, and the chippings of the buttery fly after him, to scour his gold chain!

Duch. Leave us. [*Exeunt officers*] What do you think of these?

Bos. That these are rogues that in 's prosperity, but to have waited on his fortune, could have wish'd his dirty stirrup riveted through their noses, and follow'd after 's mule, like a bear in a ring; would have prostituted their daughters to his lust; made their first-born intelligencers; thought none happy but such as were born under his blest planet, and wore his livery: and do these lice drop off now? Well, never look to have the like again: he hath left a sort of flattering rogues behind him; their doom must follow. Princes pay flatterers in their own money: flatterers dissemble their vices, and they dissemble their lies;[1] that 's justice. Alas, poor gentleman!

Duch. Poor? he hath amply fill'd his coffers.

Bos. Sure, he was too honest. Pluto,[2] the god of riches, when he 's sent by Jupiter to any man, he goes limping, to signify that wealth that comes on God's name comes slowly; but when he 's sent on the devil's errand, he rides post and comes in by scuttles.[3] Let me show you what a most un-

[1] i. e. Flatterers pretend that kings have no vices, and kings pretend that flatterers tell no lies.
[2] Put for Plutus.
[3] Short, hurried runs.

valued jewel you have in a wanton humour thrown away, to bless the man shall find him. He was an excellent courtier and most faithful; a soldier that thought it as beastly to know his own value too little as devilish to acknowledge it too much. Both his virtue and form deserv'd a far better fortune: his discourse rather delighted to judge itself than show itself: his breast was fill'd with all perfection, and yet it seem'd a private whispering-room, it made so little noise of 't.

Duch. But he was basely descended.

Bos. Will you make yourself a mercenary herald, rather to examine men's pedigrees than virtues? You shall want him: for know, an honest statesman to a prince is like a cedar planted by a spring; the spring bathes the tree's root, the grateful tree rewards it with his shadow: you have not done so. I would sooner swim to the Bermoothes on two politicians' rotten bladders, tied together with an intelligencer's heart-string, than depend on so changeable a prince's favour. Fare thee well, Antonio! since the malice of the world would needs down with thee, it cannot be said yet that any ill happened unto thee, considering thy fall was accompanied with virtue.

Duch. Oh, you render me excellent music!

Bos. Say you?

Duch. This good one that you speak of is my husband.

Bos. Do I not dream? can this ambitious age
Have so much goodness in 't as to prefer
A man merely for worth, without these shadows
Of wealth and painted honours? possible?

Duch. I have had three children by him.

Bos. Fortunate lady!
For you have made your private nuptial bed
The humble and fair seminary of peace.
No question but many an unbeneficed scholar
Shall pray for you for this deed, and rejoice
That some preferment in the world can yet

Arise from merit. The virgins of your land
That have no dowries shall hope your example
Will raise them to rich husbands. Should you want
Soldiers, 'twould make the very Turks and Moors
Turn Christians, and serve you for this act.
Last, the neglected poets of your time,
In honour of this trophy of a man,
Raised by that curious engine, your white hand,
Shall thank you, in your grave, for 't; and make that
More reverend than all the cabinets
Of living princes. For Antonio,
His fame shall likewise flow from many a pen,
When heralds shall want coats to sell to men.

Duch. As I taste comfort in this friendly speech,
So would I find concealment.

Bos. Oh, the secret of my prince,
Which I will wear on th' inside of my heart!

Duch. You shall take charge of all my coin and jewels,
And follow him; for he retires himself
To Ancona.

Bos. So.

Duch. Whither, within few days,
I mean to follow thee.

Bos. Let me think:
I would wish your grace to feign a pilgrimage
To our Lady of Loretto, scarce seven leagues
From fair Ancona; so may you depart
Your country with more honour, and your flight
Will seem a princely progress, retaining
Your usual train about you.

Duch. Sir, your direction
Shall lead me by the hand.

Car. In my opinion,
She were better progress to the baths at Lucca,
Or go visit the Spa in Germany;
For, if you will believe me, I do not like

This jesting with religion, this feigned
Pilgrimage.

Duch. Thou art a superstitious fool:
Prepare us instantly for our departure.
Past sorrows, let us moderately lament them;
For those to come, seek wisely to prevent them.

Exeunt DUCHESS *and* CARIOLA

Bos. A politician is the devil's quilted[1] anvil;
He fashions all sins on him, and the blows
Are never heard: he may work in a lady's chamber,
As here for proof. What rests but I reveal
All to my lord? Oh, this base quality
Of intelligencer! why, every quality i' th' world
Prefers[2] but gain or commendation:
Now for this act I am certain to be rais'd,
And men that paint weeds to the life are prais'd. *Exit*

[SCENE III]

[*A Room in the Cardinal's Palace at Rome*]

Enter CARDINAL, FERDINAND, MALATESTE, PESCARA, SILVIO, *and* DELIO

Card. Must we turn soldier, then?

Mal. The emperor,
Hearing your worth that way, ere you attain'd
This reverend garment, joins you in commission
With the right fortunate soldier the Marquis of Pescara,
And the famous Lannoy.

Card. He that had the honour
Of taking the French king prisoner?

Mal. The same.
Here 's a plot[3] drawn for a new fortification

[1] i. e. muffled.
[2] Produces.
[3] Plan.

At Naples. *They talk apart*

Ferd. This great Count Malateste, I perceive,
Hath got employment?

Del. No employment, my lord;
A marginal note in the muster-book, that he is
A voluntary lord.

Ferd. He 's no soldier?

Del. He has worn gunpowder in 's hollow tooth for the toothache.

Sil. He comes to the leaguer [1] with a full intent
To eat fresh beef and garlic, means to stay
Till the scent be gone, and straight return to court.

Del. He hath read all the late service as the city chronicle relates it; and keeps two pewterers going, only to express battles in model.

Sil. Then he'll fight by the book.

Del. By the almanac, I think, to choose good days and shun the critical; that 's his mistress's scarf.

Sil. Yes, he protests he would do much for that taffeta.

Del. I think he would run away from a battle, to save it from taking [2] prisoner.

Sil. He is horribly afraid gunpowder will spoil the perfume on 't.

Del. I saw a Dutchman break his pate once for calling him pot-gun; he made his head have a bore in 't like a musket.

Sil. I would he had made a touchhole to 't. He is indeed a guarded sumpter-cloth,[3] only for the remove of the court.

Enter BOSOLA *and speaks to* FERDINAND *and the* CARDINAL

Pes. Bosola arriv'd? what should be the business?

[1] Camp.
[2] i. e. being taken.
[3] An ornamental horse-cloth.

Some falling-out amongst the cardinals.
These factions amongst great men, they are like
Foxes; when their heads are divided,
They carry fire in their tails, and all the country
About them goes to wrack for 't.

Sil. What 's that Bosola?

Del. I knew him in Padua—a fantastical scholar, like such who study to know how many knots was in Hercules' club, of what colour Achilles' beard was, or whether Hector were not troubled with the toothache. He hath studied himself half blear-ey'd to know the true symmetry of Caesar's nose by a shoeing-horn; and this he did to gain the name of a speculative man.[1]

Pes. Mark Prince Ferdinand:
A very salamander lives in 's eye,
To mock the eager violence of fire.

Sil. That Cardinal hath made more bad faces with his oppression than ever Michael Angelo made good ones: he lifts up 's nose, like a foul porpoise before a storm.

Pes. The Lord Ferdinand laughs.

Del. Like a deadly cannon that lightens
Ere it smokes.

Pes. These are your true pangs of death,
The pangs of life, that struggle with great statesmen.

Del. In such a deformed silence witches whisper
Their charms.

Card. Doth she make religion her riding-hood
To keep her from the sun and tempest?

Ferd. That,
That damns her. Methinks her fault and beauty,
Blended together, show like leprosy,
The whiter, the fouler. I make it a question
Whether her beggarly brats were ever christened.

Card. I will instantly solicit the state of Ancona
To have them banish'd.

[1] i. e. a student.

Ferd. You are for Loretto?
I shall not be at your ceremony; fare you well.—
Write to the Duke of Malfi, my young nephew
She had by her first husband, and acquaint him
With 's mother's honesty.

Bos. I will.

Ferd. Antonio!
A slave that only smell'd of ink and counters,
And never in 's life look'd like a gentleman,
But in the audit-time.—Go, go presently,
Draw me out an hundred and fifty of our horse,
And meet me at the fort-bridge. ***Exeunt***

[SCENE IV]

[*The Shrine of Our Lady of Loretto*]

Enter Two Pilgrims

1 *Pil.* I have not seen a goodlier shrine than this;
Yet I have visited many.

2 *Pil.* The Cardinal of Arragon
Is this day to resign his cardinal's hat:
His sister duchess likewise is arriv'd
To pay her vow of pilgrimage. I expect
A noble ceremony.

1 *Pil.* No question.
—They come.

Here the ceremony of the CARDINAL'S *instalment, in the habit of a soldier,* [*is*] *performed in delivering up his cross, hat, robes, and ring, at the shrine, and investing him with sword, helmet, shield, and spurs; then* ANTONIO, *the* DUCHESS, *and their children, having presented themselves at the shrine, are, by a form of banishment in dumb-show expressed towards them by the* CARDINAL *and the state of Ancona, banished: during all which ceremony, this ditty is sung, to very solemn music, by divers churchmen.*

Arms and honours deck thy story,
To thy fame's eternal glory!
Adverse fortune ever fly thee;
No disastrous fate come nigh thee!

I alone will sing thy praises,
Whom to honour virtue raises;
And thy study, that divine is,
Bent to martial discipline is.
Lay aside all those robes lie by thee;
Crown thy arts with arms, they'll beautify thee.

O worthy of worthiest name, adorn'd in this manner,
Lead bravely thy forces on under war's warlike banner!
Oh, mayst thou prove fortunate in all martial courses!
Guide thou still by skill in arts and forces!
Victory attend thee nigh, whilst fame sings loud thy powers;
Triumphant conquest crown thy head, and blessings pour down showers![1] *Exeunt all except the Two Pilgrims*

1 *Pil.* Here 's a strange turn of state! who would have thought
So great a lady would have match'd herself
Unto so mean a person? yet the Cardinal
Bears himself much too cruel.

2 *Pil.* They are banish'd.

1 *Pil.* But I would ask what power hath this state
Of Ancona to determine of a free prince?

2 *Pil.* They are a free state, sir, and her brother show'd
How that the Pope, fore-hearing of her looseness,
Hath seiz'd into th' protection of the Church
The dukedom which she held as dowager.

1 *Pil.* But by what justice?

[1] 'The Author disclaims this Ditty to be his.'—(Note in the 1623 quarto.)

2 *Pil.* Sure, I think by none,
Only her brother's instigation.
1 *Pil.* What was it with such violence he took
Off from her finger?
2 *Pil.* 'Twas her wedding-ring;
Which he vow'd shortly he would sacrifice
To his revenge.
1 *Pil.* Alas, Antonio!
If that a man be thrust into a well,
No matter who sets hands to 't, his own weight
Will bring him sooner to th' bottom. Come, let 's hence.
Fortune makes this conclusion general,
All things do help th' unhappy man to fall. *Exeunt*

[SCENE V]

[*Near Loretto*]

Enter Duchess, Antonio, Children, Cariola, *and* Servants

Duch. Banish'd Ancona?
Ant. Yes, you see what power
Lightens in great men's breath.
Duch. Is all our train
Shrunk to this poor remainder?
Ant. These poor men,
Which have got little in your service, vow
To take your fortune: but your wiser buntings,
Now they are fledg'd, are gone.
Duch. They have done wisely.
This puts me in mind of death: physicians thus,
With their hands full of money, use to give o'er
Their patients.
Ant. Right the fashion of the world:
From decayed fortunes every flatterer shrinks;
Men cease to build where the foundation sinks.
Duch. I had a very strange dream to-night.

Ant. What was 't?
Duch. Methought I wore my coronet of state,
And on a sudden all the diamonds
Were chang'd to pearls.
Ant. My interpretation
Is, you'll weep shortly; for to me the pearls
Do signify your tears.
Duch. The birds that live
I' th' field on the wild benefit of nature
Live happier than we; for they may choose their mates,
And carol their sweet pleasures to the spring.

Enter BOSOLA *with a letter*

Bos. You are happily o'erta'en.
Duch. From my brother?
Bos. Yes, from the Lord Ferdinand your brother
All love and safety.
Duch. Thou dost blanch mischief,
Wouldst make it white. See, see, like to calm weather
At sea before a tempest, false hearts speak fair
To those they intend most mischief. *Reads*
'Send Antonio to me; I want his head in a business.'
A politic equivocation!
He doth not want your counsel, but your head;
That is, he cannot sleep till you be dead.
And here 's another pitfall that 's strew'd o'er
With roses: mark it, 'tis a cunning one: *Reads*
'I stand engaged for your husband for several debts at Naples: let not that trouble him; I had rather have his heart than his money:'—
And I believe so too.
Bos. What do you believe?
Duch. That he so much distrusts my husband's love,
He will by no means believe his heart is with him
Until he see it: the devil is not cunning
Enough to circumvent us in riddles.

Bos. Will you reject that noble and free league
Of amity and love which I present you?
Duch. Their league is like that of some politic kings,
Only to make themselves of strength and power
To be our after-ruin: tell them so.
Bos. And what from you?
Ant. Thus tell him; I will not come.
Bos. And what of this? *Pointing to the letter*
Ant. My brothers have dispers'd
Blood-hounds abroad; which till I hear are muzzl'd,
No truce, though hatch'd with ne'er such politic skill,
Is safe, that hangs upon our enemies' will.
I'll not come at them.
Bos. This proclaims your breeding:
Every small thing draws a base mind to fear,
As the adamant draws iron. Fare you well, sir
You shall shortly hear from 's. *Exit*
Duch. I suspect some ambush:
Therefore by all my love I do conjure you
To take your eldest son, and fly towards Milan.
Let us not venture all this poor remainder
In one unlucky bottom.
Ant. You counsel safely.
Best of my life, farewell. Since we must part,
Heaven hath a hand in 't; but no otherwise
Than as some curious artist takes in sunder
A clock or watch, when it is out of frame,
To bring 't in better order.
Duch. I know not
Which is best, to see you dead, or part with you.
—Farewell, boy:
Thou art happy that thou hast not understanding
To know thy misery; for all our wit
And reading brings us to a truer sense
Of sorrow.—In the eternal church, sir,
I do hope we shall not part thus.

Ant. Oh, be of comfort!
Make patience a noble fortitude,
And think not how unkindly we are used:
Man, like to cassia, is prov'd best being bruised.
Duch. Must I, like to a slave-born Russian,
Account it praise to suffer tyranny?
And yet, O heaven, thy heavy hand is in 't!
I have seen my little boy oft scourge his top,
An compar'd myself to 't: naught made me e'er
Go right but heaven's scourge-stick.
Ant. Do not weep:
Heaven fashion'd us of nothing, and we strive
To bring ourselves to nothing.—Farewell, Cariola,
And thy sweet armful.—If I do never see thee more,
Be a good mother to your little ones,
And save them from the tiger: fare you well.
Duch. Let me look upon you once more; for that speech
Came from a dying father.—Your kiss is colder
Than that I have seen an holy anchorite
Give to a dead man's skull.
Ant. My heart is turn'd to a heavy lump of lead,
With which I sound my danger: fare you well.
Exeunt ANTONIO *and his* Son
Duch. My laurel is all withered.
Car. Look, madam, what a troop of armèd men
Make toward us.
Duch. Oh, they are very welcome:
When Fortune's wheel is over-charg'd with princes,
The weight makes it move swift: I would have my ruin
Be sudden.

Re-enter BOSOLA *visarded, with a* Guard

I am your adventure, am I not?
Bosola. You are: you must see your husband no more.
Dutch. What devil art thou that counterfeits heaven's thunder?

Bos. Is that terrible? I would have you tell me whether
Is that note worse that frights the silly birds
Out of the corn, or that which doth allure them
To the nets? you have hearkened to the last too much.

Duch. Oh, misery! like to a rusty o'ercharg'd cannon,
Shall I never fly in pieces?—Come, to what prison?

Bos. To none.

Duch. Whither, then?

Bos. To your palace.

Duch. I have heard
That Charon's boat serves to convey all o'er
The dismal lake, but brings none back again.

Bos. Your brothers mean you safety and pity.

Duch. Pity!
With such a pity men preserve alive
Pheasants and quails, when they are not fat enough
To be eaten.

Bos. These are your children?

Duch. Yes.

Bos. Can they prattle?

Duch. No;
But I intend, since they were born accurs'd,
Curses shall be their first language.

Bos. Fie, madam!
Forget this base, low fellow,—

Duch. Were I a man
I'd beat that counterfeit face into thy other.

Bos. One of no birth.

Duch. Say that he was born mean,
Man is most happy when 's own actions
Be arguments and examples of his virtue.

Bos. A barren, beggarly virtue!

Duch. I prithee, who is greatest? can you tell?
Sad tales befit my woe: I'll tell you one.
A salmon, as she swam unto the sea,
Met with a dog-fish, who encounters her

With this rough language: 'Why art thou so bold
To mix thyself with our high state of floods,
Being no eminent courtier, but one
That for the calmest and fresh time o' the year
Dost live in shallow rivers, rank'st thyself
With silly smelts and shrimps? and darest thou
Pass by our dog-ship without reverence?'
'Oh!' quoth the salmon, 'sister, be at peace:
Thank Jupiter we both have pass'd the net!
Our value never can be truly known,
Till in the fisher's basket we be shown:
I' th' market then my price may be the higher,
Even when I am nearest to the cook and fire.'
So to great men the moral may be stretchèd;
Men oft are valued high, when they're most wretched.—
But come, whither you please. I am arm'd 'gainst misery;
Bent to all sways of the oppressor's will:
There 's no deep valley but near some great hill. *Exeunt*

ACT THE FOURTH

[SCENE I]

[*A Room in the Duchess's Palace at Malfi*]

Enter FERDINAND *and* BOSOLA

Ferd. How doth our sister duchess bear herself
In her imprisonment?
Bosola. Nobly: I'll describe her.
She 's sad as one long used to 't, and she seems
Rather to welcome the end of misery
Than shun it; a behaviour so noble
As gives a majesty to adversity:
You may discern the shape of loveliness
More perfect in her tears than in her smiles:
She will muse four hours together; and her silence,

Methinks, expresseth more than if she spake.

Ferd. Her melancholy seems to be fortified
With a strange disdain.

Bos. 'Tis so; and this restraint,
Like English mastiffs that grow fierce with tying,
Makes her too passionately apprehend
Those pleasures she 's kept from.

Ferd. Curse upon her!
I will no longer study in the book
Of another's heart. Inform her what I told you. *Exit*

Enter DUCHESS

Bos. All comfort to your grace!

Duch. I will have none.
Pray thee, why dost thou wrap thy poison'd pills
In gold and sugar?

Bos. Your elder brother, the Lord Ferdinand,
Is come to visit you, and sends you word,
'Cause once he rashly made a solemn vow
Never to see you more, he comes i' th' night;
And prays you gently neither torch nor taper
Shine in your chamber: he will kiss your hand,
And reconcile himself; but for his vow
He dares not see you.

Duch. At his pleasure.—Take hence
the lights.—
He 's come.

Enter FERDINAND

Ferd. Where are you?

Duch. Here, sir.

Ferd. This darkness suits you well.

Duch. I would ask you pardon.

Ferd. You have it; for I account it
The honorabl'st revenge, where I may kill,

To pardon.—Where are your cubs?

Duch. Whom?

Ferd. Call them your children;
For though our national law distinguish bastards
From true legitimate issue, compassionate nature
Makes them all equal.

Duch. Do you visit me for this?
You violate a sacrament o' th' Church
Shall make you howl in hell for 't.

Ferd. It had been well
Could you have liv'd thus always; for, indeed,
You were too much i' th' light:—but no more;
I come to seal my peace with you. Here 's a hand

Gives her a dead man's hand

To which you have vow'd much love; the ring upon 't
You gave.

Duch. I affectionately kiss it.

Ferd. Pray, do, and bury the print of it in your heart.
I will leave this ring with you for a love-token;
And the hand as sure as the ring; and do not doubt
But you shall have the heart too: when you need a friend,
Send it to him that owned it; you shall see
Whether he can aid you.

Duch. You are very cold:
I fear you are not well after your travel.—
Ha! lights!——Oh, horrible!

Ferd. Let her have lights enough. *Exit*

Duch. What witchcraft doth he practise, that he hath left
A dead man's hand here?

[*Here is discovered, behind a traverse,*[1] *the artificial figures of Antonio and his Children, appearing as if they were dead.*]

Bos. Look you, here 's the piece from which 'twas ta'en.

[1] Curtain.

He doth present you this sad spectacle,
That, now you know directly they are dead,
Hereafter you may wisely cease to grieve
For that which cannot be recovered.

Duch. There is not between heaven and earth one wish
I stay for after this: it wastes me more
Than were 't my picture, fashion'd out of wax,
Stuck with a magical needle, and then buried
In some foul dunghill; and yond 's an excellent property
For a tyrant, which I would account mercy.

Bos. What 's that?

Duch. If they would bind me to that lifeless trunk,
And let me freeze to death.

Bos. Come, you must live.

Duch. That 's the greatest torture souls feel in hell,
In hell, that they must live, and cannot die.
Portia, I'll new kindle thy coals again,
And revive the rare and almost dead example
Of a loving wife.

Bos. Oh, fie! despair? remember
You are a Christian.

Duch. The Church enjoins fasting:
I'll starve myself to death.

Bos. Leave this vain sorrow.
Things being at the worst begin to mend: the bee
When he hath shot his sting into your hand, may then
Play with your eyelid.

Duch. Good comfortable fellow,
Persuade a wretch that 's broke upon the wheel
To have all his bones new set; entreat him live
To be executed again. Who must dispatch me?
I account this world a tedious theatre,
For I do play a part in 't 'gainst my will.

Bos. Come, be of comfort; I will save your life.

Duch. Indeed,
I have not leisure to tend so small a business.

Bos. Now, by my life, I pity you.
Duch. Thou art a fool, then,
To waste thy pity on a thing so wretched
As cannot pity it[self]. I am full of daggers.
Puff, let me blow these vipers from me.

Enter Servant

What are you?
Serv. One that wishes you long life.
Duch. I would thou wert hang'd for the horrible curse
Thou hast given me: I shall shortly grow one
Of the miracles of pity. I'll go pray;—
No, I'll go curse.
Bos. Oh, fie!
Duch. I could curse the stars—
Bos. Oh, fearful!
Duch. And those three smiling seasons of the year
Into a Russian winter: nay, the world
To its first chaos.
Bos. Look you, the stars shine still.
Duch. Oh, but you must
Remember, my curse hath a great way to go.—
Plagues, that make lanes through largest families
Consume them!—
Bos. Fie, lady!
Duch. Let them, like tyrants,
Never be remembered but for the ill they have done;
Let all the zealous prayers of mortified
Churchmen forget them!—
Bos. Oh, uncharitable!
Duch. Let Heaven a little while cease crowning martyrs,
To punish them!—
Go, howl them this, and say, I long to bleed:
It is some mercy when men kill with speed.
Exeunt DUCHESS *and* Servant

Re-enter FERDINAND

Ferd. Excellent, as I would wish; she 's plagued in art:
These presentations are but fram'd in wax
By the curious master in that quality,
Vincentio Lauriola, and she takes them
For true substantial bodies.
Bos. Why do you do this?
Ferd. To bring her to despair.
Bos. 'Faith, end here,
And go no farther in your cruelty:
Send her a penitential garment to put on
Next to her delicate skin, and furnish her
With beads and prayer-books.
Ferd. Damn her! that body of hers,
While that my blood ran pure in 't, was more worth
Than that which thou wouldst comfort, called a soul.
I will send her masks of common courtezans,
Have her meat serv'd up by bawds and ruffians,
And, 'cause she'll needs be mad, I am resolv'd
To remove forth the common hospital
All the mad-folk, and place them near her lodging;
There let them practise together, sing and dance,
And act their gambols to the full o' th' moon:
If she can sleep the better for it, let her.
Your work is almost ended.
Bos. Must I see her again?
Ferd. Yes.
Bos. Never.
Ferd. You must.
Bos. Never in mine own shape;
That 's forfeited by my intelligence
And this last cruel lie: when you send me next,
The business shall be comfort.
Ferd. Very likely;
Thy pity is nothing of kin to thee. Antonio

Lurks about Milan: thou shalt shortly thither
To feed a fire as great as my revenge,
Which ne'er will slack till it have spent his fuel:
Intemperate agues make physicians cruel. *Exeunt*

[SCENE II]

[*Another Room in the Duchess's Lodging*]

Enter DUCHESS *and* CARIOLA

Duch. What hideous noise was that?
Car. 'Tis the wild consort[1]
Of madmen, lady, which your tyrant brother
Hath plac'd about your lodging: this tyranny,
I think, was never practis'd till this hour.
Duch. Indeed, I thank him: nothing but noise and folly
Can keep me in my right wits; whereas reason
And silence make me stark mad. Sit down;
Discourse to me some dismal tragedy.
Car. Oh, 'twill increase your melancholy.
Duch. Thou art deceived:
To hear of greater grief would lessen mine.
This is a prison?
Car. Yes, but you shall live
To shake this durance off.
Duch. Thou art a fool:
The robin-redbreast and the nightingale
Never live long in cages.
Car. Pray, dry your eyes.
What think you of, madam?
Duch. Of nothing; when I muse thus,
I sleep.
Car. Like a madman, with your eyes open?
Duch. Dost thou think we shall know one another in th' other world?

[1] Band.

Car. Yes, out of question.
Duch. Oh, that it were possible
We might but hold some two days' conference
With the dead! From them I should learn somewhat, I am sure,
I never shall know here. I'll tell thee a miracle;
I am not mad yet, to my cause of sorrow:
Th' heaven o'er my head seems made of molten brass,
The earth of flaming sulphur, yet I am not mad.
I am acquainted with sad misery
As the tann'd galley-slave is with his oar;
Necessity makes me suffer constantly,
And custom makes it easy. Who do I look like now?
Car. Like to your picture in the gallery,
A deal of life in show, but none in practice;
Or rather like some reverend monument
Whose ruins are even pitied.
Duch. Very proper;
And Fortune seems only to have her eyesight
To behold my tragedy.—
How now! what noise is that?

Enter Servant

Serv. I am come to tell you
Your brother hath intended you some sport.
A great physician, when the Pope was sick
Of a deep melancholy, presented him
With several sorts of madmen, which wild object
Being full of change and sport, forc'd him to laugh,
And so the imposthume broke: the self-same cure
The duke intends on you.
Duch. Let them come in.
Serv. There 's a mad lawyer; and a secular priest;
A doctor that hath forfeited his wits
By jealousy; an astrologian
That in his works said such a day o' th' month

Should be the day of doom, and, failing of 't,
Ran mad; an English tailor crazed i' th' brain
With the study of new fashions; a gentleman-usher
Quite beside himself with care to keep in mind
The number of his lady's salutations
Or 'How do you['s]' she employ'd him in each morning;
A farmer, too, an excellent knave in grain,
Mad 'cause he was hindered transportation:
And let one broker that 's mad loose to these,
You'd think the devil were among them.

Duch. Sit, Cariola.—Let them loose when you please,
For I am chain'd to endure all your tyranny.

Enter Madmen

Here this Song is sung by a Madman to a dismal kind of music

Oh, let us howl some heavy note,
  Some deadly dogged howl,
Sounding as from the threatening throat
  Of beasts and fatal fowl!
As ravens, screech-owls, bulls, and bears,
  We'll bell,[1] and bawl our parts,
Till irksome noise have cloy'd your ears
  And corrosived your hearts.
At last, whenas our quire wants breath,
  Our bodies being blest,
We'll sing, like swans, to welcome death,
  And die in love and rest.

1 *Madman.* Doom's-day not come yet? I'll draw it nearer by a perspective, or make a glass that shall set all the world on fire upon an instant. I cannot sleep; my pillow is stuffed with a litter of porcupines.

2 *Madman.* Hell is a mere glass-house, where the devils

[1] Bellow.

are continually blowing up women's souls on hollow irons, and the fire never goes out.

3 *Madman.* I will lie with every woman in my parish the tenth night; I will tithe them over like haycocks.

4 *Madman.* Shall my pothecary out-go me because I am a cuckold? I have found out his roguery; he makes alum of his wife's urine, and sells it to Puritans that have sore throats with overstraining.

1 *Madman.* I have skill is heraldry.

2 *Madman.* Hast?

1 *Madman.* You do give for your crest a woodcock's head with the brains picked out on 't; you are a very ancient gentleman.

3 *Madman.* Greek is turn'd Turk: we are only to be sav'd by the Helvetian translation.[1]

1 *Madman.* Come on, sir, I will lay the law to you.

2 *Madman.* Oh, rather lay a corrosive: the law will eat to the bone.

3 *Madman.* He that drinks but to satisfy nature is damned.

4 *Madman.* If I had my glass here, I would show a sight should make all the women here call me mad doctor.

1 *Madman.* What's he? a rope-maker?

2 *Madman.* No, no, no, a snuffling knave that, while he shows the tombs, will have his hand in a wench's placket.

3 *Madman.* Woe to the caroche [2] that brought home my wife from the masque at three o'clock in the morning! it had a large feather-bed in it.

4 *Madman.* I have pared the devil's nails forty times, roasted them in raven's eggs, and cur'd agues with them.

3 *Madman.* Get me three hundred milchbats, to make possets to procure sleep.

4 *Madman.* All the college may throw their caps at me:

[1] Sc. of the Bible, made by English refugees at Geneva and published in 1560.

[2] Coach.

I have made a soap-boiler costive; it was my masterpiece.

Here the dance, consisting of Eight Madmen, *with music answerable thereunto; after which* BOSOLA, *like an Old Man, enters.*

Duch. Is he mad too?

Serv. Pray, question him. I'll leave you.

Exeunt Servant *and* Madmen

Bos. I am come to make thy tomb.

Duch. Ha! my tomb?
Thou speak'st as if I lay upon my death-bed,
Gasping for breath: dost thou perceive me sick?

Bos. Yes, and the more dangerously, since thy sickness
Is insensible.

Duch. Thou art not mad, sure: dost know me?

Bos. Yes.

Duch. Who am I?

Bos. Thou art a box of worm-seed, at best but a salvatory [1] of green mummy. What's this flesh? a little crudded [2] milk, fantastical puff-paste. Our bodies are weaker than those paper-prisons boys use to keep flies in; more contemptible, since ours is to preserve earthworms. Didst thou ever see a lark in a cage? Such is the soul in the body: this world is like her little turf of grass, and the heaven o'er our heads, like her looking-glass, only gives us a miserable knowledge of the small compass of our prison.

Duch. Am not I thy duchess?

Bos. Thou art some great woman, sure, for riot begins to sit on thy forehead (clad in grey hairs) twenty years sooner than on a merry milk-maid's. Thou sleep'st worse than if a mouse should be forc'd to take up her lodging in a cat's ear: a little infant that breeds its teeth, should it lie with thee, would cry out, as if thou wert the more unquiet bed-fellow.

[1] Ointment-box.
[2] Curded.

Duch. I am Duchess of Malfi still.

Bos. That makes thy sleeps so broken:
Glories, like glow-worms, afar off shine bright,
But looked to near, have neither heat nor light.

Duch. Thou art very plain.

Bos. My trade is to flatter the dead, not the living; I am a tomb-maker.

Duch. And thou com'st to make my tomb?

Bos. Yes.

Duch. Let me be a little merry:—of what stuff wilt thou make it?

Bos. Nay, resolve me first, of what fashion?

Duch. Why, do we grow fantastical in our death-bed? do we affect fashion in the grave?

Bos. Most ambitiously. Princes' images on their tombs do not lie, as they were wont, seeming to pray up to heaven; but with their hands under their cheeks, as if they died of the toothache: they are not carved with their eyes fix'd upon the stars; but as their minds were wholly bent upon the world, the self-same way they seem to turn their faces.

Duch. Let me know fully therefore the effect
Of this thy dismal preparation,
This talk fit for a charnel.

Bos. Now I shall:—

Enter Executioners, *with a coffin, cords, and a bell*

Here is a present from your princely brothers;
And may it arrive welcome, for it brings
Last benefit, last sorrow.

Duch. Let me see it:
I have so much obedience in my blood,
I wish it in their veins to do them good.

Bos. This is your last presence-chamber.

Car. O my sweet lady!

Duch. Peace; it affrights not me.

Bos. I am the common bellman,

That usually is sent to condemn'd persons
The night before they suffer.
Duch. Even now
Thou said'st thou wast a tomb-maker.
Bos. 'Twas to bring you
By degrees to mortification. Listen.

Hark, now every thing is still
The screech-owl and the whistler shrill
Call upon our dame aloud,
And bid her quickly don her shroud!
Much you had of land and rent:
Your length in clay's now competent:[1]
A long war disturb'd your mind;
Here your perfect peace is sign'd.
Of what is 't fools make such vain keeping?
Sin their conception, their birth weeping,
Their life a general mist of error,
Their death a hideous storm of terror.
Strew your hair with powders sweet,
Don clean linen, bathe your feet,
And (the foul fiend more to check)
A crucifix let bless your neck:
'Tis now full tide 'tween night and day;
End your groan, and come away.

Car. Hence, villains, tyrants, murderers! alas!
What will you do with my lady?—Call for help.
Duch. To whom? to our next neighbours? they are mad-folks.
Bos. Remove that noise.
Duch. Farewell, Cariola.
In my last will I have not much to give:
A many hungry guests have fed upon me;
Thine will be a poor reversion.

[1] i. e. all you require.

Car. I will die with her.

Duch. I pray thee, look thou giv'st my little boy
Some syrup for his cold, and let the girl
Say her prayers ere she sleep.

CARIOLA *is forced out by the* Executioners

Now what you please:
What death?

Bos. Strangling;
Here are your executioners.

Duch. I forgive them:
The apoplexy, catarrh, or cough o' th' lungs,
Would do as much as they do.

Bos. Doth not death fright you?

Duch. Who would be afraid on 't,
Knowing to meet such excellent company
In th' other world?

Bos. Yet, methinks,
The manner of your death should much afflict you:
This cord should terrify you.

Duch. Not a whit:
What would it pleasure me to have my throat cut
With diamonds? or to be smothered
With cassia? or to be shot to death with pearls?
I know death hath ten thousand several doors
For men to take their exits; and 'tis found
They go on such strange geometrical hinges,
You may open them both ways.—Any way, for heaven sake,
So I were out of your whispering. Tell my brothers
That I perceive death, now I am well awake,
Best gift is they can give or I can take.
I would fain put off my last woman's fault,
I'd not be tedious to you.

First Executioner. We are ready.

Duch. Dispose my breath how please you; but my body
Bestow upon my women, will you?

First Executioner. Yes.

Duch. Pull, and pull strongly, for your able strength
Must pull down heaven upon me:—
Yet stay; heaven-gates are not so highly arch'd
As princes' palaces; they that enter there
Must go upon their knees [*Kneels*].—Come, violent death,
Serve for mandragora to make me sleep!—
Go tell my brothers, when I am laid out,
They then may feed in quiet. *They strangle her*

Bos. Where's the waiting woman? Fetch her: some other
Strangle the children.

Exeunt Executioners, *some of whom return with* CARIOLA

Look you, there sleeps your mistress.

Car. Oh, you are damn'd
Perpetually for this! My turn is next,
Is 't not so order'd?

Bos. Yes, and I am glad
You are so well prepar'd for 't.

Car. You are deceiv'd, sir,
I am not prepar'd for 't, I will not die;
I will first come to my answer, and know
How I have offended.

Bos. Come, dispatch her.—
You kept her counsel; now you shall keep ours.

Car. I will not die, I must not; I am contracted
To a young gentleman.

First Executioner. Here's your wedding-ring.

Car. Let me but speak with the duke; I'll discover
Treason to his person.

Bos. Delays:—throttle her.

First Executioner. She bites and scratches.

Car. If you kill me now,
I am damn'd; I have not been at confession
This two years.

Bos. [*To* Executioners] When? [1]

[1] A common exclamation of impatience.

Car. I am quick with child.

Bos. Why, then,
Your credit's sav'd. *They strangle* CARIOLA
Bear her into th' next room;
Let this lie still.

Exeunt the Executioners *with the body of* CARIOLA

Enter FERDINAND

Ferd. Is she dead?

Bos. She is what
You'd have her. But here begin your pity:
Shows the Children *strangled* [1]
Alas, how have these offended?

Ferd. The death
Of young wolves is never to be pitied.

Bos. Fix
Your eye here.

Ferd. Constantly.

Bos. Do you not weep?
Other sins only speak; murder shrieks out:
The element of water moistens the earth,
But blood flies upwards and bedews the heavens.

Ferd. Cover her face; mine eyes dazzle: she died young.

Bos. I think not so; her infelicity
Seem'd to have years too many.

Ferd. She and I were twins;
And should I die this instant, I had liv'd
Her time to a minute.

Bos. It seems she was born first:
You have bloodily approv'd the ancient truth,
That kindred commonly do worse agree
Than remote strangers.

Ferd. Let me see her face
Again. Why didst not thou pity her? what

[1] Probably by drawing a curtain, as on p. 501.

An excellent honest man mightst thou have been,
If thou hadst borne her to some sanctuary!
Or, bold in a good cause, oppos'd thyself,
With thy advancèd sword above thy head,
Between her innocence and my revenge!
I bade thee, when I was distracted of my wits,
Go kill my dearest friend, and thou hast done 't.
For let me but examine well the cause:
What was the meanness of her match to me?
Only I must confess I had a hope,
Had she continu'd widow, to have gain'd
An infinite mass of treasure by her death:
And that was the main cause; her marriage,
That drew a stream of gall quite through my heart.
For thee, as we observe in tragedies
That a good actor many times is curs'd
For playing a villain's part, I hate thee for 't,
And, for my sake, say thou hast done much ill well.

Bos. Let me quicken your memory, for I perceive
You are falling into ingratitude: I challenge
The reward due to my service.

Ferd. I'll tell thee
What I'll give thee.

Bos. Do.

Ferd. I'll give thee a pardon
For this murder.

Bos. Ha!

Ferd. Yes, and 'tis
The largest bounty I can study to do thee.
By what authority didst thou execute
This bloody sentence?

Bos. By yours.

Ferd. Mine? was I her judge?
Did any ceremonial form of law
Doom her to not-being? did a complete jury
Deliver her conviction up i' th' court?

Where shalt thou find this judgement register'd,
Unless in hell? See, like a bloody fool,
Thou'st forfeited thy life, and thou shalt die for 't.

Bos. The office of justice is perverted quite
When one thief hangs another. Who shall dare
To reveal this?

Ferd. Oh, I'll tell thee;
The wolf shall find her grave, and scrape it up,
Not to devour the corpse, but to discover
The horrid murder.

Bos. You, not I, shall quake for 't.

Ferd. Leave me.

Bos. I will first receive my pension.

Ferd. You are a villain.

Bos. When your ingratitude
Is judge, I am so.

Ferd. Oh, horror, that not the fear
Of him which binds the devils can prescribe man
Obedience!—Never look upon me more.

Bos. Why, fare thee well.
Your brother and yourself are worthy men:
You have a pair of hearts are hollow graves,
Rotten, and rotting others; and your vengeance,
Like two chain'd bullets, still goes arm in arm:
You may be brothers; for treason, like the plague,
Doth take much in a blood. I stand like one
That long hath ta'en a sweet and golden dream:
I am angry with myself, now that I wake.

Ferd. Get thee into some unknown part o' th' world,
That I may never see thee.

Bos. Let me know
Wherefore I should be thus neglected. Sir,
I serv'd your tyranny, and rather strove
To satisfy yourself than all the world:
And though I loath'd the evil, yet I lov'd
You that did counsel it; and rather sought

To appear a true servant than an honest man.

Ferd. I'll go hunt the badger by owl-light:
'Tis a deed of darkness. *Exit*

Bos. He's much distracted. Off, my painted honour!
While with vain hopes our faculties we tire,
We seem to sweat in ice and freeze in fire.
What would I do, were this to do again?
I would not change my peace of conscience
For all the wealth of Europe.—She stirs; here's life:—
Return, fair soul, from darkness, and lead mine
Out of this sensible hell:—she's warm, she breathes:—
Upon thy pale lips I will melt my heart,
To store them with fresh colour.—Who's there!
Some cordial drink!—Alas! I dare not call:
So pity would destroy pity.—Her eye opes,
And heaven in it seems to ope, that late was shut,
To take me up to mercy.

Duch. Antonio!

Bos. Yes, madam, he is living;
The dead bodies you saw were but feign'd statues:
He's reconcil'd to your brothers: the Pope hath wrought
The atonement.

Duch. Mercy! *Dies*

Bos. Oh, she's gone again! there the cords of life broke.
Oh, sacred innocence, that sweetly sleeps
On turtles' feathers, whilst a guilty conscience
Is a black register wherein is writ
All our good deeds and bad, a perspective
That shows us hell! That we cannot be suffer'd
To do good when we have a mind to it!
This is manly sorrow; these tears, I am very certain,
Never grew in my mother's milk: my estate
Is sunk below the degree of fear: where were
These penitent fountains while she was living?
Oh, they were frozen up! Here is a sight
As direful to my soul as is the sword

Unto a wretch hath slain his father. Come, I'll bear thee
Hence, and execute thy last will; that's deliver
Thy body to the reverend dispose
Of some good women: that the cruel tyrant
Shall not deny me. Then I'll post to Milan,
Where somewhat I will speedily enact
Worth my dejection. *Exit with the body*

ACT THE FIFTH

[SCENE I]

[*A Public Place in Milan*]

Enter ANTONIO *and* DELIO

Ant. What think you of my hope of reconcilement
To the Arragonian brethren?
Del. I misdoubt it;
For though they have sent their letters of safe-conduct
For your repair to Milan, they appear
But nets to entrap you. The Marquis of Pescara,
Under whom you hold certain land in cheat,[1]
Much 'gainst his noble nature hath been mov'd
To seize those lands; and some of his dependants
Are at this instant making it their suit
To be invested in your revenues.
I cannot think they mean well to your life
That do deprive you of your means of life,
Your living.
Ant. You are still an heretic
To any safety I can shape myself.
Del. Here comes the marquis: I will make myself
Petitioner for some part of your land,
To know whither it is flying.

[1] Escheat, subject to forfeiture on the outlawry of the tenant.

Ant. I pray do.

Withdraws to back

Enter PESCARA

Del. Sir, I have a suit to you.

Pesc. To me?

Del. An easy one:

There is the citadel of Saint Bennet,
With some demesnes, of late in the possession
Of Antonio Bologna,—please you bestow them on me.

Pesc. You are my friend; but this is such a suit,
Nor fit for me to give, nor you to take.

Del. No, sir?

Pesc. I will give you ample reason for 't
Soon in private:—here's the Cardinal's mistress.

Enter JULIA

Jul. My lord, I am grown your poor petitioner,
And should be an ill beggar, had I not
A great man's letter here, the Cardinal's,
To court you in my favour. *Gives a letter*

Pesc. He entreats for you
The citadel of Saint Bennet, that belong'd
To the banish'd Bologna.

Jul. Yes.

Pesc. I could not
Have thought of a friend I could rather pleasure with it:
'Tis yours.

Jul. Sir, I thank you; and he shall know
How doubly I am engag'd both in your gift,
And speediness of giving, which makes your grant
The greater. *Exit*

Ant. [*Aside*] How they fortify themselves
With my ruin!

Del. Sir, I am little bound to you.

Pesc. Why?

Del. Because you denied this suit to me, and gave 't
To such a creature.
Pesc. Do you know what it was?
It was Antonio's land; not forfeited
By course of law, but ravish'd from his throat
By the Cardinal's entreaty: it were not fit
I should bestow so main a piece of wrong
Upon my friend; 'tis a gratification
Only due to a strumpet, for it is injustice.
Shall I sprinkle the pure blood of innocents
To make those followers I call my friends
Look ruddier upon me? I am glad
This land, ta'en from the owner by such wrong,
Returns again unto so foul an use
As salary for his lust. Learn, good Delio,
To ask noble things of me, and you shall find
I'll be a noble giver.
Del. You instruct me well.
Ant. [*Aside*] Why, here's a man who would fright impudence
From sauciest beggars.
Pesc. Prince Ferdinand's come to Milan,
Sick, as they give out, of an apoplexy;
But some say 'tis a frenzy: I am going
To visit him. *Exit*
Ant. 'Tis a noble old fellow.
Del. What course do you mean to take, Antonio?
Ant. This night I mean to venture all my fortune,
Which is no more than a poor lingering life,
To the Cardinal's worst of malice: I have got
Private access to his chamber; and intend
To visit him about the mid of night,
As once his brother did our noble duchess.
It may be that the sudden apprehension
Of danger,—for I'll go in mine own shape,—

When he shall see it fraight [1] with love and duty,
May draw the poison out of him, and work
A friendly reconcilement: if it fail,
Yet it shall rid me of this infamous calling;
For better fall once than be ever falling.

Del. I'll second you in all danger; and, howe'er,
My life keeps rank with yours.

Ant. You are still my lov'd
And best friend. *Exeunt*

[SCENE II]

[*A Gallery in the Cardinal's Palace at Milan*]

Enter PESCARA *and* Doctor

Pesc. Now, doctor, may I visit your patient?

Doc. If't please your lordship: but he's instantly
To take the air here in the gallery
By my direction.

Pesc. Pray thee, what's his disease?

Doc. A very pestilent disease, my lord,
They call [it] lycanthropia.

Pesc. What's that?
I need a dictionary to 't.

Doc. I'll tell you.
In those that are possess'd with 't there o'erflows
Such melancholy humour they imagine
Themselves to be transformed into wolves;
Steal forth to churchyards in the dead of night,
And dig dead bodies up: as two nights since
One met the duke 'bout midnight in a lane
Behind Saint Mark's Church, with the leg of a man
Upon his shoulder; and he howl'd fearfully;
Said he was a wolf, only the difference
Was, a wolf's skin was hairy on the outside,

[1] Fraught.

His on the inside; bade them take their swords,
Rip up his flesh, and try: straight I was sent for,
And, having minister'd to him, found his grace
Very well recovered.

Pesc. I am glad on 't.

Doc. Yet not without some fear
Of a relapse. If he grow to his fit again,
I'll go a nearer way to work with him
Than ever Paracelsus dream'd of; if
They'll give me leave, I'll buffet his madness
Out of him. Stand aside; he comes.

Enter FERDINAND, CARDINAL, MALATESTE, *and* BOSOLA

Ferd. Leave me.

Mal. Why doth your lordship love this solitariness?

Ferd. Eagles commonly fly alone: they are crows, daws, and starlings that flock together. Look, what's that follows me?

Mal. Nothing, my lord.

Ferd. Yes.

Mal. 'Tis your shadow.

Ferd. Stay it; let it not haunt me.

Mal. Impossible, if you move, and the sun shine.

Ferd. I will throttle it.

Throws himself on the ground

Mal. O, my lord, you are angry with nothing.

Ferd. You are a fool: how is 't possible I should catch my shadow, unless I fall upon 't? When I go to hell, I mean to carry a bribe; for, look you, good gifts evermore make way for the worst persons.

Pesc. Rise, good my lord.

Ferd. I am studying the art of patience.

Pesc. 'Tis a noble virtue.

Ferd. To drive six snails before me from this town to Moscow; neither use goad nor whip to them, but let them take their own time;—the patient'st man i' th' world match me for an experiment;—and I'll crawl after like a sheep-biter.

Card. Force him up. *They raise him*

Ferd. Use me well, you were best. What I have done, I have done: I'll confess nothing.

Doc. Now let me come to him.—Are you mad, my lord? are you out of your princely wits?

Ferd. What's he?

Pesc. Your doctor.

Ferd. Let me have his beard saw'd off, and his eyebrows fil'd more civil.

Doc. I must do mad tricks with him, for that's the only way on 't.—I have brought your grace a salamander's skin to keep you from sunburning.

Ferd. I have cruel sore eyes.

Doc. The white of a cockatrix's egg is present remedy.

Ferd. Let it be a new laid one, you were best.—Hide me from him: physicians are like kings,—they brook no contradiction.

Doc. Now he begins to fear me: now let me alone with him.

Card. How now? put off your gown?

Doc. Let me have some forty urinals fill'd with rose-water: he and I'll go pelt one another with them.—Now he begins to fear me.—Can you fetch a frisk,[1] sir?—Let him go, let him go, upon my peril: I find by his eye he stands in awe of me; I'll make him as tame as a dormouse.

Ferd. Can you fetch your frisks, sir?—I will stamp him into a cullis, flay off his skin, to cover one of the anatomies[2] this rogue hath set i' th' cold yonder in Barber-Chirurgeon's-hall.—Hence, hence! you are all of you like beasts for sacrifice: there's nothing left of you but tongue and belly, flattery and lechery. *Exit*

Pesc. Doctor, he did not fear you throughly.

Doc. True;

[1] Cut a caper.
[2] Skeletons.

I was somewhat too forward.

Bos. Mercy upon me,
What a fatal judgement hath fall'n upon this Ferdinand!

Pesc. Knows your grace what accident hath brought
Unto the prince this strange distraction?

Card. [*Aside*] I must feign somewhat.—Thus they say it grew.
You have heard it rumour'd, for these many years
None of our family dies but there is seen
The shape of an old woman, which is given
By tradition to us to have been murder'd
By her nephews for her riches. Such a figure
One night, as the prince sat up late at 's book,
Appear'd to him; when crying out for help,
The gentlemen of's chamber found his grace
All on a cold sweat, alter'd much in face
And language: since which apparition,
He hath grown worse and worse, and I much fear
He cannot live.

Bos. Sir, I would speak with you.

Pesc. We'll leave your grace,
Wishing to the sick prince, our noble lord,
All health of mind and body.

Card. You are most welcome.

Exeunt PESCARA, MALATESTE, *and* Doctor

Are you come? so.—[*Aside*] This fellow must not know
By any means I had intelligence
In our duchess' death; for, though I counsell'd it,
The full of all th' engagement seem'd to grow
From Ferdinand.—Now, sir, how fares our sister?
I do not think but sorrow makes her look
Like to an oft-dyed garment: she shall now
Taste comfort from me. Why do you look so wildly?
Oh, the fortune of your master here the prince
Dejects you; but be you of happy comfort:
If you'll do one thing for me I'll entreat,

Though he had a cold tombstone o'er his bones,
I'd make you what you would be.

Bos. Anything;
Give it me in a breath, and let me fly to 't:
They that think long small expedition win,
For musing much o' th' end cannot begin.

Enter JULIA

Jul. Sir, will you come in to supper?

Card. I am busy;
Leave me.

Jul. [*Aside*] What an excellent shape hath that fellow!

Exit

Card. 'Tis thus. Antonio lurks here in Milan:
Inquire him out, and kill him. While he lives,
Our sister cannot marry; and I have thought
Of an excellent match for her. Do this, and style me
Thy advancement.

Bos. But by what means shall I find him out?

Card. There is a gentleman called Delio
Here in the camp, that hath been long approv'd
His loyal friend. Set eye upon that fellow;
Follow him to mass; maybe Antonio,
Although he do account religion
But a school-name, for fashion of the world
May accompany him; or else go inquire out
Delio's confessor, and see if you can bribe
Him to reveal it. There are a thousand ways
A man might find to trace him; as to know
What fellows haunt the Jews for taking up
Great sums of money, for sure he 's in want;
Or else to go to th' picture-makers, and learn
Who bought [1] her picture lately: some of these
Happily may take.

[1] 'Brought', in the early editions.

Bos. Well, I'll not freeze i' th' business:
I would see that wretched thing, Antonio,
Above all sights i' th' world.
Card. Do, and be happy. *Exit*
Bos. This fellow doth breed basilisks in 's eyes,
He's nothing else but murder; yet he seems
Not to have notice of the duchess' death.
'Tis his cunning: I must follow his example;
There cannot be a surer way to trace
Than that of an old fox.

Re-enter JULIA, *with a pistol*

Jul. So, sir, you are well met.
Bos. How now?
Jul. Nay, the doors are fast enough: Now, sir,
I will make you confess your treachery.
Bos. Treachery?
Jul. Yes,
Confess to me which of my women 'twas
You hired to put love-powder into my drink?
Bos. Love-powder?
Jul. Yes, when I was at Malfi.
Why should I fall in love with such a face else?
I have already suffer'd for thee so much pain,
The only remedy to do me good
Is to kill my longing.
Bos. Sure, your pistol holds
Nothing but perfumes or kissing-comfits.[1]
Excellent lady! You have a pretty way on 't
To discover your longing. Come, come, I'll disarm you,
And arm you thus: yet this is wondrous strange.
Jul. Compare thy form and my eyes together, you'll find
My love no such great miracle. Now you'll say
I am wanton: this nice modesty in ladies

[1] Perfumed sugar-plums, to sweaten the breath.

Is but a troublesome familiar that haunts them.

Bos. Know you me, I am a blunt soldier.

Jul. The better:
Sure, there wants fire where there are no lively sparks
Of roughness.

Bos. And I want compliment.

Jul. Why, ignorance
In courtship cannot make you do amiss,
If you have a heart to do well.

Bos. You are very fair.

Jul. Nay, if you lay beauty to my charge,
I must plead unguilty.

Bos. Your bright eyes carry
A quiver of darts in them sharper than sunbeams.

Jul. You will mar me with commendation,
Put yourself to the charge of courting me,
Whereas now I woo you.

Bos. [*Aside*] I have it, I will work upon this creature.—
Let us grow most amorously familiar:
If the great Cardinal now should see me thus,
Would he not count me a villain?

Jul. No; he might
Count me a wanton, not lay a scruple
Of offence on you; for if I see and steal
A diamond, the fault is not i' th' stone,
But in me the thief that purloins it. I am sudden
With you: we that are great women of pleasure
Use to cut off these uncertain wishes
And unquiet longings, and in an instant join
The sweet delight and the pretty excuse together.
Had you been i' th' street, under my chamber-window,
Even there I should have courted you.

Bos. Oh, you are
An excellent lady!

Jul. Bid me do somewhat for you
Presently to express I love you.

Bos. I will;
And if you love me, fail not to effect it.
The Cardinal is grown wondrous melancholy;
Demand the cause, let him not put you off
With feign'd excuse; discover the main ground on 't.
Jul. Why would you know this?
Bos. I have depended on him,
And I hear that he is fall'n in some disgrace
With the emperor: if he be, like the mice
That forsake falling houses, I would shift
To other dependence.
Jul. You shall not need
Follow the wars: I'll be your maintenance.
Bos. And I your loyal servant: but I cannot
Leave my calling.
Jul. Not leave an ungrateful
General for the love of a sweet lady?
You are like some cannot sleep in feather-beds,
But must have blocks for their pillows.
Bos. Will you do this?
Jul. Cunningly.
Bos. To-morrow I'll expect th' intelligence.
Jul. To-morrow? get you into my cabinet;
You shall have it with you. Do not delay me,
No more than I do you: I am like one
That is condemn'd; I have my pardon promis'd,
But I would see it seal'd. Go, get you in:
You shall see me wind my tongue about his heart
Like a skein of silk. *Exit* BOSOLA

Re-enter CARDINAL

Card. Where are you?

Enter Servants

Servants. Here.
Card. Let none, upon your lives, have conference

With the Prince Ferdinand, unless I know it.—
[*Aside*] In this distraction he may reveal
The murder. *Exeunt* Servants
Yond's my lingering consumption:
I am weary of her, and by any means
Would be quit of.
Jul. How now, my lord? what ails you?
Card. Nothing.
Jul. Oh, you are much alter'd: come, I must be
Your secretary, and remove this lead
From off your bosom: what's the matter?
Card. I may not
Tell you.
Jul. Are you so far in love with sorrow
You cannot part with part of it? or think you
I cannot love your grace when you are sad
As well as merry? or do you suspect
I, that have been a secret to your heart
These many winters, cannot be the same
Unto your tongue?
Card. Satisfy thy longing,—
The only way to make thee keep my counsel
Is, not to tell thee.
Jul. Tell your echo this,
Or flatterers, that like echoes still report
What they hear though most imperfect, and not me;
For if that you be true unto yourself,
I'll know.
Card. Will you rack me?
Jul. No, judgement shall
Draw it from you: it is an equal fault,
To tell one's secrets unto all or none.
Card. The first argues folly.
Jul. But the last tyranny.
Card. Very well: why, imagine I have committed
Some secret deed which I desire the world

May never hear of.

Jul. Therefore may not I know it?
You have conceal'd for me as great a sin
As adultery. Sir, never was occasion
For perfect trial of my constancy
Till now: sir, I beseech you——

Card. You'll repent it.

Jul. Never.

Card. It hurries thee to ruin: I'll not tell thee.
Be well advis'd, and think what danger 'tis
To receive a prince's secrets: they that do,
Had need have their breasts hoop'd with adamant
To contain them. I pray thee, yet be satisfi'd;
Examine thine own frailty; 'tis more easy
To tie knots than unloose them: 'tis a secret
That, like a lingering poison, may chance lie
Spread in thy veins, and kill thee seven year hence.

Jul. Now you dally with me.

Card. No more; thou shalt know it.
By my appointment the great Duchess of Malfi
And two of her young children, four nights since,
Were strangled.

Jul. O Heaven! sir, what have you done!

Card. How now? how settles this? think you your bosom
Will be a grave dark and obscure enough
For such a secret?

Jul. You have undone yourself, sir.

Card. Why?

Jul. It lies not in me to conceal it.

Card. No?
Come, I will swear you to 't upon this book.

Jul. Most religiously.

Card. Kiss it. *She kisses the book*
Now you shall
Never utter it; thy curiosity
Hath undone thee: thou'rt poison'd with that book;

Because I knew thou couldst not keep my counsel,
I have bound thee to 't by death.

Re-enter BOSOLA

Bos. For pity sake,
Hold!

Card. Ha! Bosola?

Jul. I forgive you
This equal piece of justice you have done;
For I betray'd your counsel to that fellow:
He overheard it; that was the cause I said
It lay not in me to conceal it.

Bos. O foolish woman,
Couldst not thou have poison'd him?

Jul. 'Tis weakness,
Too much to think what should have been done. I go,
I know not whither. *Dies*

Card. Wherefore com'st thou hither?

Bos. That I might find a great man like yourself,
Not out of his wits as the Lord Ferdinand,
To remember my service.

Card. I'll have thee hew'd in pieces.

Bos. Make not yourself such a promise of that life
Which is not yours to dispose of.

Card. Who plac'd thee here?

Bos. Her lust, as she intended.

Card. Very well:
Now you know me for your fellow-murderer.

Bos. And wherefore should you lay fair marble colours
Upon your rotten purposes to me?
Unless you imitate some that do plot great treasons,
And when they have done, go hide themselves i' th' graves
Of those were actors in 't?

Card. No more; there is
A fortune attends thee.

Bos. Shall I go sue

To Fortune any longer? 'Tis the fool's
Pilgrimage.

Card. I have honours in store for thee.

Bos. There are a many ways that conduct to seeming
Honour, and some of them very dirty ones.

Card. Throw
To the devil thy melancholy. The fire burns well:
What need we keep a stirring of 't, and make
A greater smother? Thou wilt kill Antonio?

Bos. Yes.

Card. Take up that body.

Bos. I think I shall
Shortly grow the common beare[r] for churchyards.

Card. I will allow thee some dozen of attendants
To aid thee in the murder.

Bos. Oh, by no means. Physicians that apply horse-leeches to any rank swelling use to cut off their tails, that the blood may run through them the faster: let me have no train when I go to shed blood, lest it make me have a greater when I ride to the gallows.

Card. Come to me after midnight, to help to remove
That body to her own lodging: I'll give out
She died o' th' plague; 'twill breed the less inquiry
After her death.

Bos. Where's Castruchio her husband?

Card. He's rode to Naples, to take possession
Of Antonio's citadel.

Bos. Believe me, you have done
A very happy turn.

Card. Fail not to come:
There is the master-key of our lodgings; and by that
You may conceive what trust I plant in you.

Bos. You shall find me ready. *Exit* CARDINAL

O poor Antonio,
Though nothing be so needful to thy estate
As pity, yet I find nothing so dangerous;

I must look to my footing:
In such slippery ice-pavements men had need
To be frost-nailed well, they may break their necks else;
The precedent's here afore me. How this man
Bears up in blood! seems fearless! Why, 'tis well:
Security some men call the suburbs of hell,
Only a dead wall between. Well, good Antonio,
I'll seek thee out; and all my care shall be
To put thee into safety from the reach
Of these most cruel biters that have got
Some of thy blood already. It may be,
I'll join with thee in a most just revenge:
The weakest arm is strong enough that strikes
With the sword of justice. Still methinks the duchess
Haunts me.—There, there, 'tis nothing but my melancholy.
O Penitence, let me truly taste thy cup,
That throws men down only to raise them up! *Exit*

[SCENE III]

[*A Fortification at Milan*]

Enter ANTONIO *and* DELIO

Del. Yond's the Cardinal's window. This fortification
Grew from the ruins of an ancient abbey;
And to yond side o' th' river lies a wall,
Piece of a cloister, which in my opinion
Gives the best echo that you ever heard,
So hollow and so dismal, and withal
So plain in the distinction of our words,
That many have suppos'd it is a spirit
That answers.
Ant. I do love these ancient ruins.
We never tread upon them but we set
Our foot upon some reverend history:
And, questionless, here in this open court,

Which now lies naked to the injuries
Of stormy weather, some men lie interr'd
Lov'd the church so well, and gave so largely to 't,
They thought it should have canopied their bones
Till doomsday; but all things have their end:
Churches and cities, which have diseases
Like to men, must have like death that we have.

Echo. 'Like death that we have.'

Del. Now the echo hath caught you.

Ant. It groaned, methought, and gave
A very deadly accent.

Echo. 'Deadly accent.'

Del. I told you 'twas a pretty one: you may make it
A huntsman, or a falconer, a musician,
Or a thing of sorrow.

Echo. 'A thing of sorrow.'

Ant. Aye, sure, that suits it best.

Echo. 'That suits it best.'

Ant. 'Tis very like my wife's voice.

Echo. 'Aye, wife's voice.'

Del. Come, let's walk further from 't. I would not have you
Go to th' Cardinal's to-night: do not.

Echo. 'Do not.'

Del. Wisdom doth not more moderate wasting sorrow
Than time: take time for 't; be mindful of thy safety.

Echo. 'Be mindful of thy safety.'

Ant. Necessity compels me:
Make scrutiny throughout the passes of
Your own life, you'll find it impossible
To fly your fate.

Echo. 'Oh, fly your fate.'

Del. Hark!
The dead stones seem to have pity on you, and give you
Good counsel.

Ant. Echo, I will not talk with thee,

For thou art a dead thing.
Echo. 'Thou art a dead thing.'
Ant. My duchess is asleep now,
And her little ones, I hope sweetly: O Heaven,
Shall I never see her more?
Echo. 'Never see her more.'
Ant. I mark'd not one repetition of the echo
But that; and on the sudden a clear light
Presented me a face folded in sorrow.
Del. Your fancy merely.
Ant. Come, I'll be out of this ague,
For to live thus is not indeed to live;
It is a mockery and abuse of life:
I will not henceforth save myself by halves;
Lose all, or nothing.
Del. Your own virtue save you!
I'll fetch your eldest son, and second you:
It may be that the sight of his own blood
Spread in so sweet a figure may beget
The more compassion. However, fare you well.
Though in our miseries Fortune have a part,
Yet in our noble sufferings she hath none:
Contempt of pain, that we may call our own. *Exeunt*

[SCENE IV]

[*A Room in the Cardinal's Palace*]

Enter CARDINAL, PESCARA, MALATESTE, RODERIGO, *and* GRISOLAN

Card. You shall not watch to-night by the sick prince;
His grace is very well recover'd.
Mal. Good my lord, suffer us.
Card. Oh, by no means;
The noise, and change of object in his eye,
Doth more distract him: I pray, all to bed;

And though you hear him in his violent fit,
Do not rise, I entreat you.

Pesc. So, sir; we shall not.

Card. Nay, I must have you promise upon your honours,
For I was enjoin'd to 't by himself; and he seem'd
To urge it sensibly.

Pesc. Let our honours bind
This trifle.

Card. Nor any of your followers.

Mal. Neither.

Card. It may be, to make trial of your promise,
When he's asleep, myself will rise and feign
Some of his mad tricks, and cry out for help,
And feign myself in danger.

Mal. If your throat were cutting,
I'd not come at you, now I have protested against it.

Card. Why, I thank you.

Gris. 'Twas a foul storm to-night.

Rod. The Lord Ferdinand's chamber shook like an osier.

Mal. 'Twas nothing but pure kindness in the devil,
To rock his own child. *Exeunt all except the* CARDINAL

Card. The reason why I would not suffer these
About my brother, is, because at midnight
I may with better privacy convey
Julia's body to her own lodging. Oh, my conscience!
I would pray now; but the devil takes away my heart
For having any confidence in prayer.
About this hour I appointed Bosola
To fetch the body: when he hath serv'd my turn,
He dies. *Exit*

Enter BOSOLA

Bos. Ha! 'twas the Cardinal's voice; I heard him name
Bosola and my death. Listen; I hear
One's footing.

Enter FERDINAND

Ferd. Strangling is a very quiet death.

Bos. [*Aside*] Nay, then, I see I must stand upon my guard.

Ferd. What say to that? whisper softly; do you agree to 't? So; it must be done i' th' dark: the Cardinal would not for a thousand pounds the doctor should see it.

Bos. My death is plotted; here 's the consequence of murder.
We value not desert nor Christian breath,
When we know black deeds must be cur'd with death.

Enter ANTONIO *and* Servant

Serv. Here stay, sir, and be confident, I pray:
I'll fetch you a dark lantern. *Exit*

Ant. Could I take him
At his prayers, there were hope of pardon.

Bos. Fall right, my sword!— *Stabs him*
I'll not give thee so much leisure as to pray.

Ant. Oh, I am gone! Thou hast ended a long suit
In a minute.

Bos. What art thou?

Ant. A most wretched thing,
That only have thy benefit in death,
To appear myself.

Re-enter Servant *with a lantern*

Serv. Where are you, sir?

Ant. Very near my home.—Bosola?

Serv. Oh, misfortune!

Bos. Smother thy pity, thou art dead else.—Antonio?
The man I would have saved 'bove mine own life!
We are merely the stars' tennis-balls, struck and bandied
Which way please them.—O good Antonio,
I'll whisper one thing in thy dying ear

Shall make thy heart break quickly! thy fair duchess
And two sweet children——

Ant. Their very names
Kindle a little life in me.

Bos. Are murder'd.

Ant. Some men have wish'd to die
At the hearing of sad tidings; I am glad
That I shall do 't in sadness:[1] I would not now
Wish my wounds balm'd nor heal'd, for I have no use
To put my life to. In all our quest of greatness,
Like wanton boys, whose pastime is their care,
We follow after bubbles blown in th' air.
Pleasure of life, what is 't? only the good
Hours of an ague; merely a preparative
To rest, to endure vexation. I do not ask
The process of my death; only commend me
To Delio.

Bos. Break, heart!

Ant. And let my son
Fly the courts of princes. *Dies*

Bos. Thou seem'st
To have lov'd Antonio?

Serv. I brought him hither,
To have reconcil'd him to the Cardinal.

Bos. I do not ask thee that.
Take him up, if thou tender thine own life,
And bear him where the lady Julia
Was wont to lodge.—Oh, my fate moves swift;
I have this Cardinal in the forge already;
Now I'll bring him to th' hammer. O direful misprision![2]
I will not imitate things glorious,
No more than base; I'll be mine own example.—
On, on, and look thou represent, for silence,
The thing thou bear'st. *Exeunt*

[1] i. e. in earnest.
[2] Mistake.

[SCENE V]

[*Another Room in the same*]

Enter CARDINAL, *with a book*

Card. I am puzzled in a question about hell:
He says, in hell there 's one material fire,
And yet it shall not burn all men alike.
Lay him by. How tedious is a guilty conscience!
When I look into the fish-ponds in my garden,
Methinks I see a thing arm'd with a rake,
That seems to strike at me.

Enter BOSOLA, *and* Servant *bearing* ANTONIO'S *body*

Now, art thou come?
Thou look'st ghastly:
There sits in thy face some great determination
Mix'd with some fear.

Bos. Thus it lightens into action:
I am come to kill thee.

Card. Ha!—Help! our guard!

Bos. Thou art deceived; they are out of thy howling.

Card. Hold; and I will faithfully divide
Revenues with thee.

Bos. Thy prayers and proffers
Are both unseasonable.

Card. Raise the watch!
We are betrayed!

Bos. I have confin'd your flight:
I'll suffer your retreat to Julia's chamber,
But no further.

Card. Help! we are betrayed!

Enter, above, PESCARA, MALATESTE, RODERIGO, *and* GRISOLAN

Mal. Listen.

Card. My dukedom for rescue!

Rod. Fie upon
His counterfeiting!

Mal. Why, 'tis not the Cardinal.

Rod. Yes, yes, 'tis he: but I'll see him hang'd
Ere I'll go down to him.

Card. Here 's a plot upon me;
I am assaulted! I am lost, unless some rescue.

Gris. He doth this pretty well; but it will not serve
To laugh me out of mine honour.

Card. The sword 's at my throat!

Rod. You would not bawl so loud then.

Mal. Come, come,
Let 's go to bed: he told us thus much aforehand.

Pesc. He wish'd you should not come at him; but, believe 't,
The accent of the voice sounds not in jest:
I'll down to him, howsoever, and with engines
Force ope the doors. *Exit above*

Rod. Let 's follow him aloof,
And note how the Cardinal will laugh at him.

Exeunt, above, MALATESTE, RODERIGO, *and* GRISOLAN

Bos. There's for first, *Kills the* Servant
'Cause you shall not unbarricade the door
To let in rescue.

Card. What cause hast thou to pursue my life?

Bos. Look there.

Card. Antonio?

Bos. Slain by my hand unwittingly.
Pray, and be sudden: when thou killed'st thy sister,
Thou took'st from Justice her most equal balance,
And left her naught but her sword.

Card. Oh, mercy!

Bos. Now, it seems thy greatness was only outward;
For thou fall'st faster of thyself than calamity

Can drive thee. I'll not waste longer time; there!

Stabs him

Card. Thou hast hurt me.

Bos. Again! *Stabs him again*

Card. Shall I die like a leveret,
Without any resistance?—Help, help, help!
I am slain!

Enter FERDINAND

Ferd. Th' alarum? give me a fresh horse;
Rally the vaunt-guard, or the day is lost.
Yield, yield! I give you the honour of arms,
Shake my sword over you; will you yield?

Card. Help me;
I am your brother!

Ferd. The devil! My brother fight
Upon the adverse party?

He wounds the CARDINAL, *and, in the scuffle, gives* BOSOLA *his death-wound.*

There flies your ransom.

Card. O justice!
I suffer now for what hath former bin:
Sorrow is held the eldest child of sin.

Ferd. Now you 're brave fellows. Caesar's fortune was harder than Pompey's; Caesar died in the arms of prosperity, Pompey at the feet of disgrace. You both died in the field. The pain 's nothing: pain many times is taken away with the apprehension of greater, as the toothache with the sight of a barber that comes to pull it out: there's philosophy for you.

Bos. Now my revenge is perfect.—Sink, thou main cause

Kills FERDINAND

Of my undoing!—The last part of my life
Hath done me best service.

Ferd. Give me some wet hay; I am broken-winded. I

do account this world but a dog-kennel: I will vault credit[1] and affect high pleasures beyond death,

Bos. He seems to come to himself, now he 's so near
The bottom.

Ferd. My sister, O my sister! there 's the cause on 't.
Whether we fall by ambition, blood, or lust,
Like diamonds we are cut with our own dust. *Dies*

Card. Thou hast thy payment too.

Bos. Yes, I hold my weary soul in my teeth.
'Tis ready to part from me. I do glory
That thou, which stood'st like a huge pyramid
Begun upon a large and ample base,
Shalt end in a little point, a kind of nothing.

Enter, below, PESCARA, MALATESTE, RODERIGO, *and* GRISOLAN

Pesc. How now, my lord?

Mal. O sad disaster!

Rod. How
Comes this?

Bos. Revenge for the Duchess of Malfi murdered
By th' Arragonian brethren; for Antonio
Slain by [t]his hand; for lustful Julia
Poison'd by this man; and lastly for myself,
That was an actor in the main of all,
Much 'gainst mine own good nature, yet i' th' end
Neglected.

Pesc. How now, my lord?

Card. Look to my brother: he gave us these large wounds
As we were struggling here i' the rushes. And now,
I pray, let me be laid by and never thought of. *Dies*

Pesc. How fatally, it seems, he did withstand
His own rescue!

[1] Do incredible deeds.

Mal. Thou wretched thing of blood,
How came Antonio by his death?
Bos. In a mist;
I know not how: such a mistake as I
Have often seen in a play. Oh, I am gone!
We are only like dead walls or vaulted graves,
That, ruin'd, yield no echo. Fare you well.
It may be pain, but no harm, to me to die
In so good a quarrel. Oh, this gloomy world!
In what a shadow, or deep pit of darkness,
Doth, womanish and fearful, mankind live!
Let worthy minds ne'er stagger in distrust
To suffer death or shame for what is just:
Mine is another voyage. *Dies*
Pesc. The noble Delio, as I came to the palace,
Told me of Antonio's being here, and show'd me
A pretty gentleman, his son and heir.

Enter DELIO *and* ANTONIO'S *Son*

Mal. O sir,
You come too late!
Del. I heard so, and was arm'd for 't,
Ere I came. Let us make noble use
Of this great ruin; and join all our force
To establish this young hopeful gentleman
In 's mother's right. These wretched eminent things
Leave no more fame behind 'em, than should one
Fall in a frost, and leave his print in snow;
As soon as the sun shines, it ever melts,
Both form and matter. I have ever thought
Nature doth nothing so great for great men
As when she 's pleas'd to make them lords of truth:
Integrity of life is fame's best friend,
Which nobly, beyond death, shall crown the end. *Exeunt*

A NEW WAY TO PAY OLD DEBTS

by

PHILIP MASSINGER

DRAMATIS PERSONÆ

[LORD] LOVELL
SIR GILES OVERREACH, *a cruel Extortioner*
[FRANK] WELLBORN, *a Prodigal*
[TOM] ALLWORTH, *a young Gentleman, Page to Lord Lovell*
GREEDY, *a hungry Justice of Peace*
ORDER, [*Steward*]
AMBLE, [*Usher*]
FURNACE, [*Cook*]
WATCHALL, [*Porter*]
} *Servants to the Lady Allworth*
MARRALL, *a Term-Driver; a creature of Sir Giles Overreach*
WILLDO, *a Parson*
TAPWELL, *an Alehouse Keeper*
Three Creditors, Servants, etc.
LADY ALLWORTH, *a rich Widow*
MARGARET OVERREACH, *Sir Giles' Daughter*
FROTH, *Tapwell's Wife*
Chambermaid
Waiting Woman

[SCENE: The Country near Nottingham]

A NEW WAY TO PAY OLD DEBTS

[ACT I, SCENE I]

[*Before Tapwell's House*]

Enter Wellborn *in tattered apparel,* Tapwell, *and* Froth

Well. No bouse? nor no tobacco?
Tap. Not a suck, sir;
Nor the remainder of a single can
Left by a drunken porter, all night palled too.
Froth. Not the dropping of the tap for your morning's draught, sir.
'Tis verity, I assure you.
Well. Verity, you brach!
The devil turned precisian! Rogue, what am I?
Tap. Troth, durst I trust you with a looking-glass,
To let you see your trim shape, you would quit me,
And take the name yourself.
Well. How, dog!
Tap. Even so, sir.
And I must tell you, if you but advance
Your Plymouth cloak you shall be soon instructed
There dwells, and within call, if it please your worship,
A potent monarch called the constable,
That does command a citadel called the stocks;
Whose guards are certain files of rusty billmen
Such as with great dexterity will hale
Your tattered, lousy—
Well. Rascal! Slave!

Froth. No rage, sir.
Tap. At his own peril.—Do not put yourself
In too much heat, there being no water near
To quench your thirst; and sure, for other liquor,
As mighty ale, or beer, they are things, I take it,
You must no more remember; not in a dream, sir.
Well. Why, thou unthankful villain, dar'st thou talk thus!
Is not thy house, and all thou hast, my gift?
Tap. I find it not in chalk; and Timothy Tapwell
Does keep no other register.
Well. Am not I he
Whose riots fed and clothed thee? Wert thou not
Born on my father's land, and proud to be
A drudge in his house?
Tap. What I was, sir, it skills not;
What you are, is apparent. Now, for a farewell,
Since you talk of father, in my hope it will torment you,
I'll briefly tell your story. Your dead father,
My quondam master, was a man of worship,
Old Sir John Wellborn, justice of peace and *quorum,*
And stood fair to be *custos rotulorum;*
Bore the whole sway of the shire, kept a great house,
Relieved the poor, and so forth; but he dying,
And the twelve hundred a year coming to you,
Late Master Francis, but now forlorn Wellborn—
Well. Slave, stop! or I shall lose myself.
Froth. Very hardly;
You cannot out of your way.
Tap. But to my story.
You were then a lord of acres, the prime gallant,
And I your under-butler. Note the change now.
You had a merry time of 't; hawks and hounds,
With choice of running horses; mistresses
Of all sorts and all sizes, yet so hot,
As their embraces made your lordship melt;
Which your uncle, Sir Giles Overreach, observing—

Resolving not to lose a drop of them—
On foolish mortgages, statutes, and bonds,
For a while supplied your looseness, and then left you.

Well. Some curate hath penned this invective, mongrel,
And you have studied it.

Tap. I have not done yet.
Your land gone, and your credit not worth a token,
You grew the common borrower; no man 'scaped
Your paper-pellets, from the gentleman
To the beggars on highways, that sold you switches
In your gallantry.

Well. I shall switch your brains out.

Tap. Where poor Tim Tapwell, with a little stock,
Some forty pounds or so, bought a small cottage;
Humbled myself to marriage with my Froth here,
Gave entertainment—

Well. Yes, to whores and canters,
Clubbers by night.

Tap. True, but they brought in profit,
And had a gift to pay for what they called for,
And stuck not like your mastership. The poor income
I gleaned from them hath made me in my parish
Thought worthy to be scavenger, and in time
I may rise to be overseer of the poor;
Which if I do, on your petition, Wellborn,
I may allow you thirteen-pence a quarter.
And you shall thank my worship.

Well. Thus, you dog-bolt,
And thus— *Beats and kicks him*

Tap. [*to* Froth] Cry out for help!

Well. Stir, and thou diest!
Your potent prince, the constable, shall not save you.
Hear me, ungrateful hell-hound! Did not I
Make purses for you? Then you licked my boots,
And thought your holiday cloak too coarse to clean them.
'Twas I that, when I heard thee swear if ever

Thou couldst arrive at forty pounds, thou wouldst
Live like an emperor,—'twas I that gave it
In ready gold. Deny this, wretch!

Tap. I must, sir;
For, from the tavern to the taphouse, all,
On forfeiture of their licenses, stand bound
Ne'er to remember who their best guests were,
If they grew poor like you.

Well. They are well rewarded
That beggar themselves to make such cuckolds rich.
Thou viper, thankless viper! Impudent bawd!
But since you are grown forgetful, I will help
Your memory, and tread you into mortar,
Nor leave one bone unbroken. *Beats him again*

Tap. O!

Froth. Ask mercy.

Enter ALLWORTH

Well. 'Twill not be granted.

All. Hold—for my sake, hold.
Deny me, Frank! They are not worth your anger.

Well. For once thou hast redeemed them from this scepter.
But let them vanish, creeping on their knees,
And, if they grumble, I revoke my pardon.

Froth. This comes of your prating, husband; you presumed
On your ambling wit, and must use your glib tongue,
Though you are beaten lame for 't.

Tap. Patience, Froth.
There's law to cure our bruises.

They go off on their hands and knees

Well. Sent to your mother?

All. My lady, Frank, my patroness, my all!
She 's such a mourner for my father's death,
And, in her love to him, so favors me,

That I cannot pay too much observance to her.
There are few such stepdames.

Well. 'Tis a noble widow,
And keeps her reputation pure and clear
From the least taint of infamy; her life,
With the splendor of her actions, leaves no tongue
To envy or detraction. Prithee tell me,
Has she no suitors?

All. Even the best of the shire, Frank,
My lord excepted; such as sue and send,
And send and sue again, but to no purpose.
Their frequent visits have not gained her presence.
Yet she 's so far from sullenness and pride,
That I dare undertake you shall meet from her
A liberal entertainment. I can give you
A catalogue of her suitors' names.

Well. Forbear it,
While I give you good counsel; I am bound to it.
Thy father was my friend, and that affection
I bore to him, in right descends to thee.
Thou art a handsome and a hopeful youth,
Nor will I have the least affront stick on thee,
If I with any danger can prevent it.

All. I thank your noble care. But, pray you, in what
Do I run the hazard?

Well. Art thou not in love?
Put it not off with wonder.

All. In love, at my years!

Well. You think you walk in clouds, but are transparent.
I have heard all, and the choice that you have made,
And, with my finger, can point out the north star
By which the loadstone of your folly's guided;
And, to confirm this true, what think you of
Fair Margaret, the only child and heir
Of Cormorant Overreach? Does it blush and start,
To hear her only named? blush at your want

Of wit and reason.

All. You are too bitter, sir.

Well. Wounds of this nature are not to be cured
With balms, but corrosives. I must be plain.
Art thou scarce manumised from the porter's lodge
And yet sworn servant to the pantofle,
And dar'st thou dream of marriage? I fear
'Twill be concluded for impossible
That there is now, or e'er shall be hereafter,
A handsome page or player's boy of fourteen
But he either loves a wench or drabs love him,
Court-waiters not exempted.

All. This is madness.
Howe'er you have discovered my intents,
You know my aims are lawful; and if ever
The queen of flowers, the glory of the spring,
The sweetest comfort to our smell, the rose,
Sprang from an envious briar, I may infer
There's such disparity in their conditions
Between the goodness of my soul, the daughter,
And the base churl her father.

Well. Grant this true,
As I believe it, canst thou ever hope
To enjoy a quiet bed with her whose father
Ruined thy state?

All. And yours too.

Well. I confess it;
True; I must tell you as a friend, and freely,
That, where impossibilities are apparent,
'Tis indiscretion to nourish hopes.
Canst thou imagine—let not self-love blind thee—
That Sir Giles Overreach, that, to make her great
In swelling titles, without touch of conscience
Will cut his neighbor's throat, and I hope his own too,
Will e'er consent to make her thine? Give o'er,
And think of some course suitable to thy rank,

And prosper in it.
All. You have well advised me.
But in the mean time you that are so studious
Of my affairs wholly neglect your own.
Remember yourself, and in what plight you are.
Well. No matter, no matter.
All. Yes, 'tis much material.
You know my fortune and my means; yet something
I can spare from myself to help your wants.
Well. How 's this?
All. Nay, be not angry; there 's eight pieces
To put you in better fashion.
Well. Money from thee!
From a boy! a stipendiary! one that lives
At the devotion of a stepmother,
And the uncertain favor of a lord!
I'll eat my arms first. Howsoe'er blind Fortune
Hath spent the utmost of her malice on me—
Though I am vomited out of an alehouse,
And thus accoutred—know not where to eat,
Or drink, or sleep, but underneath this canopy—
Although I thank thee, I despise thy offer:
And as I in my madness broke my state
Without the assistance of another's brain,
In my right wits I'll piece it; at the worst,
Die thus and be forgotten.
All. A strange humor!
Exeunt

[SCENE II]

[*A Room in Lady Allworth's House*]

Enter Order, Amble, Furnace, *and* Watchall

Ord. Set all things right, or, as my name is Order,
And by this staff of office that commands you,

This chain and double ruff, symbols of power,
Whoever misses in his function,
For one whole week makes forfeiture of his breakfast,
And privilege in the wine-cellar.

Amb. You are merry,
Good master steward.

Furn. Let him; I'll be angry.

Amb. Why, fellow Furnace, 'tis not twelve o'clock yet,
Nor dinner taking up; then, 'tis allowed,
Cooks, by their places, may be choleric.

Furn. You think you have spoke wisely, goodman Amble,
My lady's go-before!

Ord. Nay, nay, no wrangling.

Furn. Twit me with the authority of the kitchen!
At all hours, and all places, I'll be angry;
And thus provoked, when I am at my prayers
I will be angry.

Amb. There was no hurt meant.

Furn. I am friends with thee; and yet I will be angry.

Ord. With whom?

Furn. No matter whom. Yet now I think on it,
I am angry with my lady.

Watch. Heaven forbid, man!

Ord. What cause has she given thee?

Furn. Cause enough, master steward.
I was entertained by her to please her palate,
And, till she forswore eating, I performed it.
Now, since our master, noble Allworth, died,
Though I crack my brains to find out tempting sauces,
And raise fortifications in the pastry
Such as might serve for models in the Low Countries;
Which, if they had been practised at Breda,
Spinola might have thrown his cap at it, and ne'er took it.

Amb. But you had wanted matter there to work on.

Furn. Matter! With six eggs, and a strike of rye meal,
I had kept the town till doomsday, perhaps longer.

Ord. But what 's this to your pet against my lady?
Furn. What 's this? Marry, this: when I am three parts roasted
And the fourth part parboiled, to prepare her viands
She keeps her chamber, dines with a panada
Or water-gruel, my sweat never thought on.
Ord. But your art is seen in the dining-room.
Furn. By whom?
By such as pretend love to her, but come
To feed upon her. Yet, of all the harpies
That do devour her, I am out of charity
With none so much as the thin-gutted squire
That's stolen into commission.
Ord. Justice Greedy?
Furn. The same, the same. Meat's cast away upon him;
It never thrives. He holds this paradox,
Who eats not well, can ne'er do justice well.
His stomach's as insatiate as the grave,
Or strumpets' ravenous appetites. *Knocking*
Watch. One knocks.
Ord. Our late young master!

Enter ALLWORTH

Amb. Welcome, sir.
Furn. Your hand.
If you have a stomach, a cold bake-meat's ready.
Ord. His father's picture in little.
Furn. We are all your servants.
Amb. In you he lives.
All. At once, my thanks, to all.
This is yet some comfort. Is my lady stirring?

Enter Lady ALLWORTH, Waiting Woman, *and* Chambermaid

Ord. Her presence answers for us.
L. All. Sort those silks well.

I'll take the air alone. *Exeunt* Waiting Woman *and* Chambermaid

Furn. You air and air;
But will you never taste but spoon-meat more?
To what use serve I?

L. All. Prithee, be not angry;
I shall ere long. I' the mean time, there is gold
To buy thee aprons, and a summer suit.

Furn. I am appeased, and Furnace now grows cool.

L. All. And, as I gave directions, if this morning
I am visited by any, entertain them
As heretofore. But say, in my excuse,
I am indisposed.

Ord. I shall, madam.

L. All. Do, and leave them.
Nay, stay you, Allworth. *Exeunt* ORDER, AMBLE, FURNACE, *and* WATCHALL

All. I shall gladly grow here,
To wait on your commands.

L. All. So soon turned courtier!

All. Style not that courtship, madam, which is duty
Purchased on your part.

L. All. Well, you shall o'ercome;
I'll not contend in words. How is it with
Your noble master?

All. Ever like himself,
No scruple lessened in the full weight of honor,
He did command me, pardon my presumption,
As his unworthy deputy, to kiss
Your ladyship's fair hands.

L. All. I am honored in
His favor to me. Does he hold his purpose
For the Low Countries?

All. Constantly, good madam;
But he will in person first present his service.

L. All. And how approve you of his course? You are yet

Like virgin parchment, capable of any
Inscription, vicious or honorable.
I will not force your will, but leave you free
To your own election.

All. Any form you please,
I will put on. But, might I make my choice,
With humble emulation I would follow
The path my lord marks to me.

L. All. 'Tis well answered,
And I commend your spirit. You had a father—
Blessed be his memory—that some few hours
Before the will of heaven took him from me,
Who did commend you, by the dearest ties
Of perfect love between us, to my charge;
And, therefore, what I speak, you are bound to hear
With such respect as if he lived in me.
He was my husband, and howe'er you are not
Son of my womb, you may be of my love,
Provided you deserve it.

All. I have found you,
Most honored madam, the best mother to me,
And, with my utmost strengths of care and service,
Will labor that you never may repent
Your bounties showered upon me.

L. All. I much hope it.
These were your father's words: 'If e'er my son
Follow the war, tell him it is a school
Where all the principles tending to honor
Are taught, if truly followed. But for such
As repair thither as a place in which
They do presume they may with license practise
Their lusts and riots, they shall never merit
The noble name of soldiers. To dare boldly,
In a fair cause, and for their country's safety,
To run upon the cannon's mouth undaunted;
To obey their leaders, and shun mutinies;

To bear with patience the winter's cold
And summer's scorching heat, and not to faint,
When plenty of provision fails, with hunger;
Are the essential parts make up a soldier,
Not swearing, dice, or drinking.'

All. There 's no syllable
You speak, but is to me an oracle,
Which but to doubt were impious.

L. All. To conclude:
Beware ill company, for often men
Are like to those with whom they do converse;
And, from one man I warn you, and that 's Wellborn,—
Not 'cause he's poor, that rather claims your pity;
But that he's in his manners so debauched,
And hath to vicious courses sold himself.
'Tis true, your father loved him, while he was
Worthy the loving; but if he had lived
To have seen him as he is, he had cast him off,
As you must do.

All. I shall obey in all things.

L. All. Follow me to my chamber; you shall have gold
To furnish you like my son, and still supplied,
As I hear from you.

All. I am still your creature.

Exeunt

[SCENE III]

[*A Hall in the same*]

Enter OVERREACH, GREEDY, ORDER, AMBLE, FURNACE, WATCHALL, *and* MARRALL

Greedy. Not to be seen!

Over. Still cloistered up! Her reason,
I hope, assures her, though she make herself
Close prisoner ever for her husband's loss,

'Twill not recover him.

Ord. Sir, it is her will,
Which we, that are her servants, ought to serve it,
And not dispute. Howe'er, you are nobly welcome;
And, if you please to stay, that you may think so,
There came, not six days since, from Hull, a pipe
Of rich Canary, which shall spend itself
For my lady's honor.

Greedy. Is it of the right race?

Ord. Yes, Master Greedy.

Amb. How his mouth runs o'er!

Furn. I'll make it run, and run. Save your good worship!

Greedy. Honest Master Cook, thy hand; again. How I love thee!
Are the good dishes still in being? Speak, boy.

Furn. If you have a mind to feed, there is a chine
Of beef, well seasoned.

Greedy. Good!

Furn. A pheasant, larded.

Greedy. That I might now give thanks for 't!

Furn. Other kickshaws.
Besides, there came last night, from the forest of Sherwood,
The fattest stag I ever cooked.

Greedy. A stag, man!

Furn. A stag, sir; part of it prepared for dinner,
And baked in puff-paste.

Greedy. Puff-paste too! Sir Giles,
A ponderous chine of beef! a pheasant larded!
And red deer too, Sir Giles, and baked in puff-paste!
All business set aside, let us give thanks here.

Furn. How the lean skeleton's rapt!

Over. You know we cannot.

Mar. Your worships are to sit on a commission,
And if you fail to come, you lose the cause.

Greedy. Cause me no causes. I'll prove 't, for such dinner.

We may put off a commission; you shall find it
Henrici decimo quarto.

Over. Fie, Master Greedy!
Will you lose me a thousand pounds for a dinner?
No more, for shame! We must forget the belly
When we think of profit.

Greedy. Well, you shall o'er-rule me;
I could e'en cry now.—Do you hear, Master Cook,
Send but a corner of that immortal pasty,
And I, in thankfulness, will, by your boy,
Send you,—a brace of three-pences.

Furn. Will you be so prodigal?

Enter WELLBORN

Over. Remember me to your lady. Who have we here?

Well. You know me.

Over. I did once, but now I will not;
Thou art no blood of mine. Avaunt, thou beggar!
If ever thou presume to own me more,
I'll have thee caged and whipped.

Greedy. I'll grant the warrant.
Think of Pie-corner, Furnace!

Exeunt OVERREACH, GREEDY, *and* MARRALL

Watch. Will you out, sir?
I wonder how you durst creep in.

Ord. This is rudeness,
And saucy impudence.

Amb. Cannot you stay
To be served, among your fellows, from the basket,
But you must press into the hall?

Furn. Prithee, vanish
Into some outhouse, though it be the pigsty.
My scullion shall come to thee.

Enter ALLWORTH

Well. This is rare.

O, here's Tom Allworth. Tom!

All. We must be strangers,
Nor would I have you seen here for a million. *Exit*

Well. Better and better. He contemns me too!

Enter Waiting Woman *and* Chambermaid

Woman. Foh, what a smell's here! What thing's this?

Cham. A creature
Made out of the privy. Let us hence, for love's sake,
Or I shall swoon.

Woman. I begin to faint already.

Exeunt Waiting Woman *and* Chambermaid

Watch. Will you know your way?

Amb. Or shall we teach it you,
By the head and shoulders?

Well. No; I will not stir;
Do you mark, I will not. Let me see the wretch
That dares attempt to force me. Why, you slaves,
Created only to make legs, and cringe;
To carry in a dish, and shift a trencher;
That have not souls only to hope a blessing
Beyond black-jacks or flagons; you, that were born
Only to consume meat and drink, and batten
Upon reversions!—Who advances? Who
Shows me the way?

Ord. My lady!

Enter Lady Allworth, Waiting Woman, *and* Chambermaid

Cham. Here 's the monster.

Woman. Sweet madam, keep your glove to your nose.

Cham. Or let me
Fetch some perfumes may be predominant;
You wrong yourself else.

Well Madam, my designs

Bear me to you.
L. All. To me!
Well. And though I have met with
But ragged entertainment from your grooms here,
I hope from you to receive that noble usage
As may become the true friend of your husband,
And then I shall forget these.
L. All. I am amazed
To see and hear this rudeness. Darest thou think,
Though sworn, that it can ever find belief,
That I, who to the best men of this country
Denied my presence since my husband's death,
Can fall so low as to change words with thee,
Thou son of infamy! Forbear my house,
And know and keep the distance that's between us;
Or, though it be against my gentler temper,
I shall take order you no more shall be
An eyesore to me.
Well. Scorn me not, good lady,
But, as in form you are angelical,
Imitate the heavenly natures, and vouchsafe
At the least a while to hear me. You will grant
The blood that runs in this arm is as noble
As that which fills your veins. Those costly jewels,
And those rich clothes you wear, your men's observance,
And women's flattery, are in you no virtues,
Nor these rags, with my poverty, in me vices.
You have a fair fame, and, I know, deserve it;
Yet, lady, I must say, in nothing more
Than in the pious sorrow you have shown
For your late noble husband.
Ord. How she starts!
Furn. And hardly can keep finger from the eye,
To hear him named.
L. All. Have you aught else to say?
Well. That husband, madam, was once in his fortune

Almost as low as I; want, debts, and quarrels
Lay heavy on him. Let it not be thought
A boast in me, though I say, I relieved him.
'Twas I that gave him fashion; mine the sword,
That did on all occasions second his.
I brought him on and off with honor, lady;
And when in all men's judgments he was sunk,
And, in his own hopes, not to be buoyed up,
I stepped unto him, took him by the hand,
And set him upright.

Furn. Are not we base rogues,
That could forget this?

Well. I confess, you made him
Master of your estate; nor could your friends,
Though he brought no wealth with him, blame you for it;
For he had a shape, and to that shape a mind
Made up of all parts, either great or noble;
So winning a behavior, not to be
Resisted, madam.

L. All. 'Tis most true, he had.

Well. For his sake, then, in that I was his friend,
Do not contemn me.

L. All. For what's past excuse me,
I will redeem it. Order, give the gentleman
A hundred pounds.

Well. No, madam, on no terms.
I will nor beg nor borrow sixpence of you,
But be supplied elsewhere, or want thus ever.
Only one suit I make, which you deny not
To strangers; and 'tis this. *Whispers to her*

L. All. Fie! nothing else?

Well. Nothing, unless you please to charge your servants
To throw away a little respect upon me.

L. All. What you demand is yours.

Well. I thank you, lady.
Now what can be wrought out of such a suit

Is yet in supposition. I have said all;
When you please, you may retire. *Exit* Lady ALL.
Nay, all 's forgotten;
To the Servants
And, for a lucky omen to my project,
Shake hands, and end all quarrels in the cellar.
Ord. Agreed, agreed.
Furn. Still merry Master Wellborn. *Exeunt*

[ACT II, SCENE I]

[*A Room in Overreach's House*]

Enter OVERREACH *and* MARRALL

Over. He 's gone, I warrant thee; this commission crushed him.
Mar. Your worships have the way on 't, and ne'er miss
To squeeze these unthrifts into air; and yet,
The chapfallen justice did his part, returning
For your advantage the certificate,
Against his conscience, and his knowledge too,
With your good favor, to the utter ruin
Of the poor farmer.
Over. 'Twas for these good ends
I made him a justice. He that bribes his belly,
Is certain to command his soul.
Mar. I wonder,
Still with your license, why, your worship having
The power to put his thin-gut in commission,
You are not in 't yourself?
Over. Thou art a fool.
In being out of office I am out of danger;
Where, if I were a justice, besides the trouble,
I might or out of wilfulness or error
Run myself finely into a *prœmunire*,

And so become a prey to the informer.
No, I'll have none of 't; 'tis enough I keep
Greedy at my devotion. So he serve
My purposes, let him hang or damn, I care not.
Friendship is but a word.

Mar. You are all wisdom.

Over. I would be worldly wise. For the other wisdom,
That does prescribe us a well-governed life,
And to do right to others as ourselves,
I value not an atom.

Mar. What course take you,
With your good patience, to hedge in the manor
Of your neighbor, Master Frugal? As 'tis said
He will nor sell, nor borrow, nor exchange;
And his land, lying in the midst of your many lordships,
Is a foul blemish.

Over. I have thought on 't, Marrall,
And it shall take. I must have all men sellers,
And I the only purchaser.

Mar. 'Tis most fit, sir.

Over. I'll therefore buy some cottage near his manor,
Which done, I'll make my men break ope his fences,
Ride o'er his standing corn, and in the night
Set fire on his barns, or break his cattle's legs.
These trespasses draw on suits, and suits expenses,
Which I can spare, but will soon beggar him.
When I have harried him thus two or three year,
Though he sue *in forma pauperis,* in spite
Of all his thrift and care, he'll grow behind-hand.

Mar. The best I ever heard! I could adore you.

Over. Then, with the favor of my man of law,
I will pretend some title. Want will force him
To put it to arbitrament; then, if he sell
For half the value, he shall have ready money,
And I possess his land.

Mar. 'Tis above wonder!

Wellborn was apt to sell, and needed not
These fine arts, sir, to hook him in.

Over. Well thought on.
This varlet, Marrall, lives too long, to upbraid me
With my close cheat put upon him. Will nor cold
Nor hunger kill him?

Mar. I know not what to think on 't.
I have used all means; and the last night I caused
His host, the tapster, to turn him out of doors;
And have been since with all your friends and tenants,
And, on the forfeit of your favor, charged them,
Though a crust of mouldy bread would keep him from starving,
Yet they should not relieve him. This is done, sir.

Over. That was something, Marrall; but thou must go further,
And suddenly, Marrall.

Mar. Where, and when you please, sir.

Over. I would have thee seek him out, and, if thou canst,
Persuade him that 'tis better steal than beg.
Then, if I prove he has but robbed a henroost,
Not all the world shall save him from the gallows.
Do any thing to work him to despair,
And 'tis thy masterpiece.

Mar. I will do my best, sir.

Over. I am now on my main work with the Lord Lovell,
The gallant-minded, popular Lord Lovell,
The minion of the people's love. I hear
He's come into the country, and my aims are
To insinuate myself into his knowledge,
And then invite him to my house.

Mar. I have you;
This points at my young mistress.

Over. She must part with
That humble title, and write honorable,
Right honorable, Marrall, my right honorable daughter,

If all I have, or e'er shall get, will do it.
I'll have her well attended; there are ladies
Of errant knights decayed and brought so low,
That for cast clothes and meat will gladly serve her.
And 'tis my glory, though I come from the city,
To have their issue whom I have undone,
To kneel to mine as bondslaves.
Mar. 'Tis fit state, sir.
Over. And therefore, I'll not have a chambermaid
That ties her shoes, or any meaner office,
But such whose fathers were right worshipful.
'Tis a rich man's pride! there having ever been
More than a feud, a strange antipathy,
Between us and true gentry.

Enter WELLBORN

Mar. See, who 's here, sir.
Over. Hence, monster! prodigy!
Well. Sir, your wife's nephew.
She and my father tumbled in one belly.
Over. Avoid my sight! Thy breath's infectious, rogue!
I shun thee as a leprosy, or the plague.
Come hither, Marrall. [*Aside*] This is the time to work him. *Exit*
Mar. I warrant you, sir.
Well. By this light I think he 's mad.
Mar. Mad! Had you ta'en compassion on yourself,
You long since had been mad.
Well. You have ta'en a course,
Between you and my venerable uncle,
To make me so.
Mar. The more pale-spirited you,
That would not be instructed. I swear deeply—
Well. By what?
Mar. By my religion.
Well. Thy religion!

The devil's creed. But what would you have done?

Mar. Had there been but one tree in all the shire,
Nor any hope to compass a penny halter,
Before, like you, I had outlived my fortunes,
A withe had served my turn to hang myself.
I am zealous in your cause; pray you hang yourself,
And presently, as you love your credit.

Well. I thank you.

Mar. Will you stay till you die in a ditch, or lice devour you?
Or, if you dare not do the feat yourself,
But that you'll put the state to charge and trouble,
Is there no purse to be cut, house to be broken,
Or market-woman with eggs, that you may murder,
And so dispatch the business?

Well. Here's variety,
I must confess. But I'll accept of none
Of all your gentle offers, I assure you.

Mar. Why, have you hope ever to eat again,
Or drink, or be the master of three farthings?
If you like not hanging, drown yourself! Take some course
For your reputation.

Well. 'Twill not do, dear tempter,
With all the rhetoric the fiend hath taught you.
I am as far as thou art from despair.
Nay, I have confidence, which is more than hope,
To live, and suddenly, better than ever—

Mar. Ha! ha! These castles you build in the air
Will not persuade me or to give or lend
A token to you.

Well. I'll be more kind to thee.
Come, thou shalt dine with me.

Mar. With you!

Well. Nay more, dine gratis.

Mar. Under what hedge, I pray you? or at whose cost?
Are they padders or abram-men that are your consorts?

Well. Thou art incredulous; but thou shalt dine
Not alone at her house, but with a gallant lady;
With me, and with a lady.
Mar. Lady! what lady?
With the Lady of the Lake, or queen of fairies?
For I know it must be an enchanted dinner.
Well. With the Lady Allworth, knave.
Mar. Nay, now there's hope
Thy brain is cracked.
Well. Mark there, with what respect
I am entertained.
Mar. With choice, no doubt, of dogwhips
Why, dost thou ever hope to pass her porter?
Well. 'Tis not far off, go with me; trust thine own eyes.
Mar. Troth, in my hope, or my assurance rather,
To see thee curvet, and mount like a dog in a blanket,
If ever thou presume to pass her threshold,
I will endure thy company.
Well. Come along then. *Exeunt*

[SCENE II]

[*A Room in Lady Allworth's House*]

Enter Allworth, Waiting Woman, Chambermaid, Order, Amble, Furnace, *and* Watchall

Woman. Could you not command your leisure one hour longer?
Cham. Or half an hour?
All. I have told you what my haste is:
Besides, being now another's, not mine own,
Howe'er I much desire to enjoy you longer,
My duty suffers, if, to please myself,
I should neglect my lord.
Woman. Pray you do me the favor

To put these few quince-cakes into your pocket;
They are of mine own preserving

Cham. And this marmalade;
'Tis comfortable for your stomach.

Woman. And, at parting,
Excuse me if I beg a farewell from you.

Cham. You are still before me. I move the same suit, sir.

ALLWORTH *kisses them severally*

Furn. How greedy these chamberers are of a beardless chin!
I think the tits will ravish him.

All. My service
To both.

Woman. Ours waits on you.

Cham. And shall do ever.

Ord. You are my lady's charge; be therefore careful
That you sustain your parts.

Woman. We can bear, I warrant you.

Exeunt Waiting Woman *and* Chambermaid

Furn. Here, drink it off; the ingredients are cordial,
And this the true elixir. It hath boiled
Since midnight for you. 'Tis the quintessence
Of five cocks of the game, ten dozen of sparrows,
Knuckles of veal, potato-roots and marrow,
Coral and ambergris. Were you two years older,
And I had a wife, or gamesome mistress,
I durst trust you with neither. You need not bait
After this, I warrant you, though your journey's long;
You may ride on the strength of this till to-morrow morning.

All. Your courtesies overwhelm me. I much grieve
To part from such true friends, and yet find comfort.
My attendance on my honorable lord,
Whose resolution holds to visit my lady,
Will speedily bring me back. *Knocking at the gate*

Exit WATCHALL

Mar. [*within*] Dar'st thou venture further?

Well. [*within*] Yes, yes, and knock again.
Ord. 'Tis he; disperse!
Amb. Perform it bravely.
Furn. I know my cue, ne'er doubt me.
Exeunt all but ALLWORTH

[*Re-*]*enter* WATCHALL, *ceremoniously introducing* WELLBORN *and* MARRALL

Watch. Beast that I was, to make you stay! Most welcome.
You were long since expected.
Well. Say so much
To my friend, I pray you.
Watch. For your sake, I will, sir.
Mar. For his sake!
Well. Mum; this is nothing.
Mar. More than ever
I would have believed, though I had found it in my primer.
All. When I have given you reasons for my late harshness,
You'll pardon and excuse me; for, believe me,
Though now I part abruptly, in my service
I will deserve it.
Mar. Service! with a vengeance!
Well. I am satisfied. Farewell, Tom.
All. All joy stay with you!
Exit

Re-enter AMBLE

Amb. You are happily encountered; I yet never
Presented one so welcome as I know
You will be to my lady.
Mar. This is some vision,
Or, sure, these men are mad, to worship a dunghill;
It cannot be a truth.
Well. Be still a pagan,

An unbelieving infidel. Be so miscreant,
And meditate on 'blankets, and on dogwhips!'

Re-enter FURNACE

Furn. I am glad you are come; until I know your pleasure
I knew not how to serve up my lady's dinner.
Mar. His pleasure! Is it possible?
Well. What's thy will?
Furn. Marry, sir, I have some grouse, and turkey chicken,
Some rails and quails, and my lady willed me ask you,
What kind of sauces best affect your palate,
That I may use my utmost skill to please it.
Mar. [*Aside*] The devil's entered this cook. Sauce for his palate!
That, on my knowledge, for almost this twelvemonth,
Durst wish but cheese-parings and brown bread on Sundays.
Well. That way I like them best.
Furn. It shall be done, sir. *Exit*
Well. What think you of 'the hedge we shall dine under?'
Shall we feed gratis?
Mar. I know not what to think;
Pray you make me not mad.

Re-enter ORDER

Ord. This place becomes you not;
Pray you walk, sir, to the dining-room.
Well. I am well here,
Till her ladyship quits her chamber.
Mar. Well here, say you?
'Tis a rare change! But yesterday you thought
Yourself well in a barn, wrapped up in pease-straw.

Re-enter Waiting Woman *and* Chambermaid

Woman. O sir, you are wished for.
Cham. My lady dreamt, sir, of you.
Woman. And the first command she gave, after she rose,

Was—her devotions done—to give her notice
When you approached here.

Cham. Which is done, on my virtue.

Mar. I shall be converted. I begin to grow
Into a new belief, which saints nor angels
Could have won me to have faith in.

Woman. Sir, my lady!

Enter Lady ALLWORTH

L. All. I come to meet you, and languished till I saw you.
This first kiss is for form; I allow a second
To such a friend. *Kisses* WELLBORN

Mar. To such a friend! Heaven bless me!

Well. I am wholly yours. Yet, madam, if you please
To grace this gentleman with a salute—

Mar. Salute me at his bidding!

Well. I shall receive it
As a most high favor.

L. All. Sir, you may command me.
Advances to kiss MARRALL, *who retires*

Well. Run backward from a lady! and such a lady!

Mar. To kiss her foot is, to poor me, a favor
I am unworthy of. *Offers to kiss her foot*

L. All. Nay, pray you rise;
And since you are so humble, I'll exalt you.
You shall dine with me to-day, at mine own table.

Mar. Your ladyship's table! I am not good enough
To sit at your steward's board.

L. All. You are too modest.
I will not be denied.

Re-enter FURNACE

Furn. Will you still be babbling
Till your meat freeze on the table? The old trick still;
My art ne'er thought on!

L. All. Your arm, Master Wellborn,—
Nay, keep us company. *To* MARRALL

Mar. I was ne'er so graced.

Exeunt WELLBORN, Lady ALLWORTH, AMBLE, MARRALL, Waiting Woman, *and* Chambermaid

Ord. So! We have played our parts, and are come off well;
But if I know the mystery, why my lady
Consented to it, or why Master Wellborn
Desired it, may I perish!

Furn. Would I had
The roasting of his heart that cheated him,
And forces the poor gentleman to these shifts!
By fire!—for cooks are Persians, and swear by it—
Of all the griping and extorting tyrants
I ever heard or read of, I ne'er met
A match to Sir Giles Overreach.

Watch. What will you take
To tell him so, fellow Furnace?

Furn. Just as much
As my throat is worth, for that would be the price on 't.
To have a usurer that starves himself,
And wears a cloak of one and twenty years
On a suit of fourteen groats, bought of the hangman,
To grow rich, and then purchase, is too common.
But this Sir Giles feeds high, keeps many servants,
Who must at his command do any outrage;
Rich in his habit, vast in his expenses;
Yet he to admiration still increases
In wealth and lordships.

Ord. He frights men out of their estates,
And breaks through all law-nets, made to curb ill men,
As they were cobwebs. No man dares reprove him.
Such a spirit to dare and power to do were never
Lodged so unluckily.

Re-enter AMBLE, *laughing*

Amb. Ha! ha! I shall burst.

Ord. Contain thyself, man.

Furn. Or make us partakers
Of your sudden mirth.

Amb. Ha! ha! My lady has got
Such a guest at her table—this term-driver Marrall,
This snip of an attorney—

Furn. What of him, man?

Amb. The knave thinks still he's at the cook's shop in
Ram Alley,
Where the clerks divide, and the elder is to choose;
And feeds so slovenly!

Furn. Is this all?

Amb. My lady
Drank to him for fashion sake, or to please Master Wellborn;
As I live, he rises, and takes up a dish
In which there were some remnants of a boiled capon,
And pledges her in white broth!

Furn. Nay, 'tis like
The rest of his tribe.

Amb. And when I brought him wine,
He leaves his stool, and, after a leg or two,
Most humbly thanks my worship.

Ord. Risen already!

Amb. I shall be chid.

Re-enter Lady ALLWORTH, WELLBORN, *and* MARRALL

Furn. My lady frowns.

L. All. You wait well!
To AMBLE

Let me have no more of this; I observe you jeering.
Sirrah, I'll have you know, whom I think worthy
To sit at my table, be he ne'er so mean,
When I am present, is not your companion.

Ord. Nay, she'll preserve what's due to her.

Furn. This refreshing
Follows your flux of laughter.

L. All. [*to* WELLBORN] You are master
Of your own will. I know so much of manners,
As not to inquire your purposes. In a word,
To me you are ever welcome, as to a house
That is your own.

Well. [*Aside to* MARRALL] Mark that.

Mar. With reverence, sir,
An it like your worship.

Well. Trouble yourself no further,
Dear madam; my heart's full of zeal and service,
However in my language I am sparing.
Come, Master Marrall.

Mar. I attend your worship.

Exeunt WELLBORN *and* MARRALL

L. All. I see in your looks you are sorry, and you know me
An easy mistress. Be merry; I have forgot all.
Order and Furnace, come with me. I must give you
Further directions.

Ord. What you please.

Furn. We are ready. *Exeunt*

[SCENE III]

[*The Country near Lady Allworth's House*]

Enter WELLBORN, *and* MARRALL, *bare-headed*

Well. I think I am in a good way.

Mar. Good! sir, the best way,
The certain best way.

Well. There are casualties
That men are subject to.

Mar. You are above them;
And as you are already worshipful,

I hope ere long you will increase in worship,
And be right worshipful.

Well. Prithee do not flout me:
What I shall be, I shall be. Is 't for your ease,
You keep your hat off?

Mar. Ease! an it like your worship!
I hope Jack Marrall shall not live so long,
To prove himself such an unmannerly beast
Though it hail hazel-nuts, as to be covered
When your worship's present.

Well. [*Aside*] Is not this a true rogue,
That, out of mere hope of a future cozenage,
Can turn thus suddenly? 'Tis rank already.

Mar. I know your worship's wise, and needs no counsel,
Yet if, in my desire to do you service,
I humbly offer my advice—but still
Under correction—I hope I shall not
Incur your high displeasure.

Well. No; speak freely.

Mar. Then, in my judgment, sir, my simple judgment—
Still with your worship's favor—I could wish you
A better habit, for this cannot be
But much distasteful to the noble lady—
I say no more—that loves you; for, this morning,
To me, and I am but a swine to her,
Before the assurance of her wealth perfumed you,
You savored not of amber.

Well. I do now then!

Mar. This your batoon hath got a touch of it.

Kisses the end of his cudgel

Yet, if you please, for change, I have twenty pounds here,
Which, out of my true love, I'll presently
Lay down at your worship's feet; 'twill serve to buy you
A riding-suit.

Well. But where 's the horse?

Mar. My gelding

Is at your service. Nay, you shall ride me,
Before your worship shall be put to the trouble
To walk afoot. Alas! when you are lord
Of this lady's manor, as I know you will be,
You may with the lease of glebe land, called Knave's-acre,
A place I would manure, requite your vassal.

Well. I thank thy love, but must make no use of it.
What's twenty pounds?

Mar. 'Tis all that I can make, sir.

Well. Dost thou think, though I want clothes, I could not have them,
For one word to my lady?

Mar. As I know not that!

Well. Come, I will tell thee a secret, and so leave thee.
I will not give her the advantage, though she be
A gallant-minded lady, after we are married—
There being no woman but is sometimes forward—
To hit me in the teeth, and say, she was forced
To buy my wedding-clothes, and took me on
With a plain riding-suit, and an ambling nag.
No, I'll be furnished something like myself,
And so farewell. For thy suit touching Knave's-acre,
When it is mine, 'tis thine.

Mar. I thank your worship.

Exit WELLBORN

How was I cozened in the calculation
Of this man's fortune! My master cozened too,
Whose pupil I am in the art of undoing men;
For that is our profession! Well, well, Master Wellborn,
You are of a sweet nature, and fit again to be cheated;
Which, if the Fates please, when you are possessed
Of the land and lady, you, sans question, shall be.
I'll presently think of the means. *Walks by, musing*

Enter OVERREACH, *speaking to a* Servant *within*

Over. Sirrah, take my horse.

I'll walk to get me an appetite. 'Tis but a mile,
And exercise will keep me from being pursy.
Ha! Marrall! Is he conjuring? Perhaps
The knave has wrought the prodigal to do
Some outrage on himself, and now he feels
Compunction in his conscience for 't. No matter,
So it be done.—Marrall!

Mar. Sir.

Over. How succeed we
In our plot on Wellborn?

Mar. Never better, sir.

Over. Has he hanged or drowned himself?

Mar. No, sir, he lives;
Lives once more to be made a prey to you,
A greater prey than ever.

Over. Art thou in thy wits?
If thou art, reveal this miracle, and briefly.

Mar. A lady, sir, is fallen in love with him.

Over. With him. What lady?

Mar. The rich Lady Allworth.

Over. Thou dolt! How dar'st thou speak this?

Mar. I speak truth;
And I do so but once a year, unless
It be to you, sir. We dined with her ladyship,
I thank his worship.

Over. His worship!

Mar. As I live, sir,
I dined with him, at the great lady's table,
Simple as I stand here; and saw when she kissed him,
And would, at his request, have kissed me too.
But I was not so audacious as some youths are,
That dare do anything, be it ne'er so absurd,
And sad after performance.

Over. Why, thou rascal!
To tell me these impossibilities.
Dine at her table! and kiss him! or thee!

Impudent varlet, have not I myself,
To whom great countesses' doors have oft flew open,
Ten times attempted, since her husband's death,
In vain to see her, though I came, a suitor?
And yet your good solicitorship, and rogue Wellborn,
Were brought into her presence, feasted with her!
But that I know thee a dog that cannot blush,
This most incredible lie would call up one
On thy buttermilk cheeks.

Mar. Shall I not trust my eyes, sir,
Or taste? I feel her good cheer in my belly.

Over. You shall feel me, if you give not over, sirrah.
Recover your brains again, and be no more gulled
With a beggar's plot, assisted by the aids
Of serving-men and chambermaids, for beyond these
Thou never saw'st a woman, or I'll quit you
From my employments.

Mar. Will you credit this yet?
On my confidence of their marriage, I offered Wellborn—
[*Aside*] I would give a crown now I durst say his worship—
My nag, and twenty pounds.

Over. Did you so, idiot! *Strikes him down*
Was this the way to work him to despair,
Or rather to cross me?

Mar. Will your worship kill me?

Over. No, no; but drive the lying spirit out of you.

Mar. He's gone.

Over. I have done then. Now, forgetting
Your late imaginary feast and lady,
Know, my Lord Lovell dines with me tomorrow.
Be careful nought be wanting to receive him,
And bid my daughter's women trim her up,
Though they paint her, so she catch the lord, I'll thank them.
There's a piece for my late blows.

Mar. [*Aside*] I must yet suffer;
But there may be a time—

Over. Do you grumble?
Mar. No, sir.
Exeunt

[ACT III, SCENE I]

[*The Country near Overreach's House*]

Enter Lord LOVELL, ALLWORTH, *and* Servants

Lov. Walk the horses down the hill. Something in private
I must impart to Allworth. *Exeunt* Servants
All. O my lord,
What sacrifice of reverence, duty, watching,
Although I could put off the use of sleep,
And ever wait on your commands to serve 'em,
What dangers, though in ne'er so horrid shapes,
Nay death itself, though I should run to meet it,
Can I, and with a thankful willingness suffer!
But still the retribution will fall short
Of your bounties showered upon me.
Lov. Loving youth,
Till what I purpose be put into act,
Do not o'erprize it. Since you have trusted me
With your soul's nearest, nay, her dearest secret,
Rest confident 'tis in a cabinet locked
Treachery shall never open. I have found you—
For so much to your face I must profess,
Howe'er you guard your modesty with a blush for 't—
More zealous in your love and service to me
Than I have been in my rewards.
All. Still great ones,
Above my merit.
Lov. Such your gratitude calls 'em,
Nor am I of that harsh and rugged temper
As some great men are taxed with, who imagine
They part from the respect due to their honors

If they use not all such as follow 'em,
Without distinction of their births, like slaves.
I am not so conditioned. I can make
A fitting difference between my footboy
And a gentleman by want compelled to serve me.

All. 'Tis thankfully acknowledged; you have been
More like a father to me than a master.
Pray you, pardon the comparison.

Lov. I allow it.
And, to give you assurance I am pleased in 't,
My carriage and demeanor to your mistress,
Fair Margaret, shall truly witness for me
I can command my passions.

All. 'Tis a conquest
Few lords can boast of when they are tempted—O!

Lov. Why do you sigh? Can you be doubtful of me?
By that fair name I in the wars have purchased,
And all my actions, hitherto untainted,
I will not be more true to mine own honor,
Than to my Allworth!

All. As you are the brave Lord Lovell,
Your bare word only given is an assurance
Of more validity and weight to me
Than all the oaths, bound up with imprecations,
Which, when they would deceive, most courtiers practise;
Yet being a man—for, sure, to style you more
Would relish of gross flattery—I am forced,
Against my confidence of your worth and virtues,
To doubt, nay more, to fear.

Lov. So young, and jealous!

All. Were you to encounter with a single foe,
The victory were certain; but to stand
The charge of two such potent enemies,
At once assaulting you, as wealth and beauty,
And those too seconded with power, is odds
Too great for Hercules.

Lov. Speak your doubts and fears,
Since you will nourish them, in plainer language,
That I may understand them.
All. What 's your will,
Though I lend arms against myself—provided
They may advantage you—must be obeyed.
My much-loved lord, were Margaret only fair,
The cannon of her more than earthly form,
Though mounted high, commanding all beneath it,
And rammed with bullets of her sparkling eyes,
Of all the bulwarks that defend your senses
Could batter none, but that which guards your sight.
But when the well-tuned accents of her tongue
Make music to you, and with numerous sounds
Assault your hearing—such as Ulysses, if he
Now lived again, howe'er he stood the Sirens,
Could not resist—the combat must grow doubtful
Between your reason and rebellious passions.
Add this too; when you feel her touch, and breath
Like a soft western wind when it glides o'er
Arabia, creating gums and spices;
And, in the van, the nectar of her lips,
Which you must taste, bring the battalia on
Well armed, and strongly lined with her discourse,
And knowing manners, to give entertainment;—
Hippolytus himself would leave Diana,
To follow such a Venus.
Lov. Love hath made you
Poetical, Allworth.
All. Grant all these beat off,
Which if it be in man to do, you'll do it,
Mammon, in Sir Giles Overreach, steps in
With heaps of ill-got gold, and so much land,
To make her more remarkable, as would tire
A falcon's wings in one day to fly over.
O my good lord! These powerful aids which would

Make a mis-shapen negro beautiful—
Yet are but ornaments to give her luster,
That in herself is all perfection—must
Prevail for her. I here release your trust.
'Tis happiness enough for me to serve you
And sometimes, with chaste eyes, to look upon her.

Lov. Why, shall I swear?

All. O, by no means, my lord;
And wrong not so your judgment to the world
As from your fond indulgence to a boy,
Your page, your servant, to refuse a blessing
Divers great men are rivals for.

Lov. Suspend
Your judgment till the trial. How far is it
To Overreach's house?

All. At the most, some half hour's riding;
You'll soon be there.

Lov. And you the sooner freed
From your jealous fears.

All. O that I durst but hope it! *Exeunt*

[SCENE II]

[*A Room in Overreach's House*]

Enter OVERREACH, GREEDY *and* MARRALL

Over. Spare for no cost; let my dressers crack with the weight
Of curious viands.

Greedy. 'Store indeed's no sore,' sir.

Over. That proverb fits your stomach, Master Greedy.
And let no plate be seen but what's pure gold,
Or such whose workmanship exceeds the matter
That it is made of. Let my choicest linen
Perfume the room, and, when we wash, the water,

With precious powders mixed, so please my lord,
That he may with envy wish to bathe so ever.

Mar. 'Twill be very chargeable.

Over. Avaunt, you drudge!
Now all my labored ends are at the stake,
Is 't a time to think of thrift? Call in my daughter.

Exit MARRALL

And, Master Justice, since you love choice dishes,
And plenty of 'em—

Greedy. As I do, indeed, sir,
Almost as much as to give thanks for 'em.

Over. I do confer that providence, with my power
Of absolute command to have abundance,
To your best care.

Greedy. I'll punctually discharge it,
And give the best directions. Now am I,
In mine own conceit, a monarch; at the least,
Arch-president of the boiled, the roast, the baked;
For which I will eat often, and give thanks
When my belly's braced up like a drum: and that's pure justice. *Exit*

Over. It must be so. Should the foolish girl prove modest,
She may spoil all. She had it not from me,
But from her mother. I was ever forward,
As she must be, and therefore I'll prepare her.

Enter MARGARET

Alone,—and let your women without.

Marg. Your pleasure, sir?

Over. Ha! this is a neat dressing!
These orient pearls and diamonds well placed too!
The gown affects me not, it should have been
Embroidered o'er and o'er with flowers of gold;
But these rich jewels and quaint fashion help it.
And how below? since oft the wanton eye,
The face observed, descends unto the foot,

Which being well proportioned, as yours is,
Invites as much as perfect white and red,
Though without art. How like you your new woman,
The Lady Downfallen?

Marg. Well, for a companion;
Not as a servant.

Over. Is she humble, Meg?
And careful too, her ladyship forgotten?

Marg. I pity her fortune.

Over. Pity her! Trample on her.
I took her up in an old tamin gown—
Even starved for want of twopenny chops—to serve thee,
And if I understand she but repines
To do thee any duty, though ne'er so servile,
I'll pack her to her knight, where I have lodged him,
Into the counter, and there let them howl together.

Marg. You know your own ways; but for me, I blush
When I command her, that was once attended
With persons not inferior to myself
In birth.

Over. In birth! Why, art thou not my daughter,
The blest child of my industry and wealth?
Why, foolish girl, was 't not to make thee great
That I have run, and still pursue, those ways
That hail down curses on me, which I mind not?
Part with these humble thoughts, and apt thyself
To the noble state I labor to advance thee;
Or, by my hopes to see thee honorable,
I will adopt a stranger to my heir,
And throw thee from my care. Do not provoke me.

Marg. I will not, sir; mould me which way you please.

Re-enter Greedy

Over. How! interrupted!

Greedy. 'Tis matter of importance.
The cook, sir, is self-willed, and will not learn

From my experience. There's a fawn brought in, sir,
And, for my life, I cannot make him roast it
With a Norfolk dumpling in the belly of it;
And, sir, we wise men know, without the dumpling
'Tis not worth three-pence.

Over. Would it were whole in thy belly,
To stuff it out! Cook it any way. Prithee, leave me.

Greedy. Without order for the dumpling?

Over. Let it be dumpled
Which way thou wilt; or tell him, I will scald him
In his own cauldron.

Greedy. I had lost my stomach
Had I lost my mistress dumpling. I'll give thanks for 't.
Exit

Over. But to our business, Meg. You have heard who dines here?

Marg. I have, sir.

Over. 'Tis an honorable man;
A lord, Meg, and commands a regiment
Of soldiers, and, what's rare, is one himself,
A bold and understanding one. And to be
A lord, and a good leader, in one volume,
Is granted unto few but such as rise up
The kingdom's glory.

Re-enter Greedy

Greedy. I'll resign my office,
If I be not better obeyed.

Over. 'Slight, art thou frantic?

Greedy. Frantic! 'twould make me frantic, and stark mad,
Were I not a justice of peace and quorum too,
Which this rebellious cook cares not a straw for.
There are a dozen of woodcocks—

Over. Make thyself
Thirteen, the baker's dozen.

Greedy. I am contented,
So they may be dressed to my mind. He has found out
A new device for sauce, and will not dish them
With toasts and butter. My father was a tailor,
And my name, though a justice, Greedy Woodcock;
And, ere I'll see my lineage so abused,
I'll give up my commission.

Over. [*Loudly*] Cook!—Rogue, obey him!
I have given the word, pray you now remove yourself
To a collar of brawn, and trouble me no further.

Greedy. I will, and meditate what to eat at dinner. *Exit*

Over. And as I said, Meg, when this gull disturbed us,
This honorable lord, this colonel,
I would have thy husband.

Marg. There's too much disparity
Between his quality and mine, to hope it.

Over. I more than hope, and doubt not to effect it.
Be thou no enemy to thyself. My wealth
Shall weigh his titles down, and make you equals.
Now for the means to assure him thine, observe me;
Remember he's a courtier, and a soldier,
And not to be trifled with; and, therefore, when
He comes to woo you, see you do not coy it.
This mincing modesty has spoiled many a match
By a first refusal, in vain after hoped for.

Marg. You'll have me, sir, preserve the distance that
Confines a virgin?

Over. Virgin me no virgins!
I must have you lose that name, or you lose me.
I will have you private—start not—I say, private.
If thou art my true daughter, not a bastard,
Thou wilt venture alone with one man, though he came
Like Jupiter to Semele, and come off too;
And therefore, when he kisses you, kiss close.

Marg. I have heard this is the strumpet's fashion, sir,
Which I must never learn.

Over. Learn any thing
And from any creature that may make thee great;
From the devil himself.

Marg. [*Aside*] This is but devilish doctrine.

Over. Or, if his blood grow hot, suppose he offer
Beyond this, do not you stay till it cool,
But meet his ardor. If a couch be near,
Sit down on 't, and invite him.

Marg. In your house,
Your own house, sir; for heaven's sake, what are you then?
Or what shall I be, sir?

Over. Stand not on form;
Words are no substances.

Marg. Though you could dispense
With your own honor, cast aside religion,
The hopes of heaven, or fear of hell, excuse me,
In worldly policy, this is not the way
To make me his wife; his whore, I grant it may do.
My maiden honor so soon yielded up,
Nay, prostituted, cannot but assure him
I, that am light to him, will not hold weight
When tempted by others; so, in judgment,
When to his lust I have given up my honor,
He must and will forsake me.

Over. How! Forsake thee!
Do I wear a sword for fashion? or is this arm
Shrunk up or withered? Does there live a man
Of that large list I have encountered with
Can truly say I e'er gave inch of ground
Not purchased with his blood that did oppose me?
Forsake thee when the thing is done! He dares not.
Give me but proof he has enjoyed thy person,
Though all his captains, echoes to his will,
Stood armed by his side to justify the wrong,
And he himself in the head of his bold troop,
Spite of his lordship, and his colonelship,

Or the judge's favor, I will make him render
A bloody and a strict account, and force him,
By marrying thee, to cure thy wounded honor!
I have said it.

Re-enter MARRALL

Mar. Sir, the man of honor's come,
Newly alighted.
Over. In, without reply;
And do as I command, or thou art lost.
Exit MARGARET
Is the loud music I gave order for
Ready to receive him?
Mar. 'Tis, sir.
Over. Let them sound
A princely welcome. [*Exit* MARRALL] Roughness awhile leave me;
For fawning now, a stranger to my nature,
Must make way for me.

Loud music. Enter Lord LOVELL, GREEDY, ALLWORTH, *and* MARRALL

Lov. Sir, you meet your trouble.
Over. What you are pleased to style so is an honor
Above my worth and fortunes.
All. [*Aside*] Strange, so humble.
Over. A justice of peace, my lord.
Presents GREEDY *to him*
Lov. Your hand, good sir.
Greedy. [*Aside*] This is a lord, and some think this a favor;
But I had rather have my hand in my dumpling.
Over. Room for my lord.
Lov. I miss, sir, your fair daughter
To crown my welcome.

Over. May it please my lord
To taste a glass of Greek wine first, and suddenly
She shall attend my lord.

Lov. You'll be obeyed, sir.

Exeunt all but OVERREACH

Over. 'Tis to my wish. As soon as come, ask for her!
Why, Meg! Meg Overreach.—

Re-enter MARGARET

How! tears in your eyes!
Hah! dry them quickly or I'll dig 'em out.
Is this a time to whimper? Meet that greatness
That flies into thy bosom, think what 'tis
For me to say, 'My honorable daughter;'
And thou, when I stand bare, to say, 'Put on,'
Or, 'Father, you forget yourself.' No more;
But be instructed, or expect—he comes.

Re-enter Lord LOVELL, GREEDY, ALLWORTH, *and* MARRALL

A black-browed girl, my lord.

Lov. As I live, a rare one.

They salute

All. [*Aside*] He 's ta'en already. I am lost.

Over. That kiss
Came twanging off, I like it. Quit the room.

Exeunt all but OVERREACH, LOVELL, *and* MARGARET

A little bashful, my good lord, but you,
I hope, will teach her boldness.

Lov. I am happy
In such a scholar; but—

Over. I am past learning,
And therefore leave you to yourselves.—Remember.

Aside to MARGARET, *and exit*

Lov. You see, fair lady, your father is solicitous,

To have you change the barren name of virgin
Into a hopeful wife.

Marg. His haste, my lord,
Holds no power o'er my will.

Lov. But o'er your duty.

Marg. Which forced too much, may break.

Lov. Bend rather, sweetest.
Think of your years.

Marg. Too few to match with yours;
And choicest fruits too soon plucked, rot and wither.

Lov. Do you think I am old?

Marg. I am sure I am too young.

Lov. I can advance you.

Marg. To a hill of sorrow,
Where every hour I may expect to fall,
But never hope firm footing. You are noble,
I of a low descent, however rich;
And tissues matched with scarlet suit but ill.
O, my good lord, I could say more, but that
I dare not trust these walls.

Lov. Pray you, trust my ear then.

Re-enter OVERREACH, *behind, listening*

Over. Close at it! Whispering! This is excellent!
And, by their postures, a consent on both parts.

Re-enter GREEDY *behind*

Greedy. Sir Giles, Sir Giles!

Over. The great fiend stop that clapper!

Greedy. It must ring out, sir, when my belly rings noon.
The baked-meats are run out, the roast turned powder.

Over. I shall powder you.

Greedy. Beat me to dust, I care not.
In such a cause as this, I'll die a martyr.

Over. Marry, and shall, you barathrum of the shambles!
Strikes him

Greedy. How! strike a justice of peace! 'Tis petty treason,
Edwardi quinto. But that you are my friend,
I would commit you without bail or mainprize.

Over. Leave your bawling, sir, or I shall commit you
Where you shall not dine to-day. Disturb my lord,
When he is in discourse!

Greedy. Is't a time to talk
When we should be munching?

Lov. Hah! I heard some noise.

Over. Mum, villain; vanish! Shall we break a bargain
Almost made up? *Thrusts* GREEDY *off*

Lov. Lady, I understand you,
And rest most happy in your choice, believe it.
I'll be a careful pilot to direct
Your yet uncertain bark to a port of safety.

Marg. So shall your honor save two lives, and bind us
Your slaves for ever.

Lov. I am in the act rewarded,
Since it is good. Howe'er, you must put on
An amorous carriage towards me to delude
Your subtle father.

Marg. I am prone to that.

Lov. Now break we off our conference.— Sir Giles!
Where is Sir Giles? OVERREACH *comes forward*

Re-enter ALLWORTH, MARRALL, *and* GREEDY

Over. My noble lord; and how
Does your lordship find her?

Lov. Apt, Sir Giles, and coming;
And I like her the better.

Over. So do I too.

Lov. Yet should we take forts at the first assault,
'Twere poor in the defendant. I must confirm her
With a love-letter or two, which I must have
Delivered by my page, and you give way to't.

Over. With all my soul—a towardly gentleman!
Your hand, good Master Allworth. Know my house
Is ever open to you.

All. [*Aside*] 'Twas shut till now.

Over. Well done, well done, my honorable daughter!
Thou'rt so already. Know this gentle youth,
And cherish him, my honorable daughter.

Marg. I shall, with my best care.

Noise within, as of a coach

Over. A coach!

Greedy. More stops
Before we go to dinner! O my guts!

Enter Lady ALLWORTH *and* WELLBORN

L. All. If I find a welcome,
You share in it; if not, I'll back again,
Now I know your ends; for I come armed for all
Can be objected.

Lov. How! the Lady Allworth!

Over. And thus attended!

LOVELL *salutes* Lady ALLWORTH;
Lady ALLWORTH *salutes* MARGARET

Mar. No, 'I am a dolt!
The spirit of lies hath entered me!'

Over. Peace, patch,
'Tis more than wonder! an astonishment
That does possess me wholly!

Lov. Noble lady,
This is a favor, to prevent my visit,
The service of my life can never equal.

L. All. My lord, I laid wait for you, and much hoped
You would have made my poor house your first inn;
And therefore doubting that you might forget me,
Or too long dwell here, having such ample cause,
In this unequalled beauty, for your stay,
And fearing to trust any but myself

With the relation of my service to you,
I borrowed so much from my long restraint
And took the air in person to invite you.

Lov. Your bounties are so great, they rob me, madam,
Of words to give you thanks.

L. All. Good Sir Giles Overreach.—
Salutes him
How dost thou, Marrall? Liked you my meat so ill,
You'll dine no more with me?

Greedy. I will, when you please,
An it like your ladyship.

L. All. When you please, Master Greedy.
If meat can do it, you shall be satisfied.
And now, my lord, pray take into your knowledge
This gentleman; howe'er his outside's coarse,
Presents WELLBORN
His inward linings are as fine and fair
As any man's. Wonder not I speak at large;
And howsoe'er his humor carries him
To be thus accoutred, or what taint soever,
For his wild life, hath stuck upon his fame,
He may, ere long, with boldness, rank himself
With some that have contemned him. Sir Giles Overreach,
If I am welcome, bid him so.

Over. My nephew!
He has been too long a stranger. Faith you have,
Pray let it be mended.
LOVELL *confers aside with* WELLBORN

Mar. Why, sir, what do you mean?
This is 'rogue Wellborn, monster, prodigy,
That should hang or drown himself;' no man of worship,
Much less your nephew.

Over. Well, sirrah, we shall reckon
For this hereafter.

Mar. I'll not lose my jeer,
Though I be beaten dead for't.

Well. Let my silence plead
In my excuse, my lord, till better leisure
Offer itself to hear a full relation
Of my poor fortunes.

Lov. I would hear, and help 'em.

Over. Your dinner waits you.

Lov. Pray you lead, we follow.

L. All. Nay, you are my guest. Come, dear Master Wellborn.

Exeunt all but GREEDY

Greedy. 'Dear Master Wellborn!' So she said. Heaven! heaven!
If my belly would give me leave, I could ruminate
All day on this. I have granted twenty warrants
To have him committed, from all prisons in the shire,
To Nottingham jail; and now, 'Dear Master Wellborn!'
And 'My good nephew!' But I play the fool
To stand her prating, and forget my dinner.—

Re-enter MARRALL

Are they set, Marrall?

Mar. Long since. Pray you a word, sir.

Greedy. No wording now.

Mar. In troth, I must. My master,
Knowing you are his good friend, makes bold with you,
And does entreat you, more guests being come in
Than he expected, especially his nephew,
The table being full too, you would excuse him,
And sup with him on the cold meat.

Greedy. How! No dinner,
After all my care?

Mar. 'Tis but a penance for
A meal; besides, you broke your fast.

Greedy. That was
But a bit to stay my stomach. A man in commission
Give place to a tatterdemalion!

Mar. No bug words, sir.

Should his worship hear you—
Greedy. Lose my dumpling too,
And buttered toasts, and woodcocks!
Mar. Come, have patience.
If you will dispense a little with your worship,
And sit with the waiting women, you'll have dumpling,
Woodcock, and buttered toasts too.
Greedy. This revives me.
I will gorge there sufficiently.
Mar. This is the way, sir. [*Exeunt*

[SCENE III]

[*Another Room in Overreach's House*]

Enter OVERREACH, *as from dinner*

Over. She's caught! O woman! She neglects my lord,
And all her compliments applied to Wellborn!
The garments of her widowhood laid by,
She now appears as glorious as the spring,
Her eyes fixed on him, in the wine she drinks,
He being her pledge, she sends him burning kisses,
And sits on thorns, till she be private with him.
She leaves my meat to feed upon his looks,
And if in our discourse he be but named,
From her a deep sigh follows. And why grieve I
At this? It makes for me. If she prove his,
All that is hers is mine, as I will work him.

Enter MARRALL

Mar. Sir, the whole board is troubled at your rising.
Over. No matter, I'll excuse it. Prithee, Marrall,
Watch an occasion to invite my nephew
To speak with me in private.
Mar. Who? 'The rogue

The lady scorned to look on?'

Over. You are a wag.

Enter Lady ALLWORTH *and* WELLBORN

Mar. See, sir, she's come, and cannot be without him.

L. All. With your favor, sir, after a plenteous dinner,
I shall make bold to walk a turn or two,
In your rare garden.

Over. There's an arbor too,
If your ladyship please to use it.

L. All. Come, Master Wellborn.

Exeunt Lady ALLWORTH *and* WELLBORN

Over. Grosser and grosser! Now I believe the poet
Feigned not, but was historical, when he wrote
Pasiphaë was enamored of a bull.
This lady's lust's more monstrous.—My good lord,

Enter Lord LOVELL, MARGARET, *and the rest*

Excuse my manners.

Lov. There needs none, Sir Giles,
I may ere long say father, when it pleases
My dearest mistress to give warrant to it.

Over. She shall seal to it, my lord, and make me happy.

Re-enter WELLBORN *and* Lady ALLWORTH

Marg. My lady is returned.

L. All. Provide my coach,
I'll instantly away. My thanks, Sir Giles,
For my entertainment.

Over. 'Tis your nobleness
To think it such.

L. All. I must do you a further wrong
In taking away your honorable guest.

Lov. I wait on you, madam. Farewell, good Sir Giles.

L. All. Good Mistress Margaret! Nay, come, Master Wellborn,

I must not leave you behind; in sooth, I must not.

Over. Rob me not, madam, of all joys at once,
Let my nephew stay behind. He shall have my coach,
And, after some small conference between us,
Soon overtake your ladyship.

L. All. Stay not long, sir.

Lov. This parting kiss. [*Kisses* MARGARET] You shall every day hear from me,
By my faithful page.

All. 'Tis a service I am proud of.

Exeunt Lord LOVELL, Lady ALLWORTH, ALLWORTH, *and* MARRALL

Over. Daughter, to your chamber.—[*Exit* MARGARET] You may wonder, nephew,
After so long an emnity between us,
I should desire your friendship.

Well. So I do, sir.
'Tis strange to me.

Over. But I'll make it no wonder;
And what is more, unfold my nature to you.
We worldly men, when we see friends and kinsmen
Past hope sunk in their fortunes, lend no hand
To lift them up, but rather set our feet
Upon their heads, to press them to the bottom.
As, I must yield, with you I practised it.
But, now I see in you a way to rise,
I can and will assist you. This rich lady—
And I am glad of't—is enamored of you.
'Tis too apparent, nephew.

Well. No such thing.
Compassion rather, sir.

Over. Well, in a word,
Because your stay is short, I'll have you seen
No more in this base shape; nor shall she say,
She married you like a beggar, or in debt.

Well. [*Aside*] He'll run into the noose, and save my labor.

Over. You have a trunk of rich clothes, not far hence,
In pawn. I will redeem 'em; and that no clamor
May taint your credit for your petty debts,
You shall have a thousand pounds to cut 'em off,
And go a free man to the wealthy lady.

Well. This done, sir, out of love, and no ends else—

Over. As it is, nephew—

Well. Binds me still your servant.

Over. No compliments, you are stayed for. Ere you have supped
You shall hear from me. My coach, knaves, for my nephew.
To-morrow I will visit you.

Well. Here's an uncle
In a man's extremes! How much they do belie you,
That say you are hard-hearted!

Over. My deeds, nephew,
Shall speak my love. What men report I weigh not.

Exeunt

[ACT IV, SCENE I]

[*A Room in Lady Allworth's House*]

Enter Lord LOVELL *and* ALLWORTH

Lov. 'Tis well; give me my cloak. I now discharge you
From further service. Mind your own affairs,
I hope they will prove successful.

All. What is blest
With your good wish, my lord, cannot but prosper.
Let aftertimes report, and to your honor,
How much I stand engaged, for I want language
To speak my debt. Yet if a tear or two
Of joy, for your much goodness, can supply
My tongue's defects, I could—

Lov. Nay, do not melt.
This ceremonial thanks to me's superfluous.
Over. [*Within*] Is my lord stirring?
Lov. 'Tis he! O, here's your letter. Let him in.

Enter OVERREACH, GREEDY, *and* MARRALL

Over. A good day to my lord!
Lov. You are an early riser,
Sir Giles.
Over. And reason, to attend your lordship.
Lov. And you, too, Master Greedy, up so soon!
Greedy. In troth, my lord, after the sun is up,
I cannot sleep, for I have a foolish stomach
That croaks for breakfast. With your lordship's favor,
I have a serious question to demand
Of my worthy friend Sir Giles.
Lov. Pray you use your pleasure.
Greedy. How far, Sir Giles, and pray you answer me
Upon your credit, hold you it to be
From your manor-house, to this of my Lady's Allworth's?
Over. Why, some four mile.
Greedy. How! four mile, good Sir Giles—
Upon your reputation, think better.
For if you do abate but one half-quarter
Of five, you do yourself the greatest wrong
That can be in the world; for four miles' riding
Could not have raised so huge an appetite
As I feel gnawing on me.
Mar. Whether you ride,
Or go afoot, you are that way still provided,
An it please your worship.
Over. How now, sirrah? Prating
Before my lord! No difference! Go to my nephew,
See all his debts discharged, and help his worship
To fit on his rich suit.
Mar. [*Aside*] I may fit you too.

Tossed like a dog still! *Exit*

Lov. I have writ this morning
A few lines to my mistress, your fair daughter.

Over. 'Twill fire her, for she's wholly yours already.
Sweet Master Allworth, take my ring. 'Twill carry you
To her presence, I dare warrant you; and there plead
For my good lord, if you shall find occasion.
That done, pray ride to Nottingham, get a license,
Still by this token. I'll have it dispatched,
And suddenly, my lord, that I may say,
My honorable, nay, right honorable daughter.

Greedy. Take my advice, young gentleman, get your breakfast.
'Tis unwholesome to ride fasting. I'll eat with you,
And eat to purpose.

Over. Some Fury's in that gut.
Hungry again! Did you not devour, this morning,
A shield of brawn, and a barrel of Colchester oysters?

Greedy. Why, that was, sir, only to scour my stomach,
A kind of a preparative. Come, gentleman,
I will not have you feed like the hangman of Flushing,
Alone, while I am here.

Lov. Haste your return.

All. I will not fail, my lord.

Greedy. Nor I, to line
My Christmas coffer.

Exeunt GREEDY *and* ALLWORTH

Over. To my wish. We are private.
I come not to make offer with my daughter
A certain portion, that were poor and trivial;
In one word, I pronounce all that is mine,
In lands or leases, ready coin or goods,
With her, my lord, comes to you; nor shall you have
One motive to induce you to believe
I live too long, since every year I'll add
Something unto the heap, which shall be yours too.

Lov. You are a right kind father.
Over. You shall have reason
To think me such. How do you like this seat?
It is well wooded, and well watered, the acres
Fertile and rich. Would it not serve for change
To entertain your friends in a summer progress?
What thinks my noble lord?
Lov. 'Tis a wholesome air
And well-built pile; and she that's mistress of it,
Worthy the large revénue.
Over. She the mistress!
It may be so for a time. But let my lord
Say only that he likes it, and would have it,
I say, ere long 'tis his.
Lov. Impossible.
Over. You do conclude too fast, not knowing me,
Nor the engines that I work by. 'Tis not alone
The Lady Allworth's lands, for those once Wellborn's—
As by her dotage on him I know they will be—
Shall soon be mine; but point out any man's
In all the shire, and say they lie convenient,
And useful for your lordship, and once more
I say aloud, they are yours.
Lov. I dare not own
What's by unjust and cruel means extorted.
My fame and credit are more dear to me,
Than so to expose 'em to be censured by
The public voice.
Over. You run, my lord, no hazard.
Your reputation shall stand as fair,
In all good men's opinions, as now;
Nor can my actions, though condemned for ill,
Cast any foul aspersion upon yours.
For, though I do contemn report myself
As a mere sound, I still will be so tender
Of what concerns you, in all points of honor,

That the immaculate whiteness of your fame,
Nor your unquestioned integrity,
Shall e'er be sullied with one taint or spot
That may take from your innocence and candor.
All my ambition is to have my daughter
Right honorable, which my lord can make her.
And might I live to dance upon my knee
A young Lord Lovell, born by her unto you,
I write *nil ultra* to my proudest hopes.
As for possessions and annual rents,
Equivalent to maintain you in the port
Your noble birth and present state requires,
I do remove that burthen from your shoulders,
And take it on mine own. For, though I ruin
The country to supply your riotous waste,
The scourge of prodigals, want, shall never find you.
Lov. Are you not frighted with the imprecations
And curses of whole families, made wretched
By your sinister practices?
Over. Yes, as rocks are,
When foamy billows split themselves against
Their flinty ribs; or as the moon is moved
When wolves, with hunger pined, howl at her brightness.
I am of a solid temper, and, like these,
Steer on a constant course. With mine own sword,
If called into the field, I can make that right,
Which fearful enemies murmured at as wrong.
Now, for these other piddling complaints
Breathed out in bitterness; as when they call me
Extortioner, tyrant, cormorant, or intruder
On my poor neighbor's right, or grand incloser
Of what was common, to my private use;
Nay, when my ears are pierced with widows' cries,
And undone orphans wash with tears my threshold,
I only think what 'tis to have my daughter
Right honorable; and 'tis a powerful charm

Makes me insensible of remorse, or pity,
Or the least sting of conscience.

Lov. I admire
The toughness of your nature.

Over. 'Tis for you,
My lord, and for my daughter, I am marble.
Nay more, if you will have my character
In little, I enjoy more true delight
In my arrival to my wealth these dark
And crooked ways than you shall e'er take pleasure
In spending what my industry hath compassed.
My haste commands me hence. In one word, therefore,
Is it a match?

Lov. I hope, that is past doubt now.

Over. Then rest secure. Not the hate of all mankind here,
Nor fear of what can fall on me hereafter,
Shall make me study aught but your advancement
One story higher,—an earl, if gold can do it.
Dispute not my religion, nor my faith.
Though I am borne thus headlong by my will,
You may make choice of what belief you please,
To me they are equal; so, my lord, good morrow. *Exit*

Lov. He's gone. I wonder how the earth can bear
Such a portent! I, that have lived a soldier,
And stood the enemy's violent charge undaunted,
To hear this blasphemous beast am bathed all over
In a cold sweat. Yet, like a mountain, he—
Confirmed in atheistical assertions—
Is no more shaken than Olympus is
When angry Boreas loads his double head
With sudden drifts of snow.

Enter Lady ALLWORTH, Waiting Woman, *and* AMBLE

L. All. Save you, my lord!
Disturb I not your privacy?

Lov. No, good madam.

For your own sake I am glad you came no sooner,
Since this bold bad man, Sir Giles Overreach,
Made such a plain discovery of himself,
And read this morning such a devilish matins,
That I should think it a sin next to his
But to repeat it.

L. All. I ne'er pressed, my lord,
On others' privacies; yet, against my will,
Walking, for health's sake, in the gallery
Adjoining to your lodgings, I was made—
So vehement and loud he was—partaker
Of his tempting offers.

Lov. Please you to command
Your servants hence, and I shall gladly hear
Your wiser counsel.

L. All. 'Tis, my lord, a woman's,
But true and hearty.—Wait in the next room,
But be within call; yet not so near to force me
To whisper my intents.

Amb. We are taught better
By you, good madam.

Woman. And well know our distance.

L. All. Do so, and talk not. 'Twill become your breeding. *Exeunt* AMBLE *and* Woman
Now, my good lord. If I may use my freedom,
As to an honored friend—

Lov. You lessen else
Your favor to me.

L. All. I dare then say thus:
As you are noble—howe'er common men
Make sordid wealth the object and sole end
Of their industrious aims—'twill not agree
With those of eminent blood, who are engaged
More to prefer their honors than to increase
The state left to 'em by their ancestors,
To study large additions to their fortunes,

And quite neglect their births; though I must grant,
Riches, well got, to be a useful servant,
But a bad master.

Lov. Madam, 'tis confessed;
But what infer you from it?

L. All. This, my lord,
That as all wrongs, though thrust into one scale,
Slide of themselves off when right fills the other,
And cannot bide the trial; so all wealth,
I mean if ill-acquired, cemented to honor
By virtuous ways achieved, and bravely purchased,
Is but as rubbish poured into a river—
Howe'er intended to make good the bank—
Rendering the water, that was pure before,
Polluted and unwholesome. I allow
The heir of Sir Giles Overreach, Margaret,
A maid well qualified and the richest match
Our north part can make boast of. Yet she cannot,
With all that she brings with her, fill their mouths,
That never will forget who was her father;
Or that my husband Allworth's lands, and Wellborn's—
How wrung from both needs now no repetition—
Were real motives that more worked your lordship
To join your families, than her form and virtues.
You may conceive the rest.

Lov. I do, sweet madam,
And long since have considered it. I know,
The sum of all that makes a just man happy
Consists in the well choosing of his wife;
And there, well to discharge it, does require
Equality of years, of birth, of fortune;
For beauty being poor, and not cried up
By birth or wealth, can truly mix with neither;
And wealth, where there's such difference in years,
And fair descent, must make the yoke uneasy.
But I come nearer.

L. All. Pray you do, my lord.

Lov. Were Overreach's states thrice centupled, his daughter
Millions of degrees much fairer than she is,
Howe'er I might urge precedents to excuse me,
I would not so adulterate my blood
By marrying Margaret, and so leave my issue
Made up of several pieces, one part scarlet,
And the other London blue. In my own tomb
I will inter my name first.

L. All. [*Aside*] I am glad to hear this.
Why then, my lord, pretend your marriage to her?
Dissimulation but ties false knots
On that straight line by which you, hitherto,
Have measured all your actions.

Lov. I make answer,
And aptly, with a question. Wherefore have you,
That, since your husband's death, have lived a strict
And chaste nun's life, on the sudden given yourself
To visits and entertainments? Think you, madam,
'Tis not grown public conference, or the favors
Which you too prodigally have thrown on Wellborn,
Being too reserved before, incur not censure?

L. All. I am innocent here; and, on my life, I swear
My ends are good.

Lov. On my soul, so are mine
To Margaret; but leave both to the event.
And since this friendly privacy does serve
But as an offered means unto ourselves,
To search each other farther, you having shown
Your care of me, I my respect to you,
Deny me not, but still in chaste words, madam,
An afternoon's discourse.

L. All. So I shall hear you.

Exeunt

[SCENE II]

[*Before Tapwell's House*]

Enter TAPWELL *and* FROTH

Tap. Undone, undone! This was your counsel, Froth.
Froth. Mine! I defy thee. Did not Master Marrall—
He has marred all, I am sure—strictly command us,
On pain of Sir Giles Overreach's displeasure,
To turn the gentleman out of doors?
Tap. 'Tis true.
But now he's his uncle's darling, and has got
Master Justice Greedy, since he filled his belly,
At his commandment, to do anything.
Woe, woe to us!
Froth. He may prove merciful.
Tap. Troth, we do not deserve it at his hands.
Though he knew all the passages of our house,
As the receiving of stolen goods, and bawdry,
When he was rogue Wellborn no man would believe him,
And then his information could not hurt us.
But now he is right worshipful again,
Who dares but doubt his testimony? Methinks,
I see thee, Froth, already in a cart,
For a close bawd, thine eyes even pelted out
With dirt and rotten eggs; and my hand hissing,
If I scape the halter, with the letter R
Printed upon it.
Froth. Would that were the worst!
That were but nine days' wonder. As for credit,
We have none to lose, but we shall lose the money
He owes us, and his custom; there's the hell on't.
Tap. He has summoned all his creditors by the drum
And they swarm about him like so many soldiers
On the pay day; and has found out such A NEW WAY
To PAY HIS OLD DEBTS, as 'tis very likely

He shall be chronicled for it!

Froth. He deserves it

More than ten pageants. But are you sure his worship

Comes this way, to my lady's?

[*A cry within*] Brave master Wellborn!

Tap. Yes; I hear him.

Froth. Be ready with your petition, and present it

To his good grace.

Enter WELLBORN *in a rich habit,* MARRALL, GREEDY, ORDER, FURNACE, *and* Creditors; TAPWELL *kneeling, delivers his bill of debt*

Well. How's this! petitioned too?

But note what miracles the payment of

A little trash, and a rich suit of clothes,

Can work upon these rascals! I shall be,

I think, Prince Wellborn.

Mar. When your worship's married,

You may be—I know what I hope to see you.

Well. Then look thou for advancement.

Mar. To be known

Your worship's baliff, is the mark I shoot at.

Well. And thou shalt hit it.

Mar. Pray you, sir, dispatch

These needy followers, and for my admittance,

Provided you'll defend me from Sir Giles,

Whose service I am weary of, I'll say something

You shall give thanks for.

Well. Fear me not Sir Giles.

This interim, TAPWELL *and* FROTH *flattering and bribing* JUSTICE GREEDY

Greedy. Who, Tapwell? I remember thy wife brought me,

Last new-year's tide, a couple of fat turkeys.

Tap. And shall do every Christmas, let your worship

But stand my friend now.

Greedy. How! With Master Wellborn?
I can do anything with him on such terms.
See you this honest couple; they are good souls
As ever drew out faucet. Have they not
A pair of honest faces?
Well. I o'erheard you,
And the bribe he promised. You are cozened in them;
For, of all the scum that grew rich by my riots,
This, for a most unthankful knave, and this,
For a base bawd and whore, have worst deserved me,
And therefore speak not for 'em. By your place
You are rather to do me justice; lend me your ear.
Forget his turkeys, and call in his licence
And, at the next fair, I'll give you a yoke of oxen
Worth all his poultry.
Greedy. I am changed on the sudden
In my opinion! Come near; nearer, rascal.
And, now I view him better, did you e'er see
One look so like an arch-knave? His very countenance,
Should an understanding judge but look upon him,
Would hang him, though he were innocent.
Tap., Froth. Worshipful sir.
Greedy. No, though the great Turk came, instead of turkeys,
To beg my favor, I am inexorable.
Thou hast an ill name. Besides thy musty ale,
That hath destroyed many of the king's liege people,
Thou never hadst in thy house, to stay men's stomachs,
A piece of Suffolk cheese or gammon of bacon,
Or any esculent, as the learned call it,
For their emolument, but sheer drink only.
For which gross fault I here do damn thy licence,
Forbidding thee ever to tap or draw;
For, instantly, I will, in mine own person,
Command the constable to pull down thy sign,
And do it before I eat.

Froth. No mercy?

Greedy. Vanish!

If I show any, may my promised oxen gore me!

Tap. Unthankful knaves are ever so rewarded.

Exeunt GREEDY, TAPWELL, *and* FROTH

Well. Speak; what are you?

1 *Cred.* A decayed vintner, sir,
That might have thrived, but that your worship broke me
With trusting you with muscadine and eggs,
And five-pound suppers, with your after drinkings,
When you lodged upon the Bankside.

Well. I remember.

1 *Cred.* I have not been hasty, nor e'er laid to arrest you;
And therefore, sir—

Well. Thou art an honest fellow,
I'll set thee up again. See his bill paid.—
What are you?

2 *Cred.* A tailor once, but now mere botcher.
I gave you credit for a suit of clothes,
Which was all my stock, but you failing in payment,
I was removed from the shopboard, and confined
Under a stall.

Well. See him paid; and botch no more.

2 *Cred.* I ask no interest, sir.

Well. Such tailors need not.
If their bills are paid in one and twenty year,
They are seldom losers.—O, I know thy face,

To 3 Creditor

Thou wert my surgeon. You must tell no tales;
Those days are done. I will pay you in private.

Ord. A royal gentleman!

Furn. Royal as an emperor!
He'll prove a brave master. My good lady knew
To choose a man.

Well. See all men else discharged;
And since old debts are cleared by a new way,

A little bounty will not misbecome me.
There's something, honest cook, for thy good breakfasts;
And this, for your respect. [*To* ORDER] Take't, 'tis good gold,
And I able to spare it.

Ord. You are too munificent.

Furn. He was ever so.

Well. Pray you, on before.

3 *Cred.* Heaven bless you!

Mar. At four o'clock; the rest know where to meet me.

Exeunt ORDER, FURNACE, *and* Creditors

Well. Now, Master Marrall, what's the weighty secret
You promised to impart?

Mar. Sir, time nor place
Allow me to relate each circumstance,
This only, in a word: I know Sir Giles
Will come upon you for security
For his thousand pounds, which you must not consent to.
As he grows in heat, as I am sure he will,
Be you but rough, and say he's in your debt
Ten times the sum, upon sale of your land.
I had a hand in't—I speak it to my shame—
When you were defeated of it.

Well. That's forgiven.

Mar. I shall deserve it. Then urge him to produce
The deed in which you passed it over to him,
Which I know he'll have about him, to deliver
To the Lord Lovell, with many other writings,
And present monies. I'll instruct you further,
As I wait on your worship. If I play not my prize
To your full content, and your uncle's much vexation,
Hang up Jack Marrall.

Well. I rely upon thee.

Exeunt

[SCENE III]

[*A Room in Overreach's House*]

Enter ALLWORTH *and* MARGARET

All. Whether to yield the first praise to my lord's
Unequalled temperance or your constant sweetness
That I yet live, my weak hands fastened on
Hope's anchor, spite of all storms of despair,
I yet rest doubtful.
Marg. Give it to Lord Lovell;
For what in him was bounty, in me's duty.
I make but payment of a debt to which
My vows, in that high office registered,
Are faithful witnesses.
All. 'Tis true, my dearest.
Yet, when I call to mind how many fair ones
Make wilful shipwrecks of their faiths, and oaths
To God and man, to fill the arms of greatness,
And you rise up [no] less than a glorious star,
To the amazement of the world, hold out
Against the stern authority of a father,
And spurn at honor, when it comes to court you;
I am so tender of your good, that faintly,
With your wrong, I can wish myself that right
You yet are pleased to do me.
Marg. Yet, and ever.
To me what's title, when content is wanting?
Or wealth, raked up together with much care,
And to be kept with more, when the heart pines
In being dispossessed of what it longs for
Beyond the Indian mines? or the smooth brow
Of a pleasèd sire, that slaves me to his will,
And, so his ravenous humor may be feasted
By my obedience, and he see me great,

Leaves to my soul nor faculties nor power
To make her own election?
All. But the dangers
That follow the repulse—
Marg. To me they are nothing.
Let Allworth love, I cannot be unhappy.
Suppose the worst, that, in his rage, he kill me,
A tear or two, by you dropped on my hearse,
In sorrow for my fate, will call back life
So far as but to say, that I die yours:
I then shall rest in peace. Or should he prove
So cruel, as one death would not suffice
His thirst of vengeance, but with lingering torments
In mind and body I must waste to air,
In poverty joined with banishment; so you share
In my afflictions, which I dare not wish you,
So high I prize you, I could undergo 'em
With such a patience as should look down
With scorn on his worst malice.
All. Heaven avert
Such trials of your true affection to me!
Nor will it unto you, that are all mercy,
Show so much rigor. But since we must run
Such desperate hazards, let us do our best
To steer between them.
Marg. Your lord's ours, and sure;
And, though but a young actor, second me
In doing to the life what he has plotted,

Enter OVERREACH [*behind*]

The end may yet prove happy. Now, my Allworth.
Seeing her father
All. To your letter, and put on a seeming anger.
Marg. I'll pay my lord all debts due to his title;
And when with terms, not taking from his honor,
He does solicit me, I shall gladly hear him.

But in this peremptory, nay, commanding way,
To appoint a meeting, and, without my knowledge,
A priest to tie the knot can ne'er be undone
Till death unloose it, is a confidence
In his lordship will deceive him.

All. I hope better,
Good lady.

Marg. Hope, sir, what you please. For me
I must take a safe and secure course. I have
A father, and without his full consent,
Though all lords of the land kneeled for my favor,
I can grant nothing.

Over. I like this obedience.
Comes forward
But whatsoe'er my lord writes, must and shall be
Accepted and embraced. Sweet Master Allworth,
You show yourself a true and faithful servant
To your good lord; he has a jewel of you.
How! frowning, Meg? are these looks to receive
A messenger from my lord? What's this? Give me it.

Marg. A piece of arrogant paper, like the inscriptions.

Over. [*Reads*] 'Fair mistress, from your servant learn, all joys
That we can hope for, if deferred, prove toys;
Therefore this instant, and in private, meet
A husband, that will gladly at your feet
Lay down his honors, tendering them to you
With all content, the church being paid her due.'
Is this the arrogant piece of paper? Fool!
Will you still be one? In the name of madness, what
Could his good honor write more to content you?
Is there aught else to be wished, after these two,
That are already offered, marriage first,
And lawful pleasure after; what would you more?

Marg. Why, sir, I would be married like your daughter,
Not hurried away i' th' night I know not whither,

Without all ceremony; no friends invited
To honor the solemnity.

All. An't please your honor,
For so before to-morrow I must style you,
My lord desires this privacy, in respect
His honorable kinsmen are afar off,
And his desires to have it done brook not
So long delay as to expect their coming;
And yet he stands resolved, with all due pomp,
As running at the ring, plays, masks, and tilting,
To have his marriage at court celebrated,
When he has brought your honor up to London.

Over. He tells you true; 'tis the fashion, on my knowledge.
Yet the good lord, to please your peevishness,
Must put it off, forsooth, and lose a night,
In which perhaps he might get two boys on thee.
Tempt me no further, if you do, this goad
Points to his sword
Shall prick you to him.

Marg. I could be contented,
Were you but by, to do a father's part,
And give me in the church.

Over. So my lord have you,
What do I care who gives you? Since my lord
Does purpose to be private, I'll not cross him.
I know not, Master Allworth, how my lord
May be provided, and therefore there's a purse
Of gold, 'twill serve this night's expense. To-morrow
I'll furnish him with any sums. In the mean time,
Use my ring to my chaplain; he is beneficed
At my manor of Got'em, and called Parson Willdo.
'Tis no matter for a license, I'll bear him out in't.

Marg. With your favor, sir, what warrant is your ring?
He may suppose I got that twenty ways,
Without your knowledge; and then to be refused
Were such a stain upon me! If you pleased, sir,

Your presence would do better.

Over. Still perverse!
I say again, I will not cross my lord.
Yet I'll prevent you too.—Paper and ink, there!

All. I can furnish you.

Over. I thank you, I can write then.

Writes on his book

All. You may, if you please, put out the name of my lord,
In respect he comes disguised, and only write,
'Marry her to this gentleman.'

Over. Well advised.
'Tis done; away. [MARGARET *kneels*] My blessing, girl?
Thou hast it.
Nay, no reply, be gone.—Good Master Allworth,
This shall be the best night's work you ever made.

All. I hope so, sir.

Exeunt ALLWORTH *and* MARGARET

Over. Farewell!—Now all's cocksure.
Methinks I hear already knights and ladies
Say, Sir Giles Overreach, how is it with
Your honorable daughter? Has her honor
Slept well to-night? or, will her honor please
To accept this monkey, dog, or paroquet—
This is state in ladies—or my eldest son
To be her page, and wait upon her trencher?
My ends, my ends are compassed—then for Wellborn
And the lands. Were he once married to the widow—
I have him here—I can scarce contain myself,
I am so full of joy, nay, joy all over. *Exit*

[ACT V, SCENE I]

[*A Room in Lady Allworth's House*]

Enter Lord LOVELL, Lady ALLWORTH, *and* AMBLE

L. All. By this you know how strong the motives were
That did, my lord, induce me to dispense
A little, with my gravity, to advance,
In personating some few favors to him,
The plots and projects of the down-trod Wellborn.
Nor shall I e'er repent, although I suffer
In some few men's opinions for't, the action;
For he that ventured all for my dear husband
Might justly claim an obligation from me
To pay him such a courtesy; which had I
Coyly or over-curiously denied,
It might have argued me of little love
To the deceased.

Lov. What you intended, madam,
For the poor gentleman hath found good success;
For, as I understand, his debts are paid,
And he once more furnished for fair employment.
But all the arts that I have used to raise
The fortunes of your joy and mine, young Allworth,
Stand yet in supposition, though I hope well;
For the young lovers are in wit more pregnant
Than their years can promise; and for their desires,
On my knowledge, they are equal.

L. All. As my wishes
Are with yours, my lord, yet give me leave to fear
The building, though well grounded. To deceive
Sir Giles, that's both a lion and a fox
In his proceedings, were a work beyond
The strongest undertakers; not the trial
Of two weak innocents.

Lov. Despair not, madam.

Hard things are compassed oft by easy means;
And judgment, being a gift derived from heaven,
Though sometimes lodged i' th' hearts of worldly men,
That ne'er consider from whom they receive it,
For sakes such as abuse the giver of it.
Which is the reason that the politic
And cunning statesman, that believes he fathoms
The counsels of all kingdoms on the earth,
Is by simplicity oft over-reached.

L. All. May he be so! Yet, in his name to express it,
Is a good omen.

Lov. May it to myself
Prove so, good lady, in my suit to you!
What think you of the motion?

L. All. Troth, my lord,
My own unworthiness may answer for me;
For had you, when that I was in my prime,
My virgin flower uncropped, presented me
With this great favor; looking on my lowness
Not in a glass of self-love, but of truth,
I could not but have thought it, as a blessing
Far, far beyond my merit.

Lov. You are too modest,
And undervalue that which is above
My title, or whatever I call mine.
I grant, were I a Spaniard, to marry
A widow might disparage me; but being
A true-born Englishman, I cannot find
How it can taint my honor. Nay, what's more,
That which you think a blemish is to me
The fairest lustre. You already, madam,
Have given sure proofs how dearly you can cherish
A husband that deserves you; which confirms me,
That, if I am not wanting in my care
To do you service, you'll be still the same
That you were to your Allworth. In a word,

Our years, our states, our births are not unequal,
You being descended nobly, and allied so.
If then you may be won to make me happy,
But join your lips to mine, and that shall be
A solemn contract.

L. All. I were blind to my own good,
Should I refuse it. [*Kisses him*] Yet, my lord, receive me
As such a one, the study of whose whole life
Shall know no other object but to please you.

Lov. If I return not, with all tenderness,
Equal respect to you, may I die wretched!

L. All. There needs no protestation; my lord,
To her that cannot doubt.—

Enter WELLBORN, *handsomely apparelled*

You are welcome, sir.
Now you look like yourself.

Well. And will continue
Such in my free acknowledgment, that I am
Your creature, madam, and will never hold
My life mine own, when you please to command it.

Lov. It is a thankfulness that well becomes you.
You could not make choice of a better shape
To dress your mind in.

L. All. For me, I am happy
That my endeavors prospered. Saw you of late
Sir Giles, your uncle?

Well. I heard of him, madam,
By his minister, Marrall; he's grown into strange passions
About his daughter. This last night he looked for
Your lordship at his house, but missing you,
And she not yet appearing, his wise head
Is much perplexed and troubled.

Lov. It may be,
Sweetheart, my project took.

L. All. I strongly hope.

Over. [*Within*] Ha! find her, booby, thou huge lump of nothing,
I'll bore thine eyes out else.

Well. May it please your lordship,
For some ends of mine own, but to withdraw
A little out of sight, though not of hearing,
You may, perhaps, have sport.

Lov. You shall direct me.
Steps aside

Enter OVERREACH, *with distracted looks, driving in* MARRALL *before him, with a box*

Over. I shall *sol fa* you, rogue!

Mar. Sir, for what cause
Do you use me thus?

Over. Cause, slave! why, I am angry,
And thou a subject only fit for beating,
And so to cool my choler. Look to the writing.
Let but the seal be broke upon the box
That has slept in my cabinet these three years,
I'll rack thy soul for't.

Mar. [*Aside*] I may yet cry quittance,
Though now I suffer, and dare not resist.

Over. Lady, by your leave, did you see my daughter, lady,
And the lord her husband? Are they in your house?
If they are, discover, that I may bid them joy;
And, as an entrance to her place of honor,
See your ladyship on her left hand, and make curtsies
When she nods on you; which you must receive
As a special favor.

L. All. When I know, Sir Giles,
Her state requires such ceremony, I shall pay it.
But, in the mean time, as I am myself,
I give you to understand, I neither know
Nor care where 'her honor' is.

Over. When you once see her
Supported, and led by the lord her husband,
You'll be taught better.—Nephew.

Well. Sir.

Over. No more!

Well. 'Tis all I owe you.

Over. Have your redeemed rags
Made you thus insolent?

Well. [*In scorn*] Insolent to you!
Why, what are you, sir, unless in your years,
At the best, more than myself?

Over. [*Aside*] His fortune swells him.
'Tis rank, he's married.

L. All. This is excellent!

Over. Sir, in calm language, though I seldom use it,
I am familiar with the cause that makes you
Bear up thus bravely. There's a certain buzz
Of a stolen marriage, do you hear? of a stolen marriage,
In which, 'tis said, there's somebody hath been cozened.
I name no parties.

Well. Well, sir, and what follows?

Over. Marry, this; since you are peremptory. Remember,
Upon mere hope of your great match, I lent you
A thousand pounds. Put me in good security,
And suddenly, by mortgage or by statute,
Of some of your new possessions, or I'll have you
Dragged in your lavender robes to the jail. You know me,
And therefore do not trifle.

Well. Can you be
So cruel to your nephew, now he's in
The way to rise? Was this the courtesy
You did me 'in pure love, and no ends else'?

Over. End me no ends! Engage the whole estate,
And force your spouse to sign it, you shall have
Three or four thousand more, to roar and swagger
And revel in bawdy taverns.

Well. And beg after;
Mean you not so?

Over. My thoughts are mine, and free.
Shall I have security?

Well. No, indeed you shall not,
Nor bond, nor bill, nor bare acknowledgment.
Your great looks fright not me.

Over. But my deeds shall.
Outbraved! *Both draw*

L. All. Help, murder! murder!

Enter Servants

Well. Let him come on,
With all his wrongs and injuries about him,
Armed with his cut-throat practices to guard him.
The right that I bring with me will defend me,
And punish his extortion.

Over. That I had thee
But single in the field!

L. All. You may; but make not
My house your quarrelling scene.

Over. Were't in a church,
By heaven and hell, I'll do't!

Mar. Now put him to
The showing of the deed. [*Aside to* WELLBORN]

Well. This rage is vain, sir.
For fighting, fear not, you shall have your hands full,
Upon the least incitement; and whereas
You charge me with a debt of a thousand pounds,
If there be law—howe'er you have no conscience—
Either restore my land, or I'll recover
A debt, that's truly due to me from you,
In value ten times more than what you challenge.

Over. I in thy debt! O impudence! Did I not purchase
The land left by thy father, that rich land,
That had continued in Wellborn's name

Twenty descents; which, like a riotous fool,
Thou didst make sale of it? Is not here, inclosed,
The deed that does confirm it mine?
Mar. Now, now!
Well. I do acknowledge none; I ne'er passed over
Any such land. I grant, for a year or two
You had it in trust; which if you do discharge,
Surrendering the possession, you shall ease
Yourself and me of chargeable suits in law,
Which, if you prove not honest, as I doubt it,
Must of necessity follow.
L. All. In my judgment
He does advise you well.
Over. Good! good! conspire
With your new husband, lady; second him
In his dishonest practices. But when
This manor is extended to my use,
You'll speak in an humbler key, and sue for favor.
L. All. Never; do not hope it.
Well. Let despair first seize me.
Over. Yet, to shut up thy mouth, and make thee give
Thyself the lie, the loud lie, I draw out
The precious evidence. If thou canst forswear
Thy hand and seal, and make a forfeit of
Opens the box, and displays the bond
Thy ears to the pillory, see! Here's that will make
My interest clear—ha!
L. All. A fair skin of parchment.
Well. Indented, I confess, and labels too;
But neither wax nor words. How! Thunderstruck?
Not a syllable to insult with? My wise uncle,
Is this your precious evidence, is this that makes
Your interest clear?
Over. I am o'erwhelmed with wonder!
What prodigy is this? What subtle devil
Hath razed out the inscription? The wax

Turned into dust! The rest of my deeds whole
As when they were delivered, and this only
Made nothing! Do you deal with witches, rascal?
There is a statute for you, which will bring
Your neck in an hempen circle; yes, there is.
And now 'tis better thought for, cheater, know
This juggling shall not save you.

Well. To save thee,
Would beggar the stock of mercy.

Over. Marrall!

Mar. Sir.

Over. [*Flattering him*] Though the witnesses are dead, your testimony
Help with an oath or two; and for thy master,
Thy liberal master, my good honest servant,
I know thou wilt swear anything, to dash
This cunning sleight. Besides, I know thou art
A public notary, and such stand in law
For a dozen witnesses. The deed being drawn too
By thee, my careful Marrall, and delivered
When thou wert present, will make good my title.
Wilt thou not swear this?

Mar. I! No, I assure you.
I have a conscience not seared up like yours.
I know no deeds.

Over. Wilt thou betray me?

Mar. Keep him
From using of his hands, I'll use my tongue,
To his no little torment.

Over. Mine own varlet
Rebel against me!

Mar. Yes, and uncase you too.
'The idiot, the patch, the slave, the booby,
The property fit only to be beaten
For your morning exercise,' your 'football,' or
'Th' unprofitable lump of flesh,' your 'drudge,'

Can now anatomize you, and lay open
All your black plots, and level with the earth
Your hill of pride, and, with these gabions guarded,
Unload my great artillery, and shake,
Nay pulverize, the walls you think defend you.

L. All. How he foams at the mouth with rage!

Well. To him again.

Over. O that I had thee in my gripe, I would tear thee
Joint after joint!

Mar. I know you are a tearer,
But I'll have first your fangs pared off, and then
Come nearer to you when I have discovered,
And made it good before the judge, what ways
And devilish practices, you used to cozen with
An army of whole families, who, yet alive,
And but enrolled for soldiers, were able
To take in Dunkirk.

Well. All will come out.

L. All. The better.

Over. But that I will live, rogue, to torture thee,
And make thee wish, and kneel in vain, to die,
These swords that keep thee from me should fix here,
Although they made my body but one wound,
But I would reach thee.

Lov. [*Aside*] Heaven's hand is in this;
One bandog worry the other!

Over. I play the fool,
And make my anger but ridiculous.
There will be a time and place, there will be, cowards,
When you shall feel what I dare do.

Well. I think so.
You dare do any ill, yet want true valor
To be honest, and repent.

Over. They are words I know not,
Nor e'er will learn. Patience, the beggar's virtue,

Enter GREEDY *and* Parson WILLDO

Shall find no harbor here. After these storms
At length a calm appears. Welcome, most welcome!
There's comfort in thy looks. Is the deed done?
Is my daughter married? Say but so, my chaplain,
And I am tame.
Willdo. Married! Yes, I assure you.
Over. Then vanish all sad thoughts! There's more gold for thee.
My doubts and fears are in the titles drowned
Of my honorable, my right honorable daughter.
Greedy. Here will I be feasting, at least for a month!
I am provided. Empty guts, croak no more.
You shall be stuffed like bagpipes, not with wind,
But bearing dishes.
Over. Instantly be here?
Whispering to WILLDO
To my wish! to my wish! Now you that plot against me,
And hoped to trip my heels up, that contemned me,
Think on't and tremble. [*Loud music*] They come! I hear the music.
A lane there for my lord!
Well. This sudden heat
May yet be cooled, sir.
Over. Make way there for my lord!

Enter ALLWORTH *and* MARGARET

Marg. Sir, first your pardon, then your blessing, with
Your full allowance of the choice I have made.
As ever you could make use of your reason, *Kneeling*
Grow not in passion; since you may as well
Call back the day that's past, as untie the knot
Which is too strongly fastened. Not to dwell
Too long on words, this is my husband.
Over. How!

All. So I assure you; all the rites of marriage,
With every circumstance, are past. Alas, sir,
Although I am no lord, but a lord's page,
Your daughter and my loved wife mourns not for it;
And, for right honorable son-in-law, you may say,
Your dutiful daughter.

Over. Devil! Are they married?

Willdo. Do a father's part, and say, heaven give them joy!

Over. Confusion and ruin! Speak, and speak quickly,
Or thou art dead.

Willdo. They are married.

Over. Thou hadst better
Have made a contract with the king of fiends,
Than these. My brain turns!

Willdo. Why this rage to me?
Is not this your letter, sir, and these the words?
'Marry her to this gentleman.'

Over. It cannot—
Nor will I e'er believe it, 'sdeath! I will not.
That I, that in all passages I touched
At worldly profit have not left a print
Where I have trod for the most curious search
To trace my footsteps, should be gulled by children,
Baffled and fooled, and all my hopes and labors
Defeated and made void.

Well. As it appears.
You are so, my grave uncle.

Over. Village nurses
Revenge their wrongs with curses. I'll not waste
A syllable but thus I take the life
Which, wretched, I gave to thee.

Offers to kill MARGARET

Lov. [*Coming forward*] Hold, for your own sake!
Though charity to your daughter hath quite left you,
Will you do an act, though in your hopes lost here,

Can leave no hope for peace or rest hereafter?
Consider; at the best you are but a man,
And cannot so create your aims, but that
They may be crossed.

Over. Lord! Thus I spit at thee,
And at thy counsel; and again desire thee,
And as thou art a soldier, if thy valor
Dares show itself where multitude and example
Lead not the way, let's quit the house, and change
Six words in private.

Lov. I am ready.

L. All. Stay, sir,
Contest with one distracted!

Well. You'll grow like him,
Should you answer his vain challenge.

Over. Are you pale?
Borrow his help, though Hercules call it odds,
I'll stand against both as I am, hemmed in—
Thus!
Since, like a Libyan lion in the toil,
My fury cannot reach the coward hunters,
And only spends itself, I'll quit the place.
Alone I can do nothing. But I have servants
And friends to second me; and if I make not
This house a heap of ashes—by my wrongs,
What I have spoke I will make good—or leave
One throat uncut,—if it be possible,
Hell, add to my afflictions! *Exit*

Mar. Is't not brave sport?

Greedy. Brave sport! I am sure it has ta'en away my stomach;
I do not like the sauce.

All. Nay, weep not, dearest,
Though it express your pity. What's decreed
Above, we cannot alter.

L. All. His threats move me
No scruple, madam.
Mar. Was it not a rare trick,
An it please your worship, to make the deed nothing?
I can do twenty neater, if you please
To purchase and grow rich; for I will be
Such a solicitor and steward for you,
As never worshipful had.
Well. I do believe thee.
But first discover the quaint means you used
To raze out the conveyance?
Mar. They are mysteries
Not to be spoke in public. Certain minerals
Incorporated in the ink and wax—
Besides, he gave me nothing, but still fed me
With hopes and blows; but that was the inducement
To this conundrum. If it please your worship
To call to memory, this mad beast once caused me
To urge you or to drown or hang yourself;
I'll do the like to him, if you command me.
Well. You are a rascal! He that dares be false
To a master, though unjust, will ne'er be true
To any other. Look not for reward
Or favor from me. I will shun thy sight
As I would do a basilisk's. Thank my pity,
If thou keep thy ears. Howe'er, I will take order
Your practice shall be silenced.
Greedy. I'll commit him,
If you'll have me, sir.
Well. That were to little purpose;
His conscience be his prison. Not a word,
But instantly be gone.
Ord. Take this kick with you.
Amb. And this.
Furn. If that I had my cleaver here,
I would divide your knave's head.

Mar. This is the haven
False servants still arrive at. *Exit*

Re-enter OVERREACH

L. All. Come again!

Lov. Fear not, I am your guard.

Well. His looks are ghastly.

Willdo. Some little time I have spent, under your favors,
In physical studies, and if my judgment err not,
He's mad beyond recovery. But observe him,
And look to yourselves.

Over. Why, is not the whole world
Included in myself? To what use then
Are friends and servants? Say there were a squadron
Of pikes, lined through with shot, when I am mounted
Upon my injuries, shall I fear to charge them?
No. I'll through the battalia, and that routed,
Flourishing his sword sheathed
I'll fall to execution. Ha! I am feeble.
Some undone widow sits upon mine arm,
And takes away the use of't; and my sword,
Glued to my scabbard with wronged orphans' tears,
Will not be drawn. Ha, what are these? Sure, hangmen,
That come to bind my hands, and then to drag me
Before the judgment-seat. Now they are new shapes,
And do appear like Furies, with steel whips
To scourge my ulcerous soul. Shall I then fall
Ingloriously, and yield? No; spite of Fate,
I will be forced to hell like to myself.
Though you were legions of accursèd spirits,
Thus would I fly among you.
Rushes forward, and flings himself on the ground

Well. There's no help.
Disarm him first, then bind him.

Greedy. Take a *mittimus,*
And carry him to Bedlam.

Lov. How he foams!

Well. And bites the earth!

Willdo. Carry him to some dark room,
There try what art can do for his recovery.

Marg. O my dear father!

They force OVERREACH *off*

All. You must be patient, mistress.

Lov. Here is a precedent to teach wicked men,
That when they leave religion, and turn atheists,
Their own abilities leave 'em. Pray you take comfort,
I will endeavor you shall be his guardians
In his distractions; and for your land, Master Wellborn,
Be it good or ill in law, I'll be an umpire
Between you, and this, th' undoubted heir
Of Sir Giles Overreach. For me, here's the anchor
That I must fix on.

All. What you shall determine,
My lord, I will allow of.

Well. 'Tis the language
That I speak too. But there is something else
Beside the repossession of my land,
And payment of my debts, that I must practise.
I had a reputation, but 'twas lost
In my loose course; and until I redeem it
Some noble way, I am but half made up.
It is a time of action. If your lordship
Will please to confer a company upon me
In your command, I doubt not in my service
To my king and country but I shall do something
That may make me right again.

Lov. Your suit is granted,
And you loved for the motion.

Well. [*Coming forward*] Nothing wants then
But your allowance—

THE EPILOGUE

But your allowance, and in that our all
Is comprehended; it being known, nor we,
Nor he that wrote the comedy, can be free,
Without your manumission; which if you
Grant willingly, as a fair favor due
To the poet's and our labors—as you may,
For we despair not, gentlemen, of the play—
We jointly shall profess your grace hath might
To teach us action, and him how to write. *Exeunt.*

'TIS PITY SHE'S A WHORE

by

JOHN FORD

To my Friend the Author

With admiration I beheld this Whore,
Adorned with beauty such as might restore
(If ever being, as thy Muse hath famed)
Her Giovanni, in his love unblamed:
The ready Graces lent their willing aid;
Pallas herself now played the chambermaid,
And helped to put her dressings on. Secure
Rest thou that thy name herein shall endure
To the end of age; and Annabella be
Gloriously fair, even in her infamy.

THOMAS ELLICE

To the Truly Noble

JOHN, EARL OF PETERBOROUGH, LORD MORDAUNT, BARON OF TURVEY [1]

My Lord,

Where a truth of merit hath a general warrant, there love is but a debt, acknowledgment a justice. Greatness cannot often claim virtue by inheritance; yet, in this, yours appears most eminent, for that you are not more rightly heir to your fortunes than glory shall be to your memory. Sweetness of disposition ennobles a freedom of birth; in both your lawful interest adds honour to your own name, and mercy to my presumption. Your noble allowance of these first fruits of my leisure in the action emboldens my confidence of your as noble construction in this presentment; especially since my service must ever owe particular duty to your favours by a particular engagement. The gravity of the subject may easily excuse the lightness of the title, otherwise I had been a severe judge against mine own guilt. Princes have vouchsafed grace to trifles offered from a purity of devotion; your lordship may likewise please to admit into your good opinion, with these weak endeavours, the constancy of affection from the sincere lover of your deserts in honour,

JOHN FORD

[1] John, first Earl of Peterborough, obtained that title in the year 1627-8. He was brought up in the Roman Catholic faith, but was converted by a disputation at his own house between Bishop Usher and a Catholic, who confessed himself silenced by the just hand of God for presuming to dispute without leave from his superiors. He joined the Parliamentary army in 1642, was made General of the Ordnance and colonel of a regiment of foot, under Essex, and died in the same year.

PERSONS IN THE PLAY

BONAVENTURA, *a Friar*
A CARDINAL, *Nuncio to the Pope*
SORANZO, *a Nobleman*
FLORIO, } *Citizens of Parma*
DONADO, } *Citizens of Parma*
GRIMALDI, *a Roman Gentleman*
GIOVANNI, *Son of Florio*
BERGETTO, *Nephew of Donato*
RICHARDETTO, *a supposed Physician*
VASQUES, *Servant to Soranzo*
POGGIO, *Servant to Bergetto*
Banditti, Officers, Attendants, Servants, &c.
ANNABELLA, *Daughter of Florio*
HIPPOLITA, *Wife of Richardetto*
PHILOTIS, *Niece of Richardetto*
PUTANA, *Tutoress to Annabella*

[SCENE—Parma]

'TIS PITY SHE'S A WHORE

ACT THE FIRST

[SCENE I]

[*Friar Bonaventura's Cell*]

Enter Friar *and* GIOVANNI

Friar. Dispute no more in this; for know, young man,
These are no school-points; nice philosophy
May tolerate unlikely arguments,
But Heaven admits no jest: wits that presumed
On wit too much, by striving how to prove
There was no God with foolish grounds of art,
Discovered first the nearest way to hell,
And filled the world with devilish atheism.
Such questions, youth, are fond: [1] far better 'tis
To bless the sun than reason why it shines;
Yet He thou talk'st of is above the sun.
No more! I may not hear it.
Gio. Gentle father,
To you I have unclasped my burdened soul,
Emptied the storehouse of my thoughts and heart,
Made myself poor of secrets; have not left
Another word untold, which hath not spoke
All what I ever durst or think or know;
And yet is here the comfort I shall have?
Must I not do what all men else may,—love?

[1] Vain.

Friar. Yes, you may love, fair son.
Gio. Must I not praise
That beauty which, if framed anew, the gods
Would make a god of, if they had it there,
And kneel to it, as I do kneel to them?
Friar. Why, foolish madman,—
Gio. Shall a peevish [1] sound,
A customary form, from man to man,
Of brother and of sister, be a bar
'Twixt my perpetual happiness and me?
Say that we had one father; say one womb—
Curse to my joys!—gave both us life and birth;
Are we not therefore each to other bound
So much the more by nature? by the links
Of blood, of reason? nay, if you will have't,
Even of religion, to be ever one,
One soul, one flesh, one love, one heart, one all?
Friar. Have done, unhappy youth! for thou art lost.
Gio. Shall, then, for that I am her brother born,
My joys be ever banished from her bed?
No, father; in your eyes I see the change
Of pity and compassion; from your age,
As from a sacred oracle, distils
The life of counsel: tell me, holy man,
What cure shall give me ease in these extremes?
Friar. Repentance, son, and sorrow for this sin:
For thou hast moved a Majesty above
With thy unrangèd almost blasphemy.
Gio. O, do not speak of that, dear confessor!
Friar. Art thou, my son, that miracle of wit
Who once, within these three months, wert esteemed
A wonder of thine age throughout Bononia?
How did the University applaud
Thy government, behaviour, learning, speech,

[1] Trifling.

Sweetness, and all that could make up a man!
I was proud of my tutelage, and chose
Rather to leave my books than part with thee;
I did so:—but the fruits of all my hopes
Are lost in thee, as thou art in thyself.
O, Giovanni! [1] hast thou left the schools
Of knowledge to converse with lust and death?
For death waits on thy lust. Look through the world,
And thou shalt see a thousand faces shine
More glorious than this idol thou ador'st:
Leave her, and take thy choice, 'tis much less sin;
Though in such games as those they lose that win.

Gio. It were more ease to stop the ocean
From floats and ebbs than to dissuade my vows.

Friar. Then I have done, and in thy wilful flames
Already see thy ruin; Heaven is just.
Yet hear my counsel.

Gio. As a voice of life.

Friar. Hie to thy father's house; there lock thee fast
Alone within thy chamber; then fall down
On both thy knees, and grovel on the ground;
Cry to thy heart; wash every word thou utter'st
In tears—and if't be possible—of blood:
Beg Heaven to cleanse the leprosy of lust
That rots thy soul; acknowledge what thou art,
A wretch, a worm, a nothing; weep, sigh, pray
Three times a-day and three times every night:
For seven days' space do this; then, if thou find'st
No change in thy desires, return to me:
I'll think on remedy. Pray for thyself
At home, whilst I pray for thee here.—Away!
My blessing with thee! we have need to pray.

[1] Our old dramatists appear to have learned Italian entirely from books; few, if any, of them pronounced it correctly. Giovanni is here used by Ford as a quadrisyllable, as it was by Massinger and others of his contemporaries.—*Gifford.*

Gio. All this I'll do, to free me from the rod
Of vengeance; else I'll swear my fate's my god. *Exeunt*

[SCENE II]

[*The Street before Florio's House*]

Enter GRIMALDI *and* VASQUES, *with their swords drawn*

Vas. Come, sir, stand to your tackling; if you prove craven, I'll make you run quickly.

Grim. Thou art no equal match for me.

Vas. Indeed, I never went to the wars to bring home news; nor cannot play the mountebank for a meal's meat, and swear I got my wounds in the field. See you these gray hairs? they'll not flinch for a bloody nose. Wilt thou to this gear?

Grim. Why, slave, thinkest thou I'll balance my reputation with a cast-suit?[1] Call thy master; he shall know that I dare—

Vas. Scold like a cot-quean;[2]—that's your profession. Thou poor shadow of a soldier, I will make thee know my master keeps servants thy betters in quality and performance. Comest thou to fight or prate?

Grim. Neither, with thee. I am a Roman and a gentleman; one that have got mine honour with expense of blood.

Vas. You are a lying coward and a fool. Fight, or by these hilts, I'll kill thee:—brave my lord!—you'll fight?

Grim. Provoke me not, for if thou dost—

Vas. Have at you!

They fight; GRIMALDI *is worsted*

Enter FLORIO, DONADO, *and* SORANZO, *from opposite sides*

[1] *i.e.* Cast-off.
[2] A contemptuous term for one who concerns himself with female affairs.

Flo. What mean these sudden broils so near my doors?
Have you not other places but my house
To vent the spleen of your disordered bloods?
Must I be haunted still with such unrest
As not to eat or sleep in peace at home?
Is this your love, Grimaldi? Fie! 'tis naught.

Don. And, Vasques, I may tell thee, 'tis not well
To broach these quarrels; you are ever forward
In seconding contentions.

Enter ANNABELLA *and* PUTANA *above*

Flo. What's the ground?

Sor. That, with your patience, signiors, I'll resolve:
This gentleman, whom fame reports a soldier,—
For else I know not,—rivals me in love
To Signior Florio's daughter; to whose ears
He still prefers his suit, to my disgrace;
Thinking the way to recommend himself
Is to disparage me in his report:—
But know, Grimaldi, though, may be, thou art
My equal in thy blood, yet this bewrays
A lowness in thy mind, which, wert thou noble,
Thou wouldst as much disdain as I do thee
For this unworthiness:—and on this ground
I willed my servant to correct his tongue,
Holding a man so base no match for me.

Vas. And had not your sudden coming prevented us, I had let my gentleman blood under the gills:—I should have wormed you, sir, for running mad.[1]

Grim. I'll be revenged, Soranzo.

Vas. On a dish of warm broth to stay your stomach—do, honest innocence, do! spoon-meat is a wholesomer diet than a Spanish blade.

[1] The illusion is to the practice of cutting what is called the worm from under a dog's tongue, as a preventive of madness.—*Gifford.*

Grim. Remember this!

Sor. I fear thee not, Grimaldi.

Exit GRIMALDI

Flo. My Lord Soranzo, this is strange to me,
Why you should storm, having my word engaged;
Owing [1] her heart, what need you doubt her ear?
Losers may talk by law of any game.

Vas. Yet the villany of words, Signior Florio, may be such as would make any unspleened dove choleric. Blame not my lord in this.

Flo. Be you more silent:
I would not for my wealth, my daughter's love
Should cause the spilling of one drop of blood.
Vasques, put up, let's end this fray in wine. *Exeunt*

Put. How like you this, child? here's threatening, challenging, quarrelling, and fighting on every side; and all is for your sake: you had need look to yourself, charge; you'll be stolen away sleeping else shortly.

Ann. But, tutoress, such a life gives no content
To me; my thoughts are fixed on other ends.
Would you would leave me!

Put. Leave you! no marvel else; leave me no leaving, charge; this is love outright. Indeed, I blame you not; you have choice fit for the best lady in Italy.

Ann. Pray do not talk so much.

Put. Take the worst with the best, there's Grimaldi the soldier, a very well-timbered fellow. They say he is a Roman, nephew to the Duke Montferrato; they say he did good service in the wars against the Milanese; but, 'faith, charge, I do not like him, an't be for nothing but for being a soldier: not one amongst twenty of your skirmishing captains but have some privy maim or other that mars their standing upright. I like him the worse, he crinkles so much

[1] *i.e.* Owning.

in the hams: though he might serve if there were no more men, yet he's not the man I would choose.

Ann. Fie, how thou pratest.

Put. As I am a very woman, I like Signior Soranzo well; he is wise, and what is more, rich; and what is more than that, kind; and what is more that all this, a nobleman: such a one, were I the fair Annabella myself, I would wish and pray for. Then he is bountiful; besides, he is handsome, and, by my troth, I think, wholesome,—and that's news in a gallant of three-and-twenty; liberal, that I know; loving, that you know; and a man sure, else he could never ha' purchased such a good name with Hippolita, the lusty widow, in her husband's lifetime: an 'twere but for that report, sweetheart, would 'a were thine! Commend a man for his qualities, but take a husband as he is a plain, sufficient, naked man: such a one is for your bed, and such a one is Signior Soranzo, my life for't.

Ann. Sure the woman took her morning's draught too soon.

Enter BERGETTO *and* POGGIO

Put. But look, sweetheart, look what thing come now! Here's another of your ciphers to fill up the number: O, brave old ape in a silken coat! Observe.

Berg. Didst thou think, Poggio, that I would spoil my new clothes, and leave my dinner, to fight?

Pog. No, sir, I did not take you for so arrant a baby.

Berg. I am wiser than so: for I hope, Poggio, thou never heardst of an elder brother that was a coxcomb; didst, Poggio?

Pog. Never, indeed, sir, as long as they had either land or money left them to inherit.

Berg. Is it possible, Poggio? O, monstrous! Why, I'll undertake with a handful of silver to buy a headful of wit at any time: but, sirrah, I have another purchase in hand; I shall have the wench, mine uncle says. I will but wash my face and shift socks, and then have at her, i'faith!—Mark my pace, Poggio! *Passes over the stage, and exit*

Pog. Sir,—I have seen an ass and a mule trot the Spanish pavin[1] with a better grace, I know not how often.

Aside, and follows him

Ann. This idiot haunts me too.

Put. Ay, ay, he needs no description. The rich magnifico that is below with your father, charge, Signior Donado his uncle, for that he means to make this, his cousin,[2] a golden calf, thinks that you will be a right Israelite, and fall down to him presently: but I hope I have tutored you better. They say a fool's bauble is a lady's playfellow; yet you, having wealth enough, you need not cast upon the dearth of flesh, at any rate. Hang him, innocent![3]

GIOVANNI *passes over the stage*

Ann. But see, Putana, see! what blessèd shape
Of some celestial creature now appears!—
What man is he, that with such sad aspéct
Walks careless of himself?

Put. Where?

Ann. Look below.

Put. O, 'tis your brother, sweet.

Ann. Ha!

Put. 'Tis your brother.

Ann. Sure, 'tis not he; this is some woful thing
Wrapped up in grief, some shadow of a man.
Alas, he beats his breast and wipes his eyes,
Drowned all in tears: methinks I hear him sigh:
Let's down, Putana, and partake the cause.

[1] "A grave and majestic dance; the method of performing it was anciently by gentlemen dressed with a cap and sword; by those of the long robe, in their gowns; by princes, in their mantles; and by ladies, in gowns with long trains, the motion whereof in the dance resembled that of a peacock's tail."—*Hawkins.*

[2] *i.e.* Nephew.

[3] Idiot.

I know my brother, in the love he bears me,
Will not deny me partage in his sadness.—
My soul is full of heaviness and fear. [*Aside*]
Exit above with PUTANA

[SCENE III]

[*A Hall in Florio's House*]

Enter GIOVANNI

Gio. Lost! I am lost! my fates have doomed my death:
The more I strive, I love; the more I love,
The less I hope: I see my ruin certain.
What judgment or endeavours could apply
To my incurable and restless wounds,
I throughly have examined, but in vain.
O, that it were not in religion sin
To make our love a god, and worship it!
I have even wearied Heaven with prayers, dried up
The spring of my continual tears, even starved
My veins with daily fasts: what wit or art
Could counsel, I have practised; but, alas,
I find all these but dreams, and old men's tales,
To fright unsteady youth; I'm still the same:
Or I must speak, or burst. 'Tis not, I know,
My lust, but 'tis my fate that leads me on.
Keep fear and low faint-hearted shame with slaves!
I'll tell her that I love her, though my heart
Were rated at the price of that attempt.—
O me! she comes.

Enter ANNABELLA *and* PUTANA

Ann. Brother!
Gio. [*Aside*] If such a thing
As courage dwell in men, ye heavenly powers,
Now double all that virtue in my tongue!

Ann. Why, brother
Will you not speak to me?

Gio. Yes: how d'ye, sister?

Ann. Howe'er I am, methinks you are not well.

Put. Bless us! Why are you so sad, sir?

Gio. Let me entreat you, leave us a while, Putana.—
Sister, I would be private with you.

Ann. Withdraw, Putana.

Put. I will.—If this were any other company for her, I should think my absence an office of some credit: but I will leave them together. *Aside, and exit*

Gio. Come, sister, lend your hand: let's walk together!
I hope you need not blush to walk with me;
Here's none but you and I.

Ann. How's this?

Gio. I'faith,
I mean no harm.

Ann. Harm?

Gio. No, good faith.
How is't with ye?

Ann. [*Aside*] I trust he be not frantic.—
I am very well, brother.

Gio. Trust me, but I am sick; I fear so sick
'Twill cost my life.

Ann. Mercy forbid it! 'tis not so, I hope.

Gio. I think you love me, sister.

Ann. Yes, you know
I do.

Gio. I know't, indeed.—You're very fair.

Ann. Nay, then I see you have a merry sickness.

Gio. That's as it proves. The poets feign, I read,
That Juno for her forehead did exceed
All other goddesses; but I durst swear
Your forhead exceeds hers, as hers did theirs.

Ann. 'Troth, this is pretty!

Gio. Such a pair of stars
As are thine eyes would, like Promethean fire,
If gently glanced, give life to senseless stones.
Ann. Fie upon ye!
Gio. The lily and the rose, most sweetly strange,
Upon your dimpled cheeks do strive for change:
Such lips would tempt a saint; such hands as those
Would make an anchorite lascivious.
Ann. D'ye mock me or flatter me?
Gio. If you would see a beauty more exact
Than art can counterfeit or nature frame,
Look in your glass, and there behold your own.
Ann. O, you are a trim youth!
Gio. Here! *Offers his dagger to her*
Ann. What to do?
Gio. And here's my breast; strike home!
Rip up my bosom; there thou shalt behold
A heart in which is writ the truth I speak.
Why stand ye?
Ann. Are you earnest?
Gio. Yes, most earnest.
You cannot love?
Ann. Whom?
Gio. Me. My tortured soul
Hath felt affliction in the heat of death.
O, Annabella, I am quite undone!
The love of thee, my sister, and the view
Of thy immortal beauty have untuned
All harmony both of my rest and life.
Why d'ye not strike?
Ann. Forbid it, my just fears!
If this be true, 'twere fitter I were dead.
Gio. True, Annabella! 'tis no time to jest.
I have too long suppressed the hidden flames
That almost have consumed me: I have spent
Many a silent night in sighs and groans;

Ran over all my thoughts, despised my fate,
Reasoned against the reasons of my love,
Done all that smoothed-cheeked virtue could advise;
But found all bootless: 'tis my destiny
That you must either love, or I must die.

Ann. Comes this in sadness[1] from you?

Gio. Let some mischief
Befall me soon, if I dissemble aught.

Ann. You are my brother Giovanni.

Gio. You
My sister Annabella; I know this,
And could afford you instance why to love
So much the more for this; to which intent
Wise nature first in your creation meant
To make you mine; else't had been sin and foul
To share one beauty to a double soul.
Nearness in birth and blood doth but persuade
A nearer nearness in affection.
I have asked counsel of the holy church,
Who tells me I may love you; and 'tis just
That, since I may, I should; and will, yes, will.
Must I now live or die?

Ann. Live; thou hast won
The field, and never fought: what thou hast urged
My captive heart had long ago resolved.
I blush to tell thee,—but I'll tell thee now,—
For every sigh that thou hast spent for me
I have sighed ten; for every tear shed twenty:
And not so much for that I loved, as that
I durst not say I loved, nor scarcely think it.

Gio. Let not this music be a dream, ye gods,
For pity's sake, I beg ye!

Ann. On my knees, *She kneels*
Brother, even by our mother's dust, I charge you,

[1] Earnest.

Do not betray me to your mirth or hate:
Love me or kill me, brother.

Gio. On my knees, *He kneels*
Sister, even by my mother's dust, I charge you,
Do not betray me to your mirth or hate:
Love me or kill me, sister.

Ann. You mean good sooth, then?

Gio. In good troth, I do;
And so do you, I hope: say, I'm in earnest.

Ann. I'll swear it, I.

Gio. And I; and by this kiss,— *Kisses her*
Once more, yet once more: now let's rise [*They rise*],—by this,
I would not change this minute for Elysium.
What must we now do?

Ann. What you will.

Gio. Come, then;
After so many tears as we have wept,
Let's learn to court in smiles, to kiss, and sleep. *Exeunt*

[SCENE IV]

[*A Street*]

Enter FLORIO *and* DONADO

Flo. Signior Donado, you have said enough,
I understand you; but would have you know
I will not force my daughter 'gainst her will.
You see I have but two, a son and her;
And he is so devoted to his book,
As I must tell you true, I doubt his health:
Should he miscarry, all my hopes rely
Upon my girl.[1] As for worldly fortune,

[1] "Girl" is here, and almost everywhere else in these plays, a dissyllable. The practice is not peculiar to our poet; for Fanshaw, and others of that age, have numerous examples of it.—*Gifford.*

I am, I thank my stars, blessed with enough.
My care is, how to match her to her liking:
I would not have her marry wealth, but love
And if she like your nephew, let him have her.
Here's all that I can say.

Don. Sir, you say well.
Like a true father; and, for my part, I,
If the young folks can like,—'twixt you and me,—
Will promise to assure my nephew presently
Three thousand florins yearly during life,
And after I am dead my whole estate.

Flo. 'Tis a fair proffer, sir; meantime your nephew
Shall have free passage to commence his suit:
If he can thrive, he shall have my consent.
So for this time I'll leave you, signior. *Exit*

Don. Well,
Here's hope yet, if my nephew would have wit;
But he is such another dunce, I fear
He'll never win the wench. When I was young,
I could have done't, i'faith; and so shall he,
If he will learn of me; and, in good time,
He comes himself.

Enter BERGETTO *and* POGGIO

How now, Bergetto, whither away so fast?

Berg. O, uncle, I have heard the strangest news that ever came out of the mint!—Have I not, Poggio?

Pog. Yes, indeed, sir.

Don. What news, Bergetto?

Berg. Why, look ye, uncle, my barber told me just now that there is a fellow come to town who undertakes to make a mill go without the mortal help of any water or wind, only with sand-bags: and this fellow hath a strange horse, a most excellent beast, I'll assure you, uncle, my barber says; whose head, to the wonder of all Christian people, stands just behind where his tail is.—Is't not true, Poggio?

Pog. So the barber swore, forsooth.

Don. And you are running thither?

Berg. Ay, forsooth, uncle.

Don. Wilt thou be a fool still? Come, sir, you shall not go: you have more mind of a puppet-play than on the business I told ye. Why, thou great baby, wilt never have wit? wilt make thyself a May-game to all the world?

Pog. Answer for yourself, master.

Berg. Why, uncle, should I sit at home still, and not go abroad to see fashions like other gallants?

Don. To see hobby-horses! What wise talk, I pray, had you with Annabella, when you were at Signior Florio's house?

Berg. O, the wench,—Ud's sa'me, uncle, I tickled her with a rare speech, that I made her almost burst her belly with laughing.

Don. Nay, I think so; and what speech was't?

Berg. What did I say, Poggio?

Pog. Forsooth, my master said, that he loved her almost as well as he loved parmasent; [1] and swore—I'll be sworn for him—that she wanted but such a nose as his was, to be as pretty a young woman as any was in Parma.

Don. O, gross!

Berg. Nay, uncle:—then she asked me whether my father had any more children than myself; and I said "No; 'twere better he should have had his brains knocked out first."

Don. This is intolerable.

Berg. Then said she, "Will Signior Donado, your uncle, leave you all his wealth?"

Don. Ha! that was good; did she harp upon that string?

Berg. Did she harp upon that string! ay, that she did. I answered, "Leave me all his wealth! why, woman, he hath no other wit; if he had, he should hear on't to his everlasting glory and confusion: I know," quoth I, "I am his

[1] *i.e.* Parmesan, the cheese of Parma.

white-boy,[1] and will not be gulled:" and with that she fell into a great smile, and went away. Nay, I did fit her.

Don. Ah, sirrah, then I see there is no changing of nature. Well, Bergetto, I fear thou wilt be a very ass still.

Berg. I should be sorry for that, uncle.

Don. Come, come you home with me: since you are no better a speaker, I'll have you write to her after some courtly manner, and enclose some rich jewel in the letter.

Berg. Ay, marry, that will be excellent.

Don. Peace, innocent![2]
Once in my time I'll set my wits to school:
If all fail, 'tis but the fortune of a fool.

Berg. Poggio, 'twill do, Poggio. *Exeunt*

Act The Second

[SCENE I]

[An Apartment in Florio's House]

Enter Giovanni *and* Annabella

Gio. Come, Annabella,—no more sister now,
But love, a name more gracious,—do not blush,
Beauty's sweet wonder, but be proud to know
That yielding thou hast conquered, and inflamed
A heart whose tribute is thy brother's life.

Ann. And mine is his. O, how these stol'n contents
Would print a modest crimson on my cheeks,
Had any but my heart's delight prevailed!

Gio. I marvel why the chaster of your sex

[1] A term of endearment. It is said that this and similar terms are still used in some parts of Ireland. Under the ancient Irish Geilfine system of land tenure the homestead itself, in the division of the family property, fell to the lot of the fifth son, who was called the fair-haired or white-headed boy, *geil* meaning white.

[2] Idiot.

Should think this pretty toy called maidenhead
So strange a loss, when, being lost, 'tis nothing,
And you are still the same.

Ann. 'Tis well for you;
Now you can talk.

Gio. Music as well consists
In the ear as in the playing.

Ann. O, you're wanton!
Tell on't, you're best; do.

Gio. Thou wilt chide me, then.
Kiss me:—so! Thus hung Jove on Leda's neck,
And sucked divine ambrosia from her lips.
I envy not the mightiest man alive;
But hold myself in being king of thee,
More great than were I king of all the world.
But I shall lose you, sweetheart.

Ann. But you shall not.

Gio. You must be married, mistress.

Ann. Yes! to whom?

Gio. Some one must have you.

Ann. You must.

Gio. Nay, some other.

Ann. Now, prithee do not speak so: without jesting
You'll make me weep in earnest.

Gio. What, you will not!
But tell me, sweet, canst thou be dared to swear
That thou wilt live to me, and to no other?

Ann. By both our loves I dare; for didst thou know,
My Giovanni, how all suitors seem
To my eyes hateful, thou wouldst trust me then.

Gio. Enough, I take thy word: sweet, we must part:
Remember what thou vow'st; keep well my heart.

Ann. Will you be gone?

Gio. I must.

Ann. When to return?

Gio. Soon.

Ann. Look you do.

Gio. Farewell.

Ann. Go where thou wilt, in mind I'll keep thee here.
And where thou art, I know I shall be there.

Exit GIOVANNI

Guardian!

Enter PUTANA

Put. Child, how is't, child? well, thank Heaven, ha!

Ann. O guardian, what a paradise of joy
Have I passed over!

Put. Nay, what a paradise of joy have you passed under! Why, now I commend thee, charge. Fear nothing, sweetheart: what though he be your brother? your brother's a man, I hope; and I say still, if a young wench feel the fit upon her, let her take any body, father or brother, all is one.

Ann. I would not have it known for all the world.

Put. Nor I, indeed; for the speech of the people: else 'twere nothing.

Flo. [*Within*] Daughter Annabella!

Ann. O me, my father!—Here, sir!—Reach my work.

Flo. [*Within*] What are you doing?

Ann. So: let him come now.

Enter FLORIO, *followed by* RICHARDETTO *as a* Doctor of Physic, *and* PHILOTIS *with a lute*

Flo. So hard at work! that's well; you lose no time.
Look, I have brought you company; here's one,
A learnèd doctor lately come from Padua,
Much skilled in physic; and, for that I see
You have of late been sickly, I entreated
This reverend man to visit you some time.

Ann. You're very welcome, sir.

Rich. I thank you, mistress.
Loud fame in large report hath spoke your praise

As well for virtue as perfection: [1]
For which I have been bold to bring with me
A kinswoman of mine, a maid, for song
And music one perhaps will give content:
Please you to know her.

Ann. They are parts I love.
And she for them most welcome.

Phi. Thank you, lady.

Flo. Sir, now you know my house, pray make not strange;
And if you find my daughter need your art,
I'll be your pay-master.

Rich. Sir, what I am
She shall command.

Flo. Sir, you shall bind me to you.—
Daughter, I must have conference with you
About some matters that concern us both.—
Good Master Doctor, please you but walk in,
We'll crave a little of your cousin's cunning: [2]
I think my girl hath not quite forgot
To touch an instrument; she could have done't:
We'll hear them both.

Rich. I'll wait upon you, sir. *Exeunt*

[SCENE II]

[*A Room in Soranzo's House*]

Enter SORANZO *with a book*

Sor. [*Reads*] "Love's measure is extreme, the comfort pain,
The life unrest, and the reward disdain."
What's here? look't o'er again.—'Tis so; so writes
This smooth, licentious poet in his rhymes:
But, Sannazar, thou liest; for, had thy bozom

[1] Beauty.
[2] *i.e.* Skill.

Felt such oppression as is laid on mine,
Thou wouldst have kissed the rod that made thee smart.—
To work, then, happy Muse, and contradict
What Sannazar hath in his envy writ. *Writes*
"Love's measure is the mean, sweet his annoys,
His pleasures life, and his reward all joys."
Had Annabella lived when Sannazar
Did, in his brief Encomium,[1] celebrate
Venice, that queen of cities, he had left
That verse which gained him such a sum of gold,
And for one only look from Annabel
Had writ of her and her diviner cheeks.
O, how my thoughts are—

Vas. [*Within*] Pray, forbear; in rules of civility, let me give notice on't: I shall be taxed of my neglect of duty and service.

Sor. What rude intrusion interrupts my peace?
Can I be no where private?

Vas. [*Within*] Troth, you wrong your modesty.

Sor. What's the matter, Vasques? who is't?

Enter HIPPOLITA *and* VASQUES

Hip. 'Tis I;
Do you know me now? Look, perjured man, on her
Whom thou and thy distracted lust have wronged.
Thy sensual rage of blood hath made my youth
A scorn to men and angels; and shall I
Be now a foil to thy unsated change?

[1] This is the well-known epigram, beginning
"Viderat Hadriacis Venetam Neptunus in undis
Stare urbem," &c.
It is given by Coryat, who thus speaks of it: "I heard in Venice that a certain Italian poet, called Jacobus Sannazarius, had a hundred crownes bestowed upon him by the Senate of Venice for each of these verses following. I would to God my poeticall friend Master Benjamin Johnson were so well rewarded for his poems here in England, seeing he hath made many as good verses (in my opinion) as these of Sannazarius."—*Gifford.*

Thou know'st, false wanton, when my modest fame
Stood free from stain or scandal, all the charms
Of hell or sorcery could not prevail
Against the honour of my chaster bosom.
Thine eyes did plead in tears, thy tongue in oaths,
Such and so many, that a heart of steel
Would have been wrought to pity, as was mine:
And shall the conquest of my lawful bed,
My husband's death, urged on by his disgrace,
My loss of womanhood, be ill-rewarded
With hatred and contempt? No; know, Soranzo,
I have a spirit doth as much distaste
The slavery of fearing thee, as thou
Dost loathe the memory of what hath passed.

Sor. Nay, dear Hippolita,—

Hip. Call me not dear,
Nor think with supple words to smooth the grossness
Of my abuses: 'tis not your new mistress,
Your goodly madam-merchant, shall triumph
On my dejection; tell her thus from me,
My birth was nobler and by much more free.

Sor. You are too violent.

Hip. You are too double
In your dissimulation. Seest thou this,
This habit, these black mourning weeds of care?
'Tis thou art cause of this; and hast divorced
My husband from his life, and me from him,
And made me widow in my widowhood.

Sor. Will you yet hear?

Hip. More of thy perjuries?
Thy soul is drowned too deeply in those sins;
Thou need'st not add to the number.

Sor. Then I'll leave you;
You're past all rules of sense.

Hip. And thou of grace.

Vas. Fie, mistress, you are not near the limits of reason:

if my lord had a resolution as noble as virtue itself, you take the course to unedge it all.—Sir, I beseech you do not perplex her; griefs, alas, will have a vent: I dare undertake Madam Hippolita will now freely hear you.

Sor. Talk to a woman frantic!—Are these the fruits of your love?

Hip. They are the fruits of thy untruth, false man!
Didst thou not swear, whilst yet my husband lived,
That thou wouldst wish no happiness on earth
More than to call me wife? didst thou not vow,
When he should die, to marry me? for which
The devil in my blood, and thy protests,
Caused me to counsel him to undertake
A voyage to Ligorne, for that we heard
His brother there was dead, and left a daughter
Young and unfriended, who, with much ado,
I wished him to bring hither: he did so,
And went; and, as thou know'st, died on the way.
Unhappy man, to buy his death so dear,
With my advice! yet thou, for whom I did it,
Forgett'st thy vows, and leav'st me to my shame.

Sor. Who could help this?

Hip. Who! perjured man, thou couldst,
If thou hadst faith or love.

Sor. You are deceived:
The vows I made, if you remember well,
Were wicked and unlawful; 'twere more sin
To keep them than to break them: as for me,
I cannot mask my penitence. Think thou
How much thou hast digressed from honest shame
In bringing of a gentleman to death
Who was thy husband; such a one as he,
So noble in his quality, condition,
Learning, behaviour, entertainment, love,
As Parma could not show a braver man.

Vas. You do not well; this was not your promise.

Sor. I care not; let her know her monstrous life.
Ere I'll be servile to so black a sin,
I'll be a curse.—Woman, come here no more;
Learn to repent, and die; for, by my honour,
I hate thee and thy lust: you've been too foul. *Exit.*

Vas. [*Aside*] This part has been scurvily played.

Hip. How foolishly this beast contemns his fate,
And shuns the use of that which I more scorn
Than I once loved, his love! But let him go;
My vengeance shall give comfort to his woe.[1] *Going*

Vas. Mistress, mistress, Madam Hippolita! pray, a word or two.

Hip. With me, sir?

Vas. With you, if you please.

Hip. What is't?

Vas. I know you are infinitely moved now, and you think you have cause: some I confess you have, but sure not so much as you imagine.

Hip. Indeed!

Vas. O, you were miserably bitter, which you followed even to the last syllable; 'faith, you were somewhat too shrewd: by my life, you could not have took my lord in a worse time since I first knew him; to-morrow you shall find him a new man.

Hip. Well, I shall wait his leisure.

Vas. Fie, this is not a hearty patience; it comes sourly from you: 'troth, let me persuade you for once.

Hip. [*Aside*] I have it, and it shall be so; thanks, opportunity!—Persuade me! to what?

Vas. Visit him in some milder temper. O, if you could but master a little your female spleen, how might you win him!

Hip. He will never love me. Vasques, thou hast been a too trusty servant to such a master, and I believe thy reward in the end will fall out like mine.

[1] *i.e.* To the woe occasioned by his falsehood.

Vas. So perhaps too.

Hip. Resolve[1] thyself it will. Had I one so true, so truly honest, so secret to my counsels, as thou hast been to him and his, I should think it a slight acquittance, not only to make him master of all I have, but even of myself.

Vas. O, you are a noble gentlewoman!

Hip. Wilt thou feed always upon hopes? well, I know thou art wise, and seest the reward of an old servant daily, what it is.

Vas. Beggary and neglect.

Hip. True; but, Vasques, wert thou mine, and wouldst be private to me and my designs, I here protest, myself and all what I can else call mine should be at thy dispose.

Vas. [*Aside*] Work you that way, old mole? then I have the wind of you.—I were not worthy of it by any desert that could lie within my compass: if I could—

Hip. What then?

Vas. I should then hope to live in these my old years with rest and security.

Hip. Give me thy hand: now promise but thy silence,
And help to bring to pass a plot I have,
And here, in sight of heaven, that being done,
I make the lord of me and mine estate.

Vas. Come, you are merry; this is such a happiness that I can neither think or believe.

Hip. Promise thy secrecy, and 'tis confirmed.

Vas. Then here I call our good genii for witnesses, whatsoever your designs are, or against whomsoever, I will not only be a special actor therein, but never disclose it till it be effected.

Hip. I take thy word, and, with that, thee for mine;
Come, then, let's more confer of this anon.—
On this delicious bane my thoughts shall banquet;

[1] Assure.

Revenge shall sweeten what my griefs have tasted.

Aside, and exit with VASQUES

[SCENE III]

[*The Street*]

Enter RICHARDETTO *and* PHILOTIS

Rich. Thou seest, my lovely niece, these strange mishaps,
How all my fortunes turn to my disgrace;
Wherein I am but as a looker-on,
Whiles others act my shame, and I am silent.

Phi. But, uncle, wherein can this borrowed shape
Give you content?

Rich. I'll tell thee, gentle niece:
Thy wanton aunt in her lascivious riots
Lives now secure, thinks I am surely dead
In my late journey to Ligorne for you,—
As I have caused it to be rumoured out.
Now would I see with what an impudence
She gives scope to her loose adultery,
And how the common voice allows hereof:
Thus far I have prevailed.

Phi. Alas, I fear
You mean some strange revenge.

Rich. O, be not troubled;
Your ignorance shall plead for you in all:
But to our business.—What! you learned for certain
How Signior Florio means to give his daughter
In marriage to Soranzo?

Phi. Yes, for certain.

Rich. But how find you young Annabella's love
Inclined to him?

Phi. For aught I could perceive,
She neither fancies him or any else.

Rich. There's mystery in that, which time must show.
She used you kindly?
Phi. Yes.
Rich. And craved your company?
Phi. Often.
Rich. 'Tis well; it goes as I could wish.
I am the doctor now; and as for you,
None knows you: if all fail not, we shall thrive.—
But who comes here? I know him; 'tis Grimaldi,
A Roman and a soldier, near allied
Unto the Duke of Montferrato, one
Attending on the nuncio of the pope
That now resides in Parma; by which means
He hopes to get the love of Annabella.

Enter GRIMALDI

Grim. Save you, sir.
Rich. And you, sir.
Grim. I have heard
Of your approvèd skill, which through the city
Is freely talked of, and would crave your aid.
Rich. For what, sir?
Grim. Marry, sir, for this—
But I would speak in private.
Rich. Leave us, cousin.[1] *Exit* PHILOTIS
Grim. I love fair Annabella, and would know
Whether in art there may not be receipts
To move affection.
Rich. Sir, perhaps there may;
But these will nothing profit you.
Grim. Not me?
Rich. Unless I be mistook, you are a man
Greatly in favour with the cardinal.
Grim. What of that?

[1] "Cousin" was frequently used for nephew or niece.

Rich. In duty to his grace,
I will be bold to tell you, if you seek
To marry Florio's daughter, you must first
Remove a bar 'twixt you and her.

Grim. Who's that?

Rich. Soranzo is the man that hath her heart;
And while he lives, be sure you cannot speed.

Grim. Soranzo! what, mine enemy? is't he?

Rich. Is he your enemy?

Grim. The man I hate
Worse than confusion; I will to him straight.

Rich. Nay, then, take mine advice,
Even for his grace's sake the cardinal:
I'll find a time when he and she do meet,
Of which I'll give you notice; and, to be sure
He shall not 'scape you, I'll provide a poison
To dip your rapier's point in: if he had
As many heads as Hydra had, he dies.

Grim. But shall I trust thee, doctor?

Rich. As yourself;
Doubt not in aught. [*Exit* GRIMALDI]—Thus shall the fates decree
By me Soranzo falls, that ruined me. *Exit*

[SCENE IV]

[*Another part of the Street*]

Enter DONADO *with a letter,* BERGETTO, *and* POGGIO

Don. Well, sir, I must be content to be both your secretary and your messenger myself. I cannot tell what this letter may work; but, as sure as I am alive, if thou come once to talk with her, I fear thou wilt mar whatsoever I make.

Ber. You make, uncle! why, am not I big enough to carry mine own letter, I pray?

Don. Ay, ay, carry a fool's head o' thy own! why, thou dunce, wouldst thou write a letter, and carry it thyself?

Ber. Yes, that I would, and read it to her with my own mouth; for you must think, if she will not believe me myself when she hears me speak, she will not believe another's handwriting. O, you think I am a blockhead, uncle. No, sir, Poggio knows I have indited a letter myself; so I have.

Pog. Yes, truly, sir; I have it in my pocket.

Don. A sweet one, no doubt; pray let's see't.

Ber. I cannot read my own hand very well, Poggio; read it, Poggio.

Don. Begin.

Pog. [*Reads*] "Most dainty and honey-sweet mistress; I could call you fair, and lie as fast as any that loves you; but my uncle being the elder man, I leave it to him, as more fit for his age and the colour of his beard. I am wise enough to tell you I can bourd[1] where I see occasion; or if you like my uncle's wit better than mine you shall marry me; if you like mine better than his, I will marry you, in spite of your teeth. So, commending my best parts to you, I rest

Yours upwards and downwards, or you may choose,

Bergetto."

Ber. Ah, ha! here's stuff, uncle!

Don. Here's stuff indeed—to shame us all. Pray, whose advice did you take in this learned letter?

Pog. None, upon my word, but mine own.

Ber. And mine, uncle, believe it, nobody's else; 'twas mine own brain, I thank a good wit for't.

Don. Get you home, sir, and look you keep within doors till I return.

Ber. How! that were a jest indeed! I scorn it, i'faith.

Don. What! you do not?

Ber. Judge me, but I do now.

Pog. Indeed, sir, 'tis very unhealthy.

Don. Well, sir, if I hear any of your apish running to

[1] Jest.

motions [1] and fopperies, till I come back, you were as good no; look to't. *Exit*

Ber. Poggio, shall's steal to see this horse with the head in't tail?

Pog. Ay, but you must take heed of whipping.

Ber. Dost take me for a child, Poggio? Come, honest Poggio. *Exeunt*

[SCENE V]

[*Friar Bonaventura's Cell*]

Enter Friar *and* GIOVANNI

Friar. Peace! thou hast told a tale whose every word
Threatens eternal slaughter to the soul;
I'm sorry I have heard it: would mine ears
Had been one minute deaf, befor the hour
That thou cam'st to me! O young man, castaway,
By the religious number [2] of mine order,
I day and night have waked my agèd eyes
Above my strength, to weep on thy behalf;
But Heaven is angry, and be thou resolved [3]
Thou art a man remarked [4] to taste a mischief.
Look for't; though it come late, it will come sure.

Gio. Father, in this you are uncharitable;
What I have done I'll prove both fit and good.
It is a principle which you have taught,
When I was yet your scholar, that the frame
And composition of the mind doth follow
The frame and composition of the body:
So, where the body's furniture is beauty,
The mind's must needs be virtue; which allowed,
Virtue itself is reason but refined,

[1] Puppet-shows.
[2] Gifford proposed "founder."
[3] Satisfied.
[4] Marked out.

And love the quintessence of that: this proves,
My sister's beauty being rarely fair
Is rarely virtuous; chiefly in her love,
And chiefly in that love, her love to me:
If hers to me, then so is mine to her;
Since in like causes are effects alike.

Friar. O ignorance in knowledge! Long ago,
How often have I warned thee this before!
Indeed, if we were sure there were no Deity,
Nor Heaven nor Hell, then to be led alone
By Nature's light—as were philosophers
Of elder times—might instance some defence.
But 'tis not so: then, madman, thou wilt find
That Nature is in Heaven's positions blind.

Gio. Your age o'errules you; had you youth like mine,
You'd make her love your heaven, and her divine.

Friar. Nay, then I see thou'rt too far sold to hell:
It lies not in the compass of my prayers
To call thee back, yet let me counsel thee;
Persuade thy sister to some marriage.

Gio. Marriage! why, that's to damn her; that's to prove
Her greedy variety of lust.

Friar. O, fearful! if thou wilt not, give me leave
To shrive her, lest she should die unabsolved.

Gio. At your best leisure, father: then she'll tell you
How dearly she doth prize my matchless love;
Then you will know what pity 'twere we two
Should have been sundered from each other's arms.
View well her face, and in that little round
You may observe a world of variety;
For colour, lips; for sweet perfumes, her breath;
For jewels, eyes; for threads of purest gold,
Hair; for delicious choice of flowers, cheeks;
Wonder in every portion of that form.[1]

[1] "Throne" in the old edition.

Hear her but speak, and you will swear the spheres
Make music to the citizens in Heaven.
But, father, what is else for pleasure framed
Lest I offend your ears, shall go unnamed.

Friar. The more I hear, I pity thee the more,
That one so excellent should give those parts
All to a second death. What I can do
Is but to pray; and yet—I could advise thee,
Wouldst thou be ruled.

Gio. In what?

Friar. Why leave her yet:
The throne of mercy is above your trespass;
Yet time is left you both—

Gio. To embrace each other,
Else let all time be struck quite out of number:
She is like me, and I like her, resolved.

Friar. No more! I'll visit her.—This grieves me most,
Things being thus, a pair of souls are lost. *Exeunt*

[SCENE VI]

[*A Room in Florio's House*]

Enter FLORIO, DONADO, ANNABELLA, *and* PUTANA

Flo. Where's Giovanni?

Ann. Newly walked abroad,
And, as I heard him say, gone to the friar,
His reverend tutor.

Flo. That's a blessèd man,
A man made up of holiness: I hope
He'll teach him how to gain another world.

Don. Fair gentlewoman, here's a letter sent
To you from my young cousin; I dare swear
He loves you in his soul: would you could hear
Sometimes what I see daily, sighs and tears,
As if his breast were prison to his heart!

Flo. Receive it, Annabella.

Ann. Alas, good man! *Takes the letter*

Don. What's that she said?

Put. An't please you, sir, she said, "Alas, good man!" Truly I do commend him to her every night before her first sleep, because I would have her dream of him; and she hearkens to that most religiously.

Don. Sayest so? God-'a-mercy, Putana! there's something for thee [*Gives her money*]: and prithee do what thou canst on his behalf; 'shall not be lost labour, take my word for't.

Put. Thank you most heartily, sir: now I have a feeling of your mind, let me alone to work.

Ann. Guardian,—

Put. Did you call?

Ann. Keep this letter.

Don. Signior Florio, in any case bid her read it instantly.

Flo. Keep it! for what? pray, read it me hereright.

Ann. I shall, sir. *She reads the letter*

Don. How d'ye find her inclined, signior?

Flo. Troth, sir, I know not how; not all so well
As I could wish.

Ann. Sir, I am bound to rest your cousin's debtor.
The jewel I'll return; for if he love,
I'll count that love a jewel.

Don. Mark you that?
Nay, keep them both, sweet maid.

Ann. You must excuse me,
Indeed I will not keep it.

Flo. Where's the ring,
That which your mother, in her will, bequeathed,
And charged you on her blessing not to give 't
To any but your husband? send back that.

Ann. I have it not.

Flo. Ha! have it not! where is't?

Ann. My brother in the morning took it from me,
Said he would wear't to day.

Flo. Well, what do you say
To young Bergetto's love? are you content to
Match with him? speak.

Don. There is the point, indeed.

Ann. [*Aside*] What shall I do? I must say something now.

Flo. What say? why d'ye not speak?

Ann. Sir, with your leave—
Please you to give me freedom?

Flo. Yes, you have it.

Ann. Signior Donado, if your nephew mean
To raise his better fortunes in his match,
The hope of me will hinder such a hope:
Sir, if you love him, as I know you do,
Find one more worthy of his choice than me:
In short, I'm sure I shall not be his wife.

Don. Why, here's plain dealing; I commend thee for't;
And all the worst I wish thee is, Heaven bless thee!
Your father yet and I will still be friends:—
Shall we not, Signior Florio?

Flo. Yes; why not?
Look, here your cousin comes.

Enter BERGETTO *and* POGGIO

Don. [*Aside*] O, coxcomb! what doth he make here?

Ber. Where's my uncle, sirs?

Don. What's the news now?

Ber. Save you, uncle, save you!—You must not think I come for nothing, masters.—And how, and how is't? what, you have read my letter? ah, there I—tickled you, i'faith.

Pog. [*Aside to* BERGETTO] But 'twere better you had tickled her in another place.

Ber. Sirrah sweetheart, I'll tell thee a good jest; and riddle what 'tis.

Ann. You say you'll tell me.

Ber. As I was walking just now in the street, I met a swaggering fellow would needs take the wall of me; and because he did thrust me, I very valiantly called him rogue. He hereupon bade me draw; I told him I had more wit than so; but when he saw that I would not, he did so maul me with the hilts of his rapier, that my head sung whilst my feet capered in the kennel.

Don. [*Aside*] Was ever the like ass seen!

Ann. And what did you all this while?

Ber. Laugh at him for a gull, till I saw the blood run about mine ears, and then I could not choose but find in my heart to cry; till a fellow with a broad beard—they say he is a new-come doctor—called me into his house, and gave me a plaster, look you, here 'tis:—and, sir, there was a young wench washed my face and hands most excellently; i' faith, I shall love her as long as I live for't.—Did she not, Poggio?

Pog. Yes, and kissed him too.

Ber. Why, la, now, you think I tell a lie, uncle, I warrant.

Don. Would he that beat thy blood out of thy head had beaten some wit into it! for I fear thou never wilt have any.

Ber. O, uncle, but there was a wench would have done a man's heart good to have looked on her.—By this light, she had a face methinks worth twenty of you, Mistress Annabella.

Don. [*Aside*] Was ever such a fool born!

Ann. I am glad she liked [1] you, sir.

Ber. Are you so? by my troth, I thank you, forsooth.

Flo. Sure, 'twas the doctor's niece, that was last day with us here.

Ber. 'Twas she, 'twas she.

Don. How do you know that, simplicity?

Ber. Why, does not he say so? if I should have said no,

[1] *i.e.* Pleased.

I should have given him the lie, uncle, and so have deserved a dry beating again: I'll none of that.

Flo. A very modest well-behaved young maid
As I have seen.

Don. Is she indeed?

Flo. Indeed she is, if I have any judgment.

Don. Well, sir, now you are free: you need not care for sending letters now; you are dismissed, your mistress here will none of you.

Ber. No! why, what care I for that? I can have wenches enough in Parma for half-a-crown a-piece: — cannot I, Poggio?

Pog. I'll warrant you, sir.

Don. Signior Florio,
I thank you for your free recourse you gave
For my admittance: and to you, fair maid,
That jewel I will give you 'gainst your marriage.—
Come, will you go, sir?

Ber. Ay, marry, will I.—Mistress, farewell, mistress; I'll come again to-morrow; farewell, mistress.

Exeunt DONADO, BERGETTO, *and* POGGIO

Enter GIOVANNI

Flo. Son, where have you been? what, alone, alone still?
I would not have it so; you must forsake
This over-bookish humour. Well, your sister
Hath shook the fool off.

Gio. 'Twas no match for her.

Flo. 'Twas not indeed; I meant it nothing less;
Soranzo is the man I only like:—
Look on him, Annabella.—Come, 'tis supper-time,
And it grows late. *Exit*

Gio. Whose jewel's that?

Ann. Some sweetheart's.

Gio. So I think.

Ann. A lusty youth,
Signior Donado, gave it me to wear
Against my marriage.

Gio. But you shall not wear it:
Send it him back again.

Ann. What, you are jealous?

Gio. That you shall know anon, at better leisure.
Welcome sweet night! the evening crowns the day.

Exeunt

Act The Third

[SCENE I]

[*A Room in Donado's House*]

Enter Bergetto *and* Poggio

Ber. Does my uncle think to make me a baby still? No, Poggio; he shall know I have a sconce [1] now.

Pog. Ay, let him not bob you off like an ape with an apple.

Ber. 'Sfoot, I will have the wench, if he were ten uncles, in despite of his nose, Poggio.

Pog. Hold him to the grindstone, and give not a jot of ground: she hath in a manner promised you already.

Ber. True, Poggio; and her uncle, the doctor, swore I should marry her.

Pog. He swore; I remember.

Ber. And I will have her, that's more: didst see the cod-piece-point she gave me and the box of marmalade?

Pog. Very well; and kissed you, that my chops watered at the sight on't. There's no way but to clap-up a marriage in hugger-mugger.

Ber. I will do't; for I tell thee, Poggio, I begin to grow valiant methinks, and my courage begins to rise.

Pog. Should you be afraid of your uncle?

[1] Head.

Ber. Hang him, old doting rascal! no: I say I will have her.

Pog. Lose no time, then.

Ber. I will beget a race of wise men and constables that shall cart whores at their own charges; and break the duke's peace ere I have done myself. Come away. *Exeunt*

[SCENE II]

[*A Room in Florio's House*]

Enter FLORIO, GIOVANNI, SORANZO, ANNABELLA, PUTANA, *and* VASQUES

Flo. My Lord Soranza, though I must confess
The proffers that are made me have been great
In marriage of my daughter, yet the hope
Of your still rising honours have prevailed
Above all other jointures: here she is;
She knows my mind; speak for yourself to her,—
And hear, you, daughter, see you use him nobly:
For any private speech I'll give you time.—
Come, son, and you the rest; let them alone;
Agree they as they may.

Sor. I thank you, sir.

Gio. [*Aside to* ANNABELLA] Sister, be not all woman; think on me.

Sor. Vasques,—

Vas. My lord?

Sor. Attend me without.

Exeunt all but SORANZO *and* ANNABELLA

Ann. Sir, what's your will with me?

Sor. Do you not know
What I should tell you?

Ann. Yes; you'll say you love me.

Sor. And I will swear it too; will you believe it?

Ann. 'Tis no point of faith.

Enter GIOVANNI *in the Gallery above*

Sor. Have you not will to love?
Ann. Not you.
Sor. Whom then?
Ann. That's as the fates infer.
Gio. [*Aside*] Of those I'm regent now.
Sor. What mean you, sweet?
Ann. To live and die a maid.
Sor. O, that's unfit.
Gio. [*Aside*] Here's one can say that's but a woman's note.
Sor. Did you but see my heart, then would you swear—
Ann. That you were dead.
Gio. [*Aside*] That's true, or somewhat near it.
Sor. See you these true love's tears?
Ann. No.
Gio. [*Aside*] Now she winks.
Sor. They plead to you for grace.
Ann. Yet nothing speak.
Sor. O, grant my suit!
Ann. What is it?
Sor. To let me live—
Ann. Take it.
Sor. Still yours.
Ann. That is not mine to give.
Gio. [*Aside*] One such another word would kill his hopes.
Sor. Mistress, to leave those fruitless strifes of wit,
Know I have loved you long and loved you truly:
Not hope of what you have, but what you are,
Hath drawn me on; then let me not in vain
Still feel the rigour of your chaste disdain:
I'm sick, and sick to the heart.
Ann. Help, aqua-vitæ!
Sor. What mean you?
Ann. Why, I thought you had been sick.

Sor. Do you mock my love?

Gio. [*Aside*] There, sir, she was too nimble.

Sor. [*Aside*] 'Tis plain she laughs at me.—These scornful taunts
Neither become your modesty or years.

Ann. You are no looking-glass: or if you were,
I'd dress my language by you.

Gio. [*Aside*] I'm confirmed.

Ann. To put you out of doubt, my lord, methinks
Your common sense should make you understand
That if I loved you, or desired your love,
Some way I should have given you better taste:
But since you are a nobleman, and one
I would not wish should spend his youth in hopes,
Let me advise you to forbear your suit,
And think I wish you well, I tell you this.

Sor. Is't you speak this?

Ann. Yes, I myself; yet know,—
Thus far I give you comfort,—if mine eyes
Could have picked out a man amongst all those
That sued to me to make a husband of,
You should have been that man: let this suffice;
Be noble in your secrecy and wise.

Gio. [*Aside*] Why, now I see she loves me.

Ann. One word more.
As ever virtue lived within your mind,
As ever noble courses were your guide,
As ever you would have me know you loved me,
Let not my father know hereof by you:
If I hereafter find that I must marry,
It shall be you or none.

Sor. I take that promise.

Ann. O, O my head!

Sor. What's the matter? not well?

Ann. O, I begin to sicken!

Gio. Heaven forbid!

Aside, and exit from above

Sor. Help, help, within there, ho!

Re-enter FLORIO, GIOVANNI, *and* PUTANA

Look to your daughter, Signior Florio.

Flo. Hold her up, she swoons.

Gio. Sister, how d'ye?

Ann. Sick,—brother, are you there?

Flo. Convey her to her bed instantly, whilst I send for a physician: quickly, I say.

Put. Alas, poor child! *Exeunt all but* SORANZO

Re-enter VASQUES

Vas. My lord,—

Sor. O, Vasques, now I doubly am undone
Both in my present and my future hopes!
She plainly told me that she could not love,
And thereupon soon sickened; and I fear
Her life's in danger.

Vas. [*Aside*] By'r lady, sir, and so is yours, if you knew all.—'Las, sir, I am sorry for that: may be 'tis but the maid's sickness, an over-flux of youth; and then, sir, there is no such present remedy as present marriage. But hath she given you an absolute denial?

Sor. She hath, and she hath not; I'm full of grief:
But what she said I'll tell thee as we go. *Exeunt*

[SCENE III]

[*Another Room in the same*]

Enter GIOVANNI *and* PUTANA

Put. O, sir, we are all undone, quite undone, utterly undone, and shamed for ever! your sister, O, your sister!

Gio. What of her? for Heaven's sake, speak; how does she?

Put. O, that ever I was born to see this day!

Gio. She is not dead, ha? is she?

Put. Dead! no, she is quick; 'tis worse, she is with child. You know what you have done; Heaven forgive ye! 'tis too late to repent now, Heaven help us!

Gio. With child? how dost thou know't?

Put. How do I know't! am I at these years ignorant what the meanings of qualms and water-pangs be? of changing of colours, queasiness of stomachs, pukings, and another thing that I could name? Do not, for her and your credit's sake, spend the time in asking how, and which way, 'tis so: she is quick, upon my word: if you let a physician see her water, you're undone.

Gio. But in what case is she?

Put. Prettily amended: 'twas but a fit, which I soon espied, and she must look for often henceforward.

Gio. Commend me to her, bid her take no care; [1]
Let not the doctor visit her, I charge you;
Make some excuse, till I return.—O, me!
I have a world of business in my head.—
Do not discomfort her.—
How do these news perplex me!—If my father
Come to her, tell him she's recovered well;
Say 'twas but some ill diet—d'ye hear, woman?
Look you to't.

Put. I will, sir. *Exeunt*

[SCENE IV]

[*Another Room in the same*]

Enter FLORIO *and* RICHARDETTO

Flo. And how d'ye find her, sir?

Rich. Indifferent well;
I see no danger, scarce perceive she's sick,

[1] Not be too anxious.

But that she told me she had lately eaten
Melons, and, as she thought, those disagreed
With her young stomach.

Flo. Did you give her aught?

Rich. An easy surfeit-water, nothing else.
You need not doubt her health: I rather think
Her sickness is a fulness of the blood,—
You understand me?

Flo. I do; you counsel well;
And once, within these few days, will so order 't
She shall be married ere she know the time.

Rich. Yet let not haste, sir, make unworthy choice;
That were dishonour.

Flo. Master Doctor, no;
I will not do so neither: in plain words,
My Lord Soranzo is the man I mean.

Rich. A noble and a virtuous gentleman.

Flo. As any is in Parma. Not far hence
Dwells Father Bonaventura, a grave friar,
Once tutor to my son: now at his cell
I'll have 'em married.

Rich. You have plotted wisely.

Flo. I'll send one straight to speak with him to-night.

Rich. Soranzo's wise; he will delay no time.

Flo. It shall be so.

Enter Friar *and* Giovanni

Friar. Good peace be here and love!

Flo. Welcome, religious friar; you are one
That still bring blessing to the place you come to.

Gio. Sir, with what speed I could, I did my best
To draw this holy man from forth his cell
To visit my sick sister; that with words
Of ghostly comfort, in this time of need,
He might absolve her, whether she live or die.

Flo. 'Twas well done, Giovanni; thou herein

Hast showed a Christian's care, a brother's love.
Come, father, I'll conduct you to her chamber,
And one thing would entreat you.

Friar. Say on, sir.

Flo. I have a father's dear impression
And wish, before I fall into my grave,
That I might see her married, as 'tis fit:
A word from you, grave man, will win her more
Than all our best persuasions.

Friar. Gentle sir,
All this I'll say, that Heaven may prosper her.

Exeunt

[SCENE V]

[*A Room in Richardetto's House*]

Enter GRIMALDI

Grim. Now if the doctor keep his word, Soranzo,
Twenty to one you miss your bride. I know
'Tis an unnoble act, and not becomes
A soldier's valour; but in terms of love,
Where merit cannot sway, policy must:
I am resolved, if this physician
Play not on both hands, then Soranzo falls.

Enter RICHARDETTO

Rich. You're come as I could wish; this very night
Soranzo, 'tis ordained, must be affied [1]
To Annabella, and, for aught I know,
Married.

Grim. How!

Rich. Yet your patience:—
The place, 'tis Friar Bonaventura's cell.
Now I would wish you to bestow this night
In watching thereabouts; 'tis but a night:

[1] Contracted.

If you miss now, to-morrow I'll know all.

Grim. Have you the poison?

Rich. Here 'tis, in this box:
Doubt nothing, this will do't; in any case,
As you respect your life, be quick and sure.

Grim. I'll speed him.

Rich. Do.—Away; for 'tis not safe
You should be seen much here. Ever my love!

Grim. And mine to you. *Exit*

Rich. So! if this hit, I'll laugh and hug revenge;
And they that now dream of a wedding-feast
May chance to mourn the lusty bridegroom's ruin.
But to my other business.—Niece Philotis!

Enter PHILOTIS

Phi. Uncle?

Rich. My lovely niece!
You have bethought ye?

Phi. Yes,—and, as you counselled,
Fashioned my heart to love him: but he swears
He will to-night be married: for he fears
His uncle else, if he should know the drift,
Will hinder all, and call his coz to shrift.

Rich. To-night! why, best of all: but, let me see—
Ay—ha! yes, so it shall be—in disguise
We'll early to the friar's; I have thought on't.

Phi. Uncle, he comes.

Enter BERGETTO *and* POGGIO

Rich. Welcome, my worthy coz.

Ber. Lass, pretty lass, come buss, lass!—A-ha, Poggio!
Kisses her

Rich. [*Aside*] There's hope of this yet.—
You shall have time enough; withdraw a little;
We must confer at large.

Ber. Have you not sweetmeats or dainty devices for me?

Phi. You shall have enough, sweetheart.

Ber. Sweetheart! mark that, Poggio.—By my troth, I cannot choose but kiss thee once more for that word, "sweetheart."—Poggio, I have a monstrous swelling about my stomach, whatsoever the matter be.

Pog. You shall have physic for't, sir.

Rich. Time runs apace.

Ber. Time's a blockhead.

Rich. Be ruled: when we have done what's fit to do,
Then you may kiss your fill, and bed her too. *Exeunt*

[SCENE VI]

[*Annabella's Chamber*]

A table with wax lights; Annabella *at confession before the* Friar; *she weeps and wrings her hands*

Friar. I'm glad to see this penance; for, believe me,
You have unripped a soul so foul and guilty,
As, I must tell you true, I marvel how
The earth hath borne you up: but weep, weep on,
These tears may do you good; weep faster yet,
Whiles I do read a lecture.

Ann. Wretched creature!

Friar. Ay, you are wretched, miserably wretched,
Almost condemned alive. There is a place,—
List, daughter!—in a black and hollow vault,
Where day is never seen; there shines no sun,
But flaming horror of consuming fires,
A lightless sulphur, choked with smoky fogs
Of an infected darkness: in this place
Dwell many thousand thousand sundry sorts
Of never-dying deaths: there damnèd souls
Roar without pity; there are gluttons fed
With toads and adders; there is burning oil

Poured down the drunkard's throat; the usurer
Is forced to sup whole draughts of molten gold;
There is the murderer for ever stabbed,
Yet can he never die; there lies the wanton
On racks of burning steel, whiles in his soul
He feels the torment of his raging lust.

Ann. Mercy! O, mercy!

Friar. There stand these wretched things
Who have dreamed out whole years in lawless sheets
And secret incests, cursing one another.
Then you will wish each kiss your brother gave
Had been a dagger's point; then you shall hear
How he will cry, "O, would my wicked sister
Had first been damned, when she did yield to lust!"—
But soft, methinks I see repentance work
New motions in your heart: say, how is't with you?

Ann. Is there no way left to redeem my miseries?

Friar. There is, despair not; Heaven is merciful,
And offers grace even now. 'Tis thus agreed:
First, for your honour's safety, that you marry
My Lord Soranzo; next, to save your soul,
Leave off this life, and henceforth live to him.

Ann. Ay me!

Friar. Sigh not; I know the baits of sin
Are hard to leave; O, 'tis a death to do't:
Remember what must come. Are you content?

Ann. I am.

Friar. I like it well; we'll take the time.—
Who's near us there?

Enter FLORIO *and* GIOVANNI

Flo. Did you call, father?

Friar. Is Lord Soranzo come?

Flo. He stays below.

Friar. Have you acquainted him at full?

Flo. I have,

And he is overjoyed.

Friar. And so are we.

Bid him come near.

Gio. [*Aside*] My sister weeping! Ha!

I fear this friar's falsehood.—I will call him. *Exit*

Flo. Daughter, are you resolved?

Ann. Father, I am.

Re-enter GIOVANNI *with* SORANZO *and* VASQUES

Flo. My Lord Soranzo, here

Give me your hand; for that I give you this.

Joins their hands

Sor. Lady, say you so too?

Ann. I do, and vow

To live with you and yours.

Friar. Timely resolved:

My blessing rest on both! More to be done,
You may perform it on the morning sun. *Exeunt*

[SCENE VII]

[*A Street before the Monastery*]

Enter GRIMALDI *with his rapier drawn and a dark lantern*

Grim. 'Tis early night as yet, and yet too soon

To finish such a work; here I will lie

To listen who comes next. *He lies down*

Enter BERGETTO *and* PHILOTIS *disguised, followed at a short distance by* RICHARDETTO *and* POGGIO

Ber. We are almost at the place, I hope, sweetheart.

Grim. [*Aside*] I hear them near, and heard one say "sweetheart."

'Tis he; now guide my hand, some angry justice,

Home to his bosom!—Now have at you, sir!

Stabs BERGETTO *and exit*

Ber. O, help, help! here's a stitch fallen in my guts: O for a flesh-tailor quickly!—Poggio!

Phi. What ails my love?

Ber. I am sure I cannot piss forward and backward, and yet I am wet before and behind.—Lights! lights! ho, lights!

Phi. Alas, some villain here has slain my love!

Rich. O, Heaven forbid it!—Raise up the next neighbours
Instantly, Poggio, and bring lights. *Exit* POGGIO
How is't, Bergetto? slain! It cannot be;
Are you sure you're hurt?

Ber. O, my belly seethes likes a porridge-pot! Some cold water, I shall boil over else; my whole body is in a sweat, that you may wring my shirt; feel here.—Why, Poggio!

Re-enter POGGIO *with* Officers *and lights*

Pog. Here. Alas, how do you?

Rich. Give me a light.—What's here? all blood!—O, sirs,
Signior Donado's nephew now is slain.
Follow the murderer with all the haste
Up to the city, he cannot be far hence:
Follow, I beseech you.

Officers. Follow, follow, follow! *Exeunt*

Rich. Tear off thy linen, coz, to stop his wounds.—Be of good comfort, man.

Ber. Is all this mine own blood? nay, then, good night with me.—Poggio, commend me to my uncle, dost hear? bid him, for my sake, make much of this wench.—O, I am going the wrong way sure, my belly aches so.—O, farewell, Poggio!—O, O! *Dies*

Phi. O, he is dead!

Pog. How! dead!

Rich. He's dead indeed:
'Tis now too late to weep: let's have him home,
And with what speed we may find out the murderer.

Pog. O, my master! my master! my master! *Exeunt*

[SCENE VIII]

[*A Room in Hippolita's House*]

Enter VASQUES *and* HIPPOLITA

Hip. Betrothed?
Vas. I saw it.
Hip. And when's the marriage-day?
Vas. Some two days hence.
Hip. Two days! why, man, I would but wish two hours
To send him to his last and lasting sleep;
And, Vasques, thou shalt see I'll do it bravely.

Vas. I do not doubt your wisdom, nor, I trust, you my secrecy; I am infinitely yours.

Hip. I will be thine in spite of my disgrace.—
So soon? O wicked man, I durst be sworn
He'd laugh to see me weep.

Vas. And that's a villanous fault in him.

Hip. No, let him laugh; I'm armed in my resolves: Be thou still true.

Vas. I should get little by treachery against so hopeful a preferment as I am like to climb to.

Hip. Even to—my bosom, Vasques. Let my youth
Revel in these new pleasures: if we thrive,
He now hath but a pair of days to live. *Exeunt*

[SCENE IX]

[*The Street before the Cardinal's Gates*]

Enter FLORIO, DONADO, RICHARDETTO, POGGIO, *and* Officers

Flo. 'Tis bootless now to show yourself a child,
Signior Donado; what is done, is done:
Spend not the time in tears, but seek for justice.

Rich. I must confess somewhat I was in fault
That had not first acquainted you what love
Passed 'twixt him and my niece; but, as I live,
His fortune grieves me as it were mine own.

Don. Alas, poor creature! he meant no man harm,
That I am sure of.

Flo. I believe that too.
But stay, my masters: are you sure you saw
The murderer pass here?

1st Off. An it please you, sir, we are sure we saw a ruffian, with a naked weapon in his hand all bloody, get into my lord cardinal's grace's gate; that we are sure of; but for fear of his grace—bless us!—we durst go no farther.

Don. Know you what manner of man he was?

1st Off. Yes, sure, I know the man; they say he is a soldier; he that loved your daughter, sir, an't please ye; 'twas he for certain.

Flo. Grimaldi, on my life!

1st Off. Ay, ay, the same.

Rich. The cardinal is noble; he no doubt
Will give true justice.

Don. Knock some one at the gate.

Pog. I'll knock, sir. *Knocks*

Serv. [*Within*] What would ye?

Flo. We require speech with the lord cardinal
About some present business: pray inform
His grace that we are here.

Enter the Cardinal, *followed by* GRIMALDI

Car. Why, how now, friends! what saucy mates are you
That know nor duty nor civility?
Are we a person fit to be your host;
Or is our house become your common inn,
To beat our doors at pleasure? What such haste
Is yours, as that it cannot wait fit times?
Are you the masters of this commonwealth,

And know no more discretion? O, your news
Is here before you; you have lost a nephew,
Donado, last night by Grimaldi slain:
Is that your business? well, sir, we have knowledge on't;
Let that suffice.

Grim. In presence of your grace,
In thought I never meant Bergetto harm:
But, Florio, you can tell with how much scorn
Soranzo, backed with his confederates,
Hath often wronged me; I to be revenged, —
For that I could not win him else to fight,—
Had thought by way of ambush to have killed him
But was unluckily therein mistook;
Else he had felt what late Bergetto did:
And though my fault to him were merely chance,
Yet humbly I submit me to your grace, *Kneeling*
To do with me as you please.

Car. Rise up, Grimaldi.— *He rises*
You citizens of Parma, if you seek
For justice, know, as nuncio from the pope,
For this offence I here receive Grimaldi
Into his holiness' protection:
He is no common man, but nobly born,
Of princes' blood, though you, Sir Florio,
Thought him too mean a husband for your daughter.
If more you seek for, you must go to Rome,
For he shall thither: learn more wit, for shame.—
Bury your dead.—Away, Grimaldi; leave 'em!

Exeunt Cardinal *and* GRIMALDI

Don. Is this a churchman's voice? dwells justice here?

Flo. Justice is fled to Heaven, and comes no nearer.
Soranzo!—was't for him? O, impudence!
Had he the face to speak it, and not blush?

Come, come, Donado, there's no help in this,
When cardinals think murder's not amiss.
Great men may do their wills, we must obey;

But Heaven will judge them for't another day.

Exeunt

Act The Fourth

[SCENE I]

[*A Room in Florio's House*]

A banquet set out; hautboys. Enter the Friar, Giovanni, Annabella, Philotis, Soranzo, Donado, Florio, Richardetto, Putana, *and* Vasques

Friar. These holy rites performed, now take your times
To spend the remnant of the day in feast:
Such fit repasts are pleasing to the saints,
Who are your guests, though not with mortal eyes
To be beheld.—Long prosper in this day,
You happy couple, to each other's joy!

Sor. Father, your prayer is heard; the hand of goodness
Hath been a shield for me against my death:
And, more to bless me, hath enriched my life
With this most precious jewel; such a prize
As earth hath not another like to this. —
Cheer up, my love:—and, gentlemen my friends,
Rejoice with me in mirth: this day we'll crown
With lusty cups to Annabella's health.

Gio. [*Aside*] O torture! were the marriage yet undone,
Ere I'd endure this sight, to see my love
Clipt [1] by another, I would dare confusion,
And stand the horror of ten thousand deaths.

Vas. Are you not well, sir?

Gio. Prithee, fellow, wait;
I need not thy officious diligence.

Flo. Signior Donado, come, you must forget
Your late mishaps, and drown your cares in wine.

[1] Embraced.

Sor. Vasques!

Vas. My lord?

Sor. Reach me that weighty bowl.
Here, brother Giovanni, here's to you;
Your turn come next, though now a bachelor;
Here's to your sister's happiness and mine!

Drinks and offers him the bowl

Gio. I cannot drink.

Sor. What!

Gio. 'Twill indeed offend me.

Ann. Pray, do not urge him, if he be not willing.

Hautboys

Flo. How now! what noise[1] is this?

Vas. O, sir, I had forgot to tell you; certain young maidens of Parma, in honour to Madam Annabella's marriage, have sent their loves to her in a Masque, for which they humbly crave your patience and silence.

Sor. We are much bound to them; so much the more
As it comes unexpected: guide them in.

Enter HIPPOLITA, *followed by* Ladies *in white robes with garlands of willows, all masked. Music and a dance*

Thanks, lovely virgins! now might we but know
To whom we've been beholding for this love,
We shall acknowledge it.

Hip. Yes, you shall know. *Unmasks*
What think you now?

All. Hippolita!

Hip. 'Tis she;
Be not amazed; nor blush, young lovely bride;
I come not to defraud you of your man:
'Tis now no time to reckon-up the talk
What Parma long hath rumoured of us both:
Let rash report run on; the breath that vents it

[1] Music.

Will, like a bubble, break itself at last.
But now to you, sweet creature; lend's your hand:—
Perhaps it hath been said that I would claim
Some interest in Soranzo, now your lord;
What I have right to do, his soul knows best:
But in my duty to your noble worth,
Sweet Annabella, and my care of you,—
Here, take, Soranzo, take this hand from me;
I'll once more join what by the holy church
Is finished and allowed.—Have I done well?

Sor. You have too much engaged us.

Hip. One thing more.
That you may know my single[1] charity,
Freely I here remit all interest
I e'er could claim, and give you back your vows;
And to confirm't,—reach me a cup of wine,—

VASQUES *gives her a poisoned cup*

My Lord Soranzo, in this draught I drink
Long rest t'ye! [*She drinks*]—[*Aside to* VASQUES] Look to it, Vasques.

Vas. [*Aside to* HIPPOLITA] Fear nothing.

Sor. Hippolita, I thank you; and will pledge
This happy union as another life.—
Wine, there!

Vas. You shall have none; neither shall you pledge her.

Hip. How!

Vas. Know now, Mistress She-devil, your own mischievous treachery hath killed you; I must not marry you.

Hip. Villain!

All. What's the matter?

Vas. Foolish woman, thou art now like a firebrand that hath kindled others and burnt thyself:—*troppo sperar, inganna,*[2]—thy vain hope hath deceived thee; thou art but dead; if thou hast any grace, pray.

[1] Single-minded.
[2] Too much hope brings disappointment.

Hip. Monster!

Vas. Die in charity, for shame.—This thing of malice, this woman, had privately corrupted me with promise of marriage, under this politic reconciliation, to poison my lord, whiles she might laugh at his confusion on his marriage-day. I promised her fair; but I knew what my reward should have been, and would willingly have spared her life, but that I was acquainted with the danger of her disposition; and now have fitted her a just payment in her own coin: there she is, she hath yet [1]——and end thy days in peace, vile woman; as for life, there's no hope; think not on't.

All. Wonderful justice!

Rich. Heaven, thou art righteous.

Hip. O, 'tis true;
I feel my minute coming. Had that slave
Kept promise,—O, my torment!—thou this hour
Hadst died, Soranzo;—heat above hell-fire!—
Yet, ere I pass away,—cruel, cruel flames!—
Take here my curse amongst you: may thy bed
Of marriage be a rack unto thy heart,
Burn blood, and boil in vengeance;—O, my heart,
My flame's intolerable!—mayst thou live
To father bastards; may her womb bring forth
Monsters,—and die together in your sins,
Hated, scorned, and unpitied!—O, O! *Dies*

Flo. Was e'er so vile a creature!

Rich. Here're the end
Of lust and pride.

Ann. It is a fearful sight.

Sor. Vasques, I know thee now a trusty servant,
And never will forget thee.—Come, my love,
We'll home, and thank the heavens for this escape,—
Father and friends, we must break up this mirth;
It is too sad a feast.

[1] The old copy has a considerable double break here, probably from some defect in the MS.

Don. Bear hence the body.

Friar. [*Aside to* GIOVANNI] Here's an ominous change!
Mark this, my Giovanni, and take heed!—
I fear the event: that marriage seldom's good
Where the bride-banquet so begins in blood.

Exeunt

[SCENE II]

[*A Room in Richardetto's House*]

Enter RICHARDETTO *and* PHILOTIS

Rich. My wretched wife, more wretched in her shame
Than in her wrongs to me, hath paid too soon
The forfeit of her modesty and life.
And I am sure, my niece, though vengeance hover,
Keeping aloof yet from Soranzo's fall,
Yet he will fall, and sink with his own weight.
I need not now—my heart persuades me so—
To further his confusion; there is One
Above begins to work: for, as I hear,
Debates already 'twixt his wife and him
Thicken and run to head; she, as 'tis said,
Slightens his love, and he abandons hers:
Much talk I hear. Since things go thus, my niece,
In tender love and pity of your youth,
My counsel is, that you should free your years
From hazard of these woes by flying hence
To fair Cremona, there to vow your soul
In holiness, a holy votaress:
Leave me to see the end of these extremes.
All human worldly courses are uneven;
No life is blessèd but the way to Heaven.

Phi. Uncle, shall I resolve to be a nun?

Rich. Ay, gentle niece; and in your hourly prayers
Remember me, your poor unhappy uncle.
Hie to Cremona now, as fortune leads,

Your home your cloister, your best friends your beads:
Your chaste and single life shall crown your birth:
Who dies a virgin lives a saint on earth.

Phi. Then farewell, world, and worldly thoughts, adieu!
Welcome, chaste vows; myself I yield to you. *Exeunt*

[SCENE III]

[*A Chamber in Soranzo's House*]

Enter SORANZO *unbraced, and dragging in* ANNABELLA

Sor. Come, strumpet, famous whore! were every drop
Of blood that runs in thy adulterous veins
A life, this sword—dost see't?—should in one blow
Confound them all. Harlot, rare, notable harlot,
That with thy brazen face maintain'st thy sin,
Was there no man in Parma to be bawd
To your loose cunning whoredom else but I?
Must your hot itch and plurisy of lust,
The heyday of your luxury,[1] be fed
Up to a surfeit, and could none but I
Be picked out to be cloak to your close tricks,
Your belly sports? Now I must be the dad
To all that gallimaufry that is stuffed
In thy corrupted bastard-bearing womb!
Say, must I?

Ann. Beastly man! why, 'tis thy fate.
I sued not to thee; for, but that I thought
Your over-loving lordship would have run
Mad on denial, had ye lent me time,
I would have told ye in what case I was:
But you would needs be doing.

Sor. Whores of whores!
Darest thou tell me this?

Ann. O, yes; why not?

[1] Luxury was commonly used in the sense of lust.

You were deceived in me; 'twas not for love
I chose you, but for honour: yet know this,
Would you be patient yet, and hide your shame,
I'd see whether I could love you.

Sor. Excellent quean!
Why, art thou not with child?

Ann. What needs all this,
When 'tis superfluous? I confess I am.

Sor. Tell me by whom.

Ann. Soft! 'twas not in my bargain.
Yet somewhat, sir, to stay your longing stomach,
I am content t' acquaint you with; the man,
The more than man, that got this sprightly boy,—
For 'tis a boy, and therefore glory, sir,
Your heir shall be a son—

Sor. Damnable monster!

Ann. Nay, an you will not hear, I'll speak no more.

Sor. Yes, speak, and speak thy last.

Ann. A match! a match!
This noble creature was in every part
So angel-like, so glorious, that a woman
Who had not been but human, as was I,
Would have kneeled to him, and have begged for love.—
You! why, you are not worthy once to name
His name without true worship, or, indeed,
Unless you kneeled, to hear another name him.

Sor. What was he called?

Ann. We are not come to that;
Let it suffice that you shall have the glory
To father what so brave a father got.
In brief, had not this chance fall'n out as't doth,
I never had been troubled with a thought
That you had been a creature:—but for marriage,
I scarce dream yet of that.

Sor. Tell me his name.

Ann. Alas, alas, there's all! will you believe?

Sor. What?

Ann. You shall never know,

Sor. How!

Ann. Never: if
You do, let me cursed!

Sor. Not know it, strumpet! I'll rip up thy heart,
And find it there.

Ann. Do, do.

Sor. And with my teeth
Tear the prodigious lecher joint by joint.

Ann. Ha, ha, ha! the man's merry.

Sor. Dost thou laugh?
Come, whore, tell me your lover, or, by truth,
I'll hew thy flesh to shreds; who is't?

Ann. [*Sings*] *Che morte più dolce che morire per amore?*[1]

Sor. Thus will I pull thy hair, and thus I'll drag
Thy lust-be-lepered body through the dust.

Hales her up and down

Yet tell his name.

Ann. [*Sings*] *Morendo in grazia dee morire senza dolore.*[2]

Sor. Dost thou triumph? The treasures of the earth
Shall not redeem thee; were there kneeling kings
Did beg thy life, or angels did come down
To plead in tears, yet should not all prevail
Against my rage: dost thou not tremble yet?

Ann. At what? to die! no, be a gallant hangman;[3]
I dare thee to the worst: strike, and strike home;
I leave revenge behind, and thou shalt feel't.

Sor. Yet tell me ere thou diest, and tell me truly,
Knows thy old father this?

Ann. No, by my life.

Sor. Wilt thou confess, and I will spare thy life?

Ann. My life! I will not buy my life so dear.

[1] What death sweeter than to die for love?
[2] To die in grace is to die without sorrow.
[3] Executioner.

Sor. I will not slack my vengeance. *Draws his sword*

Enter VASQUES

Vas. What d'ye mean, sir?

Sor. Forbear, Vasques; such a damnèd whore
Deserves no pity.

Vas. Now the gods forfend:
And would you be her executioner, and kill her in your rage too? O, 'twere most unmanlike. She is your wife: what faults have been done by her before she married you were not against you: alas, poor lady, what hath she committed, which any lady in Italy, in the like case, would not? Sir, you must be ruled by your reason, and not by your fury; that were unhuman and beastly.

Sor. She shall not live.

Vas. Come, she must. You would have her confess the author of her present misfortunes, I warrant ye; 'tis an unconscionable demand, and she should lose the estimation that I, for my part, hold of her worth, if she had done it: why, sir, you ought not, of all men living, to know it. Good sir, be reconciled: alas, good gentlewoman!

Ann. Pish, do not beg for me; I prize my life
As nothing; if the man will needs be mad,
Why, let him take it.

Sor. Vasques, hear'st thou this?

Vas. Yes, and commend her for it; in this she shows the nobleness of a gallant spirit, and beshrew my heart, but it becomes her rarely.—[*Aside to* SORANZO] Sir, in any case, smother your revenge; leave the scenting-out your wrongs to me: be ruled, as you respect your honour, or you mar all.—[*Aloud*] Sir, if ever my service were of any credit with you, be not so violent in your distractions: you are married now; what a triumph might the report of this give to other neglected suitors! 'Tis as manlike to bear extremities as godlike to forgive.

Sor. O, Vasques, Vasques, in this piece of flesh,

This faithless face of hers, had I laid up
The treasure of my heart!—Hadst thou been virtuous,
Fair, wicked woman, not the matchless joys
Of life itself had made we wish to live
With any saint but thee: deceitful creature,
How hast thou mocked my hopes, and in the shame
Of thy lewd womb even buried me alive!
I did too dearly love thee.

Vas. [*Aside to* SORANZO] This is well; follow this temper with some passion: be brief and moving; 'tis for the purpose.

Sor. Be witness to my words thy soul and thoughts;
And tell me, didst not think that in my heart
I did too superstitiously adore thee?

Ann. I must confess I know you loved me well.

Sor. And wouldst thou use me thus! O Annabella,
Be thou assured, whoe'er the villain was
That thus hath tempted thee to this disgrace,
Well he might lust, but never loved like me:
He doted on the picture that hung out
Upon thy cheeks to please his humorous eye;
Not on the part I loved, which was thy heart,
And, as I thought, thy virtues.

Ann. O, my lord!
These words wound deeper than your sword could do.

Vas. Let me not ever take comfort, but I begin to weep myself, so much I pity him: why, madam, I knew, when his rage was over-past, what it would come to.

Sor. Forgive me, Annabella. Though thy youth
Hath tempted thee above thy strength to folly,
Yet will not I forget what I should be,
And what I am—a husband; in that name
Is hid divinity: if I do find
That thou wilt yet be true, here I remit
All former faults, and take thee to my bosom.

Vas. By my troth, and that's a point of noble charity.

Ann. Sir, on my knees,—

Sor. Rise up, you shall not kneel.
Get you to your chamber; see you make no show
Of alteration; I'll be with you straight:
My reason tells me now that " 'tis as common
To err in frailty as to be a woman."
Go to your chamber. *Exit* ANNABELLA

Vas. So! this was somewhat to the matter: what do you think of your heaven of happiness now, sir?

Sor. I carry hell about me; all my blood
Is fired in swift revenge.

Vas. That may be; but know you how, or on whom? Alas, to marry a great woman, being made great in the stock to your hand, is a usual sport in these days; but to know what ferret it was that hunted your coney-berry,—there's the cunning.

Sor. I'll make her tell herself, or—

Vas. Or what? you must not do so; let me yet persuade your sufferance a little while: go to her, use her mildly; win her, if it be possible, to a voluntary, to a weeping tune: for the rest, if all hit, I will not miss my mark. Pray, sir, go in: the next news I tell you shall be wonders.

Sor. Delay in vengeance gives a heavier blow. *Exit*

Vas. Ah, sirrah, here's work for the nonce! I had a suspicion of a bad matter in my head a pretty whiles ago; but after my madam's scurvy looks here at home, her waspish perverseness and loud fault-finding, then I remembered the proverb, that "where hens crow, and cocks hold their peace, there are sorry houses." 'Sfoot, if the lower parts of a she-tailor's cunning can cover such a swelling in the stomach, I'll never blame a false stitch in a shoe whiles I live again. Up, and up so quick? and so quickly too? 'twere a fine policy to learn by whom: this must be known; and I have thought on't:—

Enter PUTANA *in tears*

Here's the way, or none.—What, crying, old mistress! alas,

alas, I cannot blame ye; we have a lord, Heaven help us, is so mad as the devil himself, the more shame for him.

Put. O, Vasques, that ever I was born to see this day! Doth he use thee so too sometimes, Vasques?

Vas. Me? why he makes a dog of me: but if some were of my mind, I know what we would do. As sure as I am an honest man, he will go near to kill my lady with unkindness: say she be with child, is that such a matter for a young woman of her years to be blamed for?

Put. Alas, good heart, it is against her will full sore.

Vas. I durst be sworn all his madness is for that she will not confess whose 'tis, which he will know; and when he doth know it, I am so well acquainted with his humour, that he will forget all straight. Well, I could wish she would in plain terms tell all, for that's the way, indeed.

Put. Do you think so?

Vas. Foh, I know't; provided that he did not win her to 't by force. He was once in a mind that you could tell, and meant to have wrung it out of you; but I somewhat pacified him for that: yet, sure, you know a great deal.

Put. Heaven forgive us all! I know a little, Vasques.

Vas. Why should you not? who else should? Upon my conscience, she loves you dearly; and you would not betray her to any affliction for the world.

Put. Not for all the world, by my faith and troth, Vasques.

Vas. 'Twas pity of your life if you should; but in this you should both relieve her present discomforts, pacify my lord, and gain yourself everlasting love and preferment.

Put. Dost think so, Vasques?

Vas. Nay, I know't; sure 'twas some near and entire friend.

Put. 'Twas a dear friend indeed; but—

Vas. But what? fear not to name him; my life between you and danger: 'faith, I think 'twas no base fellow.

Put. Thou wilt stand between me and harm?

Vas. 'Ud's pity, what else? you shall be rewarded too, trust me.

Put. 'Twas even no worse than her own brother.

Vas. Her brother Giovanni, I warrant ye!

Put. Even he, Vasques; as brave a gentleman as ever kissed fair lady. O, they love most perpetually.

Vas. A brave gentleman indeed! why, therein I commend her choice.—[*Aside*] Better and better.—You are sure 'twas he?

Put. Sure; and you shall see he will not be long from her too.

Vas. He were to blame if he would: but may I believe thee?

Put. Believe me! why, dost think I am a Turk or a Jew? No, Vasques, I have known their dealings too long to belie them now.

Vas. Where are you there? within, sirs!

Enter Banditti

Put. How now! what are these?

Vas. You shall know presently.—Come, sirs, take me this old damnable hag, gag her instantly, and put out her eyes, quickly, quickly!

Put. Vasques! Vasques!—

Vas. Gag her, I say; 'sfoot, d'ye suffer her to prate? what d'ye fumble about? let me come to her. I'll help your old gums, you toad-bellied bitch! [*They gag her*] Sirs, carry her closely into the coal-house, and put out her eyes instantly; if she roars, slit her nose: d'ye hear, be speedy and sure. [*Exeunt* Banditti *with* PUTANA] Why, this is excellent and above expectation—her own brother! O, horrible! to what a height of liberty in damnation hath the devil trained our age! her brother, well! there's yet but a beginning; I must to my lord, and tutor him better in his points of vengeance: now I see how a smooth tale goes beyond a smooth tail.—But soft! what thing comes next? Giovanni! as I would wish: my belief is strengthened, 'tis as firm as winter and summer.

Enter GIOVANNI

Gio. Where's my sister?

Vas. Troubled with a new sickness, my lord; she's somewhat ill.

Gio. Took too much of the flesh, I believe.

Vas. Troth, sir, and you, I think, have e'en hit it: but my virtuous lady—

Gio. Where's she?

Vas. In her chamber; please you visit her; she is alone. [GIOVANNI *gives him money*] Your liberality hath doubly made me your servant, and ever shall, ever. *Exit* GIOVANNI

Re-enter SORANZO

Sir, I am made a man; I have plied my cue with cunning and success: I beseech you let's be private.

Sor. My lady's brother's come; now he'll know all.

Vas. Let him know't; I have made some of them fast enough. How have you dealt with my lady?

Sor. Gently, as thou hast counselled; O, my soul
Runs circular in sorrow for revenge:
But, Vasques, thou shalt know—

Vas. Nay, I will know no more, for now comes your turn to know: I would not talk so openly with you.—[*Aside*] Let my young master take time enough, and go at pleasure; he is sold to death, and the devil shall not ransom him.—Sir, I beseech you, your privacy.

Sor. No conquest can gain glory of my fear. *Exeunt*

ACT THE FIFTH

[SCENE I]

[*The Street before Soranzo's House*]

ANNABELLA *appears at a window above*

Ann. Pleasures, farewell, and all ye thriftless minutes
Wherein false joys have spun a weary life!
To these my fortunes now I take my leave.
Thou, precious Time, that swiftly rid'st in post
Over the world, to finish-up the race
Of my last fate, here stay thy restless course,
And bear to ages that are yet unborn
A wretched, woeful woman's tragedy!
My conscience now stands up against my lust
With depositions charactered in guilt,

Enter Friar *below*

And tells me I am lost: now I confess
Beauty that clothes the outside of the face
Is cursèd if it be not clothed with grace.
Here like a turtle mewed-up in a cage,
Unmated, I converse with air and walls,
And descant on my vile unhappiness.
O, Giovanni, thou hast had the spoil
Of thine own virtues and my modest fame,
Would thou hadst been less subject to those stars
That luckless reigned at my nativity!
O, would the scourge due to my black offence
Might pass from thee, that I alone might feel
The torment of an uncontrollèd flame!
Friar. [*Aside*] What's this I hear?
Ann. That man, that blessèd friar,
Who joined in ceremonial knot my hand
To him whose wife I now am, told me oft

I trod the path to death, and showed me how.
But they who sleep in lethargies of lust
Hug their confusion, making Heaven unjust;
And so did I.

Friar. [*Aside*] Here's music to the soul!

Ann. Forgive me, my good genius, and this once
Be helpful to my ends: let some good man
Pass this way, to whose trust I may commit
This paper, double-lined with tears and blood;
Which being granted, here I sadly vow
Repentance, and a leaving-of that life
I long have died in.

Friar. Lady, Heaven hath heard you,
And hath by providence ordained that I
Should be his minister for your behoof.

Ann. Ha, what are you?

Friar. Your brother's friend, the friar;
Glad in my soul that I have lived to hear
This free confession 'twixt your peace and you.
What would you, or to whom? fear not to speak.

Ann. Is Heaven so bountiful? then I have found
More favour than I hoped. Here, holy man:

Throws down a letter

Commend me to my brother; give him that.
That letter; bid him read it, and repent.
Tell him that I, imprisoned in my chamber,
Barred of all company, even of my guardian,—
Who gives me cause of much suspect,—have time
To blush at what hath passed; bid him be wise,
And not believe the friendship of my lord:
I fear much more than I can speak: good father,
The place is dangerous, and spies are busy.
I must break off. You'll do't?

Friar. Be sure I will,
And fly with speed. My blessing ever rest
With thee, my daughter; live, to die more blest! *Exit*

Ann. Thanks to the heavens, who have prolonged my breath
To this good use! now I can welcome death.

Withdraws from the window

[SCENE II]

[*A Room in Soranzo's House*]

Enter SORANZO *and* VASQUES

Vas. Am I to be believed now? first marry a strumpet, that cast herself away upon you but to laugh at your horns, to feast on your disgrace, riot in your vexations, cuckold you in your bride-bed, waste your estate upon panders and bawds!—

Sor. No more, I say, no more!

Vas. A cuckold is a goodly tame beast, my lord.

Sor. I am resolved; urge not another word;
My thoughts are great, and all as resolute
As thunder: in mean time I'll cause our lady
To deck herself in all her bridal robes;
Kiss her, and fold her gently in my arms.
Begone,—yet, hear you, are the banditti ready
To wait in ambush?

Vas. Good sir, trouble not yourself about other business than your own resolution; remember that time lost cannot be recalled.

Sor. With all the cunning words thou canst, invite
The states [1] of Parma to my birthday's feast.
Haste to my brother-rival and his father,
Entreat them gently, bid them not to fail.
Be speedy, and return.

Vas. Let not your pity betray you till my coming back; think upon incest and cuckoldry.

Sor. Revenge is all the ambition I aspire.

[1] *i.e.* Nobles.

To that I'll climb or fall: my blood's on fire. *Exeunt*

[SCENE III]

[*A Room in Florio's House*]

Enter GIOVANNI

Gio. Busy opinion is an idle fool,
That, as a school-rod keeps a child in awe,
Frights the unexperienced temper of the mind
So did it me, who, ere my precious sister
Was married, thought all taste of love would die
In such a contract; but I find no change
Of pleasure in this formal law of sports.
She is still one to me, and every kiss
As sweet and as delicious as the first
I reaped, when yet the privilege of youth
Entitled her a virgin. O, the glory
Of two united hearts like hers and mine!
Let poring book-men dream of other worlds;
My world and all of happiness is here,
And I'd not change it for the best to come:
A life of pleasure is elysium.

Enter Friar

Father, you enter on the jubilee
Of my retired delights: now I can tell you,
The hell you oft have prompted is nought else
But slavish and fond superstitious fear;
And I could prove it too—
Friar. Thy blindness slays thee:
Look there, 'tis writ to thee. *Gives him the letter*
Gio. From whom?
Friar. Unrip the seals and see;
The blood's yet seething hot, that will anon
Be frozen harder than congealèd coral.—

Why d'ye change colour, son?

Gio. 'Fore Heaven, you make
Some petty devil factor 'twixt my love
And your religion-maskèd sorceries.
Where had you this?

Friar. Thy conscience, youth, is seared,
Else thou wouldst stoop to warning.

Gio. 'Tis her hand,
I know't; and 'tis all written in her blood.
She writes I know not what. Death! I'll not fear
An armèd thunderbolt aimed at my heart.
She writes, we are discovered:—Pox on dreams
Of low faint-hearted cowardice!—discovered?
The devil we are! which way is't possible?
Are we grown traitors to our own delights?
Confusion take such dotage! 'tis but forged:
This is your peevish chattering, weak old man.

Enter VASQUES

Now, sir, what brings you?

Vas. My lord, according to his yearly custom, keeping this day a feast in honour of his birthday, by me invites you thither. Your worthy father, with the pope's reverend nuncio, and other magnificoes of Parma, have promised their presence: will't please you to be of the number?

Gio. Yes, tell him I dare come.

Vas. "Dare come!"

Gio. So I said; and tell him more, I will come.

Vas. These words are strange to me.

Gio. Say, I will come.

Vas. You will not miss?

Gio. Yet more! I'll come, sir. Are you answered?

Vas. So I'll say.—My service to you. *Exit*

Friar. You will not go, I trust.

Gio. Not go! for what?

Friar. O, do not go: this feast, I'll gage my life,

Is but a plot to train you to your ruin.
Be ruled, you shall not go.

Gio. Not go! stood Death
Threatening his armies of confounding plagues
With hosts of dangers hot as blazing stars,
I would be there: not go! yes, and resolve
To strike as deep in slaughter as they all;
For I will go.

Friar. Go where thou wilt: I see
The wildness of thy fate draws to an end,
To a bad fearful end. I must not stay
To know thy fall: back to Bononia I
With speed will haste, and shun this coming blow.—
Parma, farewell; would I had never known thee,
Or aught of thine!—Well, young man, since no prayer
Can make thee safe, I leave thee to despair. *Exit*

Gio. Despair, or tortures of a thousand hells;
All's one to me: I have set up my rest.[1]
Now, now, work serious thoughts on baneful plots;
Be all a man, my soul; let not the curse
Of old prescription rend from me the gall
Of courage, which enrols a glorious death:
If I must totter like a well-grown oak,
Some under-shrubs shall in my weighty fall
Be crushed to splits; with me they all shall perish! *Exit*

[SCENE IV]

[*A Hall in Soranzo's House*]

Enter SORANZO, VASQUES *with masks, and* Banditti

Sor. You will not fail, or shrink in the attempt?

Vas. I will undertake for their parts.—Be sure, my masters, to be bloody enough, and as unmerciful as if you were preying upon a rich booty on the very mountains of Liguria:

[1] *i.e.* I have taken my resolution.

for your pardons trust to my lord; but for reward you shall trust none but your own pockets.

Band. We'll make a murder.

Sor. Here's gold [*Gives them money*]; here's more; want nothing; what you do
Is noble, and an act of brave revenge:
I'll make ye rich, banditti, and all free.

Band. Liberty! liberty!

Vas. Hold, take every man a vizard [*Gives them masks*]: when ye are withdrawn, keep as much silence as you can possibly. You know the watchword; till which be spoken, move not; but when you hear that, rush in like a stormy flood; I need not instruct ye in your own profession.

Band. No, no, no.

Vas. In, then: your ends are profit and preferment: away!

Exeunt Banditti

Sor. The guests will all come, Vasques?

Vas. Yes, sir. And now let me a little edge your resolution: you see nothing is unready to this great work, but a great mind in you; call to your remembrance your disgraces, your loss of honour, Hippolita's blood, and arm your courage in your own wrongs; so shall you best right those wrongs in vengeance, which you may truly call your own.

Sor. 'Tis well: the less I speak, the more I burn.
And blood shall quench that flame.

Vas. Now you begin to turn Italian. This beside:—when my young incest-monger comes, he will be sharp set on his old bit: give him time enough, let him have your chamber and bed at liberty; let my hot hare have law ere he be hunted to his death, that, if it be possible, he post to hell in the very act of his damnation.

Sor. It shall be so; and see, as we would wish,
He comes himself first.

Enter GIOVANNI

Welcome, my much-loved brother:
Now I perceive you honour me; you're welcome.
But where's my father?

Gio. With the other states,[1]
Attending on the nuncio of the pope,
To wait upon him hither. How's my sister?

Sor. Like a good housewife, scarcely ready yet;
You're best walk to her chamber.

Gio. If you will.

Sor. I must expect my honourable friends;
Good brother, get her forth.

Gio. You're busy, sir. *Exit*

Vas. Even as the great devil himself would have it! let him go and glut himself in his own destruction.—[*Flourish*] Hark, the nuncio is at hand: good sir, be ready to receive him.

Enter Cardinal, FLORIO, DONADO, RICHARDETTO, *and* Attendants

Sor. Most reverend lord, this grace hath made me proud,
That you vouchsafe my house; I ever rest
Your humble servant for this noble favour.

Car. You are our friend, my lord: his holiness
Shall understand how zealously you honour
Saint Peter's vicar in his substitute:
Our special love to you.

Sor. Signiors, to you
My welcome, and my ever best of thanks
For this so memorable courtesy.—
Pleaseth your grace walk near?

Car. My lord, we come
To celebrate your feast with civil mirth,
As ancient custom teacheth: we will go.

[1] Nobles.

Sor. Attend his grace there!—Signiors, keep your way.
Exeunt

[SCENE V]

[*Annabella's Bed-chamber in the same*]

ANNABELLA *richly dressed and* GIOVANNI *discovered lying on a bed*

Gio. What, changed so soon! hath your new sprightly lord
Found out a trick in night-games more than we
Could know in our simplicity? Ha! is't so?
Or does the fit come on you, to prove treacherous
To your past vows and oaths?
Ann. Why should you jest
At my calamity, without all sense
Of the approaching dangers you are in?
Gio. What danger's half so great as thy revolt?
Thou art a faithless sister, else thou know'st
Malice, or any treachery beside,
Would stoop to my bent brows: why, I hold fate
Clasped in my fist, and could command the course
Of time's eternal motion, hadst thou been
One thought more steady than an ebbing sea.
And what? you'll now be honest, that's resolved?
Ann. Brother, dear brother, know what I have been,
And know that now there's but a dining-time
'Twixt us and our confusion: let's not waste
These precious hours in vain and useless speech.
Alas, these gay attires were not put on
But to some end; this sudden solemn feast
Was not ordained to riot in expense;
I, that have now been chambered here alone,
Barred of my guardian or of any else,
Am not for nothing at an instant freed
To fresh access. Be not deceived, my brother;
This banquet is an harbinger of death

To you and me; resolve yourself it is,
And be prepared to welcome it.
Gio. Well, then;
The schoolmen teach that all this globe of earth
Shall be consumed to ashes in a minute.
Ann. So I have read too.
Gio. But 'twere somewhat strange
To see the waters burn: could I believe
This might be true, I could believe as well
There might be hell or Heaven.
Ann. That's most certain.
Gio. A dream, a dream! else in this other world
We should know one another.
Ann. So we shall.
Gio. Have you heard so?
Ann. For certain.
Gio. But d'ye think
That I shall see you there?—You look on me.—
May we kiss one another, prate or laugh,
Or do as we do here?
Ann. I know not that.
But, brother, for the present, what d'ye mean
To free yourself from danger? some way think
How to escape: I'm sure the guests are come.
Gio. Look up, look here; what see you in my face?
Ann. Distraction and a troubled conscience.
Gio. Death, and a swift repining wrath:—yet look;
What see you in mine eyes?
Ann. Methinks you weep.
Gio. I do indeed: these are the funeral tears
Shed on your grave; these furrowed-up my cheeks
When first I loved and knew not how to woo.
Fair Annabella, should I here repeat
The story of my life, we might lose time.
Be record all the spirits of the air,
And all things else that are, that day and night,

Early and late, the tribute which my heart
Hath paid to Annabella's sacred love
Hath been these tears, which are her mourners now!
Never till now did Nature do her best
To show a matchless beauty to the world,
Which in an instant, ere it scarce was seen,
The jealous Destinies required again.
Pray, Annabella, pray! Since we must part,
Go thou, white in thy soul, to fill a throne
Of innocence and sanctity in Heaven.
Pray, pray, my sister!

Ann. Then I see your drift.—
Ye blessèd angels, guard me!

Gio. So say I.
Kiss me. If ever after-times should hear
Of our fast-knit affections, though perhaps
The laws of conscience and of civil use
May justly blame us, yet when they but know
Our loves, that love will wipe away that rigour
Which would in other incests be abhorred.
Give me your hand: how sweetly life doth run
In these well-coloured veins! how constantly
These palms do promise health! but I could chide
With Nature for this cunning flattery.
Kiss me again:—forgive me.

Ann. With my heart.

Gio. Farewell!

Ann. Will you be gone?

Gio. Be dark, bright sun,
And make this mid-day night, that thy gilt rays
May not behold a deed will turn their splendour
More sooty than the poets feign their Styx!—
One other kiss, my sister.

Ann. What means this?

Gio. To save thy fame, and kill thee in a kiss.

Stabs her

Thus die, and die by me, and by my hand!
Revenge is mine; honour doth love command.

Ann. O, brother, by your hand!

Gio. When thou art dead
I'll give my reasons for't; for to dispute
With thy—even in thy death—most lovely beauty,
Would make me stagger to perform this act,
Which I most glory in.

Ann. Forgive him, Heaven—and me my sins! Farewell,
Brother unkind, unkind—Mercy, great Heaven!
O, O! *Dies*

Gio. She's dead, alas, good soul! The hapless fruit
That in her womb received its life from me
Hath had from me a cradle and a grave.
I must not dally. This sad marriage-bed,
In all her best, bore her alive and dead.
Soranzo, thou hast missed thy aim in this:
I have prevented now thy reaching plots,
And killed a love, for whose each drop of blood
I would have pawned my heart.—Fair Annabella,
How over-glorious art thou in thy wounds,
Triumphing over infamy and hate!—
Shrink not, courageous hand, stand up, my heart,
And boldly act my last and greater part! *The scene closes*

[SCENE VI]

[*A Banqueting-room* [1] *in the same*]

A banquet set out. Enter the Cardinal, FLORIO, DONADO, SORANZO, RICHARDETTO, VASQUES, *and* Attendants

Vas. [*Aside to* SORANZO] Remember, sir, what you have to do; be wise and resolute.

[1] They had dined in another room, and, according to the usual practice, repaired to the apartment in which the confectionery was set out.—*Gifford.*

Sor. [*Aside to* VASQUES] Enough: my heart is fixed.—
Pleaseth your grace
To taste these coarse confections: though the use
Of such set entertainments more consists
In custom than in cause, yet, reverend sir,
I am still made your servant by your presence.
Car. And we your friend.
Sor. But where's my brother Giovanni?

Enter GIOVANNI *with a heart upon his dagger*

Gio. Here, here, Soranzo! trimmed in reeking blood,
That triumphs over death, proud in the spoil
Of love and vengeance! Fate, or all the powers
That guide the motions of immortal souls,
Could not prevent me.
Car. What means this?
Flo. Son Giovanni!
Sor. [*Aside*] Shall I be forestalled?
Gio. Be not amazed: if your misgiving hearts
Shrink at an idle sight, what bloodless fear
Of coward passion would have seized your senses,
Had you beheld the rape of life and beauty
Which I have acted!—My sister, O, my sister!
Flo. Ha! what of her?
Gio. The glory of my deed
Darkened the mid-day sun, made noon as night.
You came to feast, my lords, with dainty fare:
I came to feast too; but I digged for food
In a much richer mine than gold or stone
Of any value balanced; 'tis a heart,
A heart, my lords, in which is mine entombed:
Look well upon't; d'ye know't?
Vas. [*Aside*] What strange riddle's this?
Gio. 'Tis Annabella's heart, 'tis:—why d'ye startle?—
I vow 'tis hers: this dagger's point ploughed up
Her fruitful womb, and left to me the fame

Of a most glorious executioner.

Flo. Why, madman, art thyself?

Gio. Yes, father; and, that times to come may know
How, as my fate, I honoured my revenge,
List, father; to your ears I will yield up
How much I have deserved to be your son.

Flo. What is't thou say'st?

Gio. Nine moons have had their changes
Since I first throughly viewed and truly loved
Your daughter and my sister.

Flo. How!—Alas, my lords,
He is a frantic madman!

Gio. Father, no.
For nine months' space in secret I enjoyed
Sweet Annabella's sheets; nine months I lived
A happy monarch of her heart and her.—
Soranzo, thou know'st this: thy paler cheek
Bears the confounding print of thy disgrace;
For her too-fruitful womb too soon bewrayed
The happy passage of our stol'n delights,
And made her mother to a child unborn.

Car. Incestuous villain!

Flo. O, his rage belies him.

Gio. It does not, 'tis the oracle of truth;
I vow it is so.

Sor. I shall burst with fury,—
Bring the strumpet forth!

Vas. I shall, sir. *Exit*

Gio. Do, sir.—Have you all no faith
To credit yet my triumphs? Here I swear
By all that you call sacred, by the love
I bore my Annabella whilst she lived,
These hands have from her bosom ripped this heart.

Re-enter VASQUES

Is't true, or no, sir?

Vas. 'Tis most strangely true.

Flo. Cursèd man!—Have I lived to— *Dies*

Car. Hold up, Florio.—
Monster of children! see what thou hast done,
Broke thy old father's heart.—Is none of you
Dares venture on him?

Gio. Let 'em!—O, my father,
How well his death becomes him in his griefs!
Why, this was done with courage: now survives
None of our house but I, gilt in the blood
Of a fair sister and a hapless father.

Sor. Inhuman scorn of men, hast thou a thought
T' outlive thy murders? *Draws*

Gio. Yes, I tell thee, yes;
For in my fists I bear the twists of life.
Soranzo, see this heart, which was thy wife's;
Thus I exchange it royally for thine. *They fight*
And thus, and thus! SORANZO *falls*
Now brave revenge is mine.

Vas. I cannot hold any longer.—You, sir, are you grown insolent in your butcheries? have at you!

Gio. Come, I am armed to meet thee. *They fight*

Vas. No! will it not be yet? if this will not, another shall. Not yet? I shall fit you anon.—Vengeance! [1]

The Banditti *rush in*

Gio. Welcome! come more of you; whate'er you be,
I dare your worst. *They surround and wound him*
O, I can stand no longer! feeble arms,
Have you so soon lost strength? *Falls*

Vas. Now you are welcome, sir!—[*Aside to* Banditti] Away, my masters, all is done; shift for yourselves, your reward is your own; shift for yourselves.

Band. Away, away! *Exeunt*

[1] The watchword previously agreed on.

Vas. How d'ye, my lord?—See you this? [*Pointing to* GIOVANNI] How is't?

Sor. Dead; but in death well pleased that I have lived
To see my wrongs revenged on that black devil.
O, Vasques, to thy bosom let me give
My last of breath; let not that lecher live.
O! *Dies*

Vas. The reward of peace and rest be with him, my ever dearest lord and master!

Gio. Whose hand gave me this wound?

Vas. Mine, sir; I was your first man: have you enough?

Gio. I thank thee; thou hast done for me
But what I would have else done on myself.
Art sure thy lord is dead?

Vas. O, impudent slave!
As sure as I am sure to see thee die.

Car. Think on thy life and end, and call for mercy.

Gio. Mercy! why, I have found it in this justice.

Car. Strive yet to cry to Heaven.

Gio. O, I bleed fast!
Death, thou'rt a guest long looked for; I embrace
Thee and thy wounds: O, my last minute comes!
Where'er I go, let me enjoy this grace,
Freely to view my Annabella's face. *Dies*

Don. Strange miracle of justice!

Car. Raise up the city; we shall be murdered all!

Vas. You need not fear, you shall not: this strange task being ended, I have paid the duty to the son which I have vowed to the father.

Car. Speak, wretched villain, what incarnate fiend
Hath led thee on to this?

Vas. Honesty, and pity of my master's wrongs: for know, my lord, I am by birth a Spaniard, brought forth my country in my youth by Lord Soranzo's father, whom whilst he lived I served faithfully: since whose death I have been to this man as I was to him. What I have done was duty, and I repent nothing, but that the loss of my life had not ransomed his.

Car. Say, fellow, know'st thou any yet unnamed
Of counsel in this incest?

Vas. Yes, an old woman, sometimes[1] guardian to this murdered lady.

Car. And what's become of her?

Vas. Within this room she is! whose eyes, after her confession, I caused to be put out, but kept alive, to confirm what from Giovanni's own mouth you have heard. Now, my lord, what I have done you may judge of; and let your own wisdom be a judge in your own reason.

Car. Peace!—First this woman, chief in these effects,
My sentence is, that forthwith she be ta'en
Out of the city, for example's sake,
There to be burnt to ashes.

Don. 'Tis most just.

Car. Be it your charge, Donado, see it done.

Don. I shall.

Vas. What for me? if death, 'tis welcome: I have been honest to the son, as I was to the father.

Car. Fellow, for thee, since what thou didst was done
Not for thyself, being no Italian,
We banish thee for ever; to depart
Within three days: in this we do dispense
With grounds of reason, not of thine offence.

Vas. 'Tis well: this conquest is mine, and I rejoice that a Spaniard outwent an Italian in revenge. *Exit*

Car. Take up these slaughtered bodies, see them buried;
And all the gold and jewels, or whatsoever,
Confiscated by the canons of the church,
We seize upon to the pope's proper use.

Rich. [*Discovers himself*] Your grace's pardon: thus long I lived disguised,

[1] i.e. Formerly.

To see the effect of pride and lust at once
Brought both to shameful ends.

Car. What! Richardetto, whom we thought for dead?

Don. Sir, was it you—

Rich. Your friend.

Car. We shall have time
To talk at large of all: but never yet
Incest and murder have so strangely met.
Of one so young, so rich in nature's store,
Who could not say, 'TIS PITY SHE'S A WHORE? *Exeunt*